New Perspectives on

Microsoft® Office Access™ 2007

Introductory

New Perspectives on

Microsoft® Office Access™ 2007

Introductory

Joseph J. Adamski

Grand Valley State University

Kathleen T. Finnegan

THOMSON

COURSE TECHNOLOGY

Australia • Canada • Mexico • Singapore • Spain • United Kingdom • United States

THOMSON
COURSE TECHNOLOGY

New Perspectives on Microsoft Office Access 2007—Introductory

is published by Thomson Course Technology.

Acquisitions Editor:
Kristina Matthews

Senior Product Manager:
Kathy Finnegan

Product Manager:
Erik Herman

Associate Product Manager:
Brandi Henson

Editorial Assistant:
Leigh Robbins

Senior Marketing Manager:
Joy Stark

Marketing Coordinator:
Jennifer Hankin

Developmental Editor:
Jessica Evans

Senior Content Project Manager:
Jennifer Goguen McGrail

Content Project Manager:
Matthew Hutchinson

Composition:
GEX Publishing Services

Text Designer:
Steve Deschene

Cover Designer:
Elizabeth Paquin

Cover Art:
Bill Brown

ISBN-13: 978-1-4239-0588-2
ISBN-10: 1-4239-0588-1

Preface

The New Perspectives Series' critical-thinking, problem-solving approach is the ideal way to prepare students to transcend point-and-click skills and take advantage of all that Microsoft Office 2007 has to offer.

In developing the New Perspectives Series for Microsoft Office 2007, our goal was to create books that give students the software concepts and practical skills they need to succeed beyond the classroom. We've updated our proven case-based pedagogy with more practical content to make learning skills more meaningful to students.

With the New Perspectives Series, students understand *why* they are learning *what* they are learning, and are fully prepared to apply their skills to real-life situations.

"I really love the Margin Tips, which add 'tricks of the trade' to students' skills package. In addition, the Reality Check exercises provide for practical application of students' knowledge. I can't wait to use them in the classroom when we adopt Office 2007."

—Terry Morse Colucci
Institute of Technology, Inc.

About This Book

This book provides thorough, hands-on coverage of the new Microsoft Office Access 2007 software, and includes the following:

- A new "Getting Started with Microsoft Office 2007" tutorial that familiarizes students with the new Office 2007 features and user interface
- Complete instruction on Access 2007 basics, including creating and maintaining a database, querying a database, and creating forms and reports
- Expanded and in-depth coverage of higher level skills, including creating advanced queries, enhancing table design, creating custom forms and reports, and integrating Access with other programs
- A solid and complete presentation of important database concepts, including guidelines for designing databases and setting field properties, defining table relationships, object dependencies, normalization, and Access naming conventions
- Coverage of the exciting new features of Access 2007, including working in Layout view, applying conditional formats, managing database objects with the Navigation Pane, designating a trusted folder, using control layouts for forms and reports, and working with the Group, Sort, and Total pane for reports
- New business case scenarios throughout, which provide a rich and realistic context for students to apply the concepts and skills presented

System Requirements

This book assumes a typical installation of Microsoft Office Access 2007 and Microsoft Windows Vista Ultimate with the Aero feature turned off (or Windows Vista Home Premium or Business edition). Note that you can also complete the tutorials in this book using Windows XP; you will notice only minor differences if you are using Windows XP. Refer to the tutorial "Getting Started with Microsoft Office 2007" for Tips noting these differences. The browser used in this book for any steps that require a browser is Internet Explorer 7.

The New Perspectives Approach

Context

Each tutorial begins with a problem presented in a "real-world" case that is meaningful to students. The case sets the scene to help students understand what they will do in the tutorial.

Hands-on Approach

Each tutorial is divided into manageable sessions that combine reading and hands-on, step-by-step work. Colorful screenshots help guide students through the steps. **Trouble?** tips anticipate common mistakes or problems to help students stay on track and continue with the tutorial.

InSight

InSight Boxes

New for Office 2007! InSight boxes offer expert advice and best practices to help students better understand how to work with the software. With the information provided in the InSight boxes, students achieve a deeper understanding of the concepts behind the software features and skills.

Tip

Margin Tips

New for Office 2007! Margin Tips provide helpful hints and shortcuts for more efficient use of the software. The Tips appear in the margin at key points throughout each tutorial, giving students extra information when and where they need it.

Reality Check

Reality Checks

New for Office 2007! Comprehensive, open-ended Reality Check exercises give students the opportunity to practice skills by creating practical, real-world documents, such as resumes and budgets, which they are likely to use in their everyday lives at school, home, or work.

Review

In New Perspectives, retention is a key component to learning. At the end of each session, a series of Quick Check questions helps students test their understanding of the concepts before moving on. Each tutorial also contains an end-of-tutorial summary and a list of key terms for further reinforcement.

Apply

Assessment

Engaging and challenging Review Assignments and Case Problems have always been a hallmark feature of the New Perspectives Series. Colorful icons and brief descriptions accompany the exercises, making it easy to understand, at a glance, both the goal and level of challenge a particular assignment holds.

Reference Window

Task Reference

Reference

While contextual learning is excellent for retention, there are times when students will want a high-level understanding of how to accomplish a task. Within each tutorial, Reference Windows appear before a set of steps to provide a succinct summary and preview of how to perform a task. In addition, a complete Task Reference at the back of the book provides quick access to information on how to carry out common tasks. Finally, each book includes a combination Glossary/Index to promote easy reference of material.

Brief

Introductory

Comprehensive

Our Complete System of Instruction

Coverage To Meet Your Needs

Whether you're looking for just a small amount of coverage or enough to fill a semester-long class, we can provide you with a textbook that meets your needs.

- Brief books typically cover the essential skills in just 2 to 4 tutorials.
- Introductory books build and expand on those skills and contain an average of 5 to 8 tutorials.
- Comprehensive books are great for a full-semester class, and contain 9 to 12+ tutorials.

So if the book you're holding does not provide the right amount of coverage for you, there's probably another offering available. Go to our Web site or contact your Thomson Course Technology sales representative to find out what else we offer.

Student Online Companion

This book has an accompanying online companion Web site designed to enhance learning. This Web site includes:

- Internet Assignments for selected tutorials
- Student Data Files
- PowerPoint presentations

COURSECASTS

CourseCasts – Learning on the Go. Always available…always relevant.

Want to keep up with the latest technology trends relevant to you? Visit our site to find a library of podcasts, CourseCasts, featuring a "CourseCast of the Week," and download them to your mp3 player at http://coursecasts.course.com.

Our fast-paced world is driven by technology. You know because you're an active participant—always on the go, always keeping up with technological trends, and always learning new ways to embrace technology to power your life.

Ken Baldauf, host of CourseCasts, is a faculty member of the Florida State University Computer Science Department where he is responsible for teaching technology classes to thousands of FSU students each year. Ken is an expert in the latest technology trends; he gathers and sorts through the most pertinent news and information for CourseCasts so your students can spend their time enjoying technology, rather than trying to figure it out. Open or close your lecture with a discussion based on the latest CourseCast.

Visit us at http://coursecasts.course.com to learn on the go!

Skills Assessment and Training

SAM 2007 helps bridge the gap between the classroom and the real world by allowing students to train and test on important computer skills in an active, hands-on environment.

SAM 2007's easy-to-use system includes powerful interactive exams, training or projects on critical applications such as Word, Excel, Access, PowerPoint, Outlook, Windows, the Internet, and much more. SAM simulates the application environment, allowing students to demonstrate their knowledge and think through the skills by performing real-world tasks.

Designed to be used with the New Perspectives Series, SAM 2007 includes built-in page references so students can print helpful study guides that match the New Perspectives textbooks used in class. Powerful administrative options allow instructors to schedule exams and assignments, secure tests, and run reports with almost limitless flexibility.

Blackboard

Instructor Resources

We offer more than just a book. We have all the tools you need to enhance your lectures, check students' work, and generate exams in a new, easier-to-use and completely revised package. This book's Instructor's Manual, ExamView testbank, PowerPoint presentations, data files, solution files, figure files, and a sample syllabus are all available on a single CD-ROM or for downloading at www.course.com.

Online Content

Blackboard is the leading distance learning solution provider and class-management platform today. Thomson Course Technology has partnered with Blackboard to bring you premium online content. Content for use with *New Perspectives on Microsoft Office Access 2007, Introductory* is available in a Blackboard Course Cartridge and may include topic reviews, case projects, review questions, test banks, practice tests, custom syllabi, and more. Thomson Course Technology also has solutions for several other learning management systems. Please visit http://www.course.com today to see what's available for this title.

Acknowledgments

Our sincere thanks to the following reviewers for their helpful feedback and valuable insights: Steve Belville, Bryant & Stratton College; Bashar Elkhatib, Grantham University; Diane M. Larson, Indiana University Northwest; Ryan Murphy, Sinclair Community College; Diane Perreault, California State University, Sacramento; Debi Revelle, Sanford-Brown College; Lynne Stuhr, Trident Technical College; and Robert Van Cleave, Laramie County Community College. Many thanks to all the Thomson Course Technology staff, especially Kristina Matthews for her leadership, dedication, and good humor; Brandi Henson, for ensuring the quality and timely delivery of the supplements that accompany this text; Leigh Robbins, for her support throughout the development of this text; and Matthew Hutchinson, for his excellent management of the production process. Thanks as well to the following Manuscript Quality Assurance staff members for their diligent efforts in ensuring the quality and accuracy of this text: Christian Kunciw, MQA Project Leader; and John Freitas, Serge Palladino, Danielle Shaw, Marianne Snow, Teresa Storch, and Susan Whalen, MQA Testers. Many thanks to Lisa Ruffolo and Holly Ben-Joseph for their special contributions to this book. To Jen Goguen McGrail, more thanks than can be expressed for her exceptional work and tireless efforts in all matters related to the production of this text and the entire New Perspectives Series. To Jessica Evans, Developmental Editor, very special thanks for her outstanding editorial skills, incredible attention to detail, going above and beyond more times than I can recall, and for her friendship and "can-do" attitude that helped us overcome many hurdles to complete this text. Finally, I'm extremely grateful to Joe Adamski for his expertise, guidance, patience, and above all, friendship.

This book is dedicated with love to my parents, Ed and Mary Curran, for all their support and encouragement throughout the years; and to my two amazing sons, Connor and Devon, who demonstrated such patience and true "endurance" (go Blue Team!) during the many long hours I worked on this text; you both make me very proud.
–Kathleen T. Finnegan

Thank you to all the people who contributed to the challenge of completing of this book, with special thanks to Kathy Finnegan for her writing and friendship and for all the support she gives me in my writing; to Jessica Evans for her positive personality and influences, unlimited talents, friendship, and considerable contributions to the book; and to my wife, Judy, for everything.
–Joseph J. Adamski

Brief Contents

Table of Contents

Access Level II Tutorials

Tutorial 5 Creating Advanced Queries and Enhancing Table Design
Making the Panorama Database Easier to Use . . . . .AC 201

Objectives

- Explore the programs that comprise Microsoft Office
- Start programs and switch between them
- Explore common window elements
- Minimize, maximize, and restore windows
- Use the Ribbon, tabs, and buttons
- Use the contextual tabs, Mini toolbar, and shortcut menus
- Save, close, and open a file
- Use the Help system
- Print a file
- Exit programs

Getting Started with Microsoft Office 2007

Preparing a Meeting Agenda

Case | Recycled Palette

Recycled Palette, a company in Oregon founded by Ean Nogella in 2006, sells 100 percent recycled latex paint to both individuals and businesses in the area. The high-quality recycled paint is filtered to industry standards and tested for performance and environmental safety. The paint is available in both 1 gallon cans and 5 gallon pails, and comes in colors ranging from white to shades of brown, blue, green, and red. The demand for affordable recycled paint has been growing each year. Ean and all his employees use Microsoft Office 2007, which provides everyone in the company with the power and flexibility to store a variety of information, create consistent files, and share data. In this tutorial, you'll review how the company's employees use Microsoft Office 2007.

Starting Data Files

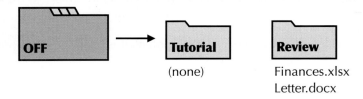

OFF → Tutorial (none)

Review
Finances.xlsx
Letter.docx

Exploring Microsoft Office 2007

Microsoft Office 2007, or **Office**, is a collection of Microsoft programs. Office is available in many suites, each of which contains a different combination of these programs. For example, the Professional suite includes Word, Excel, PowerPoint, Access, Outlook, and Publisher. Other suites are available and can include more or fewer programs (for additional information about the available suites, go to the Microsoft Web site). Each Office program contains valuable tools to help you accomplish many tasks, such as composing reports, analyzing data, preparing presentations, compiling information, sending e-mail, and planning schedules.

Microsoft Office Word 2007, or **Word**, is a computer program you use to enter, edit, and format text. The files you create in Word are called **documents**, although many people use the term *document* to refer to any file created on a computer. Word, often called a word processing program, offers many special features that help you compose and update all types of documents, ranging from letters and newsletters to reports, brochures, faxes, and even books—all in attractive and readable formats. You can also use Word to create, insert, and position figures, tables, and other graphics to enhance the look of your documents. For example, the Recycled Palette employees create business letters using Word.

Microsoft Office Excel 2007, or **Excel**, is a computer program you use to enter, calculate, analyze, and present numerical data. You can do some of this in Word with tables, but Excel provides many more tools for recording and formatting numbers as well as performing calculations. The graphics capabilities in Excel also enable you to display data visually. You might, for example, generate a pie chart or a bar chart to help people quickly see the significance of and the connections between information. The files you create in Excel are called **workbooks** (commonly referred to as spreadsheets), and Excel is often called a spreadsheet program. The Recycled Palette accounting department uses a line chart in an Excel workbook to visually track the company's financial performance.

Microsoft Office Access 2007, or **Access**, is a computer program used to enter, maintain, and retrieve related information (or data) in a format known as a database. The files you create in Access are called **databases**, and Access is often referred to as a database or relational database program. With Access, you can create forms to make data entry easier, and you can create professional reports to improve the readability of your data. The Recycled Palette operations department tracks the company's inventory in a table in an Access database.

Microsoft Office PowerPoint 2007, or **PowerPoint**, is a computer program you use to create a collection of slides that can contain text, charts, pictures, sound, movies, multimedia, and so on. The files you create in PowerPoint are called **presentations**, and PowerPoint is often called a presentation graphics program. You can show these presentations on your computer monitor, project them onto a screen as a slide show, print them, share them over the Internet, or display them on the World Wide Web. You can also use PowerPoint to generate presentation-related documents such as audience handouts, outlines, and speakers' notes. The Recycled Palette marketing department has created an effective slide presentation with PowerPoint to promote its paints to a wider audience.

Microsoft Office Outlook 2007, or **Outlook**, is a computer program you use to send, receive, and organize e-mail; plan your schedule; arrange meetings; organize contacts; create a to-do list; and jot down notes. You can also use Outlook to print schedules, task lists, phone directories, and other documents. Outlook is often referred to as an information management program. The Recycled Palette staff use Outlook to send and receive e-mail, plan their schedules, and create to-do lists.

Although each Office program individually is a strong tool, their potential is even greater when used together.

Integrating Office Programs

One of the main advantages of Office is **integration**, the ability to share information between programs. Integration ensures consistency and accuracy, and it saves time because you don't have to reenter the same information in several Office programs. The staff at Recycled Palette uses the integration features of Office daily, including the following examples:

- The accounting department created an Excel bar chart on the previous two years' fourth-quarter results, which they inserted into the quarterly financial report created in Word. They included a hyperlink in the Word report that employees can click to open the Excel workbook and view the original data.
- The operations department included an Excel pie chart of sales percentages by paint colors on a PowerPoint slide, which is part of a presentation to stockholders.
- The marketing department produced a mailing to promote its recycled paints to local contractors and designers by combining a form letter created in Word with an Access database that stores the names and addresses of these potential customers.
- A sales representative wrote a letter in Word about an upcoming promotion for new customers and merged the letter with an Outlook contact list containing the names and addresses of prospective customers.

These are just a few examples of how you can take information from one Office program and integrate it with another.

Starting Office Programs

You can start any Office program by clicking the Start button on the Windows taskbar, and then selecting the program you want from the All Programs menu. As soon as the program starts, you can immediately begin to create new files or work with existing ones. If an Office program appears in the most frequently used programs list on the left side of the Start menu, you can click the program name to start the program.

Starting Office Programs | Reference Window

- Click the Start button on the taskbar.
- Click All Programs.
- Click Microsoft Office.
- Click the name of the program you want to start.
or
- Click the name of the program you want to start in the most frequently used programs list on the left side of the Start menu.

You'll start Excel using the Start button.

To start Excel and open a new, blank workbook:

▶ **1.** Make sure your computer is on and the Windows desktop appears on your screen.

Trouble? If your screen varies slightly from those shown in the figures, your computer might be set up differently. The figures in this book were created while running Windows Vista with the Aero feature turned off, but how your screen looks depends on the version of Windows you are using, the background settings, and so forth.

Windows XP Tip

The Start button is the green button with the word "start" on it, located at the bottom left of the taskbar.

▶ **2.** Click the **Start** button 🔘 on the taskbar, and then click **All Programs** to display the All Programs menu.

▶ **3.** Click **Microsoft Office** on the All Programs list, and then point to **Microsoft Office Excel 2007**. Depending on how your computer is set up, your desktop and menu might contain different icons and commands.

> **Trouble?** If you don't see Microsoft Office on the All Programs list, click Microsoft Office Excel 2007 on the All Programs list. If you still don't see Microsoft Office Excel 2007, ask your instructor or technical support person for help.

▶ **4.** Click **Microsoft Office Excel 2007**. Excel starts, and a new, blank workbook opens. See Figure 1.

Figure 1	New, blank Excel workbook

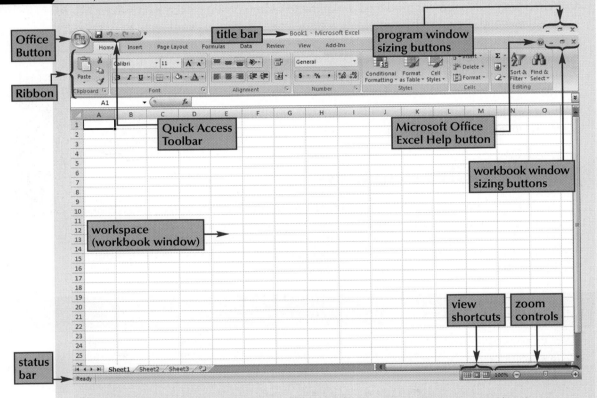

> **Trouble?** If the Excel window doesn't fill your entire screen, the window is not maximized, or expanded to its full size. You'll maximize the window shortly.

You can have more than one Office program open at once. You'll use this same method to start Word and open a new, blank document.

To start Word and open a new, blank document:

▶ **1.** Click the **Start** button 🔘 on the taskbar, click **All Programs** to display the All Programs list, and then click **Microsoft Office**.

> **Trouble?** If you don't see Microsoft Office on the All Programs list, click Microsoft Office Word 2007 on the All Programs list. If you still don't see Microsoft Office Word 2007, ask your instructor or technical support person for help.

▶ **2.** Click **Microsoft Office Word 2007**. Word starts, and a new, blank document opens. See Figure 2.

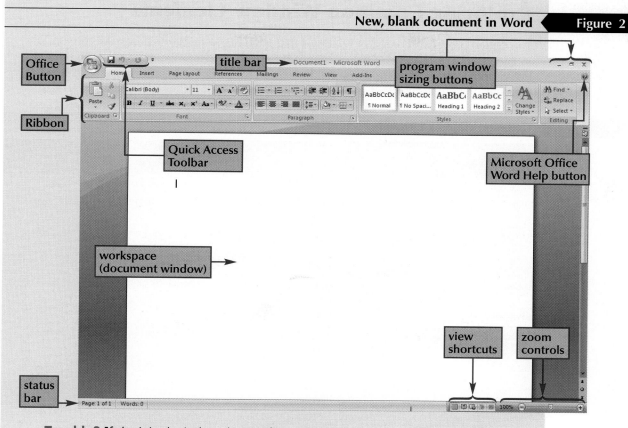

New, blank document in Word ◄ **Figure 2**

Trouble? If the Word window doesn't fill your entire screen, the window is not maximized. You'll maximize the window shortly.

Switching Between Open Programs and Files

Two programs are running at the same time—Excel and Word. The taskbar contains buttons for both programs. When you have two or more programs running or two files within the same program open, you can use the taskbar buttons to switch from one program or file to another. The button for the active program or file is darker. The employees at Recycled Palette often work in several programs at once.

To switch between Word and Excel files:

▶ **1.** Click the **Microsoft Excel – Book1** button on the taskbar. The active program switches from Word to Excel. See Figure 3.

Excel and Word programs opened simultaneously ◄ **Figure 3**

Tip

You can also press the Alt+Tab keys to switch between open files.

▶ **2.** Click the **Document1 – Microsoft Word** button on the taskbar to return to Word.

Exploring Common Window Elements

The Office programs consist of windows that have many similar features. As you can see in Figures 1 and 2, many of the elements in both the Excel program window and the Word program window are the same. In fact, all the Office programs have these same elements. Figure 4 describes some of the most common window elements.

Figure 4   **Common window elements**

Element	Description
Office Button	Provides access to document-level features and program settings
Quick Access Toolbar	Provides one-click access to commonly used commands, such as Save, Undo, and Repeat
Title bar	Contains the name of the open file, the program name, and the sizing buttons
Sizing buttons	Resize and close the program window or the workspace
Ribbon	Provides access to the main set of commands organized by task into tabs and groups
Microsoft Office Help button	Opens the Help window for that program
Workspace	Displays the file you are working on (Word document, Excel workbook, Access database, or PowerPoint slide)
Status bar	Provides information about the program, open file, or current task as well as the view shortcuts and zoom controls
View shortcuts	Change how a file is displayed in the workspace
Zoom controls	Magnify or shrink the content displayed in the workspace

Because these elements are the same in each program, after you've learned one program, it's easy to learn the others. The next sections explore these common features.

Resizing the Program Window and Workspace

There are three different sizing buttons. The Minimize button ▬ , which is the left button, hides a window so that only its program button is visible on the taskbar. The middle button changes name and function depending on the status of the window—the Maximize button ▣ expands the window to the full screen size or to the program window size, and the Restore Down button ▣ returns the window to a predefined size. The Close button ✖ , on the right, exits the program or closes the file. Excel has two sets of sizing buttons. The top set controls the program window and the lower set controls the workspace. The workspace sizing buttons look and function in exactly the same way as the program window sizing buttons, except the button names change to Minimize Window and Restore Window when the workspace is maximized.

Most often, you'll want to maximize the program window and workspace to take advantage of the full screen size you have available. If you have several files open, you might want to restore down their windows so that you can see more than one window at a time, or you might want to minimize programs or files you are not working on at the moment. You'll try minimizing, maximizing, and restoring down windows and workspaces now.

To resize windows and workspaces:

▶ **1.** Click the **Minimize** button ▭ on the Word title bar. The Word program window reduces to a taskbar button. The Excel program window is visible again.

▶ **2.** If necessary, click the **Maximize** button ▭ on the Excel title bar. The Excel program window expands to fill the screen.

▶ **3.** Click the **Restore Window** button ▭ in the lower set of Excel sizing buttons. The workspace is resized and is now smaller than the full program window. See Figure 5.

Resized Excel window and workspace ◀ **Figure 5**

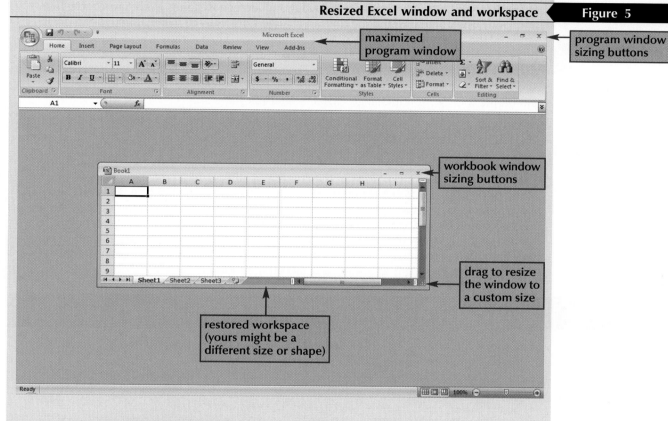

maximized program window

program window sizing buttons

workbook window sizing buttons

drag to resize the window to a custom size

restored workspace (yours might be a different size or shape)

▶ **4.** Click the **Maximize** button ▭ on the Excel workbook window title bar. The Excel workspace expands to fill the program window.

▶ **5.** Click the **Document1 - Microsoft Word** button on the taskbar. The Word program window returns to its previous size.

▶ **6.** If necessary, click the **Maximize** button ▭ on the Word title bar. The Word program window expands to fill the screen.

The sizing buttons give you the flexibility to arrange the program and file windows on your screen to best fit your needs.

Getting Information from the Status Bar

The **status bar** at the bottom of the program window provides information about the open file and current task or selection. It also has buttons and other controls for working with the file and its content. The status bar buttons and information displays are specific to the individual programs. For example, the Excel status bar displays summary information about a selected range of numbers (such as their sum or average), whereas the Word status bar shows the current page number and total number of words in a document. The right side of the status bar includes buttons that enable you to switch the workspace view in Word, Excel, PowerPoint, and Access as well as zoom the workspace in Word, Excel, and PowerPoint. You can customize the status bar to display other information or hide the **default** (original or preset) information.

Switching Views

Each program has a variety of views, or ways to display the file in the workspace. For example, Word has five views: Print Layout, Full Screen Reading, Web Layout, Outline, and Draft. The content of the file doesn't change from view to view, although the presentation of the content will. In Word, for example, Page Layout view shows how a document would appear as the printed page, whereas Web Layout view shows how the document would appear as a Web page. You can quickly switch between views using the shortcuts at the right side of the status bar. You can also change the view from the View tab on the Ribbon. You'll change views in later tutorials.

Zooming the Workspace

Zooming is a way to magnify or shrink the file content displayed in the workspace. You can zoom in to get a closer look at the content of an open document, worksheet, or slide, or you can zoom out to see more of the content at a smaller size. There are several ways to change the zoom percentage. You can use the Zoom slider at the right of the status bar to quickly change the zoom percentage. You can click the Zoom level button to the left of the Zoom slider in the status bar to open the Zoom dialog box and select a specific zoom percentage or size based on your file. You can also change the zoom settings using the Zoom group in the View tab on the Ribbon.

Reference Window	**Zooming the Workspace**

- Click the Zoom Out or Zoom In button on the status bar (or drag the Zoom slider button left or right) to the desired zoom percentage.

or

- Click the Zoom level button on the status bar.
- Select the appropriate zoom setting, and then click the OK button.

or

- Click the View tab on the Ribbon, and then in the Zoom group, click the zoom setting you want.

The figures shown in these tutorials are zoomed to enhance readability. You'll zoom the Word and Excel workspaces.

To zoom the Word and Excel workspaces:

▶ **1.** On the Zoom slider on the Word status bar, drag the **slider button** to the left until the Zoom percentage is **10%**. The document reduces to its smallest size, which makes the entire page visible but unreadable. See Figure 6.

Word document zoomed to 10% — **Figure 6**

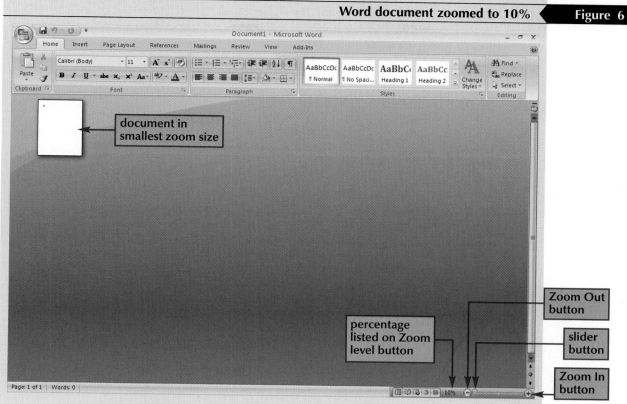

You'll zoom the document so its page width fills the workspace.

2. Click the **Zoom level** button `10%` on the Word status bar. The Zoom dialog box opens. See Figure 7.

Zoom dialog box — **Figure 7**

3. Click the **Page width** option button, and then click the **OK** button. The Word document magnifies to its page width to match the rest of the Word figures shown in these tutorials.

Now, you'll zoom the workbook to 120%.

▶ **4.** Click the **Microsoft Excel – Book1** button on the taskbar. The Excel program window is displayed.

▶ **5.** Click the **Zoom In** button ⊕ on the status bar two times. The workspace magnifies to 120%. This is the zoom percentage that matches the rest of the Excel figures shown in these tutorials.

▶ **6.** Click the **Document1 – Microsoft Word** button on the taskbar. The Word program window is displayed.

Using the Ribbon

The **Ribbon** at the top of the program window just below the title bar is the main set of commands that you click to execute tasks. The Ribbon is organized into tabs. Each **tab** has commands related to particular activities. For example, in Word, the Insert tab on the Ribbon provides access to all the commands for adding objects such as shapes, pages, tables, illustrations, text, and symbols to a document. Although the tabs differ from program to program, the first tab in each program, called the Home tab, contains the commands for the most frequently performed activities, including cutting and pasting, changing fonts, and using editing tools. In addition, the Insert, Review, View, and Add-Ins tabs appear on the Ribbon in all the Office programs except Access, although the commands they include might differ from program to program. Other tabs are program specific, such as the Design tab in PowerPoint and the Datasheet tab in Access.

To use the Ribbon tabs:

▶ **1.** In Word, point to the **Insert** tab on the Ribbon. The Insert tab is highlighted, though the Home tab with the options for using the Clipboard and formatting text remains visible.

▶ **2.** Click the **Insert** tab. The Ribbon displays the Insert tab, which provides access to all the options for adding objects such as shapes, pages, tables, illustrations, text, and symbols to a document. See Figure 8.

Figure 8 ▶ **Insert tab on the Ribbon**

▶ **3.** Click the **Home** tab on the Ribbon. The Ribbon displays the Home options.

Clicking Button Icons

Each **button**, or icon, on the tabs provides one-click access to a command. Most buttons are labeled so that you can easily find the command you need. For the most part, when you click a button, something happens in your file. If you want to repeat that action, you click the button again. Buttons for related commands are organized on a tab in **groups**. For example, the Clipboard group on the Home tab includes the Cut, Copy, Paste, and Format Painter buttons—the commands for moving or copying text, objects, and formatting.

Buttons can be toggle switches: one click turns on the feature and the next click turns off the feature. While the feature is on, the button remains colored or highlighted to remind you that it is active. For example, in Word, the Show/Hide button on the Home tab in the Paragraph group displays the nonprinting screen characters when toggled on and hides them when toggled off.

Some buttons have two parts: a button that accesses a command and an arrow that opens a menu of all the commands available for that task. For example, the Paste button on the Home tab includes the default Paste command and an arrow that opens the menu of all the Paste commands—Paste, Paste Special, and Paste as Hyperlink. To select a command on the menu, you click the button arrow and then click the command on the menu.

The buttons and groups change based on your monitor size, your screen resolution, and the size of the program window. With smaller monitors, lower screen resolutions, and reduced program windows, buttons can appear as icons without labels and a group can be condensed into a button that you click to display the group options. The figures in these tutorials were created using a screen resolution of 1024 × 768 and, unless otherwise specified, the program and workspace windows are maximized. If you are using a different screen resolution or window size, the button icons on the Ribbon might show more or fewer button names, and some groups might be condensed into buttons.

You'll type text in the Word document, and then use the buttons on the Ribbon.

To use buttons on the Ribbon:

1. Type **Recycled Palette**, and then press the **Enter** key. The text appears in the first line of the document and the insertion point moves to the second line.

   Trouble? If you make a typing error, press the Backspace key to delete the incorrect letters, and then retype the text.

2. In the Paragraph group on the Home tab, click the **Show/Hide** button ¶. The nonprinting screen characters appear in the document, and the Show/Hide button remains toggled on. See Figure 9.

   Trouble? If the nonprinting characters are removed from your screen, the Show/Hide button ¶ was already selected. Repeat Step 2 to show the nonprinting screen characters.

Button toggled on Figure 9

3. Drag to select all the text in the first line of the document (but not the paragraph mark).

4. In the Clipboard group on the Home tab, click the **Copy** button. The selected text is copied to the Clipboard.

▶ 5. Press the ↓ key. The text is deselected and the insertion point moves to the second line in the document.

▶ 6. In the Clipboard group on the Home tab, point to the top part of the **Paste** button. Both parts of the Paste button are highlighted, but the icon at top is darker to indicate it will be clicked if you press the mouse button.

▶ 7. Point to the **Paste button arrow**. The button arrow is now darker.

▶ 8. Click the **Paste button arrow**. A menu of paste commands opens. See Figure 10. To select one of the commands on the list, you click it.

Figure 10 — **Two-part Paste button**

Paste button

click the Paste button arrow to open a menu with additional options

Paste commands

▶ 9. Click **Paste**. The menu closes, and the text is duplicated in the second line of the document.

As you can see, you can quickly access commands and turn features on and off with the buttons on the Ribbon.

InSight | **Using Keyboard Shortcuts and Key Tips**

Keyboard shortcuts can help you work faster and more efficiently. A **keyboard shortcut** is a key or combination of keys you press to access a tool or perform a command. To quickly access options on the Ribbon, the Quick Access Toolbar, and the Office Button without removing your hands from the keyboard:

1. Press the Alt key. Key Tips appear that list the keyboard shortcut for each Ribbon tab, each Quick Access Toolbar button, and the Office Button.
2. Press the key for the tab or button you want to use. An action is performed or Key Tips appear for the buttons on the selected tab or the commands for the selected button.
3. Continue to press the appropriate key listed in the Key Tip until the action you want is performed.

You can also use keyboard shortcuts to perform specific commands. For example, Ctrl+S is the keyboard shortcut for the Save command (you hold down the Ctrl key while you press the S key). This type of keyboard shortcut appears in ScreenTips next to the command's name. Not all commands have this type of keyboard shortcut. Identical commands in each Office program use the same keyboard shortcut.

Using Galleries and Live Preview

A button can also open a **gallery**, which is a grid or menu that shows a visual representation of the options available for that command. For example, the Bullet Library gallery in Word shows an icon of each bullet style you can select. Some galleries include a More button that you click to expand the gallery to see all the options in it. When you hover the pointer over an option in a gallery, **Live Preview** shows the results you would achieve in your file if you clicked that option. To continue the bullets example, when you hover over a bullet style in the Bullet Library gallery, the current paragraph or selected text previews that bullet style. By moving the pointer from option to option, you can quickly see the text set with different bullet styles; you can then select the style that works best for your needs.

To use a gallery and Live Preview:

▶ **1.** In the Paragraph group on the Home tab, click the **Bullets button arrow** . The Bullet Library gallery opens.

▶ **2.** Point to the **check mark bullet** style. Live Preview shows the selected bullet style in your document, so you can determine if you like that bullet style. See Figure 11.

Live Preview of bullet style ◀ **Figure 11**

▶ **3.** Place the pointer over each of the remaining bullet styles and preview them in your document.

You don't want to add bullets to your document right now, so you'll close the Bullet Library gallery and deselect the Bullets button.

▶ **4.** Press the **Esc** key on the keyboard. The Bullet Library gallery closes and the Bullets button is deselected.

▶ **5.** Press the **Backspace** key on the keyboard to delete the text "Recycled Palette" on the second line.

Galleries and Live Preview let you quickly see how your file will be affected by a selection.

Opening Dialog Boxes and Task Panes

The button to the right of the group names is the **Dialog Box Launcher**, which you click to open a task pane or dialog box that provides more advanced functionality for that group of tasks. A **task pane** is a window that helps you navigate through a complex task or feature. For example, the Clipboard task pane allows you to paste some or all of the items that have been cut or copied from any Office program during the current work session and the Research task pane allows you to search a variety of reference resources from within a file. A **dialog box** is a window from which you enter or choose settings for how you want to perform a task. For example, the Page Setup dialog box in Word contains options for how you want a document to look. Some dialog boxes organize related information into tabs, and related options and settings are organized into groups, just as they are on the Ribbon. You select settings in a dialog box using option buttons, check boxes, text boxes, lists, and other controls to collect information about how you want to perform a task.

In Excel, you'll use the Dialog Box Launcher for the Page Setup group to open the Page Setup dialog box.

To open the Page Setup dialog box using the Dialog Box Launcher:

▶ **1.** Click the **Microsoft Excel – Book1** button on the taskbar to switch from Word to Excel.

▶ **2.** Click the **Page Layout** tab on the Ribbon.

▶ **3.** In the Page Setup group, click the **Dialog Box Launcher**, which is the small button to the right of the Page Setup group name. The Page Setup dialog box opens with the Page tab displayed. See Figure 12.

Figure 12 | Page tab in the Page Setup dialog box

▶ **4.** Click the **Landscape** option button. The workbook's page orientation changes to a page wider than it is long.

▶ **5.** Click the **Sheet** tab. The dialog box displays options related to the worksheet. You can click a check box to turn an option on (checked) or off (unchecked). You can check more than one check box in a group, whereas you can select only one option button in a group.

▶ **6.** In the Print group, click the **Gridlines** check box and the **Row and column headings** check box. Check marks appear in both check boxes, indicating that these options are selected.

You don't want to change the page setup right now, so you'll close the dialog box.

▶ **7.** Click the **Cancel** button. The dialog box closes without making any changes to the page setup.

Using Contextual Tools

Some tabs, toolbars, and menus come into view as you work. Because these tools become available only as you might need them, the workspace on your screen remains more open and less cluttered. However, tools that appear and disappear as you work can be distracting and take some getting used to.

Displaying Contextual Tabs

Any object that you can select in a file has a related contextual tab. An **object** is anything that appears on your screen that can be selected and manipulated as a whole, such as a table, a picture, a text box, a shape, a chart, WordArt, an equation, a diagram, a header, or a footer. A **contextual tab** is a Ribbon tab that contains commands related to the selected object so you can manipulate, edit, and format that object. Contextual tabs appear to the right of the standard Ribbon tabs just below a title label. For example, Figure 13 shows the Table Tools contextual tabs that appear when you select a table in a Word document. Although the contextual tabs appear only when you select an object, they function in the same way as standard tabs on the Ribbon. Contextual tabs disappear when you click elsewhere on the screen and deselect the object. Contextual tabs can also appear as you switch views. You'll use contextual tabs in later tutorials.

Table Tools contextual tabs ◀ **Figure 13**

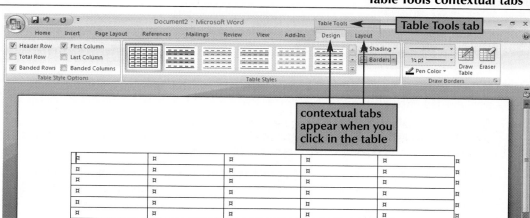

Accessing the Mini Toolbar

The **Mini toolbar** is a toolbar that appears next to the pointer whenever you select text, and it contains buttons for the most commonly used formatting commands, such as font, font size, styles, color, alignment, and indents that may appear in different groups or tabs on the Ribbon. The Mini toolbar buttons differ in each program. A transparent version of the Mini toolbar appears immediately after you select text. When you move the pointer over the Mini toolbar, it comes into full view so you can click the appropriate formatting button or buttons. The Mini toolbar disappears if you move the pointer away from the toolbar, press a key, or press a mouse button. The Mini toolbar can help you format your text faster, but initially you might find that the toolbar disappears unexpectedly. All the commands on the Mini toolbar are also available on the Ribbon. Be aware that Live Preview of selected styles does not work in the Mini toolbar.

You'll use the Mini toolbar to format text you enter in the workbook.

Tip

You can turn off the Mini toolbar and Live Preview in Word, Excel, and PowerPoint. Click the Office Button, click the Options button at the bottom of the Office menu, uncheck the first two check boxes in the Popular category, and then click the OK button.

To use the Mini toolbar to format text:

▶ **1.** If necessary, click cell **A1** (the rectangle in the upper-left corner of the worksheet).

▶ **2.** Type **Budget**. The text appears in the cell.

▶ **3.** Press the **Enter** key. The text is entered in cell A1 and cell A2 is selected.

▶ **4.** Type **2008**, and then press the **Enter** key. The year is entered in cell A2 and cell A3 is selected.

You'll use the Mini toolbar to make the word in cell A1 boldface.

▶ **5.** Double-click cell **A1** to place the insertion point in the cell. Now you can select the text you typed.

▶ **6.** Double-click **Budget** in cell A1. The selected text appears white in a black background, and the transparent Mini toolbar appears directly above the selected text. See Figure 14.

| Figure 14 | Transparent Mini toolbar |

Tip

You can redisplay the Mini toolbar if it disappears by right-clicking the selected text.

▶ **7.** Move the pointer over the Mini toolbar. The Mini toolbar is now completely visible, and you can click buttons.

Trouble? If the Mini toolbar disappears, you probably moved the pointer to another area of the worksheet. To redisplay the Mini toolbar, repeat Steps 5 through 7, being careful to move the pointer directly over the Mini toolbar in Step 7.

▶ **8.** Click the **Bold** button on the Mini toolbar. The text in cell A1 is bold and the Mini toolbar remains visible so you can continue formatting the selected text. See Figure 15.

| Figure 15 | Mini toolbar with the Bold button selected |

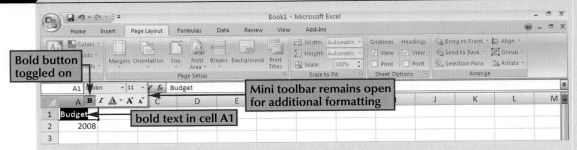

You don't want to make any other changes, so you'll close the Mini toolbar.

▶ **9.** Press the **Enter** key. The Mini toolbar disappears and cell A2 is selected.

Opening Shortcut Menus

A **shortcut menu** is a list of commands related to a selection that opens when you click the right mouse button. Each shortcut menu provides access to the commands you'll most likely want to use with the object or selection you right-click. The shortcut menu includes commands that perform actions, commands that open dialog boxes, and galleries of options that provide Live Preview. The Mini toolbar also opens when you right-click. If you click a button on the Mini toolbar, the rest of the shortcut menu closes while the Mini toolbar remains open so you can continue formatting the selection. Using a shortcut menu provides quick access to the commands you need without having to access the tabs on the Ribbon. For example, you can right-click selected text to open a shortcut menu with a Mini toolbar, text-related commands, such as Cut, Copy, and Paste, as well as other program-specific commands.

You'll use a shortcut menu in Excel to delete the content you entered in cell A1.

To use a shortcut menu to delete content:

▶ **1.** Right-click cell **A1**. A shortcut menu opens, listing commands related to common tasks you'd perform in a cell, along with a Mini toolbar. See Figure 16.

Shortcut menu with Mini toolbar ◀ Figure 16

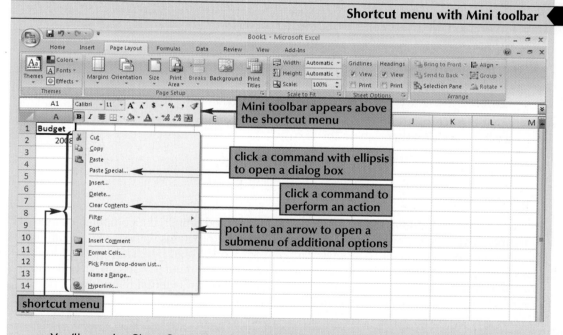

You'll use the Clear Contents command to delete the bold text from cell A1.

▶ **2.** Click **Clear Contents** on the shortcut menu. The shortcut menu closes, the Mini toolbar disappears, and the formatted text is removed from cell A1.

You'll use the Clear Contents command again to delete the year from cell A2.

▶ **3.** Right-click cell **A2**, and then click **Clear Contents** on the shortcut menu. The year is removed from cell A2.

Shortcut menus enable you to quickly access commands that you're most likely to need in the context of the task you're performing.

Tip

Press the Esc key to close an open menu, shortcut menu, list, gallery, and so forth without selecting an option.

Working with Files

The most common tasks you perform in any Office program are to create, open, save, and close files. The processes for these tasks are basically the same in all the Office programs. In addition, there are several methods for performing most tasks in Office. This flexibility enables you to use Office in a way that best fits how you like to work.

The **Office Button** provides access to document-level features, such as creating new files, opening existing files, saving files, printing files, and closing files, as well as the most common program options, called **application settings**. The **Quick Access Toolbar** is a collection of buttons that provide one-click access to commonly used commands, such as Save, Undo, and Repeat.

To begin working in a program, you need to create a new file or open an existing file. When you start Word, Excel, or PowerPoint, the program opens along with a blank file—ready for you to begin working on a new document, workbook, or presentation. When you start Access, the Getting Started with Microsoft Access window opens, displaying options for creating a new database or opening an existing one.

Ean has asked you to continue working on the agenda for the stockholder meeting. You already started typing in the document that opened when you started Word. Next, you will enter more text in the Word document.

To enter text in the Word document:

▶ **1.** Click the **Document1 – Microsoft Word** button on the taskbar to activate the Word program window.

▶ **2.** Type **Meeting Agenda** on the second line of the document, and then press the **Enter** key. The text you typed appears in the document.

Trouble? If you make a typing error, press the Backspace key to delete the incorrect letters, and then retype the text.

Saving a File

As you create and modify Office files, your work is stored only in the computer's temporary memory, not on a hard disk. If you were to exit the programs without saving, turn off your computer, or experience a power failure, your work would be lost. To prevent losing work, save your file to a disk frequently—at least every 10 minutes. You can save files to the hard disk located inside your computer, a floppy disk, an external hard drive, a network storage drive, or a portable storage disk, such as a USB flash drive.

Reference Window | **Saving a File**

To save a file the first time or with a new name or location:
- Click the Office Button, and then click Save As (or for an unnamed file, click the Save button on the Quick Access Toolbar or click the Office Button, and then click Save).
- In the Save As dialog box, navigate to the location where you want to save the file.
- Type a descriptive title in the File name box, and then click the Save button.

To resave a named file to the same location:
- Click the Save button on the Quick Access Toolbar (or click the Office Button, and then click Save).

The first time you save a file, you need to name it. This **filename** includes a descriptive title you select and a file extension assigned by Office. You should choose a descriptive title that accurately reflects the content of the document, workbook, presentation, or database, such as "Shipping Options Letter" or "Fourth Quarter Financial Analysis." Your descriptive title can include uppercase and lowercase letters, numbers, hyphens, and spaces in any combination, but not the following special characters: ? " / \ < > * | and :. Each filename ends with a **file extension**, a period followed by several characters that Office adds to your descriptive title to identify the program in which that file was created. The default file extensions for Office 2007 are .docx for Word, .xlsx for Excel, .pptx for PowerPoint, and .accdb for Access. Filenames (the descriptive title and the file extension) can include a maximum of 255 characters. You might see file extensions depending on how Windows is set up on your computer. The figures in these tutorials do not show file extensions.

You also need to decide where to save the file—on which disk and in what folder. A **folder** is a container for your files. Just as you organize paper documents within folders stored in a filing cabinet, you can organize your files within folders stored on your computer's hard disk or a removable disk, such as a USB flash drive. Store each file in a logical location that you will remember whenever you want to use the file again. The default storage location for Office files is the Documents folder; you can create additional storage folders within that folder or navigate to a new storage location.

You can navigate the Save As dialog box by clicking a folder or location on your computer in the Navigation pane along the left side of the dialog box, and then double-clicking folders in the file list until you display the storage location you want. You can also navigate to a storage location with the Address bar, which displays the current file path. Each location in the file path has a corresponding arrow that you can click to quickly select a folder within that location. For example, you can click the Documents arrow in the Address bar to open a list of all the folders in the Documents folder, and then click the folder you want to open. If you want to return to a specific spot in the file hierarchy, you click that folder name in the Address bar. The Back and Forward buttons let you quickly move between folders.

Tip

Office adds the correct file extension when you save a file. Do not type one in the descriptive title, or you will create a duplicate (such as Meeting Agenda. docx.docx).

Windows XP Tip

The default storage location for Office files is the My Documents folder.

Saving and Using Files with Earlier Versions of Office | InSight

The default file types in Office 2007 are different from those used in earlier versions. This means that someone using Office 2003 or earlier cannot open files created in Office 2007. Files you want to share with earlier Office users must be saved in the earlier formats, which use the following extensions: .doc for Word, .xls for Excel, .mdb for Access, and .ppt for PowerPoint. To save a file in an earlier format, open the Save As dialog box, click the Save as type list arrow, and then click the appropriate 97-2003 format. A compatibility checker reports which Office 2007 features or elements are not supported by the earlier version of Office, and you can choose to remove them before saving. You can use Office 2007 to open and work with files created in earlier versions of Office. You can then save the file in its current format or update it to the Office 2007 format.

The lines of text you typed are not yet saved on disk. You'll do that now.

To save a file for the first time:

Windows XP Tip

To navigate to a location in the Save As dialog box, you use the Save in arrow.

1. Click the **Save** button 📄 on the Quick Access Toolbar. The Save As dialog box opens because you have not yet saved the file and need to specify a storage location and filename. The default location is set to the Documents folder, and the first few words of the first line appear in the File name box as a suggested title.

2. In the Navigation pane, click the link for the location that contains your Data Files, if necessary.

   Trouble? If you don't have the starting Data Files, you need to get them before you can proceed. Your instructor will either give you the Data Files or ask you to obtain them from a specified location (such as a network drive). In either case, make a backup copy of the Data Files before you start so that you will have the original files available in case you need to start over. If you have any questions about the Data Files, see your instructor or technical support person for assistance.

3. Double-click the **OFF** folder in the file list, and then double-click the **Tutorial** folder. This is the location where you want to save the document.

   Next, you'll enter a more descriptive title for the filename.

4. Type **Meeting Agenda** in the File name box. See Figure 17.

Figure 17 **Completed Save As dialog box**

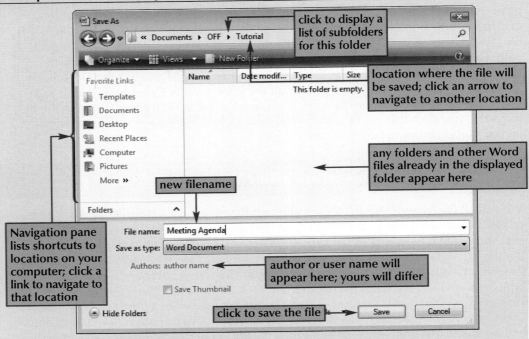

   Trouble? If the .docx file extension appears after the filename, your computer is configured to show file extensions. Continue with Step 5.

5. Click the **Save** button. The Save As dialog box closes, and the name of your file appears in the title bar.

The saved file includes everything in the document at the time you last saved it. Any new edits or additions you make to the document exist only in the computer's memory and are not saved in the file on the disk. As you work, remember to save frequently so that the file is updated to reflect the latest content of the document.

Because you already named the document and selected a storage location, the Save As dialog box doesn't open whenever you save the document again. If you want to save a copy of the file with a different filename or to a different location, you reopen the Save As dialog box by clicking the Office Button, and then clicking Save As. The previous version of the file remains on your disk as well.

You need to add your name to the agenda. Then, you'll save your changes.

To modify and save the Word document:

▶ 1. Type your name, and then press the **Enter** key. The text you typed appears on the next line.

▶ 2. Click the **Save** button 🔲 on the Quick Access Toolbar to save your changes.

Closing a File

Although you can keep multiple files open at one time, you should close any file you are no longer working on to conserve system resources as well as to ensure that you don't inadvertently make changes to the file. You can close a file by clicking the Office Button and then clicking the Close command. If that's the only file open for the program, the program window remains open and no file appears in the window. You can also close a file by clicking the Close button in the upper-right corner of the title bar or double-clicking the Office Button. If that's the only file open for the program, the program also closes.

As a standard practice, you should save your file before closing it. However, Office has an added safeguard: If you attempt to close a file without saving your changes, a dialog box opens, asking whether you want to save the file. Click the Yes button to save the changes to the file before closing the file and program. Click the No button to close the file and program without saving changes. Click the Cancel button to return to the program window without saving changes or closing the file and program. This feature helps to ensure that you always save the most current version of any file.

You'll add the date to the agenda. Then, you'll attempt to close it without saving.

To modify and close the Word document:

▶ 1. Type today's date, and then press the **Enter** key. The text you typed appears below your name in the document.

▶ 2. In the upper-left corner of the program window, click the **Office Button** . A menu opens with commands for creating new files, opening existing files, saving files, printing files, and closing files.

▶ 3. Click **Close**. A dialog box opens, asking whether you want to save the changes you made to the document.

▶ 4. Click the **Yes** button. The current version of the document is saved to the file, and then the document closes. Word is still running.

After you have a program open, you can create additional new files for the open program or you can open previously created and saved files.

Opening a File

When you want to open a blank document, workbook, presentation, or database, you create a new file. When you want to work on a previously created file, you must first open it. Opening a file transfers a copy of the file from the storage disk (either a hard disk or a portable disk) to the computer's memory and displays it on your screen. The file is then in your computer's memory and on the disk.

Reference Window | **Opening an Existing File or Creating a New File**

- Click the Office Button, and then click Open.
- In the Open dialog box, navigate to the storage location of the file you want to open.
- Click the filename of the file you want to open.
- Click the Open button.

or

- Click the Office Button, and then click a filename in the Recent Documents list.

or

- Click the Office Button, and then click New.
- In the New dialog box, click Blank Document, Blank Workbook, Blank Presentation, or Blank Database (depending on the program).
- Click the Create button.

Ean asks you to print the agenda. To do that, you'll reopen the file.

To open the existing Word document:

1. Click the **Office Button** , and then click **Open**. The Open dialog box, which works similarly to the Save As dialog box, opens.

2. Use the Navigation pane or the Address bar to navigate to the **OFF\Tutorial** folder included with your Data Files. This is the location where you saved the agenda document.

3. Click **Meeting Agenda** in the file list. See Figure 18.

Figure 18 **Open dialog box**

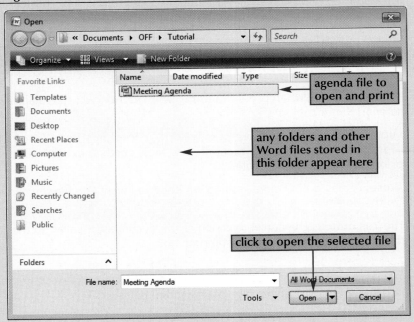

4. Click the **Open** button. The agenda file opens in the Word program window.

Next, you'll use Help to get information about printing files in Word.

Getting Help

If you don't know how to perform a task or want more information about a feature, you can turn to Office itself for information on how to use it. This information, referred to simply as **Help**, is like a huge encyclopedia available from your desktop. You can get Help in ScreenTips, from the Help window, and in Microsoft Office Online.

Viewing ScreenTips

ScreenTips are a fast and simple method you can use to get help about objects you see on the screen. A **ScreenTip** is a box with the button's name, its keyboard shortcut if it has one, a description of the command's function, and, in some cases, a link to more information. Just position the mouse pointer over a button or object to view its ScreenTip. If a link to more information appears in the ScreenTip, press the F1 key while the Screen-Tip is displayed to open the Help window with the appropriate topic displayed.

To view ScreenTips:

▶ **1.** Point to the **Microsoft Office Word Help** button 📷 . The ScreenTip shows the button's name, its keyboard shortcut, and a brief explanation of the button. See Figure 19.

ScreenTip for the Help button ◀ Figure 19

▶ **2.** Point to other buttons on the Ribbon to display their ScreenTips.

Using the Help Window

For more detailed information, you can use the **Help window** to access all the Help topics, templates, and training installed on your computer with Office and available on Microsoft Office Online. **Microsoft Office Online** is a Web site maintained by Microsoft that provides access to the latest information and additional Help resources. For example, you can access current Help topics, templates of predesigned files, and training for Office. To connect to Microsoft Office Online, you need Internet access on your computer. Otherwise, you see only those topics stored locally.

Reference Window | Getting Help

- Click the Microsoft Office Help button (the button name depends on the Office program).
- Type a keyword or phrase in the "Type words to search for" box, and then click the Search button.
- Click a Help topic in the search results list.
- Read the information in the Help window. For more information, click other topics or links.
- Click the Close button on the Help window title bar.

You open the Help window by clicking the Microsoft Office Help button located below the sizing buttons in every Office program. Each program has its own Help window from which you can find information about all the Office commands and features as well as step-by-step instructions for using them. You can search for information in the Help window using the "Type words to search for" box and the Table of Contents pane.

The "Type words to search for" box enables you to search the Help system using keywords or phrases. You type a specific word or phrase about a task you want to perform or a topic you need help with, and then click the Search button to search the Help system. A list of Help topics related to the keyword or phrase you entered appears in the Help window. If your computer is connected to the Internet, your search results come from Microsoft Office Online rather than only the Help topics stored locally on your computer. You can click a link to open a Help topic with step-by-step instructions that will guide you through a specific procedure and/or provide explanations of difficult concepts in clear, easy-to-understand language. For example, if you type "format cell" in the Excel Help window, a list of Help topics related to the words you typed appears in the Help window. You can navigate through the topics you've viewed using the buttons on the Help window toolbar. These buttons—including Back, Forward, Stop, Refresh, Home, and Print—are the same as those in the Microsoft Internet Explorer Web browser.

You'll use the "Type words to search for" box in the Help window to obtain more information about printing a document in Word.

To use the "Type words to search for" box:

► 1. Click the **Microsoft Office Word Help** button . The Word Help window opens.

► 2. Click the **Type words to search for** box, if necessary, and then type **print document**. You can set where you want to search.

► 3. Click the **Search button arrow**. The Search menu shows the online and local content available.

4. If your computer is connected to the Internet, click **All Word** in the Content from Office Online list. If your computer is not connected to the Internet, click **Word Help** in the Content from this computer list.

5. Click the **Search** button. The Help window displays a list of topics related to your keywords. See Figure 20.

Search results displaying Help topics ◀ Figure 20

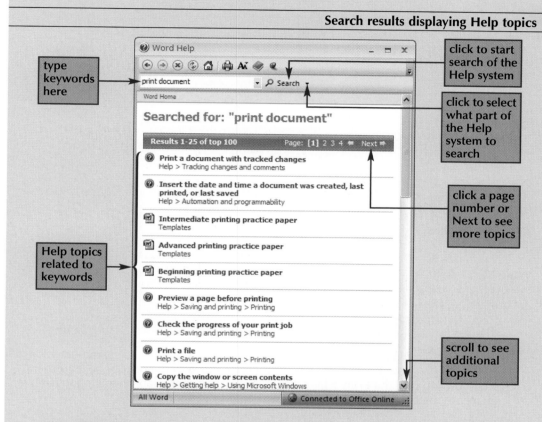

Trouble? If your search results list differs from the one shown in Figure 20, your computer is not connected to the Internet or Microsoft has updated the list of available Help topics since this book was published. Continue with Step 6.

6. Scroll through the list to review the Help topics.

7. Click **Print a file**. The Help topic is displayed in the Help window so you can learn more about how to print a document. See Figure 21.

Figure 21 **Print a file Help topic**

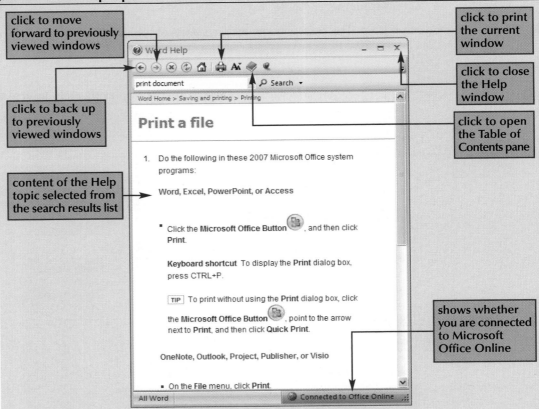

click to move forward to previously viewed windows

click to print the current window

click to back up to previously viewed windows

click to close the Help window

content of the Help topic selected from the search results list

click to open the Table of Contents pane

shows whether you are connected to Microsoft Office Online

Trouble? If you don't see the Print a file Help topic on page 1, its current location might be on another page. Click the Next link to move to the next page, and then scroll down to find the Print a file topic, repeating to search additional pages until you locate the topic.

8. Read the information.

Another way to find information in the Help system is to use the Table of Contents pane. The Show Table of Contents button on the Help window toolbar opens a pane that displays a list of the Help system content organized by subjects and topics, similar to a book's table of contents. You click main subject links to display related topic links. You click a topic link to display that Help topic in the Help window. You'll use the Table of Contents to find information about getting help in Office.

To use the Help window table of contents:

1. Click the **Show Table of Contents** button 🗐 on the Help window toolbar. The Table of Contents pane opens on the left side of the Help window.

2. Click **Getting help** in the Table of Contents pane, scrolling up if necessary. The Getting help "book" opens, listing the topics related to that subject.

3. Click the **Work with the Help window** topic, and then click the **Maximize** button 🗖 on the title bar. The Help topic is displayed in the maximized Help window, and you can read the text to learn more about the various ways to obtain help in Word. See Figure 22.

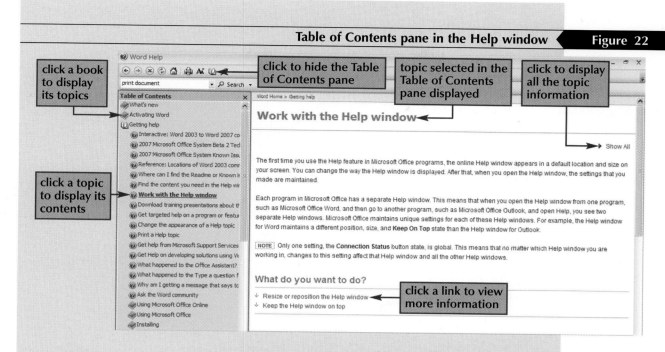

Table of Contents pane in the Help window | Figure 22

Trouble? If your search results list differs from the one shown in Figure 22, your computer is not connected to the Internet or Microsoft has updated the list of available Help topics since this book was published. Continue with Step 4.

4. Click **Using Microsoft Office Online** in the Table of Contents pane, click the **Get online Help, templates, training, and additional content** topic to display information about that topic, and then read the information.

5. Click the links within this topic and read the information.

6. Click the **Close** button ⊠ on the Help window title bar to close the window.

Printing a File

At times, you'll want a paper copy of your Office file. The first time you print during each session at the computer, you should use the Print command to open the Print dialog box so you can verify or adjust the printing settings. You can select a printer, the number of copies to print, the portion of the file to print, and so forth; the printing settings vary slightly from program to program. If you want to use the same default settings for subsequent print jobs, you can use the Quick Print button to print without opening the dialog box.

Printing a File | Reference Window

- Click the Office Button, and then click Print.
- Verify the print settings in the Print dialog box.
- Click the OK button.

or

- Click the Office Button, point to Print, and then click Quick Print.

Now that you know how to print, you'll print the agenda for Ean.

To print the Word document:

► **1.** Make sure your printer is turned on and contains paper.

► **2.** Click the **Office Button** 🔘, and then click **Print**. The Print dialog box opens. See Figure 23.

Figure 23 ► Print dialog box

Trouble? If a menu of Print commands opens, you clicked the Print button arrow on the two-part Print button. Click Print on the menu to open the Print dialog box.

► **3.** Verify that the correct printer appears in the Name box in the Printer group. If necessary, click the **Name** arrow, and then click the correct printer from the list of available printers.

► **4.** Verify that **1** appears in the Number of copies box.

► **5.** Click the **OK** button to print the document.

Trouble? If the document does not print, see your instructor or technical support person for help.

Exiting Programs

When you finish working with a program, you should exit it. As with many other aspects of Office, you can exit programs with a button or a command. You'll use both methods to exit Word and Excel. You can use the Exit command to exit a program and close an open file in one step. If you haven't saved the final version of the open file, a dialog box opens, asking whether you want to save your changes. Clicking the Yes button saves the open file, closes the file, and then exits the program.

To exit the Word and Excel programs:

► **1.** Click the **Close** button 🗙 on the Word title bar to exit Word. The Word document closes and the Word program exits. The Excel window is visible again.

> **Trouble?** If a dialog box opens, asking if you want to save the document, you might have inadvertently made a change to the document. Click the No button.
>
> ▶ **2.** Click the **Office Button** 🔘, and then click **Exit Excel**. A dialog box opens, asking whether you want to save the changes you made to the workbook. If you click the Yes button, the Save As dialog box opens and Excel exits after you finish saving the workbook. This time, you don't want to save the workbook.
>
> ▶ **3.** Click the **No** button. The workbook closes without saving a copy, and the Excel program exits.

Exiting programs after you are done using them keeps your Windows desktop uncluttered for the next person using the computer, frees up your system's resources, and prevents data from being lost accidentally.

Quick Check | Review

1. What Office program would be best to use to create a budget?
2. How do you start an Office program?
3. Explain the difference between Save and Save As.
4. How do you open an existing Office file?
5. What happens if you open a file, make edits, and then attempt to close the file or exit the program without saving the current version of the file?
6. What are two ways to get Help in Office?

Tutorial Summary | Review

You have learned how to use features common to all the programs included in Microsoft Office 2007, including starting and exiting programs; resizing windows; using the Ribbon, dialog boxes, shortcut menus, and the Mini toolbar; opening, closing, and printing files; and getting Help.

Key Terms

Access	Help window	Office Button
application settings	integration	Outlook
button	keyboard shortcut	PowerPoint
contextual tab	Live Preview	presentation
database	Microsoft Office 2007	Quick Access Toolbar
default	Microsoft Office Access 2007	Ribbon
dialog box	Microsoft Office Excel 2007	ScreenTip
Dialog Box Launcher	Microsoft Office Online	shortcut menu
document	Microsoft Office	status bar
Excel	Outlook 2007	tab
file extension	Microsoft Office	task pane
filename	PowerPoint 2007	Word
folder	Microsoft Office Word 2007	workbook
gallery	Mini toolbar	zoom
group	object	
Help	Office	

Practice	**Review Assignments**

Practice the skills you learned in the tutorial.

Data Files needed for the Review Assignments: Finances.xlsx, Letter.docx

You need to prepare for an upcoming meeting at Recycled Palette. You'll open and print documents for the presentation. Complete the following:

1. Start PowerPoint.
2. Use the Help window to search Office Online for the PowerPoint demo "Demo: Up to Speed with PowerPoint 2007." (*Hint:* Use "demo" as the keyword to search for, and make sure you search All PowerPoint in the Content from Office Online list. If you are not connected to the Internet, continue with Step 3.) Open the Demo topic, and then click the Play Demo link to view it. Close Internet Explorer and the Help window when you're done.
3. Start Excel.
4. Switch to the PowerPoint window using the taskbar, and then close the presentation but leave open the PowerPoint program. (*Hint:* Click the Office Button and then click Close.)
5. Open a new, blank PowerPoint presentation from the New Presentation dialog box.
6. Close the PowerPoint presentation and program using the Close button on the PowerPoint title bar; do not save changes if asked.
7. Open the **Finances** workbook located in the OFF\Review folder included with your Data Files.
8. Use the Save As command to save the workbook as **Recycled Palette Finances** in the OFF\Review folder.
9. Type your name, press the Enter key to insert your name at the top of the worksheet, and then save the workbook.
10. Print one copy of the worksheet using the Print button on the Office Button menu.
11. Exit Excel using the Office Button.
12. Start Word, and then open the **Letter** document located in the OFF\Review folder included with your Data Files.
13. Use the Save As command to save the document with the filename **Recycled Palette Letter** in the OFF\Review folder.
14. Press and hold the Ctrl key, press the End key, and then release both keys to move the insertion point to the end of the letter, and then type your name.
15. Use the Save button on the Quick Access Toolbar to save the change to the Recycled Palette Letter document.
16. Print one copy of the document, and then close the document.
17. Exit the Word program using the Close button on the title bar.

Assess | SAM Assessment and Training

If you have a SAM user profile, you may have access to hands-on instruction, practice, and assessment of the skills covered in this tutorial. Log in to your SAM account (**http://sam2007.course.com**) to launch any assigned training activities or exams that relate to the skills covered in this tutorial.

Review | Quick Check Answers

1. Excel
2. Click the Start button on the taskbar, click All Programs, click Microsoft Office, and then click the name of the program you want to open.
3. Save updates a file to reflect its latest contents using its current filename and location. Save As enables you to change the filename and storage location of a file.
4. Click the Office Button, and then click Open.
5. A dialog box opens asking whether you want to save the changes to the file.
6. Two of the following: ScreenTips, Help window, Microsoft Office Online

Ending Data Files

Meeting Agenda.docx

Recycled Palette Finances.xlsx
Recycled Palette Letter.docx

Reality Check

At home, school, or work, you probably complete many types of tasks, such as writing letters and balancing a checkbook, on a regular basis. You can use Microsoft Office to streamline many of these tasks.

Note: Please be sure *not* to include any personal information of a sensitive nature in the documents you create to be submitted to your instructor for this exercise. Later on, you can update the documents with such information for your own personal use.

1. Start Word, and open a new document, if necessary.
2. In the document, type a list of all the personal, work, and/or school tasks you do on a regular basis.
3. For each task, identify the type of Office file (document, workbook, presentation, or database) you would create to complete that task. For example, you would create a Word document to write a letter.
4. For each file, identify the Office program you would use to create that file, and explain why you would use that program. For example, Word is the best program to use to create a document for a letter.
5. Save the document with an appropriate filename in an appropriate folder location.
6. Use a Web browser to visit the Microsoft Web site at *www.microsoft.com* and research the different Office 2007 suites available. Determine which suite includes all the programs you need to complete the tasks on your list.
7. At the end of the task list you created in your Word document, type which Office suite you decided on and a brief explanation of why you chose that suite. Then save the document.
8. Double-click the Home tab on the Ribbon to minimize the Ribbon to show only the tab names and extend the workspace area. At the end of the Word document, type your opinion of whether minimizing the Ribbon is a helpful feature. When you're done, double-click the Home tab to display the full Ribbon.
9. Print the finished document, and then submit it to your instructor.

Objectives

Session 1.1
- Define the terms field, record, table, relational database, primary key, and foreign key
- Create a blank database
- Identify the components of the Microsoft Access window
- Create and save a table in Datasheet view
- Enter field names and records in a table datasheet
- Open a table using the Navigation Pane

Session 1.2
- Open an Access database
- Copy and paste records from another Access database
- Navigate a table datasheet
- Create and navigate a simple query
- Create and navigate a simple form
- Create, preview, navigate, and print a simple report
- Learn how to manage a database by compacting, backing up, and restoring a database

Creating a Database

Creating a Database to Contain Customer, Contract, and Invoice Data

Case | Belmont Landscapes

Soon after graduating with a degree in Landscape Architecture from nearby Michigan State University, Oren Belmont returned to his hometown of Holland, on the shores of Lake Michigan. There, Oren worked for a local firm that provided basic landscaping services to residential customers. After several years, Oren started his own landscape architecture firm, Belmont Landscapes, which specializes in landscape designs for residential and commercial customers and numerous public agencies.

Belmont Landscapes provides a wide range of services—from site analyses and feasibility studies, to drafting and administering construction documents—for projects of various scales. Oren and his staff depend on computers to help manage all aspects of the firm's operations, including financial and information management. Several months ago the company upgraded to Microsoft Windows and **Microsoft Office Access 2007** (or simply **Access**), a computer program used to enter, maintain, and retrieve related data in a format known as a database. Oren and his staff want to use Access to maintain such data as information about customers, contracts, and invoices. He asks for your help in creating the necessary Access database.

Starting Data Files

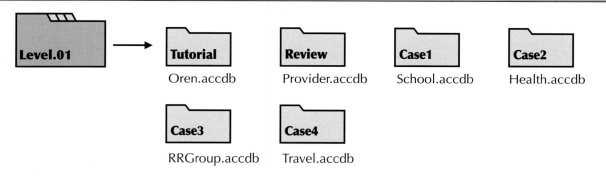

Level.01 → Tutorial — Oren.accdb

Review — Provider.accdb

Case1 — School.accdb

Case2 — Health.accdb

Case3 — RRGroup.accdb

Case4 — Travel.accdb

Session 1.1

Introduction to Database Concepts

Before you begin using Access to create the database for Oren, you need to understand a few key terms and concepts associated with databases.

Organizing Data

Data is a valuable resource to any business. At Belmont Landscapes, for example, important data includes customers' names and addresses and contract amounts and dates. Organizing, storing, maintaining, retrieving, and sorting this type of data are critical activities that enable a business to find and use information effectively. Before storing data on a computer, however, you must organize the data.

Your first step in organizing data is to identify the individual fields. A **field** is a single characteristic or attribute of a person, place, object, event, or idea. For example, some of the many fields that Belmont Landscapes tracks are customer ID, first name, last name, company name, address, phone number, contract amount, contract signing date, and contract type.

Next, you group related fields together into tables. A **table** is a collection of fields that describe a person, place, object, event, or idea. Figure 1-1 shows an example of a Customer table that contains four fields named Customer ID, First Name, Last Name, and Phone.

| Figure 1-1 | Data organization for a table of customers |

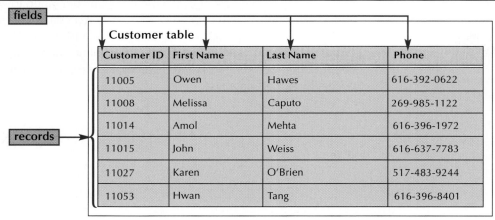

The specific value, or content, of a field is called the **field value**. In Figure 1-1, the first set of field values for Customer ID, First Name, Last Name, and Phone are, respectively: 11005; Owen; Hawes; and 616-392-0622. This set of field values is called a **record**. In the Customer table, the data for each customer is stored as a separate record. Figure 1-1 shows six records; each row of field values is a record.

Databases and Relationships

A collection of related tables is called a **database**, or a **relational database**. In this tutorial, you will create the database for Belmont Landscapes and a table named Contract to store data about contracts. In Tutorial 2, you will create two more tables, named Customer and Invoice, to store related information about customers and their invoices.

As Oren and his staff use the database that you will create, they will need to access information about customers and their contracts. To obtain this information, you must have a way to connect records in the Customer table to records in the Contract table. You connect the records in the separate tables through a **common field** that appears in both tables.

In the sample database shown in Figure 1-2, each record in the Customer table has a field named Customer ID, which is also a field in the Contract table. For example, Owen Hawes is the first customer in the Customer table and has a Customer ID field value of 11005. This same Customer ID field value, 11005, appears in three records in the Contract table. Therefore, Owen Hawes is the customer with these three contracts.

Database relationship between tables for customers and contracts Figure 1-2

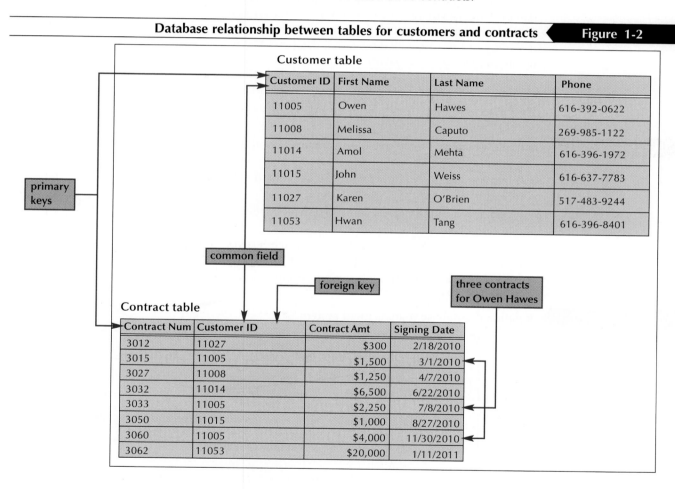

Each Customer ID value in the Customer table must be unique so that you can distinguish one customer from another. These unique Customer ID values also identify each customer's specific contracts in the Contract table. The Customer ID field is referred to as the primary key of the Customer table. A **primary key** is a field, or a collection of fields, whose values uniquely identify each record in a table. No two records can contain the same value for the primary key field. In the Contract table, the Contract Num field is the primary key because Belmont Landscapes assigns each contract a unique contract number.

When you include the primary key from one table as a field in a second table to form a relationship between the two tables, it is called a **foreign key** in the second table, as shown in Figure 1-2. For example, Customer ID is the primary key in the Customer table and a foreign key in the Contract table. Although the primary key Customer ID contains unique values in the Customer table, the same field as a foreign key in the Contract table does not necessarily contain unique values. The Customer ID value 11005, for example, appears three times in the Contract table because Owen Hawes has three contracts. Each foreign key value, however, must match one of the field values for the primary key in the other table. In the example shown in Figure 1-2, each Customer ID value in the Contract table must match a Customer ID value in the Customer table. The two tables are related, enabling users to connect the facts about customers with the facts about their contracts.

Relational Database Management Systems

To manage its databases, a company purchases a database management system. A **database management system (DBMS)** is a software program that lets you create databases and then manipulate data in them. Most of today's database management systems, including Access, are called relational database management systems. In a **relational database management system**, data is organized as a collection of tables. As stated earlier, a relationship between two tables in a relational DBMS is formed through a common field.

A relational DBMS controls the storage of databases on disk and facilitates the creation, manipulation, and reporting of data, as illustrated in Figure 1-3. Specifically, a relational DBMS provides the following functions:

- It allows you to create database structures containing fields, tables, and table relationships.
- It lets you easily add new records, change field values in existing records, and delete records.
- It contains a built-in query language, which lets you obtain immediate answers to the questions you ask about your data.
- It contains a built-in report generator, which lets you produce professional-looking, formatted reports from your data.
- It protects databases through security, control, and recovery facilities.

Figure 1-3	Relational database management system

A company such as Belmont Landscapes benefits from a relational DBMS because it allows users working in different groups to share the same data. More than one user can enter data into a database, and more than one user can retrieve and analyze data that other users entered. For example, the database for Belmont Landscapes will contain only one copy of the Contract table, and all employees will use it to meet their specific requests for contract information.

Finally, unlike other software programs, such as spreadsheet programs, a DBMS can handle massive amounts of data and can be used to create relationships among multiple tables. Each Access database, for example, can be up to two gigabytes in size, can contain up to 32,768 objects (tables, queries, forms, and so on), and can have up to 255 people using the database at the same time. For instructional purposes, the databases you will create and work with throughout this text contain a relatively small number of records compared to most databases you would encounter outside the classroom, which likely contain tables with very large numbers of records.

Creating a Database

Now that you've learned some database terms and concepts, you're ready to start Access and create the Belmont database for Oren.

To start Access:

▶ 1. Click the **Start** button 🅱 on the taskbar, click **All Programs**, click **Microsoft Office**, and then click **Microsoft Office Access 2007**. The Getting Started with Microsoft Office Access page opens. See Figure 1-4.

   Trouble? If you don't see the Microsoft Office Access 2007 option on the Microsoft Office submenu, look for it on a different submenu or as an option on the All Programs menu. If you still cannot find the Microsoft Office Access 2007 option, ask your instructor or technical support person for help.

Getting Started with Microsoft Office Access page ◀ Figure 1-4

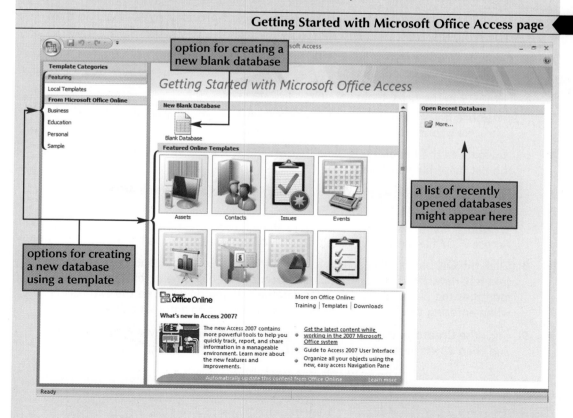

Trouble? If the Microsoft Access program window on your computer is not maximized, click the Maximize button 🔲 on the program window title bar.

The Getting Started with Microsoft Office Access page contains options for creating a new database, opening an existing database, or viewing content from Microsoft Office Online. You can create a new database that does not contain any data or objects by using the Blank Database option. If the database you need to create contains objects that match the ones found in common databases, such as ones that store data about contacts or events, you can use a template that Access installs (listed in the "Template Categories" section on the left side of the page) or download a template from Microsoft Office Online (listed in the "Featured Online Templates" section in the middle of the page). A **template** is a predesigned database that includes professionally designed tables, reports, and other database objects that can make it quick and easy for you to create a database.

In this case, the templates provided do not match Oren's needs for the Belmont Land-scapes database, so you need to create a new database from scratch. To do this, you will use the Blank Database option on the Getting Started page.

To create the new Belmont database:

▶ **1.** Make sure you have created your copy of the Access Data Files, and that your computer can access them.

   Trouble? If you don't have the starting Data Files, you need to get them before you can proceed. Your instructor will either give you the Data Files or ask you to obtain them from a specified location (such as a network drive). In either case, make a backup copy of the Data Files before you start so that you will have the original files available in case you need to start over. If you have any questions about the Data Files, see your instructor or technical support person for assistance.

▶ **2.** Click the **Blank Database** option in the center of the page. The right section of the page changes to display options for creating a blank database.

▶ **3.** In the File Name text box, select the default name provided by Access, and then type **Belmont**. Next you need to specify the location for the file.

▶ **4.** Click the **Browse** button 📁 to the right of the File Name text box. The File New Database dialog box opens.

▶ **5.** Navigate to the drive that contains your Data Files.

   Trouble? If you do not know where your Data Files are located, consult with your instructor about where to save your Data Files.

▶ **6.** Navigate to the **Level.01\Tutorial** folder. This is the folder in which you will store the database file you create.

▶ **7.** Make sure the "Save as type" text box displays "Microsoft Office Access 2007 Databases."

   Trouble? If your computer is set up to show filename extensions, you will see the Access 2007 filename extension ".accdb" in this text box as well.

▶ **8.** Click the **OK** button. You return to the Getting Started page, and the File Name text box now shows the name Belmont.accdb. The filename extension ".accdb" identifies the file as an Access 2007 database. If you do not type the extension when entering the filename, Access adds the extension automatically.

▶ **9.** Click the **Create** button. Access creates the new database, saves it to your disk, and then opens an empty table named Table1. See Figure 1-5.

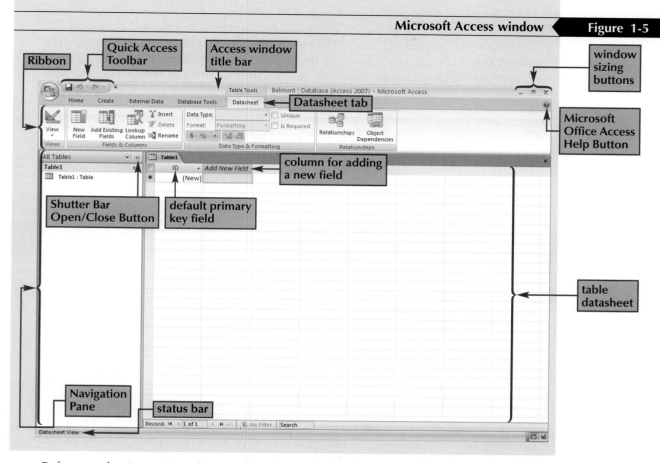

Microsoft Access window — Figure 1-5

Before you begin entering data, you need to become familiar with the components of the Microsoft Access window.

Exploring the Microsoft Access Window

The **Microsoft Access window** (or simply the **Access window**) is the program window that appears when you create a new database or open an existing database. Most of the Access window components—including the title bar, window sizing buttons, Help button, Quick Access Toolbar, Ribbon, tabs, and status bar—are the same as the components in other Microsoft Office 2007 programs.

The new blank table that Access created is displayed in **Datasheet view**, which shows a table's contents as a **datasheet** in rows and columns, similar to a table that you create in Word or an Excel spreadsheet. Each row will be a separate record in the table, and each column will contain the field values for one field in the table. Because you are in Datasheet view, the Datasheet tab is the active tab on the Ribbon. The status bar also indicates the current view.

The **Navigation Pane** is the area on the left side of the window that lists all the objects (tables, reports, and so on) in the database, and it is the main control center for opening and working with database objects. Currently, the Navigation Pane lists only the new table you are in the process of creating, which is named "Table1" by default. You will give the table a more meaningful name as part of creating it. Notice the Shutter Bar Open/Close Button at the top-right of the Navigation Pane (see Figure 1-5). You can use this button to close and open the pane. Depending on the size of your database table, you might want to close the Navigation Pane so that you have more room on the screen to view the table's contents.

When you open tables and other objects in a database, their names appear on tabbed documents. Currently, only the Table1 table is open. Notice that the table contains two columns (fields) labeled "ID" and "Add New Field." By default, Access creates the **ID column** as the primary key field for all new tables. You can choose to keep this field as the primary key or specify another field for this purpose. The **Add New Field column** is the column in which you create the first new field for your table.

Creating a Table in Datasheet View

Tables contain all the data in a database and are the fundamental objects for your work in Access. There are different ways to create a table in Access, including entering the fields and records for a table directly in Datasheet view.

Reference Window	**Creating a Table in Datasheet View**

- Click the Create tab on the Ribbon.
- In the Tables group, click the Table button.
- Accept the default ID primary key field with the AutoNumber data type, or rename the field and change its data type, if necessary.
- Double-click the Add New Field column heading, and then type the name for the field you are adding to the table.
- Press the Tab key or the Enter key.
- Add all the fields to your table by typing the field names in the column headings and pressing the Tab key or the Enter key to move to the next column.
- In the first row below the field names, enter the value for each field in the first record, pressing the Tab key or the Enter key to move from field to field.
- After entering the value for the last field in the first record, press the Tab key or the Enter key to move to the next row, and then enter the values for the next record. Continue this process until you have entered all the records for the table.
- Click the Save button on the Quick Access Toolbar, enter a name for the table, and then click the OK button.

For Belmont Landscapes, Oren needs to track information about the company's contracts with its customers. He asks you to create the Contract table according to the plan shown in Figure 1-6.

Figure 1-6	Plan for the Contract table

Field	Purpose
Contract Num	Unique number assigned to each contract; will serve as the table's primary key
Customer ID	Unique number assigned to each customer; common field that will be a foreign key to connect to the Customer table
Contract Amt	Dollar amount for the full contract
Signing Date	Date on which the customer signed the contract
Contract Type	Brief description of the contract

As shown in Oren's plan, he wants to store data about contracts in five fields, including fields to contain the amount of each contract, when it was signed, and the type of contract. These are the most important aspects of a contract and, therefore, must be tracked. Also, notice that the Contract Num field will be the primary key for the table; each contract at Belmont Landscapes has a unique contract number, so this field is the logical choice for the primary key. Finally, the Customer ID field is needed in the Contract table as a foreign key to tie the information about contracts to customers. The data about customers and their invoices will be stored in separate tables, which you will create in Tutorial 2.

Notice the name of each field in Figure 1-6. You need to name each field, table, and other object in an Access database.

Guidelines for Naming Fields | InSight

Keep the following guidelines in mind when you name fields:

- A field name can consist of up to 64 characters, including letters, numbers, spaces, and special characters, except for a period (.), exclamation mark (!), accent grave (`), and square brackets ([ ]).
- A field name cannot begin with a space.
- Capitalize the first letter of each word in the field name so it is clear which words are part of the name.
- Use concise field names that are easy to remember and reference, and that won't take up a lot of space in the table datasheet.
- Use standard abbreviations, such as Num for Number, Amt for Amount, and Qty for Quantity.
- Give fields descriptive names so that you can easily identify them when you view or edit records.
- Different DBMSs and some organizations have specific rules for naming fields. For example, many experienced database users do not include spaces in field names for ease of use when working with fields and other objects to perform more complex tasks, such as programming.

Renaming the Default Primary Key Field

As noted earlier, Access provides the ID field as a default primary key for a new table you create in Datasheet view. Recall that a primary key is a field, or a collection of fields, whose values uniquely identify each record in a table. However, according to Oren's plan, the Contract Num field should be the primary key for the Contract table. You'll begin by renaming the default ID field to create the Contract Num field.

To rename the ID field to the Contract Num field:

▶ **1.** Right-click the **ID** column heading to display the shortcut menu, and then click **Rename Column**. The column heading ID is selected, so that whatever text you type next will replace it.

▶ **2.** Type **Contract Num** and then press the **Enter** key. The column heading changes to Contract Num and the insertion point moves to the row below the heading. See Figure 1-7.

Trouble? Your instructor might ask you to omit spaces in field names as you create the tables in this book so your table designs will conform to standard field naming conventions. If so, your field names will not match the ones shown in the figures exactly, but this discrepancy will not cause problems.

Figure 1-7 | ID field renamed to Contract Num

Trouble? If you make a mistake when typing the field name, use the Backspace key to delete characters to the left of the insertion point or the Delete key to delete characters to the right of the insertion point. Then type the correct text. To correct a field name by replacing it entirely, press the Esc key, and then type the correct text.

Trouble? The entire field name "Contract Num" might not be visible on your screen. You'll learn how to resize columns to display the full field names later in this tutorial.

You have renamed the default primary key field, ID, to Contract Num. However, the Contract Num field still maintains the characteristics of the ID field, including its data type. Your next task is to change the data type of this field.

Changing the Data Type of the Default Primary Key Field

Notice the Data Type & Formatting group on the Datasheet tab. One of the options available in this group is the Data Type option (see Figure 1-7). Each field in an Access table must be assigned a data type. The **data type** determines what field values you can enter for the field. In this case, the AutoNumber data type is displayed. Access assigns the AutoNumber data type to the default ID primary key field because the **AutoNumber** data type automatically inserts a unique number in this field for every record. Therefore, it can serve as the primary key for any table you create.

Contract numbers at Belmont Landscapes are specific, four-digit numbers, so the AutoNumber data type is not appropriate for the Contract Num field, which is the new primary key field in the table you are creating. A better choice is the **Text** data type, which allows field values containing letters, digits, and other characters, and which is appropriate for identifying numbers, such as contract numbers, that are never used in calculations. So, Oren asks you to change the data type for the Contract Num field from AutoNumber to Text.

To change the data type for the Contract Num field:

▶ **1.** Make sure that the Contract Num column is selected (the column heading should have an orange background).

Trouble? If the background color of the Contract Num column heading is not orange, click the Contract Num column to select it.

▶ **2.** In the Data Type & Formatting group on the Datasheet tab, click the **Data Type arrow**, and then click **Text**. The Contract Num field is now a Text field. See Figure 1-8.

Text data type assigned to the Contract Num field ◄ **Figure 1-8**

Note the Unique check box in the Data Type & Formatting group. This check box is selected because the Contract Num field assumed the characteristics of the default primary key field, ID, including the fact that each value in the field must be unique. No two records in the Contract table will be allowed to have the same value in the Contract Num field.

With the Contract Num field created and established as the primary key, you can now enter the field names for the rest of the fields in the Contract table. (In Tutorial 2, you'll learn more about the different data types in Access and how to work with them.)

Entering Field Names

When you create a table in Datasheet view, you type the field names as the column headings, and enter the field values for each record in a row. Oren requests that you enter eight records in the Contract table, as shown in Figure 1-9.

Contract table records ◄ **Figure 1-9**

Contract Num	Customer ID	Contract Amt	Signing Date	Contract Type
3011	11001	$4,000	2/9/2010	Residential landscape plan
3026	11038	$165,000	3/11/2010	Landscape plans for large-scale housing development
3012	11027	$300	2/18/2010	Consultation for backyard, residential
3015	11005	$1,500	3/1/2010	Schematic plan for backyard, residential
3022	11043	$22,000	4/14/2010	Landscape design for two entrances
3017	11012	$2,250	3/1/2010	Peer plan review for town
3023	11070	$39,000	3/22/2010	Renovation of large multifamily housing open space
3021	11040	$28,000	5/3/2010	Landscape plans for multifamily housing site

To enter the rest of the field names for the Contract table:

1. Double-click the column heading **Add New Field**. The insertion point replaces the text "Add New Field" in the column heading and is ready for you to type the field name for the second field in the table.

2. Type **Customer ID**. Notice that the field name is displayed in italics while you type, signifying this is a new field name you are entering. See Figure 1-10.

Figure 1-10 | Customer ID field name entered in column heading

3. Press the **Tab** key. The insertion point moves to the next column and is ready for you to enter the next field name.

4. Type **Contract Amt** and then press the **Tab** key. Like the Contract Num field name, the Contract Amt field name might not be completely visible. You will resize all the columns to fully display the field names after you finish entering them.

5. Type **Signing Date**, press the **Tab** key, type **Contract Type**, and then press the **Tab** key. The datasheet now contains the five fields for the Contract table.

Several of the field names are not completely visible, so you need to resize the datasheet columns.

6. Place the pointer on the vertical line between the Contract Num and Customer ID field names until the pointer changes to a ↔ shape.

7. Double-click the pointer. The Contract Num column is resized and now displays the full field name.

Trouble? If you click the arrow immediately to the right of the Contract Num column heading by mistake, a menu will open. Simply click the arrow again to close the menu, and then repeat Steps 6 and 7.

8. Double-click the ↔ pointer on the vertical line to the right of the Customer ID, Contract Amt, Signing Date, and Contract Type column headings to resize the columns in the datasheet. Your datasheet should now look like the one shown in Figure 1-11.

Figure 1-11 | Table with field names entered

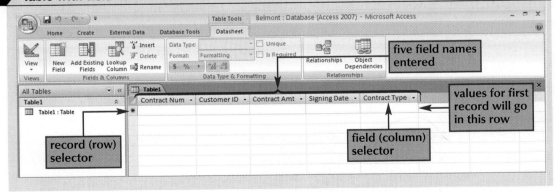

As noted earlier, Datasheet view shows a table's contents in rows (records) and columns (fields). Each column is headed by a field name inside a field selector, and each row has a record selector to its left (see Figure 1-11). Clicking a **field selector** or a **record selector** selects that entire column or row (respectively), which you then can manipulate. A field selector is also called a **column selector**, and a record selector is also called a **row selector**.

With the field names in place, you can now enter the records for the Contract table (see Figure 1-9).

Entering Records

To enter records in a table datasheet, you type the field values below the column headings for the fields. As shown in Figure 1-11, the first record you enter will go in the first row below the field names.

To enter the first record for the Contract table:

▶ 1. Click in the first row for the Contract Num field, type **3011** (the Contract Num field value for the first record), and then press the **Tab** key. Access adds the field value and moves the insertion point to the right, in the Customer ID column. See Figure 1-12.

First field value entered ◀ **Figure 1-12**

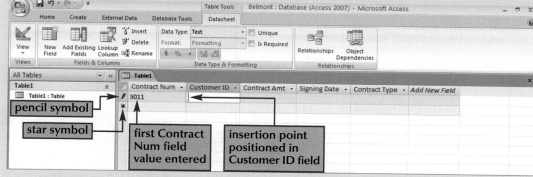

Trouble? If you make a mistake when typing a value, use the Backspace key to delete characters to the left of the insertion point or the Delete key to delete characters to the right of the insertion point. Then type the correct value. To correct a value by replacing it entirely, press the Esc key, and then type the correct value.

Notice the pencil symbol that appears in the row selector for the new record. The **pencil symbol** indicates that the record is being edited. Also notice the star symbol that appears in the row selector for the second row. The **star symbol** identifies the second row as the next row available for a new record.

▶ 2. Type **11001** (the Customer ID field value for the first record), and then press the **Tab** key. Access enters the field value and moves the insertion point to the Contract Amt column.

▶ 3. Type **$4,000** (the Contract Amt field value for the first record), and then press the **Tab** key. Notice that Access formats the field value with two decimal places, displaying it as "$4,000.00" even though you did not enter the value this way. You'll learn more about formatting field values later in this text.

Trouble? If Access does not change the value $4,000 to $4,000.00 when you press the Tab key and go to the next field, click the Contract Amt field value, click the Data Type arrow in the Data Type & Formatting group, and then click Currency in the list. Press the Tab key and continue with Step 4.

▶ 4. Type **2/9/2010** (the Signing Date field value for the first record), and then press the **Tab** key.

Trouble? If your date value is left-aligned in the column after you press the Tab key and go to the next field, instead of right-aligned, click the Signing Date field value, click the Data Type arrow in the Data Type & Formatting group, and then click Date/Time in the list. Press the Tab key and continue with Step 5.

▶ 5. Type **Residential landscape plan** (the Contract Type field value for the first record), and then press the **Tab** key. The first record is entered into the table, and the insertion point is positioned in the Contract Num field for the second record. The table is now ready for you to enter the second record. See Figure 1-13.

Figure 1-13 ▸ **Datasheet with first record entered**

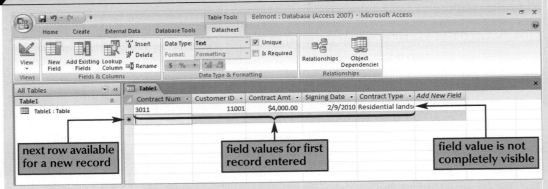

Trouble? Depending on your Windows date setting, your Signing Date field values might be displayed in a different format. This difference will not cause any problems.

Note that the Contract Type field value is not completely displayed. Again, you'll resize the columns, as necessary, after you enter all the data.

InSight | **Understanding How Access Interprets Values Entered**

When you create a table by entering field names and records directly into the table in Datasheet view, Access automatically assigns each field a data type based on the field values you enter. Access also formats the field values accordingly. For example, when you entered the value "$4,000" for the first record in the Contract Amt field, Access interpreted the value as a currency value because you typed a dollar sign and comma in the value. Likewise, when you entered the value "2/9/2010" in the Signing Date field, Access interpreted the value as a date value. After you've entered the first record in this way, Access will continue to format the field values for subsequent records, making data entry easier for you. So, as you continue to enter Contract Amt field values, you don't have to type the dollar sign or comma every time; Access will insert them automatically for you because it "knows" that the Contract Amt field contains currency values. Similarly, as you continue to enter Signing Date field values, you don't have to type the complete year "2010" but can instead type only the final two digits, "10," and Access will automatically insert the full four digits for each year.

As you enter field values in a datasheet, you should verify that Access is assigning them the data type you plan to use. If Access does not correctly interpret the field values you enter, you can easily assign the correct data type using the Data Type option in the Data Type & Formatting group on the Datasheet tab.

Now you can enter the remaining seven records in the Contract table.

To enter the remaining records in the Contract table:

Tip

You can also press the Enter key instead of the Tab key to move from one field to another, and to the next row.

1. Referring to Figure 1-9, enter the values for records 2 through 8, pressing the **Tab** key to move from field to field and to the next row for a new record. Keep in mind that you do not have to type the dollar sign or comma in the Contract Amt values, because Access will add them automatically; also, you can type just the final two digits of the year in the Signing Date values, and Access will display the full four digits in each year value.

Trouble? If you enter a value in the wrong field by mistake, such as entering a Contract Type field value in the Contract Amt field, a menu will open with options for addressing the problem. If this happens, choose the "Enter new value" option on the menu. You'll return to the field with the incorrect value highlighted, which you can then replace by typing the correct value.

To see more of the table datasheet and the full field values, you'll close the Navigation Pane and resize the Contract Type column.

▸ **2.** Click the **Shutter Bar Open/Close Button** [«] at the top of the Navigation Pane. The Navigation Pane closes, and the window displays the complete table datasheet.

▸ **3.** Place the pointer on the vertical line to the right of the Contract Type field name until the pointer changes to a ↔ shape, and then double-click the pointer. All the Contract Type field values are now fully displayed. See Figure 1-14.

Datasheet with eight records entered | **Figure 1-14**

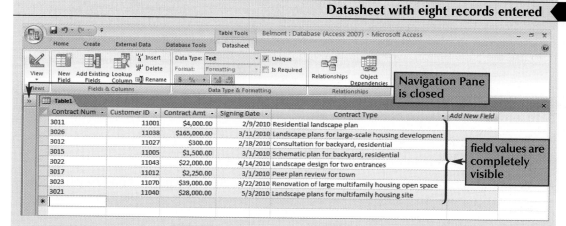

Trouble? If any of the field values on your screen do not match those shown in the figure, you can correct a field value by clicking to position the insertion point in the value, and then using the Backspace key or Delete key to delete incorrect text. Then type the correct text and press the Enter key.

Saving a Table

After you add fields and records to a table, you need to save the table's design. The records you enter are immediately stored in the database as soon as you enter them; however, the table's design—the field names and characteristics of the fields themselves—are not saved until you save the table. When you save a new table for the first time, you should give it a name that best identifies the information it contains. Like a field name, a table name can be up to 64 characters long, including spaces.

Saving a Table | Reference Window

- Click the Save button on the Quick Access Toolbar. The Save As dialog box opens.
- In the Table Name text box, type the name for the table.
- Click the OK button.

Now you need to save the table and give it the name "Contract."

To save and name the Contract table:

▶ **1.** Click the **Save** button 🖫 on the Quick Access Toolbar. The Save As dialog box opens.

▶ **2.** With the default name Table1 selected in the Table Name text box, type **Contract**, and then click the **OK** button. The tab for the table now displays the name "Contract," and the Contract table design is saved in the Belmont database.

Notice that after you saved and named the Contract table, Access reordered the records in the table so that they appear in order by the values in the Contract Num field, because it is the primary key. If you compare your screen to Figure 1-9, which shows the records in the order you entered them, you'll see that the current screen shows the records in order by the Contract Num field values.

Oren asks you to add two more records to the Contract table. When you add a record to an existing table, you must enter the new record in the next row available for a new record; you cannot insert a row between existing records for the new record. In a table with just a few records, such as the Contract table, the next available row is visible on the screen. However, in a table with hundreds of records, you would need to scroll the datasheet to see the next row available. The easiest way to add a new record to a table is to use the New button, which scrolls the datasheet to the next row available so you can enter the new record.

To enter additional records in the Contract table:

▶ **1.** Click in the first record's Contract Num field value (3011) to make it the current record.

▶ **2.** Click the **Home** tab on the Ribbon.

▶ **3.** In the Records group, click the **New** button. The insertion point is positioned in the next row available for a new record, which in this case is row 9. See Figure 1-15.

Figure 1-15	Entering a new record

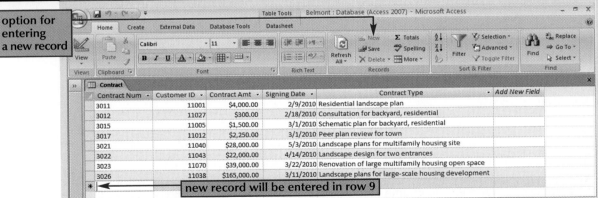

▶ **4.** With the insertion point in the Contract Num field for the new record, type **3020**, and then press the **Tab** key.

▶ **5.** Complete the entry of this record by entering each value shown below, pressing the Tab key to move from field to field:

Customer ID = **11055**
Contract Amt = **6500**
Signing Date = **2/19/10**
Contract Type = **Landscape design for restaurant**

6. Enter the values for the next new record, as follows:

Contract Num = **3025**
Customer ID = **11083**
Contract Amt = **15500**
Signing Date = **3/25/10**
Contract Type = **Landscape renovation for plaza**

Your datasheet should now look like the one shown in Figure 1-16.

Datasheet with additional records entered ◀ Figure 1-16

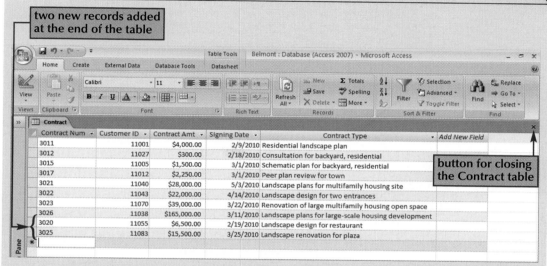

The new records you added appear at the end of the table, and are not in the correct primary key order. For example, Contract Num 3020 should be the fifth record in the table, placed between Contract Num 3017 and Contract Num 3021. When you add records to a table datasheet, they appear at the end of the table. The records are not displayed in primary key order until you close and reopen the table, or switch between views.

7. Click the **Close 'Contract'** button [X] on the table window bar (see Figure 1-16 for the location of this button). The table closes, and the main portion of the Access window is now blank because no database object is currently open.

Opening a Table

Any table you create and save is listed in the Navigation Pane. You open a table, or any Access object (query, form, report), by simply double-clicking the object name in the Navigation Pane. Next, you'll open the Contract table so you can see the order of all the records you've entered.

To open the Contract table:

1. On the Navigation Pane, click the **Shutter Bar Open/Close Button** [»] to open the pane. Note that the Contract table is listed.

2. Double-click **Contract : Table** to open the table in Datasheet view. See Figure 1-17.

Figure 1-17 | Table with 10 records entered and displayed in primary key order

Tip

Each record contains a unique Contract Num value because this field is the primary key. Other fields, however, can contain the same value in multiple records; for example, note the two values of 3/1/2010 in the Signing Date field.

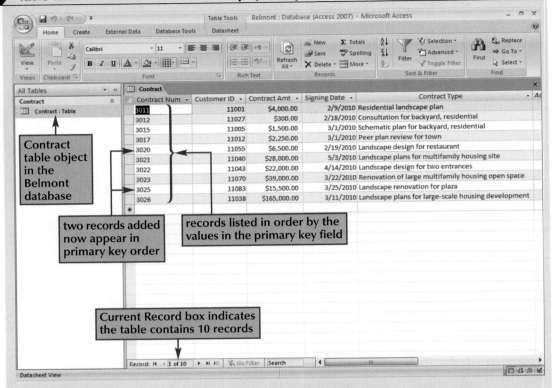

The two records you added, with Contract Num field values of 3020 and 3025, now appear in the correct primary key order. The table now contains a total of 10 records, as indicated by the Current Record box at the bottom of the datasheet. The **Current Record box** displays the number of the current record as well as the total number of records in the table.

Tip

To close an open database without exiting the Access program, click the Office Button, and then click Close Database.

3. If you are not continuing on to Session 1.2, click the **Close** button [X] on the program window title bar. Access closes the Contract table and the Belmont database, and then the Access program closes.

Saving a Database | InSight

Notice the Save button on the Quick Access Toolbar. Unlike the Save buttons in other Office programs, this Save button does not save the active document (database) to your disk. Instead, you use the Save button to save the design of an Access object, such as a table (as you saw earlier), or to save datasheet format changes, such as resizing columns. Access does not have a button or option you can use to save the active database. Similarly, you cannot use the Save As option on the Office menu to save the active database file with a new name, as you can with other Office programs.

Access saves changes to the active database to your disk automatically when you change or add a record or close the database. If your database is stored on a removable medium, such as a USB drive, you should never remove the drive while the database file is open. If you do, Access will encounter problems when it tries to save the database, which might damage the database.

Now that you've become familiar with database concepts and Access, and created the Belmont database and the Contract table, Oren wants you to add more records to the table and work with the data stored in it to create database objects including a query, form, and report. You will complete these tasks in Session 1.2.

Session 1.1 Quick Check | Review

1. A(n) _____ is a single characteristic of a person, place, object, event, or idea.
2. You connect the records in two separate tables through a(n) _____ that appears in both tables.
3. The _____ , whose values uniquely identify each record in a table, is called a(n) _____ when it is placed in a second table to form a relationship between the two tables.
4. The _____ is the area of the Access window that lists all the objects in a database, and it is the main control center for opening and working with database objects.
5. Which field does Access create, by default, as the primary key field for all new datasheets?
6. What does a pencil symbol at the beginning of a record represent? A star symbol?
7. Explain how the saving process in Access is different from saving in other Office programs.

Session 1.2

Copying Records from Another Access Database

When you created the Contract table, you entered records directly into the table datasheet. There are many other ways to enter records in a table, including copying and pasting records from a table in the same database or in a different database. To use this method, however, the tables must have the same structure—that is, the tables must contain the same fields, with the same design and characteristics, in the same order.

Oren has already created a table named Agreement that contains additional records with contract data. The Agreement table is contained in a database named "Oren" located in the Level.01\Tutorial folder included with your Data Files. The Agreement table has the same table structure as the Contract table you created. Your next task is to copy the records from the Agreement table and paste them into your Contract table. To do so, you need to open the Oren database.

| Reference Window | **Opening a Database** |

- Start Access and display the Getting Started with Microsoft Office Access page.
- Click the More option to display the Open dialog box.
- Navigate to the database file you want to open, and then click the file.
- Click the Open button.

To copy the records from the Agreement table:

▶ 1. If you took a break after the previous session, make sure that the Belmont database is open, and the Contract table is open in Datasheet view.

▶ 2. In the Navigation Pane, click the **Shutter Bar Open/Close Button** « to close the pane (if necessary) and display more of the table datasheet.

  To open a second database, you need to start Access again.

▶ 3. Click the **Start** button 🟢 on the taskbar, click **All Programs**, click **Microsoft Office**, and then click **Microsoft Office Access 2007**. The Getting Started with Microsoft Office Access page opens.

  To open an existing database, you use the More option in the Open Recent Database section on the right side of the page.

▶ 4. Click **More** to display the Open dialog box.

▶ 5. Navigate to the drive that contains your Data Files.

▶ 6. Navigate to the **Level.01\Tutorial** folder, click the database file named **Oren**, and then click the **Open** button. The Oren database opens in a second Access window. Note that the database contains only one object, the Agreement table.

  Trouble? A Security Warning might appear below the Ribbon; this warning cautions you about opening databases that could contain content that might harm your computer. Because the Oren database does not contain objects that could be harmful, you can open it safely. Click the Options button next to the Security Warning. In the dialog box that opens, click the "Enable this content" option button, and then click the OK button.

▶ 7. In the Navigation Pane, double-click **Agreement : Table** to open the Agreement table in Datasheet view. The table contains 55 records and the same five fields, with the same characteristics, as the fields in the Contract table. See Figure 1-18.

Agreement table in the Oren database ◀ **Figure 1-18**

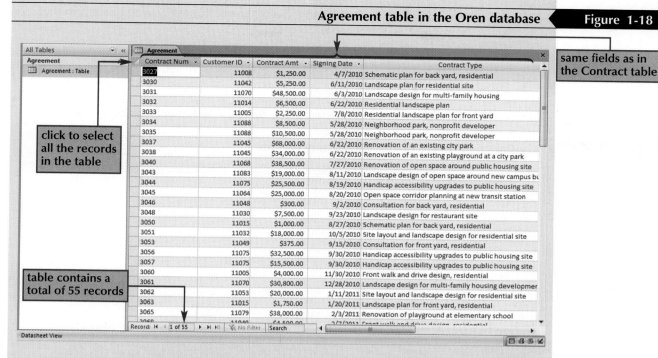

same fields as in the Contract table

click to select all the records in the table

table contains a total of 55 records

Oren wants you to copy all the records in the Agreement table. You can select all the records by clicking the **datasheet selector**, which is the box to the left of the first field name in the table datasheet (see Figure 1-18).

▶ **8.** Click the datasheet selector to the left of the Contract Num field. Access selects all the records in the table.

▶ **9.** In the Clipboard group on the Home tab, click the **Copy** button 🗎. All the records are copied to the Clipboard.

▶ **10.** Click the **Close 'Agreement'** button ✕ on the table window bar. A dialog box opens asking if you want to save the data you copied to the Clipboard.

▶ **11.** Click the **Yes** button in the dialog box. The dialog box closes, and then the table closes.

▶ **12.** Click the **Close** button ✕ on the Access window title bar to close the Oren database and the second Access program window.

With the records copied to the Clipboard, you can now paste them into the Contract table.

To paste the records into the Contract table:

▶ **1.** With the Belmont database's Contract table open in Datasheet view, position the pointer on the row selector for row 11, the next row available for a new record, until the pointer changes to a ➡ shape, and then click to select the row.

Trouble? If you have difficulty displaying the correct pointer shape, click in an empty area of the table datasheet to establish the window as the active window. Then repeat Step 1.

▶ **2.** In the Clipboard group on the Home tab, click the **Paste** button. The pasted records are added to the table, and a dialog box opens asking you to confirm that you want to paste all the records (55 total).

Trouble? If the Paste button isn't active, click the pointer on the row selector for row 11, making sure the entire row is selected, and then repeat Step 2.

▶ **3.** Click the **Yes** button. The dialog box closes, and the pasted records are highlighted. See Figure 1-19. Notice that the table now contains a total of 65 records—10 records that you entered and 55 records that you copied and pasted.

| Figure 1-19 | Contract table after copying and pasting records |

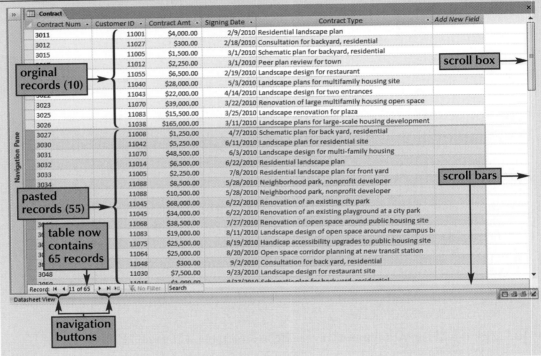

Navigating a Datasheet

The Contract table now contains 65 records, but only some of the records are visible on the screen. To view fields or records not currently visible in the datasheet, you can use the horizontal and vertical scroll bars shown in Figure 1-19 to navigate the data. The **navigation buttons**, also shown in Figure 1-19, provide another way to move vertically through the records. The Current Record box appears between the two sets of navigation buttons and displays the number of the current record as well as the total number of records in the table. Figure 1-20 shows which record becomes the current record when you click each navigation button. Note the New (blank) record button, which works in the same way as the New button on the Home tab you used earlier to enter a new record in the table.

Navigation buttons ◄ **Figure 1-20**

Navigation Button	Record Selected	Navigation Button	Record Selected
◄◄	First record	►►	Last record
◄	Previous record	►*	New (blank) record
►	Next record		

Oren suggests that you use the various navigation techniques to move through the Contract table and become familiar with its contents.

To navigate the Contract datasheet:

1. Click in the first record's Contract Num field value (3011). The Current Record box shows that record 1 is the current record.

2. Click the **Next record** navigation button ► . The second record is now highlighted, which identifies it as the current record. Also, notice that the second record's value for the Contract Num field is selected, and the Current Record box displays "2 of 65" to indicate that the second record is the current record.

3. Click the **Last record** navigation button ►► . The last record in the table, record 65, is now the current record.

4. Drag the scroll box in the vertical scroll bar (see Figure 1-19) up to the top of the bar. Notice that record 65 is still the current record, as indicated in the Current Record box. Dragging the scroll box changes the display of the table datasheet, but does not change the current record.

5. Drag the scroll box in the vertical scroll bar back down so that you can see the end of the table and the current record (record 65).

6. Click the **Previous record** navigation button ◄ . Record 64 is now the current record.

7. Click the **First record** navigation button ◄◄ . The first record is now the current record.

Tip

You can make a field the current field by clicking anywhere within the column for that field.

The Contract table now contains all the data about the customer contracts for Belmont Landscapes. To better understand how to work with this data, Oren asks you to create simple objects for the other main types of database objects—queries, forms, and reports.

Creating a Simple Query

A **query** is a question you ask about the data stored in a database. In response to a query, Access displays the specific records and fields that answer your question. When you create a query, you tell Access which fields you need and what criteria Access should use to select the records. Then Access displays only the information you want, so you don't have to navigate through the entire database for the information. In the Contract table, for example, Oren might create a query to display only those records for contracts that were signed in a specific month. Even though a query can display table information in a different way, the information still exists in the table as it was originally entered.

Oren wants to focus on the amount of each contract and the contract type. He doesn't want the list to include all the fields in the Contract table (such as Customer ID and Signing Date). To produce this list for Oren, you need to create a query based on the Contract table.

You can design your own queries or use an Access Query Wizard, which guides you through the steps to create a query. The **Simple Query Wizard** allows you to select records and fields quickly, and is an appropriate choice for producing the contract list Oren wants.

To start the Simple Query Wizard:

▶ **1.** Click the **Create** tab on the Ribbon. The Create tab provides options for creating database objects—tables, forms, reports, queries, and so on. See Figure 1-21.

| Figure 1-21 | Create tab on the Ribbon |

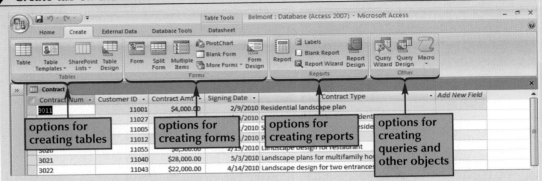

▶ **2.** In the Other group on the Create tab, click the **Query Wizard** button. The New Query dialog box opens.

▶ **3.** Make sure **Simple Query Wizard** is selected, and then click the **OK** button. The first Simple Query Wizard dialog box opens. See Figure 1-22.

| Figure 1-22 | First Simple Query Wizard dialog box |

Because the Contract table is the only object in the Belmont database, it is listed in the Tables/Queries box by default. If the database contained more objects, you could click the Tables/Queries arrow and choose another table or a query as the basis for the new query you are creating. The Available Fields list box lists all the fields in the Contract table.

You need to select fields from the Available Fields list box to include them in the query. To select fields one at a time, click a field and then click the [>] button. The selected field moves from the Available Fields list box on the left to the Selected Fields list box on the right. To select all the fields, click the [>>] button. If you change your mind or make a mistake, you can remove a field by clicking it in the Selected Fields list box and then clicking the [<] button. To remove all selected fields, click the [<<] button.

Each Simple Query Wizard dialog box contains buttons on the bottom that allow you to move to the previous dialog box (Back button), move to the next dialog box (Next button), or cancel the creation process (Cancel button). You can also finish creating the object (Finish button) and accept the wizard's defaults for the remaining options.

Oren wants his list to include data from only the following fields: Contract Num, Contract Amt, and Contract Type. You need to select these fields to include them in the query.

To create the query using the Simple Query Wizard:

▶ **1.** Click **Contract Num** in the Available Fields list box to select the field (if necessary), and then click the [>] button. The Contract Num field moves to the Selected Fields list box.

▶ **2.** Repeat Step 1 for the fields **Contract Amt** and **Contract Type**, and then click the **Next** button. The second Simple Query Wizard dialog box opens and asks if you want a detail or summary query. This dialog box opens when the values in one of the fields selected for the query could be used in calculations—in this case, the Contract Amt field. Oren wants to see every field of every record and does not want to perform summary calculations on the Contract Amt field values, so you need to create a detail query.

▶ **3.** Make sure the **Detail** option button is selected, and then click the **Next** button. The third, and final, Simple Query Wizard dialog box opens and asks you to choose a name (title) for your query. Access suggests the name "Contract Query" because the query you are creating is based on the Contract table. You'll change the suggested name to "Contract List."

▶ **4.** Click at the end of the suggested name, use the **Backspace** key to delete the word "Query," and then type **List**. Now you can view the query results.

▶ **5.** Click the **Finish** button to complete the query. Access displays the query results in Datasheet view, on a new tab named "Contract List." A query datasheet is similar to a table datasheet, showing fields in columns and records in rows—but only for those fields and records you want to see, as determined by the query specifications you select.

▶ **6.** Place the pointer on the vertical line to the right of the Contract Type field name until the pointer changes to a ✛ shape, and then double-click the pointer. All the Contract Type field values are now fully displayed. See Figure 1-23.

Tip

You can also double-click a field to move it from the Available Fields list box to the Selected Fields list box.

Figure 1-23

Query results

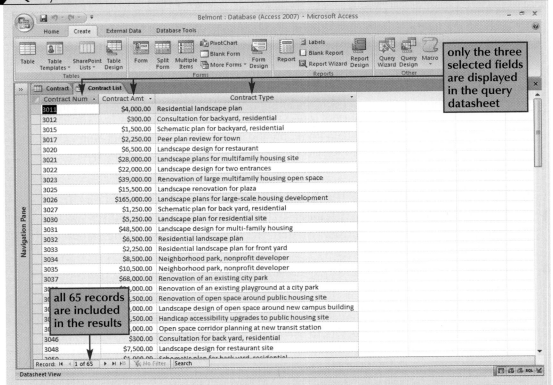

The Contract List query datasheet displays the three selected fields for each record in the Contract table. The fields are shown in the order you selected them in the Simple Query Wizard, from left to right. The records are listed in order by the primary key field, Contract Num. Even though the datasheet displays only the three fields you chose for the query, the Contract table still includes all the fields for all records.

Notice that the navigation buttons are located at the bottom of the window. You navigate a query datasheet in the same way that you navigate a table datasheet.

▶ 7. Click the **Last record** navigation button ▶|. The last record in the query datasheet is now the current record.

▶ 8. Click the **Previous record** navigation button ◀. Record 64 in the query datasheet is now the current record.

▶ 9. Click the **First record** navigation button |◀. The first record is now the current record.

▶ 10. Click the **Close 'Contract List'** button ✕ on the table window bar. A dialog box opens asking if you want to save the changes to the layout of the query. This dialog box opens because you resized the Contract Type column.

▶ 11. Click the **Yes** button to save the query layout changes and close the query.

The query results are not stored in the database; however, the query design is stored as part of the database with the name you specified. You can re-create the query results at any time by opening the query again. You'll learn more about creating and working with queries in Tutorial 3.

Next, Oren asks you to create a form for the Contract table so that Belmont Land-scapes employees can use the form to enter and work with data in the table easily.

Creating a Simple Form

A **form** is an object you use to enter, edit, and view records in a database. Although you can perform these same functions with tables and queries, forms can present data in many customized and useful ways. In Access, there are many different ways to create a form. You can design your own forms, use the Form Wizard (which guides you through the process of creating a form), or use the Form tool to create a simple form with one mouse click. The **Form tool** creates a form containing all the fields in the table or other database object on which you're basing the form.

Oren wants a form for the Contract table that shows all the fields for one record at a time, with fields listed one below another in a column. This type of form will make it easier for his staff to focus on all the data for a particular contract. You'll use the Form tool to create this form quickly and easily.

To create the form using the Form tool:

▶ 1. Make sure the Contract table is still open in Datasheet view. The table or other database object you're using as the basis for the form must either be open or selected in the Navigation Pane when you use the Form tool.

   Trouble? If the Contract table is not open, click the Shutter Bar Open/Close Button ⏵⏵ to open the Navigation Pane. Then double-click Contract : Table to open the Contract table in Datasheet view. Click the Shutter Bar Open/Close Button ⏴⏴ again to close the pane.

▶ 2. In the Forms group on the Create tab, click the **Form** button. The Form tool creates a simple form showing every field in the Contract table and places it on a tab named "Contract." Access assigns the name "Contract" because the form is based on the Contract table. See Figure 1-24.

Form created by the Form tool ◀ **Figure 1-24**

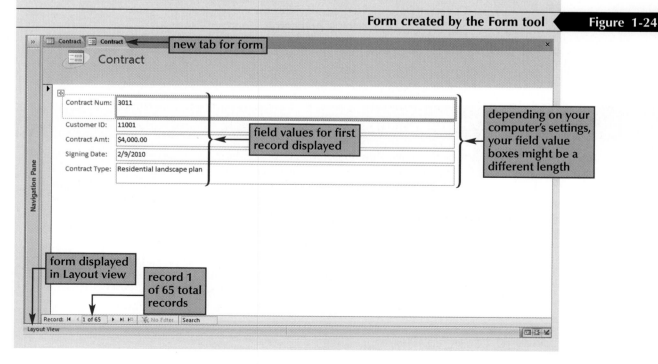

The form displays one record at a time in the Contract table, providing another view of the data that is stored in the table and allowing you to focus on the values for one record. Access displays the field values for the first record in the table and selects the first field value (Contract Num) by placing a border around the value. Each field name appears on a separate line and on the same line as its field value, which appears in a box to the right. Depending on your computer's settings, the field value boxes in your form might be shorter or longer than those shown in the figure. As indicated in the status bar, the form is displayed in Layout view. In **Layout view**, you can make design changes to the form while it is displaying data, so that you can see the effects of the changes you make immediately.

To view and maintain data using a form, you must know how to move from field to field and from record to record. Notice that the form contains navigation buttons, similar to those available in Datasheet view, which you can use to display different records in the form. You'll use these now to navigate the form; then you'll save and close the form.

To navigate, save, and close the form:

1. Click the **Next record** navigation button ▶. The form now displays the values for the second record in the Contract table.

2. Click the **Last record** navigation button ▶| to move to the last record in the table. The form displays the information for contract number 3110.

3. Click the **Previous record** navigation button ◀ to move to record 64.

4. Click the **First record** navigation button |◀ to return to the first record in the Contract table.

   Next, you'll save the form with the name "Contract Data" in the Belmont database. Then the form will be available for later use.

5. Click the **Save** button 🖫 on the Quick Access Toolbar. The Save As dialog box opens.

6. In the Form Name text box, click at the end of the highlighted word "Contract," press the **spacebar**, type **Data**, and then press the **Enter** key. Access saves the form as Contract Data in the Belmont database and closes the dialog box. The tab containing the form now displays the name "Contract Data."

7. Click the **Close 'Contract Data'** button ✕ on the form window bar to close the form.

InSight | Saving Database Objects

In general, it is best to save a database object—query, form, or report—only if you anticipate using the object frequently or if it is time consuming to create, because these objects use storage space on your disk. For example, a form you create with the Form tool would most likely not be saved, since you can re-create it easily with one mouse click. (However, for the purposes of this text, you need to save the objects you create.)

After attending a staff meeting, Oren returns with another request. He would like to see the information in the Contract table presented in a more readable format. You'll help Oren by creating a report.

Creating a Simple Report

A **report** is a formatted printout (or screen display) of the contents of one or more tables in a database. As with forms, you can design your own reports, use a Report Wizard to guide you through the steps of creating a report, or use the Report tool to create a simple report with one mouse click.

To produce the report for Oren, you'll use the Report tool, which is similar to the Form tool you used earlier to create the Contract Data form. The **Report tool** places all the fields from a selected table (or query) on a report, making it the quickest way to create a report.

To create the report using the Report tool:

▶ 1. With the Contract table open in Datasheet view, click the **Create** tab on the Ribbon.

▶ 2. In the Reports group on the Create tab, click the **Report** button. The Report tool creates a simple report showing every field in the Contract table and places it on a tab named "Contract." Again, Access assigns this name because the object you created (the report) is based on the Contract table. See Figure 1-25.

Report created by the Report tool ◀ Figure 1-25

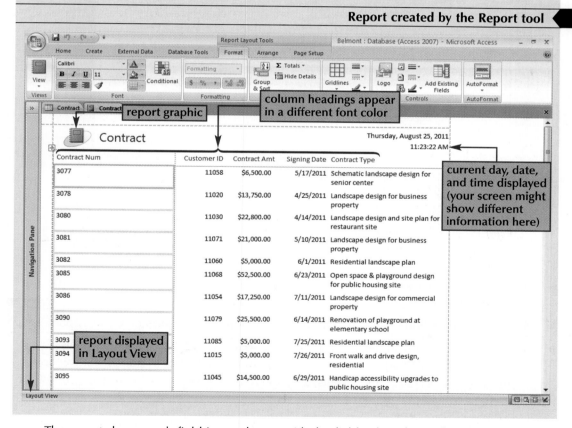

The report shows each field in a column, with the field values for each record in a row, similar to a datasheet. However, the report offers a more visually appealing format for the data, with the column headings in a different color and a line separating them from the records, a graphic of a report at the top left, and the current day, date, and time at the top right. The report is displayed in Layout view, which doesn't show how many pages there are in the report. To see this, you need to switch to Print Preview.

To view the report in Print Preview:

▶ **1.** In the Views group on the Report Layout Tools Format tab, click the **View button arrow**, and then click **Print Preview**. The first page of the report is displayed in Print Preview. See Figure 1-26.

Figure 1-26   First page of the report in Print Preview

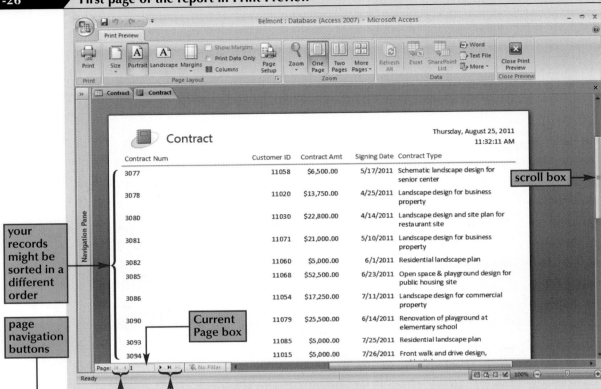

Print Preview shows exactly how the report will look when printed. Notice that Print Preview provides page navigation buttons at the bottom of the window, similar to the navigation buttons you've used to move through records in a table, query, and form.

▶ **2.** Click the **Next Page** navigation button ▶. The second page of the report is displayed in Print Preview.

▶ **3.** Click the **Last Page** navigation button ▶ to move to the last page of the report.

▶ **4.** Drag the scroll box in the vertical scroll bar (see Figure 1-26) down until the bottom of the report page is displayed. The notation "Page 3 of 3" appears at the bottom of the page, indicating that you are on page 3 out of a total of 3 pages in the report. See Figure 1-27.

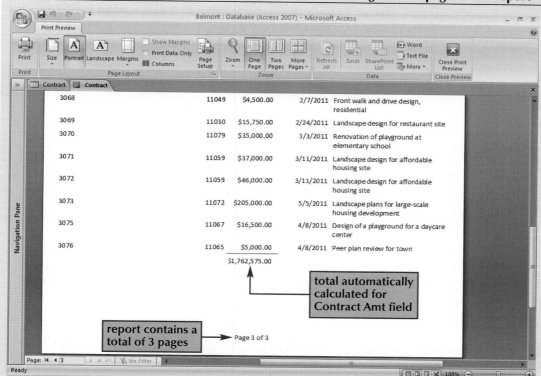

Trouble? Depending on the printer you are using, your report might have more or fewer pages, and some of the pages might be blank. If so, don't worry. Different printers format reports in different ways, sometimes affecting the total number of pages and the number of records printed per page.

Notice the total amount shown at the end of the report for the Contract Amt field. The Report tool calculated this amount and displayed it on the report. Often, you want to include such information as summaries and totals in a report; in this case, the Report tool generated it for you automatically.

▶ **5.** Click the **First Page** navigation button ◄ to return to the first page of the report, and then drag the scroll box in the vertical scroll bar back up so that the top of the report is displayed.

Next you'll save the report as "Contract Details," and then close it.

▶ **6.** Click the **Save** button 🖫 on the Quick Access Toolbar. The Save As dialog box opens.

▶ **7.** In the Report Name text box, click at the end of the highlighted word "Contract," press the **spacebar**, type **Details**, and then press the **Enter** key. Access saves the report as Contract Details in the Belmont database and closes the dialog box. The tab containing the report now displays the name "Contract Details."

Printing a Report

After creating a report, you typically print it to distribute it to others who need to view the report's contents. You use the Print command available from the Office menu to print a report.

Printing a Report

- Open the report in any view, or select the report in the Navigation Pane.
- To print the report with the default print settings, click the Office Button, point to Print, and then click Quick Print.

or

- To display the Print dialog box and select the options you want for printing the report, click the Office Button, point to Print, and then click Print (or, if the report is displayed in Print Preview, click the Print button in the Print group on the Print Preview tab).

Oren asks you to print the entire report, so you'll use the Quick Print option available from the Office Button menu.

Note: To complete the following steps, your computer must be connected to a printer.

To print the report:

▶ 1. Click the **Office Button** 🗐, point to **Print**, and then click **Quick Print**. The report prints with the default print settings.

   Trouble? If your report did not print, make sure that your computer is connected to a printer, and that the printer is turned on and ready to print. Then repeat Step 1.

▶ 2. Click the **Close 'Contract Details'** button ☒ on the report window bar to close the report.

▶ 3. Click the **Close 'Contract'** button ☒ on the table window bar to close the Contract table.

You can also use the Print dialog box to print other database objects, such as table and query datasheets. Most often, these objects are used for viewing and entering data, and reports are used for printing the data in a database.

Viewing Objects in the Navigation Pane

The Belmont database now contains four objects—the Contract table, the Contract List query, the Contract Data form, and the Contract Details report. You can view and work with these objects in the Navigation Pane.

To view the objects in the Belmont database:

▶ 1. Click the **Shutter Bar Open/Close Button** ≫ on the Navigation Pane to open the pane. See Figure 1-28.

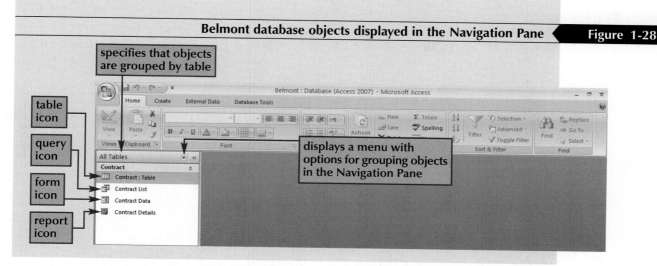

Belmont database objects displayed in the Navigation Pane — Figure 1-28

The Navigation Pane currently displays the default view, **All Tables**, which groups objects according to the tables in the database. Note the bar containing the word "Contract" in the pane; this bar is a heading for the Contract table, which is the only table in the Belmont database. Below the bar, all the objects related to the Contract table, including the table itself, are listed. Each database object—the Contract table, the Contract List query, the Contract Data form, and the Contract Details report—has a unique icon to its left to indicate the type of object. This makes it easy for you to identify the objects and choose which one you want to open and work with.

The arrow on the All Tables bar displays a menu with options for various ways to group and display objects in the Navigation Pane. As you continue to build the Belmont database and add more objects to it in later tutorials, you'll learn how to use the options in this menu.

Managing a Database

One of the main tasks involved in working with database software is managing your databases and the data they contain. By managing your databases, you can ensure that they operate in the most efficient way, that the data they contain is secure, and that you can work with the data effectively. Some of the activities involved in database management include compacting and repairing a database and backing up and restoring a database.

Compacting and Repairing a Database

Whenever you open an Access database and work in it, the size of the database increases. Further, when you delete records and when you delete or replace database objects—such as queries, forms, and reports—the space that had been occupied on the disk by the deleted or replaced records or objects does not automatically become available for other records or objects. To make the space available, you must compact the database. **Compacting** a database rearranges the data and objects in a database to decrease its file size, thereby making more space available on your disk and letting you open and close the database more quickly. Figure 1-29 illustrates the compacting process.

Figure 1-29 | Compacting a database

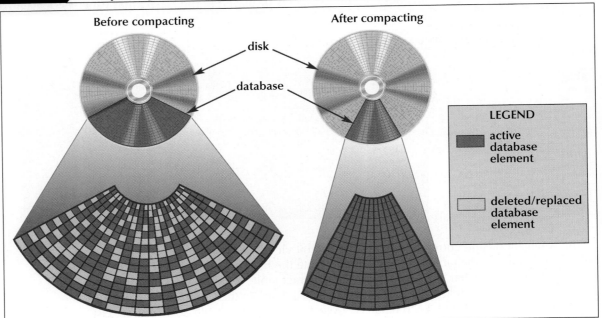

When you compact a database, Access repairs the database at the same time. In many cases, Access detects that a database is damaged when you try to open it and gives you the option to compact and repair it at that time. For example, the data in your database might become damaged, or corrupted, if you exit the Access program suddenly by turning off your computer. If you think your database might be damaged because it is behaving unpredictably, you can use the "Compact and Repair Database" option to fix it.

Reference Window | **Compacting and Repairing a Database**

- Make sure the database file you want to compact and repair is open.
- Click the Office Button, point to Manage, and then click Compact and Repair Database.

Access also allows you to set an option for your database file so that every time you close the database, it will be compacted automatically. The Compact on Close option is available in the Current Database section of the Access Options dialog box, which you open by clicking the Office Button and then clicking the Access Options button. By default, the Compact on Close option is off.

Next, you'll compact the Belmont database manually using the Compact and Repair Database option. This will make the database a much smaller and more manageable size. After compacting the database, you'll close it.

To compact and repair the Belmont database:

▶ **1.** Click the **Office Button** 🔘, and then point to **Manage**.

   Trouble? Check with your instructor before selecting the option to compact and repair the database. If your instructor tells you not to select this option, click the Exit Access button on the Office menu.

▶ **2.** Click **Compact and Repair Database**. Although nothing visible happens on screen, Access compacts the Belmont database, making it smaller, and repairs it at the same time.

▶ **3.** Click the **Close** button ☒ on the program window title bar. Access closes the Belmont database. Then the Access program window closes.

Backing Up and Restoring a Database

Backing up a database is the process of making a copy of the database file to protect your database against loss or damage. Experienced database users make it a habit to back up a database before they work with it for the first time, keeping the original data intact, and to make frequent backups while continuing to work with a database. Most users back up their databases on tapes, USB drives, recordable CDs or DVDs, or hard disks. Also, it is recommended to store the backup copy in a different location from the original. For example, if the original database is stored on a USB drive, you should not store the backup copy on the same USB drive. If you lose the drive, the original database and its backup copy would both be lost.

The Back Up Database command enables you to back up your database file from within the Access program, while you are working on your database. To use this option, you click the Office Button, point to the Manage option, and then choose Back Up Database. In the resulting Save As dialog box, Access provides a default filename for the backup copy that consists of the same filename as the database you are backing up (for example, "Belmont") plus the current date. This filenaming system makes it easy for you to keep track of your database backups and when they were created.

To restore a backup database file, you simply copy the backup from the drive on which it is stored to your hard drive, or whatever device you use to work in Access, and start working with the restored database file. If the original database file and the backup copy have the same name, restoring the backup copy might replace the original. If you want to save the original file, rename it before you restore the backup copy. To ensure that the restored database has the most current data, you should update the restored database with any changes made to the original between the time it became damaged or lost and the time you created the backup copy. (You will not actually back up the Belmont database in this tutorial.)

With the Contract table in place, you can continue to build the Belmont database so that Oren and his staff members can use it to store, manipulate, and retrieve important data for Belmont Landscapes. In the following tutorials, you'll help Oren complete and maintain the database, and you'll use it to meet the specific information needs of the firm's employees.

Review | Session 1.2 Quick Check

1. True or False: You can copy records from any Access database table and paste them in another table.
2. A(n) _____ is a question you ask about the data stored in a database.
3. The quickest way to create a form is to use the _____ .
4. To see the total number of pages in a report and navigate through the report pages, you need to display the report in _____ .
5. In the Navigation Pane, each database object has a unique _____ to its left that identifies the object's type.
6. _____ a database rearranges the data and objects in a database to decrease its file size.
7. _____ a database is the process of making a copy of the database file to protect the database against loss or damage.

Review | Tutorial Summary

In this tutorial, you learned the basic concepts associated with databases, including how data is organized in a database and the functions of a relational database management system. You also learned how to create a new blank database, and how to create a table in Datasheet view by entering field names and records. You learned the function of the primary key and its role in the design of a table. To complete the table, you copied and pasted records from another Access database table with the same design. You used the Simple Query Wizard to display only certain fields and their values. Using the Form tool and the Report tool, you learned how to create simple forms and reports quickly in order to view and work with the data stored in a table in different ways. Finally, you were introduced to some of the important tasks involved in managing a database, including compacting and backing up a database.

Key Terms

Access	Datasheet view	query
Access window	field	record
Add New Field column	field selector	record selector
All Tables (view)	field value	relational database
AutoNumber	foreign key	relational database manage-
backing up	form	ment system
column selector	Form tool	report
common field	ID column	Report tool
compacting	Layout view	row selector
Current Record box	Microsoft Access window	Simple Query Wizard
data type	Microsoft Office Access 2007	star symbol
database	navigation buttons	table
database management	Navigation Pane	template
system (DBMS)	pencil symbol	Text (data type)
datasheet	primary key	
datasheet selector	Print Preview	

| Practice | | Review Assignments |

Take time to practice the skills you learned in the tutorial using the same case scenario.

Data File needed for the Review Assignments: Provider.accdb

In the Review Assignments, you'll create a new database to contain information about the suppliers that Belmont Landscapes works with on its landscape design projects. Complete the following steps:

1. Create a new blank database named **Supplier**, and save it in the Level.01\Review folder provided with your Data Files.
2. In Datasheet view for the Table1 table, rename the default ID primary key field to **Company ID**. Change the data type of the Company ID field to Text.
3. Add the following 10 fields to the new table in the order shown: **Company Name**, **Product Type**, **Address**, **City**, **State**, **Zip**, **Phone**, **Contact First Name**, **Contact Last Name**, and **Initial Contact Date**. Resize the columns as necessary so that the complete field names are displayed. Save the table as **Company**.
4. Enter the records shown in Figure 1-30 in the Company table. As you enter the field values for the first record, use the Data Type option in the Data Type & Formatting group on the Datasheet tab to confirm that all the fields use the Text data type, except for the Zip field (which should have the Number data type) and the Initial Contact Date field (which should have the Date/Time data type). If necessary, make any changes so the fields have the correct data types.

Figure 1-30

Company ID	Company Name	Product Type	Address	City	State	Zip	Phone	Contact First Name	Contact Last Name	Initial Contact Date
AND225	Anderson OnSite	Site furnishings	200 Lincoln Dr	Kalamazoo	MI	49007	269-337-9266	Matt	Anderson	6/3/2009
HOL292	Holland Nursery	Plants	380 W 20th St	Holland	MI	49424	616-396-9330	Brenda	Ehlert	9/2/2010
BES327	Best Paving	Pavers	780 N Main St	Rockford	MI	49341	616-866-6364	Shirley	Hauser	2/14/2010
MID312	Midwest Lighting	Outdoor lighting	435 Central Dr	Battle Creek	MI	49014	269-979-3970	Weston	Caldwell	5/15/2009
BAC200	Backyard Structures	Play equipment	105 E 8th St	Holland	MI	49423	616-396-3989	Alan	Bastian	4/15/2009

5. Oren created a database named Provider that contains a Business table with supplier data. The Company table you created has the same design as the Business table. Copy all the records from the **Business** table in the **Provider** database (located in the Level.01\Review folder provided with your Data Files) to the end of the Company table in the Supplier database.
6. Resize all the columns in the datasheet so that all the field values are completely displayed, and then save the Company table.
7. Close the Company table, and then use the Navigation Pane to reopen it. Note that the records are displayed in primary key order.
8. Use the Simple Query Wizard to create a query that includes the Company Name, Product Type, Contact First Name, Contact Last Name, and Phone fields (in that order) from the Company table. Name the query **Company List**, and then close the query.
9. Use the Form tool to create a form for the Company table. Save the form as **Company Info**, and then close it.

10. Use the Report tool to create a report based on the Company table. Save the report as **Company Details**, and then close it.
11. Close the Company table, and then compact and repair the Supplier database.
12. Close the Supplier database.

Apply	**Case Problem 1**

Use the skills you learned in the tutorial to create a database for a small music school.

Data File needed for this Case Problem: School.accdb

Pine Hill Music School   After giving private piano lessons from her home for several years, Yuka Koyama founded the Pine Hill Music School in Portland, Oregon. Because of her popularity as a music teacher, Yuka attracted top-notch students, and her school quickly established a reputation for excellence. During the past two years, other qualified teachers have joined Yuka to offer instruction in voice, violin, cello, guitar, percussion, and other instruments. As her school continues to grow, Yuka wants to use Access to keep track of information about students, teachers, and contracts. You'll help Yuka create and maintain an Access database to store data about her school. Complete the following:

1. Create a new blank database named **Pinehill**, and save it in the Level.01\Case1 folder provided with your Data Files.
2. In Datasheet view for the Table1 table, rename the default primary key ID field to **Teacher ID**. Change the data type of the Teacher ID field to Text.
3. Add the following five fields to the new table in the order shown: **First Name**, **Last Name**, **Degree**, **School**, and **Hire Date**. Save the table as **Teacher**.
4. Enter the records shown in Figure 1-31 in the Teacher table. As you enter the field values for the first record, use the Data Type option in the Data Type & Formatting group on the Datasheet tab to confirm that all the fields use the Text data type, except for the Hire Date field, which should have the Date/Time data type. If necessary, make any changes so the fields have the correct data types.

Figure 1-31

Teacher ID	First Name	Last Name	Degree	School	Hire Date
13-1100	Yuka	Koyama	MM	Pacific University	1/13/2009
17-1798	Richard	Jacobson	PhD	Pacific University	1/15/2009
55-5310	Annamaria	Romano	BA	Lewis & Clark College	4/21/2009
22-0102	Andre	Dvorak	BM	University of Portland	3/3/2009
34-4506	Marilyn	Schwartz	BM	University of Portland	5/1/2009

5. Yuka created a database named School that contains a Faculty table with teacher data. The Teacher table you created has the same design as the Faculty table. Copy all the records from the **Faculty** table in the **School** database (located in the Level.01\Case1 folder provided with your Data Files) to the end of the Teacher table in the Pinehill database.
6. Resize all the columns in the datasheet so that all the field values are completely displayed, and then save the Teacher table.
7. Close the Teacher table, and then use the Navigation Pane to reopen it. Note that the records are displayed in primary key order.

8. Use the Simple Query Wizard to create a query that includes the First Name, Last Name, and Hire Date fields (in that order) from the Teacher table. Name the query **Start Date**, and then close the query.

9. Use the Form tool to create a form for the Teacher table. Save the form as **Teacher Info**, and then close it.

10. Use the Report tool to create a report based on the Teacher table. Save the report as **Teacher List**, print the report (only if asked by your instructor to do so), and then close it.

11. Close the Teacher table, and then compact and repair the Pinehill database.

12. Close the Pinehill database.

Apply | **Case Problem 2**

Apply what you learned in the tutorial to create a database for a new business in the health and fitness industry.

Data File needed for this Case Problem: Health.accdb

Parkhurst Health & Fitness Center After many years working in various corporate settings, Martha Parkhurst decided to turn her lifelong interest in health and fitness into a new business venture and opened the Parkhurst Health & Fitness Center in Richmond, Virginia. In addition to providing the usual fitness classes and weight training facilities, the center also offers specialized programs designed to meet the needs of athletes—both young and old—who participate in certain sports or physical activities. Martha's goal in establishing such programs is twofold: to help athletes gain a competitive edge through customized training, and to ensure the health and safety of all participants through proper exercises and physical preparation. Martha wants to use Access to maintain information about the members who have joined the center and the types of programs offered. She needs your help in creating this database. Complete the following:

1. Create a new blank database named **Fitness**, and save it in the Level.01\Case2 folder provided with your Data Files.

2. In Datasheet view for the Table1 table, rename the default primary key ID field to **Program ID**. Change the data type of the Program ID field to Text.

3. Add the following three fields to the new table in the order shown: **Program Type**, **Monthly Fee**, and **Physical Required**. Resize the columns as necessary so that the complete field names are displayed. Save the table as **Program**.

4. Enter the records shown in Figure 1-32 in the Program table. As you enter the field values for the first record, use the Data Type option in the Data Type & Formatting group on the Datasheet tab to confirm that all the fields use the Text data type, except for the Monthly Fee field, which should have the Currency data type. If necessary, make any changes so the fields have the correct data types.

Figure 1-32

Program ID	Program Type	Monthly Fee	Physical Required
201	Junior Full (ages 13-17)	$35.00	Yes
202	Junior Limited (ages 13-17)	$25.00	Yes
203	Young Adult Full (ages 18-25)	$45.00	No
204	Young Adult Limited (ages 18-25)	$30.00	No

5. Martha created a database named Health that contains a Class table with program data. The Program table you created has the same design as the Class table. Copy all the records from the **Class** table in the **Health** database (located in the Level.01\Case2 folder provided with your Data Files) to the end of the Program table in the Fitness database.

6. Resize all the columns in the datasheet so that all the field values are completely displayed, and then save the Program table.

7. Use the Simple Query Wizard to create a query that includes all the fields from the Program table. In the second Simple Query Wizard dialog box, select the Detail option. Resize the columns in the query datasheet so that all the field values are completely displayed, save the query as **Program Data**, and then close the query.

8. Use the Form tool to create a form for the Program table. Save the form as **Program Info**, and then close it.

9. Use the Report tool to create a report based on the Program table. Save the report as **Program List**, print the report (only if asked by your instructor to do so), and then close it.

10. Close the Program table, and then compact and repair the Fitness database.

11. Close the Fitness database.

| Challenge | **Case Problem 3** |

Use what you've learned, and expand your skills, to create a database containing information about an agency that recycles household goods.

Data File needed for this Case Problem: RRGroup.accdb

Rossi Recycling Group   The Rossi Recycling Group is a not-for-profit agency in Salina, Kansas that provides recycled household goods to needy people and families at no charge. Residents of Salina and surrounding communities donate cash and goods, such as appliances, furniture, and tools, to the Rossi Recycling Group. The group's volunteers then coordinate with local human services agencies to distribute the goods to those in need. The Rossi Recycling Group was established by Mary and Tom Rossi, who live on the outskirts of Salina on a small farm. Mary and Tom organize the volunteers to collect the goods and store the collected items in their barn for distribution. Tom wants to create an Access database to keep track of information about donors, their donations, and the human services agencies. Complete the following:

1. Create a new blank database named **Rossi**, and then save it in the Level.01\Case3 folder provided with your Data Files.

2. In Datasheet view for the Table1 table, rename the default primary key ID field to **Donor ID**. Change the data type of the Donor ID field to Text.

3. Add the following four fields to the new table in the order shown: **Title**, **First Name**, **Last Name**, and **Phone**. Resize the columns as necessary so that the complete field names are displayed. Save the table as **Donor**.

4. Enter the records shown in Figure 1-33 in the Donor table. As you enter the field values for the first record, use the Data Type option in the Data Type & Formatting group on the Datasheet tab to confirm that all the fields use the Text data type. If necessary, make any changes so the fields have the correct data types.

Figure 1-33

Donor ID	Title	First Name	Last Name	Phone
36012	Mr.	Joel	Martinson	785-823-9275
36016	Mr.	Doug	Showers	620-793-8477
36001	Mrs.	Janis	Fendrick	785-452-8736
36020	Mrs.	JoAnn	Randolph	785-309-6540
36019	Ms.	Connie	Springen	785-452-1178

5. Tom created a database named RRGroup that contains a Contributors table with data about donors. The Donor table you created has the same design as the Contributors table. Copy all the records from the **Contributors** table in the **RRGroup** database (located in the Level.01\Case3 folder provided with your Data Files) to the end of the Donor table in the Rossi database.

6. Resize all the columns in the datasheet so that all the field values are completely displayed, and then save the Donor table.

7. Close the Donor table, and then use the Navigation Pane to reopen it. Note that the records are displayed in primary key order.

◆ EXPLORE 8. Use the Simple Query Wizard to create a query that includes all the fields in the Donor table *except* the Title field. (*Hint*: Use the `>>` and `<` buttons to select the necessary fields.) Save the query using the name **Donor Phone List**.

◆ EXPLORE 9. The query results are displayed in order by the Donor ID field values. You can specify a different order by sorting the query. Display the Home tab. Then, click the insertion point anywhere within the Last Name column to make it the current field. In the Sort & Filter group on the Home tab, click the Ascending button. The records are now listed in order by the values in the Last Name field. Save and close the query.

◆ EXPLORE 10. Use the Form tool to create a form for the Donor table. In the new form, navigate to record 8, and then print the form *for the current record only*. (*Hint*: You must use the Print dialog box in order to print only the current record. Click the Office Button, point to Print, and then click Print to open the Print dialog box. Click the Selected Record(s) option button and then click the OK button to print the current record.) Save the form as **Donor Info**, and then close it.

11. Use the Report tool to create a report based on the Donor table. Save the report as **Donor List**. Print the report (only if asked by your instructor to do so), and then close it.

12. Close the Donor table, and then compact and repair the Rossi database.

13. Close the Rossi database.

Challenge	**Case Problem 4**

Work with the skills you've learned, and explore some new skills, to create a database for a luxury rental company.

Data File needed for this Case Problem: Travel.accdb

GEM Ultimate Vacations   As guests of a friend, Griffin and Emma MacElroy spent two weeks at a magnificent villa in the south of France. This unforgettable experience stayed with them upon returning to their home in a suburb of Chicago, Illinois. As a result, they decided to open their own agency, GEM Ultimate Vacations, which specializes in locating and booking luxury rental properties, primarily in Europe. Recently, Griffin and Emma expanded their business to include properties in Africa as well. From the beginning, Griffin and Emma used computers to help them manage all aspects of their business. They recently installed Access and now would like you to create a database to store information about guests, properties, and reservations. Complete the following:

1. Create a new blank database named **GEM**, and then save it in the Level.01\Case4 folder provided with your Data Files.

2. In Datasheet view for the Table1 table, rename the default primary key ID field to **Guest ID**. Change the data type of the Guest ID field to Text.

3. Add the following eight fields to the new table in the order shown: **Guest First Name**, **Guest Last Name**, **Address**, **City**, **State/Prov**, **Postal Code**, **Country**, and **Phone**. Resize the columns as necessary so that the complete field names are displayed. Save the table as **Guest**.

⊕ EXPLORE
4. Enter the records shown in Figure 1-34 in the Guest table. As you enter the field values for the first record, use the Data Type option in the Data Type & Formatting group on the Datasheet tab to confirm that all the fields use the Text data type, except for the Postal Code field, which should have the Number data type. If necessary, make any changes so the fields have the correct data types. When you type the Postal Code value for the fourth record, Access will open an error menu because you entered letters into a field that is formatted with the Number data type, which stores numbers that will be used in calculations. Because the postal codes will not be used in calculations, choose the option on the menu to convert the data in this column to the Text data type to continue.

Figure 1-34

Guest ID	Guest First Name	Guest Last Name	Address	City	State/Prov	Postal Code	Country	Phone
201	Michael	Miskowsky	153 Summer Ave	Evanston	IL	60201	USA	847-623-0975
203	Tom	Davis	5003 Wilson Blvd	Chicago	IL	60603	USA	312-897-4515
206	Li	Zhu	6509 Great Rd	Gary	IN	46401	USA	219-655-8109
202	Ingrid	Gorman	207 Riverside Dr West	Windsor	ON	N9A 5K4	Canada	519-977-8577
205	Richard	Nelson	34 Settlers Dr	Tinley Park	IL	60477	USA	708-292-4441

5. Emma created a database named Travel that contains a Client table with data about guests. The Guest table you created has the same design as the Client table. Copy all the records from the **Client** table in the **Travel** database (located in the Level.01\Case4 folder provided with your Data Files) to the end of the Guest table in the GEM database.

6. Resize all the columns in the datasheet so that all the field values are completely displayed, and then save the Guest table.

7. Close the Guest table, and then use the Navigation Pane to reopen it. Note that the records are displayed in primary key order.

8. Use the Simple Query Wizard to create a query that includes the following fields from the Guest table, in the order shown: Guest ID, Guest Last Name, Guest First Name, City, and Phone. Name the query **Guest Data**.

⊕ EXPLORE
9. The query results are displayed in order by the Guest ID field values. You can specify a different order by sorting the query. Display the Home tab. Then, click the insertion point anywhere within the Guest Last Name column to make it the current field. In the Sort & Filter group on the Home tab, click the Ascending button. The records are now listed in order by the values in the Guest Last Name field. Save and close the query.

EXPLORE 10. Use the Form tool to create a form for the Guest table. In the new form, navigate to record 12, and then print the form *for the current record only*. (*Hint*: You must use the Print dialog box in order to print only the current record. Click the Office Button, point to Print, and then click Print to open the Print dialog box. Click the Selected Record(s) option button and then click the OK button to print the current record.) Save the form as **Guest Info**, and then close it.

11. Use the Report tool to create a report based on the Guest table. Save the report as **Guest List**.

EXPLORE 12. Display the report in Print Preview. Use the Two Pages button in the Zoom group on the Print Preview tab to view both pages of the report at the same time. Use the Landscape button in the Page Layout group to change the orientation of the report to landscape. Print the report (only if asked by your instructor to do so), and then close it.

13. Close the Guest table, and then compact and repair the GEM database.

14. Close the GEM database.

Research | **Internet Assignments**

Use the Internet to find and work with data related to the topics presented in this tutorial.

The purpose of the Internet Assignments is to challenge you to find information on the Internet that you can use to work effectively with this software. The actual assignments are updated and maintained on the Course Technology Web site. Log on to the Internet and use your Web browser to go to the Student Online Companion for New Perspectives Office 2007 at **www.course.com/np/office2007**. Then navigate to the Internet Assignments for this tutorial.

Assess | **SAM Assessment and Training**

If you have a SAM user profile, you may have access to hands-on instruction, practice, and assessment of the skills covered in this tutorial. Log in to your SAM account (**http://sam2007.course.com**) to launch any assigned training activities or exams that relate to the skills covered in this tutorial.

Review | **Quick Check Answers**

Session 1.1

1. field
2. common field
3. primary key; foreign key
4. Navigation Pane
5. ID field
6. the record being edited; the next row available for a new record
7. Access saves changes to the active database to disk automatically, when a record is changed or added and when you close the database. You use the Save button in Access only to save changes to the design of an object, such as a table, or to the format of a datasheet—not to save the database file.

Session 1.2

1. False; to copy and paste records from one table to another, the tables must have the same structure—that is, the tables must contain the same fields, with the same characteristics, in the same order.
2. query
3. Form tool
4. Print Preview
5. icon
6. Compacting
7. Backing up

Ending Data Files

Level.01 → Tutorial
Belmont.accdb

Review
Supplier.accdb

Case1
Pinehill.accdb

Case2
Fitness.accdb

Case3
Rossi.accdb

Case4
GEM.accdb

Objectives

Session 2.1
- Learn the guidelines for designing databases and setting field properties
- View and modify field data types and formatting
- Create a table in Design view
- Define fields and specify a table's primary key
- Modify the structure of a table

Session 2.2
- Import data from an Excel worksheet
- Create a table by importing an existing table structure
- Delete, rename, and move fields
- Add data to a table by importing a text file
- Define a relationship between two tables

Building a Database and Defining Table Relationships

Creating the Invoice and Customer Tables

Case | Belmont Landscapes

The Belmont database currently contains one table, the Contract table. Oren also wants to track information about the firm's customers, both residential and commercial, and the invoices sent to customers for services provided by Belmont Landscapes. This information includes such items as each customer's name and address and the invoice amount and invoice date.

In this tutorial, you'll create two new tables in the Belmont database—Invoice and Customer—to contain the data Oren wants to track. You will use two different methods for creating the tables, and learn how to modify the fields. After adding records to the tables, you will define the necessary relationships between the tables in the Belmont database to relate the tables, enabling Oren and his staff to work with the data more efficiently.

Starting Data Files

Level.01 → **Tutorial**

Belmont.accdb (*cont.*)
Customer.txt
Invoices.xlsx
Sarah.accdb

Review

Goods.xlsx
Supplier.accdb (*cont.*)

Case1

Lessons.xlsx
Music.accdb
Pinehill.accdb (*cont.*)
Student.txt

Case2

Center.xlsx
Fitness.accdb (*cont.*)

Case3

Agency.txt
Gifts.xlsx
Recycle.accdb
Rossi.accdb (*cont.*)

Case4

Bookings.txt
GEM.accdb (*cont.*)
Overseas.accdb

Session 2.1

Guidelines for Designing Databases

A database management system can be a useful tool, but only if you first carefully design the database so that it meets the needs of its users. In database design, you determine the fields, tables, and relationships needed to satisfy the data and processing requirements. When you design a database, you should follow these guidelines:

- **Identify all the fields needed to produce the required information.** For example, Oren needs information about contracts, invoices, and customers. Figure 2-1 shows the fields that satisfy these information requirements.

Figure 2-1	Oren's data requirements

Contract Num	Contract Amt
Customer ID	Signing Date
Company	Invoice Date
First Name	Contract Type
Last Name	Phone
Address	Invoice Paid
City	Invoice Num
State	Invoice Amt
Zip	

- **Organize each piece of data into its smallest useful part.** For example, Oren could store each customer's complete name in one field called Customer Name instead of using two fields called First Name and Last Name, as shown in Figure 2-1. However, doing so would make it more difficult to work with the data. If Oren wanted to view the records in alphabetical order by last name, he wouldn't be able to do so with field values such as "Tom Cotter" and "Ray Yost" stored in a Customer Name field. He could do so with field values such as "Cotter" and "Yost" stored separately in a Last Name field.
- **Group related fields into tables.** For example, Oren grouped the fields related to contracts into the Contract table, which you created in Tutorial 1. The fields related to invoices are grouped into the Invoice table, and the fields related to customers are grouped into the Customer table. Figure 2-2 shows the fields grouped into all three tables for the Belmont database.

Figure 2-2	Oren's fields grouped into tables

Contract table	Invoice table	Customer table
Contract Num	Invoice Num	Customer ID
Customer ID	Contract Num	Company
Contract Amt	Invoice Amt	First Name
Signing Date	Invoice Date	Last Name
Contract Type	Invoice Paid	Phone
		Address
		City
		State
		Zip

- **Determine each table's primary key.** Recall that a primary key uniquely identifies each record in a table. Although a primary key is not mandatory in Access, it's a good idea to include one in each table. Without a primary key, selecting the exact record that you want can be a problem. For some tables, one of the fields, such as a Social Security or credit card number, naturally serves the function of a primary key. For other tables, two or more fields might be needed to function as the primary key. In these cases, the primary key is called a **composite key**. For example, a school grade table would use a combination of student number and course code to serve as the primary key. For a third category of tables, no single field or combination of fields can uniquely identify a record in a table. In these cases, you need to add a field whose sole purpose is to serve as the table's primary key. For Oren's tables, Contract Num is the primary key for the Contract table, Invoice Num is the primary key for the Invoice table, and Customer ID is the primary key for the Customer table.

- **Include a common field in related tables.** You use the common field to connect one table logically with another table. For example, Oren's Contract and Customer tables include the Customer ID field as a common field. Recall that when you include the primary key from one table as a field in a second table to form a relationship, the field is called a foreign key in the second table; therefore, the Customer ID field is a foreign key in the Contract table. With this common field, Oren can find all contracts for a particular customer; he can use the Customer ID value for a customer and search the Contract table for all records with that Customer ID value. Likewise, he can determine which customer has a particular contract by searching the Customer table to find the one record with the same Customer ID value as the corresponding value in the Contract table. Similarly, the Contract Num field is a common field, serving as the primary key in the Contract table and a foreign key in the Invoice table.

- **Avoid data redundancy.** When you store the same data in more than one place, **data redundancy** occurs. With the exception of common fields to connect tables, you should avoid redundancy because it wastes storage space and can cause inconsistencies. An inconsistency would exist, for example, if you type a field value one way in one table and a different way in the same table or in a second table. Figure 2-3, which contains portions of potential data stored in the Customer and Contract tables, shows an example of incorrect database design that has data redundancy in the Contract table. In Figure 2-3, the Company field in the Contract table is redundant, and one value for this field was entered incorrectly, in three different ways.

Figure 2-3 ▶ **Incorrect database design with data redundancy**

Customer table

Customer ID	Company	First Name	Last Name
11067	Blossom Day Care Center	Christina	Garrett
11068	Grand Rapids Housing Authority	Jessica	Ropiak
11070	Legacy Companies, LTD.	Michael	Faraci
11071	Blue Star Mini Golf	Vanetta	Walker
11072	Sierra Investment Company	Rodrigo	Valencia

data redundancy

Contract table

Contract Num	Customer ID	Company	Contract Amt	Signing Date
3023	11070	Legacy Company	$39,000.00	3/22/2010
3040	11068	Grand Rapids Housing Authority	$38,500.00	7/27/2010
3042	11070	Legacies Co. Limited	$48,500.00	6/3/2010
3073	11072	Sierra Investment Company	$205,000.00	5/5/2011
3081	11071	Blue Star Mini Golf	$21,000.00	5/10/2011
3085	11070	Legacy Corp. Ltd	$30,800.00	12/28/2010
3099	11067	Blossom Day Care Center	$6,500.00	7/25/2011

inconsistent data

- **Determine the properties of each field.** You need to identify the **properties**, or charac-teristics, of each field so that the DBMS knows how to store, display, and process the field values. These properties include the field's name, maximum number of characters or digits, description, valid values, and other field characteristics. You will learn more about field properties later in this tutorial.

   The Invoice and Customer tables you need to create will contain the fields shown in Figure 2-2. Before you create these new tables in the Belmont database, you first need to learn some guidelines for setting field properties.

Guidelines for Setting Field Properties

As just noted, the last step of database design is to determine which values to assign to the properties, such as the name and data type, of each field. When you select or enter a value for a property, you **set** the property. Access has rules for naming fields, choosing data types, and setting other properties for fields.

Naming Fields and Objects

You must name each field, table, and other object in an Access database. Access then stores these items in the database, using the names you supply. It's best to choose a field or object name that describes the purpose or contents of the field or object so that later you can easily remember what the name represents. For example, the three tables in the Belmont database will be named Contract, Invoice, and Customer, because these names suggest their contents. Note that a table or query name must be unique within a database. A field name must be unique within a table, but it can be used again in another table. Refer to the "Guidelines for Naming Fields" InSight box in Tutorial 1 for a reminder of these guidelines, which apply to naming all database objects.

Assigning Field Data Types

Each field must have a data type, which is either assigned automatically by Access or specifically by the table designer. The **data type** determines what field values you can enter for the field and what other properties the field will have. For example, the Invoice table will include an Invoice Date field, which will store date values, so you will assign the Date/Time data type to this field. Then Access will allow you to enter and manipulate only dates or times as values in the Invoice Date field.

Figure 2-4 lists the data types available in Access, describes the field values allowed for each data type, explains when you should use each data type, and indicates the field size of each data type.

Data types for fields | **Figure 2-4**

Data Type	Description	Field Size
Text	Allows field values containing letters, digits, spaces, and special characters. Use for names, addresses, descriptions, and fields containing digits that are not used in calculations.	0 to 255 characters; default is 255
Memo	Allows field values containing letters, digits, spaces, and special characters. Use for long comments and explanations.	1 to 65,535 characters; exact size is determined by entry
Number	Allows positive and negative numbers as field values. Numbers can contain digits, a decimal point, commas, a plus sign, and a minus sign. Use for fields that will be used in calculations, except those involving money.	1 to 15 digits
Date/Time	Allows field values containing valid dates and times from January 1, 100 to December 31, 9999. Dates can be entered in month/day/year format, several other date formats, or a variety of time formats, such as 10:35 PM. You can perform calculations on dates and times, and you can sort them. For example, you can determine the number of days between two dates.	8 bytes
Currency	Allows field values similar to those for the Number data type, but is used for storing monetary values. Unlike calculations with Number data type decimal values, calculations performed with the Currency data type are not subject to round-off error.	Accurate to 15 digits on the left side of the decimal point and to 4 digits on the right side
AutoNumber	Consists of integer values created automatically by Access each time you create a new record. You can specify sequential numbering or random numbering, which guarantees a unique field value, so that such a field can serve as a table's primary key.	9 digits
Yes/No	Limits field values to yes and no, on and off, or true and false. Use for fields that indicate the presence or absence of a condition, such as whether an order has been filled or whether an invoice has been paid.	1 character
OLE Object	Allows field values that are created in other Microsoft Windows programs as objects, such as spreadsheets and word-processing documents. These objects can be linked or embedded. Each field value is limited to a single file.	1 gigabyte maximum; exact size depends on object size
Hyperlink	Consists of text used as a hyperlink address, which can have up to four parts: the text that appears in a field or control; the path to a file or page; a location within the file or page; and text displayed as a ScreenTip.	Up to 65,535 characters total for the four parts of the Hyperlink data type
Attachment	Allows field values with one or more attached files, such as images, videos, documents, charts, and other supported files, similar to e-mail attachments. Provides greater flexibility than the OLE Object data type and uses storage space more efficiently.	2 gigabytes maximum; individual attached files cannot exceed 256 MB
Lookup Wizard	Creates a field that lets you look up a value in another table or in a predefined list of values.	Same size as the primary key field used to perform the lookup

Setting Field Sizes

The **Field Size property** defines a field value's maximum storage size for Text, Number, and AutoNumber fields only. The other data types have no Field Size property because their storage size is either a fixed, predetermined amount or is determined automatically by the field value itself, as shown in Figure 2-4. A Text field has a default field size of 255 characters; you can also set its field size by entering a number from 0 to 255. For example, the First Name and Last Name fields in the Customer table will be Text fields with a size of 20 characters and 25 characters, respectively. These field sizes will accommodate the values that will be entered in each of these fields.

InSight		**Understanding the Field Size Property for Number Fields**

When you use the Number data type to define a field, you should set the field's Field Size property based on the largest value that you expect to store in that field. Access processes smaller data sizes faster, using less memory, so you can optimize your database's performance and its storage space by selecting the correct field size for each field. Field Size property settings for Number fields are as follows:

- **Byte:** Stores whole numbers (numbers with no fractions) from 0 to 255 in one byte
- **Integer:** Stores whole numbers from −32,768 to 32,767 in two bytes
- **Long Integer** (default): Stores whole numbers from −2,147,483,648 to 2,147,483,647 in four bytes
- **Single:** Stores positive and negative numbers to precisely seven decimal places and uses four bytes
- **Double:** Stores positive and negative numbers to precisely 15 decimal places and uses eight bytes
- **Replication ID:** Establishes a unique identifier for replication of tables, records, and other objects in databases created using Access 2003 and earlier versions and uses 16 bytes
- **Decimal:** Stores positive and negative numbers to precisely 28 decimal places and uses 12 bytes

For example, it would be wasteful to use the Long Integer field size for a Number field that will store only whole numbers ranging from 0 to 255, because the Long Integer field size uses four bytes of storage space. A better choice would be the Byte field size, which uses one byte of storage space to store the same values.

In Tutorial 1, you created the Belmont database and the Contract table. Access assigned the data types and field formatting for the fields you created in the Contract table based on the data you entered into each field in Datasheet view. Oren suggests that you view the data types and formatting of the fields in the Contract table to determine if you need to modify any of them to better store and format the data they contain.

Viewing and Modifying Field Data Types and Formatting

When you create a table in Datasheet view, such as the Contract table, you enter field (column) headings and field values in the rows below the headings. Access then determines what data type to assign to each field based on the values you enter for the field. If the values entered do not provide enough information for Access to "guess" the data type, the default type assigned is the Text data type.

Now, you'll open the Contract table in the Belmont database to view the data type and formatting for each field in Datasheet view.

To view the data type and formatting of the Contract table's fields:

▶ **1.** Start Access and open the **Belmont** database you created in Tutorial 1. This database file should be located in the Level.01\Tutorial folder provided with your Data Files.

Trouble? If the Security Warning is displayed below the Ribbon, click the Options button next to the Security Warning. In the dialog box that opens, click the "Enable this content" option button, and then click the OK button.

▶ **2.** In the Navigation Pane, double-click **Contract : Table** to open the Contract table in Datasheet view.

▶ **3.** On the Navigation Pane, click the **Shutter Bar Open/Close Button** ≪ to close the pane and view more of the table datasheet.

You can view the data type and some properties for each field using the Datasheet tab.

▶ **4.** Click in the first field value for the **Contract Num** field to make it the current field, and then click the **Datasheet** tab on the Ribbon. The Data Type option in the Data Type & Formatting group indicates that the current field, Contract Num, has the Text data type. In Tutorial 1, you changed the data type for this field to Text after you created this field by renaming the default primary key ID field.

▶ **5.** Press the **Tab** key to move to the Customer ID field and make it the active field. This field has the Number data type. See Figure 2-5.

Data type for the Customer ID field ◀ Figure 2-5

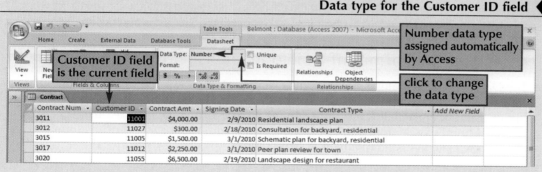

Access automatically assigned the Number data type to the Customer ID field when you created the Contract table in Tutorial 1. Because you entered numeric values in the field, such as 11001, Access determined that the field should be a Number field. However, the Number data type is best used for fields that will be used in mathematical calculations (except those involving money), or for numeric values that require a high degree of accuracy. The Customer ID field values will not be used in calculations; therefore, the Text data type is a better choice for this field.

Changing the Data Type of a Field in Datasheet View

As you learned in Tutorial 1, you can easily change the data type for a field in Datasheet view. Next, you'll change the data type of the Customer ID field to Text.

To change the data type of the Customer ID field:

▶ **1.** Make sure the Customer ID field is still the active field.

▶ **2.** In the Data Type & Formatting group on the Datasheet tab, click the **Data Type arrow**, and then click **Text**. The Customer ID field is now a Text field. See Figure 2-6.

Figure 2-6   Customer ID field data type changed to Text

field values are now left-aligned

Notice that the values in the Customer ID field now appear left-aligned within their boxes, as opposed to their previous right-aligned format (see Figure 2-5). In Access, values for Text fields are left-aligned, and values for Number, Date/Time, and Currency fields are right-aligned.

The next field in the Contract table, Contract Amt, contains dollar values representing the total amount of each Belmont Landscapes contract. Oren knows that these dollar amounts will never contain cents, because the contracts are drawn up in whole amounts only; therefore, the two decimal places currently shown for the values are unnecessary. Furthermore, Oren feels that the dollar signs clutter the datasheet and are also unnecessary. He asks you to modify the format of the Contract Amt field to remove the dollar signs and decimal places.

Changing the Format of a Field in Datasheet View

The Data Type & Formatting group on the Datasheet tab allows you to modify some formatting for certain field types. When you format a field, you change the way data is displayed, but not the actual values stored in the table. Next, you'll use the options provided to modify the format of the Contract Amt field. You'll also check the format of the Signing Date field and modify it, if necessary.

To modify the format of the Contract Amt and Signing Date fields:

1. With the Customer ID field still active, press the **Tab** key to move to the Contract Amt field. The options in the Data Type & Formatting group indicate that this field has the Currency data type and the Currency format. See Figure 2-7.

Figure 2-7   Contract Amt field with the Currency data type

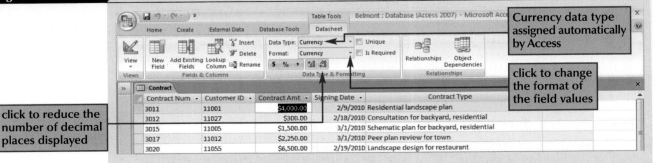

click to reduce the number of decimal places displayed

When you first entered the field values for the Contract Amt field in Tutorial 1, you included the dollar sign and commas; therefore, Access determined that this field should have the Currency data type, which is correct. The Currency format specifies that the values appear with dollar signs and two decimal places. You need to change this format to the Standard format, which does not contain dollar signs.

▶ **2.** In the Data Type & Formatting group, click the **Format arrow**, and then click **Standard**. The dollar signs are removed, but the two decimal places are still displayed.

▶ **3.** In the Data Type & Formatting group, click the **Decrease Decimals** button ![icon]. Access decreases the decimal places by one, and the values now display only one decimal place.

▶ **4.** Click the **Decrease Decimals** button ![icon] again to remove the second decimal place and the decimal point. The Contract Amt field values are now displayed without dollar signs or decimal places. See Figure 2-8.

Contract Amt field values after modifying the format ◀ Figure 2-8

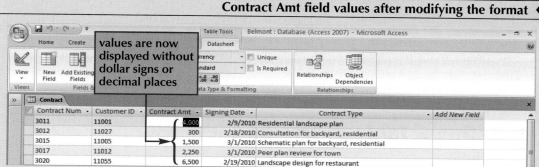

▶ **5.** Press the **Tab** key to move to the Signing Date field. The Data Type option shows that this field is a Date/Time field. In Tutorial 1, when you entered date values in this field, Access automatically assigned the Date/Time data type to the field.

By default, Access assigns the General Date format to Date/Time fields. This format includes settings for date or time values, or a combination of date and time values. However, Oren wants only date values to appear in the Signing Date field, so he asks you to specify the Short Date format for the field.

▶ **6.** In the Data Type & Formatting group, click the **Format arrow**, and then click **Short Date**. See Figure 2-9.

Signing Date field after modifying the format ◀ Figure 2-9

Tip

When working with date values, you can type dates directly or click the calendar button shown in Figure 2-9 to select a date from an interactive calendar.

Although no change is apparent in the worksheet—the Signing Date field values already appear with the Short Date setting (for example, 2/9/2010), as part of the default format—the field now has the Short Date format applied to it. This ensures that only date field values, and not time or date/time values, are allowed in the field.

▶ 7. Press the **Tab** key to move to the Contract Type field. Notice that Access assigned the Text data type to this field, which is correct because this field stores values with fewer than 255 characters.

Each of the three Text fields in this table—Contract Num, Customer ID, and Contract Type—has the default field size of 255. To change the field size, you need to work in Design view. You'll change the field sizes for these fields later in this session, after you learn more about Design view. For now, you can close the Contract table.

To close the Contract table:

▶ 1. Click the **Close 'Contract'** button ⊠ on the table window bar.

According to his plan for the Belmont database, Oren wants to track information about the invoices the firm sends to its customers. Next, you'll create the Invoice table for Oren—this time, working directly in Design view.

Creating a Table in Design View

Creating a table in Design view involves entering the field names and defining the properties for the fields, specifying a primary key for the table, and then saving the table structure.

Oren documented the design for the new Invoice table by listing each field's name, data type, size (if applicable), and description, as shown in Figure 2-10.

| Figure 2-10 | Design for the Invoice table |

Field Name	Data Type	Field Size	Description	Other
Invoice Num	Text	4	Primary key	
Contract Num	Text	4	Foreign key	
Invoice Amt	Currency			Format = Currency
				Decimal Places = 2
Invoice Date	Date/Time			Format = mm/dd/yyyy
Invoice Paid	Yes/No			

You will use Oren's design as a guide for creating the Invoice table in the Belmont database.

To begin creating the Invoice table:

▶ 1. Click the **Create** tab on the Ribbon.

▶ 2. In the Tables group on the Create tab, click the **Table Design** button. A new table named Table1 opens in Design view. See Figure 2-11.

Table window in Design view ◄ Figure 2-11

You use **Design view** to define or modify a table structure or the properties of the fields in a table.

Defining Fields

Initially, the default table name, Table1, appears on the tab for the new table, and the insertion point is located in the first row's Field Name box. After you type the field's name and press the Tab key to move to the Data Type box for the field, the purpose or characteristics of the current property (Field Name, in this case) will appear in the Field Properties pane. You can display more complete Help information about the current property by pressing the **F1 key**.

You enter values for the Field Name, Data Type, and Description field properties in the **Table Design grid**. You select values for all other field properties, most of which are optional, in the **Field Properties pane**. These other properties will appear when you move to the first row's Data Type box.

Defining a Field in Design View | Reference Window

- In the Field Name box, type the name for the field, and then press the Tab key.
- Accept the default Text data type, or click the arrow and select a different data type for the field. Press the Tab key.
- Enter an optional description for the field, if necessary.
- Use the Field Properties pane to type or select other field properties, as appropriate.

The first field you need to define is the Invoice Num field. This field will be the primary key for the Invoice table.

To define the Invoice Num field:

▶ **1.** Type **Invoice Num** in the first row's Field Name box, and then press the **Tab** key to advance to the Data Type box. The default data type, Text, appears highlighted in the Data Type box, which now also contains an arrow, and the field properties for a Text field appear in the Field Properties pane. See Figure 2-12.

| Figure 2-12 | Table window after entering the first field name |

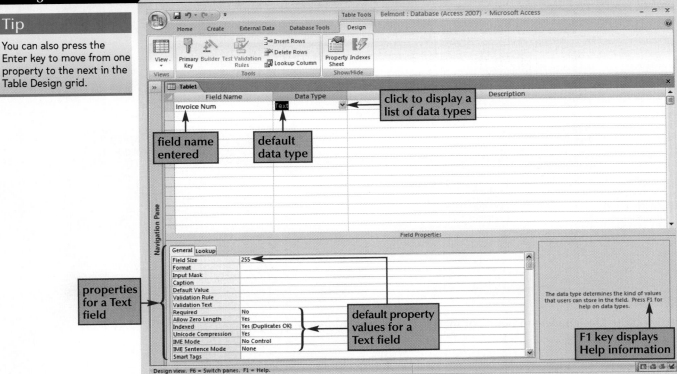

Notice that the right side of the Field Properties pane now provides an explanation for the current property, Data Type. You can display Help information about the current property by pressing the F1 key.

Trouble? If you make a typing error, you can correct it by clicking to position the insertion point, and then using either the Backspace key to delete characters to the left of the insertion point or the Delete key to delete characters to the right of the insertion point. Then type the correct text.

Because the Invoice Num field values will not be used in calculations, you will accept the default Text data type for the field.

▶ **2.** Press the **Tab** key to accept Text as the data type and to advance to the Description box.

Next you'll enter the Description property value as "Primary key." You can use the **Description property** to enter an optional description for a field to explain its purpose or usage. A field's Description property can be up to 255 characters long, and its value appears on the status bar when you view the table datasheet. Note that specifying "Primary key" for the Description property does *not* establish the current field as the primary key; you use a button on the Ribbon to specify the primary key in Design view, which you will do later in this session.

▶ **3.** Type **Primary key** in the Description box.

Notice the Field Size property for the field. The default setting of 255 for Text fields is displayed. You need to change this number to 4 because all invoice numbers at Belmont Landscapes contain only four digits.

▶ **4.** Double-click the number **255** in the Field Size property box to select it, and then type **4**. The definition of the first field is complete. See Figure 2-13.

Invoice Num field defined ◀ Figure 2-13

Oren's Invoice table design (Figure 2-10) shows Contract Num as the second field. Because Oren and other staff members want to relate information about invoices to the contract data in the Contract table, the Invoice table must include the Contract Num field, which is the Contract table's primary key. Recall that when you include the primary key from one table as a field in a second table to connect the two tables, the field is a foreign key in the second table. The field must be defined in the same way in both tables.

Next, you will define Contract Num as a Text field with a Field Size of 4. Later in this session, you will change the Field Size of the Contract Num field in the Contract table to 4 so that the field definition is the same in both tables.

To define the Contract Num field:

▶ **1.** In the Table Design grid, click in the second row's Field Name box, type **Contract Num** in the box, and then press the **Tab** key to advance to the Data Type box.

▶ **2.** Press the **Tab** key to accept Text as the field's data type. Because the Contract Num field is a foreign key to the Contract table, you'll enter "Foreign key" in the Description property to help users of the database understand the purpose of this field.

▶ **3.** Type **Foreign key** in the Description box.

Next, you'll change the Field Size property to 4. When defining the fields in a table, you can move between the Table Design grid and the Field Properties pane of the Table window by pressing the **F6** key.

▶ **4.** Press the **F6** key to move to the Field Properties pane. The current entry for the Field Size property, 255, is highlighted.

▶ **5.** Type **4** to set the Field Size property. You have completed the definition of the second field.

The third field in the Invoice table is the Invoice Amt field, which will display currency values, similar to the Contract Amt field in the Contract table. However, for this field, Oren wants the values to appear with two decimal places, because invoice amounts might include cents. He also wants the values to include dollar signs, so that the values will be formatted as currency when they are printed in reports sent to customers.

To define the Invoice Amt field:

▶ **1.** Click in the third row's Field Name box, type **Invoice Amt** in the box, and then press the **Tab** key to advance to the Data Type box.

▶ **2.** Click the **Data Type** arrow, click **Currency** in the list box, and then press the **Tab** key to advance to the Description box.

According to Oren's design (Figure 2-10), you do not need to enter a description for this field. If you've assigned a descriptive field name and the field does not fulfill a special function (such as primary key), you usually do not enter a value for the optional Description property. Invoice Amt is a field that does not require a value for its Description property.

Oren wants the Invoice Amt field values to be displayed with two decimal places, even if he decides to change the format for this field later. The **Decimal Places property** specifies the number of decimal places that are displayed to the right of the decimal point.

Tip

You can display the arrow and the list box simultaneously if you click the right side of a box.

▶ **3.** In the Field Properties pane, click the **Decimal Places** box to position the insertion point there. An arrow appears on the right side of the Decimal Places box. When you position the insertion point or select text in many Access boxes, Access displays an arrow, which you can click to display a list box with options.

▶ **4.** Click the **Decimal Places** arrow, and then click **2** in the list box to specify two decimal places for the Invoice Amt field values. The definition of the third field is now complete. See Figure 2-14.

Figure 2-14	Table window after defining the first three fields

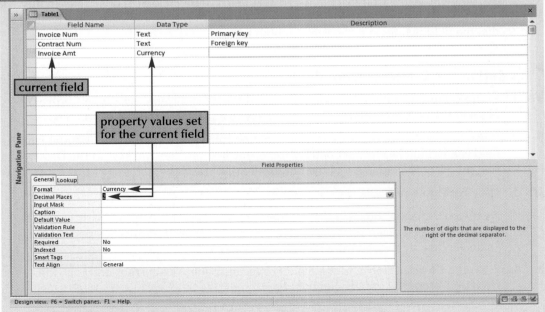

The next field you'll define in the Invoice table is Invoice Date. This field will contain the dates on which invoices are generated for Belmont Landscapes customers. When Belmont Landscapes first draws up contracts with its customers, the firm establishes invoice dates based on the different phases of the projects. For long-term projects with multiple phases, some of these dates are months or years in the future. You'll define the Invoice Date field using the Date/Time data type. Also, according to Oren's design (Figure 2-10), the date values should be displayed in the format mm/dd/yyyy, which is a two-digit month, a two-digit day, and a four-digit year.

To define the Invoice Date field:

1. Click in the fourth row's Field Name box, type **Invoice Date**, and then press the **Tab** key to advance to the Data Type box.

   You can select a value from the Data Type list box as you did for the Invoice Amt field. Alternately, you can type the property value in the box or type just the first character of the property value.

2. Type **d**. The value in the fourth row's Data Type box changes to "date/Time," with the letters "ate/Time" highlighted. See Figure 2-15.

Selecting a value for the Data Type property **Figure 2-15**

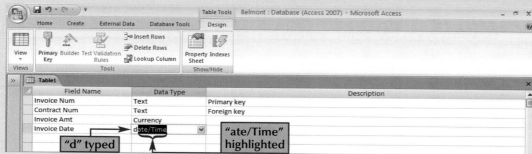

3. Press the **Tab** key to advance to the Description box. Note that Access changes the value for the Data Type property to "Date/Time."

   Oren wants the values in the Invoice Date field to be displayed in a format showing the month, the day, and a four-digit year, as in the following example: 03/11/2010. You use the Format property to control the display of a field value.

4. In the Field Properties pane, click the right side of the **Format** box to display the list of predefined formats for Date/Time fields. As noted in the right side of the Field Properties pane, you can either choose a predefined format or enter a custom format.

   Trouble? If you see an arrow instead of a list of predefined formats, click the arrow to display the list.

   None of the predefined formats matches the exact layout Oren wants for the Invoice Date values. Therefore, you need to create a custom date format. Figure 2-16 shows some of the symbols available for custom date and time formats.

Tip

A complete description of all the custom formats is available in Access Help.

Figure 2-16 ▶ **Symbols for some custom date formats**

Symbol	Description
/	date separator
d	day of the month in one or two numeric digits, as needed (1 to 31)
dd	day of the month in two numeric digits (01 to 31)
ddd	first three letters of the weekday (Sun to Sat)
dddd	full name of the weekday (Sunday to Saturday)
w	day of the week (1 to 7)
ww	week of the year (1 to 53)
m	month of the year in one or two numeric digits, as needed (1 to 12)
mm	month of the year in two numeric digits (01 to 12)
mmm	first three letters of the month (Jan to Dec)
mmmm	full name of the month (January to December)
yy	last two digits of the year (01 to 99)
yyyy	full year (0100 to 9999)

Oren wants the dates to be displayed with a two-digit month (mm), a two-digit day (dd), and a four-digit year (yyyy). You'll enter this custom format now.

▶ **5.** Click the **Format** arrow to close the list of predefined formats, and then type **mm/dd/yyyy** in the Format property box. See Figure 2-17.

Figure 2-17 ▶ **Specifying the custom date format**

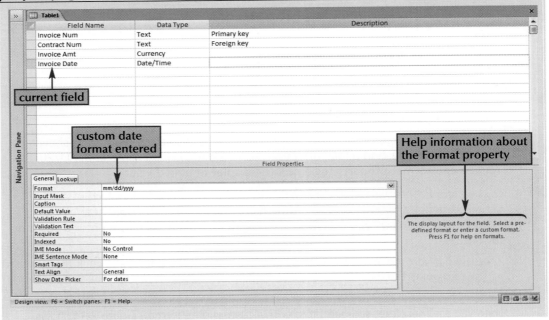

The fifth, and final, field to be defined in the Invoice table is Invoice Paid. This field will be a Yes/No field to indicate the payment status of each invoice record stored in the Invoice table.

To define the Invoice Paid field:

▶ **1.** Click in the fifth row's Field Name box, type **Invoice Paid**, and then press the **Tab** key to advance to the Data Type box.

▶ **2.** Type **y**. Access completes the data type as "yes/No."

▶ **3.** Press the **Tab** key to select the Yes/No data type and move to the Description box.

According to Oren's table design (see Figure 2-10), the Invoice Paid field does not have a description, so you've finished defining the fields for the Invoice table. Next, you need to specify the primary key for the table.

Specifying the Primary Key

As you learned in Tutorial 1, the primary key for a table uniquely identifies each record in a table.

Understanding the Importance of the Primary Key | InSight

Although Access does not require a table to have a primary key, including a primary key offers several advantages:

- A primary key uniquely identifies each record in a table.
- Access does not allow duplicate values in the primary key field. For example, if a record already exists in the Contract table with a Contract Num value of 3020, Access prevents you from adding another record with this same value in the Contract Num field. Preventing duplicate values ensures the uniqueness of the primary key field.
- When a primary key has been specified, Access forces you to enter a value for the primary key field in every record in the table. This is known as **entity integrity**. If you do not enter a value for a field, you have actually given the field a **null value**. You cannot give a null value to the primary key field because entity integrity prevents Access from accepting and processing that record.
- Access stores records on disk as you enter them. You can enter records in any order, but Access displays them by default in order by the field values of the primary key. If you enter records in no specific order, you are ensured that you will later be able to work with them in a more meaningful, primary key sequence.
- Access responds faster to your requests for specific records based on the primary key.

According to Oren's design, you need to specify Invoice Num as the primary key for the Invoice table. You can do so while the table is in Design view.

Specifying a Primary Key in Design View | Reference Window

- In the Table window in Design view, click in the row for the field you've chosen to be the primary key. If the primary key will consist of two or more fields, click the row selector for the first field, press and hold down the Ctrl key, and then click the row selector for each additional primary key field.
- In the Tools group on the Table Tools Design tab, click the Primary Key button.

To specify Invoice Num as the primary key:

▶ **1.** Click in the row for the Invoice Num field to make it the current field.

▶ **2.** In the Tools group on the Table Tools Design tab, click the **Primary Key** button. A key symbol appears in the row selector for the first row, indicating that the Invoice Num field is the table's primary key. See Figure 2-18.

Figure 2-18 Invoice Num field selected as the primary key

Tip

The Primary Key button works as a toggle; you can click it to remove the key symbol from the selected field if you want to specify a different field as the primary key.

You've defined the fields for the Invoice table and specified its primary key, so you can now save the table structure.

Saving the Table Structure

The last step in creating a table is to name the table and save the table's structure. When you save a table structure, the table is stored in the database file (in this case, the Belmont database file). Once the table is saved, you can use it to enter data in the table. According to Oren's plan, you need to save the table you've defined as "Invoice."

To name and save the Invoice table:

▶ 1. Click the **Save** button 🖫 on the Quick Access Toolbar. The Save As dialog box opens.

▶ 2. Type **Invoice** in the Table Name text box, and then press the **Enter** key. Access saves the table with the name Invoice in the Belmont database. Notice that the tab for the table now displays the name "Invoice" instead of Table1.

Modifying the Structure of an Access Table

Even a well-designed table might need to be modified. Access allows you to modify a table's structure in Design view: you can change the order of fields, add and delete fields, and change field properties.

After meeting with Sarah Fisher, the office manager at Belmont Landscapes, and reviewing the structure of the Invoice table, Oren has changes he wants you to make to the table. First, he wants the Invoice Amt field to be moved so that it appears right before the Invoice Paid field. Then, he wants you to add a new Text field, named Invoice Item, to the table to include information about what the invoice is for, such as schematic landscape plans, construction documents, and so on. Oren would like the Invoice Item field to be inserted between the Invoice Date and Invoice Amt fields.

Moving a Field

To move a field, you use the mouse to drag it to a new location in the Table window in Design view. Next, you'll move the Invoice Amt field so that it is before the Invoice Paid field.

To move the Invoice Amt field:

▶ **1.** Position the pointer on the row selector for the Invoice Amt field until the pointer changes to a ➡ shape.

▶ **2.** Click the **row selector** to select the entire Invoice Amt row.

▶ **3.** Place the pointer on the row selector for the Invoice Amt field, click the ⬚ pointer, and then drag the ⬚ pointer to the row selector for the Invoice Paid field. See Figure 2-19.

Moving the Invoice Amt field in the table structure ◀ Figure 2-19

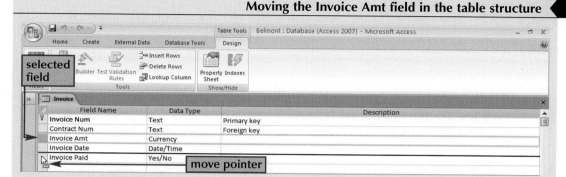

▶ **4.** Release the mouse button. Access moves the Invoice Amt field between the Invoice Date and Invoice Paid fields in the table structure.

Trouble? If the Invoice Amt field did not move, repeat Steps 1 through 4, making sure you hold down the mouse button during the drag operation.

Adding a Field

Next, you need to add the Invoice Item field to the table structure between the Invoice Date and Invoice Amt fields. To add a new field between existing fields, you must insert a row. You begin by selecting the field that will be below the new field you want to insert.

Adding a Field Between Two Existing Fields | Reference Window

- In the Table window in Design view, select the row for the field above which you want to add a new field.
- In the Tools group on the Table Tools Design tab, click the Insert Rows button.
- Define the new field by entering the field name, data type, optional description, and any property specifications.

To add the Invoice Item field to the Invoice table:

▶ **1.** Click in the Field Name box for the Invoice Amt field. You need to establish this field as the current field so that the row for the new record will be inserted above this field.

▶ **2.** In the Tools group on the Table Tools Design tab, click the **Insert Rows** button. Access adds a new, blank row between the Invoice Date and Invoice Amt fields. The insertion point is positioned in the Field Name box for the new row, ready for you to type the name for the new field. See Figure 2-20.

Figure 2-20 ▶ Table structure after inserting a row

You'll define the Invoice Item field in the new row of the Invoice table. This field will be a Text field with a Field Size of 40.

▶ **3.** Type **Invoice Item**, press the **Tab** key to move to the Data Type property, and then press the **Tab** key again to accept the default Text data type and to move to the Description property.

▶ **4.** Press the **F6** key to move to the Field Size property and to select the default field size, and then type **40**. The definition of the new field is complete. See Figure 2-21.

Figure 2-21 ▶ Invoice Item field added to the Invoice table

▶ **5.** Click the **Save** button on the Quick Access Toolbar to save the changes to the Invoice table structure.

Changing Field Properties

With the Invoice table design complete, you can now go back and modify the Field Size property for the three Text fields in the Contract table. Recall that each of these fields still has the default field size of 255, which is too large for the data contained in these fields.

To modify the Field Size property of the Contract table's Text fields:

▶ **1.** Click the **Close 'Invoice'** button ☒ on the table window bar to close the Invoice table.

▶ **2.** On the Navigation Pane, click the **Shutter Bar Open/Close Button** ⏩ to open the pane. Notice that the Invoice table is listed below the bar containing the word "Invoice." Because the Navigation Pane is set to All Tables view, the pane organizes objects by table and displays each table name in its own bar. See Figure 2-22.

Navigation Pane with two tables ◀ **Figure 2-22**

objects are organized by tables in the Navigation Pane

new Invoice table object

▶ **3.** Double-click **Contract : Table** to open the Contract table in Datasheet view. To change the Field Size property, you need to display the table in Design view.

▶ **4.** In the Views group on the Home tab, click the **View** button. The table is displayed in Design view with the Contract Num field selected. You need to change the Field Size property for this field to 4, because each contract number at Belmont Landscapes consists of four digits.

▶ **5.** Press the **F6** key to move to and select the default setting of 255 for the Field Size property, and then type **4**.

Next you need to set the Customer ID Field Size property to 5, because each Customer ID number at Belmont Landscapes consists of five digits.

▶ **6.** Click in the **Customer ID** Field Name box to make this the active field, press the **F6** key, and then type **5**.

Finally, for the Contract Type field, you will set the Field Size property to 75. This size can accommodate the values for the Contract Type field, some of which are lengthy.

▶ **7.** Click in the **Contract Type** Field Name box, press the **F6** key, and then type **75**. Now you can save the modified table.

▶ **8.** Click the **Save** button 🖫 on the Quick Access Toolbar. A dialog box opens informing you that some data may be lost because you decreased the field sizes. Because you know that all of the values in the Contract Num, Customer ID, and Contract Type fields include fewer characters than the new Field Size properties that you set for each field, you can ignore this message.

▶ **9.** Click the **Yes** button, and then close the Contract table.

▶ **10.** If you are not continuing to Session 2.2, click the **Close** button ☒ on the program window title bar. Access closes the Belmont database, and then the Access program closes.

You have created the Invoice table and made modifications to its design. In the next session, you'll add records to the Invoice table and create the new Customer table in the Belmont database.

Review | **Session 2.1 Quick Check**

1. What guidelines should you follow when designing a database?
2. What is the purpose of the Data Type property for a field?
3. For which three types of fields can you assign a field size?
4. The default Field Size property setting for a Text field is _____ .
5. In Design view, which key do you press to move from the Table Design grid to the Field Properties pane?
6. A(n) _____ value, which results when you do not enter a value for a field, is not permitted for a primary key.

Session 2.2

Adding Records to a New Table

The Invoice table design is complete. Now, Oren would like you to add records to the table so it will contain the invoice data for Belmont Landscapes. You add records to a table in Datasheet view as you did in Tutorial 1, by typing the field values in the rows below the column headings for the fields. You'll begin by entering the records shown in Figure 2-23.

Figure 2-23	Records to be added to the Invoice table

Invoice Num	Contract Num	Invoice Date	Invoice Item	Invoice Amt	Invoice Paid
2011	3011	03/23/2010	Schematic Plan	$1,500.00	Yes
2031	3020	04/19/2010	Schematic Plan	$1,500.00	Yes
2073	3023	09/21/2012	Construction Observation	$10,000.00	No
2062	3026	09/12/2011	Permitting	$10,000.00	No

To add the first record to the Invoice table:

▶ 1. If you took a break after the previous session, make sure that the **Belmont** database is open, and the Navigation Pane is open.

▶ 2. In the Navigation Pane, double-click **Invoice : Table** to open the Invoice table in Datasheet view.

▶ 3. Close the Navigation Pane, and then use the ↔ pointer to resize each column so that the field names are completely visible.

▶ 4. In the Invoice Num field, type **2011**, press the **Tab** key, type **3011** in the Contract Num field, and then press the **Tab** key.

Next you need to enter the Invoice Date field value. Recall that you specified a custom date format, mm/dd/yyyy, for this field. You do not need to type each digit; for example, you can type just "3" instead of "03" for the month, and you can type "10" instead of "2010" for the year. Access will display the full value according to the custom date format.

5. Type **3/23/10**, press the **Tab** key, type **Schematic Plan** in the Invoice Item field, and then press the **Tab** key. Notice that Access displays the date "03/23/2010" in the Invoice Date field.

   Next you need to enter the Invoice Amt value for the first record. This is a Currency field with the Currency format and two decimal places specified. Because of the field's set properties, you do not need to type the dollar sign, comma, or zeroes for the decimal places; Access will display these items automatically for you.

6. Type **1500** and then press the **Tab** key. Access displays the value as "$1,500.00."

   The last field in the table, Invoice Paid, is a Yes/No field. Notice the check box displayed in the field. By default, the value for any Yes/No field is "No"; therefore, the check box is initially empty. For Yes/No fields with check boxes, you press the Tab key to leave the check box unchecked, and you press the spacebar to insert a check mark in the check box. For the record you are entering in the Invoice table, the invoice has been paid, so you need to insert a check mark in the check box.

7. Press the **spacebar** to insert a check mark, and then press the **Tab** key. The values for the first record are entered. See Figure 2-24.

First record entered in the Invoice table   **Figure 2-24**

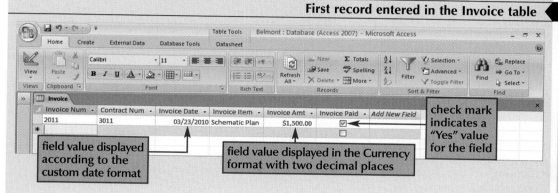

field value displayed according to the custom date format

field value displayed in the Currency format with two decimal places

check mark indicates a "Yes" value for the field

Tip

The spacebar works as a toggle for check boxes in Yes/No fields; you press the spacebar to insert a check mark in an empty check box and to remove an existing check mark. You can also change a check box to select it or deselect it by clicking it with the mouse.

Now you can add the remaining three records. As you do, you'll learn a shortcut for inserting the value from the same field in the previous record.

To add the next three records to the Invoice table:

1. Refer to Figure 2-23 and enter the values for the second record's Invoice Num, Contract Num, and Invoice Date fields.

   Notice the value for the second record's Invoice Item field, "Schematic Plan." This value is the exact same value as this field in the first record. You can quickly insert the value from the same field in the previous record using the **Ctrl + '** (apostrophe) keyboard shortcut.

2. In the Invoice Item field, press the **Ctrl + '** keys. Access inserts the value "Schematic Plan" in the Invoice Item field for the second record.

3. Press the **Tab** key to move to the Invoice Amt field. Again, the value you need to enter for this field—$1,500.00—is the same as the value for this field in the previous record. So, you can use the keyboard shortcut again.

4. In the Invoice Amt field, press the **Ctrl + '** keys. Access inserts the value $1,500.00 in the Invoice Amt field for the second record.

5. Press the **Tab** key to move to the Invoice Paid field, press the **spacebar** to insert a check mark in the check box, and then press the **Tab** key. The second record is entered in the Invoice table.

> **6.** Refer to Figure 2-23 to enter the values for the third and fourth records, using the Ctrl + ' keys to enter the fourth record's Invoice Amt value. Also, for both records, the invoices have not been paid. Therefore, be sure to press the Tab key to leave the Invoice Paid field values unchecked (signifying "No").

> **7.** Resize the columns, as necessary, so that all field values are completely visible. Your table should look like the one in Figure 2-25.

Figure 2-25 | **Invoice table with four records added**

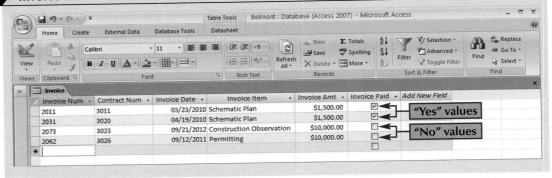

To complete the entry of records in the Invoice table, you'll use a method that allows you to import the data.

Importing Data from an Excel Worksheet

Often, the data you want to add to an Access table exists in another file, such as a Word document or an Excel workbook. You can bring the data from other files into Access in different ways. For example, you can copy and paste the data from an open file, or you can **import** the data, which is a process that allows you to copy the data from a source without having to open the source file.

Oren had been using Excel to track invoice data for Belmont Landscapes and already created a worksheet, named "Invoices," containing this data. You'll import this Excel worksheet into your Invoice table to complete the entry of data in the table. To use the import method, the columns in the Excel worksheet must match the names and data types of the fields in the Access table. The Invoices worksheet contains the following columns: Invoice Num, Contract Num, Invoice Date, Invoice Item, Invoice Amt, and Invoice Paid. These column headings match the fields names in the Invoice table exactly, so you can import the data. Before you import data into a table, you need to close the table.

To import the Invoices worksheet into the Invoice table:

> **1.** Click the **Close 'Invoice'** button ☒ on the table window bar to close the Invoice table. A dialog box opens asking if you want to save the changes to the table layout. This dialog box opens because you resized the table columns.

> **2.** Click the **Yes** button in the dialog box.

> **3.** Click the **External Data** tab on the Ribbon.

> **4.** In the Import group on the External Data tab, click the **Excel** button (with the ScreenTip "Import Excel spreadsheet"). The Get External Data - Excel Spreadsheet dialog box opens. See Figure 2-26.

Get External Data - Excel Spreadsheet dialog box | Figure 2-26

The dialog box provides options for importing the entire worksheet as a new table in the current database, adding the data from the worksheet to an existing table, or linking the data in the worksheet to the table. You need to add, or append, the worksheet data to the Invoice table.

▶ **5.** Click the **Browse** button. The File Open dialog box opens. The Excel workbook file is named "Invoices" and is located in the Level.01\Tutorial folder provided with your Data Files.

▶ **6.** Navigate to the **Level.01\Tutorial** folder, where your starting Data Files are stored, and then double-click the **Invoices** Excel file. You return to the dialog box.

▶ **7.** Click the **Append a copy of the records to the table** option button. The list box to the right of this option becomes active. Next, you need to select the table to which you want to add the data.

▶ **8.** Click the **arrow** on the list box, and then click **Invoice**.

▶ **9.** Click the **OK** button. The first Import Spreadsheet Wizard dialog box opens. See Figure 2-27.

Figure 2-27 ▶ **First Import Spreadsheet Wizard dialog box**

The dialog box shows all the worksheets in the selected Excel workbook. In this case, the Invoices workbook contains only one worksheet, which is also named "Invoices." The bottom section of the dialog box displays some of the data contained in the selected worksheet.

▶ **10.** Click the **Next** button. The second Import Spreadsheet Wizard dialog box opens and indicates that the column headings from the Invoices worksheet will be used as field names in the table.

▶ **11.** Click the **Next** button. The third, and final, Import Spreadsheet Wizard dialog box opens. Notice that the Import to Table text box shows that the data from the spreadsheet will be imported into the Invoice table.

▶ **12.** Click the **Finish** button. A dialog box opens asking if you want to save the import steps. If you needed to repeat this same import procedure many times, it would be a good idea to save the steps for the procedure. However, you don't need to save these steps because you'll be importing the data only this one time. Once the data is in the Access table, Oren will no longer use Excel to track invoice data.

▶ **13.** Click the **Close** button in the dialog box to close it without saving the steps.

The data from the Invoices worksheet has been added to the Invoice table. Next, you'll open the table to view the new records.

To open the Invoice table and view the imported data:

▶ **1.** Open the Navigation Pane, and then double-click **Invoice : Table** to open the table in Datasheet view.

▶ **2.** Resize the Invoice Item column so that all field values are fully displayed. Notice that the table now contains a total of 176 records—four records you entered plus 172 records imported from the Invoices worksheet. The records are displayed in primary key order by the values in the Invoice Num field. See Figure 2-28.

Invoice table after importing data from Excel ◀ Figure 2-28

records are displayed in order by the Invoice Num field values

table contains a total of 176 records

▶ **3.** Save and close the Invoice table, and then close the Navigation Pane.

Two of the tables—Contract and Invoice—are now complete. According to Oren's plan for the Belmont database, you need to create a third table, named "Customer," to track data about Belmont Landscapes' residential and commercial customers. You'll use a different method to create this table.

Creating a Table by Importing an Existing Table Structure

If another Access database contains a table—or even just the design, or structure, of a table—that you want to include in your database, you can easily import the table and any records it contains or import only the table structure into your database.

Oren documented the design for the new Customer table by listing each field's name, data type, size (if applicable), and description, as shown in Figure 2-29. Note that each field in the Customer table will be a Text field, and the Customer ID field will be the table's primary key.

Figure 2-29 ▶ **Design for the Customer table**

Field Name	Data Type	Field Size	Description
Customer ID	Text	5	Primary key
Company	Text	50	
Last Name	Text	25	Contact's last name
First Name	Text	20	Contact's first name
Phone	Text	14	
Address	Text	35	
City	Text	25	
State	Text	2	
Zip	Text	10	
E-mail Address	Text	50	

Sarah already created an Access database containing a Customer table design. She never entered any records into the table because she wasn't sure if the table design was correct. After reviewing the table design, both Sarah and Oren agree that it contains many of the fields Oren wants to track, but that some changes are needed. Therefore, you can import the table structure in Sarah's database to create the Customer table in the Belmont database, and then modify it to produce the final table structure Oren wants.

To create the Customer table by importing the structure of another table:

▶ 1. Make sure the **External Data** tab is the active tab on the Ribbon.

▶ 2. In the Import group, click the **Access** button. The Get External Data - Access Database dialog box opens. This dialog box is similar to the one you used earlier when importing the Excel spreadsheet.

▶ 3. Click the **Browse** button. The File Open dialog box opens. The Access database file from which you need to import the table structure is named "Sarah" and is located in the Level.01\Tutorial folder provided with your Data Files.

▶ 4. Navigate to the **Level.01\Tutorial** folder, where your starting Data Files are stored, and then double-click the **Sarah** database file. You return to the dialog box.

▶ 5. Make sure the **Import tables, queries, forms, reports, macros, and modules into the current database** option button is selected, and then click the **OK** button. The Import Objects dialog box opens. The dialog box contains tabs for importing all the different types of Access database objects—tables, queries, forms, and so on. The Tables tab is the current tab.

▶ 6. Click the **Options** button in the dialog box to see all the options for importing tables. See Figure 2-30.

Figure 2-30

Import Objects dialog box

Note the Import Tables section of the dialog box, which contains options for importing the definition and data—that is, the structure of the table and any records contained in the table—or the definition only. You need to import only the structure of the Customer table Sarah created.

▶ 7. On the Tables tab, click **Customer** to select this table.

▶ 8. In the Import Tables section of the dialog box, click the **Definition Only** option button, and then click the **OK** button. Access creates the Customer table in the Belmont database using the structure of the Customer table in the Sarah database, and opens a dialog box asking if you want to save the import steps.

▶ 9. Click the **Close** button to close the dialog box without saving the import steps.

▶ 10. Open the Navigation Pane and note that the Customer table is listed.

▶ 11. Double-click **Customer : Table** to open the table, and then close the Navigation Pane. See Figure 2-31.

Figure 2-31

Imported Customer table in Datasheet view

The Customer table opens in Datasheet view. The table contains no records.

The table structure you imported contains more fields than Oren wants to include in the Customer table (see Figure 2-29). Also, he wants to rename and reorder some of the fields. You'll begin to modify the table structure by deleting fields.

Deleting Fields from a Table Structure

After you've created a table using any method, you might need to delete one or more fields. When you delete a field, you also delete all the values for the field from the table. Therefore, before you delete a field you should make sure that you want to do so and that you choose the correct field to delete. You can delete fields from either Datasheet view or Design view.

Reference Window | Deleting a Field from a Table Structure

- In Datasheet view, select the column heading for the field you want to delete.
- In the Fields & Columns group on the Datasheet tab, click the Delete button.

or

- In Design view, click in the Field Name box for the field you want to delete.
- In the Tools group on the Table Tools Design tab, click the Delete Rows button.

Refer back to Figure 2-29. Notice that Oren's design does not specify a Cell Phone field. Oren doesn't think it's necessary to track customers' cell phone numbers because his employees typically contact customers using either their home or business phone numbers. You'll begin to modify the Customer table sturcture by deleting the Cell Phone field.

To delete the Cell Phone field from the table in Datasheet view:

1. Click the **Datasheet** tab on the Ribbon.

2. Click the **Cell Phone** column heading to select the Cell Phone field.

3. In the Fields & Columns group on the Datasheet tab, click the **Delete** button. The Cell Phone field is removed.

You can also delete fields from a table structure in Design view. You'll switch to Design view to delete the rest of the unnecessary fields.

To delete the fields in Design view:

1. In the Views group on the Datasheet tab, click the **View** button. The Customer table opens in Design view. See Figure 2-32.

Figure 2-32 | **Customer table in Design view**

▶ **2.** Click in the **Fax Number** Field Name box to make it the current field.

▶ **3.** In the Tools group on the Table Tools Design tab, click the **Delete Rows** button. The Fax Number field is removed from the Customer table structure.

You'll delete the County, Web Page, and Notes fields next. Instead of deleting these fields individually, you'll use the pointer to select them and then delete them at the same time.

▶ **4.** Click and hold down the mouse button on the row selector for the **County** field, and then drag the mouse to select the **Web Page** and **Notes** fields.

▶ **5.** Release the mouse button. The rows for the three fields are selected.

▶ **6.** In the Tools group on the Table Tools Design tab, click the **Delete Rows** button. See Figure 2-33.

Customer table after deleting fields ◀ Figure 2-33

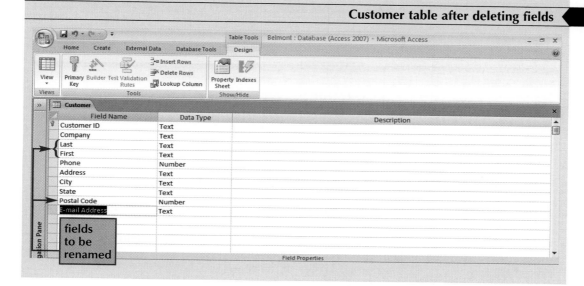

Renaming Fields in Design View

To match Oren's design for the Customer table, you need to rename several fields. In Tutorial 1, you renamed the default primary key field, ID, in Datasheet view. You can also rename fields in Design view by simply editing the names in the Table Design grid.

To rename the fields in Design view:

▶ **1.** Click to position the insertion point to the right of the word **Last** in the third row's Field Name box, press the **spacebar**, and then type **Name**. The name of the third field is now Last Name.

2. Click to position the insertion point to the right of the word **First** in the fourth row's Field Name box, press the **spacebar**, and then type **Name**. The name of the fourth field is now First Name.

You can also select an entire field name and then type new text to replace it.

3. In the ninth field's Field Name box, drag to select the text **Postal Code**, and then type **Zip**. The text you type replaces the original text. See Figure 2-34.

Figure 2-34 | **Customer table after renaming fields**

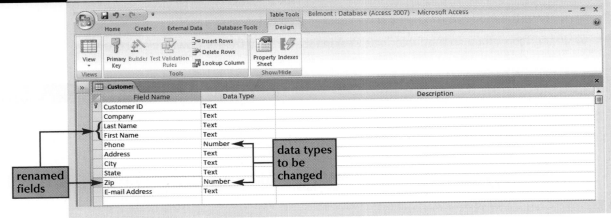

Changing the Data Type for Fields in Design View

According to Oren's plan, all of the fields in the Customer table should be Text fields. The table structure you imported specifies the Number data type for the Phone and the Zip fields. In Tutorial 1, you used an option in Datasheet view to change a field's data type. You can also change the data type for a field in Design view.

To change the data type of the fields in Design view:

1. Click the right side of the **Data Type** box for the Phone field to display the list of data types.

2. Click **Text** in the list. The Phone field is now a Text field. Note that, by default, the Field Size property is set to 255. According to Oren's plan, the Phone field should have a Field Size property of 14. You'll make this change next.

3. Press the **F6** key to move to and select the default Field Size property, and then type **14**.

4. Click the right side of the **Data Type** box for the Zip field, and then click **Text** in the list. The Zip field is now a Text field. According to Oren's plan, you need to change the Field Size property to 10.

5. Press the **F6** key to move to and select the default Field Size property, and then type **10**.

Finally, Oren would like descriptions entered for the Customer ID, Last Name, and First Name fields. You'll enter those now.

To enter the Description property values:

▶ **1.** Click in the Description box for the Customer ID field, and then type **Primary key**.

▶ **2.** Press the ↓ key to move to the Description property for the Company field. After you press the ↓ key, a Property Update Options button 🖅 appears near the Description box for the Company field. When you change a field's property in Design view, you can use this button to update the corresponding property on forms and reports that include the field you've modified. For example, if the Belmont database included a form that contained the Customer ID field, you could choose to **propagate**, or update, the modified Description property in the form by clicking the Property Update Options button, and then choosing the option to make the update everywhere the field is used. The text on the Property Update Options button varies depending on the task; in this case, if you click the button, the option is "Update Status Bar Text everywhere Customer ID is used."

Because the Belmont database does not include any forms or reports that are based on the Customer table, you do not need to update the properties, so you can ignore the button for now.

▶ **3.** Press the ↓ key to move to the Description box for the Last Name field, and then type **Contact's last name**.

▶ **4.** Press the ↓ key to move to the Description box for the First Name field, and then type **Contact's first name**. See Figure 2-35.

| Customer table after changing data types and entering descriptions | Figure 2-35 |

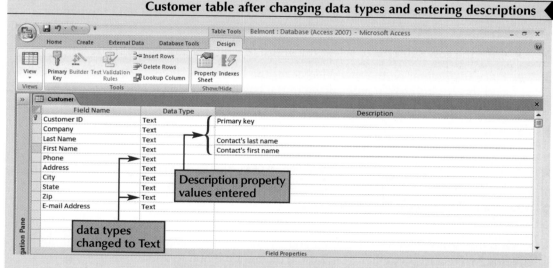

▶ **5.** Click the **Save** button 🖫 on the Quick Access Toolbar to save your changes to the Customer table.

▶ **6.** In the Views group on the Table Tools Design tab, click the **View** button to display the table in Datasheet view. See Figure 2-36.

Figure 2-36   Modified Customer table in Datasheet view

After viewing the Customer table datasheet, Oren decides that he would like the First Name field to appear before the Last Name field. Earlier in this tutorial, when you created the Invoice table, you learned how to change the order of fields in Design view. Although you can reorder fields in Datasheet view by dragging a field's column heading to a new location, doing so rearranges only the *display* of the table's fields; the table structure is not changed. To move a field, you must display the table in Design view.

To move the Last Name field to follow the First Name field:

▶ **1.** In the Views group on the Datasheet tab, click the **View** button. The Customer table opens in Design view.

▶ **2.** Position the pointer on the row selector for the Last Name field until the pointer changes to a ➡ shape.

▶ **3.** Click the **row selector** to select the entire row for the Last Name field.

▶ **4.** Place the pointer on the row selector for the Last Name field, click the ⬚ pointer, and then drag the ⬚ pointer down to the line below the row selector for the First Name field.

▶ **5.** Release the mouse button. The Last Name field now appears below the First Name field in the table structure.

▶ **6.** Click the **Save** button ⬚ on the Quick Access Toolbar to save the change to the Customer table design.

▶ **7.** Display the table in Datasheet view.

With the Customer table design set, you can now enter records in it. You'll begin by entering two records, and then you'll use a different method to add the remaining records.

To add two records to the Customer table:

▶ **1.** Enter the following values for the fields in the first record (these values are for a residential customer with no company name):

Customer ID = **11001**
Company = [do not enter a value; leave blank]
First Name = **Sharon**
Last Name = **Maloney**
Phone = **616-866-3901**
Address = **49 Blackstone Dr**
City = **Rockford**

> State = **MI**
> Zip = **49341**
> E-mail Address = **smaloney2@milocal123.com**

▶ **2.** Enter the following values for the fields in the second record, for a commercial customer:

> Customer ID = **11012**
> Company = **Grand Rapids Engineering Dept.**
> First Name = **Anthony**
> Last Name = **Rodriguez**
> Phone = **616-454-9801**
> Address = **225 Summer St**
> City = **Grand Rapids**
> State = **MI**
> Zip = **49503**
> E-mail Address = **arod24@gred11.gov**

▶ **3.** Close the Customer table.

Before Belmont Landscapes decided to store data using Access, Sarah managed the company's customer data in a different system. She exported that data into a text file and asks you to import it into the new Customer table. You can import the data contained in this text file to add the remaining records to the Customer table.

Adding Data to a Table by Importing a Text File

There are many ways to import data into an Access database. So far, you've learned how to add data to an Access table by importing an Excel spreadsheet, and you've created a new table by importing the structure of an existing table. You can also import data contained in text files.

To complete the entry of records in the Customer table, you'll import the data contained in Sarah's text file. The file is named Customer.txt and is located in the Level.01\Tutorial folder provided with your Data Files.

To import the data contained in the Customer.txt file:

▶ **1.** Click the **External Data** tab on the Ribbon.

▶ **2.** In the Import group, click the **Text File** button (with the ScreenTip "Import text file"). The Get External Data - Text File dialog box opens. This dialog box is similar to the one you used earlier when importing the Excel spreadsheet and the Access table structure.

▶ **3.** Click the **Browse** button. The File Open dialog box opens.

▶ **4.** Navigate to the **Level.01\Tutorial** folder, where your starting Data Files are stored, and then double-click the **Customer** text file. You return to the dialog box.

▶ **5.** Click the **Append a copy of the records to the table** option button. The list box to the right of this option becomes active. Next, you need to select the table to which you want to add the data.

▶ **6.** Click the **arrow** on the list box, and then click **Customer**.

▶ **7.** Click the **OK** button. The first Import Text Wizard dialog box opens. The dialog box indicates that the data to be imported is in a "Delimited" format. A **delimited** text file is one in which fields of data are separated by a character such as a comma or a tab. In this case, the dialog box shows that data is separated by the comma character in the text file.

▶ **8.** Make sure the **Delimited** option button is selected in the dialog box, and then click the **Next** button. The second Import Text Wizard dialog box opens. See Figure 2-37.

| Figure 2-37 | ▶ | **Second Import Text Wizard dialog box** |

This dialog box asks you to confirm the delimiter character that separates the fields in the text file you're importing. Access detects that the comma character is used in the Customer text file and selects this option. The bottom area of the dialog box gives you a preview of the data you're importing.

▶ **9.** Make sure the **Comma** option button is selected, and then click the **Next** button. The third, and final, Import Text Wizard dialog box opens. Notice that the Import to Table text box shows that the data from the text file will be imported into the Customer table.

▶ **10.** Click the **Finish** button. A dialog box opens asking if you want to save the import steps. You'll only import the customer data once, so you can close the dialog box without saving the import steps.

▶ **11.** Click the **Close** button in the dialog box to close it without saving the import steps.

Oren asks you to open the Customer table in Datasheet view so he can see the results of importing the text file.

To view the Customer table datasheet:

▶ **1.** Open the Navigation Pane, and then double-click **Customer : Table** to open the Customer table in Datasheet view. The Customer table contains a total of 40 records.

▶ **2.** Close the Navigation Pane.

Next, you need to resize all the columns in the datasheet, both to make sure all the field values are fully displayed and to reduce the width of any fields that are wider than the values they contain, such as the Zip field. When you resize a column by double-clicking the pointer on the column dividing line, you are sizing the column to its **best fit**—that is, so the column is just wide enough to display the longest visible value in the column, including the field name.

▶ **3.** Resize all the columns to their best fit, scrolling the table datasheet as necessary. When finished, scroll back to display the first fields in the table. See Figure 2-38.

Customer table after importing data from the text file | **Figure 2-38**

Customer ID	Company	First Name	Last Name	Phone	Address	City	State
11001		Sharon	Maloney	616-866-3901	49 Blackstone Dr	Rockford	MI
11005		Owen	Hawes	616-392-0622	102 Pineview Rd	Holland	MI
11008		Melissa	Caputo	269-985-1122	302 Main St	Saint Joseph	MI
11012	Grand Rapids Engineering Dept.	Anthony	Rodriguez	616-454-9801	225 Summer St	Grand Rapids	MI
11014		Amol	Mehta	616-396-1972	54 Lakeshore Ave	Holland	MI
11015		John	Weiss	616-637-7783	456 Winchester St	South Haven	MI
11020	Battle Creek Dental Partners	Harry	Billings	269-963-0808	587 Longmeadow Rd	Battle Creek	MI
11027		Karen	O'Brien	517-483-9244	38 Langley Rd	Lansing	MI
11030	Finn's on the Waterfront	Devin	Finnerty	616-393-1228	78 East 8th St	Holland	MI
11031	Happy Haven Day Care	Kathy	Rowe	616-842-4603	29 Graham's Ln	Grand Haven	MI
11032		Pam	Wallner	269-857-1276	80 Cedar St	Saugatuck	MI
11038	M. Grant Investment Company	Alex	Engber	517-482-1400	505 Washington Ave	Lansing	MI
11040	RiverView Development Company	Charles	Nowak	616-988-0777	144 E Tower Ave	Grand Rapids	MI
11042		Michael	Ingram	269-337-9208	10 Lincoln Dr	Kalamazoo	MI
11043	Monroe State College	Rachel	Kirk	616-988-1320	40 Monroe St	Grand Rapids	MI
11045	Kalamazoo Neighborhood Development	James	Blackhawk	269-343-7509	3047 Millbrook Ave	Kalamazoo	MI
11048		Olivia	Pappas	616-637-6591	4 N Orchard St	South Haven	MI
11049		Claire	Boucher	269-983-2255	828 Turner St	Saint Joseph	MI
11053		Hwan	Tang	616-396-8401	283 Cottrell St	Holland	MI
11054	Gilded Goose Gift Shop	Taylor	Wilson	616-355-3989	258 Briar Ln	Holland	MI
11055	Fox and Hound Grille	Steve	Gorski	269-979-2004	1440 Beadle Lake Rd	Battle Creek	MI
11058	Cherrywood Senior Center	Lisa	Hall	269-857-1771	77 Forest Hill Rd	Saugatuck	MI
11059	G.R. Neighborhood Development Corp.	Matthew	Fraser	616-392-0015	8045 Jefferson Ave	Grand Rapids	MI
11060		Jerome	Smith	616-949-3862	75 Hillcrest St	East Grand Rapids	MI
11064	Northwest Transit Station	Henry	Goldberg	517-487-4700	3572 Clinton Ave	Lansing	MI

Record: 1 of 40 | No Filter | Search

Primary key

> **Tip**
>
> When you resize a column to its best fit, only the visible field values are affected. You must scroll down the datasheet to make sure all field values for the entire column are fully displayed, resizing as you scroll, if necessary.

▶ **4.** Save and close the Customer table, and then open the Navigation Pane.

The Belmont database now contains three tables—Contract, Invoice, and Customer—and the tables contain all the necessary records. Your final task is to complete the database design by defining the necessary relationships between its tables.

Defining Table Relationships

One of the most powerful features of a relational database management system is its ability to define relationships between tables. You use a common field to relate one table to another. The process of relating tables is often called performing a **join**. When you join tables that have a common field, you can extract data from them as if they were one larger table. For example, you can join the Customer and Contract tables by using the Customer ID field in both tables as the common field. Then you can use a query, form, or report to extract selected data from each table, even though the data is contained in two separate tables, as shown in Figure 2-39. In the Customer Contracts query shown in Figure 2-39, the Customer ID, Company, First Name, and Last Name columns are fields from the Customer table, and the Contract Num and Contract Amt columns are fields from the Contract table. The joining of records is based on the common field of Customer ID. The Customer and Contract tables have a type of relationship called a one-to-many relationship.

Figure 2-39 — **One-to-many relationship and sample query**

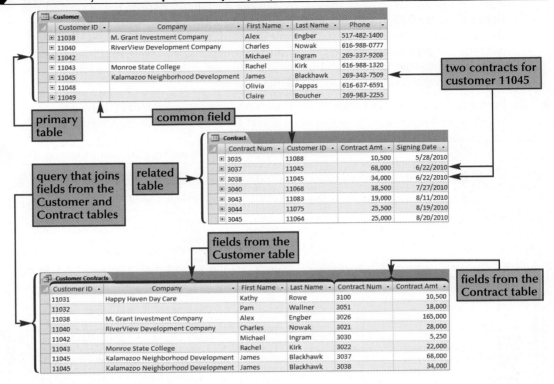

One-to-Many Relationships

A **one-to-many relationship** exists between two tables when one record in the first table matches zero, one, or many records in the second table, and when one record in the second table matches at most one record in the first table. For example, as shown in Figure 2-39, customer 11045 has two contracts in the Contract table. Other customers have one or more contracts. Every contract has a single matching customer.

Access refers to the two tables that form a relationship as the primary table and the related table. The **primary table** is the "one" table in a one-to-many relationship; in Figure 2-39, the Customer table is the primary table because there is only one customer for each contract. The **related table** is the "many" table; in Figure 2-39, the Contract table is the related table because a customer can have zero, one, or many contracts.

Because related data is stored in two tables, inconsistencies between the tables can occur. Consider the following scenarios:

• Oren adds a record to the Contract table for a new customer, Taylor McNulty, using Customer ID 12050. Oren did not first add the new customer's information to the Customer table, so this contract does not have a matching record in the Customer table. The data is inconsistent, and the contract record is considered to be an **orphaned record**.

• Oren changes the Customer ID in the Customer table for Kalamazoo Neighborhood Development from 11045 to 12090. Because there is no customer 11045 in the Customer table, this change creates two orphaned records in the Contract table, and the database is inconsistent.

- Oren deletes the record for Kalamazoo Neighborhood Development, customer 11045, from the Customer table because this customer no longer does business with Belmont Landscapes. The database is again inconsistent; two records for customer 11045 in the Contract table have no matching record in the Customer table.

You can avoid these problems by specifying referential integrity between tables when you define their relationships.

Referential Integrity

Referential integrity is a set of rules that Access enforces to maintain consistency between related tables when you update data in a database. Specifically, the referential integrity rules are as follows:

- When you add a record to a related table, a matching record must already exist in the primary table, thereby preventing the possibility of orphaned records.
- If you attempt to change the value of the primary key in the primary table, Access prevents this change if matching records exist in a related table. However, if you choose the **cascade updates option**, Access permits the change in value to the primary key and changes the appropriate foreign key values in the related table, thereby eliminating the possibility of inconsistent data.
- When you attempt to delete a record in the primary table, Access prevents the deletion if matching records exist in a related table. However, if you choose the **cascade deletes option**, Access deletes the record in the primary table and also deletes all records in related tables that have matching foreign key values.

Understanding the Cascade Deletes Option	InSight

Although there are advantages to using the cascade deletes option for enforcing referential integrity, its use does present risks as well. You should rarely select the cascade deletes option, because setting this option might cause you to inadvertently delete records you did not intend to delete. It is best to use other methods for deleting records that give you more control over the deletion process.

Now you'll define a one-to-many relationship between the Customer (primary) and Contract (related) tables. You will also define a one-to-many relationship between the Contract (primary) table and the Invoice (related) table.

Defining a Relationship Between Two Tables

When two tables have a common field, you can define a relationship between them in the Relationships window. The **Relationships window** illustrates the relationships among a database's tables. Using this window, you can view or change existing relationships, define new relationships between tables, and rearrange the layout of the tables in the window.

You need to open the Relationships window and define the relationship between the Customer and Contract tables. You'll define a one-to-many relationship between the two tables, with Customer as the primary table and Contract as the related table, and with Customer ID as the common field (the primary key in the Customer table and a foreign key in the Contract table). You'll also define a one-to-many relationship between the Contract and Invoice tables, with Contract as the primary table and Invoice as the related table, and with Contract Num as the common field (the primary key in the Contract table and a foreign key in the Invoice table).

To define the one-to-many relationship between the Customer and Contract tables:

▶ **1.** Click the **Database Tools** tab on the Ribbon.

▶ **2.** In the Show/Hide group on the Database Tools tab, click the **Relationships** button. The Show Table dialog box opens. See Figure 2-40.

Figure 2-40	Show Table dialog box

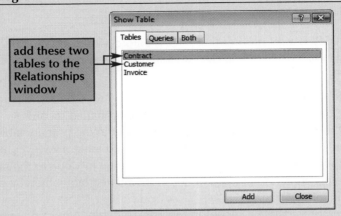

You must add each table participating in a relationship to the Relationships window. Because the Customer table is the primary table in the relationship, you'll add it first.

Tip

You can also double-click a table name in the Show Table dialog box to add it to the Relationships window.

▶ **3.** Click **Customer**, and then click the **Add** button. The Customer table is added to the Relationships window.

▶ **4.** Click **Contract**, and then click the **Add** button. The Contract table is added to the Relationships window.

▶ **5.** Click the **Close** button in the Show Table dialog box to close it.

When you add a table to the Relationships window, the fields in the table appear in a **field list**. So that you can view all the fields and complete field names, you'll resize the Customer table field list.

▶ **6.** Use the ⥮ pointer to drag the bottom of the Customer table field list to lengthen it until the vertical scroll bar disappears and all the fields are visible. See Figure 2-41.

Figure 2-41	Field list boxes for the two tables

Notice that the key symbol appears next to the Customer ID field in the Customer table field list and next to the Contract Num field in the Contract table field list to indicate that these fields are the primary key fields for their respective tables.

To form the relationship between the two tables, you drag the common field of Customer ID from the primary table to the related table. Then Access opens the Edit Relationships dialog box, in which you select the relationship options for the two tables.

7. Click **Customer ID** in the Customer field list, and then drag it to **Customer ID** in the Contract field list. When you release the mouse button, the Edit Relationships dialog box opens. See Figure 2-42.

Edit Relationships dialog box ◄ **Figure 2-42**

The primary table, related table, and common field appear at the top of the dialog box. The relationship type, One-To-Many, appears at the bottom of the dialog box. When you click the Enforce Referential Integrity check box, the two cascade options become available. If you select the Cascade Update Related Fields option, Access will update the appropriate foreign key values in the related table when you change a primary key value in the primary table. You will not select the Cascade Delete Related Records option, because doing so could cause you to delete records that you do not want to delete; this option is rarely selected.

8. Click the **Enforce Referential Integrity** check box, and then click the **Cascade Update Related Fields** check box.

9. Click the **Create** button to define the one-to-many relationship between the two tables and to close the dialog box. The completed relationship appears in the Relationships window. See Figure 2-43.

Defined relationship in the Relationships window ◄ **Figure 2-43**

> The **join line** connects the Customer ID fields, which are common to the two
> tables. The common field joins the two tables, which have a one-to-many
> relationship. The "one" side of the relationship has the digit 1 at its end, and the
> "many" side of the relationship has the infinity symbol at its end. The two tables
> are still separate tables, but you can use the data in them as if they were one table.

Now you need to define the one-to-many relationship between the Contract and
Invoice tables. In this relationship, Contract is the primary ("one") table because there is
at most one contract for each invoice. Invoice is the related ("many") table because there
are zero, one, or many invoices set up for each contract, depending on how many
project phases are involved for each contract.

To define the relationship between the Contract and Invoice tables:

▶ **1.** In the Relationships group on the Relationship Tools Design tab, click the **Show Table** button. The Show Table dialog box opens.

▶ **2.** Click **Invoice** in the list of tables, click the **Add** button, and then click the **Close** button to close the Show Table dialog box. The Invoice table's field list appears in the Relationships window to the right of the Contract table's field list.

   Because the Contract table is the primary table in this relationship, you need to drag the Contract Num field from the Contract field list to the Invoice field list.

▶ **3.** Click and drag the **Contract Num** field in the Contract field list to the **Contract Num** field in the Invoice field list. When you release the mouse button, the Edit Relationships dialog box opens.

▶ **4.** Click the **Enforce Referential Integrity** check box, and then click the **Cascade Update Related Fields** check box.

▶ **5.** Click the **Create** button to define the one-to-many relationship between the two tables and close the dialog box. The completed relationship appears in the Relationships window. See Figure 2-44.

| Figure 2-44 | ▶ Both relationships defined |

With both relationships defined, you have connected the data among the three
tables in the Belmont database.

▶ **6.** Click the **Save** button 💾 on the Quick Access Toolbar to save the layout in the Relationships window.

▶ **7.** Click the **Close 'Relationships'** button ✖ on the Relationships tab to close the Relationships window.

▶ **8.** Click the **Office Button** 🔘, point to **Manage**, and then click **Compact and Repair Database**. Access compacts the Belmont database.

▶ **9.** Click the **Close** button ⊠ on the program window title bar. Access closes the Belmont database and then the Access program window closes.

Session 2.2 Quick Check | Review

1. To insert a check mark in an empty check box for a Yes/No field, you press the
   _____ .
2. What is the keyboard shortcut for inserting the value from the same field in the previous record into the current record?
3. _____ data is a process that allows you to copy the data from a source without having to open the source file.
4. What is the effect of deleting a field from a table structure?
5. A(n) _____ text file is one in which fields of data are separated by a character such as a comma or a tab.
6. The _____ is the "one" table in a one-to-many relationship, and the
   _____ is the "many" table in the relationship.
7. _____ is a set of rules that Access enforces to maintain consistency between related tables when you update data in a database.

Tutorial Summary | Review

In this tutorial, you learned some important guidelines for designing databases and tables and for setting field properties. You put these guidelines into practice by creating two tables—one in Design view, and another by importing the structure of an existing table. You worked in Design view to define fields, set properties, specify a table's primary key, and modify a table's structure. To complete the first table, you imported data from an Excel worksheet into the table. After creating the second table, you deleted, renamed, and moved fields in the table structure. To complete the second table, you imported data from a text file into the table. This tutorial also presented one of the most important database concepts—defining table relationships. You learned how to define a one-to-many relationship between two tables in a database and how to enforce referential integrity as part of the relationship.

Key Terms

best fit	Double	one-to-many relationship
Byte	entity integrity	orphaned record
cascade deletes option	F1 key	primary table
cascade updates option	F6 key	propagate
composite key	field list	properties
Ctrl + '	Field Properties pane	referential integrity
data redundancy	Field Size property	related table
data type	import	Relationships window
Decimal	Integer	Replication ID
Decimal Places property	join	set (a property)
delimited	join line	Single
Description property	Long Integer	Table Design grid
Design view	null value	

Practice	**Review Assignments**

Practice the skills you learned in the tutorial using the same case scenario.

Data Files needed for the Review Assignments: Supplier.accdb *(cont. from Tutorial 1)* **and Goods.xlsx**

In addition to tracking information about the suppliers Belmont Landscapes works with, Oren also wants to track information about their products. He asks you to create a new table in the Supplier database by completing the following:

1. Open the **Supplier** database located in the Level.01\Review folder provided with your Data Files, and then open the **Company** table in Design view.
2. Enter **Primary key** for the Company ID field's Description property.
3. Change the Data Type property for the Zip field to Text.
4. Change the Format property for the Initial Contact Date field to Short Date. Do not propagate the field property changes.
5. Change the Field Size property for each Text field in the table, as follows:

   Company ID = **6**
   Company Name = **50**
   Product Type = **40**
   Address = **35**
   City = **25**
   State = **2**
   Zip = **10**
   Phone = **14**
   Contact First Name = **20**
   Contact Last Name = **25**

6. Save and close the Company table. Click the Yes button when a message appears indicating some data might be lost.
7. Create a new table in Design view, using the table design shown in Figure 2-45.

Figure 2-45

Field Name	Data Type	Description	Field Size	Other
Product ID	Text	Primary key	4	
Company ID	Text	Foreign key	6	
Product Type	Text		35	
Price	Currency			Format = Standard
				Decimal Places = 2
Color	Text		15	
Size	Text		15	
Material	Text		30	
Weight in Lbs	Number		Single	
Discount Offered	Yes/No			

8. Make sure Product ID is specified as the primary key, and then save the table as **Product**.
9. Modify the table structure by adding a new field named **Unit** (Text field, Field Size: 15) between the Price and Color fields. Move the Size field so that it follows the Material field.
10. Enter the records shown in Figure 2-46 in the Product table. When finished, close the Product table.

Figure 2-46

Product ID	Company ID	Product Type	Price	Unit	Color	Material	Size	Weight in Lbs	Discount Offered
5306	GEN359	Pine mulch	23.35	Cubic yard	Dark brown	Softwoods-pine			Y
5013	HOL207	Small bench	712.00	Each	Green	Steel and cast iron	8 x 2 feet	266	N

11. Use the Import Spreadsheet Wizard to add data to the Product table. The data you need to import is contained in the Goods workbook, which is an Excel file located in the Level.01\Review folder provided with your Data Files.
    a. Specify the Goods workbook as the source of the data.
    b. Select the option for appending the data.
    c. Select Product as the table.
    d. In the Import Spreadsheet Wizard dialog boxes, choose the Goods worksheet, make sure Access uses column headings as field names, and import to the Product table. Do not save the import steps.

12. Open the **Product** table and resize all columns to their best fit. Then save and close the Product table.

13. Define a one-to-many relationship between the primary Company table and the related Product table. Select the referential integrity option and the cascade updates option for the relationship.

14. Save the changes to the Relationships window, compact and repair the Supplier database, and then close the database.

Apply	**Case Problem 1**

Use the skills you learned in the tutorial to create and modify tables containing data for a small music school.

Data Files needed for this Case Problem: Pinehill.accdb (*cont. from Tutorial 1*), **Music.accdb, Lessons.xlsx, and Student.txt**

Pine Hill Music School Yuka Koyama uses the Pinehill database to maintain information about the students, teachers, and contracts for her music school. Yuka asks you to help her build the database by updating one table and creating two new tables. Complete the following:

1. Open the **Pinehill** database located in the Level.01\Case1 folder provided with your Data Files.

2. Open the **Teacher** table, and set field properties as shown in Figure 2-47.

Figure 2-47

Field Name	Data Type	Description	Field Size	Format
Teacher ID	Text	Primary key	7	
First Name	Text		20	
Last Name	Text		25	
Degree	Text		3	
School	Text		50	
Hire Date	Date/Time			Short Date

3. Add a new field as the last field in the Teacher table with the field name **Takes Beginners** and the Yes/No data type.

4. Save the Teacher table. Click the Yes button when a message appears indicating some data might be lost.

5. In the datasheet, resize the Takes Beginners field to best fit, and then specify that the following teachers can take beginners: Schwartz, Romano, Eberle, Norris, Tanaka, Culbertson, and Mueller.

6. Save and close the Teacher table.

7. Yuka created a table named Student in the Music database that is located in the Level.01\Case1 folder provided with your Data Files. Import the structure of the Student table in the Music database into a new table named Student in the Pinehill database. Do not save the import steps.

8. Delete the following fields from the **Student** table: Company, E-mail Address, Business Phone, Fax Number, and Notes.

9. Add two fields to the end of the Student table: **Birth Date** (Date/Time data type) and **Gender** (Text data type).

10. Rename the primary key field, ID, to **Student ID**, and change its data type to Text. Save the Student table.

11. Move the Last Name field so it follows the First Name field.

12. Modify the design of the Student table so that it matches the design in Figure 2-48, including the revised field names. Do not propagate the field property changes.

Figure 2-48

Field Name	Data Type	Description	Field Size
Student ID	Text	Primary key	7
First Name	Text		20
Last Name	Text		25
Address	Text		35
City	Text		25
State	Text		2
Zip	Text		10
Phone	Text		14
Birth Date	Date/Time		Short Date
Gender	Text	F(emale), M(ale)	1

13. Save your changes to the table design, add the records shown in Figure 2-49 to the Student table, and then close the Student table.

Figure 2-49

Student ID	First Name	Last Name	Address	City	State	Zip	Phone	Birth Date	Gender
APP7509	Sam	Applegate	15675 SW Greens Way	Portland	OR	97224	503-968-2245	10/10/1993	M
BAR7544	Andrea	Barreau	7660 SW 135th Ave	Beaverton	OR	97008	503-579-2227	11/28/1996	F

14. Yuka exported the student data that she was maintaining in another computer system to a text file, and she asks you to add this data to the Student table. The data you need to import is contained in the Student text file (located in the Level.01\Case1 folder provided with your Data Files).

   a. Specify the Student text file as the source of the data.

   b. Select the option for appending the data to the table.

   c. Select Student as the table.

   d. In the Import Text Wizard dialog boxes, choose the option to import delimited data, to use a comma delimiter, and to import the data into the Student table. Do not save the import steps.

15. Open the Student table, resize all the columns in the datasheet to their best fit, and then save and close the table.

16. Create a new table in Design view, using the table design shown in Figure 2-50.

Figure 2-50

Field Name	Data Type	Description	Field Size	Other Properties
Contract ID	Text	Primary key	4	
Student ID	Text	Foreign key	7	
Teacher ID	Text	Foreign key	7	
Contract Start Date	Date/Time		Short Date	
Contract End Date	Date/Time		Short Date	
Lesson Type	Text		25	
Lesson Length	Number	30 or 60 minutes	Integer	
Lesson Monthly Cost	Currency			Format: Currency Decimal Places: 0
Monthly Rental Cost	Currency	Monthly rental charge for instrument		Format: Currency Decimal Places: 0

17. Specify Contract ID as the primary key, save the table using the name **Contract**, and then close the table.

18. Use the Import Spreadsheet Wizard to add data to the Contract table. The data you need to import is contained in the Lessons workbook, which is an Excel file located in the Level.01\Case1 folder provided with your Data Files.

    a. Specify the Lessons workbook as the source of the data.

    b. Select the option for appending the data to the table.

    c. Select Contract as the table.

    d. In the Import Spreadsheet Wizard dialog boxes, choose the Sheet1 worksheet, and import to the Contract table. Do not save the import steps.

19. Open the **Contract** table and add the records shown in Figure 2-51. (*Hint*: Use the New button on the Home tab to add a new record.)

Figure 2-51

Contract ID	Student ID	Teacher ID	Contract Start Date	Contract End Date	Lesson Type	Lesson Length	Lesson Monthly Cost	Monthly Rental Cost
3176	VAR7527	91-0178	3/21/2010	3/21/2011	Violin	30	$140	$35
3179	MCE7551	70-4490	6/1/2010	6/1/2011	Guitar	60	$200	$0

20. Resize all the columns in the datasheet to their best fit, and then save and close the Contract table.

21. Define the one-to-many relationships between the database tables as follows: between the primary Student table and the related Contract table, and between the primary Teacher table and the related Contract table. Select the referential integrity option and the cascade updates option for each relationship.

22. Save the changes to the Relationships window, compact and repair the Pinehill database, and then close the database.

Challenge | Case Problem 2

Challenge yourself by using the Import Spreadsheet Wizard to create a new table to store data about fitness center members.

Data Files needed for this Case Problem: Fitness.accdb (*cont. from Tutorial 1*) and Center.xlsx

Parkhurst Health & Fitness Center Martha Parkhurst uses the Fitness database to track information about members who join the center and the program in which each member is enrolled. She asks you to help her maintain this database. Complete the following:

1. Open the **Fitness** database located in the Level.01\Case2 folder provided with your Data Files.
2. Open the **Program** table, and change the following field properties:
   Program ID: Type **Primary key** for the description, and change the field size to **3**.
   Monthly Fee: Change the Format property to Standard.
   Physical Required: Change the data type to Yes/No.
3. Save and close the Program table. Click the Yes button when a message appears indicating some data might be lost.

⊕ **EXPLORE**
4. Use the Import Spreadsheet Wizard to create a table in the Fitness database. As the source of the data, specify the Center workbook, located in the Level.01\Case2 folder provided with your Data Files. Select the option to import the source data into a new table in the current database, and then click the OK button.

⊕ **EXPLORE**
5. Complete the Import Spreadsheet Wizard as follows:
   a. Select Sheet1 as the worksheet you want to import.
   b. Accept the option specifying that the first row contains column headings.
   c. Accept the field options the wizard suggests, and do not skip any fields.
   d. Choose Member ID as your own primary key.
   e. Import the data to a table named **Member**, and do not save your import steps.
6. Open the **Member** table, and then delete the Initiation Fee Waived field.
7. Modify the design of the Member table so that it matches the design shown in Figure 2-52, including the field names and their order. (*Hint:* For Text fields, delete any formats specified in the Format property boxes.) Do not propagate the field property changes.

Figure 2-52

Field Name	Data Type	Description	Field Size	Other Properties
Member ID	Text	Primary key	4	
Program ID	Text	Foreign key	3	
First Name	Text		18	
Last Name	Text		18	
Street	Text		30	
City	Text		24	
State	Text		2	
Zip	Text		10	
Phone	Text		14	
Date Joined	Date/Time			Format: Short Date
Expiration Date	Date/Time	Date when membership expires		Format: Short Date
Membership Status	Text	Active, Inactive, or On Hold	8	

⊕ EXPLORE

8. Open the Access Help window and enter **default value** as the search text. Select the Help article titled "Set default values for fields or controls," and then select "Set a default value for a table field." Read that section of the Help article, and then scroll down and examine the examples of default values. Set the Default Value property for the Membership Status field to **"Active"** (including the quotation marks). Close the Access Help window.

9. Save the Member table. Click the Yes button when a message appears indicating some data might be lost.

10. Add the records shown in Figure 2-53 to the Member table. (*Hint*: Use the New button on the Home tab to add a new record.)

Figure 2-53

Member ID	Program ID	First Name	Last Name	Street	City	State	Zip	Phone	Date Joined	Expiration Date	Membership Status
1170	210	Ed	Curran	25 Fairway Drive	Bon Air	VA	23235	804-323-6824	6/3/2010	12/3/2010	Active
1172	206	Tung	Lin	40 Green Boulevard	Richmond	VA	23220	804-674-0227	11/16/2010	11/16/2011	Active

11. Resize all the columns in the datasheet to their best fit, and then save and close the table.

12. Define a one-to-many relationship between the primary Program table and the related Member table. Select the referential integrity option and the cascade updates option for this relationship.

13. Save the changes to the Relationships window, compact and repair the Fitness database, and then close the database.

Apply | **Case Problem 3**

Use the skills you learned in the tutorial to create and modify tables containing data for a not-for-profit agency that recycles household goods.

Data Files needed for this Case Problem: Agency.txt, Rossi.accdb (*cont. from Tutorial 1*), **Gifts.xlsx, and Recycle.accdb**

Rossi Recycling Group Tom Rossi uses the Rossi database to maintain information about the donors, agencies, and donations to his not-for-profit agency. Tom asks you to help him maintain the database by updating one table and creating two new ones. Complete the following:

1. Open the **Rossi** database located in the Level.01\Case3 folder provided with your Data Files.

2. Open the **Donor** table. For the Donor ID field, add **Primary key** as the description and set the Field Size property to **5**. Set the Field Size properties for the remaining fields as follows:
   Title: **4**
   First Name: **20**
   Last Name: **25**
   Phone: **14**

3. Save and close the Donor table. Click the Yes button when a message appears indicating some data might be lost.

4. Tom created a table named Agency in the Recycle database that is located in the Level.01\Case3 folder provided with your Data Files. Import the structure of the Agency table in the Recycle database into a new table named Agency in the Rossi database. Do not save the import steps.

5. Delete the following fields from the Agency table: Fax Number, Mobile Phone, E-mail Address, and Notes.
6. Rename the ID field to **Agency ID**, and change its data type to Text. Make sure Agency ID is the primary key.
7. Modify the design of the Agency table so that it matches the design shown in Figure 2-54, including the field names and their order. Do not propagate the field property changes.

Figure 2-54

Field Name	Data Type	Description	Field Size
Agency ID	Text	Primary key	3
Agency Name	Text		40
Contact First Name	Text		20
Contact Last Name	Text		25
Address	Text		30
City	Text		24
State	Text		2
Zip	Text		10
Phone	Text		14

8. Save your changes to the table design, add the records shown in Figure 2-55 to the Agency table, and then close the Agency table.

Figure 2-55

Agency ID	Agency Name	Contact First Name	Contact Last Name	Address	City	State	Zip	Phone
K64	Community Development	Jerri	Clarkson	223 Penn Ave	Salina	KS	67401	785-309-3351
K82	SeniorCare Program	Todd	Groverman	718 N Walnut	McPherson	KS	67460	620-241-3668

9. Tom exported the student data that he was maintaining in another computer system to a text file, and he asks you to add this data to the Agency table. The data you need to import is contained in the Agency text file (located in the Level.01\Case3 folder provided with your Data Files).
   a. Specify the Agency text file as the source of the data.
   b. Select the option for appending the data to the table.
   c. Select Agency as the table.
   d. In the Import Text Wizard dialog boxes, choose the option to import delimited data, to use a comma delimiter, and to import the data into the Agency table. Do not save the import steps.
10. Resize all the columns in the datasheet to their best fit, and then save and close the table.
11. Use Design view to create a table using the table design shown in Figure 2-56.

Figure 2-56

Field Name	Data Type	Description	Field Size	Other Properties
Donation ID	Text	Primary key	4	
Donor ID	Text	Foreign key	5	
Agency ID	Text	Foreign key	3	
Donation Date	Date/TIme			Format: Short Date
Donation Description	Text		50	
Donation Value	Currency	Cash amount donated or estimated value of goods donated		Format: Currency Decimal Places: 2
Pickup Required	Yes/No			

12. Specify Donation ID as the primary key, save the table as **Donation**, and then close the table.

13. Use the Import Spreadsheet Wizard to add data to the Donation table. The data you need to import is contained in the Gifts workbook, which is an Excel file located in the Level.01\Case3 folder provided with your Data Files.
    a. Specify the Gifts workbook as the source of the data.
    b. Select the option for appending the data to the table.
    c. Select Donation as the table.
    d. In the Import Spreadsheet Wizard dialog boxes, choose the Sheet1 worksheet, and import to the Donation table. Do not save the import steps.

14. Open the **Donation** table, and add the records shown in Figure 2-57. Whenever possible, use a keyboard shortcut to insert the same value as in the previous record.

Figure 2-57

Donation ID	Donor ID	Agency ID	Donation Date	Donation Description	Donation Value	Pickup Required
2117	36012	K82	2/20/2010	Cash	$50.00	No
2122	36016	N33	3/22/2010	Cash	$35.00	No

15. Resize all the columns in the datasheet to their best fit, and then save and close the table.

16. Define the one-to-many relationships between the database tables as follows: between the primary Donor table and the related Donation table, and between the primary Agency table and the related Donation table. Select the referential integrity option and the cascade updates option for each relationship.

17. Save the changes to the Relationships window, compact and repair the Rossi database, and then close the database.

| Challenge | **Case Problem 4** |

Work with the skills you've learned, and explore some new skills, to create a database for a luxury rental company.

Data Files needed for this Case Problem: Bookings.txt, GEM.accdb *(cont. from Tutorial 1)*, **and Overseas.accdb**

GEM Ultimate Vacations   Griffin and Emma MacElroy use the GEM database to track the data about the services they provide to the clients who book luxury vacations through their agency. They ask you to help them maintain this database. Complete the following:

1. Open the **GEM** database located in the Level.01\Case4 folder provided with your Data Files.

2. Open the **Guest** table. Add **Primary key** as the description for the Guest ID field and change its Field Size property to **3**. Change the Field Size property for the following fields:
   Guest First Name: **20**
   Guest Last Name: **25**
   Address: **32**
   City: **24**
   State/Prov: **2**
   Postal Code: **10**
   Country: **15**
   Phone: **14**

3. Save and close the Guest table. Click the Yes button when a message appears indicating some data might be lost.

⊕ **EXPLORE**   4. Open the Access Help window and enter **import table** as the search text. Select the Help article titled "Import or link to data in another Access database," and then select "Import data from another Access database." Read the steps in the "Import the data" section of the Help article. Close the Access Help window, click the External Data tab on the Ribbon, and then click the Access button (with the ScreenTip "Import Access database") in the Import group.

⊕ **EXPLORE**   5. Import the Rentals table structure and data from the Overseas database into a new table in the GEM database as follows:
   a. As the source of the data, specify the Overseas database, located in the Level.01\Case4 folder provided with your Data Files.
   b. Select the option button to import tables, queries, forms, reports, macros, and modules into the current database, and then click the OK button.
   c. In the Import Objects dialog box, click Rentals, click the Options button, and then make sure that the correct option is selected to import the table's data and structure.
   d. Do not save your import steps.

⊕ **EXPLORE**   6. Right-click the Rentals table in the Navigation Pane, click Rename on the shortcut menu, and then enter **Property** as the new name for this table.

7. In the Property table, delete the VIP Program field, and then move the Property Type field so that it appears between the Sleeps and Description fields.

8. Make sure that the Property ID field is the table's primary key. Change the data type of the Property ID field to Text with a Field Size property of **4**.

9. Resize all the columns in the datasheet to their best fit, and then save and close the table.

10. Use Design view to create a table using the table design shown in Figure 2-58.

Figure 2-58

Field Name	Data Type	Description	Field Size	Other Properties
Reservation ID	Text	Primary key	3	
Guest ID	Text	Foreign key	3	
Property ID	Text	Foreign key	4	
Start Date	Date/TIme			
End Date	Date/TIme			
People	Number	Number of people in the party	Integer	
Rental Rate	Currency	Rate per day; includes any discounts or promotions		Format: Currency Decimal Places: 0

11. Specify Reservation ID as the primary key, and then save the table as **Reservation**.

⊕ EXPLORE 12. Open the Access Help window and enter **custom date format** as the search text. Select the Help article titled "Enter a date or time value," and then scroll down and read the "Custom Date/Time format reference" section. Change the Format property of the Start Date and End Date fields to a custom format that displays dates in a format similar to 11/23/10. Save and close the Reservation table, and then close the Access Help window.

13. Griffin exported the reservation data that he was maintaining in another computer system to a text file, and he asks you to add this data to the Reservation table. The data you need to import is contained in the Bookings text file (located in the Level.01\Case4 folder provided with your Data Files).

    a. Specify the Bookings text file as the source of the data.

    b. Select the option for appending the data to the table.

    c. Select Reservation as the table.

    d. In the Import Text Wizard dialog boxes, choose the option to import delimited data, to use a comma delimiter, and to import the data into the Reservation table. Do not save the import steps.

14. Resize all the columns in the datasheet to their best fit, and then save and close the table.

15. Define the one-to-many relationships between the database tables as follows: between the primary Guest table and the related Reservation table, and between the primary Property table and the related Reservation table. Select the referential integrity option and the cascade updates option for each relationship.

16. Save the changes to the Relationships window, compact and repair the GEM database, and then close the database.

Research | Internet Assignments

Use the Internet to find and work with data related to the topics presented in this tutorial.

The purpose of the Internet Assignments is to challenge you to find information on the Internet that you can use to work effectively with this software. The actual assignments are updated and maintained on the Course Technology Web site. Log on to the Internet and use your Web browser to go to the Student Online Companion for New Perspectives Office 2007 at **www.course.com/np/office2007**. Then navigate to the Internet Assignments for this tutorial.

Review | **Quick Check Answers**

Session 2.1

1. Identify all the fields needed to produce the required information, organize each piece of data into its smallest useful part, group related fields into tables, determine each table's primary key, include a common field in related tables, avoid data redundancy, and determine the properties of each field.
2. The Data Type property determines what field values you can enter into the field and what other properties the field will have.
3. Text, Number, and AutoNumber fields
4. 255
5. F6
6. null

Session 2.2

1. spacebar
2. Ctrl + '
3. Importing
4. The field and all its values are removed from the table.
5. delimited
6. primary table; related table
7. Referential integrity

Ending Data Files

Level.01 → Tutorial — Belmont.accdb

Review — Supplier.accdb

Case1 — Pinehill.accdb

Case2 — Fitness.accdb

Case3 — Rossi.accdb

Case4 — GEM.accdb

Objectives

Session 3.1
- Find, modify, and delete records in a table
- Learn how to use the Query window in Design view
- Create, run, and save queries
- Update data using a query datasheet
- Create a query based on multiple tables
- Sort data in a query
- Filter data in a query

Session 3.2
- Specify an exact match condition in a query
- Change the font size and alternating row color in a datasheet
- Use a comparison operator in a query to match a range of values
- Use the And and Or logical operators in queries
- Create and format a calculated field in a query
- Perform calculations in a query using aggregate functions and record group calculations
- Change the display of database objects in the Navigation Pane

Maintaining and Querying a Database

Updating and Retrieving Information About Customers, Contracts, and Invoices

Case | Belmont Landscapes

At a recent meeting, Oren Belmont and his staff discussed the importance of maintaining accurate information about the firm's customers, contracts, and invoices, and regularly monitoring the business activities of Belmont Landscapes. For example, Sarah Fisher and the office staff need to make sure they have up-to-date contact information, such as phone numbers and e-mail addresses, for all the firm's customers. They also must monitor the invoice activity to ensure that invoices are paid on time and in full. Taylor Sico, the marketing manager at Belmont Landscapes, and her marketing staff track customer activity to develop new strategies for promoting the services provided by Belmont Landscapes. In addition, Oren is interested in analyzing other aspects of the business related to contracts and finances. You can satisfy all these informational needs for Belmont Landscapes by updating data in the Belmont database and by creating and using queries that retrieve information from the database.

Starting Data Files

Level.01 → Tutorial
Belmont.accdb *(cont.)*

Review
Supplier.accdb *(cont.)*

Case1
Pinehill.accdb *(cont.)*

Case2
Fitness.accdb *(cont.)*

Case3
Rossi.accdb *(cont.)*

Case4
GEM.accdb *(cont.)*

Session 3.1

Updating a Database

Updating, or **maintaining**, a database is the process of adding, modifying, and deleting records in database tables to keep them current and accurate. After reviewing the data in the Belmont database, Sarah identified some changes that need to be made to the data. She would like you to modify the field values in one record in the Customer table, and then delete a record in the Contract table.

Modifying Records

To modify the field values in a record, you must first make the record the current record. Then you position the insertion point in the field value to make minor changes or select the field value to replace it entirely. In Tutorial 1, you used the mouse with the scroll bars and the navigation buttons to navigate the records in a datasheet. You can also use key-stroke combinations and the F2 key to navigate a datasheet and to select field values. The **F2 key** is a toggle that you use to switch between navigation mode and editing mode:

- In **navigation mode**, Access selects an entire field value. If you type while you are in navigation mode, your typed entry replaces the highlighted field value.
- In **editing mode**, you can insert or delete characters in a field value based on the location of the insertion point.

Figure 3-1 shows some of the navigation mode and editing mode keystroke techniques.

| Figure 3-1 | Navigation mode and editing mode keystroke techniques |

Press	To Move the Selection in Navigation Mode	To Move the Insertion Point in Editing Mode
←	Left one field value at a time	Left one character at a time
→	Right one field value at a time	Right one character at a time
Home	Left to the first field value in the record	To the left of the first character in the field value
End	Right to the last field value in the record	To the right of the last character in the field value
↑ or ↓	Up or down one record at a time	Up or down one record at a time and switch to navigation mode
Tab or Enter	Right one field value at a time	Right one field value at a time and switch to navigation mode
Ctrl+Home	To the first field value in the first record	To the left of the first character in the field value
Ctrl+End	To the last field value in the last record	To the right of the last character in the field value

The Customer table record Sarah wants you to change is for Walker Investment Company, one of Belmont Landscapes' commercial customers. The company recently moved its office from Grand Rapids to Battle Creek, so you need to update the Customer table record with the new address and phone information.

To open the Belmont database and modify the record:

1. Start Access and open the **Belmont** database located in the Level.01\Tutorial folder.

Trouble? If the Security Warning is displayed below the Ribbon, click the Options button next to the Security Warning. In the dialog box that opens, click the "Enable this content" option button, and then click the OK button.

▶ **2.** Open the **Customer** table in Datasheet view. The first value for the Customer ID field (11001) is highlighted, indicating that the table is in navigation mode.

The record you need to modify is near the end of the table and has a Customer ID field value of 11087.

▶ **3.** Press the **Ctrl+End** keys. Access displays records from the end of the table and selects the last field value in the last record, record 40. This field value is for the E-mail Address field.

▶ **4.** Press the **Home** key. The first field value in the last record is now selected. This field value is for the Customer ID field.

▶ **5.** Press the **↑** key. The Customer ID field value for the previous record (Customer ID 11087) is selected. This record is the one you need to change.

▶ **6.** Press the **Tab** key four times to move to the Phone field and select its field value, type **269-963-0190**, press the **Tab** key, type **1752 S Main St**, press the **Tab** key, type **Battle Creek**, press the **Tab** key twice, type **49014**, and then press the **Tab** key. The changes to the record are complete. See Figure 3-2.

Table after changing field values in a record ◀ **Figure 3-2**

Tip

Access saves changes to field values when you move the insertion point to a new field or to another record, or when you close the table. It is not necessary to click the Save button to save changes to field values or records.

▶ **7.** Close the Customer table.

The next update Sarah asks you to make is to delete a record in the Contract table. The customer who signed Contract Num 3101 owns a chain of small restaurants and had planned to renovate the landscaping at each restaurant site. His plans have changed for one of these sites, and he has cancelled the contract. When you are maintaining database tables, you first need to find the data to change.

Finding Data in a Table

Access provides options you can use to locate specific field values in a table. Instead of scrolling the Contract table datasheet to find the contract that you need to delete—the record for contract number 3101—you can use the Find command to find the record. The **Find command** allows you to search a table or query datasheet, or a form, to locate a specific field value or part of a field value. This feature is particularly useful when searching a table that contains a large number of records.

To search for the record in the Contract table:

▶ **1.** Open the **Contract** table in Datasheet view. The first field value for the Contract Num field (3011) is selected. You need to search the Contract Num field to find the record containing the Contract Num field value 3101, so the insertion point is already correctly positioned in the field you want to search.

2. In the Find group on the Home tab, click the **Find** button. The Find and Replace dialog box opens. See Figure 3-3.

Figure 3-3 Find and Replace dialog box

The field value 3011 appears in the Find What text box because this value is selected in the table datasheet. Also, the Contract Num field is displayed in the Look In list box because it is the current field. The Match list box indicates that the Find command will match the whole field value, which is correct for your search. You also can choose to search for only part of a field value, such as when you need to find all contract numbers that start with a certain value. The Search list box indicates that all the records in the table will be searched for the value you want to find. You also can choose to search up or down from the currently selected record.

Trouble? Some of the settings in your dialog box might be different from those shown in Figure 3-3, depending on the last search performed on the computer you're using. If so, change the settings so that they match those in the figure.

3. Make sure the value 3011 is selected in the Find What text box, type **3101** to replace the selected value, and then click the **Find Next** button. Access moves to and selects the field value you specified.

4. Click the **Cancel** button to close the Find and Replace dialog box.

Deleting Records

To delete a record, you need to select the record in Datasheet view, and then delete it using the Delete button in the Records group on the Home tab, or the Delete Record option on the shortcut menu.

Reference Window | Deleting a Record

- With the table in Datasheet view, click the row selector for the record you want to delete.
- In the Records group on the Home tab, click the Delete button (or right-click the row selector for the record, and then click Delete Record on the shortcut menu).
- In the dialog box asking you to confirm the deletion, click the Yes button.

Now that you have found the record with Contract Num 3101, you can delete it. To delete a record, you must first select the entire row for the record.

To delete the record:

1. Click the row selector for the record containing the Contract Num field value **3101**, which should still be highlighted. The entire row is selected.

2. In the Records group on the Home tab, click the **Delete** button. A dialog box opens and indicates that you cannot delete the record. The dialog box indicates that the Invoice table contains records that are related to Contract Num 3101 and, therefore, you cannot delete the record in the Contract table. Recall that you defined a one-to-many relationship between the Contract and Invoice tables and enforced referential integrity. When you try to delete a record in the primary table (Contract), Access prevents the deletion if matching records exist in the related table (Invoice). This protection helps to maintain the integrity of the data in the database.

   To delete the record in the Contract table, you first must delete the related records in the Invoice table.

3. Click the **OK** button in the dialog box to close it. Notice the plus sign that appears at the beginning of each record in the Contract table. The **plus sign** indicates that the records have related records in another table—in this case, the Invoice table.

4. Scroll the table window down until you see the rest of the records in the table, so that you have room to view the related records for the contract record.

5. Click the **plus sign** next to Contract Num 3101. Access displays the four related records from the Invoice table for this contract. The plus sign changes to a minus sign for the current record when its related records are displayed. See Figure 3-4.

Related records from the Invoice table in the subdatasheet ◀ Figure 3-4

plus signs indicate records have related records in another table

minus sign appears when related records are displayed

subdatasheet with related records from the Invoice table

The related records from the Invoice table are displayed in a **subdatasheet**. When you first open a table that is the primary table in a one-to-many relationship, the subdatasheet containing the records from the related table is not displayed. You need to click the plus sign, also called the **expand indicator**, to display the related records in the subdatasheet. When the subdatasheet is open you can navigate and update it, just as you can using a table datasheet.

You need to delete the records in the Invoice table that are related to Contract Num 3101 so you can then delete this contract record. The four Invoice table records are for invoices set up to be paid for future phases of the contract, which has now been cancelled. You could open the Invoice table and find the related records. However, an easier way to delete the related records for Contract Num 3101 is to delete them from the subdatasheet. The records will be deleted from the Invoice table automatically.

6. Click and hold the mouse button on the row selector for the first Invoice table record in the subdatasheet, drag the pointer down to select all four records, and then release the mouse button. With the four records selected, you can delete them all at the same time.

▶ **7.** In the Records group on the Home tab, click the **Delete** button. Access opens a dialog box asking you to confirm the deletion of four records. Because the deletion of a record is permanent and cannot be undone, Access prompts you to make sure that you want to delete the records.

▶ **8.** Click the **Yes** button to confirm the deletion and close the dialog box. The records are removed from the Invoice table, and the subdatasheet is now empty.

▶ **9.** Click the **minus sign** next to Contract Num 3101 to close the subdatasheet.

Now that you have deleted all the related records in the Invoice table, you can delete the record for Contract Num 3101. You will use the shortcut menu to delete the record.

▶ **10.** Right-click the row selector for the record for Contract Num **3101**. Access selects the record and displays the shortcut menu.

▶ **11.** Click **Delete Record** on the shortcut menu, and then click the **Yes** button in the dialog box to confirm the deletion. The record is deleted from the table.

▶ **12.** Close the Contract table.

You have finished updating the Belmont database by modifying and deleting records. Next, you'll retrieve specific data from the database to meet various requests for information about Belmont Landscapes.

Introduction to Queries

As you learned in Tutorial 1, a query is a question you ask about data stored in a database. For example, Oren might create a query to find records in the Customer table for only those customers located in a specific city. When you create a query, you tell Access which fields you need and what criteria Access should use to select the records. Access provides powerful query capabilities that allow you to do the following:

• Display selected fields and records from a table.
• Sort records.
• Perform calculations.
• Generate data for forms, reports, and other queries.
• Update data in the tables in a database.
• Find and display data from two or more tables.

Most questions about data are generalized queries in which you specify the fields and records you want Access to select. These common requests for information, such as "Which customers are located in Kalamazoo?" or "How many invoices have been paid?" are called **select queries**. The answer to a select query is returned in the form of a datasheet. The result of a query is also referred to as a **recordset**, because the query produces a set of records that answers your question.

More specialized, technical queries, such as finding duplicate records in a table, are best formulated using a Query Wizard. A **Query Wizard** prompts you for information by asking a series of questions and then creates the appropriate query based on your answers. In Tutorial 1, you used the Simple Query Wizard to display only some of the fields in the Contract table; Access provides other Query Wizards for more complex queries. For common, informational queries, it is easier for you to design your own query than to use a Query Wizard.

Taylor wants you to create a query to display the customer ID, company, first name, last name, city, and e-mail address for each record in the Customer table. Her marketing staff needs this information to complete an e-mail campaign advertising a special promotion being offered to Belmont Landscapes' customers. You'll open the Query window in Design view to create the query for Taylor.

Query Window

You use the Query window in Design view to create a query. In Design view, you specify the data you want to view by constructing a query by example. When you use **query by example** (**QBE**), you give Access an example of the information you are requesting. Access then retrieves the information that precisely matches your example.

For Taylor's query, you need to display data from the Customer table.

To open the Query window in Design view:

▶ **1.** Close the Navigation Pane so that more of the workspace is displayed.

▶ **2.** Click the **Create** tab on the Ribbon. Access displays the options for creating different database objects.

▶ **3.** In the Other group on the Create tab, click the **Query Design** button. The Show Table dialog box opens on the Query window in Design view. See Figure 3-5.

Show Table dialog box ◀ Figure 3-5

The Show Table dialog box lists all the tables in the Belmont database. You can choose to base a query on one or more tables, on other queries, or on a combination of tables and queries. The query you are creating will retrieve data from the Customer table, so you need to add this table to the Query window.

▶ **4.** Click **Customer** in the Tables list box, click the **Add** button, and then click the **Close** button. Access places the Customer table's field list in the Query window and closes the Show Table dialog box. See Figure 3-6.

Figure 3-6 | Select query in Design view

Trouble? If you add the wrong table to the Query window, right-click the bar at the top of the field list containing the table name, and then click Remove Table on the shortcut menu. To add the correct table to the Query window, click the Show Table button in the Query Setup group on the Query Tools Design tab to redisplay the Show Table dialog box, and then repeat Step 4.

In Design view, the Ribbon displays the Query Tools Design tab, with options for creating and running different types of queries. In the Query Type group on the Query Tools Design tab, notice that the Select button is active; this indicates that you are creating a select query, which is the default type of query. The default query name (Query1) is displayed on the tab for the query. You'll change the default query name to a more meaningful one later when you save the query.

The top portion of the Query window in Design view contains the field list (or lists) for the table(s) used in the query, and the bottom portion contains the design grid. Each **field list** contains the fields for the table(s) you are querying. The table name appears at the top of the list box, and the fields are listed in the order in which they appear in the table. Notice that the primary key for the table is identified by the key symbol. You can scroll the field list to see more fields, or you can expand the field list box by dragging its borders to display all the fields and the complete field names. In the **design grid**, you include the fields and record selection criteria for the information you want to see. Each column in the design grid contains specifications about a field you will use in the query. You can choose a single field for your query by double-clicking the field name to place it in the next available design grid column.

Tip

You can also use the mouse to drag a field name from the field list to a column in the design grid.

When you are constructing a query, you can see the query results at any time by clicking the View button or the Run button in the Results group on the Query Tools Design tab. In response, Access displays the query datasheet (or recordset), which contains the set of fields and records that results from answering, or **running**, the query. The order of the fields in the query datasheet is the same as the order of the fields in the design grid.

Comparing Methods for Adding All Fields to the Design Grid | InSight

If the query you are creating includes every field from the specified table, you can use one of the following three methods to transfer all the fields from the field list to the design grid:

- Click and drag each field individually from the field list to the design grid. Use this method if you want the fields in your query to appear in an order that is different from the order in the field list.
- Double-click the asterisk at the top of the field list. Access places the table name followed by a period and an asterisk (as in "Customer.*") in the design grid, which signifies that the order of the fields is the same in the query as it is in the field list. Use this method if you don't need to sort the query or specify conditions for the records you want to select. The advantage of using this method is that you do not need to change the query if you add or delete fields from the underlying table structure. Such changes are reflected automatically in the query.
- Double-click the field list title bar to highlight all the fields, and then click and drag one of the highlighted fields to the design grid. Access places each field in a separate column and arranges the fields in the order in which they appear in the field list. Use this method when you need to sort your query or include record selection criteria.

Now you'll create and run Taylor's query to display selected fields from the Customer table.

Creating and Running a Query

The default table datasheet displays all the fields in the table in the same order as they appear in the table. In contrast, a query datasheet can display selected fields from a table, and the order of the fields can be different from that of the table, enabling those viewing the query results to see only the information they need and in the order they want.

Taylor wants the Customer ID, Company, First Name, Last Name, City, and E-mail Address fields from the Customer table to appear in the query results. You'll add each of these fields to the design grid. First you'll resize the Customer table field list to display all of the fields.

To select the fields for the query, and then run the query:

1. Position the pointer on the bottom border of the Customer field list until the pointer changes to a ↕ shape, and then click and drag the pointer down until the vertical scroll bar in the field list disappears and all fields in the Customer table are displayed.

2. In the Customer field list, double-click **Customer ID** to place the field in the design grid's first column Field text box. See Figure 3-7.

Figure 3-7 | Field added to the design grid

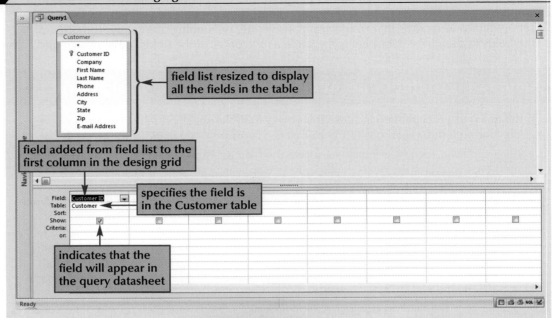

In the design grid's first column, the field name Customer ID appears in the Field text box, the table name Customer appears in the Table text box, and the check mark in the Show check box indicates that the field will be displayed in the datasheet when you run the query. Sometimes you might not want to display a field and its values in the query results. For example, if you are creating a query to list all customers located in Lansing, and you assign the name "Lansing Customers" to the query, you do not need to include the City field value for each record in the query results—the query design only lists customers with the City field value of "Lansing." Even if you choose not to include a field in the display of the query results, you can still use the field as part of the query to select specific records or to specify a particular sequence for the records in the datasheet.

▶ **3.** Double-click **Company** in the Customer field list. Access adds this field to the second column in the design grid.

▶ **4.** Repeat Step 3 for the **First Name**, **Last Name**, **City**, and **E-mail Address** fields to add these fields to the design grid in that order.

Trouble? If you double-click the wrong field and accidentally add it to the design grid, you can remove the field from the grid. Select the field's column by clicking the pointer ↓ on the field selector, which is the thin bar above the Field text box, for the field you want to delete, and then press the Delete key (or in the Query Setup group on the Query Tools Design tab, click the Delete Columns button).

Having selected the fields for Taylor's query, you can now run the query.

▶ **5.** In the Results group on the Query Tools Design tab, click the **Run** button. Access runs the query and displays the results in Datasheet view. See Figure 3-8.

Datasheet displayed after running the query

Figure 3-8

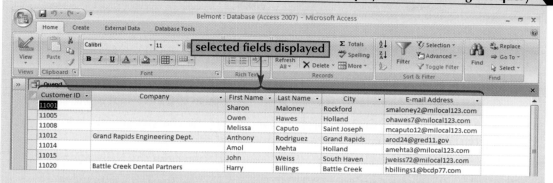

The six fields you added to the design grid appear in the datasheet, and the records are displayed in primary key sequence by Customer ID. Access selected a total of 40 records for display in the datasheet. Taylor asks you to save the query as "Customer E-mail" so that she can easily retrieve the same data again.

6. Click the **Save** button on the Quick Access toolbar. The Save As dialog box opens.

7. Type **Customer E-mail** in the Query Name text box, and then press the **Enter** key. Access saves the query with the specified name in the Belmont database and displays the name on the tab for the query.

Query Datasheet vs. Table Datasheet		InSight

Although a query datasheet looks just like a table datasheet and appears in Datasheet view, a query datasheet is temporary, and its contents are based on the criteria you establish in the design grid. In contrast, a table datasheet shows the permanent data in a table. However, you can update data while viewing a query datasheet, just as you can when working in a table datasheet or form.

When viewing the query results, Taylor noticed that the contact person for the River-View Development Company is incorrect. Charles Nowak recently retired from his position, and she asks you to update the record with the first name, last name, and e-mail address of the new contact.

Updating Data Using a Query

Although a query datasheet is temporary and its contents are based on the criteria in the query design grid, you can update the data in a table using a query datasheet. In this case, Taylor has changes she wants you to make to a record in the Customer table. Instead of making the changes in the table datasheet, you can make them in the Customer E-mail query datasheet because the query is based on the Customer table. The underlying Customer table will be updated with the changes you make.

To update data using the Customer E-mail query datasheet:

1. Locate the record with Customer ID 11040, RiverView Development Company (record 13 in the datasheet).

▶ **2.** In the First Name field for this record, double-click **Charles** to select the name, and then type **Susan**.

▶ **3.** Press the **Tab** key to move to and select the value in the Last Name field, and then type **Darcy**.

▶ **4.** Press the **Tab** key twice to move to and select the value in the E-mail Address field, type **sdarcy33@rvdc3.com**, and then press the **Tab** key.

▶ **5.** Close the Customer E-mail query, and then open the Navigation Pane. Note that the Customer E-mail query is listed in the Customer section of the Navigation Pane.

Now you'll check the Customer table to verify that the changes you made in the query datasheet were also made in the Customer table.

▶ **6.** Open the **Customer** table in Datasheet view, and then close the Navigation Pane.

▶ **7.** For the record with Customer ID 11040 (record 13), use the **Tab** key to move through the field values. Notice that the changes you made in the query datasheet to the First Name, Last Name, and E-mail Address field values were made to the record in the Customer table.

▶ **8.** Close the Customer table.

Sarah also wants to view specific information in the Belmont database. She would like to review the contract signing dates and amounts for customers while also viewing certain contact information for the customers. So, she needs to see data from both the Customer table and the Contract table at the same time.

Creating a Multitable Query

A multitable query is a query based on more than one table. If you want to create a query that retrieves data from multiple tables, the tables must have a common field. In Tutorial 2, you established a relationship between the Customer (primary) and Contract (related) tables based on the common Customer ID field that exists in both tables, so you can now create a query to display data from both tables at the same time. Specifically, Sarah wants to view the values in the City, Company, First Name, and Last Name fields from the Customer table and the Signing Date and Contract Amt fields from the Contract table.

To create the query using the Customer and Contract tables:

▶ **1.** Click the **Create** tab on the Ribbon.

▶ **2.** In the Other group on the Create tab, click the **Query Design** button. Access opens the Show Table dialog box. You need to add the Customer and Contract tables to the Query window.

▶ **3.** Click **Customer** in the Tables list box, click the **Add** button, click **Contract**, click the **Add** button, and then click the **Close** button. The Customer and Contract field lists appear in the Query window, and the Show Table dialog box closes.

▶ **4.** Use the ↕ pointer to resize the Customer field list so that all the fields in the table are displayed.

The one-to-many relationship between the two tables is shown in the Query window, in the same way that Access indicates a relationship between two tables in the Relationships window. Note that the join line is thick at both ends; this signifies that you selected the option to enforce referential integrity. If you had not selected this option, the join line would be thin at both ends and neither the "1" nor the infinity symbol would appear, even though the tables have a one-to-many relationship.

You need to place the City, Company, First Name, and Last Name fields (in that order) from the Customer field list into the design grid, and then place the Signing Date and Contract Amt fields from the Contract field list into the design grid. This is the order in which Sarah wants to view the fields in the query results.

5. In the Customer field list, double-click **City** to place this field in the design grid's first column Field text box.

6. Repeat Step 5 to add the **Company**, **First Name**, and **Last Name** fields from the Customer table to the second through fourth columns of the design grid.

7. Repeat Step 5 to add the **Signing Date** and **Contract Amt** fields (in that order) from the Contract table to the fifth and sixth columns of the design grid. The query specifications are complete, so you can now run the query.

8. In the Results group on the Query Tools Design tab, click the **Run** button. Access runs the query and displays the results in Datasheet view. See Figure 3-9.

Datasheet for query based on the Customer and Contract tables Figure 3-9

fields from the Customer table | fields from the Contract table

City	Company	First Name	Last Name	Signing Date	Contract Amt
Rockford		Sharon	Maloney	2/9/2010	4,000
Holland		Owen	Hawes	3/1/2010	1,500
Holland		Owen	Hawes	7/8/2010	2,250
Holland		Owen	Hawes	11/30/2010	4,000
Saint Joseph		Melissa	Caputo	4/7/2010	1,250
Grand Rapids	Grand Rapids Engineering Dept.	Anthony	Rodriguez	3/1/2010	2,250
Holland		Amol	Mehta	6/22/2010	6,500
South Haven		John	Weiss	8/27/2010	1,000
South Haven		John	Weiss	1/20/2011	1,750
South Haven		John	Weiss	7/26/2011	5,000
Battle Creek	Battle Creek Dental Partners	Harry	Billings	4/25/2011	13,750
Lansing		Karen	O'Brien	2/18/2010	300
Holland	Finn's on the Waterfront	Devin	Finnerty	9/23/2010	7,500
Holland	Finn's on the Waterfront	Devin	Finnerty	2/24/2011	15,750
Holland	Finn's on the Waterfront	Devin	Finnerty	4/14/2011	22,800
Grand Haven	Happy Haven Day Care	Kathy	Rowe	8/8/2011	10,500
Saugatuck		Pam	Wallner	10/5/2010	18,000
Lansing	M. Grant Investment Company	Alex	Engber	3/11/2010	165,000
Grand Rapids	RiverView Development Company	Susan	Darcy	5/3/2010	28,000
Kalamazoo		Michael	Ingram	6/11/2010	5,250
Grand Rapids	Monroe State College	Rachel	Kirk	4/14/2010	22,000
Kalamazoo	Kalamazoo Neighborhood Development	James	Blackhawk	6/22/2010	68,000
Kalamazoo	Kalamazoo Neighborhood Development	James	Blackhawk	6/22/2010	34,000
Kalamazoo	Kalamazoo Neighborhood Development	James	Blackhawk	6/29/2011	14,500
Kalamazoo	Kalamazoo Neighborhood Development	James	Blackhawk	8/2/2011	50,000

Record: 1 of 64

Only the six selected fields from the Customer and Contract tables appear in the datasheet. The records are displayed in order according to the values in the Customer ID field, because it is the primary key field in the primary table, even though this field is not included in the query datasheet.

Sarah plans on frequently tracking the data retrieved by the query, so she asks you to save the query as "Customer Contracts."

9. Click the **Save** button on the Quick Access Toolbar. The Save As dialog box opens.

10. Type **Customer Contracts** in the Query Name text box, and then press the **Enter** key. Access saves the query and displays its name on the query tab.

Sarah decides she wants the records displayed in alphabetical order by city. Because the query displays data in order by the field values in the Customer ID field, which is the primary key for the Customer table, you need to sort the records by the City field to display the data in the order Sarah wants.

Sorting Data in a Query

Sorting is the process of rearranging records in a specified order or sequence. Sometimes you might need to sort data before displaying or printing it to meet a specific request. For example, Sarah might want to review contract information arranged by the Signing Date field because she needs to know which months are the busiest for Belmont Landscapes in terms of signings. On the other hand, Oren might want to view contract information arranged by the Contract Amt field, because he monitors the financial aspects of the business.

When you sort data in a query, you do not change the sequence of the records in the underlying tables. Only the records in the query datasheet are rearranged according to your specifications.

To sort records, you must select the **sort field**, which is the field used to determine the order of records in the datasheet. In this case, Sarah wants the data sorted by city, so you need to specify City as the sort field. Sort fields can be Text, Number, Date/Time, Currency, AutoNumber, Yes/No, or Lookup Wizard fields, but not Memo, OLE object, Hyperlink, or Attachment fields. You sort records in either ascending (increasing) or descending (decreasing) order. Figure 3-10 shows the results of each type of sort for some of these data types.

Figure 3-10 | **Sorting results for different data types**

Data Type	Ascending Sort Results	Descending Sort Results
Text	A to Z	Z to A
Number	lowest to highest numeric value	highest to lowest numeric value
Date/Time	oldest to most recent date	most recent to oldest date
Currency	lowest to highest numeric value	highest to lowest numeric value
AutoNumber	lowest to highest numeric value	highest to lowest numeric value
Yes/No	yes (check mark in check box) then no values	no then yes values

Access provides several methods for sorting data in a table or query datasheet and in a form. One of the easiest ways is to use the AutoFilter feature for a field.

Using AutoFilter to Sort Data

As you've probably noticed when working in Datasheet view for a table or query, each column heading has an arrow to the right of the field name. This arrow gives you access to the **AutoFilter** feature, which enables you to quickly sort and display field values in various ways. When you click this arrow, a menu opens with options for sorting and displaying field values. The first two options on the menu enable you to sort the values in the current field in ascending or descending order. Unless you save the datasheet or form after you've sorted the records, the rearrangement of records is temporary.

Next, you'll use an AutoFilter to sort the Customer Contracts query results by the City field.

Tip

You can also use the Ascending and Descending buttons in the Sort & Filter group on the Home tab to quickly sort records based on the currently selected field in a datasheet.

To sort the records using an AutoFilter:

▶ 1. Click the arrow on the City column heading to display the AutoFilter menu. See Figure 3-11.

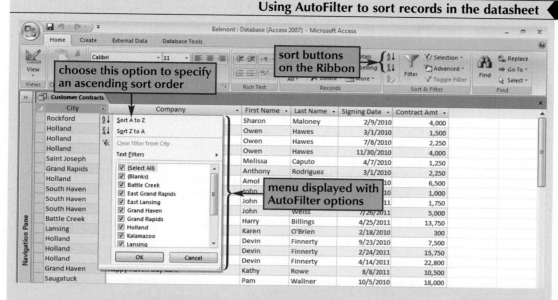

Using AutoFilter to sort records in the datasheet | Figure 3-11

Sarah wants the data sorted in ascending order by the values in the City field, so you need to select the first option in the menu.

▶ 2. Click **Sort A to Z**. The records are rearranged in ascending alphabetical order by city. A small, upward-pointing arrow appears on the right side of the City column heading. This arrow indicates that the values in the field have been sorted in ascending order. If you used the same method to sort the field values in descending order, a small downward-pointing arrow would appear there.

After viewing the query results, Sarah decides that she would also like to see the records arranged by the values in the Contract Amt field, so that she can identify the contracts with the largest amounts. She still wants the records to be arranged by the city field values as well. To produce the results Sarah wants, you need to sort using two fields.

Sorting Multiple Fields in Design View

Sort fields can be unique or nonunique. A sort field is **unique** if the value in the sort field for each record is different. The Customer ID field in the Customer table is an example of a unique sort field because each customer record has a different value in this primary key field. A sort field is **nonunique** if more than one record can have the same value for the sort field. For example, the City field in the Customer table is a nonunique sort field because more than one record can have the same City value.

When the sort field is nonunique, records with the same sort field value are grouped together, but they are not sorted in a specific order within the group. To arrange these grouped records in a specific order, you can specify a **secondary sort field**, which is a second field that determines the order of records that are already sorted by the **primary sort field** (the first sort field specified).

Access lets you select up to 10 different sort fields. When you use the buttons on the Ribbon to sort by more than one field, the sort fields must be in adjacent columns in the datasheet. (Note that you cannot use an AutoFilter to sort on more than one field. This method works for a single field only.) You can specify only one type of sort—either

> **Tip**
>
> The primary sort field is *not* the same as a table's primary key field. A table has at most one primary key, which must be unique, whereas any field in a table can serve as a primary sort field.

ascending or descending—for the selected columns in the datasheet. You highlight the adjacent columns, and Access sorts first by the first column and then by each remaining highlighted column in order from left to right.

Sarah wants the records sorted first by the City field values, as they currently are, and then by the Contract Amt field values. The two fields are in the correct left-to-right order in the query datasheet, but they are not adjacent, so you cannot use the Ascending and Descending buttons on the Ribbon to sort them. You could move the City field to the left of the Contract Amt field in the query datasheet, but both columns would be sorted with the same sort order. This is not what Sarah wants—she wants the City field values sorted in ascending order so that they are in the correct alphabetical order, for ease of reference; and she wants the Contract Amt field values to be sorted in descending order, so that she can focus on the contracts with the largest amounts. To sort the City and Contract Amt fields with different sort orders, you must specify the sort fields in Design view.

In the Query window in Design view, Access first uses the sort field that is leftmost in the design grid. Therefore, you must arrange the fields you want to sort from left to right in the design grid, with the primary sort field being the leftmost. In Design view, multiple sort fields do not have to be adjacent to each other, as they do in Datasheet view; however, they must be in the correct left-to-right order.

Reference Window | Sorting a Query Datasheet

- In the query datasheet, click the arrow on the column heading for the field you want to sort.
- In the menu that opens, click Sort A to Z for an ascending sort, or click Sort Z to A for a descending sort.

or

- In the query datasheet, select the column or adjacent columns on which you want to sort.
- In the Sort & Filter group on the Home tab, click the Ascending button or the Descending button.

or

- In Design view, position the fields serving as sort fields from left to right.
- Click the right side of the Sort text box for the field you want to sort, and then click Ascending or Descending for the sort order.

To achieve the results Sarah wants, you need to modify the query in Design view to specify the sort order for the two fields.

To select the two sort fields in Design view:

Tip

In Design view, the sort fields do not have to be adjacent, and fields that are not sorted can appear between the sort fields.

1. In the Views group on the Home tab, click the **View** button to open the query in Design view. The fields are currently in the correct left-to-right order in the design grid, so you only need to specify the sort order for the two fields.

   First, you need to specify an ascending sort order for the City field. Even though the records are already sorted by the values in this field, you need to modify the query so that this sort order, and the sort order you will specify for the Contract Amt field, are part of the query's design. Any time the query is run, the records will be sorted according to these specifications.

2. Click the right side of the **City Sort** text box to display the arrow and the sort options, and then click **Ascending**. You've selected an ascending sort order for the City field, which will be the primary sort field. The City field is a Text field, and an ascending sort order will display the field values in alphabetical order.

3. Click the right side of the **Contract Amt Sort** text box, click **Descending**, and then click in one of the empty text boxes to the right of the Contract Amt field to deselect the setting. You've selected a descending sort order for the Contract Amt field, which will be the secondary sort field, because it appears to the right of the primary sort field (City) in the design grid. The Contract Amt field is a Currency field, and a descending sort order will display the field values with the highest amounts first. See Figure 3-12.

Selecting two sort fields in Design view ◣ **Figure 3-12**

sort order for the primary sort field

sort order for the secondary sort field

You have finished your query changes, so now you can run the query and then save the modified query with the same query name.

4. In the Results group on the Query Tools Design tab, click the **Run** button. Access runs the query and displays the query datasheet. The records appear in ascending order, based on the values of the City field. Within groups of records with the same City field value, the records appear in descending order by the values of the Contract Amt field. See Figure 3-13.

Datasheet sorted on two fields ◣ **Figure 3-13**

primary sort field

secondary sort field

records grouped by City are shown in descending order by Contract Amt

When you save the query, all of your design changes—including the selection of the sort fields—are saved with the query. The next time Sarah runs the query, the records will appear sorted by the primary and secondary sort fields.

5. Click the **Save** button on the Quick Access Toolbar to save the revised Customer Contracts query.

Sarah knows that Belmont Landscapes has seen an increase in business recently for customers located in the city of Grand Rapids. She would like to focus briefly on the information for customers in that city only. Furthermore, she is interested in knowing how many contracts were signed in March, because this month has sometimes been a slow month for Belmont Landscapes in terms of contract signings. Selecting only the records with a City field value of "Grand Rapids" and a Signing Date field value beginning with "3" (for the month of March) is a temporary change that Sarah wants in the datasheet, so you do not need to switch to Design view and change the query. Instead, you can apply a filter.

Filtering Data

A **filter** is a set of restrictions you place on the records in an open datasheet or form to *temporarily* isolate a subset of the records. A filter lets you view different subsets of displayed records so that you can focus on only the data you need. Unless you save a query or form with a filter applied, an applied filter is not available the next time you run the query or open the form.

The simplest technique for filtering records is Filter By Selection. **Filter By Selection** lets you select all or part of a field value in a datasheet or form, and then display only those records that contain the selected value in the field. You can also use the AutoFilter feature to filter records. When you click the arrow on a column heading, the menu that opens provides options for filtering the display based on a field value or the selected part of a field value. Another technique for filtering records is to use **Filter By Form**, which changes your datasheet to display blank fields. Then you can select a value using the arrow that appears when you click any blank field to apply a filter that selects only those records containing that value.

Reference Window	**Using Filter By Selection**

- In the datasheet or form, select part of the field value that will be the basis for the filter; or, if the filter will be based on the entire field value, click anywhere within the field value.
- In the Sort & Filter group on the Home tab, click the Selection button, and then click the type of filter you want to apply.

For Sarah's request, you need to select a City field value of Grand Rapids, and then use Filter By Selection to display only those query records with this value. Then you will filter the records further by selecting only those records with a Signing Date value that begins with "3" (for March).

To display the records using Filter By Selection:

▶ **1.** In the query datasheet, locate the first occurrence of a City field containing the value **Grand Rapids**, and then click anywhere within that field value.

▶ **2.** In the Sort & Filter group on the Home tab, click the **Selection** button. A menu opens with options for the type of filter to apply. See Figure 3-14.

Using Filter By Selection   Figure 3-14

The menu provides options for displaying only those records with a City field value that equals the selected value (in this case, Grand Rapids); does not equal the value; contains the value somewhere within the field; or does not contain the value somewhere within the field. You want to display all the records whose City field value equals Grand Rapids.

▶ 3. In the Selection menu, click **Equals "Grand Rapids"**. Access displays the filtered results. Only the 13 records that have a City field value of "Grand Rapids" appear in the datasheet. See Figure 3-15.

Datasheet after applying the filter   Figure 3-15

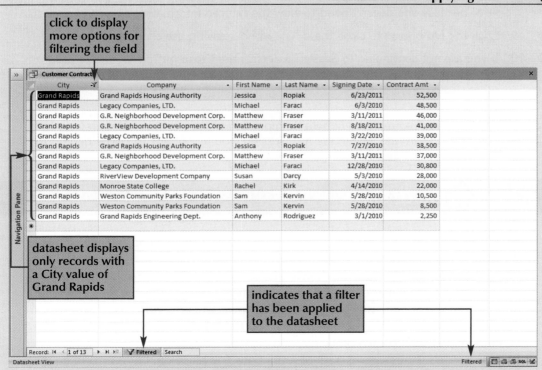

On the status bar, the button labeled "Filtered" to the right of the navigation buttons and the notation "Filtered" both indicate that a filter has been applied to the datasheet. Also, notice that the Toggle Filter button in the Sort & Filter group on the Home tab is active; you can click this button (or the Filtered button next to the navigation buttons) to toggle between the filtered and nonfiltered displays of the query datasheet. The City field also has a filtered icon to the right of the field name; you can click this icon to display additional options for filtering the field.

Next, Sarah wants to view only those records with a Signing Date value in the month of March to focus on the contracts signed in that month for customers located in Grand Rapids. So, you need to apply an additional filter to the datasheet.

▶ 4. In any Signing Date field value beginning with the number "3" (for the month of March), select only the first digit **3**.

▶ 5. In the Sort & Filter group on the Home tab, click the **Selection** button. Notice that three filters are available based on your selection: to display only those records with a Signing Date field value that begins with 3; to display only those records with a Signing Date field value that does not begin with 3; or to display only those records with a Signing Date field value that is between two dates. If you choose the between option, a dialog box opens, in which you enter the date values that you want to use.

▶ 6. Click **Begins With 3** in the Selection menu. The second filter is applied to the query datasheet, which now shows only the four records for customers located in Grand Rapids who signed contracts in the month of March.

Now you can redisplay all the query records by clicking the Toggle Filter button, which you use to switch between the filtered and nonfiltered displays.

▶ 7. In the Sort & Filter group on the Home tab, click the **Toggle Filter** button. Access redisplays all the records in the query datasheet.

▶ 8. Close the Customer Contracts query. Access asks if you want to save your changes to the design of the query—in this case, the filtered display, which is still available through the Toggle Filter button. Sarah does not want the query saved with the filter because she doesn't need to view the filtered information on a regular basis.

▶ 9. Click the **No** button to close the query without saving the changes.

▶ 10. If you are not continuing to Session 3.2, click the **Close** button ⊠ on the program window title bar. Access closes the Belmont database, and then the Access program closes.

The queries you've created will help Belmont Landscapes employees retrieve just the information they want to view. In the next session, you'll continue to create queries to meet their information needs.

Review | **Session 3.1 Quick Check**

1. In Datasheet view, what is the difference between navigation mode and editing mode?
2. What is a select query?
3. Describe the field list and the design grid in the Query window in Design view.
4. How are a table datasheet and a query datasheet similar? How are they different?
5. For a Date/Time field, how do the records appear when sorted in ascending order?
6. True or False: When you define multiple sort fields in Design view, the sort fields must be adjacent to each other.
7. A(n) _____ is a set of restrictions you place on the records in an open datasheet or form to isolate a subset of records temporarily.

Session 3.2

Defining Record Selection Criteria for Queries

Oren wants to display customer and contract information for all customers who live in Holland, Oren's hometown. He is planning to do a special local promotion for Holland customers, because Belmont Landscapes is located there, and Oren wants to increase his firm's presence in the community. For this request, you could create a query to select the correct fields and all records in the Customer and Contract tables, select a City field value of Holland in the query datasheet, and then click the Selection button and choose the appropriate filter option to filter the query results and display the information for only those customers in Holland. However, a faster way of displaying the data Oren needs is to create a query that displays the selected fields and only those records in the Customer and Contract tables that satisfy a condition.

Just as you can display selected fields from a database in a query datasheet, you can display selected records. To tell Access which records you want to select, you must specify a condition as part of the query. A **condition** is a criterion, or rule, that determines which records are selected. To define a condition for a field, you place the condition in the field's Criteria text box in the design grid.

A condition usually consists of an operator, often a comparison operator, and a value. A **comparison operator** asks Access to compare the value in a database field to the condition value and to select all the records for which the relationship is true. For example, the condition >50000 for the Contract Amt field selects all records in the Contract table with Contract Amt field values greater than $50,000. Figure 3-16 shows the Access comparison operators.

Access comparison operators | Figure 3-16

Operator	Meaning	Example
=	equal to (optional; default operator)	="Hall"
<	less than	<#1/1/99#
<=	less than or equal to	<=100
>	greater than	>"C400"
>=	greater than or equal to	>=18.75
<>	not equal to	<>"Hall"
Between ... And ...	between two values (inclusive)	Between 50 And 325
In ()	in a list of values	In ("Hall", "Seeger")
Like	matches a pattern that includes wildcards	Like "706*"

Specifying an Exact Match

For Oren's request, you need to create a query that will display only those records in the Customer table with the value Holland in the City field. This type of condition is called an **exact match** because the value in the specified field must match the condition exactly in order for the record to be included in the query results. You'll create the query in Design view.

To create the query in Design view:

▶ 1. If you took a break after the previous session, make sure that the Belmont database is open in the Access program window and that the Navigation Pane is closed.

▶ 2. Click the **Create** tab on the Ribbon.

▶ 3. In the Other group on the Create tab, click the **Query Design** button. The Show Table dialog box opens. You need to add the Customer and Contract tables to the Query window.

▶ 4. Click **Customer** in the Tables list box, click the **Add** button, click **Contract**, click the **Add** button, and then click the **Close** button.

▶ 5. Use the ⬍ pointer to resize the Customer field list so that all the fields are displayed.

▶ 6. Add the following fields from the Customer table to the design grid in the order shown: **Company**, **First Name**, **Last Name**, **Phone**, **Address**, **City**, and **E-mail Address**.

Oren also wants information from the Contract table included in the query results.

▶ 7. Add the following fields from the Contract table to the design grid in the order shown: **Contract Num**, **Contract Amt**, **Signing Date**, and **Contract Type**. See Figure 3-17.

| Figure 3-17 | ▶ | Query in Design view |

The field lists for the Customer and Contract tables appear in the top portion of the window, and the join line indicating a one-to-many relationship connects the two tables. The fields you selected appear in the design grid; to see all of the fields, you need to scroll to the right using the horizontal scroll bar.

To display the information Oren wants, you need to enter the condition for the City field in its Criteria text box. Oren wants to display only those records with a City field value of Holland.

To enter the exact match condition, and then save and run the query:

▶ 1. Click the **City Criteria** text box, type **Holland**, and then press the **Enter** key. The condition changes to "Holland".

Access automatically enclosed the condition you typed in quotation marks. You must enclose Text values in quotation marks when using them as selection criteria. If you omit the quotation marks, however, Access will include them automatically.

2. Click the **Save** button 🖫 on the Quick Access Toolbar to open the Save As dialog box.

3. Type **Holland Customers** in the Query Name text box, and then press the **Enter** key. Access saves the query with the specified name and displays the name on the query tab.

4. In the Results group on the Query Tools Design tab, click the **Run** button. Access runs the query and displays the selected field values for only those records with a City field value of Holland. A total of 12 records are selected and displayed in the datasheet. See Figure 3-18.

Datasheet displaying selected fields and records   ◄   Figure 3-18

Oren realizes that it's not necessary to include the City field values in the query results. The name of the query, Holland Customers, indicates that the query design includes all customers that are located in Holland, so the City field values are unnecessary and repetitive. Also, he decides that he would prefer the query datasheet to show the fields from the Contract table first, followed by the Customer table fields. You need to modify the query to produce the results Oren wants.

Modifying a Query

After you create a query and view the results, you might need to make changes to the query if the results are not what you expected or want to view. First, Oren asks you to modify the Holland Customers query to remove the City field values from the query results.

To remove the display of the City field values:

1. In the Views group on the Home tab, click the **View** button. The Holland Customers query opens in Design view.

You need to keep the City field as part of the query design, because it contains the defined condition for the query. You only need to remove the display of the field's values from the query results.

▶ **2.** Click the **City Show** check box to remove the check mark. The query will still find only those records with the value Holland in the City field, but the query results will not display these field values.

Next, you need to change the order of the fields in the query so that the contract information is listed first.

To move the fields from the Contract table before the fields from the Customer table:

▶ **1.** Scroll the design grid to the right until the remaining fields in the query design are visible. You need to move the Contract Num field so it becomes the first field in the query design.

▶ **2.** Position the pointer on the Contract Num field selector until the pointer changes to a ⬇ shape, and then click to select the field. See Figure 3-19.

Figure 3-19	Selected Contract Num field

▶ **3.** Position the pointer on the Contract Num field selector, and then click and drag the pointer 🔓 to the left, allowing the design grid to scroll back to the left, until the vertical line to the left of the Company field is highlighted. See Figure 3-20.

Figure 3-20	Dragging the field in the design grid

▶ **4.** Release the mouse button. The Contract Num field moves to the left of the Company field.

You can also select and move multiple fields at once.

▶ **5.** Scroll back to the right to view the remaining fields in the design grid. Now you need to select and move the Contract Amt, Signing Date, and Contract Type fields so that they follow the Contract Num field in the query design. To select multiple fields, you simply click and drag the mouse over the field selectors for the fields you want.

6. Click and hold the pointer ↓ on the Contract Amt field selector, drag the pointer to the right to select the Signing Date and Contract Type fields, and then release the mouse button. All three fields are now selected. See Figure 3-21.

Multiple fields selected to be moved ◄ Figure 3-21

7. Position the pointer ◄ anywhere near the top of the three selected fields, and then click and drag the pointer to the left until the vertical line to the right of the Contract Num field is highlighted.

8. Release the mouse button. The four fields from the Contract table are now the first four fields in the query design.

You have finished making the modifications to the query Oren requested, so you can now run the query.

9. In the Results group on the Query Tools Design tab, click the **Run** button. Access displays the results of the modified query. See Figure 3-22.

Results of modified query ◄ Figure 3-22

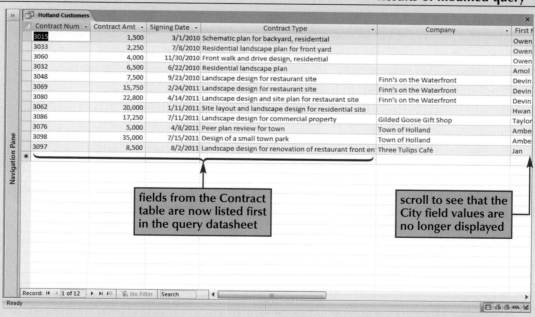

Note that the City field values are no longer displayed in the query results (you need to scroll the datasheet to the right to verify this).

Oren would like to see more fields and records on the screen at one time. He asks you to change the datasheet's font size, and then to resize all the columns to their best fit.

Changing a Datasheet's Appearance

You can change the characteristics of a datasheet, including the font type and size of text in the datasheet, to improve its appearance or readability. As you learned in earlier tutorials, you can also resize the datasheet columns to view more columns on the screen at the same time. You'll change the font size from the default 11 points to 9, and then resize the datasheet columns.

To change the font size and resize the columns in the datasheet:

▶ **1.** In the Font group on the Home tab, click the **Font Size** arrow, and then click **9**. The font size for the entire datasheet changes to 9 points.

Next, you need to resize the columns to their best fit, so that each column is just wide enough to fit the longest value in the column. Instead of resizing each column individually, you'll use the datasheet selector to select all the columns and resize them at the same time.

▶ **2.** Click the **datasheet selector**, which is the box to the left of the Contract Num field name. All the columns in the datasheet are highlighted, indicating they are selected.

▶ **3.** Position the pointer ✛ at the right edge of any column in the datasheet, and then double-click the pointer. All the columns visible on the screen are resized to their best fit. Because only the visible columns are resized, you must scroll the datasheet to the right to make sure all field values for the entire column are fully displayed, resizing as you scroll, if necessary.

▶ **4.** Scroll the datasheet to the right and verify that all columns were resized to their best fit. If necessary, resize any individual column that might not have been resized to best fit the data it contains.

▶ **5.** Scroll to the left, if necessary, so that the Contract Num field is visible, and then click any field value in the Contract Num column to make it the current field. More columns are now visible in the datasheet.

Changing the Background Color of Datasheet Rows

By default, the rows in a datasheet are displayed with alternating background colors of white and light gray to distinguish one row from another, making it easier to view and read the contents of a datasheet. The default white/gray alternate scheme provides a subtle color difference between the rows. You can change the background color for datasheet rows to something more noticeable using the **Alternate Fill/Back Color button** in the Font group. Oren suggests that you change the row colors of the query datasheet to see the effect of using this feature.

To change the background color of the datasheet rows:

▶ **1.** In the Font group on the Home tab, click the arrow on the **Alternate Fill/Back Color** button ▦ ▾ to display the gallery of color choices. See Figure 3-23.

Gallery of color choices for alternate fill color ◀ **Figure 3-23**

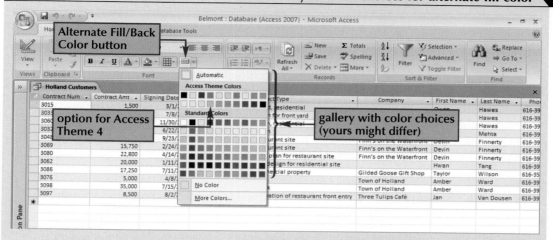

The Access Theme Colors gallery provides colors from Access themes, so that your datasheet's color scheme matches the default used for the Access program. The Standard Colors gallery provides many standard color choices. You might also see a Recent Colors gallery, with colors that you have recently used in a datasheet. On the menu, you could also choose the No Color option, which sets each row's background to white; or the More Colors option, which creates a custom color. You'll use one of the theme colors.

Tip

The name of the color appears in a ScreenTip when you point to a color in the gallery.

2. In the Access Theme Colors gallery, click the color box for **Access Theme 4** (second row, fourth color box). The alternating background color is applied to the query datasheet. See Figure 3-24.

Datasheet formatted with new fill color ◀ **Figure 3-24**

Every other row in the datasheet uses the Access Theme 4 background color. Oren likes how the datasheet looks with this color scheme, so he asks you to save the query.

3. Save and close the Holland Customers query.

After viewing the query results, Oren decides that he would like to see the same fields, but only for those records with a Contract Amt field value equal to or greater than $25,000. He is interested to know which Belmont Landscapes customers in all cities and towns have signed the largest contracts, so that he can follow up with these customers personally. To create the query that will produce the results Oren wants, you need to use a comparison operator to match a range of values—in this case, any Contract Amt value greater than or equal to $25,000.

Using a Comparison Operator to Match a Range of Values

Once you create and save a query, you can double-click the query name in the Navigation Pane to run the query again. You can then click the View button to change its design. You can also use an existing query as the basis for creating another query. Because the design of the query you need to create next is similar to the Holland Customers query, you will copy, paste, and rename this query to create the new query. Using this approach keeps the Holland Customers query intact.

To create the new query by copying the Holland Customers query:

▶ **1.** Open the Navigation Pane. Note that the Holland Customers query is listed below both the Contract and Customer groups, because the query is based on data from both tables.

You need to use the shortcut menu to copy the Holland Customers query and paste it in the Navigation Pane; then you'll give the copied query a different name. To do so, you could copy either instance of the Holland Customers query in the Navigation Pane.

▶ **2.** In the Customer group on the Navigation Pane, right-click **Holland Customers** to select it and display the shortcut menu.

▶ **3.** Click **Copy** on the shortcut menu.

▶ **4.** Right-click the empty area of the Navigation Pane, and then click **Paste** on the shortcut menu. The Paste As dialog box opens with the text "Copy Of Holland Customers" in the Query Name text box. Because Oren wants the new query to show the contracts with the largest amounts, you'll name the new query "Large Contract Amounts."

▶ **5.** Type **Large Contract Amounts** in the Query Name text box, and then press the **Enter** key. The new query appears in both the Contract and Customer groups in the Navigation Pane.

▶ **6.** In the Customer group on the Navigation Pane, double-click the **Large Contract Amounts** query to open, or run, the query. Notice that all the design changes you made to the original Holland Customers query—decreasing the font size, resizing all the columns, and applying the new alternating background row color—were saved with the query.

▶ **7.** Close the Navigation Pane.

Next, you need to open the query in Design view and modify its design to produce the results Oren wants—to display only those records with Contract Amt field values that are greater than or equal to $25,000.

To modify the design of the new query:

▶ **1.** In the Views group on the Home tab, click the **View** button to display the query in Design view.

▶ **2.** Click the **Contract Amt Criteria** text box, type **>=25000**, and then press the **Tab** key. See Figure 3-25.

Criteria entered for Contract Amt field | Figure 3-25

new condition entered

Trouble? If you receive an error message saying that you entered an expression containing invalid syntax, you might have typed a comma in the amount "25000" or a dollar sign. Commas and dollar signs are not allowed in selection criteria. Delete the comma and/or dollar sign from the Contract Amt Criteria box, and then press the Tab key.

The condition specifies that a record will be selected only if its Contract Amt field value is $25,000 or greater. Before you run the query, you need to delete the condition for the City field. Recall that the City field is part of the query, but its values are not displayed in the query results. When you modified the query to remove the City field values from the query results, Access moved the field to the end of the design grid. So, you need to locate the City field, delete its condition, specify that the City field values should be included in the query results, and then move the field back to its original position following the Address field.

3. Press the **Tab** key eight times until the condition for the City field is highlighted, and then press the **Delete** key. The condition for the City field is removed.

4. Click the **Show** check box for the City field to insert a check mark so that the field values will be displayed in the query results.

5. Use the ↓ pointer to select the City field, drag the selected field to the right of the Address field, and then click in an empty box to deselect the City field. See Figure 3-26.

Design grid after moving City field | Figure 3-26

Show check box is selected

City field moved back to its original location

condition removed from City Criteria text box

6. In the Results group on the Query Tools Design tab, click the **Run** button. Access runs the query and displays the selected fields for only those records with a Contract Amt field value of greater than or equal to $25,000. A total of 23 records are selected. See Figure 3-27.

Figure 3-27 ▶ Running the modified query

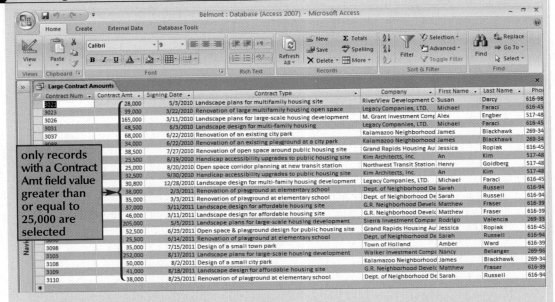

only records with a Contract Amt field value greater than or equal to 25,000 are selected

The City field values are also included in the query datasheet; you need to scroll the datasheet to the right to view them.

7. Save and close the Large Contract Amounts query.

Oren recently hired Steve Barry as a new consultant at Belmont Landscapes. Steve will focus primarily on customers located in Lansing. To help Steve prioritize his site visits in Lansing, Oren asks you to provide him with a list of all customers in Lansing who have signed contracts with values greater than $25,000. To produce this list, you need to create a query containing two conditions—one for the city and another for the contract amount.

Defining Multiple Selection Criteria for Queries

Multiple conditions require you to use **logical operators** to combine two or more conditions. When you want a record selected only if two or more conditions are met, you need to use the **And logical operator**. In this case, Oren wants to see only those records with a City field value of Lansing *and* a Contract Amt field value greater than $25,000. If you place conditions in separate fields in the *same* Criteria row of the design grid, all conditions in that row must be met in order for a record to be included in the query results. However, if you place conditions in *different* Criteria rows, a record will be selected if at least one of the conditions is met. If none of the conditions are met, Access does not select the record. When you place conditions in different Criteria rows, you are using the **Or logical operator**. Figure 3-28 illustrates the difference between the And and Or logical operators.

Logical operators And and Or for multiple selection criteria ◄ Figure 3-28

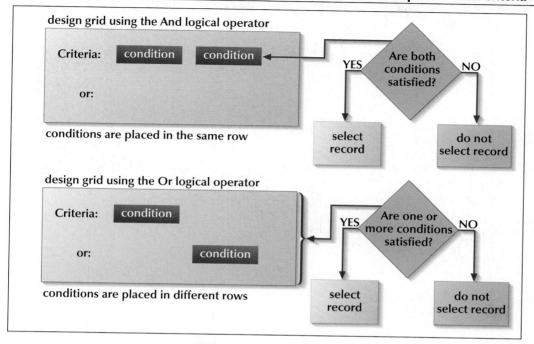

The And Logical Operator

To create the query for Oren, you need to use the And logical operator to show only the records for customers located in Lansing *and* with a contract amount greater than $25,000. You'll create a new query based on both the Customer and Contract tables to produce the necessary results. In the query design, both conditions you specify will appear in the same Criteria row; therefore, the query will select records only if both conditions are met.

To create a new query using the And logical operator:

1. Click the **Create** tab on the Ribbon.

2. In the Other group on the Create tab, click the **Query Design** button.

3. Add the **Customer** and **Contract** tables to the Query window, and then close the Show Table dialog box. Resize the Customer field list to display all the field names.

4. Add the following fields from the Customer field list to the design grid in the order shown: **Company**, **First Name**, **Last Name**, **Phone**, and **City**.

5. Add the **Contract Amt** and **Signing Date** fields from the Contract table to the design grid.

   Now you need to enter the two conditions for the query.

6. Click the **City Criteria** text box, and then type **Lansing**.

7. Press the **Tab** key to move to the **Contract Amt Criteria** text box, type **>25000**, and then press the **Tab** key. See Figure 3-29.

Figure 3-29 | Query to find customers in Lansing with large contracts

8. Run the query. Access displays only those records that meet both conditions: a City field value of Lansing and a Contract Amt field value greater than $25,000. Three records are selected, for two different customers. See Figure 3-30.

Figure 3-30 | Results of query using the And logical operator

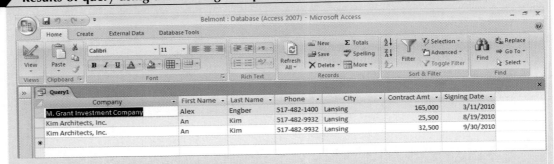

9. Click the **Save** button on the Quick Access Toolbar, and then save the query as **Key Lansing Customers**.

10. Close the query. When Steve begins working at Belmont Landscapes, he can run this query to see which customers in Lansing he should contact first.

Next, Oren and Taylor meet to discuss strategies for increasing business for Belmont Landscapes. They are interested in knowing which customers signed contracts for small amounts—less than $10,000—or which contracts were signed in the first two months of 2011, because business seemed unusually slow during those months. They want to use this information for two reasons: (1) to target specific customers who signed smaller contracts with Belmont Landscapes, to determine if these customers might have additional landscaping needs; and (2) to analyze the number and type of contracts signed during these slow months so they can develop strategies for increasing contract signings in the future. To help with their planning, Oren and Taylor have asked you to produce a list of all contracts with amounts less than $10,000 or that were signed between 1/1/2011 and 3/1/2011. To create this query, you need to use the Or logical operator.

The Or Logical Operator

To create the query that Oren and Taylor requested, your query must select a record when either one of two conditions is satisfied or when both conditions are satisfied. That is, a record is selected if the Contract Amt field value is less than $10,000 *or* if the Signing Date field value is between 1/1/2011 and 3/1/2011 *or* if both conditions are met. You will enter the condition for the Contract Amt field in the Criteria row and the condition for the Signing Date field in the "or" criteria row, thereby using the Or logical operator.

To display the information Oren and Taylor want to view, you'll create a new query containing the First Name, Last Name, Company, and City fields from the Customer table (in that order); and the Contract Amt, Signing Date, and Contract Type fields from the Contract table. Then you'll specify the conditions using the Or logical operator.

To create a new query using the Or logical operator:

▶ 1. Click the **Create** tab on the Ribbon and then, in the Other group, click the **Query Design** button.

▶ 2. Add the **Customer** and **Contract** tables to the Query window, close the Show Table dialog box, and then resize the Customer field list.

▶ 3. Add the following fields from the Customer table to the design grid in the order shown: **First Name**, **Last Name**, **Company**, and **City**.

▶ 4. Add the following fields from the Contract table to the design grid in the order shown: **Contract Amt**, **Signing Date**, and **Contract Type**.

   Now you need to specify the first condition, <10000, in the Contract Amt field.

▶ 5. Click the **Contract Amt Criteria** text box, type **<10000** and then press the **Tab** key.

   Because you want records selected if either of the conditions for the Contract Amt or Signing Date fields is satisfied, you must enter the condition for the Signing Date field in the "or" row of the design grid. To specify the date period for the query, you'll use the Between operator.

▶ 6. Press the ↓ key, type **Between 1/1/2011 And 3/1/2011** in the "or" text box for Signing Date, and then press the **Tab** key.

   To view the entire condition for the Signing Date field, you'll resize this field's column in the design grid.

▶ 7. Place the pointer on the vertical line to the right of the Signing Date field selector until the pointer changes to a ↔ shape, and then double-click to widen the column. The condition in the Signing Date field is now fully displayed. Note that Access automatically places number signs around the date values in the condition to distinguish the date values from the operators. See Figure 3-31.

Query window with the Or logical operator   Figure 3-31

Oren wants the list displayed in descending order by Signing Date, to better analyze the data.

▶ 8. Click the right side of the **Signing Date Sort** text box, and then click **Descending**.

9. Run the query. Access displays only those records that meet either condition: a Contract Amt field value less than $10,000 or a Signing Date field value between 1/1/2011 and 3/1/2011. Access also selects records that meet both conditions. A total of 29 records are selected. The records in the query datasheet appear in descending order based on the values in the Signing Date field. See Figure 3-32.

Figure 3-32 | **Results of query using the Or logical operator**

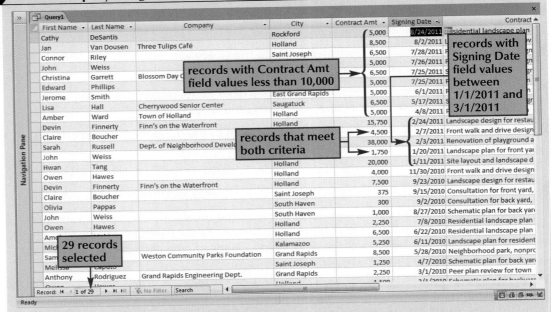

10. Save the query as **Small Contracts Or Winter Signings**, and then close it.

InSight | **Understanding the Results of Using And vs. Or**

When you use the And logical operator to define multiple selection criteria in a query, you *narrow* the results produced by the query, because a record must meet more than one condition to be included in the results. When you use the Or logical operator, you *broaden* the results produced by the query, because a record must meet only one of the conditions to be included in the results. This is an important distinction to keep in mind when you include multiple selection criteria in queries, so that the queries you create will produce the results you want.

Next, Oren turns his attention to some financial aspects of his business. He wants to use the Belmont database to perform calculations. He is considering imposing a 3% late fee on unpaid invoices and wants to know exactly what the late fee charges would be, should he decide to institute such a policy in the future. To produce the information for Oren, you need to create a calculated field.

Creating a Calculated Field

In addition to using queries to retrieve, sort, and filter data in a database, you can use a query to perform calculations. To perform a calculation, you define an **expression** containing a combination of database fields, constants, and operators. For numeric expressions, the data types of the database fields must be Number, Currency, or Date/Time; the constants are numbers such as .03 (for the 3% late fee); and the operators can be arithmetic operators (+ – * /) or other specialized operators. In complex expressions, you can enclose calculations in parentheses to indicate which one should be performed first. In expressions without parentheses, Access calculates in the following order of precedence: multiplication and division before addition and subtraction. When operators have equal precedence, Access calculates them in order from left to right.

To perform a calculation in a query, you add a calculated field to the query. A **calculated field** is a field that displays the results of an expression. A calculated field appears in a query datasheet or in a form or report; however, it does not exist in a database. When you run a query that contains a calculated field, Access evaluates the expression defined by the calculated field and displays the resulting value in the query datasheet, form, or report.

To enter an expression for a calculated field, you can type it directly in a Field text box in the design grid. Alternately, you can open the Zoom box or Expression Builder and use either one to enter the expression. The **Zoom box** is a dialog box that you can use to enter text, expressions, or other values. To use the Zoom box, however, you must know all the parts of the expression you want to create. **Expression Builder** is an Access tool that makes it easy for you to create an expression; it contains a box for entering the expression, buttons for common operators, and one or more lists of expression elements, such as table and field names. Unlike a Field text box, which is too small to show an entire expression at one time, the Zoom box and Expression Builder are large enough to display lengthy expressions. In most cases, Expression Builder provides the easiest way to enter expressions, because you don't have to know all the parts of the expression; you can choose the necessary elements from the Expression Builder dialog box.

> **Tip**
>
> If your field names include spaces in the names, as in the fields "First Name" and "Last Name," you must enclose the names in brackets when using them in an expression.

Using Expression Builder

| Reference Window

- Open the query in Design view.
- In the design grid, position the insertion point in the Field text box of the field for which you want to create an expression.
- In the Query Setup group on the Query Tools Design tab, click the Builder button.
- Use the expression elements and common operators to build the expression, or type the expression directly.
- Click the OK button.

To produce the information Oren wants, you need to create a new query based on the Invoice table and, in the query, create a calculated field that will multiply each Invoice Amt field value by .03 to calculate the proposed 3% late fee.

To create the new query that will include the calculated field:

▶ **1.** Click the **Create** tab on the Ribbon and then, in the Other group, click the **Query Design** button.

Oren wants to see data from both the Contract and Invoice tables, so you need to add these two tables to the Query window.

▶ **2.** Add the **Contract** and **Invoice** tables to the Query window, and then close the Show Table dialog box. The field lists appear in the Query window, and the one-to-many relationship between the Contract (primary) and Invoice (related) tables is displayed.

▶ **3.** Add the following fields to the design grid in the order given: **Contract Num** and **Contract Amt** from the Contract table; and **Invoice Item**, **Invoice Paid**, and **Invoice Amt** from the Invoice table.

Oren is interested in viewing data for unpaid invoices only, because a late fee would apply only to them, so you need to enter the necessary condition for the Invoice Paid field. Recall that Invoice Paid is a Yes/No field. The condition you need to enter is the word "No" in the Criteria text box for this field, so that Access will retrieve the records for unpaid invoices only.

▶ **4.** In the **Invoice Paid Criteria** text box, type **No** and then press the **Tab** key.

The query name you'll use will indicate that the data is for unpaid invoices, so you don't need to include the Invoice Paid values in the query results.

▶ **5.** Click the **Invoice Paid Show** check box to remove the check mark.

▶ **6.** Save the query with the name **Unpaid Invoices With Late Fees**.

Now you can use the Expression Builder to create the calculated field for the Invoice Amt field.

To create the calculated field:

▶ **1.** Click the blank Field text box to the right of the Invoice Amt field. This field will contain the calculated field values.

▶ **2.** In the Query Setup group on the Query Tools Design tab, click the **Builder** button. The Expression Builder dialog box opens.

The center pane in the dialog box lists the fields from the query so you can include them in the expression. You can use the common operators and expression elements to help you build an expression.

The expression for the calculated field will multiply the Invoice Amt field values by the numeric constant .03 (which represents a 3% late fee). To include a field in the expression, you select the field and then click the Paste button in the dialog box. To include a numeric constant, you simply type the constant in the expression.

▶ **3.** Click **Invoice Amt** in the field list, and then click the **Paste** button in the dialog box. The field name appears in the expression box, within brackets.

To include the multiplication operator in the expression, you click the asterisk (*) button. Note that you do not include spaces between the elements in an expression.

▶ **4.** Click the ***** button in the row of common operators, and then type **.03**. You have finished entering the expression. See Figure 3-33.

Completed expression for the calculated field ◄ Figure 3-33

expression ──

selected field used
in expression

▶ 5. Click the **OK** button. Access closes the Expression Builder dialog box and adds the expression to the design grid in the Field text box for the calculated field.

   Next, you need to specify a name for the calculated field as it will appear in the query results.

▶ 6. Press the **Home** key to position the insertion point to the left of the expression.

   You'll enter the name Late Fee, which is descriptive of the field's contents; then you'll run the query. To separate the calculated field name from the expression, you must type a colon between them.

▶ 7. Type **Late Fee:**. *Make sure you include the colon following the field name.*

▶ 8. Run the query. Access displays the query datasheet, which contains the specified fields and the calculated field with the name "Late Fee." See Figure 3-34.

Datasheet displaying the calculated field ◄ Figure 3-34

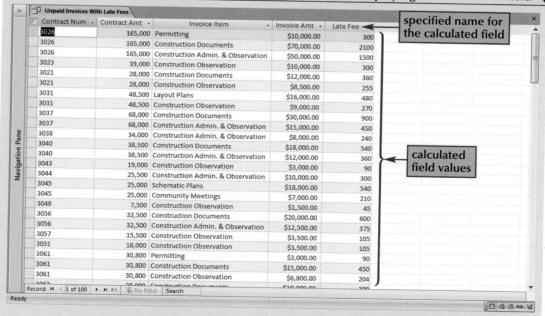

specified name for
the calculated field

Contract Num	Contract Amt	Invoice Item	Invoice Amt	Late Fee
3026	165,000	Permitting	$10,000.00	300
3026	165,000	Construction Documents	$70,000.00	2100
3026	165,000	Construction Admin. & Observation	$50,000.00	1500
3023	39,000	Construction Observation	$10,000.00	300
3021	28,000	Construction Documents	$12,000.00	360
3021	28,000	Construction Observation	$8,500.00	255
3031	48,500	Layout Plans	$16,000.00	480
3031	48,500	Construction Observation	$9,000.00	270
3037	68,000	Construction Documents	$30,000.00	900
3037	68,000	Construction Admin. & Observation	$15,000.00	450
3038	34,000	Construction Admin. & Observation	$8,000.00	240
3040	38,500	Construction Documents	$18,000.00	540
3040	38,500	Construction Admin. & Observation	$12,000.00	360
3043	19,000	Construction Observation	$3,000.00	90
3044	25,500	Construction Admin. & Observation	$10,000.00	300
3045	25,000	Schematic Plans	$18,000.00	540
3045	25,000	Community Meetings	$7,000.00	210
3048	7,500	Construction Observation	$1,500.00	45
3056	32,500	Construction Documents	$20,000.00	600
3056	32,500	Construction Admin. & Observation	$12,500.00	375
3057	15,500	Construction Observation	$3,500.00	105
3051	18,000	Construction Observation	$3,500.00	105
3061	30,800	Permitting	$3,000.00	90
3061	30,800	Construction Documents	$15,000.00	450
3061	30,800	Construction Observation	$6,800.00	204

calculated
field values

Record: 1 of 100   No Filter   Search

Ready

Trouble? If the calculated field name does not appear correctly, as shown in Figure 3-34, you might not have included the required colon. Switch to Design view, resize the column in the design grid that contains the calculated field to best fit, and then change your expression to Late Fee: [Invoice Amt]*0.03 and repeat Step 8.

The Late Fee field values are currently displayed without dollar signs and decimal places. Oren wants these values to be displayed in the same format as the Invoice Amt field values, in case he decides to produce a report for customers showing both the invoice amounts and any imposed late fees.

Formatting a Calculated Field

You can specify a particular format for a calculated field, just as you can for any field, by modifying its properties. Next, you'll change the format of the Late Fee calculated field so that all values appear in the Currency format with two decimal places.

To format the calculated field:

▶ 1. Switch to Design view.

▶ 2. Right-click the **Late Fee** calculated field in the design grid to open the shortcut menu, and then click **Properties**. The Property Sheet for the calculated field opens on the right side of the window. See Figure 3-35.

Figure 3-35 **Property Sheet for the calculated field**

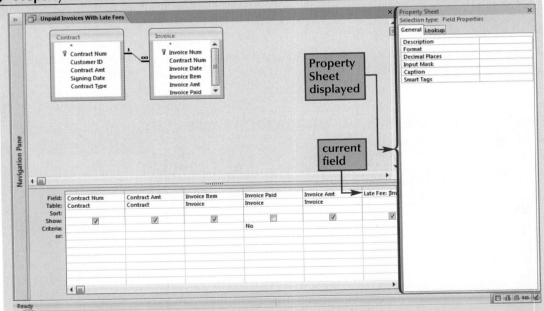

You need to change the Format property to Currency and the Decimal Places property to 2.

▶ 3. Click the right side of the **Format** text box to display the list of formats, and then click **Currency**.

▶ 4. Click the right side of the **Decimal Places** text box, and then click **2**.

▶ **5.** Close the Property Sheet for the calculated field, and then run the query. The amounts in the Late Fee calculated field are now displayed with dollar signs and two decimal places.

▶ **6.** Save and close the Unpaid Invoices With Late Fees query.

Creating Calculated Fields | InSight

Values that are produced by calculated fields should not be stored as separate fields in a database table. If you store the results of a calculated field in a table and the data produced by the calculated field becomes outdated, you would have to update the records in the table datasheet with the current data. It is best to create a query that includes a calculated field to perform the calculation you want. Then, every time you open the query, the calculation is performed and the resulting query datasheet reflects the most current data.

Oren wants to prepare a report on a regular basis that includes a summary of information about the contract amounts for Belmont Landscapes. He would like to know the minimum, average, and maximum contract amounts. He asks you to determine these statistics from data in the Contract table.

Using Aggregate Functions

You can calculate statistical information, such as totals and averages, on the records displayed in a table datasheet or selected by a query. To do this, you use the Access aggregate functions. **Aggregate functions** perform arithmetic operations on selected records in a database. Figure 3-36 lists the most frequently used aggregate functions.

Frequently used aggregate functions | Figure 3-36

Aggregate Function	Determines	Data Types Supported
Average	Average of the field values for the selected records	AutoNumber, Currency, Date/Time, Number
Count	Number of records selected	AutoNumber, Currency, Date/Time, Memo, Number, OLE Object, Text, Yes/No
Maximum	Highest field value for the selected records	AutoNumber, Currency, Date/Time, Number, Text
Minimum	Lowest field value for the selected records	AutoNumber, Currency, Date/Time, Number, Text
Sum	Total of the field values for the selected records	AutoNumber, Currency, Date/Time, Number

Working with Aggregate Functions Using the Totals Row

If you want to quickly perform a calculation using an aggregate function in a table or query datasheet, you can use the Totals button on the Home tab. When you click this button, a row labeled "Total" appears at the end of the datasheet. You can then choose one of the aggregate functions for a field in the datasheet, and the results of the calculation will be displayed in the Total row for that field.

Oren is interested to know the total amount of all contracts for the company. You can quickly display this amount using the Sum function in the Total row in the Contract table datasheet.

To display the total amount of all contracts in the Contract table:

▶ 1. Open the Navigation Pane, open the **Contract** table in Datasheet view, and then close the Navigation Pane.

▶ 2. In the Records group on the Home tab, click the **Totals** button. Access adds a row with the label "Total" to the end of the datasheet.

▶ 3. Scroll to the end of the datasheet to view the Total row. You want to display the sum of all the values in the Contract Amt field.

▶ 4. Click the **Contract Amt** field in the Total row. An arrow appears on the left side of the field.

▶ 5. Click the **arrow** to display the menu of aggregate functions. See Figure 3-37.

Figure 3-37 ▶ **Using aggregate functions in the Total row**

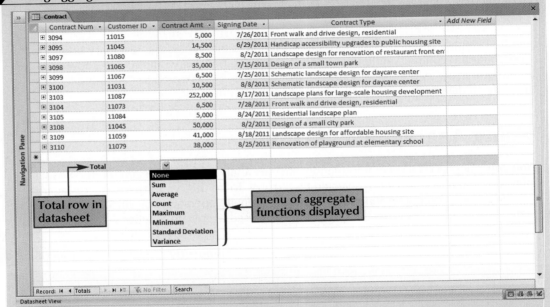

▶ 6. Click **Sum** in the menu. Access adds all the values in the Contract Amt field and displays the total 1,753,075 in the Total row for the field.

Oren doesn't want to change the Contract table to always display this total. You can remove the Total row by clicking the Totals button again; this button works as a toggle to switch between the display of the Total row and the results of any calculations in the row, and the display of the datasheet without this row.

▶ 7. In the Records group on the Home tab, click the **Totals** button. Access removes the Total row from the datasheet.

▶ 8. Close the Contract table without saving the changes.

For Oren's report, he wants to know the minimum, average, and maximum contract amounts for the company. To produce this information for Oren, you need to use aggregate functions in a query.

Creating Queries with Aggregate Functions

Aggregate functions operate on the records that meet a query's selection criteria. You specify an aggregate function for a specific field, and the appropriate operation applies to that field's values for the selected records.

To display the minimum, average, and maximum of all the contract amounts in the Contract table, you will use the Minimum, Average, and Maximum aggregate functions for the Contract Amt field.

To calculate the minimum, average, and maximum of all contract amounts:

▶ **1.** Create a new query in Design view, add the **Contract** table to the Query window, and then close the Show Table dialog box.

To perform the three calculations on the Contract Amt field, you need to add the field to the design grid three times.

▶ **2.** Double-click **Contract Amt** in the Contract field list three times to add three copies of the field to the design grid.

You need to select an aggregate function for each Contract Amt field. When you click the Totals button in the Show/Hide group on the Query Tools Design tab, a row labeled "Total" is added to the design grid. The Total row provides a list of the aggregate functions that you can select.

▶ **3.** In the Show/Hide group on the Query Tools Design tab, click the **Totals** button. A new row labeled "Total" appears between the Table and Sort rows in the design grid. The default entry for each field in the Total row is the Group By operator, which you will learn about later in this tutorial. See Figure 3-38.

Total row inserted in the design grid ◀ Figure 3-38

In the Total row, you specify the aggregate function you want to use for a field.

▶ **4.** Click the right side of the first column's **Total** text box, and then click **Min**. This field will calculate the minimum amount of all the Contract Amt field values.

When you run the query, Access automatically will assign a datasheet column name of "MinOfContract Amt" for this field. You can change the datasheet column name to a more descriptive or readable name by entering the name you want in the Field text box. However, you must also keep the field name Contract Amt in the Field text box, because it identifies the field whose values will be calculated. The Field text box will contain the datasheet column name you specify followed by the field name (Contract Amt) with a colon separating the two names.

►   5. Click to the left of Contract Amt in the first column's Field text box, and then type **Minimum Contract Amt:**. *Be sure that you type the colon following the name.*

►   6. Click the right side of the second column's **Total** text box, and then click **Avg**. This field will calculate the average of all the Contract Amt field values.

►   7. Click to the left of Contract Amt in the second column's Field text box, and then type **Average Contract Amt:**.

►   8. Click the right side of the third column's **Total** text box, and then click **Max**. This field will calculate the maximum amount of all the Contract Amt field values.

►   9. Click to the left of Contract Amt in the third column's Field text box, and then type **Maximum Contract Amt:**.

► 10. Run the query. Access displays one record containing the three aggregate function values. The single row of summary statistics represents calculations based on all the records selected for the query—in this case, all 64 records in the Contract table.

► 11. Resize all columns to their best fit so that the column names are fully displayed, and then click the field value in the first column. See Figure 3-39.

Figure 3-39   **Result of the query using aggregate functions**

► 12. Save the query as **Contract Amt Statistics**.

Oren also wants his report to include the same contract amount statistics (minimum, average, and maximum) grouped by city.

Using Record Group Calculations

In addition to calculating statistical information on all or selected records in selected tables, you can calculate statistics for groups of records. For example, you can determine the number of customers in each city or the average contract amount by city.

To create a query for Oren's latest request, you can modify the current query by adding the City field and assigning the Group By operator to it. The **Group By operator** divides the selected records into groups based on the values in the specified field. Those records with the same value for the field are grouped together, and the datasheet displays one record for each group. Aggregate functions, which appear in the other columns of the design grid, provide statistical information for each group.

You need to modify the current query to add the Group By operator to the City field from the Customer table. This will display the statistical information grouped by city for all the records in the query datasheet. To create the new query, you will save the Contract Amt Statistics query with a new name, keeping the original query intact, and then modify the new query.

To create a new query with the Group By operator:

▶ **1.** Display the **Contract Amt Statistics** query in Design view.

▶ **2.** Click the **Office Button** 🔘, point to **Save As**, and then click **Save Object As**. The Save As dialog box opens, indicating that you are saving a copy of the Contract Amt Statistics query as a new query.

▶ **3.** Type **Contract Amt Statistics By City** to replace the highlighted name, and then press the **Enter** key. The new query is saved with the name you specified.

You need to add the City field to the query. This field is in the Customer table. To include another table in an existing query, you open the Show Table dialog box.

▶ **4.** In the Query Setup group on the Query Tools Design tab, click the **Show Table** button to open the Show Table dialog box.

▶ **5.** Add the **Customer** table to the Query window, close the Show Table dialog box, and then resize the Customer field list.

▶ **6.** Drag the **City** field from the Customer field list to the first column in the design grid. When you release the mouse button, the City field appears in the design grid's first column, and the existing fields shift to the right. Group By, the default option in the Total row, appears for the City field.

▶ **7.** Run the query. Access displays 12 records—one for each City group. Each record contains the City field value for the group and the three aggregate function values. The summary statistics represent calculations based on the 64 records in the Contract table. See Figure 3-40.

Aggregate functions grouped by City   **Figure 3-40**

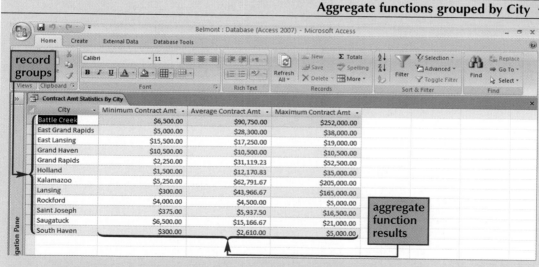

▶ **8.** Save and close the query.

▶ **9.** Open the Navigation Pane.

You have created and saved many queries in the Belmont database. The Navigation Pane provides options for opening and managing the queries you've created, as well as the other objects in the database, such as tables, forms, and reports.

Working with the Navigation Pane

As noted in Tutorial 1, the Navigation Pane is the main area for working with the objects in a database. As you continue to create objects in your database, you might want to display and work with them in different ways. The Navigation Pane provides options for grouping database objects in various ways to suit your needs. For example, you might want to view only the queries created for a certain table or all the query objects in the database.

The Navigation Pane divides database objects into categories, and each category contain groups. The groups contain one or more objects. The default category is **Tables and Related Views**, which arranges objects by tables, and the default group is **All Tables**, which includes all tables in the database in the list. You can also choose to display the objects for a specific table only.

The default group name, All Tables, appears at the top of the Navigation Pane. Currently, each table in the Belmont database—Contract, Invoice, and Customer—is displayed in a bar, and the objects related to each table are listed below the table name. Some objects appear more than once. As noted earlier, when an object is based on more than one table, that object appears in the group for each table. For example, the Holland Customers query is based on both the Contract and Customer tables, so it is listed in the group for both tables.

To group objects differently, you can select another category by using the Navigation Pane menu. You'll try this next.

Tip

You can hide the display of a group's objects by clicking the bar for the group; click the bar again to expand the group and display its objects.

To group objects differently in the Navigation Pane:

1. At the top of the Navigation Pane, click the **All Tables** bar. A menu is displayed for choosing different categories and groups. See Figure 3-41.

Figure 3-41   **Navigation Pane menu**

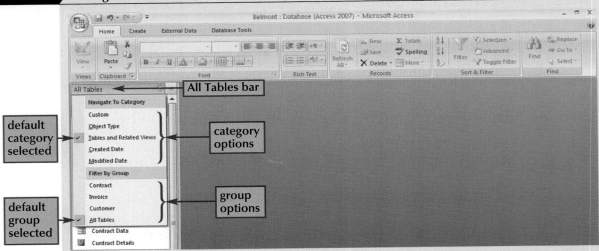

The top section of the menu provides the options for choosing a different category. The Tables and Related Views category has a check mark next to it, signifying that it is the currently selected category. The lower section of the menu provides options for choosing a different group; these options might change depending on the selected category.

2. In the top section of the menu, click **Object Type**. The Navigation Pane is now grouped into categories of object types—tables, queries, forms, and reports. See Figure 3-42.

Trouble? If your Navigation Pane doesn't show all the object types, click the bar at the top of the pane to open the Navigation Pane menu, and then click All Access Objects.

You can also select a different group for a category display.

3. Click the **All Access Objects** bar to display the Navigation Pane menu, and then click **Queries**. The Navigation Pane now shows only the query objects in the database.

4. Click the **Queries** bar, and then click **Tables and Related Views** to return to the default display of the Navigation Pane.

5. Compact and repair the Belmont database, and then close Access.

The default Tables and Related Views category is a predefined category. You can also create custom categories to group objects in the way that best suits how you want to manage your database objects. As you continue to build a database and the list of objects grows, creating a custom category can help you to work more efficiently with the objects in the database.

The queries you've created and saved will help Oren, Taylor, Sarah, and others to monitor and analyze the business activity of Belmont Landscapes and its customers. Now any staff member can run the queries at any time, modify them as needed, or use them as the basis for designing new queries to meet additional information requirements.

Review | **Session 3.2 Quick Check**

1. A(n) _____ is a criterion, or rule, that determines which records are selected for a query datasheet.
2. In the design grid, where do you place the conditions for two different fields when you use the And logical operator? The Or logical operator?
3. To perform a calculation in a query, you define a(n) _____ containing a combination of database fields, constants, and operators.
4. How does a calculated field differ from a table field?
5. What is an aggregate function?
6. The _____ operator divides selected records into groups based on the values in a field.
7. What is the default category for the display of objects in the Navigation Pane?

Review | **Tutorial Summary**

In this tutorial, you learned how to maintain a database by finding specific data, modifying values in records, and deleting records. You also learned how to create queries in Design view, based on one or more tables, and how to run and save queries. You learned different methods for sorting and filtering data to view records in a particular order. Using record selection criteria, you specified an exact match in a query, used a comparison operator to match a range of values, and used the And and Or logical operators to meet various requests for data retrieval. You also created a calculated field in the Expression Builder dialog box to display the results of an expression in a query, and you used aggregate functions and the Group By operator to calculate and display statistical information in a query. Finally, you learned how to change the display and grouping of database objects in the Navigation Pane.

Key Terms

aggregate function	Expression Builder	query by example (QBE)
All Tables	F2 key	Query Wizard
Alternate Fill/Back Color button	field list	recordset
And logical operator	filter	run (a query)
AutoFilter	Filter By Form	secondary sort field
calculated field	Filter By Selection	select query
comparison operator	Find command	sort
condition	Group By operator	sort field
datasheet selector	logical operator	subdatasheet
design grid	maintain (a database)	Tables and Related Views
editing mode	navigation mode	unique sort field
exact match	nonunique sort field	update (a database)
expand indicator	Or logical operator	Zoom box
expression	plus sign	
	primary sort field	

Practice | Review Assignments

Build on what you learned in the tutorial by practicing those skills using the same case scenario.

Data File needed for the Review Assignments: Supplier.accdb *(cont. from Tutorial 2)*

Oren asks you to update some information in the Supplier database and also to retrieve specific information from the database. Complete the following:

1. Open the **Supplier** database located in the Level.01\Review folder provided with your Data Files.

2. Open the **Company** table, and then change the following field values for the record with the Company ID MID312: Address to **2250 E Riverview St**, Phone to **269-979-0700**, Contact First Name to **Aimee**, and Contact Last Name to **Gigandet**. Close the table.

3. Open the **Product** table, find the record with Product ID 5318, and then delete the record. Close the table.

4. Create a query based on the Company table. Include the following fields, in the order shown, in the query: Company Name, Contact First Name, Contact Last Name, Phone, and Initial Contact Date. Sort the query in ascending order based on the Company Name. Save the query as **Contact List**, and then run the query.

5. Use the Contact List query datasheet to update the Company table by changing the Phone field value for Genesis Garden Center to **616-456-1783**.

6. Change the alternate background color for the rows in the Contact List query datasheet to Light Label Text, and then save and close the query.

7. Use Design view to create a query based on the Company and Product tables. Select the Company Name and City fields from the Company table, and the Product Type, Price, Unit, and Discount Offered fields from the Product table. Sort the query results in descending order based on the Price. Select only those records with a City field value of Holland, but do not display the City field values in the query results. Save the query as **Holland Companies**, and then run the query. Resize all columns in the datasheet, if necessary, and then save and close the query.

8. Use Design view to create a query that lists all products that cost more than $5,000 and are not eligible for a discount. Display the following fields from the Product table in the query results: Product ID, Product Type, Price, Unit, and Weight in Lbs. (*Hint*: The Discount Offered field is a Yes/No field that should not appear in the query results.) Save the query as **High Prices No Discount**, run the query, and then close it.

9. Use Design view to create a query that lists companies located in Grand Rapids or products that cost less than $1,000. Include the Company Name, City, Contact First Name, and Contact Last Name fields from the Company table; and the Product Type, Price, and Discount Offered fields from the Product table. Save the query as **Grand Rapids Or Low Prices**, run the query, and then close it.

10. Use Design view to create a query that lists only those products that are eligible for a discount, along with a 5% discount amount based on the current price. Include the following fields from the Product table in the query: Product ID, Product Type, and Price. (*Hint:* The Discount Offered field is a Yes/No field that should not appear in the query results.) Display the discount in a calculated field named **Discount** that determines a 5% discount based on the Price field values. Display the results in descending order by Price. Save the query as **Prices With Discount Amounts**, and then run the query.

11. Modify the format of the Discount field in the Prices With Discount Amounts query so that it uses the Standard format and two decimal places. Run the query, resize all columns in the datasheet to best fit, and then save and close the query.

12. Create a query that calculates the lowest, highest, and average prices for all products using the field names **Lowest Price**, **Highest Price**, and **Average Price**, respectively. Run the query, resize all columns in the datasheet to best fit, save the query as **Price Statistics**, and then close it.

13. In the Navigation Pane, copy the Price Statistics query, and then rename the copied query as **Price Statistics By Company**.

14. Modify the Price Statistics By Company query so that the records are grouped by the Company Name field in the Company table. Company Name should appear as the first field in the query datasheet. Save and run the query, and then close it.

15. Change the Navigation Pane so that it displays all objects grouped by object type.

16. Compact and repair the Supplier database, and then close it.

| Apply | **Case Problem 1** |

Use the skills you learned in the tutorial to update records and create queries in a database for a small music school.

Data File needed for this Case Problem: Pinehill.accdb *(cont. from Tutorial 2)*

Pine Hill Music School   After reviewing the Pinehill database, Yuka Koyama wants to modify some records and then view specific information about the students, teachers, and contracts for her music school. She asks you to update and then query the Pinehill database to perform these tasks. Complete the following:

1. Open the **Pinehill** database located in the Level.01\Case1 folder provided with your Data Files.

2. In the **Teacher** table, change the following information for the record with Teacher ID 55-5310: Degree is **BM** and Hire Date is **3/12/2009**. Close the table.

3. In the **Student** table, find the record with the Student ID HAV7535, and then delete the related record in the subdatasheet for this student. Delete the record for Student ID HAV7535, and then close the Student table.

4. Create a query based on the Student table that includes the Last Name, First Name, and Phone fields, in that order. Save the query as **Student Phone List**, and then run the query.

5. In the results of the Student Phone List query, change the phone number for Andrea Barreau to **503-579-2277**. Close the query.

6. Use Design view to create a query based on the Teacher and Contract tables. Display the Last Name field from the Teacher table, and the Student ID, Contract End Date, Lesson Type, Lesson Length, and Lesson Monthly Cost fields, in that order, from the Contract table. Sort in ascending order first on the teacher's last name, and then in ascending order by the Student ID. Save the query as **Lessons By Teacher**, and then run it.

7. Use the Office Button to save the Lessons By Teacher query as **Current Lessons**.

8. Modify the Current Lessons query to display all contracts that end on or after 7/1/2010. Save your changes, and then run the query.

9. Save the Current Lessons query as **Current Guitar Lessons**.

10. Modify the Current Guitar Lessons query to display only those records for guitar lesson contracts that end on or after 7/1/2010. Do not include the Lesson Type field values in the query results. Run and save the query.

11. In the Current Guitar Lessons query datasheet, calculate the total monthly amount for current guitar lessons.

12. Change the alternate background color for the rows in the Current Guitar Lessons query datasheet to Light Label Text and the font size to 12. Resize all columns in the datasheet to fit the data, and then save and close the query.

13. Change the Navigation Pane so that it displays all objects grouped by object type.

14. Compact and repair the Pinehill database, and then close it.

| Create | **Case Problem 2** |

Follow the steps provided and use the figures as guides to create queries for a health and fitness center.

Data File needed for this Case Problem: Fitness.accdb (*cont. from Tutorial 2*)

Parkhurst Health & Fitness Center Martha Parkhurst needs to change a few records in the Fitness database, and analyze the records for members enrolled in different programs at the fitness center. To help her perform these tasks, you'll update the Fitness database and create queries to answer her questions. Complete the following:

1. Open the **Fitness** database located in the Level.01\Case2 folder provided with your Data Files.

2. In the **Member** table, find the record for Member ID 1158, and then change the Street value to **89 Mockingbird Lane** and the Phone to **804-751-1847**. Close the table.

3. In the **Program** table, find the record for Program ID 205. In the subdatasheet, delete the related record from the Member table. Then delete the record for Program ID 205 in the Program table. Close the table.

4. Use Design view to create a query that lists members who are required to have physical examinations. In the query results, display the First Name, Last Name, and Date Joined fields from the Member table, and the Monthly Fee field from the Program table. Sort the records in descending order by the Date Joined. Select records only for members required to take a physical. (*Hint:* The Physical Required field is a Yes/No field.) Save the query as **Physicals Needed**, and then run the query.

5. Use the Physicals Needed query datasheet to update the Member table by changing the Date Joined value for Ed Curran to **10/18/2010**.

6. Use the Physicals Needed query datasheet to display the total Monthly Fee for the selected members. Save and close the query.

7. Use Design view to create a query that lists the Member ID, First Name, Last Name, Date Joined, Program Type, and Monthly Fee fields for members who joined the fitness center between June 1 and June 30, 2010. Save the query as **June Members**, run the query, and then close it.

8. Create and save the query to produce the results shown in Figure 3-43. Close the query when you are finished.

Figure 3-43

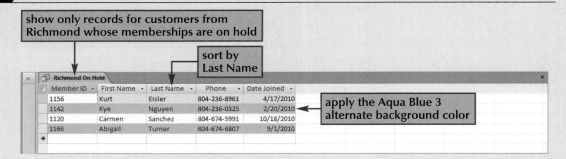

show only records for customers from Richmond whose memberships are on hold

sort by Last Name

apply the Aqua Blue 3 alternate background color

EXPLORE

9. Create and save the query to produce the results shown in Figure 3-44. Close the query when you are finished.

Figure 3-44

primary sort field

secondary sort field

show only customers from Bon Air or Glen Allen

Total row shows the sum of the Monthly Fee values

EXPLORE

10. Create and save the query to produce results that display statistics for the Monthly Fee field, as shown in Figure 3-45. Close the query when you are finished.

Figure 3-45

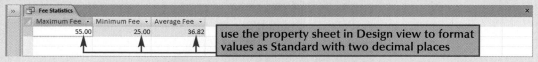

use the property sheet in Design view to format values as Standard with two decimal places

11. In the Navigation Pane, copy the Fee Statistics query and rename the copied query as **Fee Statistics By City**.

12. Modify the Fee Statistics By City query to display the same statistics grouped by City, with City appearing as the first field. (*Hint:* Add the Member table to the query.) Run the query, and then save and close it.

13. Change the Navigation Pane so that it displays all objects grouped by object type.

14. Compact and repair the Fitness database, and then close it.

Challenge | Case Problem 3

Work with the skills you've learned, and explore some new skills, to create queries for a not-for-profit agency that recycles household goods.

Data File needed for this Case Problem: Rossi.accdb (cont. from Tutorial 2)

Rossi Recycling Group Tom Rossi needs to modify some records in the Rossi database, and then he wants to find specific information about the donors, agencies, and donations to his not-for-profit agency. Tom asks you to help him update the database and create queries. Complete the following:

1. Open the **Rossi** database located in the Level.01\Case3 folder provided with your Data Files.

2. In the **Donor** table, delete the record with a Donor ID of 36065. (*Hint:* Delete the related record first.) Close the table.

3. Create a query based on the Agency table that includes the Agency Name, Contact First Name, Contact Last Name, and City fields, in that order. Save the query as **Agencies By City**, and then run it.

4. Modify the Agencies By City query so that it sorts records in ascending order first by City and then by Agency Name. Save and run the query.

5. In the Agencies By City query datasheet, change the contact for the Community Development agency to **Beth Dayton**. Close the query.

6. Use Design view to create a query that displays the Donor ID, First Name, Last Name, Donation Description, and Donation Value for all donations over $50. Sort the query in ascending order by Donation Value. Save the query as **Large Donations**, and then run the query.

7. Save the Large Donations query as **Large Cash Donations**.

EXPLORE   8. Modify the Large Cash Donations query to display only those records with donations valuing more than $50 in cash. Use the query datasheet to calculate the average large cash donation. Save and close the query.

9. Use Design view to create a query that displays the Agency ID, Donation ID, Donation Date, and Donation Description fields. Save the query as **Senior Donations**, and then run the query.

10. Filter the results of the Senior Donations query datasheet to display records for all donations to the SeniorCare Program (Agency ID K82).

EXPLORE   11. Format the datasheet of the Senior Donations query so that it does not display gridlines, uses an alternate background color for rows of Green 2, and displays a font size of 12. (*Hint*: Use the Gridlines button on the Home tab to select a gridlines option.) Resize the columns to display the complete field names and values. Save your changes.

12. Save the Senior Donations query as **Computer Or Youth Donations**.

13. Modify the Computer Or Youth Donations query to display donations of computer equipment or those to the After School Youth agency (Agency ID Y68). Sort the records in ascending order first by Donation Description and then by Agency ID. Run, save, and then close the query.

EXPLORE   14. Use Design view to create a query that displays the Donor ID, Agency Name, Donation Description, and Donation Value fields for all donations that require a pickup. (*Hint:* The Pickup Required field is a Yes/No field.) Create a calculated field named **Net Donation** that displays the results of subtracting $8.75 from the Donation Value field values. Display the results in ascending order by Donation Value. Save the query as **Donations After Pickup Charge**, and then run it. Modify the query to format the calculated field as Currency with two Decimal Places. Run the query and resize the columns in the datasheet to their best fit. Save and close the query.

EXPLORE   15. Use the **Donation** table to display the sum, average, and count of the Donation Value field for all donations. Then complete the following:

   a. Specify column names of **Total Donations**, **Average Donation**, and **Number of Donations**.

   b. Save the query as **Donation Statistics**, and then run it.

   c. Modify the field properties so that the values in the Total Donations and Average Donation columns display two decimal places and the Standard format. Run the query and resize the columns in the datasheet to their best fit. Save and close the query.

    d. In the Navigation Pane, create a copy of the Donation Statistics query named **Donation Statistics By Agency**.

    e. Modify the Donation Statistics By Agency query to display the sum, average, and count of the Donation Value field for all donations grouped by Agency Name, with Agency Name appearing as the first field. (*Hint*: Add the Agency table to the query.) Sort the records in descending order by Total Donations. Save, run, and then close the query.

16. Change the Navigation Pane so that it displays only queries. (*Hint:* Display the objects by type, and then select Queries in the Filter by Group section of the Navigation Pane menu.)

17. Compact and repair the Rossi database, and then close it.

Challenge | Case Problem 4

Work with the skills you've learned, and explore some new skills, to create queries for a luxury rental company.

Data File needed for this Case Problem: GEM.accdb *(cont. from Tutorial 2)*

GEM Ultimate Vacations   Griffin and Emma MacElroy want to modify some records, and then analyze data about their clients and the luxury properties they rent. You offer to help them update and query the GEM database. Complete the following:

1. Open the **GEM** database located in the Level.01\Case4 folder provided with your Data Files.

2. In the **Guest** table, delete the record with a Guest ID of 224, and then close the table.

3. Create a query based on the Property table that includes the Property Name, Location, Country, Nightly Rate, and Property Type fields, in that order. Sort in ascending order based on the Nightly Rate field values. Save the query as **Properties By Rate**, and then run the query.

⊕ EXPLORE   4. In the results of the Properties By Rate query, change the nightly rate for the Hartfield Country Manor property to $2,500, and then use the datasheet to display the number of properties and the average nightly rate. Save and close the query.

5. Create a query that displays the Guest Last Name, City, State/Prov, Reservation ID, Start Date, and End Date fields. Save the query as **Guest Trip Dates**, and then run the query. Change the alternate background color of the rows in the query datasheet to Access Theme 2. In Datasheet view, use an AutoFilter to sort the query results from oldest to newest Start Date. Save and close the query.

6. Create a query that displays the Guest Last Name, City, Reservation ID, People, Start Date, and End Date fields for all guests from Illinois (IL). Sort the query in ascending order by City. Save the query as **Illinois Guests**, run it, and then close the query.

⊕ EXPLORE   7. Create a query that displays the Guest Last Name, City, Reservation ID, Start Date, and Property ID fields for all guests who are not from Illinois or who are renting a property starting in the month of June 2010. Sort the query in descending order by Start Date. Save the query as **Out Of State Or June**, and then run the query.

8. Save the Out Of State Or June query as **Out Of State And June**.

9. Modify the Out Of State And June query to select all clients who are not from Illinois and who are renting a property beginning in the month of June 2010. Sort the query in ascending order by Start Date. Run the query, and then save and close it.

10. Create a query that displays the Reservation ID, Start Date, End Date, Property ID, Property Name, People, and Rental Rate fields for all reservations. Add a field to the query named **Cost Per Person** that displays the results of dividing the Rental Rate field values by the People field values. Display the results in descending order by Cost Per Person. Save the query as **Rental Cost** and then run it. Modify the query by setting the following properties for the Cost Per Person field: Format set to Currency and Decimal Places set to 2. Run the query, resize all datasheet columns to their best fit, and then save your changes.

11. Save the Rental Cost query as **Top Rental Cost**.

✦ EXPLORE
12. Open the Access Help window and use **top values query** as the search text. Select the Help article titled "Find the records with the top or bottom values in a group or field," and then read the "Find the records that contain top or bottom values" section. Close the Access Help window. Modify the Top Rental Cost query in Design view to display only the top five values for the Cost Per Person field. (*Hint:* Use the Return list box in the Query Setup group on the Query Tools Design tab.) Save, run, and then close the query.

✦ EXPLORE
13. Use the Reservation table to determine the minimum, average, and maximum Rental Rate values for all reservations. Then complete the following:
    a. Specify column names of **Lowest Rate**, **Average Rate**, and **Highest Rate**.
    b. Save the query as **Rate Statistics**, and then run the query.
    c. In Design view, use the property sheet for each column to format the results with the Standard format and two decimal places.
    d. Run the query, resize all the datasheet columns to their best fit, save your changes, and then close the query.
    e. Create a copy of the Rate Statistics query named **Rate Statistics By Country**.
    f. Revise the Rate Statistics By Country query to display the rate statistics grouped by Country of the property, with Country appearing as the first field. Save your changes and then run and close the query.

14. Change the view of the Navigation Pane to show all Access objects grouped by object type.

15. Compact and repair the GEM database, and then close it.

Research | **Internet Assignments**

Use the Internet to find and work with data related to the topics presented in this tutorial.

The purpose of the Internet Assignments is to challenge you to find information on the Internet that you can use to work effectively with this software. The actual assignments are updated and maintained on the Course Technology Web site. Log on to the Internet and use your Web browser to go to the Student Online Companion for New Perspectives Office 2007 at **www.course.com/np/office2007**. Then navigate to the Internet Assignments for this tutorial.

Assess | **SAM Assessment and Training**

If you have a SAM user profile, you may have access to hands-on instruction, practice, and assessment of the skills covered in this tutorial. Log in to your SAM account (**http://sam2007.course.com**) to launch any assigned training activities or exams that relate to the skills covered in this tutorial.

Review | **Quick Check Answers**

Session 3.1

1. In navigation mode, the entire field value is selected, and anything you type replaces the field value; in editing mode, you can insert or delete characters in a field value based on the location of the insertion point.
2. A select query is a general query in which you specify the fields and records you want Access to select.
3. The field list contains the table name at the top of the list box and the table's fields listed in the order in which they appear in the table; the design grid displays columns that contain specifications about a field you will use in the query.
4. A table datasheet and a query datasheet look the same, appearing in Datasheet view, and can be used to update data in a database. A table datasheet shows the permanent data in a table, whereas a query datasheet is temporary and its contents are based on the criteria you establish in the design grid.
5. oldest to most recent date
6. False
7. filter

Session 3.2

1. condition
2. in the same Criteria row; in different Criteria rows
3. expression
4. A calculated field appears in a query datasheet, form, or report but does not exist in a database, as does a table field.
5. a function that performs an arithmetic operation on selected records in a database
6. Group By
7. Tables and Related Views

Ending Data Files

Level.01 →	Tutorial	Review	Case1
	Belmont.accdb	Supplier.accdb	Pinehill.accdb
	Case2	Case3	Case4
	Fitness.accdb	Rossi.accdb	GEM.accdb

Objectives

Creating Forms and Reports

Creating a Customer Data Form, a Customer Contracts Form, and a Customers and Contracts Report

Case | Belmont Landscapes

Oren Belmont wants to continue enhancing the Belmont database to make it easier for his staff to enter, locate, and maintain data. In particular, he wants the database to include a form based on the Customer table to make it easier for employees to enter and change data about the firm's customers. He also wants the database to include a form that shows data from both the Customer and Contract tables at the same time. This form will show the contract information for each customer along with the corresponding customer data, providing a complete picture of Belmont Landscapes' customers and their contracts.

In addition, Taylor Sico would like the database to include a formatted report of customer and contract data so that employees will have printed output when completing market analyses and planning strategies for selling Belmont Landscapes' services to customers. She wants the information to be formatted in a professional manner, to make the report appealing and easy to use.

Starting Data Files

Level.01 →

Tutorial
Belmont.accdb *(cont.)*
Landscape.bmp

Review
Supplier.accdb *(cont.)*
Tools.bmp

Case1
Piano.bmp
Pinehill.accdb *(cont.)*

Case2
Fitness.accdb *(cont.)*
Weights.bmp

Case3
Donate.bmp
Rossi.accdb *(cont.)*

Case4
GEM.accdb *(cont.)*
Villa.bmp

Session 4.1

Creating a Form Using the Form Wizard

As you learned in Tutorial 1, a form is an object you use to enter, edit, and view records in a database. You can design your own forms or have Access create them for you automatically. In Tutorial 1, you used the Form tool to create the Contract Data form in the Belmont database. Recall that the Form tool creates a form automatically, using all the fields in the selected table or query.

Oren asks you to create a new form that his staff can use to view and maintain data in the Customer table. To create the form for the Customer table, you'll use the Form Wizard. The **Form Wizard** allows you to choose some or all of the fields in the selected table or query, choose fields from other tables and queries, and display the selected fields in any order on the form. You can also apply an existing style to the form to format its appearance quickly.

To open the Belmont database and start the Form Wizard:

▶ 1. Start Access and open the **Belmont** database located in the Level.01\Tutorial folder.

   Trouble? If the Security Warning is displayed below the Ribbon, click the Options button next to the Security Warning. In the dialog box that opens, click the "Enable this content" option button, and then click the OK button.

▶ 2. If necessary, open the Navigation Pane. To create a form based on a table or query, you can select the table or query in the Navigation Pane first, or you can select it using the Form Wizard.

▶ 3. In the Navigation Pane, click **Customer : Table** to select the Customer table as the basis for the new form.

▶ 4. Click the **Create** tab on the Ribbon. The Forms group on the Create tab provides options for creating various types of forms and designing your own forms.

▶ 5. In the Forms group, click the **More Forms** button, and then click **Form Wizard**. The first Form Wizard dialog box opens. See Figure 4-1.

| Figure 4-1 | First Form Wizard dialog box |

Because you selected the Customer table in the Navigation Pane before starting the Form Wizard, this table is selected in the Tables/Queries list box, and the fields for the Customer table are listed in the Available Fields list box.

Oren wants the form to display all the fields in the Customer table, but in a different order. He would like the Phone field to appear at the bottom of the form so that it stands out, making it easier for someone who needs to call customers to use the form and quickly identify the phone number for a customer.

To create the form using the Form Wizard:

1. Click the >> button to move all the fields to the Selected Fields list box. Next, you need to remove the Phone field, and then add it back as the last selected field so that it will appear at the bottom of the form.

2. In the Selected Fields list box, click the **Phone** field, and then click the < button to move the field back to the Available Fields list box.

   To add the Phone field to the end of the form, you need to highlight the last field in the list, and then move the Phone field back to the Selected Fields list box.

3. In the Selected Fields list box, click the **E-mail Address** field.

4. With the Phone field selected in the Available Fields list box, click the > button to move the Phone field to the end of the Selected Fields list box.

5. Click the **Next** button to display the second Form Wizard dialog box, in which you select a layout for the form. See Figure 4-2.

Choosing a layout for the form   **Figure 4-2**

The layout choices are Columnar, Tabular, Datasheet, and Justified. A sample of the selected layout appears on the left side of the dialog box.

6. Click each of the option buttons and review the corresponding sample layout.

   The Tabular and Datasheet layouts display the fields from multiple records at one time, whereas the Columnar and Justified layouts display the fields from one record at a time. Oren thinks the Columnar layout is the appropriate arrangement for displaying and updating data in the table, so that anyone using the form can focus on just one customer record at a time.

▶ 7. Click the **Columnar** option button (if necessary), and then click the **Next** button. Access displays the third Form Wizard dialog box, in which you choose a style for the form. A sample of the selected style appears in the box on the left. If you choose a style, which is called an **AutoFormat**, and decide you'd prefer a different one after the form is created, you can change it.

▶ 8. Scroll through the list of styles and click a few of them to review the corresponding sample. Oren likes the Office style and asks you to use it for the form.

▶ 9. Click **Office** in the list of styles, and then click the **Next** button. Access displays the final Form Wizard dialog box and shows the Customer table's name as the default form name. "Customer" is also the default title that will appear on the tab for the form.

You'll use "Customer Data" as the form name and, because you don't need to change the form's design at this point, you'll display the form.

▶ 10. Click the insertion point to the right of Customer in the text box, press the **spacebar**, type **Data**, and then click the **Finish** button.

▶ 11. Close the Navigation Pane to display more of the form window. The completed form is opened in Form view. See Figure 4-3.

Figure 4-3 ▶ **Customer Data form in Form view**

You use Form view to view, enter, and maintain data in the table on which the form is based. Notice that the title you specified for the form appears on the tab for the form object and as a title on the form itself. The Columnar layout you selected places the names of the fields in the Customer table in a column on the left of the form, and the corresponding field values in boxes on the right. The form currently displays the field values for the first record in the Customer table.

After viewing the form, Oren decides that he doesn't like the form's style. The font color of the field names is somewhat light, making the names a bit difficult to read. Also, he wants the colors used in the form to reflect the landscaping business. He also suggests adding a graphic to the form, for visual interest, and perhaps modifying other form elements, such as the color of certain text, the type of line used for the text boxes, and so on. You can make all of these changes working with the form in Layout view.

Modifying a Form's Design in Layout View

After you create a form, you might need to modify its design to improve its appearance or to make the form easier to use. **Layout view** allows you to modify many aspects of a form's layout and design. In Layout view, you see the form as it appears in Form view, but you can still modify the form's design; in Form view, you cannot make any design changes. Because you can see the form and its data while you are modifying the form, Layout view makes it easy for you to see the results of any design changes you make. You can continue to make changes, undo modifications, and rework the design in Layout view to achieve the look you want for the form.

The first modification you'll make to the Customer Data form is to change its AutoFormat.

Tip

Some form design changes require you to switch to Design view, which gives you a more detailed view of the form's structure.

Changing a Form's AutoFormat

You can change a form's appearance by choosing a different AutoFormat for the form. As you learned when you created the Customer Data form, an AutoFormat is a predefined style for a form (or report). The AutoFormats available for a form are the ones you saw when you selected the form's style using the Form Wizard. To change an AutoFormat, you first need to switch to Layout view.

Changing a Form's AutoFormat	Reference Window

- Display the form in Layout view.
- In the AutoFormat group on the Form Layout Tools Format tab, click the More button.
- In the displayed gallery, click the AutoFormat you want to apply; or, click AutoFormat Wizard to open the AutoFormat dialog box, click the name of the AutoFormat you want to apply, and then click the OK button.

To change the AutoFormat for the Customer Data form:

▶ **1.** In the Views group on the Home tab, click the **View** button. The form is displayed in Layout view. See Figure 4-4.

Figure 4-4 | Form displayed in Layout view

Form Layout Tools Format tab displays options for changing the form's appearance

More button

orange outline indicates the selected field

Trouble? If the Field List or Property Sheet opens on the right side of your window, click the Close button ✖ to close it.

You can use Layout view to modify an existing form. In Layout view, an orange outline identifies the currently selected object on the form; in this case, the first field, Customer ID, is selected. You need to change the AutoFormat for the Customer Data form.

▶ 2. In the AutoFormat group on the Form Layout Tools Format tab, click the **More** button (see Figure 4-4 for the location of this button). A gallery opens showing the available AutoFormats for the form. See Figure 4-5.

Figure 4-5 | Gallery of AutoFormats displayed

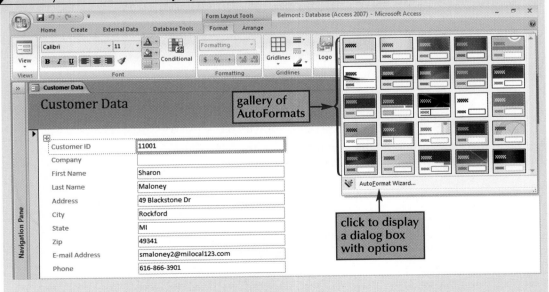

gallery of AutoFormats

click to display a dialog box with options

You can point to each option in the gallery to see its ScreenTip; or choose the Auto-Format Wizard option to open a dialog box and view a sample form with each AutoFormat applied.

▶ 3. Click **AutoFormat Wizard** at the bottom of the gallery. The AutoFormat dialog box opens. Each form AutoFormat is listed on the left, and a sample of the selected AutoFormat appears on the right.

▶ 4. Scroll the list and click several form AutoFormats to view their samples.

Oren decides that he prefers the Foundry AutoFormat, because its field names and field values are easier to read. Also, the earth tone colors provided by the AutoFormat are more reflective of the landscaping business.

▶ 5. Click **Foundry** in the Form AutoFormats list box, and then click the **OK** button. The AutoFormat dialog box closes, and the Form window in Layout view shows the new AutoFormat.

Oren is pleased with the form's new style. Next, he asks you to add a picture to the form for visual interest. The picture, which is included on various stationery items for Belmont Landscapes—business cards, flyers, and so on—is a small graphic of a piece of landscaping equipment. You'll add this picture to the form.

Adding a Picture to a Form

A picture is one of many controls you can add and modify on a form. A **control** is an item on a form, report, or other database object that you can manipulate to modify the object's appearance. The controls you can add and modify in Layout view for a form are available in the Controls group on the Form Layout Tools Format tab. The picture you need to add is contained in a file named Landscape.bmp, which is located in the Level.01\Tutorial folder provided with your Data Files.

To add the picture to the form:

▶ 1. Make sure the form is still displayed in Layout view.

▶ 2. In the Controls group on the Form Layout Tools Format tab, click the **Logo** button. The Insert Picture dialog box opens.

▶ 3. Navigate to the **Level.01\Tutorial** folder provided with your Data Files, click the **Landscape** filename, and then click the **OK** button. The picture appears as a selected object on top of the form's title.

▶ 4. Use the ⬚ pointer to move the picture to the right of the Customer Data form title, and then click in a blank area on the main form (to the right of the field values) to deselect the picture. See Figure 4-6.

Figure 4-6 ▸ **Form with new AutoFormat applied and picture added**

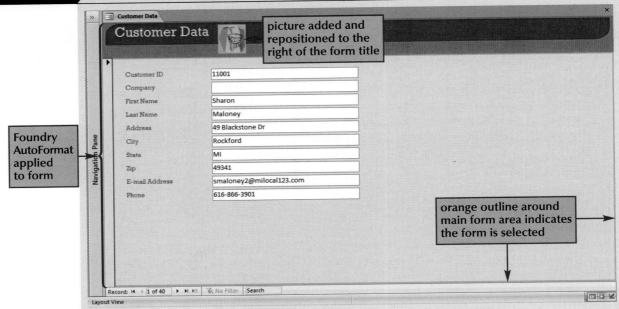

Trouble? Don't be concerned if your picture is not in the exact location as the one shown in Figure 4-6. Just make sure the picture is not blocking any part of the form title, and appears to the right of the form title and above the main part of the form.

The addition of the picture to the form provides more color and visual interest. Next, Oren asks you to change the color of the form title to a light blue so that it will coordinate better with the picture next to the title.

Changing the Color of the Form Title

The Font group on the Form Layout Tools Format tab provides many options you can use to change the appearance of text on a form. For example, you can bold, italicize, and underline text; change the font, font color, and font size; and change the alignment of text. Next, you'll change the color of the title "Customer Data" on the form to a light blue.

To change the color of the form's title text:

▸ 1. Click anywhere in the title **Customer Data** at the top of the form (not on the form tab). An orange outline appears around the words to indicate the text is selected.

   Trouble? If a white box with the insertion point appears at the location of the title, you most likely double-clicked the title by mistake and changed to editing mode. Press the Esc key to move out of editing mode. The title should now be selected and you can continue to Step 2.

▸ 2. In the Font group on the Form Layout Tools Format tab, click the arrow on the **Font Color** button to display the gallery of available colors. The gallery provides colors for Access themes and standard colors, as well as an option for creating a custom color.

▸ 3. In the Access Theme Colors gallery, place the pointer over the fourth color box in the second row of boxes. The ScreenTip indicates this is the Access Theme 4 color.

4. Click the color box for **Access Theme 4**.

5. Click in a blank area of the main form to deselect the title text. The light blue color is applied to the form title, tying it to the picture on the form. See Figure 4-7.

Form title with new color applied   Figure 4-7

You have made a couple of changes to the form, and should save it now.

6. Click the **Save** button 🔲 on the Quick Access Toolbar to save the modified form.

Oren suggests a different type of line for the boxes that contain the field values. He thinks the solid line currently used on the form somewhat overshadows the field values within the boxes, and that a more subtle type of line might look better and make the field values easier to read.

Changing the Type of Line on a Form

A line on a form, such as the box around each field value, is another type of control that you can modify in Layout view. The Controls group provides options for changing the thickness, type, and color of any line on a form. Next, you'll change the type of line for the boxes around the field values on the Customer Data form.

To change the type of line for the field value boxes:

1. Click the field value **11001** for the Customer ID field. An orange outline appears around the box to indicate it is selected. The field value is also selected and can be modified. See Figure 4-8.

Customer ID field value and box selected   Figure 4-8

2. In the Controls group on the Form Layout Tools Format tab, click the **Line Type** button, and then point to each option in the gallery of line types to see the ScreenTip for each type of line.

3. Click the **Dots** option (fourth line type option in the gallery), and then click in a blank area of the main form to deselect the box. The box around the field value for Customer ID changes to a dotted line.

Oren thinks the dotted line type is much better and makes the field value easier to see. He asks you to change the line type for the rest of the boxes on the form. To do so, you can select the remaining boxes and apply the new line type to them all at the same time.

4. Click the field value box for the **Company** field (the box is currently empty), press and hold the **Shift** key, click each of the remaining field value boxes, and then release the **Shift** key. All the field value boxes except the first one should be selected; each box is outlined in orange to indicate it is selected. See Figure 4-9.

Figure 4-9   Form with multiple field value boxes selected

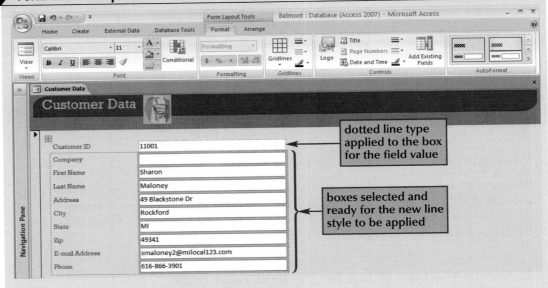

5. In the Controls group on the Form Layout Tools Format tab, click the **Line Type** button, and then click the **Dots** option.

6. Click in a blank area of the main form to deselect the field value boxes. The line type for each box is now dotted.

Oren approves of all the formatting changes you have made so far. After viewing the form and considering how his employees will use it, he realizes that the E-mail Address field should be positioned at the bottom of the form. When a new customer signs a contract with Belmont Landscapes, the customer fills out a paper form with contact information. On this paper form, the customer's e-mail address is the final piece of information provided. Because Oren's employees will enter customer information into the Customer table based on the paper forms customers fill out, the design and layout of the Customer Data form should match the paper form, for ease of data entry. Therefore, Oren asks you to move the E-mail Address field to the bottom of the form.

Moving a Field in Layout View

In Layout view, you can reposition fields on a form to improve the form's appearance or make it easier to use. You move a field by selecting it and then dragging it to a new location on the form. When you move a field, both the field name and the box for the field value are repositioned.

To move the E-mail Address field to the bottom of the form:

▶ **1.** Click the field value box for the **E-mail Address** field. An orange outline appears around the field value box, and a thin dotted line appears around the field name. This indicates both are selected.

▶ **2.** Place the pointer over the selected field until it changes to ⁺ᵏ⁺.

▶ **3.** Click and drag the pointer down until an orange line appears below the Phone field. This indicates the new location for the field you are moving. See Figure 4-10.

Moving the E-mail Address field   **Figure 4-10**

▶ **4.** Release the mouse button, and then click in a blank area of the main form to deselect the field. The E-mail Address field is now positioned below the Phone field at the bottom of the form.

▶ **5.** Click the **Save** button 🔡 on the Quick Access Toolbar to save the form.

▶ **6.** In the Views group on the Form Layout Tools Format tab, click the **View** button to display the form in Form view. See Figure 4-11.

Figure 4-11 **Modified form displayed in Form view**

Oren is pleased with the modified appearance of the form. Later, he plans to revise the existing Contract Data form and make the same changes to it, so that it matches the appearance of the Customer Data form.

| InSight | **Understanding the Importance of Form Design** |

When you create a form, it's important to consider how the form will be used, so that its design will accommodate the needs of people using the form to view, enter, and maintain data. For example, if a form in a database mimics a paper form that users will enter data from, the form in the database should have the same fields in the same order as those on the paper form. This will enable users to easily tab from one field to the next in the database form to enter the necessary information from the paper form. Also, it's important to include a meaningful title on the form to identify its purpose, and to enhance the appearance of the form. A form that is visually appealing makes working with the database more user-friendly and can improve the readability of the form, thereby helping to prevent errors in data entry. Finally, be sure to use a consistent design for all the forms in your database. Users will expect to see similar elements—titles, pictures, styles, and so on—in each form contained in a database. A mix of form styles and elements among the forms in a database could cause confusion and lead to problems when working with the forms.

Navigating a Form

Oren wants to use the Customer Data form to view some data in the Customer table. As you saw earlier, you use Layout view to modify the appearance of a form. To view, navigate, and change data using a form, you need to display the form in Form view. As you learned in Tutorial 1, you navigate a form in the same way that you navigate a table datasheet. Also, the navigation mode and editing mode keystroke techniques you used with datasheets in Tutorial 3 are the same when navigating a form.

The Customer Data form is already displayed in Form view, so you can use it to navigate through the fields and records of the Customer table.

To navigate the Customer Data form:

▶ **1.** Press the **Tab** key twice to move to the First Name field value, and then press the **End** key to move to the E-mail Address field.

▶ **2.** Press the **Home** key to move back to the Customer ID field value. The first record in the Customer table still appears in the form.

▶ **3.** Press the **Ctrl+End** keys to move to the E-mail Address field for record 40, which is the last record in the table. The record number for the current record appears in the Current Record box between the navigation buttons at the bottom of the form.

▶ **4.** Click the **Previous record** navigation button ◀ to move to the E-mail Address field in record 39.

▶ **5.** Press the ↑ key twice to move to the Zip field in record 39.

▶ **6.** Click the insertion point between the numbers "7" and "5" in the Address field value to switch to editing mode, press the **Home** key to move the insertion point to the beginning of the field value, and then press the **End** key to move the insertion point to the end of the field value.

▶ **7.** Click the **First record** navigation button ◀| to move to the Address field value in the first record. The entire field value is highlighted because you have switched from editing mode to navigation mode.

▶ **8.** Click the **Next record** navigation button ▶ to move to the Address field value in record 2, the next record.

Next, Oren asks you to display the record for the Three Tulips Café, one of Belmont Landscapes' customers. The paper form containing the original contact information for this customer was damaged. Oren recently contacted the owner of the café and obtained all the customer information again. Now Oren wants to view the data for this customer in the Customer table to make sure it is correct.

Finding Data Using a Form

As you learned in Tutorial 3, the Find command lets you search for data in a form or datasheet so you can display only those records you want to view. You choose a field to serve as the basis for the search by making that field the current field, and then you enter the value you want Access to match in the Find and Replace dialog box.

Reference Window | **Finding Data in a Form or Datasheet**

- Open the form or datasheet, and then make the field you want to search the current field.
- In the Find group on the Home tab, click the Find button to open the Find and Replace dialog box.
- In the Find What text box, type the field value you want to find.
- Complete the remaining options, as necessary, to specify the type of search to conduct.
- Click the Find Next button to begin the search.
- Click the Find Next button to continue searching for the next match.
- Click the Cancel button to stop the search operation.

You need to find the record for the Three Tulips Café. Oren doesn't recall the Customer ID value for this customer, so you'll base the search on the Company field name.

To find the record using the Customer Data form:

1. Click in the **Company** field value (which is empty for the current record) to establish Company as the current field. This is the field you need to search.

   Instead of searching for the entire company name, Three Tulips Café, you can search for a record that contains part of the name anywhere in the Company field value. Performing a partial search such as this is often easier than matching the entire field value and is useful when you don't know or can't remember the entire field value.

2. In the Find group on the Home tab, click the **Find** button. The Find and Replace dialog box opens. The Look In box shows that the Company field will be searched. You'll search for records that contain the word "tulips" in the company name.

3. In the Find What text box, type **tulips**. Note that you do not have to enter the word as "Tulips" with a capital letter "T" because the Match Case option is not selected in the Find and Replace dialog box. Access will find any record containing the word "tulips" with any combination of uppercase and lowercase letters.

4. Click the **Match** arrow to display the list of matching options, and then click **Any Part of Field**. Access will find any record that contains the word "tulips" in any part of the Company field.

5. Move the Find and Replace dialog box by dragging its title bar so that you can see both the dialog box and the form at the same time. See Figure 4-12.

Finding data using the form ◄ Figure 4-12

6. Click the **Find Next** button. The Customer Data form now displays record 35, which is the record for the Three Tulips Café (Customer ID 11080). The word "Tulips" is selected in the Company field value because you searched for this word. Oren reviews the information for the record and determines it is correct.

The search value you enter can be an exact value or it can include wildcard characters. A **wildcard character** is a placeholder you use when you know only part of a value or when you want to start or end with a specific character or match a certain pattern. Figure 4-13 shows the wildcard characters you can use when finding data.

Wildcard characters ◄ Figure 4-13

Wildcard Character	Purpose	Example
*	Match any number of characters. It can be used as the first and/or last character in the character string.	th* finds the, that, this, therefore, and so on
?	Match any single alphabetic character.	a?t finds act, aft, ant, apt, and art
[]	Match any single character within the brackets.	a[fr]t finds aft and art but not act, ant, and apt
!	Match any character not within brackets.	a[!fr]t finds act, ant, and apt but not aft and art
-	Match any one of a range of characters. The range must be in ascending order (a to z, not z to a).	a[d-p]t finds aft, ant, and apt but not act and art
#	Match any single numeric character.	#72 finds 072, 172, 272, 372, and so on

Next, Oren wants to view the customer records for any customers with phone numbers beginning with the area code 517. He is curious to know how many customers are in cities serviced by that area code, and what the cities are. You could search for any field containing the digits 517 in any part of the field, but this search would also find records with the digits 517 in any part of the phone number. To find only those records with the 517 area code, you'll use the * wildcard character.

To find the records using the * wildcard character:

▶ 1. Make sure the Find and Replace dialog box is still open.

▶ 2. Click anywhere in the Customer Data form to make it active, and then press the **Tab** key seven times to move to the Phone field. This is the field you want to search.

▶ 3. Click the title bar of the Find and Replace dialog box to make it active. The Look In box now displays Phone, indicating that the Phone field will be searched.

▶ 4. Double-click **tulips** in the Find What text box to select the entire value, and then type **517***.

▶ 5. Click the **Match** arrow, and then click **Whole Field**. Because you're using a wild-card character in the search value, you want Access to search the whole field.

With the settings you've entered, Access will find records in which any field value in the Phone field begins with the digits 517.

▶ 6. Click the **Find Next** button. Access displays record 36, which is the first record found for a customer with the area code 517. This customer is located in East Lansing. Notice that the search process started from the point of the previously displayed record in the form, which was record 35.

▶ 7. Click the **Find Next** button. Access displays record 8, which is the next record found for a customer with the area code 517. This customer is located in Lansing. Notice that the search process cycles back through the beginning of the records in the underlying table.

▶ 8. Click the **Find Next** button. Access displays record 12, the third record found; this customer is also located in Lansing.

▶ 9. Click the **Find Next** button. Access displays record 25 for another customer located in Lansing, with the area code 517.

▶ 10. Click the **Find Next** button. Access displays record 33 for another customer located in Lansing.

▶ 11. Click the **Find Next** button. Access displays a dialog box informing you that the search is finished.

▶ 12. Click the **OK** button to close the dialog box. Oren notes that all customers with an area code of 517 are located in either Lansing or East Lansing.

▶ 13. Click the **Cancel** button to close the Find and Replace dialog box.

Oren has identified some updates he wants you to make to the Customer table. You'll use the Customer Data form to update the data in the Customer table.

Maintaining Table Data Using a Form

Maintaining data using a form is often easier than using a datasheet, because you can concentrate on all the changes required to a single record at one time. In Form view, you can edit the field values for a specific record, delete a record from the underlying table, or add a new record to the table. You already know how to navigate a form and find specific records. Now you'll use the Customer Data form to make the changes Oren wants to the Customer table.

First, you'll update the record for the Cherrywood Senior Center. The center has a new contact person with a new phone number and e-mail address, so you need to update the First Name, Last Name, Phone, and E-mail Address fields for this customer. Oren happens to know that the Cherrywood Senior Center is record 22 in the Customer table. If you know the number of the record you want to view, you can enter the number in the Current Record box to move to that record.

To change the record using the Customer Data form:

1. Select **33** in the Current Record box at the bottom of the form, type **22**, and then press the **Enter** key. Record 22 (Cherrywood Senior Center) is now the current record.

   You need to update the values in the First Name, Last Name, Phone, and E-mail Address fields with the information for the new contact person at the center, Dan Lewis.

2. In the First Name field value box, double-click **Lisa** to select the entry, and then type **Dan**.

3. Press the **Tab** key to move to and select the field value in the Last Name field, and then type **Lewis**.

4. Click the insertion point at the end of the field value for the Phone field, press the **Backspace** key three times, and then type **890**. The Phone field value is now 269-857-1890.

5. Click the insertion point before the first character in the E-mail Address field, press the **Delete** key seven times to delete the characters before the @ symbol, and then type **dlewis4**. The E-mail Address field value is now dlewis4@csc77.com. The updates to the record are complete. See Figure 4-14.

> **Tip**
>
> Note that the pencil symbol appears in the upper-left corner of the form, indicating that the form is in editing mode.

Customer record after changing field values ◄ **Figure 4-14**

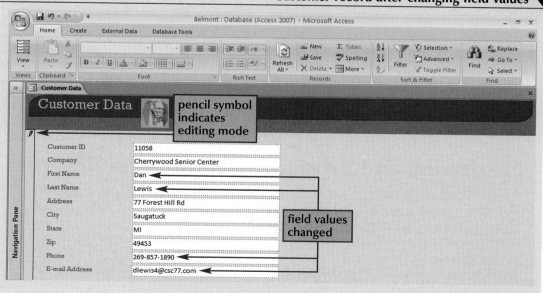

Next, Oren asks you to add a record for a new customer. The customer has not yet returned a signed contract, but Oren expects to receive the contract soon and wants to be sure the Customer table is updated first with the new customer record. You'll use the Customer Data form to add the new record.

To add the new record using the Customer Data form:

▶ **1.** In the Records group on the Home tab, click the **New** button. Record 41, the next available new record, becomes the current record. All field value boxes are empty, and the insertion point is positioned in the field value box for Customer ID.

▶ **2.** Refer to Figure 4-15 and enter the value shown for each field. Press the **Tab** key to move from field to field.

| Figure 4-15 | Completed form for the new record |

Trouble? Compare your screen with Figure 4-15. If any field value is incorrect, correct it now, using the methods described earlier for editing field values.

▶ **3.** After entering the value for the E-mail Address field, press the **Tab** key. Record 42, the next available new record, becomes the current record, and the record for Customer ID 11090 is saved in the Customer table.

Oren would like a printed copy of the record for the new customer only. He wants to give the printout to a staff member as a reminder to look for the new contract for this customer when it comes in.

Previewing and Printing Selected Form Records

Access prints as many form records as can fit on a printed page. If only part of a form record fits on the bottom of a page, the remainder of the record prints on the next page. Access allows you to print all pages or a range of pages. In addition, you can print the currently selected form record.

Before printing record 41, the record for Lily's Boutique, you'll preview the form record to see how it will look when printed.

To preview the form and print the data for record 41:

▶ **1.** Click the **Previous record** navigation button ◀ to redisplay record 41.

▶ 2. Click the **Office Button** 🔘, point to **Print**, and then click **Print Preview**. The Print Preview window opens, showing the form records for the Customer table. Notice that each record appears in its own form. See Figure 4-16.

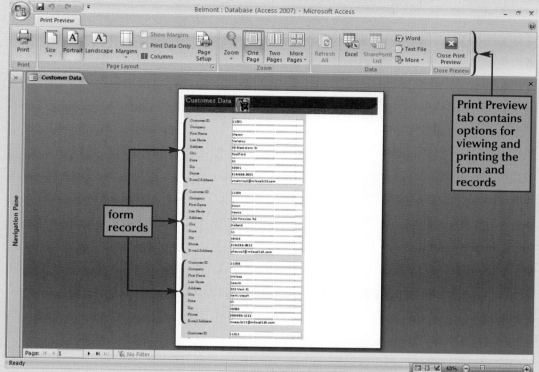

If you clicked the Print button now, all the records for the table would be printed, beginning with the first record.

▶ 3. In the Close Preview group on the Print Preview tab, click the **Close Print Preview** button. You return to the form in Form view.

The record that you need to print (for Lily's Boutique) is currently displayed in the form. To print selected records, you use the Print dialog box.

▶ 4. Click the **Office Button** 🔘, point to **Print**, and then click **Print**. The Print dialog box opens.

▶ 5. Click the **Selected Record(s)** option button to print the current form record (record 41).

Trouble? Check with your instructor to be sure you should print the form; then continue to the next step. If you should not print the form, click the Cancel button, and then skip to Step 7.

▶ 6. Click the **OK** button to close the dialog box and to print the selected record.

▶ 7. Close the Customer Data form.

▶ 8. If you are not continuing to Session 4.2, click the **Close** button ⊠ on the program window title bar. Access closes the Belmont database, and then the Access program closes.

The Customer Data form will enable Oren and his staff to enter and maintain data easily in the Customer table. In the next session, you'll create another form for working with data in both the Customer and Contract tables at the same time. You'll also create a report showing data from both tables.

1. Describe the difference between creating a form using the Form tool and creating a form using the Form Wizard.
2. What is an AutoFormat, and how do you change one for an existing form?
3. A(n) _____ is an item on a form, report, or other database object that you can manipulate to modify the object's appearance.
4. Which table record is displayed in a form when you press the Ctrl+End keys while you are in navigation mode?
5. Which wildcard character matches any single alphabetic character?
6. To print only the current record displayed in a form, you need to select the _____ option button in the Print dialog box.

Session 4.2

Oren would like you to create a form so that he can view the data for each customer and the customer's contracts at the same time. The type of form you need to create will include a main form and a subform.

Creating a Form with a Main Form and a Subform

To create a form based on two tables, you must first define a relationship between the two tables. In Tutorial 2, you defined a one-to-many relationship between the Customer (primary) and Contract (related) tables, so you can now create a form based on both tables.

When you create a form containing data from two tables that have a one-to-many relationship, you actually create a **main form** for data from the primary table and a **subform** for data from the related table. Access uses the defined relationship between the tables to join them automatically through the common field that exists in both tables.

Oren and his staff will use the form when contacting customers about their contracts. The main form will contain the customer ID, company name (if any), first and last names, phone number, and e-mail address for each customer. The subform will contain the information about the contracts for each customer.

You'll use the Form Wizard to create the form.

To create the form using the Form Wizard:

1. If you took a break after the previous session, make sure that the Belmont database is open and the Navigation Pane is closed.

2. Click the **Create** tab on the Ribbon.

3. In the Forms group on the Create tab, click the **More Forms** button, and then click **Form Wizard**. The first Form Wizard dialog box opens.

   When creating a form based on two tables, you first choose the primary table and select the fields you want to include in the main form; then you choose the related table and select fields from it for the subform.

▶ **4.** If necessary, click the **Tables/Queries** arrow, and then click **Table: Customer**.

Oren wants the form to include only the Customer ID, Company, First Name, Last Name, Phone, and E-mail Address fields from the Customer table.

▶ **5.** Click **Customer ID** in the Available Fields list box (if necessary), and then click the ⟩ button to move the field to the Selected Fields list box.

▶ **6.** Repeat Step 5 for the **Company**, **First Name**, **Last Name**, **Phone**, and **E-mail Address** fields.

The Customer ID field will appear in the main form, so you do not have to include it in the subform. Otherwise, Oren wants the subform to include all the fields from the Contract table.

▶ **7.** Click the **Tables/Queries** arrow, scroll the list up, and then click **Table: Contract**. The fields from the Contract table appear in the Available Fields list box. The quickest way to add the fields you want to include is to move all the fields to the Selected Fields list box, and then to remove the only field you don't want to include (Customer ID).

▶ **8.** Click the ⟩⟩ button to move all the fields in the Contract table to the Selected Fields list box.

▶ **9.** Click **Contract.Customer ID** in the Selected Fields list box, and then click the ⟨ button to move the field back to the Available Fields list box.

▶ **10.** Click the **Next** button. The next Form Wizard dialog box opens. See Figure 4-17.

> **Tip**
>
> Note that the table name (Contract) is included in the Customer ID field name to distinguish it from the same field (Customer ID) in the Customer table.

Choosing a format for the main form and subform	Figure 4-17

In this dialog box, the list box on the left shows the order in which you will view the selected data: first by data from the primary Customer table, and then by data from the related Contract table. The form will be displayed as shown on the right side of the dialog box, with the fields from the Customer table at the top in the main form, and the fields from the Contract table at the bottom in the subform. The selected "Form with subform(s)" option button specifies a main form with a subform. The Linked forms option creates a form structure in which only the main form fields are displayed. A button with the subform's name on it appears on the main form; you can click this button to display the associated subform records.

The default options shown in Figure 4-17 are correct for creating a form with Customer data in the main form and Contract data in the subform.

To finish creating the form:

▶ 1. Click the **Next** button. The next Form Wizard dialog box opens, in which you choose the subform layout.

The Tabular layout displays subform fields as a table, whereas the Datasheet layout displays subform fields as a table datasheet. The layout choice is a matter of personal preference. You'll use the Datasheet layout.

▶ 2. Click the **Datasheet** option button (if necessary), and then click the **Next** button. The next Form Wizard dialog box opens, in which you choose the form's style (AutoFormat).

Oren wants all forms in the Belmont database to have the same style, so you will choose Foundry, which is the same AutoFormat you applied to the Customer Data form.

▶ 3. Click **Foundry** (if necessary), and then click the **Next** button. The next Form Wizard dialog box opens, in which you choose names for the main form and the subform.

You will use the name "Customer Contracts" for the main form and the name "Contract Subform" for the subform.

▶ 4. Click the insertion point to the right of the last letter in the Form text box, press the **spacebar**, and then type **Contracts**. The main form name is now Customer Contracts. The Contract Subform name is already set.

▶ 5. Click the **Finish** button. After a few moments, the completed form opens in Form view. Next, you'll resize the columns in the subform to their best fit.

▶ 6. Double-click the pointer ✛ at the right edge of each column in the subform. The columns are resized to their best fit. See Figure 4-18.

| Figure 4-18 | Main form with subform in Form view |

In the main form, Access displays the fields from the first record in the Customer table in a columnar format. The records in the main form appear in primary key order by Customer ID. Customer ID 11001 has one related record in the Contract table; this record, for Contract Num 3011, is shown in the subform datasheet. The main form name, "Customer Contracts," appears as the form's title and on the form object tab. The name of the subform appears to the left of the subform. Note that only the word "Contract" and not the complete name "Contract Subform" appears on the form. Access displays only the table name for the subform itself, but displays the complete name of the object, "Contract Subform," when you view and work with objects in the Navigation Pane. The subform designation is necessary in a list of database objects, so that you can distinguish the Contract subform from other objects, such as the Contract table; but the subform designation is not needed in the Customer Contracts form. Only the table name is required to identify the table containing the records in the subform.

The form includes two sets of navigation buttons. You use the top set of navigation buttons to select records from the related table in the subform, and you use the set of navigation buttons at the bottom of the form window to select records from the primary table in the main form.

You'll use the navigation buttons to view different records.

To navigate to different main form and subform records:

1. In the main form, click the **Last record** navigation button [▶|]. Record 41 in the Customer table (for Lily's Boutique) becomes the current record in the main form. The subform shows that this customer currently has no contracts; recall that you just entered this customer record in the Customer table. Oren can use the subform to enter the information for this customer's contract when he receives it, and that information will be updated in the Contract table.

2. In the main form, click the **Previous record** navigation button [◀]. Record 40 in the Customer table (for Weston Community Parks Foundation) becomes the current record in the main form. The subform shows that this customer has two contracts.

3. In the main form, select **40** in the Current Record box, type **34**, and then press the **Enter** key. Record 34 in the Customer table (for Dept. of Neighborhood Development) becomes the current record in the main form. The subform shows that this customer has four contracts.

4. Double-click the pointer ↔ at the right edge of the Contract Type column in the subform so that the complete values for this field are visible.

5. In the subform, click the **Last record** navigation button [▶|]. Record 4 in the Contract table becomes the current record in the subform.

6. Save and close the Customer Contracts form.

> **Tip**
>
> As you move through the form/subform, notice that some field values in the subform are not completely visible. You can resize any subform field to its best fit to fully display the field values.

You've finished your work for Oren on the forms in the Belmont database. Next, Taylor Sico asks you to create a report that she can use to prepare a new advertising campaign.

Creating a Report Using the Report Wizard

As you learned in Tutorial 1, a report is a formatted printout of the contents of one or more tables or queries in a database. In Access, you can create your own reports or use the Report Wizard to create them for you. Like the Form Wizard, the **Report Wizard** asks you a series of questions and then creates a report based on your answers. Whether you use the Report Wizard or design your own report, you can change the report's design after you create it.

InSight		**Creating a Report Based on a Query**

You can create a report based on one or more tables or queries. When you use a query as the basis for a report, you can use criteria and other query tools to retrieve only the information you want to examine in the report. Experienced Access users often create a query just so they can create a report based on that query. When thinking about the type of report you want to create, consider creating a query first and basing the report on the query, to produce the exact results you want to see in the report.

Taylor wants you to create a report that includes selected data from the Customer table and all the data from the Contract table for each customer. Taylor has sketched a design of the report she wants (Figure 4-19). Like the Customer Contracts form you just created, which includes a main form and a subform, the report will be based on both tables, which are joined in a one-to-many relationship through the common Customer ID field. As shown in the sketch in Figure 4-19, the selected customer data from the primary Customer table includes the customer ID, company, first name, last name, city, and phone number. Below the data for each customer, the report will include the signing date, contract number, contract amount, and contract type from the related Contract table. The set of field values for each contract is called a **detail record**.

Figure 4-19	▶ **Report sketch for the Customers and Contracts report**

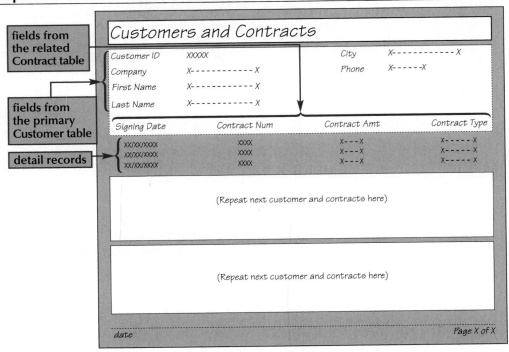

You'll use the Report Wizard to create the report according to Taylor's sketch.

To start the Report Wizard and select the fields to include in the report:

► **1.** Click the **Create** tab on the Ribbon.

► **2.** In the Reports group on the Create tab, click the **Report Wizard** button. The first Report Wizard dialog box opens.

As was the case when you created the form with a subform, initially you can choose only one table or query to be the data source for the report. Then you can include data from other tables or queries. You will select the primary Customer table first.

► **3.** If necessary, click the **Tables/Queries** arrow, and then click **Table: Customer**.

In the first Report Wizard dialog box, you select fields in the order you want them to appear on the report. Taylor wants the Customer ID, Company, First Name, Last Name, City, and Phone fields from the Customer table to appear on the report, in that order.

► **4.** Click **Customer ID** in the Available Fields list box (if necessary), and then click the [>] button. The field moves to the Selected Fields list box.

► **5.** Repeat Step 4 to add the **Company**, **First Name**, **Last Name**, **City**, and **Phone** fields to the report.

► **6.** Click the **Tables/Queries** arrow, and then scroll the list up and click **Table: Contract**. The fields from the Contract table appear in the Available Fields list box.

The Customer ID field will appear on the report with the customer data, so you do not have to include it in the detail records for each contract. Otherwise, Taylor wants all the fields from the Contract table to be included in the report.

► **7.** Click the [>>] button to move all the fields from the Available Fields list box to the Selected Fields list box.

► **8.** Click **Contract.Customer ID** in the Selected Fields list box, click the [<] button to move the selected field back to the Available Fields list box, and then click the **Next** button. The second Report Wizard dialog box opens. See Figure 4-20.

Choosing a grouped or ungrouped report ◄ **Figure 4-20**

data grouped by table →

click to display tips and examples →

Tip

You can display tips for creating reports and examples of reports by clicking the "Show me more information" button.

You can choose to arrange the selected data grouped by table, which is the default, or ungrouped. For a **grouped report**, the data from a record in the primary table appears as a group, followed on subsequent lines of the report by the joined records from the related table. For the report you are creating, data from a record in the Customer table appears in a group, followed by the related records for each customer from the Contract table. An example of an ungrouped report would be a report of records from the Customer and Contract tables in order by Contract Num. Each contract and its associated customer data would appear together on one or more lines of the report; the data would not be grouped by table.

The default options shown on your screen are correct for the report Taylor wants, so you can continue responding to the Report Wizard questions.

To finish creating the report using the Report Wizard:

▶ 1. Click the **Next** button. The next Report Wizard dialog box opens, in which you choose additional grouping levels.

   Two grouping levels are shown: one for a customer's data, and the other for a customer's contracts. Grouping levels are useful for reports with multiple levels, such as those containing monthly, quarterly, and annual totals, or for those containing city and country groups. Taylor's report contains no further grouping levels, so you can accept the default options.

▶ 2. Click the **Next** button. The next Report Wizard dialog box opens, in which you choose the sort order for the detail records. See Figure 4-21.

Figure 4-21	Choosing the sort order for detail records

The records from the Contract table for a customer represent the detail records for Taylor's report. She wants these records to appear in increasing, or ascending, order by the value in the Signing Date field, so that the contracts will be shown in chronological order. The Ascending option is already selected by default. To change to descending order, you click this button, which acts as a toggle between the two sort orders. Also, you can sort on multiple fields, as you can with queries.

3. Click the arrow on the first list box, click **Signing Date**, and then click the **Next** button. The next Report Wizard dialog box opens, in which you choose a layout and page orientation for the report. See Figure 4-22.

Choosing the report layout | Figure 4-22

4. Click each layout option and examine each sample that appears.

You'll use the Outline layout option because it resembles the layout shown in Taylor's sketch. Also, because there are few fields in the Contract table, the information will fit in portrait orientation, so you will accept the default page orientation.

5. Click the **Outline** option button, and then click the **Next** button. The next Report Wizard dialog box opens, in which you choose a style for the report.

A sample of the selected style, or AutoFormat, appears in the box on the left. You can always choose a different AutoFormat after you create the report. For consistency with the form objects you created, you'll choose the Foundry AutoFormat.

6. Click **Foundry** (if necessary), and then click the **Next** button. The final Report Wizard dialog box opens, in which you choose a report name, which also serves as the printed title on the report.

According to Taylor's sketch, the report title you need to specify is "Customers and Contracts." However, for consistency with how other objects are named in the database, you'll specify the name "Customers And Contracts," with each word capitalized. Later, you'll change the report title so that it appears with the word "and," per Taylor's sketch.

7. In the text box for the title, enter the title **Customers And Contracts** and then click the **Finish** button. The Report Wizard creates the report based on your answers and saves it as an object in the Belmont database. Then Access opens the report in Print Preview.

To view the entire page, you need to change the Zoom setting.

8. In the Zoom group on the Print Preview tab, click the arrow for the **Zoom** button, and then click **Fit to Window**. The first page of the report is displayed in Print Preview.

When a report is displayed in Print Preview, you can use the pointer to toggle between a full-page display and a close-up display of the report. Taylor asks you to check the report to see if any adjustments need to be made. For example, some of the field titles or values might not be displayed completely, or you might need to move fields to enhance the report's appearance. You need to view a close-up display of the report.

To view a close-up display of the report:

▶ **1.** Click the pointer 🔍 at the top center of the report. The display changes to show a close-up view of the report. See Figure 4-23.

Figure 4-23   **Close-up view of the report**

Trouble? Depending on your computer settings, the shading and colors used in your report might look different. This difference should not cause any problems.

The detail records for the Contract table fields appear in ascending order based on the values in the Signing Date field. Because the Signing Date field is used as the basis for sorting records, it appears as the first field in this section, even though you selected the fields in the order in which they appear in the Contract table.

All of the text in this portion of the report is displayed completely and is legible. However, you should check the entire report because some field values are longer than others and might not be fully displayed.

▶ **2.** Use the vertical scroll bar to scroll to the bottom of the first page, checking the text in the report as you scroll. Notice the current date and page number at the bottom of the first page of the report; these elements were included by the Report Wizard as part of the report's design. The first page is fine; now you need to check the second page.

▶ **3.** Click the **Next Page** navigation button ▶ to move to page 2 of the report.

▶ **4.** Use the vertical scroll bar to scroll back up the page and check the field values. All are displayed completely.

▶ **5.** Click the **Next Page** navigation button ▶ to move to page 3 of the report. Notice that the Company field value for the RiverView Development Company (Customer ID 11040) is not completely displayed.

> **6.** Continue to scroll through the pages of the report. Note that several Company field values are too long to fit within the space provided and are not fully displayed. Otherwise, all other text in the report is displayed correctly.

To fix the display of the Company field values, you first need to move the City and Phone fields to the right to provide more space for the company names. Then, you need to widen the space for the Company field values so that the complete values are displayed. The changes you need to make can be done in Layout view for the report. Also in Layout view, you can fix the report title so that it reads "Customers and Contracts."

Modifying a Report's Design in Layout View

Similar to Layout view for forms, Layout view for reports enables you to make modifications to the report's design. Many of the same options—such as those for changing the AutoFormat and changing the color of text and lines—are provided in Layout view for reports. Before moving and resizing the necessary fields, you'll fix the name of the report title to change the word "And" to "and" so that the title matches Taylor's sketch.

To edit the report title:

> **1.** Click the **Layout View** button ▦, which is located at the bottom right of the report window in Print Preview, on the status bar. The report is displayed in Layout view.
>
>   **Trouble?** If the Field List or Property Sheet opens on the right side of your wndow, click the Close button ☒ to close it.

> **2.** Click the **Customers And Contracts** report title. An orange outline appears around the title, indicating it is selected.

> **3.** Click the title again to switch to editing mode. The title now appears in a white box, and the insertion point appears at the location you clicked.

> **4.** Click to the right of the letter "A" in "And," press the **Backspace** key, and then type **a**.

> **5.** Press the **Enter** key. The title of the report is now "Customers and Contracts." Notice that the name of the report object in the database is still "Customers And Contracts," as shown on the tab for the report.

Moving a Field on a Report in Layout View

Working in Layout view, you can reposition fields to improve the appearance of the report or to address the problem of some field values not being completely displayed. In the Customers And Contracts report, you need to make space for the longer Company field values by moving the City and Phone fields to the right. To make sure all the Company field values will fit, you should make any adjustments based on the longest company name—Kalamazoo Neighborhood Development.

To move the City and Phone fields:

▸ **1.** Use the vertical scroll bar to scroll the report until the record for Customer ID 11045, Kalamazoo Neighborhood Development, is displayed.

To select and move multiple fields, you use the Shift key.

▸ **2.** Click the **City** field name for Customer ID 11045, press and hold the **Shift** key, and then click the **Phone** field name for the same record. Both fields are selected and can be moved. See Figure 4-24.

Figure 4-24 ▸ **Fields selected and ready to be moved**

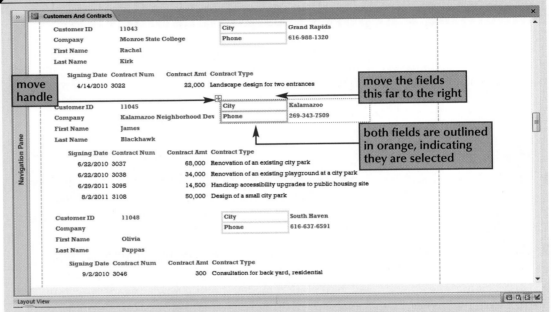

Notice the small box with two double-arrowed lines that is above the top-left corner of the selected fields. This box is called the **move handle**; you use it to reposition selected fields on a report or other database object.

▸ **3.** Position the pointer ⁺₍ on the move handle for the selected fields, and then drag them to the right. As you drag, black outlines indicate the location of both the field names and the field values.

▸ **4.** Release the mouse when the left edge of the field names is approximately aligned with the beginning of the word "two" in the Contract Type field value above (see Figure 4-24). The City and Phone fields are now positioned farther to the right. Note that *all* City and Phone fields for the entire report have been moved, not just those for the current record. See Figure 4-25.

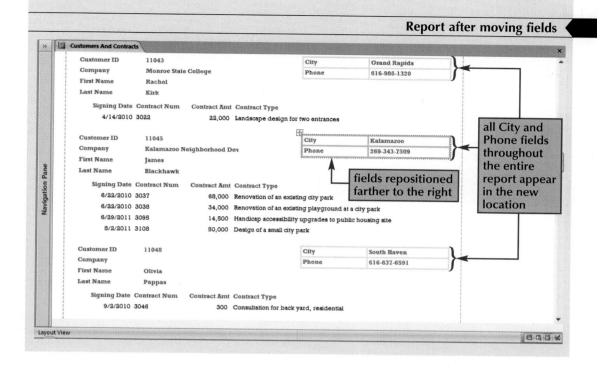

Resizing a Field on a Report in Layout View

With the City and Phone fields in the new location, there is more room on the report to display the full Company field values. Your next task is to resize the Company field value box so that the longest value (Kalamazoo Neighborhood Development) is fully displayed. This will ensure that all other company names will be completely visible in the report as well.

To widen the field value for the Company field:

► **1.** Click the field value **Kalamazoo Neighborhood Development** for Customer ID 11045. An orange outline appears around the field value, indicating it is selected.

► **2.** Position the pointer on the right side of the orange box until the pointer changes to a ↔ shape.

► **3.** Click and drag the ↔ pointer to the right until the right edge of the Company field value box is aligned approximately with the "e" in the word "design" in the Contract Type field value above it, and the complete field value is displayed. The field values for all fields in this section of the main report—Customer ID, Company, First Name, and Last Name—are resized as well. See Figure 4-26.

Trouble? When you release the mouse button after resizing the field, the screen might scroll to another location. If this happens, scroll your screen so that it matches Figure 4-26.

Figure 4-26 **Report after resizing fields**

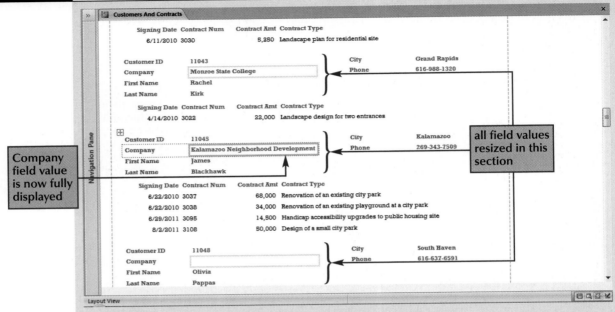

Company field value is now fully displayed

all field values resized in this section

Even though you needed to increase the width of the Company field only, it's not a problem that all the other field values in this part of the report were also resized. With the City and Phone fields moved to the right, the report can accommodate the wider field values throughout.

Earlier, when meeting with Oren, Taylor viewed and worked with the Customer Data form. She likes how the picture looks on the form, and she likes the blue color applied to the form's title. She asks you to insert the same picture on the Customers And Contracts report, and to change the color of the report title to the same blue color used on the form.

Inserting a Picture in a Report and Changing the Font Color

You can add a picture to a report for visual interest or to identify a particular section of the report. You can also change the color of text on the report to enhance its appearance. Because Taylor plans to print the report using a color printer, she asks you to include a picture in the report and change the report title color to blue.

To insert the picture and change the color of the title in the report:

1. Press the **Ctrl+Home** keys to scroll to the top of the report.

2. Make sure the **Report Layout Tools Format** tab is selected on the Ribbon. Notice that the options provided in the Controls group for reports are the same as those you worked with for forms.

3. In the Controls group, click the **Logo** button.

4. Navigate to the **Level.01\Tutorial** folder, and then double-click the **Landscape** file. The picture is inserted in the top-left corner of the report, partially covering the report title.

5. Use the pointer ⬚ to move the picture to the right of the report title.

   Now you can change the color of the report title.

6. Click the title **Customers and Contracts** to select it. An orange outline surrounds the words, indicating they are selected.

7. In the Font group on the Report Layout Tools Format tab, click the arrow for the **Font Color** button , and then click the color box for **Access Theme 4**. The color is applied to the report title. See Figure 4-27.

Report after adding the picture and changing the title font color   Figure 4-27

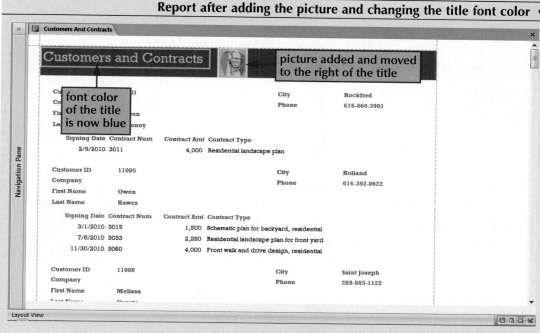

Taylor is pleased with the report's appearance, and shows it to Oren. He also approves of the report's contents and design, but has one final suggestion to enhance the report. He'd like to draw attention to the contract amounts that are greater than $25,000 by formatting them with a bold, red font. Because Oren doesn't want all the contract amounts to appear in this font, you need to use conditional formatting.

Using Conditional Formatting in a Report

Conditional formatting in a report (or form) is special formatting applied to certain field values depending on one or more conditions—similar to criteria you establish for queries. If a field value meets the condition or conditions you specify, the formatting is applied to the value.

Oren would like the Customers And Contracts report to show any contract amount that is greater than $25,000 in a bold, red font. This formatting will help to highlight the more significant contracts for Belmont Landscapes.

To apply conditional formatting to the Contract Amt field in the report:

1. Click the first Contract Amt field value, **4,000**, for Contract Num 3011. An orange outline appears around the field value, and a dotted line appears down the column for the field value throughout the entire report. Because you selected a value in the Contract Num column, the conditional formatting you specify next will affect only the values in this column. You must select a field *value*, and not the field *name*, before applying a conditional format.

2. In the Font group on the Report Layout Tools Format tab, click the **Conditional** button. The Conditional Formatting dialog box opens. See Figure 4-28.

Figure 4-28 ▶ **Conditional Formatting dialog box**

The Default Formatting section at the top of the dialog box shows how text that does not meet the condition will be formatted in the report. In the Condition 1 section of the dialog box, you enter the specifications for the condition in the text boxes provided. Then, you use the formatting buttons to determine how text in the report should be formatted when the condition is met. The preview box shows how the text will look with the conditional formatting.

3. In the Condition 1 section of the dialog box, click the arrow for the box containing the word "between," and then click **greater than**. Oren wants only those contract amounts greater than $25,000 to be formatted.

The options available in this box include the operators you used when establishing criteria in a query. For example, if you wanted to apply conditional formatting to only those field values that are equal to a specific value, you would choose the "equal to" option in the list.

4. Press the **Tab** key to move to the text box, and then type **25000**.

5. In the Condition 1 section, click the arrow for the **Font/Fore Color** button A ▾ , and then click the first color box in the last row (the dark red color).

6. In the Condition 1 section, click the **Bold** button B . The specifications for the conditional formatting are complete. See Figure 4-29.

Figure 4-29 ▶ **Conditional formatting set for the Contract Amt field**

7. Click the **OK** button. The dialog box closes, and the conditional format is applied to the Contract Amt field values.

To get a better view of the report and the formatting changes, you'll switch to Print Preview.

▶ **8.** In the Views group on the Report Layout Tools Format tab, click the arrow for the **View** button, and then click **Print Preview**. The report appears in Print Preview.

▶ **9.** Move to page 7 of the report and scroll down the window. Notice the conditional formatting applied to the Contract Amt field values that are greater than $25,000. See Figure 4-30.

Viewing the finished report in Print Preview ◀ Figure 4-30

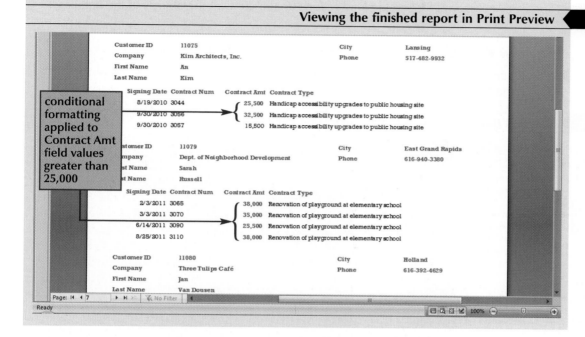

The Importance of Previewing Reports | InSight

When you create a report, it is a good idea to display the report in Print Preview repeatedly as you continue to develop the report. Doing so will give you a chance to find any formatting problems or other issues so that you can make any necessary corrections before printing the report. It is particularly important to preview a report after you've made changes to its design to ensure that the changes you made have not created new problems with the report's format. Before printing any report, you should preview it so you can determine where the pages will break, and make any necessary adjustments so that the final printed output looks exactly the way you want it to.

The report is now complete. You'll print just the first page of the report so that Oren and Taylor can view the final results and share the report design with other staff members before printing the entire report. (*Note:* Check with your instructor first to be sure you should complete the following printing steps.)

To print page 1 of the report:

▶ **1.** In the Print group on the Print Preview tab, click the **Print** button. The Print dialog box opens.

▶ **2.** In the Print Range section, click the **Pages** option button. The insertion point now appears in the From text box so that you can specify the range of pages to print.

▶ **3.** Type **1** in the From text box, press the **Tab** key to move to the To text box, and then type **1**. These settings specify that only page 1 of the report will be printed.

▶ **4.** Click the **OK** button. The Print dialog box closes, and the first page of the report is printed.

▶ **5.** Save and close the Customers And Contracts report.

You've created many different objects in the Belmont database. Before you close it and exit Access, you'll open the Navigation Pane to view all the objects in the database.

To view the Belmont database objects in the Navigation Pane:

▶ **1.** Open the Navigation Pane and scroll up, if necessary, to display the top of the pane. See Figure 4-31.

Figure 4-31 ▶ **Belmont database objects in the Navigation Pane**

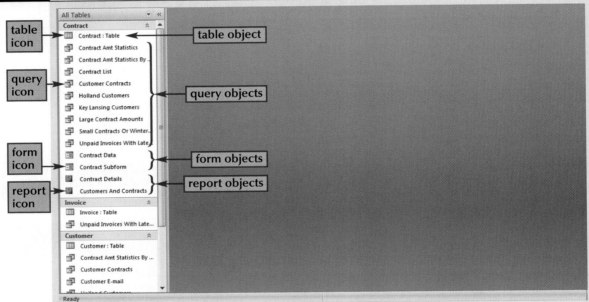

The Navigation Pane displays the objects grouped by table. Within each table group, the table itself is listed first, followed by any queries, forms, and reports you created based on the table. Each object is identified with a unique icon to help you distinguish objects with similar names or the same names. Objects you created based on more than one table appear in the list of objects for both tables. For example, note that the Customer Contracts query object is listed for both the Contract table and the Customer table because its design is based on both tables.

▶ **2.** Scroll down to the bottom of the Navigation Pane. Notice the Customer Contracts form in the Customer table list. This is the form you created containing a main form based on the Customer table and a subform based on the Contract table. The Contract Subform object is listed with the Contract table. Also, note that the database contains a query object with the same name, "Customer Contracts." The icons in the Navigation Pane help you to distinguish the Customer Contracts query (listed for both the Customer and Contract tables) from the Customer Contracts report.

▶ **3.** Compact and repair the Belmont database, and then close Access.

Oren is satisfied that the forms you created—the Customer Data form and the Customer Contracts form—will make it easier to enter, view, and update data in the Belmont database. The Customers And Contracts report presents important information about Belmont Landscapes' customers in an attractive and professional format, which will help Taylor and other staff members in their marketing efforts.

Session 4.2 Quick Check | Review

1. In a form that contains a main form and a subform, what data is displayed in the main form and what data is displayed in the subform?
2. Describe how you use the navigation buttons to move through a form containing a main form and a subform.
3. When you create a report based on two tables that are joined in a one-to-many relationship, the field values for the records from the related table are called the _____ records.
4. True or False: To move a field to another location on a report, you first need to display the report in Design view.
5. When working in Layout view for a report, which key do you press and hold down so that you can click to select multiple fields?
6. _____ in a report (or form) is special formatting applied to certain field values depending on one or more conditions.

Tutorial Summary | Review

In this tutorial, you learned how to create a form using the Form Wizard and how to modify the form's design in Layout view by changing the form's AutoFormat, adding a picture, changing the font color of the form's title, changing the type of line around field values on the form, and moving a field on the form. You also used the form's navigation buttons and various keyboard techniques to navigate through the records in a form. You used the Find command to locate specific form records, and included wildcard characters to search for records by specifying only a partial field value. In addition, you maintained table data using a form, and previewed and printed selected form records. With the one-to-many relationship already established between the necessary tables, you were able to create a form with a main form and a subform to display data from both tables at the same time. You also used the Report Wizard to create a report displaying data from two related tables. Working in Layout view, you modified the report by moving and resizing fields, and you enhanced the report by adding a picture and changing the font color of the report title. Finally, you learned how to apply conditional formatting to certain field values in the report to format them differently from other text in the report.

Key Terms

AutoFormat	Form Wizard	move handle
conditional formatting	grouped report	Report Wizard
control	Layout view	subform
detail record	main form	wildcard character

Practice	**Review Assignments**

Practice the skills you learned in the tutorial using the same case scenario.

Data Files needed for the Review Assignments: Supplier.accdb (*cont. from Tutorial 3*) **and Tools.bmp**

Oren asks you to enhance the Supplier database with forms and reports. Complete the following:

1. Open the **Supplier** database located in the Level.01\Review folder provided with your Data Files.

2. Use the Form Wizard to create a form based on the **Product** table. Select all fields for the form, the Columnar layout, and the Office style, and specify the title **Product Data** for the form.

3. In the Product Data form, change the AutoFormat to Foundry.

4. Insert the Tools picture, which is located in the Level.01\Review folder provided with your Data Files, in the Product Data form. Move the picture just to the right of the Product Data form title.

5. Change the font color of the Product Data form title to Green 3.

6. Change the type of line displayed around the Tools picture to Transparent.

7. Use the Product Data form to update the Product table as follows:

   a. Use the Find command to search for "wall" in the Product Type field and then display the record for a retaining wall (Product ID 5227). Change the Price in this record to **11.45** and the Discount Offered to **Yes**.

   b. Add a new record with the following field values, leaving the Color, Material, and Weight in Lbs fields blank:
   Product ID: **5630**
   Company ID: **GEN359**
   Product Type: **Annual**
   Price: **2.70**
   Unit: **Each**
   Color: [do not enter a value]
   Material: [do not enter a value]
   Size: **1 quart**
   Weight in Lbs: [do not enter a value]
   Discount Offered: **Yes**

   c. Save and close the form.

8. Use the Form Wizard to create a form containing a main form and a subform. Select all fields except Product Type from the Company table for the main form, and select Product ID, Product Type, Price, Unit, and Color—in that order—from the Product table for the subform. Use the Datasheet layout and the Foundry style. Specify the title **Companies And Products** for the main form and **Product Subform** for the subform.

9. Change the form title text to **Companies and Products**.

10. Resize all columns in the subform to their best fit, working left to right. Navigate through each record in the main form to make sure all the field values in the subform are completely displayed. Save and close the form.

11. Use the Report Wizard to create a report based on the primary Company table and the related Product table. Select the Company ID, Company Name, Contact First Name, Contact Last Name, and City fields—in that order—from the Company table and the Product ID, Product Type, Price, and Unit fields from the Product table. Sort the detail records in ascending order by Product ID. Choose the Stepped layout, Landscape orientation, and the Foundry style. Specify the title **Products By Company** for the report.

12. Change the report title text to **Products by Company**.

13. Resize the controls in the Products By Company report as follows, scrolling the report in Layout view to make sure your changes apply to all field values as necessary:

    a. Resize the Company ID field so that its left edge aligns with the left edge of the report. Also resize this field to its best fit.

    b. Resize the remaining column widths as necessary to fit the longest name or value they contain.

14. Insert the Tools picture, which is located in the Level.01\Review folder provided with your Data Files, in the **Products By Company** report. Position the picture just to the right of the Products by Company title so that its top edge is just below the top border of the report.

15. Apply conditional formatting so that the City field values equal to Lansing appear as dark red and bold.

16. Preview each page of the report, verifying that all the fields fit on the page. If necessary, return to Layout view and make changes so the report prints within the margins of the page and so that all field names and values are completely displayed.

17. Save the report, print its first page (only if asked by your instructor to do so), and then close the report.

18. Compact and repair the Supplier database, and then close it.

| Apply | **Case Problem 1** |

Use the skills you learned in the tutorial to create forms and a report to work with and display data about music school classes.

Data Files needed for this Case Problem: Pinehill.accdb *(cont. from Tutorial 3)* **and Piano.bmp**

Pine Hill Music School Yuka Koyama wants to use the Pinehill database to track and view information about the classes her music school offers. She asks you to create the necessary forms and a report to help her manage this data. Complete the following:

1. Open the **Pinehill** database located in the Level.01\Case1 folder provided with your Data Files.

2. Use the Form Wizard to create a form based on the Student table. Select all the fields for the form, the Columnar layout, and the Office style. Specify the title **Student Data** for the form.

3. Change the AutoFormat for the Student Data form to Technic.

4. Use the Find command to display the record for Jeff Tealey, and then change the Address field value for this record to **304 Forest Ave**.

5. Use the Student Data form to add a new record to the Student table with the following field values:
   Student ID: **NEL7584**
   First Name: **Kayla**
   Last Name: **Nelson**
   Address: **15540 Belleview Dr**
   City: **Portland**
   State: **OR**
   Zip: **97229**
   Phone: **541-563-3156**
   Birth Date: **10/13/2000**
   Gender: **F**

6. Save and close the Student Data form.

7. Use the Form Wizard to create a form containing a main form and a subform. Select all the fields from the Teacher table for the main form, and select the Contract ID, Student ID, and Lesson Type fields from the Contract table for the subform. Use the Datasheet layout and the Technic style. Specify the title **Contracts By Teacher** for the main form and the title **Contract Subform** for the subform.

8. Change the form title text for the main form to **Contracts by Teacher**, and change the font color of the title to Access Theme 2.

9. Change the type of line bordering the field values in the main form to Dots.

10. Save and close the Contracts By Teacher form.

11. Use the Report Wizard to create a report based on the primary Student table and the related Contract table. Select the Student ID, First Name, Last Name, and Phone fields from the Student table, and select all fields from the Contract table except Student ID and Contract Start Date. Sort the detail records in ascending order by Contract ID. Choose the Stepped layout, Landscape orientation, and the Technic style. Specify the title **Student Contracts** for the report.

12. Resize the fields in the report so that the field names and values are completely displayed and the report fits completely within the margins of the page. (*Hint:* Switch to Print Preview to determine whether all of the fields fit on the page.)

13. Insert the Piano picture, which is located in the Level.01\Case1 folder provided with your Data Files, in the Student Contracts report. Position the picture to the right of the Student Contracts report title so that its top edge is just below the top edge of the report.

14. Apply conditional formatting so that Contract End Date values that occur earlier than 1/1/2011 appear as bold and green (last row, sixth column in the gallery).

15. Preview the report to confirm that it is formatted correctly. If necessary, return to Layout view and make changes so the report prints within the margins of the page and so that all field names and values are completely displayed. When you are finished, save the report, print its first page (only if asked by your instructor to do so), and then close the report.

16. Compact and repair the Pinehill database, and then close it.

Challenge | Case Problem 2

Challenge yourself by creating and working with a form and report for a fitness center.

Data Files needed for this Case Problem: Fitness.accdb (*cont. from Tutorial 3*) and Weights.bmp

Parkhurst Health & Fitness Center Martha Parkhurst is using the Fitness database to track and analyze the business activity of the fitness center members and their programs. To make her work easier, you'll create a form and report in the Fitness database. Complete the following:

1. Open the **Fitness** database located in the Level.01\Case2 folder provided with your Data Files.

✦ EXPLORE

2. Use the Form Wizard to create a form containing a main form and a subform. Select all the fields from the Program table for the main form, and select the Member ID, First Name, Last Name, and Phone fields from the Member table for the subform. Use the Tabular layout and the Office style. Specify the title **Program Members** for the main form and the title **Member Subform** for the subform.

✦ EXPLORE

3. Change the AutoFormat of the Member Subform to Northwind. (*Hint:* Close the Program Members form, and then open the Member Subform. Change the AutoFormat of the subform, and then save and close the subform.)

4. In the Program Members form, change the AutoFormat to Origin. Change the font color of the main form title to Access Theme 3, and change the line type of the field boxes in the main form to Solid.

5. Save the Program Members form, navigate to the second record in the subform for the first main record, and then change the Phone field value to **804-553-7986**.

6. Navigate to the ninth record in the main form, and then change the Last Name field value for the fourth record in the subform to **Larsen**. Close the form.

✦ EXPLORE

7. Use the Report Wizard to create a report based on the primary Program table and the related Member table. Select all fields except Physical Required from the Program table, and then select the following fields from the Member table: Member ID, First Name, Last Name, City, Phone, and Date Joined. In the third Report Wizard dialog box, specify the City field as an additional grouping level. Sort the detail records by Date Joined in *descending* order. Choose the Block layout, Landscape orientation, and the Office style for the report. Specify the title **Programs And Members** for the report.

8. Revise the report title text to **Programs and Members**.

9. Change the report's AutoFormat to Origin.

10. Resize the fields as necessary so that all the field names and values are completely displayed within the margins of the report.

11. Insert the Weights picture, which is located in the Level.01\Case2 folder provided with your Data Files, in the report. Move the picture just to the right of the Programs and Members title.

✦ EXPLORE

12. Open the Access Help window and use **resize an image in a report** as the search text. Select the Help article titled "Modify, edit, or change a report," select the section titled "Modify your report in Layout view," select the topic titled "Add or modify a logo or other image," and then read the "Resize a control that contains a logo or other image" section. Verify that the Weights picture is still selected, and then resize it to about 75 percent of its original height. Close the Access Help window.

13. Apply conditional formatting so that all City field values equal to Ashland are formatted as bold and dark blue-green (sixth row, ninth column in the gallery).

14. Preview the report to confirm that it is formatted correctly. Save the report, print its first page (only if asked by your instructor to do so), and then close the report.

15. Compact and repair the Fitness database, and then close it.

Challenge | Case Problem 3

Work with the skills you've learned, and explore some new skills, to create forms and a report for a not-for-profit agency.

Data Files needed for this Case Problem: Rossi.accdb *(cont. from Tutorial 3)* **and Donate.bmp**

Rossi Recycling Group Tom Rossi wants to work with and display data about the donations made to the Rossi Recycling Group. You'll help him by creating forms and a report in the Rossi database. Complete the following:

1. Open the **Rossi** database located in the Level.01\Case3 folder provided with your Data Files.

2. Use the Form Wizard to create a form based on the Donation table. Select all the fields for the form, the Columnar layout, and the Median style. Specify the title **Donation Info** for the form.

⊕ EXPLORE 3. Use the Donation Info form to update the Donation table as follows:
   a. Use the Find command to search for the record that contains "tools" in the Donation Description field. Display the record for Power tools, and then change the Donation Value to **565**.
   b. Add a new record with the following values:
      Donation ID: **2219**
      Donor ID: **36077**
      Agency ID: **W22**
      Donation Date: **12/21/2010**
      Donation Description: **Toys**
      Donation Value: **45**
      Pickup Required: **No**
   c. Find the record with Donation ID 2150, and then delete it. (*Hint:* Select the record by clicking the record selector—the bar with a right-pointing triangle to the left of the form—and then click the Delete button in the Records group on the Home tab. When asked to confirm the deletion, click the Yes button.)

4. Change the AutoFormat of the Donation Info form to Verve, and then change the font color of the form title to Maroon 3.

⊕ EXPLORE 5. With the title text selected, drag the right title border to resize the title to fit on one line. Save and close the form.

⊕ EXPLORE 6. Use the Form Wizard to create a form containing a main form and a subform. Select all the fields from the Donor table for the main form, and select the Donation ID, Agency ID, Donation Date, Donation Description, and Donation Value fields from the Donation table for the subform. Use the Tabular layout and the Verve style. Specify the name **Donors And Donations** for the main form and the title **Donation Subform** for the subform.

7. Revise the title text in the main form to **Donors and Donations**.

8. Use the appropriate wildcard character to find all records with a Phone value that begins with the area code 316. Change the record with the Phone field value of 316-282-2226 to **316-282-2556**. Save and close the form.

⊕ EXPLORE 9. Use the Report Wizard to create a report based on the primary Agency table and the related Donation table. Select the Agency Name and Phone fields from the Agency table, and select all fields except Agency ID and Pickup Required from the Donation table. In the third Report Wizard dialog box, select Donor ID as an additional grouping level. Sort the detail records in *descending* order by Donation Value. Choose the Stepped layout, Portrait orientation, and the Verve style. Specify the name **Agencies And Donations** for the report.

10. Revise the report title text to **Agencies and Donations**.

11. Resize the fields as necessary so that all the field names and values are completely displayed on the page.

12. Insert the Donate picture, which is located in the Level.01\Case3 folder provided with your Data Files, in the report. Move the picture just to the right of the Agencies and Donations report title.

⊕ EXPLORE 13. Change the fill color of the Donate picture to Transparent. (*Hint:* Select the picture, click the arrow for the Fill/Back Color button in the Font group on the Format tab, and then click Transparent.) Change the line type of the picture border to Transparent.

⊕ EXPLORE 14. Open the Access Help window and use **add gridlines to a report** as the search text. Select the Help article titled "Modify, edit, or change a report," select the topic titled "Modify your report in Layout view," and then select and read the "Add gridlines" section. Display Horizontal gridlines for the fields from the Agency table. (*Hint:* Click an Agency Name or Phone field value, and then select a gridline option.) Close the Access Help window.

15. Apply conditional formatting so that any Donation Value greater than or equal to $200 is formatted using a bold, blue-green (top row, ninth column in the gallery) font.

16. Preview the report to confirm that it is formatted correctly. If necessary, return to Layout view and make changes so the report prints within the margins of the page and so that all field names and values are completely displayed. When you are finished, save the report, print its first page (only if asked by your instructor to do so), and then close the report.

17. Change the Navigation Pane so it displays all objects grouped by object type.

18. Compact and repair the Rossi database, and then close it.

Create | **Case Problem 4**

With the figures provided as guides, create a form and a report to display and manage data for a luxury rental agency.

Data Files needed for this Case Problem: **GEM.accdb** *(cont. from Tutorial 3)* and **Villa.bmp**

GEM Ultimate Vacations Griffin and Emma MacElroy want to use the GEM database to track and analyze data about their clients and the luxury properties they rent. You'll help them by creating forms and reports to meet this goal. Complete the following:

1. Open the **GEM** database located in the Level.01\Case4 folder provided with your Data Files.

⊕ EXPLORE 2. Create the form shown in Figure 4-32.

Figure 4-32

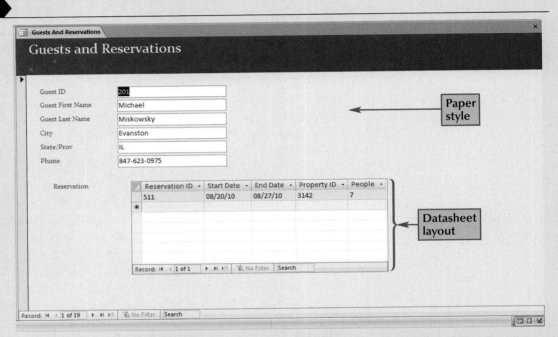

(*Hints:* To resize the subform to display all five fields, use the same technique you use to resize any form control: click the subform control to select it, and then drag the border. Widen the subform to display most of the fields in the subform, resize all columns in the subform to their best fit, and then adjust the size of the subform again.)

3. Using the form you just created, navigate to the second record in the subform for the third main record, and then change the People field value to **7**.

4. Use the Find command to move to the record for Kelly Skolnik, and then change the End Date field value for Reservation ID 507 to **5/22/10**.

5. Use the appropriate wildcard character to find all records with a Phone value that begins with the area code 630. Change the Phone field value of 630-442-4831 to **630-442-5943**. Save and close the form.

⊕ EXPLORE 6. Use the Report Wizard to create the report shown in Figure 4-33.

Figure 4-33

Title text appears with the Access Theme 8 font color

Outline layout, Landscape orientation, Paper style

detail records sorted by Reservation ID in ascending order

Villa picture inserted

Light Blue 1 Fill/Back Color applied to the field name backgrounds

Phone field resized to its best fit

(*Hint*: To display the Light Blue 1 background color with the field names from the Reservation table, press and hold down the Shift key and click to select the six field names, and then apply the Light Blue 1 Fill/Back Color.)

7. Apply conditional formatting so that all People field values greater than 7 are formatted as bold and aqua blue (top row, ninth column in the gallery).

EXPLORE

8. Preview the report so you see two pages at once. (*Hint*: Use a button on the Print Preview tab.) Print page 1 of the report (only if asked by your instructor to do so).

9. Save and close the report, compact and repair the GEM database, and then close it.

| Research | **Internet Assignments** |

Use the Internet to find and work with data related to the topics presented in this tutorial.

The purpose of the Internet Assignments is to challenge you to find information on the Internet that you can use to work effectively with this software. The actual assignments are updated and maintained on the Course Technology Web site. Log on to the Internet and use your Web browser to go to the Student Online Companion for New Perspectives Office 2007 at **www.course.com/np/office2007**. Then navigate to the Internet Assignments for this tutorial.

| Assess | **SAM Assessment and Training** |

If you have a SAM user profile, you may have access to hands-on instruction, practice, and assessment of the skills covered in this tutorial. Log in to your SAM account (**http://sam2007.course.com**) to launch any assigned training activities or exams that relate to the skills covered in this tutorial.

Review | **Quick Check Answers**

Session 4.1

1. The Form tool creates a form automatically using all the fields in the selected table or query; the Form Wizard allows you to choose some or all of the fields in the selected table or query, choose fields from other tables and queries, and display fields in any order on the form.
2. An AutoFormat is a predefined style for a form (or report). To change a form's Auto-Format, display the form in Layout view, click the More button in the AutoFormat group on the Form Layout Tools Format tab, and then click the AutoFormat you want to apply in the gallery displayed, or click AutoFormat Wizard to open the AutoFormat dialog box and select the AutoFormat you want to apply.
3. control
4. the last record in the table
5. the question mark (?)
6. Selected Record(s)

Session 4.2

1. The main form displays the data from the primary table, and the subform displays the data from the related table.
2. You use the top set of navigation buttons to select and move through records from the related table in the subform, and the bottom set to select and move through records from the primary table in the main form.
3. detail
4. False
5. Shift
6. Conditional formatting

Ending Data Files

Level.01 → **Tutorial**
Belmont.accdb

Review
Supplier.accdb

Case1
Pinehill.accdb

Case2
Fitness.accdb

Case3
Rossi.accdb

Case4
GEM.accdb

Reality Check

The Microsoft Access program is widely used in corporations to track business data, but it can also be a valuable tool to use to track data in your personal life. For example, you might want to create an Access database to track information about items in a personal collection, such as CDs, DVDs, or books; items related to a hobby, such as coin or stamp collecting, travel, or family history; or items related to sports teams, theater clubs, or other organizations to which you might belong. In this exercise, you'll use Access to create a database that will contain information of your choice, using the Access skills and features presented in Tutorials 1 through 4.

Using Templates

The Access program includes templates for creating databases and tables. A **database template** is a database containing predefined tables, queries, forms, and reports. A **table template** is a template containing predefined fields. Using a database or table template can save you time and effort in the creation process. For example, if the fields available in one of the table templates Access offers are similar to the data you want to track, you can use the table template to quickly create a table with the fields and field properties already created and set for you. You can then modify the table, as necessary, to suit your needs. Before you begin to create your own database, review the following steps for using database and table templates.

To create a database using a database template:

1. On the Getting Started with Microsoft Office Access page, click the appropriate link in the Template Categories pane; or click a link in the From Microsoft Office Online pane; or click one of the templates in the Featured Online Templates section in the middle of the page.
2. Specify the name for your database and a location in which to save the database file.
3. Click the Create button (or the Download button if you are using an Office Online template).
4. Use the resulting database objects to enter, modify, or delete data or database objects.

To create a table using a table template:

1. With your database file open, click the Create tab on the Ribbon.
2. In the Tables group, click the Table Templates button. A gallery opens listing the different table templates provided with Access.
3. Click the template you want to use.
4. Modify the resulting table as needed, by adding or deleting fields, changing field properties, and so on.

You can decide to use a database and/or table template for the following exercise if the templates fit the data you want to track. Note, however, that you still need to create the additional database objects indicated in the following steps—tables, queries, forms, and reports—to complete the exercise successfully.

Note: Please be sure *not* to include any personal information of a sensitive nature in the database you create to be submitted to your instructor for this exercise. Later on, you can update the data in your database with such information for your own personal use.

1. Create a new Access database to contain personal data you want to track.
2. Create two or three tables in the database that can be joined through one-to-many relationships.
3. Define the properties for each field in each table. Make sure you include a mix of data types for the fields (for example, do not include only Text fields in each table).
4. Specify a primary key for each table.
5. Define the necessary one-to-many relationships between the tables in the database with referential integrity enforced.
6. Enter 20 to 30 records in each table. If appropriate, you can import the data for a table from another source, such as an Excel spreadsheet or a text file.
7. Create 5 to 10 queries based on single tables and multiple tables. Be sure that some of the queries you create include some or all of the following: exact match conditions, comparison operators, and logical operators.
8. For some of the queries, use various sorting and filtering techniques to display the query results in various ways. Save these queries with the sort and/or filter applied.
9. If possible, and depending on the data you are tracking, create at least one calculated field in one of the queries.
10. If possible, and depending on the data you are tracking, use aggregate functions to produce summary statistics based on the data in at least one of your tables.
11. Create at least one form for each table in your database. Enhance each form's appearance with pictures, AutoFormats, line colors, and so on.
12. Create at least one form with a main form and subform based on related tables in your database. Enhance the form's appearance as appropriate.
13. Create at least one report based on each table in your database. Enhance each report's appearance with pictures, AutoFormats, color, and so on.
14. Apply conditional formatting to the values in at least one of your reports.
15. Submit your completed database to your instructor as requested. Include printouts of any database objects, such as reports, if required.

Objectives

Creating Advanced Queries and Enhancing Table Design

Making the Panorama Database Easier to Use

Case | Belmont Landscapes

After graduating with a university degree in Landscape Architecture and then working for a firm that provides basic landscape services to residential customers, Oren Belmont started his own landscape architecture firm in Holland, Michigan. Belmont Landscapes specializes in landscape designs for residential and commercial customers and numerous public agencies. The firm provides a wide range of services—from site analyses and feasibility studies, to drafting and administering construction documents—for projects of various scales. Oren's company developed the Panorama database of customer, contract, and invoice data; and the employees use Microsoft Office Access 2007 (or simply Access) to manage it. The Panorama database contains tables, queries, forms, and reports that Sarah Fisher, office manager, and Taylor Sico, marketing manager, use to track customers and their landscape projects.

Oren, Sarah, and Taylor are interested in taking better advantage of the power of Access to make the database easier to use and to create more sophisticated queries. For example, Taylor wants to obtain lists of employers in certain cities, and Sarah needs a summarized list of invoice amounts by city. Sarah wants to change the design of the Customer and Contract tables. In this tutorial, you'll modify and customize the Panorama database to satisfy these requirements.

Starting Data Files

Level.02 →	Tutorial	Review	Case1	Case2
	Panorama.accdb	Products.accdb	Contract.accdb	Training.accdb

Case3	Case4	Case5
Agency.accdb	Vacation.accdb	(none)

Session 5.1

Reviewing the Panorama Database

Tip

Read the Microsoft Access Naming Conventions section in the appendix titled "Relational Databases and Database Design" for more information about naming conventions.

Sarah and her staff had no previous database experience when they created the Panorama database using the wizards and other easy-to-use Access tools. As business continued to grow at Belmont Landscapes, Sarah convinced Oren that they needed to hire a computer expert to further enhance the Panorama database, and they hired Lucia Perez, who has a business information systems degree and nine years of experience developing database systems. Lucia spent a few days reviewing the Panorama database, and she decided to implement simple naming standards for the objects and field names in the database to make her future work easier.

Before implementing the enhancements for Sarah and Taylor, you'll review the naming changes Lucia made to the object and field names in the Panorama database.

To review the object naming standards in the Panorama database:

▶ 1. Make sure you have created your copy of the Access Data Files, and that your computer can access them.

   Trouble? If you don't have the Access Data Files, you need to get them before you can proceed. Your instructor will either give you the Data Files or ask you to obtain them from a specified location (such as a network drive). In either case, make a backup copy of the Data Files before you start so that you will have the original files available in case you need to start over. If you have any questions about the Data Files, see your instructor or technical support person for assistance.

▶ 2. Start Access, and then open the **Panorama** database in the Level.02\Tutorial folder provided with your Data Files.

   Trouble? If the Security Warning is displayed below the Ribbon, click the Options button next to the Security Warning. In the dialog box that opens, click the "Enable this content" option button, and then click the OK button.

The Navigation Pane displays the objects grouped by object type, as shown in Figure 5-1. Lucia added prefix tags to the object names—a tbl prefix tag for tables, a qry prefix tag for queries, a frm prefix tag for forms, and a rpt prefix tag for reports. Using object prefix tags, you can readily identify the object type, even when the objects have the same base name—for instance, tblContract, frmContract, and rptContract. In addition, Lucia removed spaces from the object names based on her experience with other database management systems, such as SQL Server and Oracle, that do not permit spaces in object and field names. If Belmont Landscapes needs to upscale to one of these other database management systems in the future, Lucia will have to do less work to make the transition.

Panorama database objects on the Navigation Pane | Figure 5-1

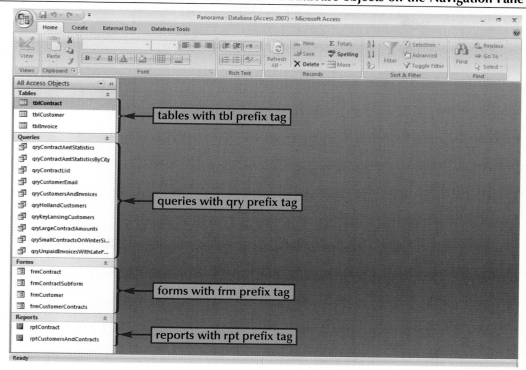

Next, you'll review the naming changes Lucia made to the tables by opening the tblContract table in Datasheet view and then in Design view.

To review the field naming standards in the tblContract table:

1. In the Tables group on the Navigation Page, double-click **tblContract** to open the tblContract table in Datasheet view.

   Notice that each column heading name contains spaces. You need to review the table in Design view to see Lucia's changes.

2. In the Views group on the Home tab, click the **View** button. The table is displayed in Design view with the ContractNum field selected. See Figure 5-2.

Figure 5-2 | **Panorama database field names and Caption property settings**

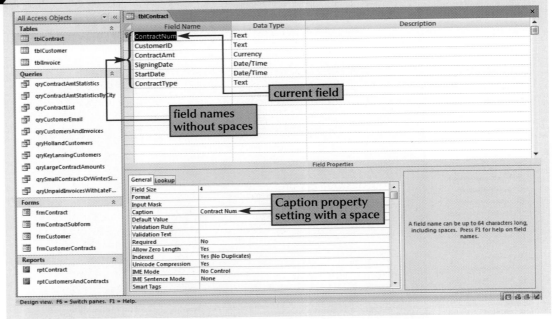

Notice that Lucia removed the spaces from each of the six field names. If the field names do not contain spaces, why do the column headings in Datasheet view contain spaces? Lucia set the Caption property for the ContractNum field to Contract Num, and she set the Caption property for the other five fields in a similar way. The **Caption property** for a field specifies its column heading value in datasheets and its label value in forms and reports. If you don't set the Caption property, Access uses the field name as the default column heading name and the default label name. Using the Caption property, you can use field names without spaces as a standard, while providing the users with more readable names on their queries, forms, and reports.

Now that you've reviewed Lucia's database changes, you'll create the queries that Sarah and Taylor need.

Using a Pattern Match in a Query

You are already familiar with queries that use an exact match or a range of values (for example, queries that use the >= or < comparison operators) to select records. Access provides many other operators for creating select queries. These operators let you create more complicated queries that are difficult or impossible to create with exact match or range of values selection criteria.

Sarah and Taylor created a list of questions they want to answer using the Panorama database:

- Which customers have the 616 area code?
- What is the customer information for customers located in Holland, Rockford, or Saugatuck?
- What is the customer information for all customers *except* those located in Holland, Rockford, or Saugatuck?
- What is the customer and contract information for contracts that have values of less than $10,000 or that were signed during the winter *and* are located in Grand Rapids or East Grand Rapids?

- What are the names of Belmont Landscapes' customers? The customer name is either the company name for nonresidential customers or the last and first names for residential customers.
- What is the customer information for customers in a particular city? For this query, the user needs to be able to specify the city.

Next, you will create the queries necessary to answer these questions. Taylor wants to view the records for all customers located in the 616 area code. She plans to travel to this area next week and wants to contact customers ahead of time to schedule appointments. To answer Taylor's question, you can create a query that uses a pattern match. A **pattern match** selects records with a value for the designated field that matches the pattern of the simple condition value, in this case, customers with the 616 area code. You do this using the Like comparison operator.

The **Like comparison operator** selects records by matching field values to a specific pattern that includes one or more of these wildcard characters: asterisk (*), question mark (?), and number symbol (#). The asterisk represents any string of characters, the question mark represents any single character, and the number symbol represents any single digit. Using a pattern match is similar to using an exact match, except that a pattern match includes wildcard characters.

To create the query, you must first place the tblCustomer table field list in the Query window in Design view.

To create the new query in Design view:

1. Close the **tblContract** table, and then click the **Shutter Bar Open/Close Button** ≪ at the top of the Navigation Pane to close it.

2. Click the **Create** tab on the Ribbon and then, in the Other group on the Create tab, click the **Query Design** button. Access opens the Show Table dialog box on top of the Query window in Design view.

3. Click **tblCustomer** in the Tables list box, click the **Add** button, and then click the **Close** button. Access places the tblCustomer table field list in the Query window and closes the Show Table dialog box.

4. Double-click the **title bar** of the tblCustomer field list to highlight all the fields, and then drag the highlighted fields to the first column's Field text box in the design grid. Access places each field in a separate column in the design grid, in the same order that the fields appear in the table. See Figure 5-3.

> **Tip**
>
> You can also double-click a table name to add the table's field list to the Query window.

| Figure 5-3 | Adding the fields for the pattern match query |

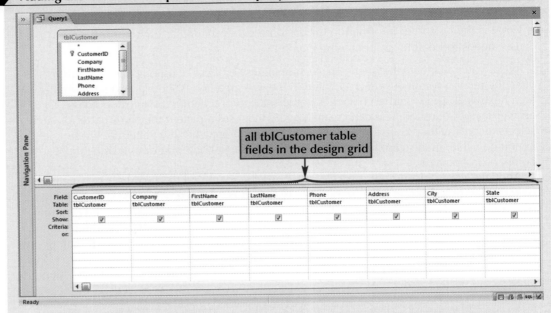

Trouble? If tblCustomer.* appears in the first column's Field text box, you dragged the * from the field list instead of the highlighted fields. Press the Delete key, and then repeat Step 4.

Now you will enter the pattern match condition Like "616*" for the Phone field. Access will select records with a Phone field value of 616 in positions one through three. The asterisk wildcard character specifies that any characters can appear in the remaining positions of the field value.

To specify records that match the specified pattern:

▶ **1.** Click the **Phone Criteria** text box, and then type **Like "616*"**. See Figure 5-4.

| Figure 5-4 | Record selection based on matching a specific pattern |

Tip

If you omit the Like operator, Access automatically adds it when you run the query.

Now you can save the query.

▶ **2.** Click the **Save** button on the Quick Access Toolbar to open the Save As dialog box.

▶ **3.** Type **qry616AreaCode** in the Query Name text box, and then press the **Enter** key. Access saves the query with the specified name and displays the name on the query tab.

▶ **4.** In the Results group on the Query Tools Design tab, click the **Run** button. The query results display the 24 records with the area code 616 in the Phone field. See Figure 5-5.

tblCustomer table records for area code 616 | Figure 5-5

Customer ID	Company	First Name	Last Name	Phone	Address	City	State
11001		Sharon	Maloney	6168663901	49 Blackstone Dr	Rockford	MI
11004		Amber	Sullivan	6168669111	2807 Fairview Dr	Rockford	MI
11005		Owen	Hawes	6163920622	102 Pineview Rd	Holland	MI
11012	Grand Rapids Engineering Dept	Anthony	Rodriguez	6164549801	225 Summer St	Grand Rapids	MI
11014		Amol	Mehta	6163961972	54 Lakeshore Ave	Holland	MI
11015		John	Weiss	6166377783	456 Winchester St	South Haven	MI
11030	Finn's on the Waterfront	Devin	Finnerty	6163931228	78 E 8th St	Holland	MI
11031	Happy Haven Day Care	Kathy	Rowe	6168424603	29 Graham's Ln	Grand Haven	MI
11040	RiverView Development Company	Susan	Darcy	6169880777	144 E Tower Ave	Grand Rapids	MI
11043	Monroe State College	Rachel	Kirk	6169881320	40 Monroe St	Grand Rapids	MI
11048		Olivia	Pappas	6166376591	4 N Orchard St	South Haven	MI
11053		Hwan	Tang	6163968401	283 Cottrell St	Holland	MI
11054	Gilded Goose Gift Shop	Taylor	Wilson	6163553989	258 Briar Ln	Holland	MI
11059	G. R. Neighborhood Development Corp	Matthew	Fraser	6163920015	8045 Jefferson Ave	Grand Rapids	MI
11060		Jerome	Smith	6169493862	75 Hillcrest St	East Grand Rapids	MI
11065	Town of Holland	Amber	Ward	6163930403	24 Prospect St	Holland	MI
11068	Grand Rapids Housing Authority	Jessica	Ropiak	6164544002	5230 Fulton St	Grand Rapids	MI
11070	Legacy Companies, LTD	Michael	Faraci	6164567093	250 Market Ave	Grand Rapids	MI
11079	Dept. of Neighborhood Development	Sarah	Russell	6169403380	722 Beechwood Dr	East Grand Rapids	MI
11080	Three Tulips Café	Jan	Van Dousen	6163924629	249 W 11th St	Holland	MI
11084		Cathy	DeSantis	6168664882	78 Spring St	Rockford	MI
11085		Edward	Phillips	6166375408	39 Water St	South Haven	MI
11088	Weston Community Parks Foundation	Sam	Kervin	6164543327	333 Pearl St	Grand Rapids	MI
11090	Lily's Boutique	Lily	Shaw	6168425361	751 E Maple St	Grand Haven	MI

Note that Lucia removed the hyphens from the Phone field values; for example, 6168663901 in the first record used to be 616-866-3901. You'll modify the Phone field later in this tutorial to format its values with hyphens.

5. Close the qry616AreaCode query.

Next, Sarah asks you to create a query that displays information about customers in Holland, Rockford, or Saugatuck. She wants a printout of the customer data for her administrative aide, who will contact these customers. To produce the results Sarah wants, you'll create a query using a list-of-values match.

Using a List-of-Values Match in a Query

A **list-of-values match** selects records whose value for the designated field matches one of two or more simple condition values. You could accomplish this by including several Or conditions in the design grid, but the In comparison operator provides an easier and clearer way to do this. The **In comparison operator** lets you define a condition with a list of two or more values for a field. If a record's field value matches one value from the list of defined values, then Access selects and includes that record in the query results.

To display the information Sarah requested, you want to select records if their City field value equals Holland, Rockford, or Saugatuck. These are the values you will use with the In comparison operator. Sarah wants the query to contain the same data as the qry616AreaCode query, so you'll make a copy of that query and modify it.

To create the query using a list-of-values match:

1. Open the Navigation Pane, then in the Queries group on the Navigation Page, right-click **qry616AreaCode**, and then click **Copy** on the shortcut menu.

2. In the Clipboard group on the Home tab, click the **Paste** button, type **qryHollandRockfordSaugatuckCustomers** in the Query Name text box, and then press the **Enter** key.

To modify the copied query, you need to open it in Design view.

▶ **3.** In the Queries group on the Navigation Pane, right-click **qryHollandRockfordSaugatuckCustomers** to select it and display the shortcut menu.

▶ **4.** Click **Design View** on the shortcut menu to open the query in Design view, and then close the Navigation Pane.

You need to delete the existing condition from the Phone field.

▶ **5.** Click the **Phone Criteria** text box, press the **F2** key to highlight the entire condition, and then press the **Delete** key to remove the condition.

Now you can enter the criteria for the new query using the In comparison operator. When you use this operator, you must enclose the list of values you want to match within parentheses and separate the values with commas. In addition, for fields defined using the Text data type, you enclose each value in quotation marks, although Access adds the quotation marks if you omit them. When using the In comparison operator for fields defined using the Number or Currency data type, you don't enclose the values in quotation marks.

▶ **6.** Right-click the **City Criteria** text box to open the shortcut menu, click **Zoom** to open the Zoom dialog box, and then type **In ("Holland","Rockford", "Saugatuck")**. See Figure 5-6.

| **Figure 5-6** | **Record selection based on matching field values to a list of values** |

Tip

After clicking in a text box, you can also open the Zoom dialog box for that text box by holding down the Shift key and pressing the F2 key.

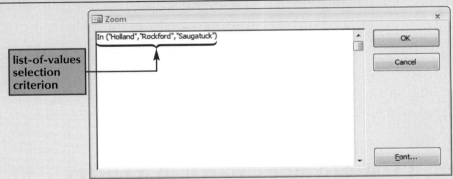

list-of-values selection criterion

▶ **7.** Click the **OK** button to close the Zoom dialog box, and then save and run the query. Access displays the recordset, which shows the 13 records with Holland, Rockford, or Saugatuck in the City field.

▶ **8.** Close the query.

Sarah asks her assistant to contact Belmont Landscapes customers who are not in Holland, Rockford, and Saugatuck. You can provide Sarah with this information by creating a query with the Not logical operator.

Using the Not Operator in a Query

The **Not logical operator** negates a criterion or selects records for which the designated field does not match the criterion. For example, if you enter Not "Holland" in the Criteria text box for the City field, the query results show records that do not have the City field value Holland, that is, records of all customers not located in Holland.

To create Sarah's query, you will combine the Not logical operator with the In comparison operator to select customers whose City field value is not in the list ("Holland", "Rockford","Saugatuck"). The qryHollandRockfordSaugatuckCustomers query has the fields that Sarah needs to see in the query results. Sarah doesn't need to keep the qryHollandRockfordSaugatuckCustomers query, so you'll rename and then modify the query.

To create the query using the Not logical operator:

▶ **1.** Open the Navigation Pane, then in the Queries group on the Navigation Page, right-click **qryHollandRockfordSaugatuckCustomers**, and then click **Rename** on the shortcut menu.

▶ **2.** Position the insertion point after "qry," type **Non**, and then press the **Enter** key. The query name is now qryNonHollandRockfordSaugatuckCustomers.

▶ **3.** Open the **qryNonHollandRockfordSaugatuckCustomers** query in Design view, and then close the Navigation Pane.

You need to change the existing condition in the City field to add the Not logical operator.

▶ **4.** Click the **City Criteria** text box, open the Zoom dialog box, click at the beginning of the expression, type **Not**, and then press the **spacebar**. See Figure 5-7.

Record selection based on not matching a list of values ◀ **Figure 5-7**

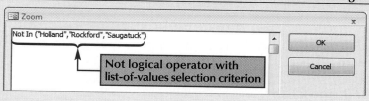

▶ **5.** Click the **OK** button, and then save and run the query. The recordset displays only those records with a City field value that is not Holland, Rockford, or Saugatuck. The recordset includes a total of 29 customer records.

▶ **6.** Scroll down the datasheet to make sure that no Holland or Rockford or Saugatuck customers appear in your results.

Now you can close and delete the query, because Sarah does not need to run this query again.

▶ **7.** Close the query, and then open the Navigation Pane.

▶ **8.** Right-click **qryNonHollandRockfordSaugatuckCustomers**, click **Delete** on the shortcut menu, and then click the **Yes** button when asked to confirm the query deletion. The query is permanently deleted from the database.

You now are ready to answer Taylor's question about Grand Rapids or East Grand Rapids customers that signed contracts for less than $10,000 or that signed contracts during the winter.

Using an AutoFilter to Filter Data

Taylor wants to view the customer last and first names, company names, cities, contract amounts, signing dates, and contract types for customers in Grand Rapids or East Grand Rapids that have signed contracts for less than $10,000 or that signed contracts during the winter. The qrySmallContractsOrWinterSignings query contains the same fields Taylor wants to view. This query also uses the Or logical operator to select records if the ContractAmt field value is less than $10,000 or if the SigningDate field value is between 1/1/2011 and 3/1/2011. These are two of the conditions needed to answer Taylor's question. You could modify the qrySmallContractsOrWinterSignings query in Design view to further restrict the records selected to customers located only in Grand Rapids and East Grand Rapids. However, you can use the AutoFilter feature to choose the city restrictions faster and more flexibly. You previously used the AutoFilter feature to sort records, and you previously used Filter By Form and Filter By Selection to filter records. Now you'll show Taylor how to use the AutoFilter feature to filter records.

To filter the records using an AutoFilter:

► **1.** Open the **qrySmallContractsOrWinterSignings** query in Design view, and then close the Navigation Pane.

The *<10000* condition for the ContractAmt field selects records whose contract amounts are less than $10,000, and the *Between #1/1/2011# And #3/1/2011#* condition for the SigningDate field selects records whose contracts were signed during the first two months of 2011. Because the conditions are in two different rows, the query uses the Or logical operator. If you wanted to answer Taylor's question in Design view, you would add a condition for the City field, using either the Or logical operator—*"Grand Rapids" Or "East Grand Rapids"*—or the In comparison operator—*In ("Grand Rapids","East Grand Rapids")*. You'd place this condition for the City field in both the Criteria row and in the or row. The query recordset would include a record only if both conditions in either row are satisfied.

Instead, you'll show Taylor how to choose the information she wants using an AutoFilter.

► **2.** Run the query, and then click the **arrow** on the City column heading to display the AutoFilter menu. See Figure 5-8.

Figure 5-8 | **Using an AutoFilter to filter records in the query recordset**

The AutoFilter menu lists all City field values that appear in the recordset. A check mark next to an entry indicates that records with that City field value appear in the recordset. To filter for selected City field values, you uncheck the cities you don't want selected and leave checked the cities you do want selected. You can click the "(Select All)" check box to select or deselect all field values. The "(Blanks)" entry includes null values when checked and excludes null values when unchecked. (Recall that a null field value is the absence of a value for the field.)

3. Click the **(Select All)** check box to deselect all check boxes, click the **East Grand Rapids** check box, and then click the **Grand Rapids** check box.

   The two check boxes indicate that the AutoFilter will include only East Grand Rapids and Grand Rapids City field values.

4. Click the **OK** button. Access displays the four records for customers in East Grand Rapids and Grand Rapids with small contract amounts or with winter signing dates. See Figure 5-9.

Using an AutoFilter to filter records in the query recordset	Figure 5-9

You click the Toggle Filter button in the Sort & Filter group on the Home tab to remove the current filter and display all records in the query. If you click the Toggle Filter button a second time, you reapply the filter.

5. In the Sort & Filter group on the Home tab, click the **Toggle Filter** button. Access removes the filter, and all 31 records appear in the recordset.

6. Click the **Toggle Filter** button. Access applies the City filter, displaying the four records for customers in East Grand Rapids and Grand Rapids.

   Taylor knows how to use the AutoFilter feature and has the information she needs. You can close the query without saving your query design changes.

7. Close the query without saving the query design changes.

Sarah wants to view all fields from the tblCustomer table, along with the customer name. The customer name is either the company name for nonresidential customers or the last and first names for residential customers.

Assigning a Conditional Value to a Calculated Field

Records for residential customers have nonnull FirstName and LastName field values and null Company field values in the tblCustomer table, while records for all other customers have nonnull values for all three fields. Sarah wants to view records from the tblCustomer table in order by the Company field value, if it's nonnull, and at the same time in order by the LastName and then FirstName field values, if the Company field value is null. To produce the information for Sarah, you need to create a query that includes all fields from the tblCustomer table and then add a calculated field that will display the customer name—either the Company field value or the LastName and FirstName field values, separated by a comma and a space.

To combine the LastName and FirstName fields, you'll use the expression *LastName &* *", " & FirstName*. The **& (ampersand) operator** is a concatenation operator that joins text expressions. If the LastName field value is Maloney and the FirstName field value is Sharon, for example, the result of the expression is *Maloney, Sharon*.

To display the correct customer value, you'll use the IIf function. The **IIf (Immediate If) function** assigns one value to a calculated field or control if a condition is true, and a second value if the condition is false. The IIf function has three parts: a condition that is true or false, the result when the condition is true, and the result when the condition is false. Each part of the IIf function is separated by a comma. The condition you'll use is *IsNull(Company)*. The **IsNull function** tests a field value or an expression for a null value; if the field value or expression is null, the result is true; otherwise, the result is false. The expression *IsNull(Company)* is true when the Company field value is null, and is false when the Company field value is not null.

For the calculated field, you'll enter *IIf(IsNull(Company),LastName & ", " & FirstName,Company)*. You interpret this expression as: If the Company field value is null, then set the calculated field value to the concatenation of the LastName field value and the text string ", " and the FirstName field value. If the Company field value is not null, then set the calculated field value to the Company field value.

Now you are ready to create Sarah's query to display the customer name.

To create the query to display the customer name:

▶ 1. Click the **Create** tab on the Ribbon and then, in the Other group on the Create tab, click the **Query Design** button to open the Show Table dialog box on top of the Query window in Design view.

▶ 2. Click **tblCustomer** in the Tables list box, click the **Add** button, and then click the **Close** button to place the tblCustomer table field list in the Query window and close the Show Table dialog box.

Sarah wants all fields from the tblCustomer table to appear in the query recordset and the new calculated field to appear in the first column.

▶ 3. Double-click the **title bar** of the tblCustomer field list to highlight all the fields, and then drag the highlighted fields to the second column's Field text box in the design grid. Access places each field in a separate column in the design grid starting with the second column in the design grid, in the same order that the fields appear in the table.

Trouble? If you accidentally drag the highlighted fields to the first column in the design grid, click the CustomerID Field text box, and then click the Insert Columns button in the Query Setup group on the Query Tools Design tab. Continue with Step 4.

Tip

After clicking in a text box, you can also open the Expression Builder dialog box for that text box by holding down the Ctrl key and pressing the F2 key.

▶ 4. Right-click the blank Field text box to the left of the CustomerID field, and then click **Build** on the shortcut menu to open the Expression Builder dialog box.

Sarah wants to use "Customer" as the name of the calculated field, so you'll type that name, followed by a colon, and then you'll choose the IIf function.

▶ 5. Type **Customer:** and then press the **spacebar**. Be sure you type the colon following Customer.

▶ 6. Double-click **Functions** in the left column, click **Built-In Functions** in the left column, scroll down the middle column and click **Program Flow**, click **IIf** in the right column, and then click the **Paste** button. Access adds the IIf function with four placeholders to the right of the calculated field name in the expression box. See Figure 5-10.

Pasted IIf function for the calculated field   Figure 5-10

The expression you will create does not need the leftmost placeholder, <<Expr>>, so you'll delete it. You'll replace the second placeholder (<<expr>>) with the condition using the IsNull function, the third placeholder (<<truepart>>) with the expression using the & operator, and the fourth placeholder (<<falsepart>>) with the Company field name.

▶ 7. Click **<<Expr>>** in the expression box, and then press the **Delete** key to delete the first placeholder.

▶ 8. Click **<<expr>>** in the expression box, click **Inspection** in the middle column, click **IsNull** in the right column, click the **Paste** button, click **<<varexpr>>** in the expression box, and then type **Company**. You've completed the entry of the condition in the IIf function. See Figure 5-11.

After entering the condition for the calculated field's IIf function   Figure 5-11

Instead of typing the field name of Company in the previous step, you could have double-clicked Tables in the left column, clicked tblCustomer, and then pasted Company.

Now you'll replace the fourth placeholder and then the third placeholder.

▶ 9. Click **<<falsepart>>** and then type **Company**.

▶ 10. Click **<<truepart>>**, and then type **LastName & ", " & FirstName** to finish creating the calculated field. Be sure you type a space after the comma within the quotation marks. See Figure 5-12.

Figure 5-12 The completed calculated field

false part expression · true part expression

Sarah wants the query sorted in ascending order by the Customer calculated field.

To sort, save, and run the query:

▶ **1.** Click the **OK** button in the Expression Builder dialog box to close it.

▶ **2.** Click the right side of the **Customer Sort** text box to display the sort order options, and then click **Ascending**. The query will display the records in alphabetical order based on the Customer field values.

The calculated field name of Customer consists of a single word, so you do not need to set the Caption property for it. However, you'll review the properties for the calculated field by opening the property sheet for it.

▶ **3.** In the Show/Hide group on the Query Tools Design tab, click the **Property Sheet** button. The property sheet opens and displays the properties for the Customer calculated field. See Figure 5-13.

Figure 5-13 Property sheet for the Customer calculated field

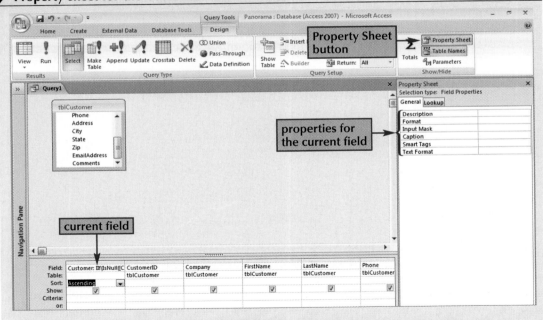

Property Sheet button · properties for the current field · current field

Among the properties for the calculated field, which is the current field, is the Caption property. Leaving the Caption property set to null means that the column name for the calculated field in the query recordset will be Customer, which is the calculated field name. The Property Sheet button is a toggle, so you'll click it again to close the property sheet.

▶ **4.** Click the **Property Sheet** button to close the property sheet.

▶ **5.** Save the query as **qryCustomersByName**, run the query, and then resize the Customer column to its best fit. Access displays all records from the tblCustomer table in alphabetical order by the Customer field. See Figure 5-14.

Completed query displaying the Customer calculated field ◀ **Figure 5-14**

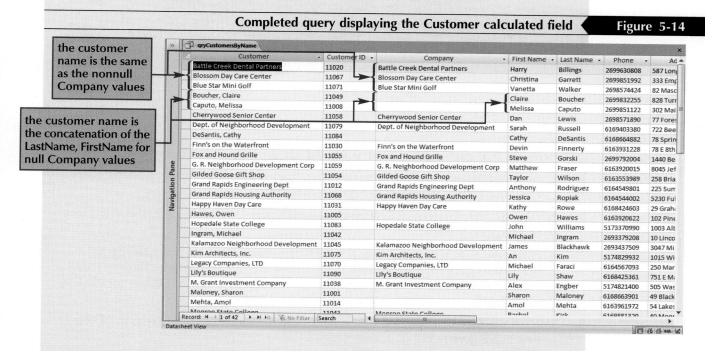

the customer name is the same as the nonnull Company values

the customer name is the concatenation of the LastName, FirstName for null Company values

▶ **6.** Save and close the query.

You are now ready to create the query to satisfy Sarah's request for information about customers in a particular city.

Creating a Parameter Query

Sarah's next request is for records in the qryCustomersByName query for customers in a particular city. For this query, she wants to specify the city, such as Battle Creek or Holland, when she executes the query.

To create this query, you will copy, rename, and modify the qryCustomersByName query. You could create a simple condition using an exact match for the City field, but you would need to change it in Design view every time you run the query. Alternatively, Sarah or a member of her staff could filter the qryCustomersByName query for the city records they want to view. Instead, you will create a parameter query. A **parameter query** displays a dialog box that prompts the user to enter one or more criteria values when the query is run. In this case, you want to create a query that prompts for the city and selects only those customer records with that City field value from the table. You will enter the prompt in the Criteria text box for the City field. When Access runs the query, it will open a dialog box and prompt you to enter the city. Access then creates the query results, just as if you had changed the criteria in Design view.

Reference Window | **Creating a Parameter Query**

- Create a select query that includes all fields to appear in the query results. Also choose the sort fields and set the criteria that do not change when you run the query.
- Decide which fields to use as prompts when the query runs. In the Criteria text box for each of these fields, type the prompt you want to appear in a message box when you run the query, and enclose the prompt in brackets.

Now you can copy and rename the qryCustomersByName query, and then change its design to create the parameter query.

To create the parameter query based on an existing query:

▶ 1. Open the Navigation Pane, copy and then paste the qryCustomersByName query, renaming it **qryCustomersByNameParameter**.

▶ 2. Open the **qryCustomersByNameParameter** query in Design view, and then close the Navigation Pane.

Next, you must enter the criteria for the parameter query. In this case, Sarah wants the query to prompt users to enter the city for the customer records they want to view. So, you need to enter the prompt in the Criteria text box for the City field. Brackets must enclose the text of the prompt.

▶ 3. Click the **City Criteria** text box, type **[Enter the city:]** and then press the **Enter** key. See Figure 5-15.

| Figure 5-15 | Specifying the prompt for the parameter query |

▶ 4. Save and run the query. Access displays a dialog box prompting you for the name of the city. See Figure 5-16.

| Figure 5-16 | Enter Parameter Value dialog box |

The bracketed text you specified in the Criteria text box of the City field appears above a text box, in which you must type a City field value. Sarah wants to see all customers in Holland.

▶ 5. Type **Holland**, press the **Enter** key, and then scroll to the right, if necessary, to display the City field values. The recordset displays the data for the seven customers in Holland. See Figure 5-17.

Results of the parameter query ◄ Figure 5-17

Sarah asks what happens if she doesn't enter a value in the dialog box when she runs the qryCustomersByNameParameter query. You can run the query again to show Sarah the answer to her question.

▶ **6.** Switch to Design view, and then run the query. The Enter Parameter Value dialog box opens.

If you click the OK button or press the Enter key, you'll run the parameter query without entering a value for the City field criterion.

▶ **7.** Click the **OK** button. Access displays no records in the query results.

When you run the parameter query and enter Holland in the dialog box, Access runs the query the same way as if you had entered *"Holland"* in the City Criteria text box in the design grid by displaying all Holland customer records. When you do not enter a value in the dialog box, Access runs the query the same way as if you had entered *null* in the City Criteria text box. Because none of the records has a null City field value, Access displays no records. Sarah asks if there's a way to display records for a selected City field value when she enters its value in the dialog box and to display all records when she doesn't enter a value.

InSight | Creating a More Flexible Parameter Query

Most users want parameter queries to display the records that match their entered parameter value or to display all records when they don't enter a parameter value. To provide this functionality, you can change the Criteria text box in the design grid for the specified column. For example, you could change an entry for a City field from *[Enter the city:]* to *Like [Enter the city:]* & "*". That is, you can prefix the Like operator to the original criterion and concatenate the criterion to a wildcard character. When you run the parameter query with this new entry, Access will display one of the following recordsets:

- If you enter a specific City field value in the dialog box, such as Saugatuck, the entry is the same as *Like "Saugatuck"* & "*", which becomes *Like "Saugatuck*"* after the concatenation operation. That is, Access selects all records whose City field values have Saugatuck in the first nine positions and any characters in the remaining positions. If the table on which the query is based contains records with City field values of Saugatuck, Access displays only those records. However, if the table on which the query is based also contains records with City field values of Saugatuck City, then Access would display both the Saugatuck and the Saugatuck City records.
- If you enter a letter in the dialog box, such as S, the entry is the same as *Like "S*"*, and the recordset displays all records with City field values that begin with the letter S.
- If you enter no value in the dialog box, the entry is the same as *Like Null* & "*", which becomes *Like "*"* after the concatenation operation, and the recordset displays all records.

Now you'll modify the parameter query to satisfy Sarah's request and test the new version of the query.

To modify and test the parameter query:

▶ 1. Switch to Design view.

▶ 2. Click the **City Criteria** text box, and then open the Zoom dialog box.

   You'll use the Zoom dialog box to modify the value in the City Criteria text box.

▶ 3. Click to the left of the expression in the Zoom dialog box, type **Like**, press the **spacebar**, press the **End** key, press the **spacebar**, and then type **& "*"**. See Figure 5-18.

| **Figure 5-18** ▶ | **Modified City Criteria value in the Zoom dialog box** |

Now you can test the modified parameter query.

▶ 4. Click the **OK** button to close the Zoom dialog box, save your query design changes, and then run the query.

   First, you'll test the query to display customers in Saugatuck.

▶ 5. Type **Saugatuck**, and then press the **Enter** key. The recordset displays the data for the three customers in Saugatuck.

   Now you'll test the query without entering a value when prompted.

▶ 6. Switch to Design view, run the query, and then click the **OK** button. The recordset displays all 42 original records from the tblCustomer table.

Finally, you'll test the query and enter S in the dialog box.

▶ **7.** Switch to Design view, run the query, type **S**, and then press the **Enter** key. The recordset displays the 10 records for customers in Saint Joseph, Saugatuck, and South Haven.

▶ **8.** Close the query.

▶ **9.** If you are not continuing on to the next session, close the Panorama database, and then exit Access, clicking the **Yes** button if you are prompted to confirm that you want to exit Access and to empty the Clipboard.

The queries you created will make the Panorama database easier to use. In the next session, you will create a top values query and use query wizards to create three additional queries.

Session 5.1 Quick Check | Review

1. You use the _____ property to specify how a field name appears in datasheet column headings and in form and report labels.
2. Which comparison operator selects records based on a specific pattern?
3. What is the purpose of the asterisk (*) in a pattern match query?
4. When do you use the In comparison operator?
5. How do you negate a selection criterion?
6. The _____ function returns one of two values based on whether the condition being tested is true or false.
7. When do you use a parameter query?

Session 5.2

Creating a Crosstab Query

Oren wants to analyze his company's invoices by city, so he can view the paid and unpaid contract amounts for all customers located in each city. He asks you to create a crosstab query using the Crosstab Query Wizard to provide the information he needs.

A **crosstab query** performs aggregate function calculations on the values of one database field and displays the results in a spreadsheet format. Recall that an aggregate function performs an arithmetic operation on selected records in a database. Figure 5-19 lists the aggregate functions you can use in a crosstab query. A crosstab query can also display one additional aggregate function value that summarizes the set of values in each row. The crosstab query uses one or more fields for the row headings on the left and one field for the column headings at the top.

Figure 5-19	Aggregate functions used in crosstab queries

Aggregate Function	Definition
Avg	Average of the field values
Count	Number of the nonnull field values
First	First field value
Last	Last field value
Max	Highest field value
Min	Lowest field value
StDev	Standard deviation of the field values
Sum	Total of the field values
Var	Variance of the field values

Figure 5-20 shows two query recordsets—the top recordset (qryCustomersAndInvoices) is from a select query and the bottom recordset (qryCitiesAndInvoicesCrosstab) is from a crosstab query based on the select query.

Figure 5-20	Comparing a select query to a crosstab query

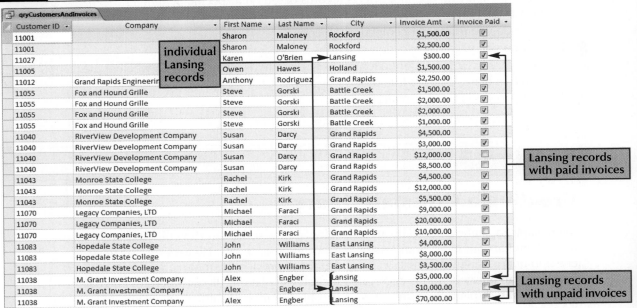

Comparing a select query to a crosstab query (continued) Figure 5-20

qryCitiesAndInvoicesCrosstab

City	Total Of InvoiceAmt	Paid	Unpaid
Battle Creek	$272,250.00	$10,250.00	$262,000.00
East Grand Rapids	$141,500.00	$6,500.00	$135,000.00
East Lansing	$34,500.00	$31,500.00	$3,000.00
Grand Haven	$15,750.00	$5,250.00	$10,500.00
Grand Rapids	$416,050.00	$118,250.00	$297,800.00
Holland	$146,050.00	$43,500.00	$102,550.00
Kalamazoo	$371,500.00	$52,000.00	$319,500.00
Lansing	$263,800.00	$62,800.00	$201,000.00
Rockford	$9,000.00	$4,000.00	$5,000.00
Saint Joseph	$34,625.00	$11,125.00	$23,500.00
Saugatuck	$45,500.00	$21,000.00	$24,500.00
South Haven	$13,050.00	$7,050.00	$6,000.00

paid invoices

unpaid invoices

one row for Lansing invoice amounts

The qryCustomersAndInvoices query, a select query, joins the tblCustomer, tblContract, and tblInvoice tables to display selected data from those tables for all invoices. The qryCitiesAndInvoicesCrosstab query, a crosstab query, uses the qryCustomersAndInvoices query as its source query and displays one row for each unique City field value. The City column in the crosstab query identifies each row. The crosstab query uses the Sum aggregate function on the InvoiceAmt field to produce the displayed values in the Paid and Unpaid columns for each City row. An entry in the Total Of InvoiceAmt column represents the total of the Paid and Unpaid values for the City field value in that row.

Select Queries versus Crosstab Queries | InSight

A select query displays several records—one for each row selected by the select query—while a crosstab query displays only one summarized record for each unique field value. If you want to analyze the records in a query to see the big picture, you would start with a crosstab query, identify which field values to analyze further, and then look in detail at the select query for specific field values. Both select and crosstab queries serve as valuable tools in tracking and analyzing a company's business, and you should use each type of query in the appropriate situation.

When you create a query in Design view or with a wizard, Access automatically constructs an equivalent SQL statement and saves only the SQL statement version of the query. **SQL (Structured Query Language)** is a standard language used in querying, updating, and managing relational databases. If you learn SQL for one relational DBMS, it's a relatively easy task to begin using SQL for other relational DBMSs. However, differences exist between DBMSs in their versions of SQL, somewhat like having different dialects in English, and in what additions they make to SQL. The SQL statement equivalent that Access creates for a crosstab query is one such SQL-language addition. If you need to convert an Access database to SQL-Server, Oracle, or another DBMS, you should know that your crosstab queries most likely will not work in these other databases.

Tip

Microsoft Office Access Help provides more information on creating a crosstab query without using a wizard.

The quickest way to create a crosstab query is to use the **Crosstab Query Wizard**, which guides you through the steps for creating one. You could also change a select query to a crosstab query in Design view using the Crosstab button in the Query Type group on the Query Tools Design tab.

Reference Window | **Using the Crosstab Query Wizard**

- In the Other group on the Create tab, click the Query Wizard button.
- In the New Query dialog box, click Crosstab Query Wizard, and then click the OK button.
- Complete the Wizard dialog boxes to select the table or query on which to base the crosstab query, select the row heading field (or fields), select the column heading field, select the calculation field and its aggregate function, and enter a name for the crosstab query.

The crosstab query you will create, which is similar to the one shown in Figure 5-20, has the following characteristics:

- The qryCustomersAndInvoices query in the Panorama database is the basis for the new crosstab query. The base query includes the CustomerID, Company, FirstName, LastName, City, InvoiceAmt, and InvoicePaid fields.
- The City field is the leftmost column in the crosstab query and identifies each crosstab query row.
- The values from the InvoicePaid field, which is a Yes/No field, identify the rightmost columns of the crosstab query.
- The crosstab query applies the Sum aggregate function to the InvoiceAmt field values and displays the resulting total values in the Paid and Unpaid columns of the query results.
- The grand total of the InvoiceAmt field values appears for each row in a column with the heading Total Of InvoiceAmt.

You are now ready to create the crosstab query for Oren.

To start the Crosstab Query Wizard:

▶ 1. If you took a break after the previous session, make sure that the Panorama database is open and the Navigation Pane is closed.

   Trouble? If the Security Warning is displayed below the Ribbon, click the Options button next to the Security Warning. In the dialog box that opens, click the "Enable this content" option button, and then click the OK button.

▶ 2. Click the **Create** tab on the Ribbon and then, in the Other group on the Create tab, click the **Query Wizard** button. The New Query dialog box opens.

▶ 3. Click **Crosstab Query Wizard**, and then click the **OK** button. The first Crosstab Query Wizard dialog box opens.

You'll now use the Crosstab Query Wizard to create the crosstab query for Oren.

To finish the Crosstab Query Wizard:

▶ 1. Click the **Queries** option button in the View section to display the list of queries in the Panorama database, and then click **Query: qryCustomersAndInvoices**. See Figure 5-21.

Choosing the query for the crosstab query

Figure 5-21

▶ **2.** Click the **Next** button to open the next Crosstab Query Wizard dialog box, in which you choose the field (or fields) for the row headings. Because Oren wants the crosstab query to display one row for each unique City field value, you will select that field for the row headings.

▶ **3.** In the Available Fields list box, click **City**, and then click the ⟩ button to move the City field to the Selected Fields list box.

▶ **4.** Click the **Next** button to open the next Crosstab Query Wizard dialog box, in which you select the field values that will serve as column headings. Oren wants to see the paid and unpaid total invoice amounts, so you need to select the InvoicePaid field for the column headings.

▶ **5.** Click **InvoicePaid** in the list box, and then click the **Next** button.

In the Crosstab Query Wizard dialog box that appears next, you choose the field that will be calculated for each row and column intersection and the function to use for the calculation. The results of the calculation will appear in the row and column intersections in the query results. Oren needs to calculate the sum of the InvoiceAmt field value for each row and column intersection.

▶ **6.** Click **InvoiceAmt** in the Fields list box, click **Sum** in the Functions list box, and then make sure that the **Yes, include row sums** check box is checked. The "Yes, include row sums" option creates a column showing the overall totals for the values in each row of the query recordset. See Figure 5-22.

Tip

When you select a field, Access changes the sample crosstab query in the dialog box to illustrate your choice.

Figure 5-22 ▶ **Completed crosstab query design**

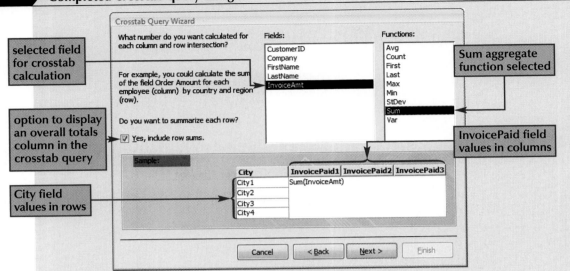

7. Click the **Next** button to open the final Crosstab Query Wizard dialog box, in which you choose the query name.

8. Click in the text box, delete the underscore character so that the query name is qryCustomersAndInvoicesCrosstab, be sure the option button for viewing the query is selected, and then click the **Finish** button. Access saves the crosstab query, and then displays the query recordset.

9. Resize all the columns in the query recordset to their best fit, and then click the City field value in the first row (**Battle Creek**). See Figure 5-23.

Figure 5-23 ▶ **Crosstab query recordset**

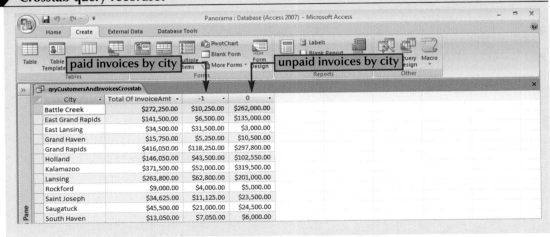

The query recordset contains one row for each City field value. The Total Of InvoiceAmt column shows the total invoice amount for the customers in each city. The columns labeled -1 and 0 show the total paid (-1 column) and unpaid (0 column) invoice amounts for customers in each city. Because the InvoicePaid field is a Yes/No field, by default, Access displays field values in datasheets, forms, and reports in a check box (either checked or unchecked), but stores a checked value in the database as a -1 and an unchecked value as a zero. Instead of displaying check boxes, the crosstab query displays the stored values as column headings.

Oren wants you to change the column headings of -1 to Paid and of zero to Unpaid. You'll use the IIf function to change the column headings, using the expression *IIf (InvoicePaid,"Paid","Unpaid")*—if the InvoicePaid field value is true (because it's a Yes/No field or a True/False field), or is checked, use Paid as the column heading; otherwise, use Unpaid as the column heading.

Tip

Because the InvoicePaid field is a Yes/No field, the condition *InvoicePaid* is the same as the condition *InvoicePaid = −1*, which uses a comparison operator and a value. For all data types except Yes/No fields, you must use a comparison operator in a condition.

To change the crosstab query column headings:

▶ 1. Click the **Home** tab on the Ribbon, and then switch to Design view. The design grid has four entries. See Figure 5-24.

Crosstab query in the design grid ◀ Figure 5-24

From left to right, the City entry produces the row headings in the crosstab query, the InvoicePaid entry produces the column headings, the InvoiceAmt entry produces the totals in each row/column intersection, and the Total Of InvoiceAmt entry produces the row total column heading and total values. Each field name is enclosed in brackets.

You need to replace the Field text box value in the second column with the IIf function expression to change the -1 and zero column headings to Paid and Unpaid. You can type the expression directly in the text box, use Expression Builder to create the expression, or type the expression in the Zoom dialog box. You'll use the last method.

▶ 2. Click the **InvoicePaid Field** text box, and then open the Zoom dialog box.

▶ 3. Delete the highlighted expression, and then type **IIf (InvoicePaid,"Paid", "Unpaid")** in the Zoom dialog box. See Figure 5-25.

IIf function for the crosstab query column headings ◀ Figure 5-25

▶ 4. Click the **OK** button, and then save and run the query. Access displays the complete crosstab query with Paid and Unpaid as column headings.

You can now close the completed query.

▶ 5. Close the query, and then open the Navigation Pane.

In the Navigation Pane, Access displays objects alphabetically by object type with tables appearing first and then queries, forms, and reports. Access displays some types of queries separately from select queries; for example, crosstab queries appear before select queries. Access uses unique icons to represent different types of queries. The crosstab query icon appears in the Queries list to the left of the qryCustomersAndInvoicesCrosstab query. This icon looks different from the icon that appears to the left of the other queries, which are all select queries.

Next, Oren wants to identify any contracts that have the same start dates as other contracts, because these are the ones that might have potential scheduling difficulties. To find the information Oren needs, you'll create a find duplicates query.

Creating a Find Duplicates Query

A **find duplicates query** is a select query that finds duplicate records in a table or query. You can create this type of query using the **Find Duplicates Query Wizard**. A find duplicates query searches for duplicate values based on the fields you select as you answer the Wizard's questions. For example, you might want to display all employers that have the same name, all students who have the same phone number, or all products that have the same description. Using this type of query, you can locate duplicates to avert potential problems (for example, you might have inadvertently assigned two different numbers to the same product), or you can eliminate duplicates that cost money (for example, you could send just one advertising brochure to all customers having the same address).

You can meet Oren's request by using the Find Duplicates Query Wizard to display records for contracts that have the same start dates in the tblContract table.

Reference Window | **Using the Find Duplicates Query Wizard**

- In the Other group on the Create tab, click the Query Wizard button.
- Click Find Duplicates Query Wizard, and then click the OK button.
- Complete the Wizard dialog boxes to select the table or query on which to base the query, select the field (or fields) to check for duplicate values, select the additional fields to include in the query results, enter a name for the query, and then click the Finish button.

You'll use the Find Duplicates Query Wizard to create and run a new query to display duplicate start dates in the tblContract table.

To create the query using the Find Duplicates Query Wizard:

▶ 1. Close the Navigation Pane, click the **Create** tab on the Ribbon and then, in the Other group on the Create tab, click the **Query Wizard** button to open the New Query dialog box.

▶ 2. Click **Find Duplicates Query Wizard**, and then click the **OK** button. The first Find Duplicates Query Wizard dialog box opens. In this dialog box, you select the table or query on which to base the new query. You'll use the tblContract table.

▶ 3. Click **Table: tblContract** (if necessary), and then click the **Next** button. Access opens the next Find Duplicates Query Wizard dialog box, in which you choose the fields you want to check for duplicate values.

4. In the Available fields list box, click **StartDate**, click the ⟨ > ⟩ button to select the StartDate field as the field to check for duplicate values, and then click the **Next** button. In the next Find Duplicates Query Wizard dialog box, you select the additional fields you want displayed in the query results.

Oren wants all remaining fields to be included in the query results.

5. Click the ⟨ >> ⟩ button to move all fields from the Available fields list box to the Additional query fields list box, and then click the **Next** button. Access opens the final Find Duplicates Query Wizard dialog box, in which you enter a name for the query. You'll use qryDuplicateContractStartDates as the query name.

6. Type **qryDuplicateContractStartDates** in the text box, be sure the option button for viewing the results is selected, and then click the **Finish** button. Access saves the query, and then displays the 10 records for contracts with duplicate start dates. See Figure 5-26.

Query recordset for contracts with the same start dates ◄ Figure 5-26

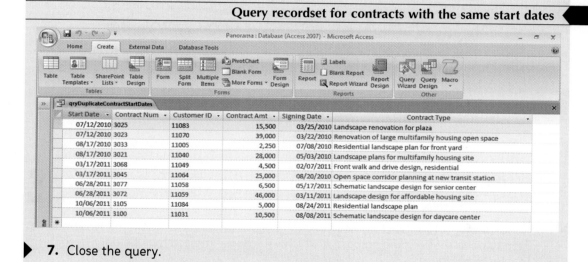

7. Close the query.

Oren now asks you to find the records for customers with no contracts. These are customers who had contracts in the past, but who have chosen not to sign a contract with Belmont Landscapes in the past year. Oren wants to contact these customers to see if there are any services that the company might be able to furnish. To provide Oren with this information, you need to create a find unmatched query.

Creating a Find Unmatched Query

A **find unmatched query** is a select query that finds all records in a table or query that have no related records in a second table or query. For example, you could display all customers who have not signed recent contracts or all students who are not currently enrolled in classes. Such a query provides information for Oren to solicit business from the inactive customers and for a school administrator to contact the students to find out their future educational plans. You can use the **Find Unmatched Query Wizard** to create this type of query.

Reference Window | **Using the Find Unmatched Query Wizard**

- In the Other group on the Create tab, click the Query Wizard button.
- Click Find Unmatched Query Wizard, and then click the OK button.
- Complete the Wizard dialog boxes to select the table or query on which to base the new query, select the table or query that contains the related records, specify the common field in each table or query, select the additional fields to include in the query results, enter a name for the query, and then click the Finish button.

Oren wants to know which customers have no open contracts. These customers are inactive, and he will contact them to determine their interest in doing further business with Belmont Landscapes. To create a list of inactive customers, you'll use the Find Unmatched Query Wizard to display only those records from the tblCustomer table with no matching CustomerID field value in the tblContract table.

To create the query using the Find Unmatched Query Wizard:

▶ 1. In the Other group on the Create tab, click the **Query Wizard** button to open the New Query dialog box.

▶ 2. Click **Find Unmatched Query Wizard**, and then click the **OK** button. The first Find Unmatched Query Wizard dialog box opens. In this dialog box, you select the table or query on which to base the new query. You'll use the qryCustomersByName query.

▶ 3. Click the **Queries** option button in the View section to display the list of queries, click **Query: qryCustomersByName** in the list box to select this query, and then click the **Next** button to open the next Find Unmatched Query Wizard dialog box, in which you choose the table that contains the related records. You'll select the tblContract table.

▶ 4. Click **Table: tblContract** in the list box (if necessary), and then click the **Next** button to open the next dialog box, in which you choose the common field for both tables. See Figure 5-27.

Figure 5-27 ▶ **Selecting the common field**

Tip

If the two objects you selected for the find unmatched query have a one-to-many relationship defined in the Relationships window, the Matching fields box will join the two correct fields automatically.

The common field between the query and the table is the CustomerID field. You need to click the common field in each list box, and then click the symbol between the two list boxes to join the two objects. The Matching fields box then will display CustomerID <=> CustomerID to indicate the joining of the two matching fields.

▶ **5.** Click **CustomerID** in the Fields in 'qryCustomersByName' list box, click **CustomerID** in the Fields in 'tblContract' list box, click the ⟨=⟩ button to connect the two selected fields, and then click the **Next** button to open the next Find Unmatched Query Wizard dialog box, in which you choose the fields you want to see in the query recordset. Oren wants the query recordset to display all available fields.

▶ **6.** Click the ⟩⟩ button to to move all fields from the Available fields list box to the Selected fields list box, and then click the **Next** button to open the final dialog box, in which you enter the query name.

▶ **7.** Type **qryInactiveCustomers**, be sure the option button for viewing the results is selected, and then click the **Finish** button. Access saves the query and then displays two records in the query recordset. See Figure 5-28.

Query recordset displaying customers without contracts ◀ **Figure 5-28**

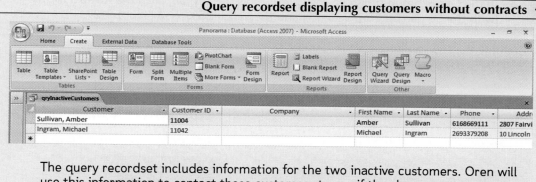

The query recordset includes information for the two inactive customers. Oren will use this information to contact these customers to see if they have any current or future landscaping needs.

▶ **8.** Close the query.

Next, Oren wants Taylor to contact those customers who have the highest contract amounts to make sure that Belmont Landscapes is providing satisfactory service. To display the information Taylor needs, you will create a top values query.

Creating a Top Values Query

Whenever a query displays a large group of records, you might want to limit the number to a more manageable size by displaying, for example, just the first 10 records. The **Top Values property** for a query lets you limit the number of records in the query results. For the Top Values property, you can click one of the preset values from a list, or enter either an integer (such as 15, to display the first 15 records) or a percentage (such as 20%, to display the first fifth of the records) to find a specific number of records.

Suppose you have a select query that displays 45 records. If you want the query recordset to show only the first five records, you can change the query by entering a Top Values property value of either 5 or 10%. If the query contains a sort and the last record that Access can display is one of two or more records with the same value for the primary sort field, Access displays all records with that matching key value.

Creating a Top Values Query | Reference Window

- Create a select query with the necessary fields and sorting and selection criteria.
- In the Query Setup group on the Query Tools Design tab, enter the number of records (or percentage of records) you want selected in the Return (Top Values) text box.

Taylor wants to view the same data that appears in the qryLargeContractAmounts query for customers with the highest 25% contract amounts. You will modify the query and then use the Top Values property to produce this information for Taylor.

Tip

Based on the number or percentage you enter, a top values query selects that number or percentage of records starting from the top of the recordset. Thus, you usually include a sort in a top values query to display the records with the highest or lowest values for the sorted field.

To set the Top Values property for the query:

1. Open the Navigation Pane, open the **qryLargeContractAmounts** in Datasheet view, and then close the Navigation Pane. Access displays 22 records, all with ContractAmt field values greater than $25,000, sorted in descending order by the ContractAmt field.

2. Click the **Home** tab, and then switch to Design view.

3. In the Query Setup group on the Query Tools Design tab, click the **Return** arrow (with the ScreenTip "Top Values"), and then click **25%**. See Figure 5-29.

Figure 5-29	Creating the top values query

If the number or percentage of records you want to select, such as 15 or 20%, doesn't appear in the Top Values list, you can type the number or percentage in the Return text box.

4. Run the query. Access displays six records in the query recordset; these records represent the customers with the highest 25% contract amounts (25% of the original 22 records). See Figure 5-30.

Figure 5-30	Top values query recordset

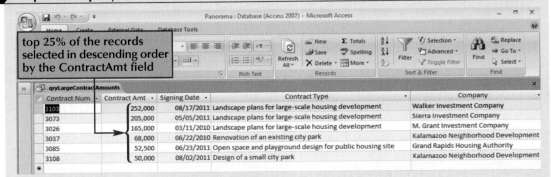

Because Taylor won't need to run this query again, you won't save it.

5. Close the query without saving it.

6. If you are not continuing on to the next session, close the Panorama database, and then exit Access, clicking the **Yes** button if you are prompted to confirm that you want to exit Access and to empty the Clipboard.

Oren and Taylor will use the information provided by the queries you created to analyze the business and to contact customers. In the next session, you will enhance the tblCustomer and tblContract tables.

Session 5.2 Quick Check | Review

1. What is the purpose of a crosstab query?
2. What are the four query wizards you can use to create a new query?
3. What is a find duplicates query?
4. What does a find unmatched query do?
5. What happens when you set a query's Top Values property?
6. What happens if you set a query's Top Values property to 2 and the first five records have the same value for the primary sort field?

Session 5.3

Creating a Lookup Field

The tblContract table in the Panorama database contains information about the contracts Belmont Landscapes has signed with its customers. Sarah wants to make entering data in the table easier for her staff. In particular, data entry is easier if they do not need to remember the correct CustomerID field values for each customer. Because the tblCustomer and tblContract tables have a one-to-many relationship, Sarah asks you to change the tblContract table's CustomerID field, which is a foreign key to the tblCustomer table, to a lookup field. A **lookup field** lets the user select a value from a list of possible values. For the CustomerID field, the user will be able to select a customer's ID number from the list of customer names in the qryCustomersByName query rather than having to remember the correct CustomerID field value. Access will store the CustomerID in the tblContract table, but both the customer name and the CustomerID field value will appear in Datasheet view when entering or changing a CustomerID field value. This arrangement makes entering and changing CustomerID field values easier for the user and guarantees that the CustomerID field value is valid. You use a **Lookup Wizard field** in Access to create a lookup field in a table.

Sarah asks you to change the CustomerID field in the tblContract table to a lookup field. You begin by opening the Panorama database and then opening the tblContract table in Design view.

To change the CustomerID field to a lookup field:

▶ 1. If you took a break after the previous session, make sure that the Panorama database is open.

   Trouble? If the Security Warning is displayed below the Ribbon, click the Options button next to the Security Warning. In the dialog box that opens, click the "Enable this content" option button, and then click the OK button.

▶ 2. If necessary, open the Navigation Pane, and then open the **tblContract** table in Design view.

3. Click the right side of the **Data Type** text box for the CustomerID field to display the list of data types, and then click **Lookup Wizard**. A message box appears, warning you to delete the relationship between the tblCustomer and tblContract tables if you want to make the CustomerID field a lookup field. See Figure 5-31.

| Figure 5-31 | | **Warning message for an existing table relationship** |

Access will use the lookup field to form the one-to-many relationship between the tblCustomer and tblContract tables, so you don't need the relationship you previously defined between the two tables.

4. Click the **OK** button, close the tblContract table, and then click the **No** button when asked if you want to save the table design changes.

5. Click the **Database Tools** tab on the Ribbon, and then, in the Show/Hide group on the Database Tools tab, click the **Relationships** button to open the Relationships window.

6. Right-click the join line between the tblCustomer and tblContract tables, click **Delete**, and then click the **Yes** button to confirm the deletion.

   Trouble? If the Delete command does not appear on the shortcut menu, click a blank area in the Relationships window to close the shortcut menu, and then repeat Step 6.

7. Close the Relationships window.

Now you can resume changing the CustomerID field to a lookup field.

To finish changing the CustomerID field to a lookup field:

1. Open the **tblContract** table in Design view.

2. Click the right side of the **Data Type** text box for the CustomerID field, and then click **Lookup Wizard**. The first Lookup Wizard dialog box opens.

   This dialog box lets you specify a list of allowed values for the CustomerID field in a record in the tblContract table. You can specify a table or query from which users select the value, or you can enter a new list of values. You want the CustomerID values to come from the qryCustomersByName query.

3. Make sure the option for looking up the values in a table or query is selected, and then click the **Next** button to display the next Lookup Wizard dialog box.

4. Click the **Queries** option button in the View section to display the list of queries, click **Query: qryCustomersByName**, and then click the **Next** button to display the next Lookup Wizard dialog box. See Figure 5-32.

This dialog box lets you select the lookup fields from the qryCustomersByName query. You need to select the CustomerID field because it's the common field that links the query and the tblContract table. You also must select the Customer field because Sarah wants the user to be able to select from a list of customer names when entering a new contract record or changing an existing CustomerID field value.

▶ **5.** Click **Customer** (if necessary), click the ⟩ button to move the Customer field to the Selected Fields list box, click **CustomerID** (if necessary), click the ⟩ button to move the CustomerID field to the Selected Fields list box, and then click the **Next** button to display the next Lookup Wizard dialog box. This dialog box lets you choose a sort order for the list box entries. Sarah wants the entries to appear in ascending Customer order. Note that ascending is the default sort order.

▶ **6.** Click the **1** arrow, click **Customer**, and then click the **Next** button to open the next dialog box.

In this dialog box, you can adjust the widths of the lookup columns. Note that when you resize a column to its best fit, Access resizes the column so that the widest column heading and the visible field values fit the column width. However, some field values that aren't visible in this dialog box might be wider than the column width, so you must scroll down the column to make sure you don't have to repeat the column resizing.

▶ **7.** Click the **Customer** column selector, press and hold down the **Shift** key, click the **CustomerID** column selector to select both columns, release the **Shift** key, and then place the pointer on the right edge of the CustomerID field column heading. When the pointer changes to a ↔ shape, double-click to resize the columns to their best fits, and then scroll down the columns, and repeat the resizing as necessary. When you are finished, press **Ctrl + Home** to scroll back to the top of the Customer column. See Figure 5-33.

Figure 5-33 | **Adjusting the widths of lookup columns**

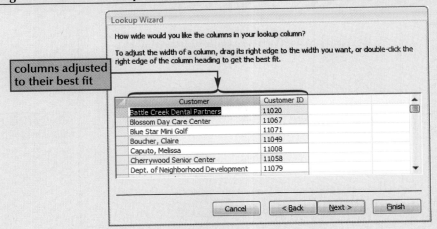

columns adjusted to their best fit

8. Click the **Next** button.

   In the dialog box that appears next, you select the field you want to store in the table. You'll store the CustomerID field in the tblContract table, because it's the foreign key to the tblCustomer table.

9. Click **CustomerID** in the Available Fields list box, and then click the **Next** button.

   In the dialog box that appears next, you specify the field name for the lookup field. Because you'll be storing the CustomerID field in the table, you'll accept the default field name, CustomerID.

10. Click the **Finish** button, and then save the table.

   The Data Type value for the CustomerID field is still Text because this field contains text data. However, when you update the field, Access uses the CustomerID field value to look up and display in the tblContract table datasheet both the Customer and CustomerID field values from the qryCustomersByName query.

In reviewing contracts recently, Sarah noticed that the CustomerID field value stored in the tblContract table for contract number 3030 is incorrect. She asks you to test the new lookup field to select the correct code. To do so, you need to switch to Datasheet view.

To change the CustomerID field value:

1. Switch to Datasheet view, and then resize the **CustomerID** column to its best fit.

   Notice that the Customer ID column displays Customer field values, even though it's the CustomerID field values that are stored in the table.

2. For Contract Num 3030, click **Lily's Boutique** in the Customer ID column, and then click the **arrow** to display the list of Customer and CustomerID field values from the qryCustomersByName query. See Figure 5-34.

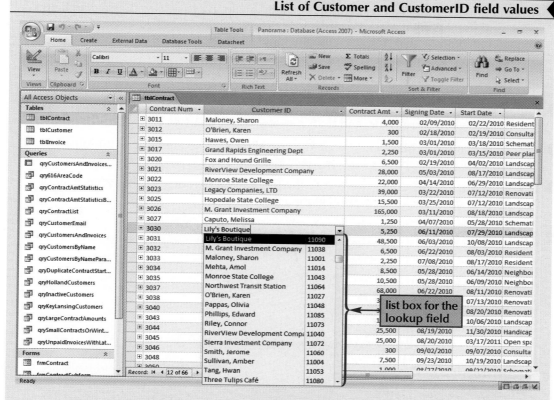

List of Customer and CustomerID field values | Figure 5-34

The customer for contract 3030 is Michael Ingram, so you need to select his entry in the list box to change the CustomerID field value.

▶ **3.** Scroll up the list box, and then click **Ingram, Michael** to select that value to display in the datasheet and to store the CustomerID field value of 11042 in the table. The list box closes and "Ingram, Michael" appears in the Customer ID text box.

▶ **4.** Save and close the tblContract table.

Sarah wants you to make changes to the design of the tblCustomer table, so you'll open the table in preparation for the changes.

▶ **5.** Open the **tblCustomer** table in Datasheet view, and then close the Navigation Pane.

Sarah asks you to change the appearance of the Phone field in the tblCustomer table to a standard telephone number format.

Using the Input Mask Wizard

The Phone field in the tblCustomer table is a 10-digit number that's difficult to read because it appears with none of the special formatting characters usually associated with a telephone number. For example, the Phone field value for Sharon Maloney, which appears as 6168663901, would be more readable in any of the following formats: 616-866-3901, 616.866.3901, 616/866-3901, or (616) 866-3901. Sarah asks you to use the (616) 866-3901 style for the Phone field.

Sarah wants the parentheses and hyphens to appear as literal display characters whenever users enter Phone field values. A **literal display character** is a special character that automatically appears in specific positions of a field value; users don't need to type literal display characters. To include these characters, you need to create an **input mask**, a pre-defined format used to enter and display data in a field. An easy way to create an input mask is to use the **Input Mask Wizard**, an Access tool that guides you in creating a pre-defined format for a field. You must use the Input Mask Wizard in Design view.

To use the Input Mask Wizard for the Phone field:

▶ **1.** Switch to Design view, and then click the **Phone Field Name** text box to make that row the current row and to display its Field Properties options.

▶ **2.** Click the **Input Mask** text box in the Field Properties pane. A Build button ⋯ appears to the right of the Input Mask text box.

▶ **3.** Click the **Build** button ⋯ next to the Input Mask text box. The first Input Mask Wizard dialog box opens. See Figure 5-35.

Figure 5-35 ▶ **Input Mask Wizard dialog box**

You can scroll the Input Mask list box, select the input mask you want, and then enter representative values to practice using the input mask.

▶ **4.** If necessary, click **Phone Number** in the Input Mask list box to select it.

▶ **5.** Click the far left side of the **Try It** text box. (__) ___-____ appears in the Try It text box. As you type a phone number, Access replaces the underscores, which are placeholder characters.

   Trouble? If your insertion point is not immediately to the right of the left parenthesis, press the ← key until it is.

▶ **6.** Type **9876543210** to practice entering a sample phone number. The input mask formats the typed value as (987) 654-3210.

▶ **7.** Click the **Next** button. The next Input Mask Wizard dialog box opens. In it, you can change the input mask and placeholder character. Because you can change an input mask easily after the Input Mask Wizard finishes, you'll accept all wizard defaults.

▶ **8.** Click the **Finish** button. The Input Mask Wizard creates the phone number input mask, placing it in the Input Mask text box for the Phone field. See Figure 5-36.

Phone number input mask created by the Input Mask Wizard ◄ **Figure 5-36**

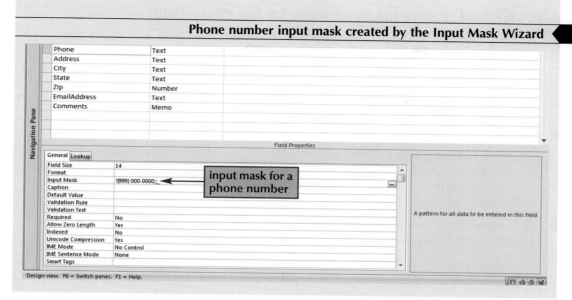

The characters used in a field's input mask restrict the data you can enter in the field, as shown in Figure 5-37. Other characters, such as the left and right parenthesis in the phone number input mask, that appear in an input mask are literal display characters.

Input mask characters ◄ **Figure 5-37**

Input Mask Character	Description
0	Digit only must be entered. Entry is required.
9	Digit or space can be entered. Entry is optional.
#	Digit, space, or a plus or minus sign can be entered. Entry is optional.
L	Letter only must be entered. Entry is required.
?	Letter only can be entered. Entry is optional.
A	Letter or digit must be entered. Entry is required.
a	Letter or digit can be entered. Entry is optional.
&	Any character or a space must be entered. Entry is required.
C	Any character or a space can be entered. Entry is optional.
>	All characters that follow are displayed in uppercase.
<	All characters that follow are displayed in lowercase.
"	Enclosed characters treated as literal display characters.
\	Following character treated as a literal display character. This is the same as enclosing a single character in quotation marks.
!	Input mask is displayed from right to left, rather than the default of left to right. Characters typed into the mask always fill in from left to right.
;;	The character between the first and second semicolon determines whether to store in the database the literal display characters. If left blank or a value of 1, do not store the literal display characters. If a value of 0, store the literal display characters. The character following the second semicolon is the placeholder character that will appear in the displayed input mask.

Sarah wants to view the Phone field with the default input mask before you change it for her.

To view and change the input mask for the Phone field:

▶ **1.** Save the table, and then switch to Datasheet view. The Phone field values now have the format specified by the input mask.

Sarah decides that she would prefer to omit the parentheses around the area codes and use only hyphens as separators in the displayed Phone field values, so you'll change the input mask in Design view.

▶ **2.** Switch to Design view.

The input mask changed from !(999) 000-0000;;_ to !\(999") "000\-0000;;_. The backslash character (\) causes the character that follows it to appear as a literal display character. Characters enclosed in quotation marks also appear as literal display characters. (See Figure 5-37.)

Tip

If you omit the backslashes preceding the hyphens, Access will automatically insert them when you press the Tab key. However, Access doesn't add backslashes automatically for other literal display characters, such as periods and slashes, so it's best to always include the backslashes.

▶ **3.** Change the input mask to **999\-000\-0000;;_** in the Input Mask text box for the Phone field, and then press the **Tab** key.

Because you've modified a field property, the Property Update Options button appears to the left of the Input Mask property.

▶ **4.** Click the **Property Update Options** button, and then click **Update Input Mask everywhere Phone is used**. The Update Properties dialog box opens. See Figure 5-38.

Figure 5-38   **Update Properties dialog box**

objects dependent on the Phone field

Because the frmCustomer and frmCustomerContracts forms display Phone field values from the tblCustomer table, Access will automatically change the Phone field's Input Mask property in these objects to your new input mask. This capability to update field properties in objects automatically when you modify a table field property is called **property propagation**. Although the Update Properties dialog box displays no queries, property propagation also does occur with queries automatically. Property propagation is limited to field properties such as the Decimal Places, Description, Format, and Input Mask properties.

▶ **5.** Click the **Yes** button, save the table, and then switch to Datasheet view. The Phone field values now have the format Sarah requested. See Figure 5-39.

Figure 5-39   **After changing the Phone field input mask**

Because Sarah wants her staff to store only standard 10-digit U.S. phone numbers for customers, the input mask you've created will enforce the standard entry and display format that Sarah desires.

Understanding When to Use Input Masks		InSight

An input mask is appropriate for a field only if all field values have a consistent format. For example, you can use an input mask with hyphens as literal display characters to store U.S. phone numbers in a consistent format of 987-654-3210. However, a multinational company would not be able to use an input mask to store phone numbers from all countries, because international phone numbers do not have a consistent format. For another example, U.S. zip codes have a consistent format, and you could use an input mask of 00000#9999 to enter and display U.S. zip codes such as 98765 and 98765-4321, but you could not use an input mask if you need to store and display foreign postal codes in the same field. If you need to store and display phone numbers, zip/postal codes, and other fields in a variety of formats, it's best to define them as Text fields without an input mask and let users enter field values and the literal display characters.

After the change to the Phone field's input mask, Access gave you the option to update, selectively and automatically, the Phone field's Input Mask property in other objects in the database. Sarah asks if there's an easy way to determine which objects are affected by changes made to other objects. To show Sarah how to determine the dependencies among objects in an Access database, you'll open the Object Dependencies pane.

Identifying Object Dependencies

An **object dependency** exists between two objects when a change to the properties of data in one object affects the properties of data in the other object. Dependencies between Access objects (tables, queries, forms, and so on) can occur in various ways. For example, the tblContract and tblInvoice tables are dependent on each other because they have a one-to-many relationship. As another example, because the tblContract table uses the qryCustomersByName query to obtain the Customer field to display along with the CustomerID field, these two tables have a dependency. Any query, form, or other object that uses fields from the tblCustomer table is dependent on the tblCustomer table. Any form or report that uses fields from a query is directly dependent on the query and is indirectly dependent on the tables that provide the data to the query. Large databases contain hundreds of objects, so it would be useful to have a way to view the dependencies among objects easily before you attempt to delete or modify an object. The **Object Dependencies pane** displays a collapsible list of the dependencies among the objects in an Access database; you click the list's expand indicators to show or hide different levels of dependencies. Next, you'll open the Object Dependencies pane to show Sarah the object dependencies in the Panorama database.

To open and use the Object Dependencies pane:

▶ **1.** Click the **Database Tools** tab on the Ribbon, and then, in the Show/Hide group, click the **Object Dependencies** button to open the Object Dependencies pane, and then drag the left edge of the pane to the left until the horizontal scroll bar at the bottom of the pane disappears. See Figure 5-40.

Figure 5-40 | **After opening the Object Dependencies pane**

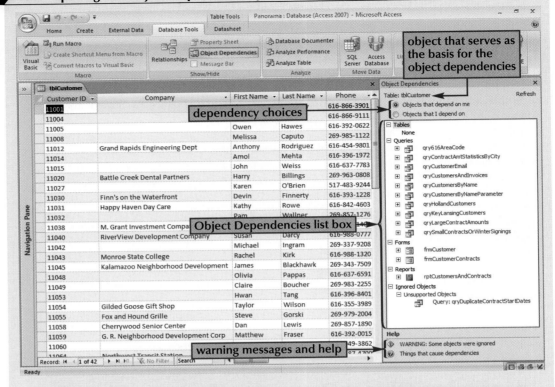

Trouble? If the "Objects that depend on me" option button is not selected, click the option button to select it.

The Object Dependencies list box displays the objects that depend on the tblCustomer table, the object name that appears at the top of the pane. If you change the design of the tblCustomer table, the change might affect objects in the list box. Changing a property for a field in the tblCustomer table that's also used by another listed object affects that other object. If the other object does not use the field you are changing, that other object is not affected.

Objects listed in the Ignored Objects portion of the pane might, or might not, have an object dependency with the tblCustomer table, and you'd have to review them yourself. The Help section at the bottom of the pane displays links for further information about object dependencies.

▶ 2. Click the **frmCustomer** link in the Object Dependencies pane. The frmCustomer form opens in Design view. All the fields in the form are fields from the tblCustomer table, which is why the form has an object dependency with the table.

▶ 3. Switch to Form view for the frmCustomer form. Note that the Phone field values are displayed using the input mask you applied to the field in the tblCustomer table. This change propagated from the table to the form.

▶ 4. Close the frmCustomer form, open the **tblContract** table in Datasheet view, and then click the **Refresh** link near the top of the Object Dependencies pane. The Object Dependencies list box now displays the objects that depend on the tblContract table.

▶ 5. Click the **Objects that I depend on** option button near the top of the pane to view the objects that affect the tblContract table.

> **6.** Click the **expand indicator** ⊞ for the qryCustomersByName query in the Object Dependencies pane. The list expands to display all the tblCustomer table, which is another table that the query depends upon.

> **7.** Close the tblContract table, close the Object Dependencies pane, and then close the Navigation Pane.

Sarah now better understands object dependencies and how to identify them by using the Object Dependencies pane.

Defining Data Validation Rules

Sarah wants to limit the entry of Zip field values in the tblCustomer table to Michigan zip codes because Belmont Landscapes customers are located only in Michigan. In addition, Sarah wants to make sure that a SigningDate field value entered in a tblContract table record is chronologically earlier than the StartDate field value in the same record. She's concerned that typing errors might produce incorrect query results and cause other problems. To provide these data-entry capabilities, you'll set field validation properties for the Zip field in the tblCustomer table and set table validation properties in the tblContract table.

Defining Field Validation Rules

To prevent a user from entering an incorrect value in the Zip field, you can create a **field validation rule** that verifies a field value by comparing it to a constant or a set of constants. You create a field validation rule by setting the Validation Rule and the Validation Text field properties. The **Validation Rule property** value specifies the valid values that users can enter in a field. The **Validation Text property** value will be displayed in a dialog box if the user enters an invalid value (in this case, a value other than a Michigan zip code). After you set these two Zip field properties in the tblCustomer table, Access will prevent users from entering an invalid Zip field value in the tblCustomer table and in all current and future queries and forms that include the Zip field.

You'll now set the Validation Rule and Validation Text properties for the Zip field in the tblCustomer table. Michigan zip codes must be between 48000 and 49999.

To create and test a field validation rule for the Zip field:

> **1.** Switch to Design view for the tblCustomer table, and then click the **Zip Field Name** text box to make that row the current row.

> To make sure that the only values entered in the Zip field are between 48000 and 49999, you'll specify a range of valid values in the Validation Rule text box. The Zip field is a Number field, so you can use this numeric range test.

> **2.** In the Field Properties pane, click the **Validation Rule** text box, type **>=48000 And <=49999**, and then press the **Tab** key.

> Instead of using the range of values test, you could also use the equivalent *Between 48000 And 49999*.

> You can set the Validation Text property to a value that appears in a dialog box that opens if a user enters a value not listed in the Validation Rule text box.

> **3.** Type **Michigan zip codes must be between 48000 and 49999** in the Validation Text text box. See Figure 5-41.

Tip

Using the numeric range test with a Text field isn't allowed; you'll get an error message. Also, enclosing the numbers in quotation marks for a Text field range test will eliminate the error message but will yield unpredictable results.

Figure 5-41 **Validation properties for the Zip field**

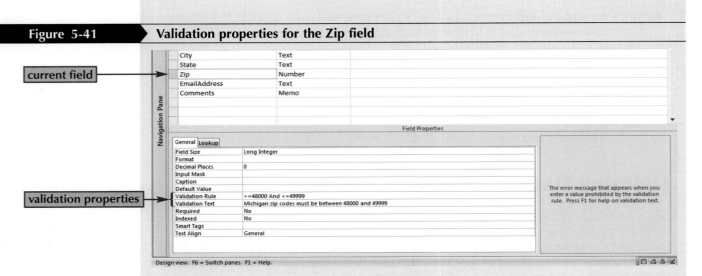

current field

validation properties

> The error message that appears when you enter a value prohibited by the validation rule. Press F1 for help on validation text.

Design view. F6 = Switch panes. F1 = Help.

You can now save the table design changes and then test the validation properties.

▶ **4.** Save the table, and then click the **Yes** button when asked if you want to test the existing Zip field values in the tblCustomer table against the new validation rule.

Access tests the existing records in the tblCustomer table against the validation rule. If any record violates the rule, you are prompted to continue testing or to revert to the previous Validation Rule property setting. Next, you'll test the validation rule.

▶ **5.** Switch to Datasheet view, and then scroll the table to the right until the Zip field is visible.

▶ **6.** Double-click **49341** in the first row's Zip field text box, type **54321**, and then press the **Tab** key. A dialog box opens containing the message "Michigan zip codes must be between 48000 and 49999," which is the Validation Text property setting you created in Step 3.

▶ **7.** Click the **OK** button, and then press the **Esc** key. The first row's Zip field value again has its original value, 49341.

▶ **8.** Close the tblCustomer table.

Now that you've finished entering the field validation rule for the Zip field in the tblCustomer table, you'll enter the table validation rule for the date fields in the tblContract table.

Defining Table Validation Rules

To make sure that a user enters a SigningDate field value in the tblContract table that is chronologically earlier than the record's StartDate field value, you can create a **table validation rule** that compares one field value in a table record to another field value in the same record to verify their relative accuracy. Once again, you'll use the Validation Rule and Validation Text properties, but this time you'll set these properties for the table instead of for an individual field.

You'll now set the Validation Rule and Validation Text properties to compare the SigningDate and StartDate field values in the tblContract table.

To create and test a table validation rule in the tblContract table:

▶ **1.** Open the Navigation Pane, open the **tblContract** table in Design view, and then, in the Show/Hide group on the Table Tools Design tab, click the **Property Sheet** button to open the property sheet for the table.

To make sure that each SigningDate field value is chronologically earlier than, or less than, each StartDate field value, you'll compare the two field values in the Validation Rule text box.

▶ **2.** In the property sheet, click the **Validation Rule** text box, type **[SigningDate]<[StartDate]**, and then press the **Tab** key.

▶ **3.** Type **The signing date must be earlier than the start date** in the Validation Text text box. See Figure 5-42.

Setting table validation properties | **Figure 5-42**

properties for the table

only part of the entered text is displayed

validation properties

You can now test the validation properties.

▶ **4.** Close the property sheet, save the table, and then click the **Yes** button when asked if you want to test the existing dates in the tblContract table against the new validation rule.

▶ **5.** Close the Navigation Pane, switch to Datasheet view, click the Signing Date column value in the first record, click the **date picker** icon to the right of the date, click **27** in the calendar control to change the date to 2/27/2010, press the **Tab** key to advance to the Start Date column, and then press the **Tab** key two more times to complete your changes to the record. A dialog box opens containing the message "The signing date must be earlier than the start date," which is the Validation Text property setting you entered in Step 3.

Unlike field validation rule violations, which Access detects immediately after you finish your field entry and advance to another field, Access detects table validation rule violations when you finish all changes to the current record and advance to another record.

▶ **6.** Click the **OK** button, and then press the **Esc** key to undo your change to the Signing Date column value.

▶ **7.** Close the tblContract table.

Based on a request from Sarah, Lucia added a Memo field to the tblCustomer table, and now you'll review Lucia's work.

Working with Memo Fields

You use a Memo field for long comments and explanations. Text fields are limited to 255 characters, but Memo fields can hold up to 65,535 characters. In addition, Text fields limit you to plain text with no special formatting, but you can define Memo fields either to store plain text similar to Text fields or to store rich text, which you can selectively format with options such as bold, italic, and different fonts and colors.

You'll review the Memo field, named Comments, that Lucia added to the tblCustomer table.

To review the Memo field in the tblCustomer table:

▶ 1. Open the Navigation Pane, open the **tblCustomer** table in Datasheet view, and then close the Navigation Pane.

If you scroll to the right to view the Comments field, you'll no longer be able to identify which customer applies to a row because the Company, First Name, and Last Name columns will be hidden. You'll freeze those three columns so they remain visible in the datasheet as you scroll to the right.

▶ 2. Click the **Company** column selector, press and hold down the **Shift** key, click the **Last Name** column selector, and then release the **Shift** key to select the Company, First Name, and Last Name columns.

▶ 3. In the Records group on the Home tab, click the **More** button, and then click **Freeze**. The three selected columns shift to the left and are now the three leftmost columns in the datasheet.

▶ 4. Scroll to the right until you see the Comments column. Notice that the Company, First Name, and Last Name columns, the three leftmost columns, remain visible. See Figure 5-43.

Figure 5-43 ▶ **Freezing three datasheet columns**

The Comments column is a Memo field that Belmont Landscapes staff members use to store notes, explanations, and other commentary about the customer. Notice that the Comments field value for Battle Creek Dental Partners displays rich text, using a bold, italic, and blue font. The Comments field values are partially hidden because the datasheet column is not wide enough. You'll view the first record's Comments field value in the Zoom dialog box.

▶ **5.** Click the **Comments** text box for the first record, hold down the **Shift** key, press the **F2** key, and then release the **Shift** key. The Zoom dialog box displays the entire Comments field value.

▶ **6.** Click the **OK** button to close the Zoom dialog box.

Table Datasheet Row and Column Resizing for Memo Fields	InSight

For Memo fields that contain many characters, you can widen the column to view more of its contents by dragging the right edge of the field's column selector to the right or by using the Column Width command when you click the More button in the Records group on the Home tab. However, increasing the column width reduces the number of other columns you can view at the same time. Further, for Memo fields containing thousands of characters, you can't widen the column enough to be able to view the entire contents of the field at one time across the width of the screen. Therefore, increasing the column width of a Memo field seldom makes sense.

Alternatively, you can increase the row height of a datasheet by dragging the bottom edge of a row selector down or by using the Row Height command when you click the More button in the Records group on the Home tab. Increasing the row height causes the text in a Memo field to wrap to the next line, so that you can view multiple lines at one time. Once again, however, for Memo fields containing thousands of characters, you can't increase the row height enough to ensure viewing the entire contents of the field at one time on screen. In addition, you'd view fewer records at one time, and the row height setting for a table propagates to all queries that have an object dependency with the table. Thus, you shouldn't increase the row height of a table datasheet to accommodate a Memo field.

What is the best way to view the contents of Memo fields that contain a large number of characters? It is best to use the Zoom dialog box in a datasheet, or to use a large scrollable text box on a form.

Now you'll review the property settings for the Comments field Lucia added to the tblCustomer table.

To review the property settings of the Memo field:

▶ **1.** Save the table, switch to Design view, click the **Comments Field Name** text box to make that row the current row, and then scroll to the bottom of the list of properties in the Field Properties pane.

▶ **2.** Click the **Text Format** text box in the Field Properties pane, and then click its **arrow**. The list of available text formats appears in the list box. See Figure 5-44.

| Figure 5-44 | Viewing the properties for a Memo field |

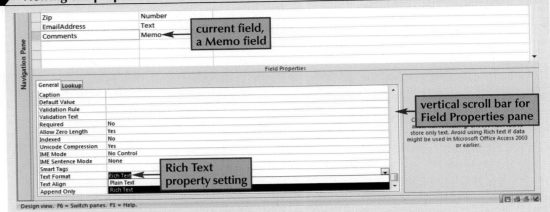

Lucia set the **Text Format property** to Rich Text, which lets you format the datasheet field contents using the options in the Font group on the Home tab. The default Text Format property setting for a Memo field is Plain Text, which doesn't allow text formatting.

3. Click the **arrow** on the Text Format text box to close the list, and then click the **Append Only** text box.

The **Append Only property**, which appears at the bottom of the list of properties, tracks the changes that you make to a Memo field. The default setting of No lets you edit the Memo field value in a normal way. Setting this property to Yes also lets you edit the Memo field value in a normal way but, additionally, causes Access to keep a historical record of all versions of the Memo field value. You can view each version of the field value, along with a date and time stamp of when each version change occurred.

You've finished your review of the Memo field, so you can close the table.

4. Close the tblCustomer table.

When employees at Belmont Landscapes open the Panorama database, a Security Warning appears below the Ribbon, and they must "enable this content" in the database before beginning their work. Sarah asks if you can eliminate this extra step when employees open the database.

Designating a Trusted Folder

A database is a file, and files can contain malicious instructions that can damage other files on your computer or files on other computers on your network. Unless you take special steps, Access treats every database as a potential threat to your computer. One such special step is to designate a folder as a trusted folder. A **trusted folder** is a folder on a drive or network that you designate as trusted and where you place databases you know are safe. When you open a database located in a trusted folder, Access treats it as a safe file and no longer displays a Security Warning. You can also place files used with other Microsoft Office programs, such as Word documents and Excel workbooks, in a trusted folder to eliminate warnings when you open them.

Because the Panorama database does not contain harmful instructions, you'll set up a trusted folder in which to store it to eliminate the Security Warning when a user opens the database.

To designate a trusted folder:

▶ 1. Click the **Office Button** , and then click the **Access Options** button. The Access Options dialog box opens.

▶ 2. In the left section of the dialog box, click **Trust Center**, click the **Trust Center Settings** button in the window on the right to open the Trust Center dialog box, and then in the left section, click **Trusted Locations**. The trusted locations for your installation of Access and other options are displayed on the right. See Figure 5-45.

Designating a trusted folder ◀ **Figure 5-45**

Existing trusted locations appear in the list at the top; and options to add, remove, and modify trusted locations appear at the bottom.

Trouble? Check with your instructor before adding a new trusted location. If your instructor tells you not to select this option, skip to Step 5.

▶ 3. Click the **Add new location** button to open the Microsoft Office Trusted Location dialog box, click the **Browse** button, navigate to the Level.02\Tutorial folder where your Data Files are stored, and then click the **OK** button.

You can also choose to designate subfolders of the selected location as trusted locations, but you won't select this option.

▶ 4. Click the **OK** button. Access adds the Level.02\Tutorial folder to the list of trusted locations.

▶ 5. Click the **OK** button to close the Trust Center dialog box, and then click the **OK** button to close the Access Options dialog box.

To show Sarah that adding the trusted location eliminates the Security Warning, you need to close and then open the database. You've created several queries and completed several table design changes, so you should compact and repair the Panorama database when you reopen it. Lucia doesn't use the Compact on Close option with the Panorama database, because it's possible to lose the database if there's a computer malfunction when the Compact on Close operation runs. As a precaution, you'll make a backup copy of the database before you reopen it. Making frequent backup copies of your critical files safeguards your data from hardware and software malfunctions, which can occur at any time.

To copy, open, and compact and repair the Panorama database:

1. Click the **Office Button** , and then click **Close Database** to close the Panorama database.

2. Make a backup copy of the Panorama database, preferably to a USB drive or other external medium, using a filename of Copy of Panorama_date, where *date* is the current date in the format 2010_02_15, for example, if you made the backup on February 15, 2010.

Tip

The date the database was last opened appears below the filename in the Open Recent Database pane.

3. Make sure the Access window is the active window, and then click **C:\Level.02\ ... \Panorama** in the Open Recent Database pane of the Getting Started window. The database opens, and no Security Warning appears below the Ribbon because the database is located in the trusted location you designated.

   Next, you'll compact and repair the database.

4. Click the **Office Button** , point to **Manage**, and then click **Compact and Repair Database**.

   You've finished the work requested by Belmont Landscapes, so you can close the database and exit Access.

5. Close the Panorama database and then exit Access, clicking the **Yes** button if you are prompted to confirm that you want to exit Access and empty the Clipboard.

You've completed the table design changes to the Panorama database that will make working with it easier and more accurate.

Review | **Session 5.3 Quick Check**

1. What is a lookup field?
2. A(n) _____ is a predefined format you use to enter and display data in a field.
3. What is property propagation?
4. Define the Validation Rule property, and give an example of when you would use it.
5. Define the Validation Text property, and give an example of when you would use it.
6. Setting a Memo field's Text Format property to _____ lets you format its contents.
7. A(n) _____ folder is a location in which you can place safe databases.

In this tutorial, you built on your earlier work with simple queries by learning how to use pattern and list-of-values matches, the Not operator, the & operator, and the IIf function. You also learned how to create parameter, crosstab, find duplicates, find unmatched, and top values queries. You enhanced the design of tables by creating lookup fields and input masks and by defining field and table validation rules. You also learned how to identify object dependencies, work with Memo fields, and designate trusted folders.

Key Terms

& (ampersand) operator
Append Only property
Caption property
crosstab query
Crosstab Query Wizard
field validation rule
find duplicates query
Find Duplicates Query
    Wizard
find unmatched query
Find Unmatched Query
    Wizard
IIf (Immediate If) function

In comparison operator
input mask
Input Mask Wizard
IsNull function
Like comparison operator
list-of-values match
literal display character
lookup field
Lookup Wizard field
Not logical operator
Object Dependencies pane
object dependency

parameter query
pattern match
property propagation
SQL (Structured Query
    Language)
table validation rule
Text Format property
Top Values property
trusted folder
Validation Rule property
Validation Text property

Practice		Review Assignments

Practice the skills you learned in the tutorial using the same case scenario.

Data File needed for the Review Assignments: Products.accdb

In the Review Assignments, you'll create several new queries and enhance the table design in a database that contains information about the suppliers that Belmont Landscapes works with on its landscape design projects. Complete the following steps:

1. Open the **Products** database, which is located in the Level.02\Review folder provided with your Data Files.

2. Modify the first record in the **tblCompany** table datasheet by changing the ContactFirstName and ContactLastName field values to your first and last names. Close the table.

3. Create a query to find all records in the tblCompany table in which the City field value starts with the letter H. Display all fields in the query recordset, and sort in ascending order by CompanyName. Save the query as **qryHSelectedCities**, run the query, and then close it.

4. Make a copy of the qryHSelectedCities query using the new name **qryOtherSelectedCities**. Modify the new query to find all records in the tblCompany table in which the City field values are not Lansing, Rockford, or Zeeland. Save and run the query, and then close it.

5. Create a query to find all records from the tblProduct table in which the Color field value is Black, White, or Grey. Use a list-of-values match for the selection criteria. Display all fields in the query recordset, and sort in descending order by Price. Save the query as **qrySelectedColors**, run the query, and then close it.

6. Create a query to display all records from the tblCompany table, selecting the CompanyName, City, and Phone fields, and sorting in ascending order by CompanyName. Add a calculated field named **ContactName** as the first column that concatenates the ContactFirstName, a space, and the ContactLastName. Set the Caption property for the ContactName field to **Contact Name**. Save the query as **qryCompanyContacts**, run the query, resize the Contact Name column to its best fit, and then save and close the query.

7. Create a parameter query to select the tblProduct table records for a Color field value that the user specifies. If the user doesn't enter a Color field value, select all records from the table. Display the ProductType, Price, Color, and DiscountOffered fields in the query recordset, sorting in ascending order by Price. Save the query as **qryColorParameter**. Run the query and enter no value as the Color field value, and then run the query again and enter **Wood** as the Color field value. Close the query.

8. Create a find duplicates query based on the tblProduct table. Select ProductType as the field that might contain duplicates, and select the ProductID, CompanyID, Price, and DiscountOffered fields as additional fields in the query recordset. Save the query as **qryDuplicateProductTypes**, run the query, and then close it.

9. Create a find unmatched query that finds all records in the tblCompany table for which there is no matching record in the tblProduct table. Display the CompanyID, CompanyName, City, Phone, ContactFirstName, and ContactLastName fields from the tblCompany table in the query recordset. Save the query as **qryCompaniesWithoutMatchingProducts**, run the query, and then close it.

10. Make a copy of the qryPricesWithDiscountAmounts query using the new name **qryTopPricesWithDiscountAmounts**. Modify the new query to use the Top Values property to select the top 25% of records. Save and run the query, and then close it.

11. In the **tblProduct** table, change the CompanyID field to a lookup field. Select the CompanyName and CompanyID fields from the tblCompany table, sort in ascending order by the CompanyName field, do not hide the key column, make sure the Company Name column is the leftmost column, resize the lookup columns to their best fit, select CompanyID as the field to store in the table, and accept the default label for the lookup column. View the tblProduct table datasheet, resize the Company ID column to its best fit, test the lookup field without changing a value permanently, and then save and close the table.

12. Use the Input Mask Wizard to add an input mask to the Phone field in the **tblCompany** table. The ending input mask should use periods as separators, as in 987.654.3210 with only the last seven digits required; do not store the literal display characters if you are asked to do so. Update the Input Mask property everywhere the Phone field is used. Test the input mask by typing over an existing Phone field value, being sure not to change the value by pressing the Esc key after you type the last digit in the Phone field.

13. Add a Memo field named **CompanyComments** as the last field in the tblCompany table. Set the Caption property to **Company Comments** and the Text Format property to Rich Text. In the table datasheet, resize the new column to its best fit, and then add your city and state in bold, italic font to the Memo field in the first record. Save and close the tblCompany datasheet.

14. Designate the Level.02\Review folder as a trusted folder. (*Note:* Check with your instructor before adding a new trusted location.)

15. Close the Products database without exiting Access, make a backup copy of the database, open the **Products** database, compact and repair the database, close the database, and then exit Access.

Apply	**Case Problem 1**

Use the skills you learned in the tutorial to work with the data contained in a database for a small music school.

Data File needed for this Case Problem: Contract.accdb

Pine Hill Music School   Yuka Koyama owns and runs the Pine Hill Music School in Portland, Oregon. She and the qualified teachers who work for her offer instruction in voice, violin, cello, guitar, percussion, and other instruments. Yuka created an Access database named Contract to store data about students, teachers, and contracts. You'll help Yuka create several new queries and make design changes to the tables. Complete the following:

1. Open the **Contract** database, which is located in the Level.02\Case1 folder provided with your Data Files.

2. Change the first record in the **tblStudent** table datasheet so the First Name and Last Name columns contain your first and last names. Close the table.

3. Create a query to find all records in the tblStudent table in which the Phone field value begins with 541. Display the FirstName, LastName, City, and Phone fields in the query recordset; and sort in ascending order by LastName. Save the query as **qry541AreaCodes**, run the query, and then close it.

4. Make a copy of the qryCurrentLessons query using the new name **qrySelectedLessons**. Modify the new query to delete the existing condition for the ContractEndDate field and to include a list-of-values criterion that finds all records in which the LessonType field value is Cello, Flute, or Violin. Save and run the query, and then close it.

5. Create a query to find all records in the tblStudent table in which the City field value is not equal to Portland. Display the FirstName, LastName, City, and Phone fields in the query recordset; and sort in ascending order by City. Save the query as **qryNonPortland**, run the query, and then close it.

6. Create a query to display all records from the tblTeacher table, selecting all fields, and sorting in ascending order by LastName and then in ascending order by FirstName. Add a calculated field named **TeacherName** as the second column that concatenates FirstName, a space, and LastName for each teacher. Set the Caption property for the TeacherName field to **Teacher Name**. Do not display the FirstName and LastName fields in the query recordset. Save the query as **qryTeacherNames**, run the query, resize the Teacher Name column to its best fit, and then save and close the query.

7. Create a parameter query to select the tblContract table records for a LessonType field value that the user specifies. If the user doesn't enter a LessonType field value, select all records from the table. Include all fields from the tblContract table in the query recordset. Save the query as **qryLessonTypeParameter**. Run the query and enter no value as the LessonType field value, and then run the query again and enter **Guitar** as the LessonType field value. Close the query.

⊕ **EXPLORE**

8. Create a crosstab query based on the tblContract table. Use the LessonType field values for the row headings, the LessonLength field values for the column headings, and the count of the ContractID field values as the summarized value, and include row sums. Save the query as **qryLessonTypeCrosstab**. Change the column heading for the row sum column to **Total Number of Lessons**, and change the column headings for the [LessonLength] columns to **Number of 30-Minute Lessons** and **Number of 60-Minute Lessons**. Resize the columns in the query recordset to their best fit, and then save and close the query.

9. Create a find duplicates query based on the tblContract table. Select StudentID and LessonType as the fields that might contain duplicates, and select all other fields in the table as additional fields in the query recordset. Save the query as **qryMultipleLessonsForStudents**, run the query, and then close it.

10. Create a find unmatched query that finds all records in the tblStudent table for which there is no matching record in the tblContract table. Display all fields from the tblStudent table in the query recordset. Save the query as **qryStudentsWithoutContracts**, run the query, and then close it.

11. In the **tblContract** table, change the TeacherID field data type to Lookup Wizard. Select the TeacherName and TeacherID fields from the qryTeacherNames query, sort in ascending order by TeacherName, resize the lookup columns to their best fit, select TeacherID as the field to store in the table, and accept the default label for the lookup column. View the tblContract table datasheet, resize the TeacherID column to its best fit, and then save and close the table.

12. Use the Input Mask Wizard to add an input mask to the Phone field in the **tblStudent** table. The ending input mask should use periods as separators, as in 987.654.3210 with only the last seven digits required; do not store the literal display characters if you are asked to do so. Update the Input Mask property everywhere the Phone field is used. Test the input mask by typing over an existing Phone field value, being sure not to change the value permanently by pressing the Esc key after you type the last digit in the Phone field.

13. Define a field validation rule for the Gender field in the tblStudent table. Acceptable field values for the Gender field are M or F. Use the message "Gender values must be M or F" to notify a user who enters an invalid Gender field value. Save your table changes, test the field validation rule for the Gender field, making sure any tested field values are the same as they were before your testing, and then close the table.

14. Define a table validation rule for the **tblContract** table to verify that ContractStartDate field values precede ContractEndDate field values in time. Use an appropriate validation message. Save your table changes, test the table validation rule, making sure any tested field values are the same as they were before your testing, and then close the table.

15. Designate the Level.02\Case1 folder as a trusted folder. (*Note:* Check with your instructor before adding a new trusted location.)

16. Close the Contract database without exiting Access, make a backup copy of the database, open the **Contract** database, compact and repair the database, close the database, and then exit Access.

| Apply | | Case Problem 2 |

Apply what you learned in the tutorial to work with the data for a new business in the health and fitness industry.

Data File needed for this Case Problem: Training.accdb

Parkhurst Health & Fitness Center Martha Parkhurst owns and operates the Parkhurst Health & Fitness Center in Richmond, Virginia. The center offers the usual weight training equipment and fitness classes and also offers specialized programs designed to meet the needs of athletes who participate in certain sports or physical activities. Martha created the Training database to maintain information about the members who have joined the center and the types of programs offered. To make the database easier to use, Martha wants you to create several queries and to make changes to its table design. Complete the following steps:

1. Open the **Training** database, which is located in the Level.02\Case2 folder provided with your Data Files.

2. Modify the first record in the **tblMember** table datasheet by changing the First Name and Last Name column values to your first and last names. Close the table.

3. Create a query to find all records in the tblProgram table in which the MonthlyFee field value is 20, 30, or 40. Use a list-of-values match for the selection criterion, and include all fields from the table in the query recordset. Sort the query in descending order by the ProgramID field. Save the query as **qrySelectedPrograms**, run the query, and then close it.

4. Make a copy of the qrySelectedPrograms query using the new name **qrySelectedProgramsModified**. Modify the new query to find all records in the tblProgram table in which the MonthlyFee field value is not 20, 30, or 40. Save and run the query, and then close it.

5. Create a query to display all records from the tblMember table, selecting the LastName, FirstName, Street, and Phone fields, and sorting in ascending order by LastName and then in ascending order by FirstName. Add a calculated field named **MemberName** as the first column that concatenates FirstName, a space, and LastName. Set the Caption property for the MemberName field to **Member Name**. Do not display the FirstName and LastName fields in the query recordset. Create a second calculated field named **CityLine**, inserting it between the Street and Phone fields. The CityLine field concatenates City, a space, State, two spaces, and Zip. Set the Caption property for the CityLine field to **City Line**. Save the query as **qryMemberNames**, run the query, resize all columns to their best fit, and then save and close the query.

⊕ EXPLORE

6. Create a query to display all matching records from the tblProgram and tblMember tables, selecting the ProgramType and MonthlyFee fields from the tblProgram table, and the FirstName and LastName fields from the tblMember table. Add a calculated field named **MonthlyFeeStatus** as the last column that equals Active if the MembershipStatus field is equal to Active and equals Not Active otherwise. Set the Caption property for the calculated field to **Monthly Fee Status**. Save the query as **qryMonthlyFeeStatus**, run the query, resize all columns to their best fit, and then save and close the query.

7. Make a copy of the qryRichmondOnHold query using the new name **qryRichmondAndChesterActive**. Modify the new query to select all records in which the City field value is Richmond or Chester and the MembershipStatus field value is Active. Save and run the query, and then close the query.

8. Create a parameter query to select the tblMember table records for a City field value that the user specifies. If the user doesn't enter a City field value, select all records from the table. Display all fields from the tblMember table in the query recordset. Save the query as **qryMemberCityParameter**. Run the query and enter no value as the City field value, and then run the query again and enter **Ashland** as the City field value. Close the query.

9. Create a crosstab query based on the qryMonthlyFeeStatus query. Use the ProgramType field values for the row headings, the MonthlyFeeStatus field values for the column headings, the sum of the MonthlyFee field values as the summarized value, and include row sums. Save the query as **qryMonthlyFeeCrosstab**, resize the columns in the query recordset to their best fit, and then save and close the query.

10. Create a find duplicates query based on the tblMember table. Select ExpirationDate as the field that might contain duplicates, and select all other fields in the table as additional fields in the query recordset. Save the query as **qryDuplicateMemberExpirationDates**, run the query, and then close it.

11. Create a find unmatched query that finds all records in the tblProgram table for which there is no matching record in the tblMember table. Select all fields from the tblProgram table. Save the query as **qryProgramsWithoutMembers**, run the query, and then close it.

12. Create a new query based on the tblMember table. Display the FirstName, LastName, Phone, ExpirationDate, MembershipStatus, and ProgramID fields in the query recordset. Sort in ascending order by the ExpirationDate field, and then use the Top Values property to select the top 25% of records. Save the query as **qryUpcomingExpirations**, run the query, and then close it.

⊕ EXPLORE

13. Use the Input Mask Wizard to add an input mask to the JoinDate field in the **tblMember** table. Select the Short Date input mask, and then modify the default Short Date input mask by changing the two slashes to dashes. Next type **mm-dd-yyyy** in the Format property text box for the JoinDate field to specify the date format. Test the input mask by typing over an existing Join Date column value, being certain not to change the value by pressing the Esc key after you type the last digit in the Join Date column. Finally, repeat the same procedure to add the same input mask and Format property setting to the ExpirationDate field, and then save and close the table.

14. Define a field validation rule for the MonthlyFee field in the **tblProgram** table. Acceptable field values for the MonthlyFee field are values between 15 and 55. Enter the message **Value must be between 15 and 55, inclusive** so it appears if a user enters an invalid MonthlyFee field value. Save your table changes and then test the field validation rule for the MonthlyFee field; be certain the field values are the same as they were before your testing.

15. Define a table validation rule for the **tblMember** table to verify that JoinDate field values precede ExpirationDate field values in time. Use an appropriate validation message. Save your table changes, test the table validation rule, making sure any tested field values are the same as they were before your testing.

16. Add a Memo field named **MemberComments** as the last field in the tblMember table. Set the Caption property to **Member Comments** and the Text Format property to Rich Text. In the table datasheet, resize the new column to its best fit, and then add a comment in the Memo field in the first record about the types of physical activities you pursue, formatting the text with blue, italic font. Save your table changes, and then close the table.

17. Designate the Level.02\Case2 folder as a trusted folder. (*Note:* Check with your instructor before adding a new trusted location.)

18. Close the Training database without exiting Access, make a backup copy of the database, open the **Training** database, compact and repair the database, close the database, and then exit Access.

| Challenge | **Case Problem 3** |

Apply the skills you've learned, and explore some new skills, to work with a database that contains data about an agency that recycles household goods.

Data File needed for this Case Problem: Agency.accdb

Rossi Recycling Group   The Rossi Recycling Group is a not-for-profit agency in Salina, Kansas that provides recycled household goods to needy people and families at no charge. Residents of Salina and surrounding communities donate cash and goods, such as appliances, furniture, and tools, to the Rossi Recycling Group. The group's volunteers then coordinate with local human services agencies to distribute the goods to those in need. The Rossi Recycling Group was established by Mary and Tom Rossi, who live on the outskirts of Salina on a small farm. Mary and Tom organize the volunteers to collect the goods and store the collected items in their barn for distribution. Tom has created an Access database to keep track of information about donors, their donations, and the human services agencies. He wants you to create several queries and to make changes to the table design of the database. To do so, you'll complete the following steps:

1. Open the **Agency** database, which is located in the Level.02\Case3 folder provided with your Data Files.

2. Modify the first record in the **tblDonor** table datasheet by changing the Title, First Name, and Last Name column values to your title and name. Close the table.

3. Create a query to find all records in the tblDonation table in which the AgencyID field value starts with either the letter R or the letter W. Display all fields in the query recordset, and sort in descending order by DonationValue. Save the query as **qryROrWAgencyDonations**, run the query, and then close it.

4. Make a copy of the qryAgenciesByCity query using the new name **qryNonSalinaAgencies**. Modify the new query to select all records in which the City field value is not Salina. Save and run the query, and then close it.

⊕ **EXPLORE**

5. The existing qryDonationsAfterPickupCharge query displays the DonorID, AgencyName, DonationDescription, and DonationValue fields for all donations that require a pickup, along with the NetDonation calculated field that displays the results of subtracting $8.75 from the DonationValue field value. Make a copy of the qryDonationsAfterPickupCharge query using the new name **qryNetDonations**. Modify the new query to select *all* records, to display the PickupRequired field, and to sort only in descending order by NetDonation. Also, change the NetDonation calculated field to subtract the delivery charge of $8.75 from the DonationField value when a pickup is required and to otherwise use the DonationValue field value. Save and run the query, and then close it.

6. Create a query to display all records from the tblAgency table, selecting all the fields except the ContactFirstName and ContactLastName fields, and sorting in ascending order by AgencyName. Add a calculated field named **ContactName** as the third column that concatenates ContactFirstName, a space, and ContactLastName. Set the Caption property for the ContactName field to **Contact Name**. Save the query as **qryAgencyContactNames**, run the query, resize the new column to its best fit, and then save and close the query.

7. Create a parameter query to select the tblDonation table records for a DonationDesc (donation description) field value that the user specifies. If the user doesn't enter a DonationDesc field value, select all records from the table. Display all fields from the tblDonation table in the query recordset, and sort in ascending order by DonationValue. Save the query as **qryDonationDescParameter**. Run the query and enter no value as the DonationDesc field value, and then run the query again and enter **Cash** as the DonationDesc field value. Close the query.

⊕ **EXPLORE**

8. Create a crosstab query based on the qryNetDonations query. Use the AgencyName field values for the row headings, the PickupRequired field values for the column headings, and the sum of the NetDonation field values as the summarized value, and include row sums. Save the query as **qryNetDonationsCrosstab**. Change the column headings for the two rightmost columns to **No Pickup** and **Pickup Required**. Change the format of the displayed values to Standard with two decimal places. Resize the columns in the query recordset to their best fit, and then save and close the query.

9. Create a find duplicates query based on the qryNetDonations query. Select DonorID and AgencyName as the fields that might contain duplicates, and select the remaining fields in the query as additional fields in the query recordset. Save the query as **qryMultipleDonorDonations**, run the query, and then close it.

10. Create a find unmatched query that finds all records in the tblDonor table for which there is no matching record in the tblDonation table. Select all fields from the tblDonor table in the query recordset. Save the query as **qryDonorsWithoutDonations**, run the query, and then close it.

⊕ **EXPLORE**

11. Make a copy of the qryNetDonations query using the new name **qryTopNetDonations**. Modify the new query by using the Top Values property to select the top 40% of the records. Save and run the query, and then close the query.

12. Use the Input Mask Wizard to add an input mask to the Phone field in the **tblDonor** table. The ending input mask should use hyphens as separators, as in 987-654-3210, with only the last seven digits required; do not store the literal display characters if you are asked to do so. Update the Input Mask property everywhere the Phone field is used. Test the input mask by typing over an existing Phone field value, being sure not to change the value permanently by pressing the Esc key after you type the last digit in the Phone field. Close the table.

13. Designate the Level.02\Case3 folder as a trusted folder. (*Note:* Check with your instructor before adding a new trusted location.)

14. Close the Agency database without exiting Access, make a backup copy of the database, open the **Agency** database, compact and repair the database, close the database, and then exit Access.

Challenge | **Case Problem 4**

Apply the skills you've learned, and explore some new skills, to work with the data for a luxury property rental company.

Data File needed for this Case Problem: Vacation.accdb

GEM Ultimate Vacations Griffin and Emma MacElroy own and operate their own agency, GEM Ultimate Vacations, which specializes in locating and booking luxury rental properties in Europe and Africa. To track their guests, properties, and reservations, they created the Vacation database. Griffin and Emma want you to create several queries and to make changes to the table design. To do so, you'll complete the following steps:

1. Open the **Vacation** database, which is located in the Level.02\Case4 folder provided with your Data Files.

2. Modify the first record in the **tblGuest** table datasheet by changing the First Name and Last Name column values to your first and last names.

3. Create a query to find all records in the tblProperty table in which the PropertyName field value starts with the word Chateau. Display all fields except the Description field in the query recordset. Save the query as **qryChateauProperties**, run the query, and then close it.

4. Make a copy of the qryChateauProperties query using the new name **qryNonChateauProperties**. Modify the new query to find all records in the tblProperty table in which the PropertyName field value starts with a word other than Chateau, and sort in ascending order by PropertyName. Save and run the query, and then close it.

5. Create a query to find all records in the tblGuest table in which the City field value is Aurora, Chicago, or Crown Point. Use a list-of-values match for the selection criterion, and display all fields from the tblGuest table in the query recordset. Save the query as **qrySelectedGuests**, run the query, and then close it.

⊕ EXPLORE
6. Create a query to select all records from the tblProperty table with nightly rates of $1,700 or $2,000 in France or Italy. Display all fields except the Description field in the query recordset. Save the query as **qryFranceItalySelectedProperties**, run the query, and then close it.

7. Create a parameter query to select the tblProperty table records for a Country field value that the user specifies. If the user doesn't enter a Country field value, select all records from the table. Display all fields from the tblProperty table in the query recordset, and sort in ascending order by PropertyName. Save the query as **qryCountryParameter**. Run the query and enter no value as the Country field value, and then run the query again and enter **Scotland** as the Country field value. Close the query.

8. Create a query that contains all records from the tblGuest table and all matching records from the tblReservation table. Display all fields from the tblGuest table and all fields except GuestID from the tblReservation table. Save the query as **qryGuestsAndReservations**, run the query, and then close it. Create a crosstab query based on the qryGuestsAndReservations query. Use the City field values for the row headings, the People field values for the column headings, and the sum of the RentalRate field as the summarized value, and include row sums. Save the query as **qryReservationsCrosstab**, resize the columns in the query recordset to their best fit, and then save and close the query.

9. Create a find duplicates query based on the tblProperty table. Select Location and Country as the fields that might contain duplicates, and select the remaining fields in the table as additional fields in the query recordset. Save the query as **qryDuplicateLocations**, run the query, and then close it.

10. Create a find unmatched query that finds all records in the tblGuest table for which there is no matching record in the tblReservation table. Display the GuestFirstName, GuestLastName, City, and Phone fields from the tblGuest table in the query recordset. Save the query as **qryGuestsWithoutReservations**, run the query, and then close it.

⊕ EXPLORE
11. Modify the **qryTopRentalCost** query to use the Top Values property to select the top 30% of the records. Save and run the query, and then close it.

12. In the **tblReservation** table, change the PropertyID field data type to Lookup Wizard. Select the PropertyID, PropertyName, and Location fields from the tblProperty table, sort in ascending order by PropertyName, do not hide the key column, resize the lookup columns to their best fit, select PropertyID as the field to store in the table, and accept the default label for the look up column. View the tblReservation datasheet, resize the PropertyID column to its best fit, test the lookup field without changing a field value permanently, and then close the table.

⊕ EXPLORE
13. Open the **tblGuest** table in Design view. Change the StateProv field data type to Lookup Wizard using a list of values that you enter. In the Lookup Wizard dialog box, create two columns and type the following pairs of values: **Illinois** and **IL**, **Indiana** and **IN**, and **Ontario** and **ON**. Resize the lookup columns to their best fit, select Col2 as the field to store in the table, and accept the default label for the lookup column. View the tblGuest table datasheet, resize the lookup column to its best fit, test the lookup field without changing permanently field values, and then save and close the table.

⊕ EXPLORE
14. Define a field validation rule for the Bedrooms field in the **tblProperty** table. Acceptable field values for the Bedrooms field are values between 3 and 25, including those two values. Display the message **Value must be between 3 and 25** when a user enters an invalid Bedrooms field value. Save your table changes and then test the field validation rule for the Bedrooms field; be certain the field values are the same as they were before your testing.

15. Define a table validation rule for the **tblReservation** table to verify that StartDate field values precede EndDate field values in time. Use an appropriate validation message. Save your table changes, test the table validation rule, making sure any tested field values are the same as they were before your testing, and then close the table.

16. Designate the Level.02\Case4 folder as a trusted folder. (*Note:* Check with your instructor before adding a new trusted location.)

17. Close the Vacation database without exiting Access, make a backup copy of the database, open the **Vacation** database, compact and repair the database, close the database, and then exit Access.

Create	Case Problem 5

Work with the skills you've learned, and explore some new skills, to create a database for an Internet service provider.

There are no Data Files needed for this Case Problem.

Always Connected Everyday   Chris and Pat Dixon own and manage Always Connected Everyday (ACE), a successful Internet service provider (ISP) in your area. ACE provides Internet access to residential and business customers and offers a variety of access plans, from dial-up and DSL to wireless. Figure 5-46 shows the pricing options for the access plans ACE offers.

Figure 5-46

Access Plan	Monthly	Annually	Setup Fee
Dial-up limited	$9.95		
Dial-up no e-mail	$14.95	$149.50	
Dial-up unlimited	$19.95	$199.50	
DSL pro	$29.95		$69.00
DSL turbo	$49.95		$69.00
DSL business	$89.95		$129.00
Wireless city economy	$39.95		$99.00
Wireless city basic	$49.95		$99.00
Wireless city advanced	$64.95		$109.00
Wireless city business	$99.95		$199.00
Wireless rural basic	$59.95		$109.00

Dial-up plans are available in all communities served by ACE, and DSL and wireless access are limited by a customer's proximity to DSL phone lines or wireless towers. Within each type of service—dial-up, DSL, and wireless—ACE offers low-cost plans with either slower access speeds or fewer capabilities and more expensive plans with either higher access speeds or greater service and features.

Chris and Pat need you to create a database to track their plans, customers, and service calls. The process of creating a complete database—including all fields, tables, relationships, queries, forms, and other database objects—for ACE is an enormous undertaking. You will start with just a few database components, and then you will create additional objects and functionality in subsequent tutorials.

Complete the following steps to create the database and its initial objects:

1. Read the appendix titled "Relational Databases and Database Design" at the end of this book.
2. If you are not familiar with ISPs, use your Web browser to find out more about them, so that you know common terminology and offerings.
3. The initial database structure includes the following tables and fields:
   a. The **tblAccessPlan** table includes the fields shown in Figure 5-46, along with a primary key field, which you can define as an AutoNumber field.
   b. The **tblCustomer** table includes a unique customer account number; an optional company name; and first name, last name, address, city, state, zip, phone, access plan ID (foreign key), next billing date, and e-mail address for the customer; and the customer's user ID and password for accessing ACE's Web site.

4. Building on Step 3, for each field, determine and set its attributes, such as data type, field size, and validation rules.

5. Create the database structure using Access. Use the database name **ACE**, and save the database in the Level.02\Case5 folder provided with your Data Files. Create the tables with their fields, following the naming standards used in this tutorial. Be sure to set each field's properties correctly, including the Caption property. Select a primary key for each table, use an input mask for one field, and then define the relationships between the tables.

6. For each table, create a form that you'll use to view, add, edit, and delete records in that table.

7. For tables with one-to-many relationships, create a form with a main form for the primary table and a subform for the related table.

8. Design test data for each table in the database. Your tblCustomer table should contain at least 15 records. Make sure your test data covers common situations. For example, your test data should include at least two access plans with multiple customers using the plans; at least two access plans with no customers using it; multiple cities, phone prefixes, and next billing dates; residential customers with no company names; and commercial customers with company names and the first and last names of the company's contact. Use your first and last names for the first record in the tblCustomer table.

9. Add the test data to your tables using the forms you created in Steps 6 and 7.

10. Open each table datasheet, and resize all datasheet columns to their best fit.

11. For the foreign key field in the tblCustomer table, change the field's data type to Lookup Wizard, including both the foreign key and its description as lookup columns. If necessary, resize the lookup column in the table datasheet.

12. Create a query named **qryCustomerNames** that contains all the fields from the tblCustomer table. Add a calculated field named **CustomerName** as the first column that is either the company name or the concatenation of the last name, a comma, a space, and the first name; set its Caption property to **Customer Name**. Sort in ascending order by CustomerName.

13. Create one parameter query, one crosstab query, and one find unmatched query, and save them using appropriate object names.

14. Designate the Level.02\Case5 folder as a trusted folder. (*Note:* Check with your instructor before adding a new trusted location.)

15. Close the ACE database without exiting Access, make a backup copy of the database, open the **ACE** database, compact and repair the database, close the database, and then exit Access.

Research | **Internet Assignments**

Use the Internet to find and work with data related to the topics presented in this tutorial.

The purpose of the Internet Assignments is to challenge you to find information on the Internet that you can use to work effectively with this software. The actual assignments are updated and maintained on the Course Technology Web site. Log on to the Internet and use your Web browser to go to the Student Online Companion for New Perspectives Office 2007 at **www.course.com/np/office2007**. Then navigate to the Internet Assignments for this tutorial.

Review | **Quick Check Answers**

Session 5.1

1. Caption
2. Like
3. a wildcard that represents any string of characters in a pattern match query
4. to define a condition with two or more values
5. Use the Not logical operator to negate a condition.
6. IIf (or Immediate If)
7. when you want to prompt the user to enter the selection criterion when the query runs

Session 5.2

1. It performs aggregate function calculations on the values of one database field and displays the results in a spreadsheet format.
2. Simple Query Wizard, Crosstab Query Wizard, Find Duplicates Query Wizard, Find Unmatched Query Wizard
3. It finds duplicate records in a table or query based on the values in one or more fields.
4. It finds all records in a table or query that have no related records in a second table or query.
5. You limit the number of records displayed in the query results.
6. Access displays the first five records.

Session 5.3

1. A field that lets you select a value from a list of possible values
2. input mask
3. an Access feature that updates control properties in objects when you modify table field properties
4. A property that specifies the valid values that users can enter in a field. You could use this property to specify that users can enter only positive numeric values in a numeric field.
5. A property value that appears in a dialog box if a user violates the field's validation rule. You could display the message "Must be a positive integer" if the user enters a value less than or equal to zero.
6. Rich Text
7. Trusted

Ending Data Files

Level.02 → Tutorial
Panorama.accdb

Review
Products.accdb

Case1
Contract.accdb

Case2
Training.accdb

Case3
Agency.accdb

Case4
Vacation.accdb

Case5
ACE.accdb

Objectives

Session 6.1
- Change a lookup field to a Text field
- View and print database documentation
- Create datasheet, multiple items, and split forms
- Modify a form and anchor form controls in Layout view

Session 6.2
- Plan, design, and create a custom form in Design view and in Layout view
- Select, move, align, resize, delete, and rename controls in a form
- Add a combo box to a form
- Add form headers and footers to a form

Session 6.3
- Add a combo box to a form to find records
- Add a subform to a form
- Add calculated controls to a form and a subform
- Change the tab order in a form
- Improve the appearance of a form

Using Form Tools and Creating Custom Forms

Creating Forms for Belmont Landscapes

Case | Belmont Landscapes

Oren Belmont hired Lucia Perez to enhance the Panorama database, and she initially concentrated on standardizing the table design and creating queries for Belmont Landscapes. Sarah Fisher and her staff created a few forms before Lucia's hiring, and Lucia's next priority is to work with Sarah to create new forms that will be more useful and easier to use.

In this tutorial, you will create new forms for Belmont Landscapes. In creating the forms, you will use many Access form customization features, such as adding controls and a subform to a form, using combo boxes and calculated controls, and adding color and special effects to a form. These features will make it easier for Sarah and her staff to interact with the Panorama database.

Starting Data Files

Level.02 → Tutorial — Panorama.accdb *(cont.)*

Review — Products.accdb *(cont.)*

Case1 — Contract.accdb *(cont.)*

Case2 — Training.accdb *(cont.)*

Case3 — Agency.accdb *(cont.)*

Case4 — Vacation.accdb *(cont.)*

Case5 — ACE.accdb *(cont.)*

Session 6.1

Designing Forms

You've used wizards to create forms, and you've modified a form's design in Layout view to create a custom form. To create a **custom form**, you can modify an existing form in Layout view or in Design view, or you can design and create a form from scratch in Layout view or in Design view. You can design a custom form to match a paper form, to display some fields side by side and others top to bottom, to highlight certain sections with color, or to add visual effects. Whether you want to create a simple or complex custom form, planning the form's content and appearance is always your first step.

InSight | **Form Design Guidelines**

When you plan a form, you should keep in mind the following form design guidelines:
- Use forms to perform all database updates, because forms provide better readability and control than do table and query recordsets.
- Determine the fields and record source needed for each form. A form's **Record Source property** specifies the table or query that provides the fields for the form.
- Group related fields and position them in a meaningful, logical order.
- If users will refer to a source document while working with the form, design the form to match the source document closely.
- Identify each field value with a label that names the field, and align field values and labels for readability.
- Size the width of each text box to fully display the values it contains and also to provide a visual clue to users about the length of those values.
- Display calculated fields in a distinctive way, and prevent users from changing and updating them.
- Use default values, list boxes, and other form controls whenever possible to reduce user errors by minimizing keystrokes and limiting entries. A **control** is an item, such as a text box or command button, that you place in a form or report.
- Use colors, fonts, and graphics sparingly to keep the form uncluttered and to keep the focus on the data.
- Use a consistent style for all forms in a database.

Sarah and her staff had created a few forms and made table design changes before learning about proper form design guidelines. The guidelines recommend performing all database updates using forms. As a result, Belmont Landscapes won't use table or query datasheets to update the database, and Sarah asks if she should reconsider any of the table design changes you made to the Panorama database in the previous tutorial.

Changing a Lookup Field to a Text Field

The input mask and validation rule changes are important table design changes, but setting the CustomerID field to a lookup field in the tblContract table is an unnecessary change. A form combo box provides the same capability in a clearer, more flexible way. A **combo box** is a control that provides the features of a text box and a list box; it lets you choose a value from the list or type an entry. Before creating the new forms for Sarah, you'll change the data type of the CustomerID field in the tblContract table from a Lookup Wizard field to a Text field.

To change the data type of the CustomerID field:

▶ **1.** Start Access, and then open the **Panorama** database in the Level.02\Tutorial folder provided with your Data Files.

Trouble? If the Security Warning is displayed below the Ribbon, either the Panorama database is not located in the Level.02\Tutorial folder or you did not designate that folder as a trusted folder. Make sure you opened the database in the Level.02\Tutorial folder, and make sure that it's a trusted folder.

▶ **2.** Open the Navigation Pane, open the **tblContract** table in Design view, and then close the Navigation Pane.

▶ **3.** Click the Field Name box for the CustomerID field, and then click the **Lookup** tab in the Field Properties pane. The Field Properties pane now displays the lookup properties for the CustomerID field. See Figure 6-1.

Tip

You can press the F11 key to open or close the Navigation Pane.

Lookup properties for the CustomerID field ◀ **Figure 6-1**

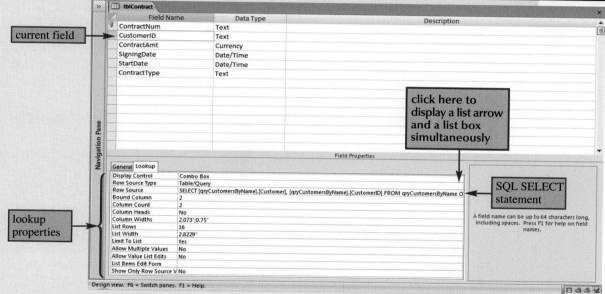

Notice the **Row Source property**, which specifies the data source for a control in a form or report or for a field in a table or query. The Row Source property is usually set to a table name, a query name, or an SQL statement. For the CustomerID field, the Row Source property is set to an SQL SELECT statement. You'll learn more about SQL later in the text.

To remove the lookup feature for the CustomerID field, you need to change the **Display Control property**, which specifies the default control used to display a field, from Combo Box to Text Box.

▶ **4.** Click the right side of the **Display Control** property box, and then click **Text Box**. All the lookup properties in the Field Properties pane disappear, and the CustomerID field changes back to a Text field without lookup properties.

▶ **5.** Click the **General** tab in the Field Properties pane and notice that the properties for a Text field still apply to the CustomerID field.

6. Save the table, switch to Datasheet view, resize the Customer ID column to its best fit, and then click one of the **CustomerID** text boxes. An arrow does not appear in the CustomerID text box because the field is no longer a lookup field.

7. Save the table, and then close the tblContract table.

Before you could change the CustomerID field in the tblContract table to a lookup field in the previous tutorial, you had to delete the one-to-many relationship between the tblCustomer and tblContract tables. Now that you've changed the data type of the CustomerID field back to a Text field, you'll view the table relationships to make sure that the tables in the Panorama database are related correctly.

To view the table relationships in the Relationships window:

1. On the Ribbon, click the **Database Tools** tab, and then in the Show/Hide group, click the **Relationships** button to open the Relationships window. See Figure 6-2.

| Figure 6-2 | Panorama database tables in the Relationships window |

The primary tblContract table and the related tblInvoice table have a one-to-many relationship with referential integrity enforced. You need to establish a similar one-to-many relationship between the tblCustomer and tblContract tables.

2. Click **CustomerID** in the tblCustomer field list, drag it to **CustomerID** in the tblContract field list, and then release the mouse button to open the Edit Relationships dialog box.

3. Click the **Enforce Referential Integrity** check box, click the **Cascade Update Related Fields** check box, and then click the **Create** button to define the one-to-many relationship between the two tables and to close the dialog box. The join line connecting the tblCustomer and tblContract tables indicates the type of relationship (one-to-many) with referential integrity enforced (bold join line).

Sarah asks you to print a copy of the database relationships to use as a reference, and she asks if other Access documentation is available.

Printing Database Relationships and Using the Documenter

You can print the Relationships window to document the fields, tables, and relationships in a database. You can also use the **Documenter**, another Access tool, to create detailed documentation of all, or selected, objects in a database. For each selected object, the Documenter lets you print documentation, such as the object's properties and relationships, and the fields used by the object and their properties. You can use the documentation to help you understand an object and to help you plan changes to that object.

Using the Documenter

- Start Access and open the database you want to document.
- In the Analyze group on the Database Tools tab, click the Database Documenter button.
- Select the object(s) you want to document.
- If necessary, click the Options button to select specific documentation options for the selected object(s), and then click the OK button.
- Click the OK button, print the documentation, and then close the Object Definition window.

Next, you'll print the Relationships window and use the Documenter to create documentation for the tblContract table. Sarah will show her staff the tblContract table documentation as a sample of the information that the Documenter provides.

To print the Relationships window and use the Documenter:

▶ **1.** In the Tools group on the Design tab, click the **Relationship Report** button to open the Relationships for Panorama report in Print Preview. See Figure 6-3.

Relationships for Panorama report | **Figure 6-3**

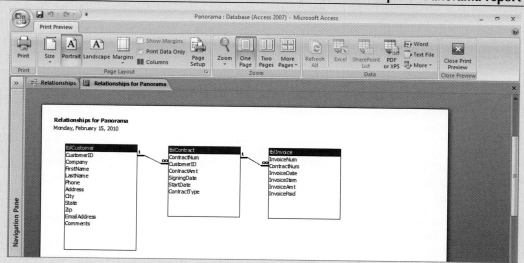

▶ **2.** In the Print group on the Print Preview tab, click the **Print** button, select your printer in the Name text box, and then click the **OK** button. Access prints the Relationships for Panorama report.

▶ **3.** Click the **Close 'Relationships for Panorama'** button ⊠ on the Relationships for Panorama tab to close the window. A dialog box opens and asks if you want to save the report. Because you can easily create the report at any time, you won't save it.

▶ **4.** Click the **No** button to close the report without saving changes, and then close the Relationships window.

Now you'll use the Documenter to create detailed documentation for the tblContract table as a sample to show Sarah.

▶ **5.** On the Ribbon, click the **Database Tools** tab. In the Analyze group, click the **Database Documenter** button, and then click the **Tables** tab (if necessary) in the Documenter dialog box. See Figure 6-4.

Figure 6-4 ▶ **Documenter dialog box**

You select which documentation you want the Documenter to include for the selected table, its fields, and its indexes. Sarah asks you to include all table documentation and the second options for fields and for indexes.

▶ **6.** Click the **tblContract** check box, and then click the **Options** button. The Print Table Definition dialog box opens. See Figure 6-5.

Figure 6-5 ▶ **Print Table Definition dialog box**

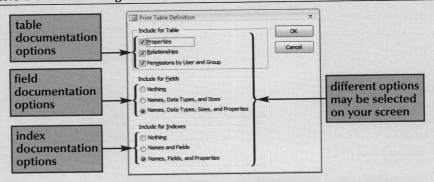

You select which documentation you want the Documenter to include for the selected table, its fields, and its indexes. Sarah asks you to include all table documentation and the second options for fields and for indexes.

▶ **7.** Make sure all check boxes are checked in the Include for Table section, click the **Names, Data Types, and Sizes** option button in the Include for Fields section (if necessary), click the **Names and Fields** option button in the Include for Indexes section (if necessary), click the **OK** button, and then click the **OK** button. The Documenter dialog box closes and the Object Definition report opens in Print Preview.

▶ **8.** In the Zoom group on the Print Preview tab, click the arrow on the **Zoom** button, and then click **Zoom 100%**.

When you need to view more of the horizontal contents of an open object, you can close the Navigation Pane. You can also minimize the Ribbon when you want to view more of the vertical contents of an open object. To minimize the Ribbon, double-click any tab on the Ribbon, or right-click a tab and then click Minimize the Ribbon. To restore the Ribbon, double-click any tab on the Ribbon, or right-click a tab and then click Minimize the Ribbon (it's a toggle option).

9. Double-click the **Print Preview** tab on the Ribbon to minimize the Ribbon, and then scroll down the report so you can see the date at the top of the window. See Figure 6-6.

Tip

After minimizing the Ribbon, if you click, instead of double-click, any tab on the Ribbon, the full Ribbon appears and then minimizes again as soon as you click anywhere outside the Ribbon.

Object Definition report for the tblContract table   Figure 6-6

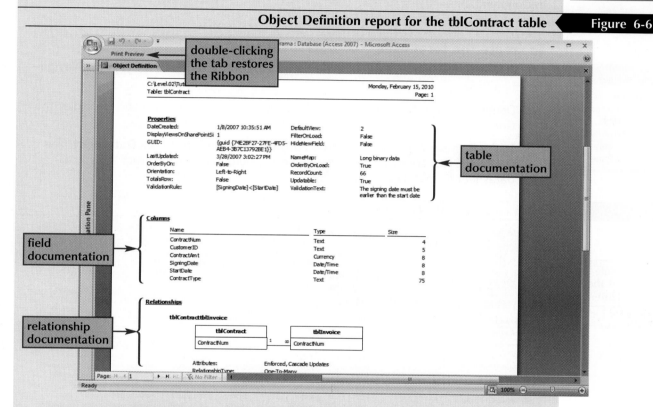

The Object Definition report displays table, field, and relationship documentation for the tblContract table.

10. Scroll down the Object Definition report to view the remaining information in the documentation, print the documentation if your instructor asks you to do so, and then close the Object Definition report. Notice that the Navigation Pane is closed and the Ribbon is minimized.

Sarah and her staff will review the printout of the Relationships window and the documentation about the tblContract table and decide if they need to view additional documentation. Next, you'll create new forms for Sarah and her staff.

Creating Forms Using Form Tools

The Panorama database currently contains four forms: the frmContract form was created using the Form tool, the frmCustomer form was created using the Form Wizard, and the frmCustomerContracts main form and its frmContractSubform subform were created using the Form Wizard. Only the frmCustomer form is a custom form. Design changes that were made to the frmCustomer form in Layout view include changing its AutoFormat, changing its form title color and its line type, adding a picture, and moving a field.

Sarah wants to view the forms that can be created using other types of form tools, so she can determine if any of the forms would be helpful to her when updating the database.

Creating a Form Using the Datasheet Tool

The **Datasheet tool** creates a form in a datasheet format that contains all the fields in the source table or query. You'll use the Datasheet tool to create a form based on the tblContract table.

Tip

When you use the Datasheet tool, the record source (either a table or query) for the form must either be open or selected in the Navigation Pane.

To create the form using the Datasheet tool:

▶ 1. Open the Navigation Pane, and then click **tblContract** (if necessary) in the Navigation Pane.

▶ 2. Double-click the **Create** tab on the Ribbon to restore the Ribbon and to display the Create tab.

▶ 3. In the Forms group, click the **More Forms** button, and then click **Datasheet**. The Datasheet tool creates a form showing every field in the tblContract table in a datasheet format. See Figure 6-7.

Figure 6-7 | **Form created by the Datasheet tool**

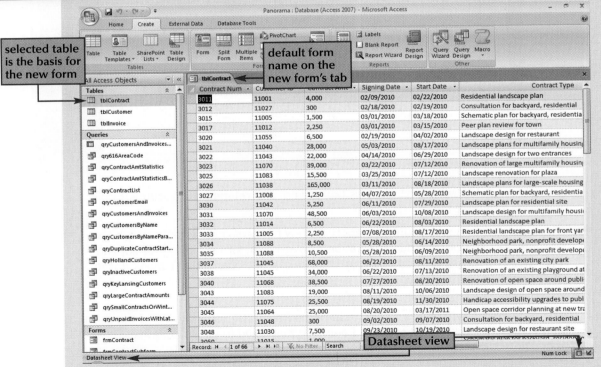

The new form displays all the records and fields from the tblContract table in Datasheet view and in the same format as a table or query recordset displayed in Datasheet view. "Datasheet View" appears on the status bar, as do two view icons, one for Datasheet view and the other for Design view. The form name, tblContract, is the same name as the table used as the basis for the form, but you should change the name when you save the form.

When working with forms, you view and update data in Form view, you view and make simple design changes in Layout view, and you make simple and complex design changes in Design view. For the form created with the Datasheet tool, you'll check the available view options.

▶ **4.** Click the **Home** tab on the Ribbon.

▶ **5.** In the Views group, click the arrow on the **View** button. See Figure 6-8.

Tip

Each table and query in a database must have a unique name. Although you could name a form or report the same as a table or query, it would cause confusion. Fortunately, using object name prefixes prevents this confusing practice.

View options for a form created by the Datasheet tool ◀ **Figure 6-8**

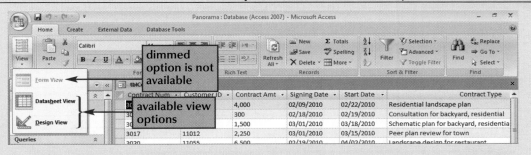

Form view is dimmed, which means that it's unavailable for this form type, and Layout view is not an option in the list. Datasheet view allows you to view and update data, and Design view is the only other view option for this form.

Sarah and her staff don't have a need for a form with a datasheet format, so you won't save it.

▶ **6.** Click the arrow on the **View** button to close the menu, and then close the form without saving it.

Next, you'll show Sarah a form created using the Multiple Items tool.

Creating a Form Using the Mulitple Items Tool

The **Multiple Items tool** creates a customizable form that displays multiple records from a source table or query in a datasheet format. You'll use the Multiple Items tool to create a form based on the tblContract table.

To create the form using the Multiple Items tool:

▶ **1.** Make sure that the tblContract table is selected in the Navigation Pane, and then click the **Create** tab on the Ribbon.

▶ **2.** In the Forms group, click the **Multiple Items** button. The Multiple Items tool creates a form showing every field in the tblContract table and opens the form in Layout view. See Figure 6-9.

Figure 6-9   Form created by the Multiple Items tool

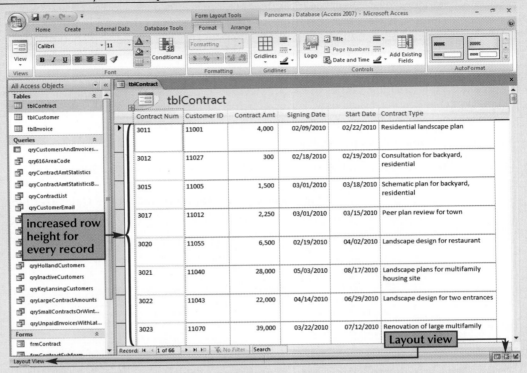

The new form displays all the records and fields from the tblContract table in a format similar to a datasheet, but the row height for every record is increased compared to a standard datasheet. Unlike a form created by the Datasheet tool, which has only Datasheet view and Design view available, a Multiple Items form is a standard form that can be displayed in Form view, Layout view, and Design view, as indicated by the buttons on the right side of the status bar.

For the form created with the Multiple Items tool, you'll check the available view options.

3. In the Views group, click the arrow on the **View** button. Form view, Layout view, and Design view are the available views for this form. See Figure 6-10.

Figure 6-10   View options for a form created by the Multiple Items tool

Sarah thinks this new form could be more useful than the form created by the Datasheet tool, but she doesn't have an immediate need for the form, so you won't save it.

4. Click the arrow on the **View** button to close the menu, and then close the form without saving it.

The final form tool you'll show Sarah is the Split Form tool.

Creating a Form Using the Split Form Tool

The **Split Form tool** creates a customizable form that displays the data in a form in both Form view and Datasheet view at the same time. The two views are synchronized with each other at all times. Selecting a field in one view selects the same field in the other view. You can add, change, or delete data from either view. Typically, you'd use Datasheet view to locate a record, and then use Form view to update the record. You'll use the Split Form tool to create a form based on the tblContract table.

To create the form using the Split Form tool:

1. Make sure that the tblContract table is selected in the Navigation Pane, and then click the **Create** tab on the Ribbon.

2. In the Forms group, click the **Split Form** button, and then close the Navigation Pane. The Split Form tool creates a split form that opens in Layout view and displays a form with the contents of the first record in the tblContract table on the top and a datasheet of the first several records in the tblContract table on the bottom. See Figure 6-11.

Form created by the Split Form tool | **Figure 6-11**

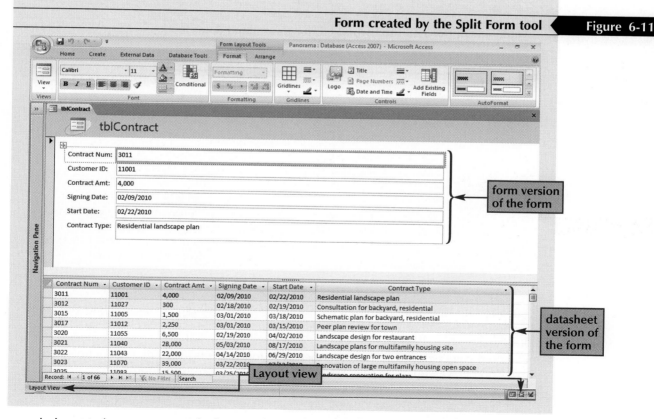

In Layout view, you can make layout and design changes to the form and layout changes to the datasheet. Sarah thinks the split form will be a useful addition to the

Panorama database, and she wants you to show her the types of design modifications that are possible with a split form.

Modifying a Split Form in Layout View

You use the Format tab on the Ribbon, as shown in Figure 6-12, to modify the format and appearance of a split form and all other form types.

Figure 6-12 | **Layout view options on the Format tab**

font options for the form and datasheet	Format property options for Currency, Date, and Number fields	gridline options for the form and datasheet	special controls for the form	AutoFormat options for the form

For a split form, some options on the Format tab apply to the form or the datasheet, other options apply to only the form, and the Add Existing Fields in the Controls group applies to both the form and the datasheet at the same time, as described in Figure 6-13.

Figure 6-13 | **Layout view options on the Format tab for a form and datasheet**

Group	Form Is Active	Datasheet Is Active
Font	Selected option applied to the selected labels and text boxes.	Selected option applied to every field value in the datasheet.
Formatting	Selected option applied to the selected text box, which must be a Currency, Date, or Number field.	Selected option applied to every field value in the active column, which must be a Currency, Date, or Number field.
Gridlines	Selected option applied to every label and text box in the form.	Only the options in the Gridlines list apply to the entire datasheet.
Controls	All options applied only to the form, except for the Add Existing Fields button, which applies to both the form and the datasheet.	Options do not apply in a datasheet, except for the Add Existing Fields button, which applies to both the form and the datasheet.
AutoFormat	Selected choice applied only to the form.	Not available.

Before selecting an option from the Format tab, you need to decide whether you want to modify the form or the datasheet, and then click in that object to select the object. Clicking anywhere in a datasheet selects the datasheet and also selects the column and the record you clicked. Clicking anywhere in a form selects the form. For controls in a form, you click a control to select it. To select several controls in a form, press and hold down the Shift key while clicking each control; a thicker, colored border appears around the selected controls. An option you choose from a group on the Format tab applies to all selected controls.

In previous tutorials, you've shown Sarah how to use some of the form modification options on the Format tab, and you'll use other options on this tab later in this tutorial, so you won't show her any Format tab options now. Instead, you'll show her some options on the Arrange tab. For a split form, options on the Arrange tab apply only to the form and do not apply to the datasheet.

To modify the form in Layout view:

▶ **1.** Click the **Arrange** tab on the Ribbon.

The form's label and text box controls for the fields from the tblContract table are grouped in a control layout. A **control layout** is a set of controls grouped together in a form or report, so that you can manipulate the set as a single control. For example, you can move and resize all the controls in a control layout as a group—moving or resizing one control in the control layout moves or resizes all controls in the control layout. You also can rearrange fields and their attached labels within the control layout.

All the text boxes in the control layout are the same width. The first five text boxes—from the ContractNum text box to the StartDate text box—are much wider than necessary. However, if you reduce the width of any text box in a control layout, all text boxes in the control layout are also resized. Sarah wants you to reduce the width of the first five text boxes and to move and resize the ContractType label and text box.

▶ **2.** Click the **layout selector** ⊞, which is located at the top-left corner of the Contract Num label, to select the entire control layout. An orange outline, which identifies the controls that you've selected, appears around the labels and text boxes in the form. See Figure 6-14.

Control layout selected in the form ◀ **Figure 6-14**

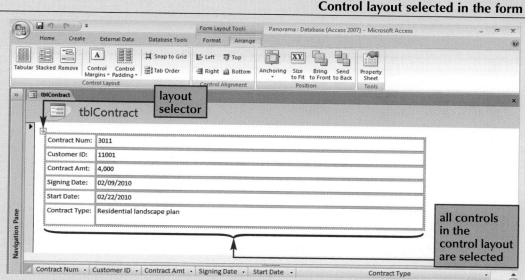

Next, you'll resize the text boxes in the control layout.

▶ **3.** Click the **ContractNum** text box (the text box that contains the value 3011) to deselect the control layout and select the ContractNum text box, hold down the **Shift** key, click each of the five text boxes below the ContractNum text box, and then release the **Shift** key to select all six text boxes in the control layout. When you resize one of the text boxes, all six selected text boxes will be resized equally.

▶ 4. Position the pointer on the right edge of the SigningDate text box until the pointer changes to a ↔ shape, click and drag to the left until the right edge is just to the right of the SigningDate field value, and then release the mouse button. You've resized all six text boxes. See Figure 6-15.

Figure 6-15 ▶ **After resizing the text boxes in the control layout**

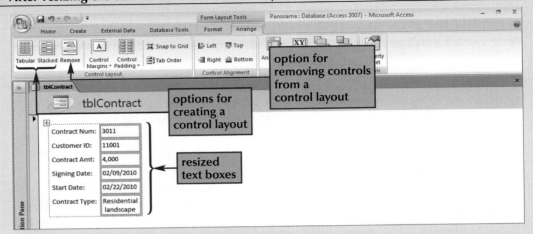

Trouble? If you resize the text boxes too far to the left, number signs appear inside the SigningDate and StartDate text boxes. Drag the right edge of the text boxes slightly to the right and repeat the process until the date values are visible inside the text boxes.

The control layout for the form is a **stacked layout**, which arranges text box controls vertically with a label to the left of each control; you click the Stacked button in the Control Layout group to place selected controls in a stacked layout. You can also choose a **tabular layout**, which arranges text box controls in a datasheet format with labels above each column; you click the Tabular button in the Control Layout group to place selected controls in a tabular layout.

You can now remove the ContractType text box and its label from the stacked layout, move the two controls, and then resize the text box.

▶ 5. Click the **ContractType** text box, and then in the Control Layout group, click the **Remove** button. An orange outline appears around the ContractType text box and its label, indicating that the two controls have been removed from the stacked layout.

▶ 6. Make sure that the ContractType text box and its label are selected, and then drag the two controls up and to the right until their tops are aligned with the top of the ContractNum controls. See Figure 6-16. (*Note:* You will resize the ContractType text box in the next step.)

▶ 7. Click the **ContractType** text box so that it's the only selected control, and then drag the right edge of the control to the right and the bottom edge of the control down to the positions shown in Figure 6-16.

After moving and resizing the ContractType controls ◀ Figure 6-16

Trouble? It won't cause any problems if the two ContractType controls on your screen are in slightly different positions than the ones shown in the figure or your ContractType text box is not exactly the same size.

You do not usually need to change the default settings for the **Control Margins property**, which controls the spacing around the text inside a control, and the **Control Padding property**, which controls the spacing around the outside of a control. However, you'll show Sarah the effects of changing these properties.

▶ **8.** Click one of the controls in the stacked layout, click the **layout selector** ⊕ to select all controls in the stacked layout, click the **Control Margins** button in the Control Layout group, and then click **Medium**. The text inside the stacked layout controls moves down and to the right.

▶ **9.** Click the **Control Margins** button, click **Wide** and observe the effect of this setting on the text inside the controls, click the **Control Margins** button, click **None** and observe the effect of this setting, click the **Control Margins** button, and then click **Narrow**. Narrow is the default setting for the Control Margins property.

Narrow is also the default setting for the Control Padding property.

▶ **10.** In the Control Layout group, click the **Control Padding** button, click **Medium** and observe the change to the spacing around the controls, and then repeat for the other settings of this property, making sure you set the property to **Narrow** as your final step.

Next, you'll show Sarah how to anchor controls.

Anchoring Controls in a Form

You can design attractive forms that use the screen dimensions effectively when all the users of a database have the same sized monitors and use the same screen resolution. How do you design attractive forms when users have a variety of monitor sizes and screen resolutions? If you design a form to fit on large monitors using high screen resolutions, then only a portion of the controls in the form fit on smaller monitors with lower resolutions, forcing users to scroll the form. If you design a form to fit on small monitors with low screen resolutions, then the form is displayed on larger monitors in a small area in the upper-left corner of the screen, making the form look unattractively cramped. As a compromise, you can anchor the controls in the form. The **Anchor property** for a control automatically resizes the control and places the control in the same relative position on the screen as the screen size and resolution change. Unfortunately, when you use the Anchor property, Access doesn't scale the control's font size to match the screen size and resolution.

Next, you'll show Sarah how to anchor controls in a form. Because all monitors at Belmont Landscapes are the same size and use the same resolution, first you'll save the split form, so that you can demonstrate anchoring and then discard those changes to the form.

To anchor controls in the form:

▶ 1. Save the form as **frmContractSplit**.

You can't anchor individual controls in a control layout; you can only anchor the entire control layout as a group. You've already removed the ContractType controls from the stacked layout, so you can anchor them separately from the stacked layout. You'll remove the SigningDate and StartDate controls from the stacked layout, so you'll have three sets of controls to anchor—the stacked layout is one set, the ContractType controls are in the second set, and the SigningDate and StartDate controls make up the third set.

▶ 2. Use **Shift + Click** to select the **SigningDate** and **StartDate** text boxes, and then click the **Remove** button in the Control Layout group to remove these two controls and their labels from the stacked layout.

First, you'll anchor the selected SigningDate and StartDate controls.

▶ 3. In the Position group on the Arrange tab, click the **Anchoring** button to open the Anchoring gallery. See Figure 6-17.

Figure 6-17	Displaying the Anchoring gallery

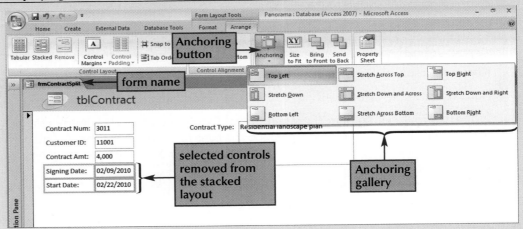

Four of the nine options in the Anchoring gallery fix the position of the selected controls in the top left (the default setting), bottom left, top right, or bottom right positions in the form. If other controls block the corner positions for controls you're anchoring for the first time, the new controls are positioned in relation to the blocking controls. The other five anchoring options resize, or stretch, and position the selected controls.

You'll anchor the SigningDate and StartDate controls in the bottom left and the ContractType controls in the top right.

▶ **4.** Click **Bottom Left** in the Anchoring gallery, click the **ContractType** text box, click the **Anchoring** button, and then click **Top Right**. The SigningDate and StartDate controls shifted down, and the ContractType controls shifted to the right.

Next, you'll open the Navigation Pane, and then increase the height of the form to simulate the effect of a larger screen for the form.

▶ **5.** Open the Navigation Pane. The two sets of controls on the left shift to the right, because the horizontal dimensions of the form decreased from the left, and these two sets of controls are anchored to the left in the form. The ContractType controls remain in the same position in the form.

▶ **6.** Position the pointer on the border between the form and the datasheet until the pointer changes to a ✛ shape, and then drag down until you see only the column headings and the first row in the datasheet. The bottom set of controls shifts down, because it's anchored to the bottom, and the two sets of controls at the top remain in the same positions in the form. See Figure 6-18.

Anchored controls in a resized form ◀ Figure 6-18

Finally, you'll show Sarah one of the anchoring options that resizes the ContractType text box as the form dimensions change.

▶ **7.** Click the **ContractType** text box, click the **Anchoring** button, and then click **Stretch Down and Right**. Because the ContractType text box is already anchored to the top right, it can't stretch any more to the right, but it does stretch down to increase the height of the text box.

▶ **8.** Position the pointer on the border between the form and the datasheet until the pointer changes to a ✛ shape, and then drag up until you can see several rows in the datasheet. The bottom set of controls shifts up, and the bottom edge of the ContractType text box shifts up, reducing its height.

You've finished showing Sarah Layout view changes to the split form, so you can close the form without saving the anchoring changes.

▶ **9.** Close the frmContractSplit form without saving your design changes.

▶ **10.** If you are not continuing on to the next session, close the Panorama database, and then exit Access.

You've used form wizards and form tools to create forms, and you've modified forms in Layout view. In the next session, you will continue your work with forms, concentrating on the techniques, tools, and options available in Design view.

Review | Session 6.1 Quick Check

1. According to the form design guidelines, which object(s) should you use to perform all database updates?
2. The _____ property specifies the data source for a control in a form or report or for a field in a table or query.
3. What is the Documenter?
4. What is the Multiple Items tool?
5. What is a split form?
6. The _____ property for a control automatically resizes the control and places the control in the same relative position on the screen as the screen's size and resolution change.

Session 6.2

Planning and Designing a Custom Form

Sarah needs a form to enter and view information about Belmont Landscapes' contracts and their related invoices. She wants the information in a single form, and she asks Lucia to design a form for her review.

After several discussions with Sarah and her staff, Lucia prepared a paper design for a custom form to display a contract and its related invoices. Lucia then used her paper design to create the form shown in Figure 6-19.

Lucia's design for the custom form | Figure 6-19

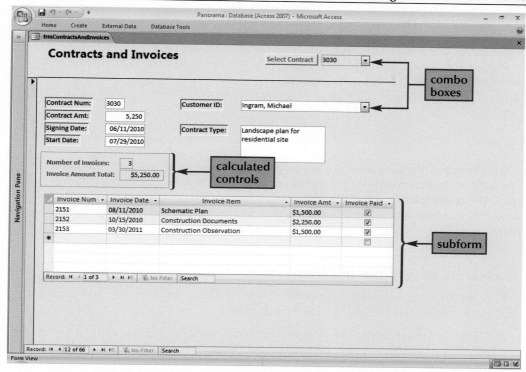

Notice that the top of the form displays a title and a combo box to select a contract record. Below these items are six field values with identifying labels from the tblContract table; these fields are the ContractNum, ContractAmt, SigningDate, StartDate, CustomerID, and ContractType fields. The CustomerID field is displayed in a combo box and the other field values are displayed in text boxes. The tblInvoice table fields appear in a subform, a separate form contained within another form. Unlike the tblContract table data, which displays identifying labels to the left of the field values in text boxes, the tblInvoice table data is displayed in datasheet format with identifying column headings above the field values. Finally, Number of Invoices and Invoice Amount Total in the main form display calculated controls based on the content of the subform.

Creating a Custom Form in Design View

To create Lucia's custom form, you could use the Form Wizard to create a basic version of the form and then customize it in Layout and Design views. However, to create Lucia's form, you would need to make many modifications to a basic form created by a wizard, so you will create the form directly in Design view. Creating forms in Design view is easy once you've done one form, and Design view allows you more control, precision, and options than creating forms in Layout view. You'll also find that you'll create forms more productively if you switch between Design view and Layout view, because some design modifications are easier to make in one of the two views than in the other view.

The Form Window in Design View

You use the Form window in Design view to create and modify forms. To create the custom form based on Lucia's design, you'll create a blank form, add the fields from the tblContract and tblInvoice tables, and then add other controls and make other form modifications.

Reference Window | Creating a Form in Design View

- Click the Create tab on the Ribbon.
- In the Forms group, click the Blank Form button.
- Click the Design View button on the status bar.
- Make sure the Field List pane is open, and then add the required fields to the form.
- Add other required controls to the form.
- Modify the size, position, and other properties as necessary for the fields and other controls in the form.
- Save the form.

The form you'll create will be a bound form. A **bound form** is a form that has a table or query as its record source. You use bound forms for maintaining and displaying table data. **Unbound forms** are forms that do not have a record source and are usually used for forms that help users navigate among the objects in a database. Now you'll create a blank bound form based on the tblContract table.

To create a blank form in Design view:

► 1. If you took a break after the previous session, make sure that the Panorama database is open and the Navigation Pane is open.

► 2. Click the **Create** tab on the Ribbon and then, in the Forms group on the Create tab, click the **Blank Form** button. Access opens the Form window in Layout view.

► 3. Click the **Design View** button 🖼 on the status bar to switch to Design view, and then close the Navigation Pane. See Figure 6-20.

| Figure 6-20 | Blank form in Design view |

Trouble? If the Field List pane displays the "No fields available to be added to the current view" message, click the "Show all tables" link to display the tables in the Panorama database, and then click the plus sign next to tblContract in the Field List pane to display the fields in the table.

Trouble? If the tblContract table in the Field List pane is not expanded to show the fields in the table, click the plus sign next to tblContract to display the fields.

Design view contains the tools necessary to create a custom form. You create the form by placing controls in the blank form. You can place three kinds of controls in a form:

- A **bound control** is connected, or bound, to a field in the database based on the record source, or the underlying table or query. You use bound controls to display and maintain table field values.
- An **unbound control** is not connected to a field in the database. You use unbound controls to display text, such as a form title or instructions; to display lines, rectangles, and other objects; or to display graphics and pictures created using other software programs. An unbound control that displays text is called a **label**.
- A **calculated control** displays a value that is the result of an expression. The expression usually contains one or more fields, and the calculated control is recalculated each time any value in the expression changes.

To create a bound control, you add fields from the Field List pane to the Form window, and position the bound controls where you want them to appear in the form. To place other controls in a form or a report, you use the buttons in the Controls group on the Design tab; ScreenTips are available for each control in the Controls group. The buttons in the Controls group let you add to the form controls such as lines, rectangles, images, buttons, check boxes, and list boxes.

Design view for a form contains a **Detail section**, which is a rectangular area consisting of a grid with a section bar above the grid. You click the **section bar** to select the section in preparation for setting properties for the entire section. The **grid** consists of the area with dotted and solid lines that help you position controls precisely in a form. In the Detail section, you place bound controls, unbound controls, and calculated controls for your form. You can change the size of the Detail section by dragging its edges.

Rulers at the top and left edges of the Detail section define the horizontal and vertical dimensions of the form and serve as guides for placing controls in a form.

Your first task is to add bound controls to the Detail section for the six fields from the tblContract table.

Adding Fields to a Form

When you add a bound control to a form, Access adds a text box and, to its left, an attached label. The text box displays a field value from the record source. The attached label displays either the Caption property value for the field, if the Caption property value has been set, or the field name. To create a bound control, you first display the Field List pane by clicking the Add Existing Fields button in the Tools group on the Design tab. Then you double-click a field in the Field List pane to add the bound control to the Detail section. You can also drag a field from the Field List pane to the Detail section.

Next, you'll add bound controls to the Detail section for the six fields in the Field List pane. The Field List pane displays the three tables in the Panorama database, and the six fields in the tblContract table.

To add bound controls from the tblContract table to the grid:

▶ **1.** Double-click **ContractNum** in the Field List pane. Access adds a bound control in the Detail section of the form, removes the tblCustomer and tblInvoice tables from the "Fields available for this view" section of the Field List pane, and places the two tables in the "Fields available in related tables" section of the Field List pane.

▶ **2.** Repeat Step 1 for the **ContractAmt**, **SigningDate**, **StartDate**, **CustomerID**, and **ContractType** fields, in this order, in the Field List pane. Six bound controls—one for each of the six fields in the Field List pane—have been added in the Detail section of the form. See Figure 6-21.

Figure 6-21	Adding text boxes and attached labels as bound controls to a form

six attached labels

six text boxes are bound controls connected to the table field values

tables related to the tblContract table

You should periodically save your work as you create a form, so you'll now save the form.

▶ **3.** Click the **Save** button 🖫 on the Quick Access Toolbar. The Save As dialog box opens.

▶ **4.** With the default name Form1 selected in the Form Name text box, type **frmContractsAndInvoices**, and then press the **Enter** key. The tab for the form now displays the form name, and the form design is saved in the Panorama database.

You've added the fields you need to the grid, so you can close the Field List pane.

▶ **5.** In the Tools group on the Design tab, click the **Add Existing Fields** button to close the Field List pane.

Creating and modifying a form in Design view might seem awkward at first. With practice you will become comfortable working with custom forms.

To design a form productively, you should keep in mind the following suggestions:

- You can click the Undo button one or more times immediately after you make one or more errors or make undesired form adjustments.
- You should back up your database frequently, especially before you create new objects or customize existing objects. If you run into difficulty, you can revert to your most recent backup copy of the database.
- You should save your form after you've completed a portion of your work successfully and before you need to perform steps you've never done before. If you're not satisfied with subsequent steps, close the form without saving the changes you made since your last save, and then open the form and perform the steps again.
- You can always close the form, make a copy of the form in the Navigation Pane, and practice with the copy.
- Adding controls, setting properties, and performing other tasks in Access in the correct way should work all the time with consistent results, but in rare instances, you might find a feature doesn't work properly. If a feature you've used succesfully doesn't work suddenly, you should save your work, close the database, make a backup copy of the database, open the database, and then compact and repair the database. Performing a compact and repair resolves most of these types of problems.

Compare your form's Detail section with Sarah's design, and notice that you need to move the ContractType bound control up and to the right. To do so, you must select and move the bound control.

Selecting, Moving, and Aligning Controls

Six text boxes now appear in the form's Detail section, one below the other. Each text box is a bound control connected to a field in the underlying table. Each text box has an attached label to its left. Each text box and attached label pair is a control in the form, and each individual text box is also a control in the form, as is each individual label. When you select a control, the control becomes outlined in orange, and eight squares, called handles, appear on its four corners and at the midpoints of its four edges. The larger handle in a control's upper-left corner is its **move handle**, which you use to move the control. You use the other seven handles, called **sizing handles**, to resize the control. When you work in Design view, controls you place in the form do not become part of a control layout, so you can individually select, move, resize, and otherwise manipulate one control without also changing the other controls. However, at any time you can select a group of controls and place them in a control layout—either a stacked layout or a tabular layout.

Reference Window | **Selecting and Moving Controls**

- Click the control to select it. To select several controls at once, press and hold down the Shift key while clicking each control. Handles appear around all selected controls.
- To move a single selected control, drag the control's move handle, which is the handle in the upper-left corner, to its new position.
- To move a group of selected controls, point to any selected control until the pointer changes to a move pointer, and then drag the group of selected controls to its new position.
- To move selected controls in small increments, press the appropriate arrow key.
- To move selected controls to the next nearest grid dot, hold down the Ctrl key and press the appropriate arrow key.

Based on Lucia's design for the custom form, you must select the ContractType bound control and move it up and to the right in the Detail section. The ContractType bound control consists of a field-value text box, labeled ContractType, and an attached label, labeled Contract Type, to its left.

To select the ContractType bound control:

1. If necessary, click the **ContractType** text box to select it. Move handles, which are the larger handles, appear on the upper-left corners of the selected text box control and its attached label. Sizing handles also appear, but only on the text box. See Figure 6-22.

| Figure 6-22 | Selecting the ContractType bound control |

You can move a text box and its attached label together. To move them, place the pointer anywhere on the border of the text box, but not on a move handle or a sizing handle. When the pointer changes to a ⭍ shape, you can drag the text box and its attached label to the new location. As you move a control, an outline of the control moves on the rulers to indicate the current position of the control as you drag it. To move a group of selected controls, point to any selected control until the pointer changes to a ⭍ shape, and then drag the group of selected controls to its new position. You can move controls with more precision when you use the arrow keys instead of the mouse. To move selected controls in small increments, press the appropriate arrow key. To move selected controls to the next nearest grid dot, hold down the Ctrl key and press the appropriate arrow key.

You can also move either a text box or its label individually. If you want to move the text box but not its label, for example, place the pointer on the text box's move handle. When the pointer changes to a ⁺ℕ shape, drag the text box to the new location. You use the label's move handle in a similar way to move only the label.

You'll now arrange the controls to match Lucia's design.

To move the ContractType bound control:

▶ **1.** Position the pointer on one of the edges of the ContractType text box, but not on a move handle or a sizing handle. When the pointer changes to a ⁺ℕ shape, drag the control to the right until the left edge of the highlight on the horizontal ruler is at the 3-inch mark, drag the control up until the top of the highlight on the vertical ruler is just below the top of the SigningDate bound control, and then release the mouse button. See Figure 6-23.

After moving the ContractType bound control ◀ **Figure 6-23**

Trouble? If you need to make major adjustments to the placement of the ContractType bound control, click the Undo button on the Quick Access Toolbar one or more times until the bound control is back to its starting position, and then repeat Step 1. If you need to make minor adjustments to the placement of the ContractType bound control, use the arrow keys.

Now you need to align the ContractType and SigningDate bound controls on their top edges. If you've selected a column of controls, you can align the left edges or the right edges of the controls. If you've selected a row of controls, you can align the top edges or the bottom edges of the controls. A fifth alignment option, To Grid, aligns selected controls with the dots in the grid. You can find the five alignment options on the Arrange tab of the Ribbon or on the shortcut menu. You'll use the shortcut menu to align the two bound controls. Then you'll save the modified form and review your work in Form view.

To align the ContractType and SigningDate bound controls:

▶ **1.** Make sure the ContractType bound control is selected, hold down the **Shift** key, click the **Contract Type** label, click the **SigningDate** text box, click the **Signing Date** label, and then release the **Shift** key. This action selects the four controls; each selected control has an orange border.

▶ **2.** Right-click one of the selected controls, point to **Align** on the shortcut menu, and then click **Top**. The four selected controls are aligned on their top edges. See Figure 6-24.

Figure 6-24 ▶ **After top-aligning four controls in the Detail section**

As you create a form, you should periodically save your modifications to the form and review your progress in Form view.

▶ **3.** Save your form design changes, and then switch to Form view. See Figure 6-25.

Figure 6-25 ▶ **Form displayed in Form view**

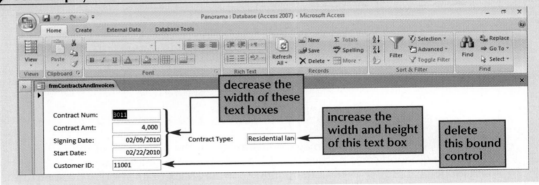

The value in the ContractType text box is not fully displayed, so you need to increase the size of the text box. The widths of the other four text boxes are wider than necessary, so you'll reduce their widths. Also, the CustomerID bound control consists of a label and a text box, but the plan for the form shows a combo box for the CustomerID positioned above the ContractType bound control. You'll delete the CustomerID bound control in preparation for adding it to the form as a combo box.

Resizing and Deleting Controls

A selected control displays seven sizing handles: four at the midpoints on each edge of the control and one at each corner except the upper-left corner. Recall that the upper-left corner displays the move handle. Positioning the pointer over a sizing handle changes the pointer to a two-headed arrow; the directions in which the arrows point indicate in which direction you can resize the selected control. When you drag a sizing handle, you resize the control. As you resize the control, a thin line appears inside the sizing handle to guide you in completing the task accurately, as do the outlines that appear on the horizontal and vertical rulers.

Resizing a Control

- Click the control to select it and display the sizing handles.
- Place the pointer over the sizing handle you want, and then drag the edge of the control until it is the size you want.
- To resize selected controls in small increments, hold down the Shift key and press the appropriate arrow key. This technique applies the resizing to the right edge and the bottom edge of the control.

You'll begin by deleting the CustomerID bound control. Then you'll resize the ContractType text box, which is too narrow and too short to display ContractType field values. Then you'll resize the remaining four text boxes to reduce their widths.

To delete a bound control and resize the text boxes:

▶ **1.** Switch to Design view, click an unused portion of the grid to deselect all controls, and then click the **CustomerID** text box to select it.

▶ **2.** Right-click the **CustomerID** text box to open the shortcut menu, and then click **Delete**. The label and the text box for the CustomerID bound control are deleted.

▶ **3.** Click the **ContractType** text box to select it.

▶ **4.** Place the pointer on the middle-right handle of the ContractType text box. When the pointer changes to a ↔ shape, drag the right border horizontally to the right to the 6-inch mark on the horizontal ruler.

▶ **5.** Place the pointer on the middle-bottom handle of the ContractType text box. When the pointer changes to a ↕ shape, drag the bottom border down to the 1.75-inch mark on the vertical ruler. See Figure 6-26.

> **Tip**
>
> If you want to delete a label but not its associated text box, right-click the label, and then click Delete on the shortcut menu.

After resizing the ContractType text box ◀ **Figure 6-26**

Resizing controls in Design view is a trial-and-error process, in which you resize a control in Design view, switch to Form view to observe the effect of the resizing, switch back to Design view to make further refinements to the control's size, and continue until the control is sized correctly. It's easier to resize controls in Layout view, because you can see actual field values while you resize the controls. You'll resize the other four text boxes in Layout view.

▶ **6.** Switch to Layout view, and then click the **ContractNum** text box (if necessary) to select it.

▶ **7.** Position the pointer on the right edge of the **ContractNum** text box. When the pointer changes to a ↔ shape, drag the right border horizontally to the left until the text box is slightly wider than the field value it contains. See Figure 6-27.

The sizes of the ContractAmt, SigningDate, and StartDate text boxes will look fine if you reduce them to have the same widths, so you'll select all three text boxes and resize them as a group.

▶ **8.** Select the **ContractAmt**, **SigningDate**, and **StartDate** text boxes.

▶ **9.** Position the pointer on the right edge of any of the three selected controls. When the pointer changes to a ↔ shape, drag the right border horizontally to the left until the SigningDate and StartDate text boxes are slightly wider than the field values they contain. See Figure 6-27.

Figure 6-27 ▶ **After resizing text boxes in Layout view**

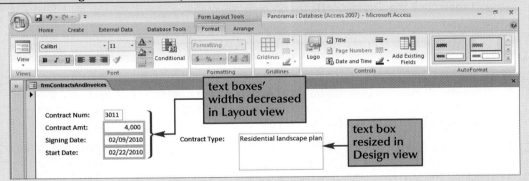

Trouble? If you resized the text boxes too far to the left, number signs will be displayed inside the SigningDate and StartDate text boxes. Drag the right edge of the text boxes slightly to the right and repeat the process until the date values are visible inside the text boxes.

▶ **10.** Navigate through the first several records to make sure the five text boxes are sized properly to display the full field values. If any text box is too small, select the text box and increase its width the appropriate amount.

▶ **11.** Save your form design changes, switch to Design view, and then deselect all controls by clicking in an unused portion of the grid.

InSight | **Making Form Design Modifications**

When you design forms and other objects, you'll find it helpful to switch frequently between Design view and Layout view. Some form modifications are easier to make in Layout view, other form modifications are easier to make in Design view, and still other form modifications can be made only in Design view. You should check your progress frequently in either Layout view or Form view, and you should save your modifications after completing a set of changes successfully.

Recall that you removed the lookup feature from the CustomerID field because a combo box provides the same lookup capability in a form. Next, you'll add a combo box for the CustomerID field to the custom form.

Adding a Combo Box to a Form

The tblCustomer and tblContract tables are related in a one-to-many relationship. The CustomerID field in the tblContract table is a foreign key to the tblCustomer table, and you can use a combo box in the custom form to view and maintain CustomerID field values more easily and accurately than using a text box. Recall that a combo box is a control that provides the features of a text box and a list box; you can choose a value from the list or type an entry.

You use the **Combo Box tool** in Design view to add a combo box to a form. If you want help when adding the combo box, you can select one of the Access Control Wizards. A **Control Wizard** asks a series of questions and then uses your answers to create a control in a form or report. Access offers Control Wizards for the Combo Box, List Box, Option Group, Command Button, Subform/Subreport, and other control tools.

You will use the Combo Box Wizard to add a combo box to the form for the CustomerID field.

To add a combo box to the form:

▶ **1.** In the Controls group on the Design tab, make sure the Use Control Wizards button ⊠ is selected.

▶ **2.** In the Controls group on the Design tab, click the **Combo Box** button 🛅 (with the ScreenTip "Combo Box (Form Control)"). After you click the Combo Box tool or most other tools in the Controls group, nothing happens until you move the pointer over the form. When you move the pointer over the form, the pointer changes to a shape that is unique for the tool with a plus symbol in its upper-left corner. You position the plus symbol in the location where you want to place the upper-left corner of the control.

You'll place the combo box near the top of the form above the ContractType bound control, and then position it more precisely after you've finished the wizard.

▶ **3.** Position the + portion of the pointer three grid dots from the top of the grid and at the 4-inch mark on the horizontal ruler, and then click the mouse button. Access places a combo box control in the form and opens the first Combo Box Wizard dialog box.

You can use an existing table or query as the source for a new combo box or type the values for the combo box. In this case, you'll use the qryCustomersByName query as the basis for the new combo box. This query includes the Customer calculated field, whose value equals the Company field value, if it's nonnull, or the concatenation of the LastName and FirstName field values in all other cases.

▶ **4.** Click the **I want the combo box to look up the values in a table or query** option button (if necessary), click the **Next** button to open the next Combo Box Wizard dialog box, click the **Queries** option button in the View group, click **Query: qryCustomersByName**, and then click the **Next** button. Access opens the third Combo Box Wizard dialog box. This dialog box lets you select the fields from the query to appear as columns in the combo box. You'll select the first two fields.

▶ **5.** Double-click **Customer** to move this field to the Selected Fields list box, double-click **CustomerID**, and then click the **Next** button. This dialog box lets you choose a sort order for the combo box entries. Sarah wants the entries to appear in ascending Customer order.

▶ **6.** Click the **arrow** for the first list box, click **Customer**, and then click the **Next** button to open the next Combo Box Wizard dialog box.

▶ **7.** Resize the columns to their best fit, scrolling down the columns to make sure all values are visible and resizing again if they're not, and then click the **Next** button.

In this dialog box, you select the foreign key, which is the CustomerID field.

▶ **8.** Click **CustomerID** and then click the **Next** button.

In this dialog box, you specify the field in the tblContract table where you will store the selected CustomerID value from the combo box. You'll store the value in the CustomerID field in the tblContract table.

▶ **9.** Click the **Store that value in this field** option button, click its **arrow**, click **CustomerID**, and then click the **Next** button.

Trouble? If CustomerID doesn't appear in the list, click the Cancel button, press the Delete key to delete the combo box, click the Add Existing Fields button in the Tools group on the Ribbon, double-click CustomerID in the Field List pane, press the Delete key to delete CustomerID, close the Field List pane, and then repeat Steps 1-9.

In this dialog box, you specify the name for the combo box control. You'll use the field name of CustomerID.

▶ **10.** Type **CustomerID** and then click the **Finish** button. The completed CustomerID combo box appears in the form.

You need to position and resize the combo box control, but first you'll change the text for the attached label from CustomerID to Customer ID with a terminating colon to match the format used for other label controls in the form. To change the text for a label control, you set the control's **Caption property** value.

Reference Window	**Changing a Label's Caption**

- Right-click the label to select it and to display the shortcut menu, and then click Properties to display the property sheet.
- If necessary, click the All tab to display the All page in the property sheet.
- Edit the existing text in the Caption text box; or click the Caption text box and press the F2 key to select the current value, and then type a new caption.
- In the Tools group on the Design tab, click the Property Sheet button to close the property sheet.

Next, you'll change the text that appears in the combo box label.

To set the Caption property value for the Customer ID label:

▶ **1.** Right-click the **Customer ID** label, which is the control to the left of the CustomerID text box, to select it and to display the shortcut menu, and then click **Properties** on the shortcut menu. The property sheet for the Customer ID label opens.

▶ **2.** If necessary, click the **All** tab to display all properties for the selected Customer ID label.

 Trouble? If the Selection type entry below the Property Sheet title bar is not "Label," then you selected the wrong control in Step 1. Click the Customer ID label to change to the property sheet for this control.

▶ **3.** Click before the "ID" in the Caption text box, press the **spacebar**, press the **End** key, type a colon, and then press the **Tab** key to move to the next property in the property sheet. The Caption property value should now be Customer ID: and the label for the CustomerID bound control now displays Customer ID:. See Figure 6-28.

> **Tip**
>
> After selecting a control, you can press the F4 key to open and close the property sheet for the control.

> **Tip**
>
> After you've set a property value, you won't see the effects of the new setting until you select another property in the property sheet, select another control in the form, or close the property sheet.

CustomerID combo box added to the form | **Figure 6-28**

Trouble? Some property values in your property sheet, such as the Width and Top property values, might differ if your label's position slightly differs from the label position used as the basis for Figure 6-28. These differences cause no problems.

Tip

You should always check that the Selection type entry is the correct control type and the Control list box displays the correct name for the control whose properties you are changing.

The Selection type entry, which is the line below the property sheet title bar, displays the control type (Label in this case) for the selected control. Below the Selection type entry in the property sheet is the Control list box, which you can use to select another control in the form and then change its properties in the property sheet. Or you can simply click the control to change to its properties in the property sheet. The first property in the property sheet, the **Name property**, is the property that specifies the name of a control, section, or object (CustomerID_Label in this case). The Name property value is the same as the value displayed in the Control list box. For bound controls, the Name property value matches the field name. For unbound controls, Access sets the Name property to the control type (for example, Label) followed by a number (for example, Label2). For unbound controls, you can set the Name property to another, more meaningful value at any time.

▶ 4. Close the property sheet, and then save your design changes.

Now that you've added the combo box to the form, you can view the form in Layout view, and then position the combo box and its attached label and resize the combo box. You'll need to view the form in Form view to determine any fine-tuning necessary for the width of the combo box.

To view and modify the combo box in Layout view:

▶ 1. Switch to Layout view to view the form, and then click the **CustomerID** combo box, hold down the **Shift** key, click the **Customer ID** label, and then release the **Shift** key to select both controls.

First, you'll align the CustomerID combo box and its label with the ContractType and ContractNum bound controls. You'll move the selected controls to the right of the Contract Type label, align the Customer ID and Contract Type labels on their left edges, align the CustomerID and ContractType controls on their left edges, and then align the bottom edges of the combo box and its label with the bottom edges of the ContractNum bound control.

▶ 2. Drag the selected controls to the right until the Customer ID label is approximately one inch to the right of the Contract Type label, making sure the two controls remain above the ContractNum bound control.

▶ 3. Select the **Customer ID** label and the **Contract Type** label, click the **Arrange** tab on the Ribbon, and then in the Control Alignment group on the Arrange tab, click the **Left** button. The selected controls are aligned on their left edges.

▶ 4. Repeat Step 3 to align the **CustomerID** combo box and the **ContractType** text boxes on their left edges.

▶ 5. Select the **Contract Num** label, **ContractNum** text box, **Customer ID** label, and **CustomerID** combo box, and then in the Control Alignment group on the Arrange tab, click the **Bottom** button. The four selected controls are aligned on their bottom edges.

▶ 6. Switch to Form view, and then click the **CustomerID** arrow to open the control's list box. See Figure 6-29.

CustomerID combo box in Form view ◄ Figure 6-29

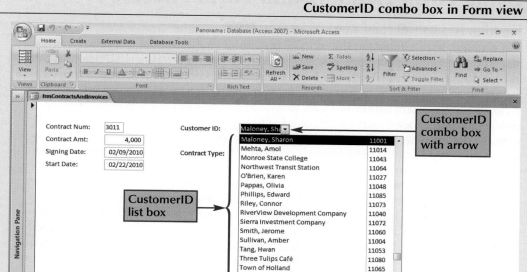

You need to widen the CustomerID combo box, so that the widest customer value in the list is displayed in the combo box. You can widen the combo box in Layout view or in Design view. Because Layout view displays live data, you'll use Layout view instead of Design view to make this change because you can determine the proper width more accurately in Layout view.

▶ 7. Switch to Layout view, and then navigate to record 16. Weston Community Parks Foundation, which is the customer value for this record, is the widest value that is displayed in the combo box. You want to widen the combo box, so that the value in record 16 is completely visible.

▶ 8. Make sure that only the combo box is selected, and then pointing to the right edge, widen the combo box until the entire customer value is visible. See Figure 6-30.

After resizing the CustomerID combo box in Layout view ◄ Figure 6-30

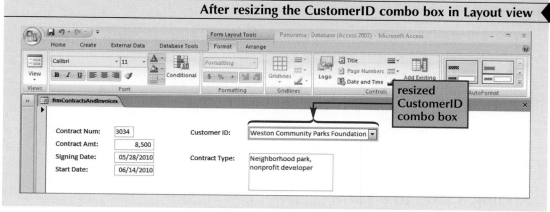

Now you'll add the title to the top of the form.

Using Form Headers and Form Footers

The **Form Header** and **Form Footer sections** let you add titles, instructions, command buttons, and other controls to the top and bottom of your form, respectively. Controls placed in the Form Header or Form Footer sections remain on the screen whenever the form is displayed in Form view or Layout view; they do not change when the contents of the Detail section change as you navigate from one record to another record.

To add either a form header or footer to your form, you must first add both the Form Header and Form Footer sections as a pair to the form. If your form needs one of these sections but not the other, you can remove a section by setting its height to zero, which is the same method you would use to remove any form section. You can also prevent a section from appearing in Form view or in Print Preview by setting its Visible property to No. The **Visible property** determines if Access displays a control or section. Set the Visible property to Yes to display the control or section, and set the Visible property to No to hide it.

You can add the Form Header and Form Footer sections as a pair to a form either directly or indirectly. The direct way to add these sections is to click the Form Header/Footer button in the Show/Hide group on the Arrange tab. This direct method is available only in Design view. The indirect way to add the Form Header and Form Footer sections in Layout view or Design view is to use one of these four buttons in the Controls group on the Design tab: the Logo button, the Title button, the Page Numbers button (Insert Page Number button in Design view), or the Date and Time button (Date & Time button in Design view). Clicking any of these four buttons causes Access to add the Form Header and Form Footer sections to the form and to place an appropriate control in the Form Header section. If you use the indirect method in Layout view, Access sets the Form Footer section's height to zero. In Design view, the indirect method creates a nonzero height Form Footer section. Note that the Page Numbers button is dimmed, and thus inactive, in Layout view. Many forms contain a title and possibly a picture, but forms rarely display a page number or the date and time, so an inactive Page Numbers button is not a problem, especially because you can add page numbers in Design view.

Reference Window | **Adding and Removing Form Header and Form Footer Sections**

- In Design view, click the Form Header/Footer button in the Show/Hide group on the Arrange tab.

  or

- In Layout view or Design view, click a button in the Controls group to add a logo, title, page numbers, or date and time to the form.
- To remove a Form Header or Form Footer section, drag its bottom edge up until the section area disappears or set the section's Visible property to No.

Lucia's design includes a title at the top of the form. Because the title will not change as you navigate through the form records, you will add the title to the Form Header section in the form.

Adding a Title to a Form

You'll add the title to Sarah's form in Layout view. When you add the title to the form in Layout view, Access adds the Form Header section to the form and places the title in the Form Header section. At the same time, Access adds the Page Footer section to the form and sets its height to zero.

To add a title to the form:

▶ **1.** In the Controls group on the Format tab, click the **Title** button. Access adds the title to the form, displaying it in the upper-left corner of the form and using the form name as the title.

You need to change the title. Because the title is already selected, you can type over or edit the selected title.

▶ **2.** Press the **Home** key to move to the start of the title, press the **Delete** key three times to delete the first three characters, click before the word "And," press the **spacebar**, type the letter **a**, press the **Delete** key, press the → key twice, press the **spacebar**, and then press the **Enter** key. You've changed the title to Contracts and Invoices. See Figure 6-31.

Title placed in the Form Header section ◀ Figure 6-31

Sarah wants the title to be prominent in the form. The title is already a larger font size than the font used for the form's labels and text boxes, so you'll change the title's font weight to bold to increase its prominence.

▶ **3.** Make sure the title control is still selected, and then in the Font group on the Format tab, click the **Bold** button **B**. The title is displayed in 18-point, bold text.

It is not obvious in Layout view that the title is displayed in the Form Header section, so you'll view the form design in Design view.

▶ **4.** Switch to Design view, and then save your design changes. The title is displayed in the Form Header section. See Figure 6-32.

Tip

Keep in mind that a form's total height includes the heights of the Form Header, Detail, and Form Footer sections. If you set the form's total height to more than the screen size, users will need to use scroll bars to view the content of your form, which is less productive for users and isn't good form design.

Figure 6-32 ▶ **Form Header and Form Footer sections in Design view**

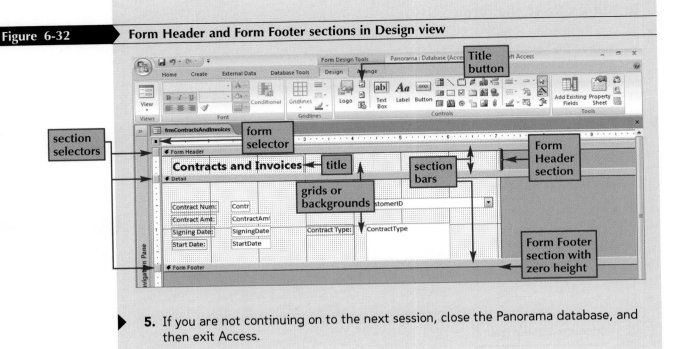

5. If you are not continuing on to the next session, close the Panorama database, and then exit Access.

The form now contains a Form Header section that displays the title, a Detail section that displays the bound controls and combo box, and a Form Footer section that is set to a height of zero. Each section consists of a **section selector** and a section bar, either of which you can click to select and set properties for the entire section, and a grid or background, which is where you place controls that you want display in the form. The **form selector** is the selector at the intersection of the horizontal and vertical rulers; you click the form selector when you want to select the form and set its properties. The vertical ruler is segmented into sections for the Form Header section, the Detail section, and the Form Footer section.

So far, you've added controls to the form and modified the controls by selecting, moving, aligning, resizing, and deleting them. You've added and modified a combo box and added a title in the Form Header section. In the next session, you will continue your work with the custom form by adding a combo box to find records, adding a subform, adding calculated controls, changing form and section properties, and changing control properties.

Review | Session 6.2 Quick Check

1. What is a bound form, and when do you use bound forms?
2. What is the difference between a bound control and an unbound control?
3. The _____ consists of the dotted and solid lines that appear in the Detail section to help you position controls precisely in a form.
4. The handle in a selected object's upper-left corner is the _____ handle.
5. How do you move a selected text box and its label at the same time?
6. How do you resize a control?
7. A(n) _____ control provides the features of a text box and a list box.
8. How do you change a label's caption?
9. What is the Form Header section?

Session 6.3

Adding a Combo Box to Find Records

Most combo boxes, such as the CustomerID combo box, are used to display and update data. You can also use combo boxes to find records. You will add a combo box to the Form Header section to find a specific record in the tblContract table to display in the form.

Adding a Combo Box to Find Records | Reference Window

- Open the property sheet for the form in Design view, make sure the record source is a table or query, and then close the property sheet.
- In the Controls section on the Design tab, click the Combo Box button, and then click the position in the form where you want to place the control.
- Click the third option button (Find a record on my form based on the value I selected in my combo box) in the first Combo Box Wizard dialog box, and then complete the remaining Combo Box Wizard dialog boxes.

You can use the Combo Box Wizard to add a combo box to find records in a form. However, the Combo Box Wizard provides this find option only if the form's record source is a table or query. You'll view the property sheet for the form to view the Record Source property, and you'll change the property setting, if necessary.

To add a combo box to find records to the form:

▶ **1.** If you took a break after the previous session, make sure that the Panorama database is open, the frmContractsAndInvoices form is open in Design view, and the Navigation Pane is closed.

▶ **2.** Click the **form selector** (located to the left of the horizontal ruler) to select the form, open the property sheet, and then click the **All** tab (if necessary). The property sheet displays the properties for the form. See Figure 6-33.

Property sheet settings for the form | Figure 6-33

The Record Source property is set to an SQL SELECT statement. You need to change the Record Source property to a table or query, or the Combo Box Wizard will not present you with the option to find records in a form. You'll change the Record Source property to the tblContract table, because this table is the record source for all the bound controls you added to the Detail section.

▶ **3.** Click the **Record Source** text box, press the **F2** key to select the entire property setting, type **tblContract**, and then close the property sheet.

You'll now use the Combo Box Wizard to add a combo box to the form's Form Header section to find a record in the tblContract table to display in the form.

▶ **4.** In the Controls group on the Design tab, click the **Combo Box** button 🔲 (with the ScreenTip "Combo Box (Form Control)"), position the + portion of the pointer at the top of the Form Header section and at the 5-inch mark on the horizontal ruler (see Figure 6-33), and then click the mouse button. Access places a combo box control in the form and opens the first Combo Box Wizard dialog box.

The dialog box now displays a third option to "Find a record on my form based on the value I selected in my combo box," which you'll use for this combo box. You choose the first option, which you used for the CustomerID combo box, when you want to select a value from a list of foreign key values from an existing table or query. You choose the second option when you want users to select a value from a short fixed list of values that don't change. For example, if Belmont Landscapes wanted to include a field in the tblCustomer table to classify each customer, you could use a combo box with this second option to display a list of values such as Residential, Commercial, Nonprofit, and Government.

▶ **5.** Click the **Find a record on my form based on the value I selected in my combo box** option button, and then click the **Next** button to open the next dialog box. This dialog box lets you select the fields from the tblContract table to appear as columns in the combo box. You'll select the first field.

▶ **6.** Double-click **ContractNum** to move this field to the Selected Fields list box, and then click the **Next** button.

▶ **7.** The column is already resized properly, so click the **Next** button.

In this dialog box, you specify the name for the combo box's label. You'll use Select Contract as the label.

▶ **8.** Type **Select Contract**, and then click the **Finish** button. The completed unbound combo box is displayed in the form. See Figure 6-34.

| Figure 6-34 | Unbound combo box added to the form |

You'll align the right edges of the two combo boxes, move the attached label close to the combo box, and then align the bottoms of the combo box and its attached label with the bottom of the title in the Form Header section.

▶ **9.** Deselect all controls, select the two combo boxes (one in the Form Header section and the other in the Detail section), right-click one of the selected controls, point to **Align**, and then click **Right**. The two combo boxes are aligned on their right edges.

▶ **10.** Click the **Select Contract** label, point to the label's move handle, and then drag the label to the right until it is two grid dots to the left of the combo box.

▶ **11.** Select the combo box in the Form Header section, the **Select Contract** label, and the title, right-click one of the selected controls, point to **Align**, click **Bottom**, and then click the **Select Contract** label. The three controls are aligned on their bottom edges. See Figure 6-35.

After aligning the combo box and its label	Figure 6-35

You'll save your form changes and view the new combo box in Form view.

To find contract records using the combo box:

▶ **1.** Save the form design changes, and then switch to Form view.

▶ **2.** Click the **Select Contract** combo box arrow to open the combo box's list box. See Figure 6-36.

Displaying the combo box's list of contract numbers	Figure 6-36

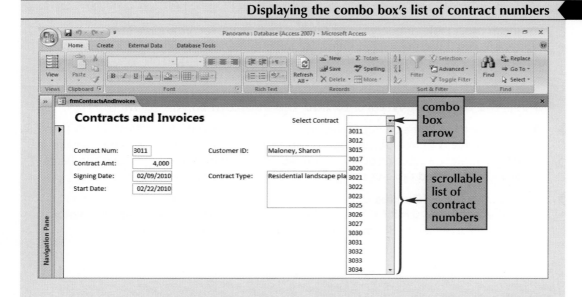

▶ **3.** Scroll down the list, and then click **3073**. The current record changes from record 1 to record 41, which is the record for contract number 3073.

The form design is very plain at this point with no color, special effects, or visual contrast among the controls. Before making the form more attractive and useful, you'll add the remaining controls to the form: a subform and two calculated controls.

Adding a Subform to a Form

Lucia's design for the form includes a subform that displays the related invoices for the displayed contract. The form you've been creating is the main form for records from the primary tblContract table (the "one" side of the one-to-many relationship), and the subform will display records from the related tblInvoice table (the "many" side of the one-to-many relationship). You use the **Subform/Subreport tool** in Design view to add a subform to a form. You can add the subform on your own, or you can get help adding the subform by using the SubForm Wizard.

You will use the SubForm Wizard to add the subform for the Invoice table records to the bottom of the form. First, you'll increase the height of the Detail section to make room for the subform.

To add the subform to the form:

▶ **1.** Switch to Design view.

<table>
<tr><td rowspan="10" valign="top">

Tip

When you increase a section's height, you might need to go slightly beyond the desired ending position to expose the vertical ruler measurement, and then decrease the height back to the correct position.

</td></tr>
</table>

▶ **2.** Place the pointer on the bottom edge of the Detail section. When the pointer changes to a ╋ shape, drag the section's edge down until it is at the 4-inch mark on the vertical ruler.

▶ **3.** In the Controls group on the Design tab, make sure the Use Control Wizards tool ▧ is selected.

▶ **4.** In the Controls group on the Design tab, click the **Subform/Subreport** button ▤.

▶ **5.** Position the + portion of the pointer in the Detail section at the 2.5-inch mark on the vertical ruler and at the 1-inch mark on the horizontal ruler, and then click the mouse button. Access places a subform control in the form's Detail section and opens the first SubForm Wizard dialog box.

You can use a table or query, or an existing form as the record source for a subform. In this case, you'll use the related tblInvoice table as the record source for a new subform.

To use the SubForm Wizard to add the subform to the form:

▶ **1.** Make sure the Use existing Tables and Queries option button is selected, and then click the **Next** button. Access opens the next SubForm Wizard dialog box, which lets you select a table or query as the record source for the subform and the fields from the selected table or query.

▶ **2.** Click the **Tables/Queries** arrow to display the list of tables and queries in the Panorama database, scroll to the top of the list box, and then click **Table: tblInvoice**. The Available Fields list box shows the fields in the tblInvoice table.

Lucia's form design includes all fields from the tblInvoice table in the subform, except the ContractNum field, which is already placed in the Detail section of the form from the tblContract table.

3. Click the `>>` button to move all available fields to the Selected Fields list box, click **ContractNum** in the Selected Fields list box, click the `<` button, and then click the **Next** button to open the next SubForm Wizard dialog box. See Figure 6-37.

In this dialog box, you select the link between the primary tblContract table and the related tblInvoice table. The common field in the two tables, ContractNum, links the tables. Access uses the ContractNum field to display a record in the main form, which displays data from the primary tblContract table, and to select and display the related records for that contract in the subform, which displays data from the related tblInvoice table.

4. Make sure the Choose from a list option button is selected and that the first link is highlighted, and then click the **Next** button. The next SubForm Wizard dialog box lets you specify a name for the subform.

5. Type **frmInvoiceSubform** and then click the **Finish** button. Access increases the height and width of the subform in the form. The subform is where the related tblInvoice records will appear. The subform label appears above the subform and displays the subform name.

6. Deselect all controls, save your form changes, switch to Form view, and then click the **ContractNum** text box to deselect the value. See Figure 6-38.

Figure 6-38 **Viewing the subform in Form view**

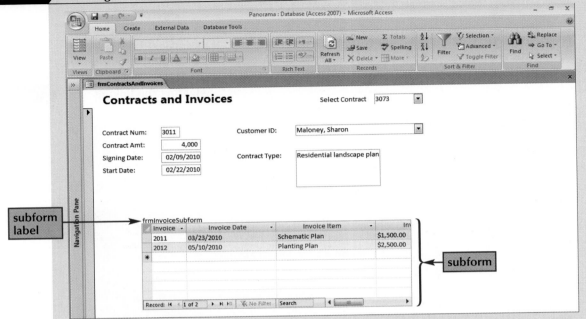

The subform displays the two invoices related to the first contract record for contract number 3011.

Trouble? If the size of the columns in your datasheet differs or the position of your subform is different, don't worry. You'll resize all columns to their best fit and move the subform later.

After viewing the form, Sarah identifies some modifications she wants you to make. The subform is not properly sized and the columns in the subform are not sized to their best fit. She wants you to resize the subform and its columns, so that all columns in the subform are entirely visible. Also, she asks you to delete the subform label, because the label is unnecessary for identifying the subform contents. You'll switch to Design view to make these changes.

To modify the subform's design:

▶ **1.** Switch to Design view. Notice that in Design view, the subform data does not appear in a datasheet format as it does in Form view. That difference causes no problem; you can ignore it.

   First, you'll delete the subform label.

▶ **2.** Deselect all controls, right-click the subform label to open the shortcut menu (make sure no other controls have handles), and then click **Cut**.

   Next, you'll open the subform in another window, and then resize the columns to their best fit in Datasheet view.

3. Move the pointer to the edge of the subform border, click the border's edge to select the subform (an orange border and handles appear on the subform's border when the subform is selected), position the pointer on the border and right-click the border when the pointer changes to a ⬚ shape, and then click **Subform in New Window** on the shortcut menu. The subform opens in Design view. You'll switch to Datasheet view to resize the columns to their best fit.

4. Switch to Datasheet view, and then resize all columns to their best fit, scrolling down the datasheet to resize the Invoice Item column again, as necessary.

5. Save your design changes, and then close the frmInvoiceSubform form.

   Trouble? If the subform in the frmContractsAndInvoices form appears to be blank after you close the frmInvoiceSubform, don't worry. This is a temporary effect; the subform's controls do still exist.

   Next, you'll move and resize the subform in Layout view, where you can more easily observe the effects of your changes.

6. Switch to Layout view, click the edge of the subform to select it, hold down the **Shift** key, click the **Start Date** label, and then release the **Shift** key. The subform and the Start Date label are selected, and you'll align the two controls on their left edges.

7. Click the **Arrange** tab on the Ribbon, and then in the Control Alignment group on the Arrange tab, click **Left**. The two controls are aligned on their left edges.

   Next, you'll widen the subform on its right side.

8. Hold down the **Shift** key, click the **Start Date** label to deselect it, release the **Shift** key, leaving only the subform selected, and then drag the right edge of the subform to the right until all five datasheet columns are fully visible. See Figure 6-39.

After moving and resizing the subform in Layout view ◄ Figure 6-39

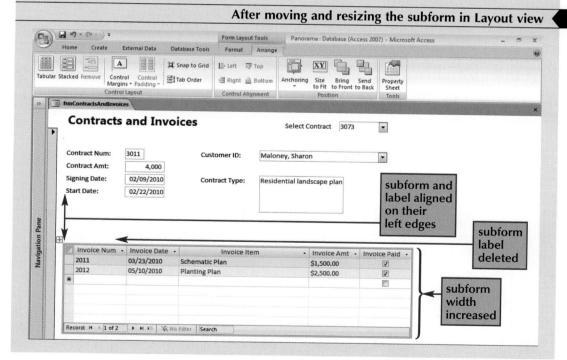

You've finished your work with the subform, and now you need to add two calculated controls to the main form. The first calculated control will display the number of invoices displayed in the subform, and the other will display the total of the invoice amounts displayed in the subform.

Displaying a Subform's Calculated Controls in the Main Form

For the invoices displayed in the subform, Lucia's form design includes calculated controls in the main form for the number of invoices and for the total of the invoice amounts for the related records displayed in the subform. To display these calculated controls in a form or report, you use the Count and Sum functions. The **Count function** determines the number of occurrences of an expression, and its general format as a control in a form or report is =Count(*expression*). The **Sum function** calculates the total of an expression, and its general format as a control in a form or report is =Sum(*expression*). The invoices and invoice amounts are displayed in the subform's Detail section, so you'll need to place calculated controls for the number of invoices and the total invoice amounts in the subform's Form Footer section. However, your design has these two calculated controls displayed in the main form, not in the subform. Fortunately, the subform appears in Datasheet view, and Form Headers and Footers do not appear in Datasheet view, so the subform's calculated controls will not appear in the subform. Although the calculated controls are not displayed in the subform, the calculations occur, and you can add calculated controls in the main form that reference the subform's calculated controls and display these values.

Adding Calculated Controls to a Subform's Form Footer Section

First, you'll open the subform in Design view in another window and add the calculated controls to the subform's Form Footer section.

To add calculated controls to the subform's Form Footer section:

1. Save your form design changes, switch to Design view, click the subform border to select the subform, right-click the border, and then click **Subform in New Window** on the shortcut menu. The subform opens in Design view. See Figure 6-40.

Figure 6-40	Subform in Design view

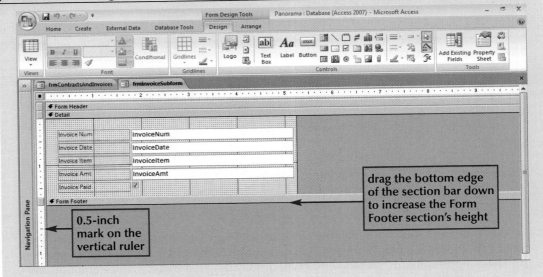

The subform's Detail section contains the tblInvoice table fields. As a subform in the main form, the fields appear as a datasheet even though the fields do not appear that way in Design view. The heights of the subform's Form Header and Form Footer sections are zero, meaning that these sections have been removed from the subform. You'll increase the height of the Form Footer section so that you can add the two calculated controls to the section.

▶ **2.** Place the pointer at the bottom edge of the Form Footer section bar. When the pointer changes to a ✛ shape, drag the bottom edge of the section down to the 0.5-inch mark on the vertical ruler.

Now you'll add the first calculated control to the Form Footer section. To create the text box for the calculated control, you use the **Text Box tool** in the Controls group on the Design tab. Because the Form Footer section is not displayed in a datasheet, you do not need to position the control precisely.

▶ **3.** In the Controls group on the Design tab, click the **Text Box** button.

▶ **4.** Position the + portion of the pointer near the top of the Form Footer section and at the 1-inch mark on the horizontal ruler, and then click the mouse button. Access places a text box control and an attached label control to its left in the Form Footer section.

Next, you'll set the Name and Control Source properties for the text box. Recall that the Name property specifies the name of an object or control. Later, when you add the calculated control in the main form, you'll reference the subform's calculated control value by using its Name property value. The **Control Source property** specifies the source of the data that appears in the control; the Control Source property setting can be either a field name or an expression. You precede expressions with an equal sign to distinguish them from field names, which do not have an equal sign.

▶ **5.** Open the property sheet for the text box in the Form Footer section (the word "Unbound" is displayed inside the text box), click the **All** tab (if necessary), select the entry in the Name text box, type **txtInvoiceAmtSum** in the Name text box, press the **Tab** key, type **=Sum(InvoiceAmt)** in the Control Source text box, and then press the **Tab** key. See Figure 6-41.

Setting properties for the subform calculated control ◀ **Figure 6-41**

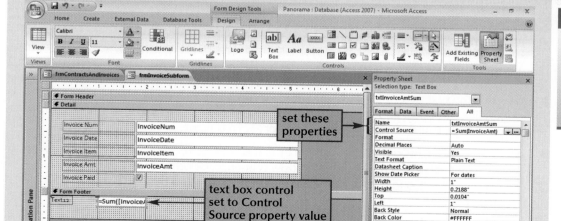

The calculated control's Name property setting (txtInvoiceAmtSum) follows a common naming convention: txt is a prefix tag to identify the control type (a text box), InvoiceAmt is the name for the related field, and Sum is a suffix tag to identify the control as a summary control.

You've finished creating the first calculated control, and now you'll create the other calculated control.

▶ **6.** Repeat Steps 3 through 5, positioning the + portion of the pointer near the top of the Form Footer section and at the 4-inch mark on the horizontal ruler, setting the Name property value to **txtInvoiceNumCount**, and setting the Control Source property value to **=Count(InvoiceNum)**.

When you use the Count function, you are counting the number of displayed records—in this case, the number of records displayed in the subform. Instead of using InvoiceNum as the expression for the Count function, you could use any of the other fields displayed in the subform.

You've finished creating the subform's calculated controls, so you can close the property sheet, save your subform design changes, and return to the main form.

▶ **7.** Close the property sheet, save your subform changes, and then close the subform. You return to Design view for the main form.

Next, you'll add two calculated controls in the main form to display the values of the two calculated controls from the subform.

Adding Calculated Controls to a Main Form

The subform's calculated controls now contain a count of the number of invoices and a total of the invoice amounts. You need to add two calculated controls in the main form that reference the values in the subform's calculated controls. Because it's easy to make a typing mistake with these references, you'll use Expression Builder to set the Control Source property for the two main form calculated controls.

To add a calculated control to the main form's Detail section:

▶ **1.** In the Controls group on the Design tab, click the **Text Box** button, and then add the text box and its attached label in the Detail section, clicking the + portion of the pointer at the 2-inch mark on the horizontal ruler and the 2-inch mark on the vertical ruler. Don't be concerned about positioning the control precisely, because you'll resize and move the label and text box later.

▶ **2.** Select the label and open the property sheet, set its Caption property to **Number of Invoices:**, right-click an edge of the label to open the shortcut menu, point to **Size**, and then click **To Fit**. Don't be concerned if the label now overlaps the text box.

You'll use Expression Builder to set the Control Source property for the text box.

▶ **3.** Click the text box (the word "Unbound" is displayed inside the text box) to select it, click the **Control Source** text box in the property sheet, and then click the property's **Build** button ⌐...⌐ to open Expression Builder.

▶ **4.** Double-click **frmContractsAndInvoices** in the left column, click **frmInvoiceSubform** in the left column, scroll down the middle column, click **txtInvoiceNumCount** in the middle column, and then click the **Paste** button. See Figure 6-42.

Text box control's expression in the Expression Builder dialog box ◀ Figure 6-42

Access changed the pasted txtInvoiceNumCount to [frmInvoiceSubform].Form!
[txtInvoiceNumCount]. This expression asks Access to display the value of the
txtInvoiceNumCount control that is located in the frmInvoiceSubform form, which
is a form object.

You need to add an equal sign to the start of the expression.

▶ **5.** Press the **Home** key, click the **=** button in the row of operators to the left of the
Paste button, and then click the **OK** button. Access closes the Expression Builder
dialog box and sets the Control Source property.

Next, you'll add a second text box to the main form, set the Caption property for
the label, and use Expression Builder to set the text box's Control Source property.

▶ **6.** Repeat Steps 1 through 3 to add a text box to the main form, clicking the + portion of
the pointer at the 5-inch mark on the horizontal ruler and the 2-inch mark on the vertical ruler, and setting the label's Caption property to **Invoice Amount Total:**.

▶ **7.** With the Expression Builder dialog box open for the new text box, click the **=** button to
insert an equal sign in the large text box, double-click **frmContractsAndInvoices** in
the left column, click **frmInvoiceSubform** in the left column, scroll down the middle
column, click **txtInvoiceAmtSum** in the middle column, and then click the **Paste**
button. Access changed the pasted txtInvoiceAmtSum to the expression
[frmInvoiceSubform].Form![txtInvoiceAmtSum].

Next, you'll save your form changes and view the form in Layout view.

▶ **8.** Close the Expression Builder dialog box, close the property sheet, save your form
changes, and then switch to Layout view. See Figure 6-43.

Figure 6-43 ▶ **After adding two calculated controls**

Next, you need to resize, move, and format the two calculated controls and their attached labels.

Resizing, Moving, and Formatting Calculated Controls

In addition to resizing and repositioning the two calculated controls and their attached labels, you need to change the format of the rightmost calculated control to Currency and to set the following properties for both calculated controls:

- Set the Tab Stop property to a value of No. The **Tab Stop property** specifies whether users can use the Tab key to move to a control on a form. If the Tab Stop property is set to No, users can't tab to the control.
- Set the ControlTip Text property to a value of "Calculated total number of invoices for this contract" for the leftmost calculated control and "Calculated invoice total for this contract" for the rightmost calculated control. The **ControlTip Text property** specifies the text that appears in a ScreenTip when users hold the mouse pointer over a control on a form.

InSight | **Setting Properties in the Property Sheet**

You can set many properties in the property sheet by typing a value in the property's text box, by selecting a value from the property's list box, or by double-clicking the property name. If you need to set a property by typing a long text entry, you can open the Zoom dialog box and type the entry in the dialog box. You can also use Expression Builder to help you enter expressions.

Now you'll resize, move, and format the calculated controls and their attached labels, and you'll set other properties for the calculated controls.

To modify the calculated controls and their attached labels:

1. Right-click the rightmost calculated control, click **Properties** on the shortcut menu to open the property sheet, click the **All** tab in the property sheet (if necessary), set the Format property to **Currency**, and then close the property sheet. The value displayed in the calculated control changes from 4000 to $4,000.00.

   Now you'll resize the calculated controls, adjust the positions of each label and text box pair with respect to each other, and then move the controls into their final positions in the form.

2. Individually, reduce the widths of the two calculated controls. See Figure 6-44.

3. Click the **Number of Invoices** label, use the arrow keys to move the label into position next to its related calculated control, repeat the process for the **Invoice Amount Total** label and its related calculated control, and then deselect all controls. See Figure 6-44.

After modifying the calculated controls and their labels | Figure 6-44

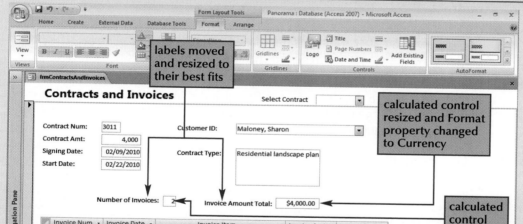

4. Use **Shift + Click** to select the **Start Date** label and the **Number of Invoices** label, click the **Arrange** tab on the Ribbon, click the **Left** button in the Control Alignment group to align the labels on their left edges, press the **Shift** key, click the **Start Date** label to deselect it, release the **Shift** key, and then move the **Number of Invoices** label up to the position shown in Figure 6-45.

5. Select the **Number of Invoices** label and its related calculated control, and then in the Control Alignment group, click the **Top** button to align the two controls on their top edges.

6. Repeat Steps 4 and 5 for the **Invoice Amount Total** label and its related calculated control. See Figure 6-45.

7. Move the bottom calculated control to the left to the position shown in Figure 6-45, align the two calculated controls on their left edges, and then deselect all controls.

Figure 6-45 **After moving and aligning the calculated controls and their labels**

8. Right-click the bottom calculated control, click **Properties** on the shortcut menu, click the **Other** tab in the property sheet, set the Tab Stop property to **No**, and then set the ControlTip Text property to **Calculated invoice total for this contract**.

9. Click the top calculated control, set the Tab Stop property to **No**, set the ControlTip Text property to **Calculated total number of invoices for this contract**, close the property sheet, save your form design changes, and then switch to Form view.

10. Click the **Number of Invoices** text box, position the pointer on the Number of Invoices text box to display its ScreenTip, click the **Invoice Amount Total** text box, and then position the pointer on the Invoice Amount Total text box to display its ScreenTip. See Figure 6-46.

Figure 6-46 **Displaying a control's ScreenTip**

Trouble? Do not be concerned if the ScreenTips do not display on your screen.

Sarah asks you to verify that users can't update the calculated controls in the main form and that users will tab in the correct order through the controls in the form.

Changing the Tab Order in a Form

Pressing the Tab key in Form view moves the focus from one control to another. **Focus** refers to the control that is currently active and awaiting user action; focus also refers to the object and record that is currently active. The order in which you move from control to control, or change the focus, in a form when you press the Tab key is called the **tab order**. Sarah wants to verify that the tab order in the main form is top-to-bottom, left-to-right. First, you'll verify that users can't update the calculated controls.

To test the calculated controls and modify the tab order:

▶ 1. Select **2** in the Number of Invoices text box, and then press the **8** key. The Number of Invoices value remains at 2, and a message is displayed on the status bar. See Figure 6-47.

After attempting to update a calculated control — Figure 6-47

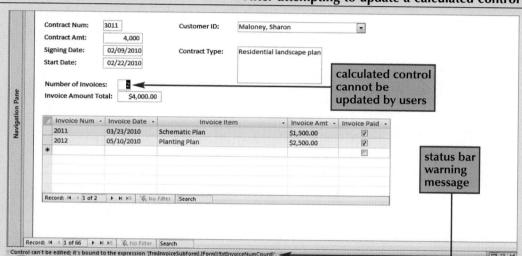

The status bar message warns you that you can't update, or edit, the calculated control because it's bound to an expression. The calculated control in the main form changes in value only when the value of the expression changes.

▶ 2. Click the **Invoice Amount Total** text box, and then press any key. The value remains unchanged, and a message displays on the status bar, because you cannot edit a calculated control.

Next, you'll determine the tab order of the fields in the main form. Sarah wants the tab order to be down and then across.

▶ 3. Select **3011** in the ContractNum text box, press the **Tab** key to advance to the ContractAmt text box, and then press the **Tab** key five more times to advance to the SigningDate, StartDate, ContractType, CustomerID text boxes, in order, and then to the subform.

You tab through the text boxes in a main form before tabbing through the fields in a subform. In the main form, tabbing bypasses the two calculated controls because you set their Tab Stop property to No, and you bypass the Select Contract combo box because it's an unbound control. Also, you tab through only the text boxes in a form, not the labels.

The tab order Sarah wants for the text boxes in the main form (top-to-bottom, left-to-right) is correct for the first four text boxes (ContractNum, ContractAmt, SigningDate, and StartDate text boxes). Then you should tab from the StartDate text box to the CustomerID text box and finally to the ContractType text box, but tabbing is reversed for the last two text boxes. The default tab order doesn't match the order Sarah wants, so you'll change the tab order. You can change the tab order in Layout view or in Design view.

4. Switch to Design view, click the **Arrange** tab on the Ribbon, and then in the Control Layout group on the Arrange tab, click the **Tab Order** button. The Tab Order dialog box opens. See Figure 6-48.

Figure 6-48 | **Changing the tab order for the main form**

Because you did not set the Name property for the combo box control and the calculated controls, Access assigned their names: Combo6 (your name might be different) for the CustomerID combo box, Text13 (your name might be different) for the Number of Invoices calculated control, and Text15 (your name might be different) for the Invoice Amount Total calculated control. The Auto Order button lets you create a left-to-right, top-to-bottom tab order automatically, which is not the order Sarah wants. You need to move the Combo6 entry above the ContractType entry.

5. Click the **row selector** to the left of Combo6, and then drag the row selector above the ContractType entry. The entries are now correct in the correct order.

6. Click the **OK** button, save your form design changes, switch to Form view, and then tab through the controls in the main form to make sure the tab order is correct.

   Trouble? If the tab order is incorrect, switch to Design view, click the Arrange tab on the Ribbon, click Tab Order in the Control Layout group, move appropriate entries in the Tab Order dialog box, and then repeat Step 6.

You've finished adding controls to the form, but the form is plain looking and lacks visual clues for the different controls in the form. You'll complete the form by making it more attractive and easier for Sarah and her staff to use.

Improving a Form's Appearance

The frmContractsAndInvoices form has four distinct areas: the Form Header section containing the title and the Select Contract combo box, the six bound controls in the Detail section, the two calculated controls in the Detail section, and the subform in the Detail section. To visually separate these four areas, you'll increase the height of the Form Header section, add a horizontal line at the bottom of the Form Header section, and draw a rectangle around the calculated controls.

Adding a Line to a Form

You can use lines in a form to improve the form's readability, to group related information, or to underline important values. You use the **Line tool** in Design view to add a line to a form or report.

Adding a Line to a Form or Report | Reference Window

- Display the form or report in Design view.
- In the Controls group on the Design tab, click the Line button.
- Position the pointer where you want the line to begin.
- Drag the pointer to the position for the end of the line, and then release the mouse button. If you want to ensure that you draw a straight horizontal or vertical line, hold down the Shift key before and during the drag operation.
- To make small adjustments to the line length, select the line, hold down the Shift key, and then press an arrow key. To make small adjustments in the placement of a line, select the line, hold down the Ctrl key, and then press an arrow key.

You will add a horizontal line to the Form Header section to separate the controls in the this section from the controls in the Detail section.

To add a line to the form:

▶ **1.** Switch to Design view, and then drag down the bottom of the Form Header section to the 1-inch mark on the vertical ruler to make room to draw a horizontal line at the bottom of the Form Header section.

▶ **2.** In the Controls group on the Design tab, click the **Line** button �️.

▶ **3.** Position the pointer's plus symbol (+) at the left edge of the Form Header section and at the 0.75-inch mark on the vertical ruler.

▶ **4.** Hold down the **Shift** key, drag a horizontal line from left to right, so the end of the line aligns with the right edge of the grid in the Form Header section, release the mouse button, and then release the **Shift** key. See Figure 6-49.

Figure 6-49 **Adding a line to the form**

Trouble? If the line is not straight or not positioned correctly, click the Undo button on the Quick Access Toolbar, and then repeat Steps 2 through 4. If the line is not the correct length, hold down the Shift key, and press one or more of the arrow keys until the line's length is the same as that of the line shown in Figure 6-49.

▶ **5.** Drag up the bottom of the Form Header section to just below the line at the 0.75-inch mark on the vertical ruler.

▶ **6.** Save your form design changes.

Next, you'll add a Rectangle around the calculated controls in the Detail section.

Adding a Rectangle to a Form

You can use a rectangle in a form to group related controls and to separate the group from other controls. You use the **Rectangle tool** in Design view to add a rectangle to a form or report.

Reference Window | **Adding a Rectangle to a Form or Report**

- Display the form or report in Design view.
- In the Controls group on the Design tab, click the Rectangle button.
- Click in the form or report to create a default-sized rectangle, or drag a rectangle in the position and size you want.

You will add a rectangle to the Detail section around the calculated controls and their labels to separate them from the subform and from the other controls in the Detail section.

To add a rectangle to the form:

▶ **1.** In the Controls group on the Design tab, click the **Rectangle** button ☐.

▶ **2.** Position the pointer's plus symbol (+) approximately two grid dots above and two grid dots to the left of the Number of Invoices label.

3. Drag a rectangle down and to the right until all four sides of the rectangle are approximately two grid dots from the two calculated controls and their labels. See Figure 6-50.

Adding a rectangle to the form ◄ Figure 6-50

Trouble? If the rectangle is not sized or positioned correctly, use the sizing handles to adjust its size and the move handle to adjust its position.

Next, you'll set the thickness of the rectangle's lines.

4. In the Controls group on the Design tab, click the **Line Thickness** button ≡ ▾, click the line with the ScreenTip **2 pt** in the list, and then deselect the control.

Next, you'll add color and visual effects to the controls in the Detail and Form Header sections.

Modifying the Visual Effects of the Controls in a Form

Distinguishing one group of controls in a form from other groups is an important visual cue to the users of the form. For example, users should be able to distinguish the bound controls in the form from the calculated controls and from the Select Contract control in the Form Header section. You'll now modify the controls in the form to provide these visual cues. You'll start by setting font properties for the calculated control's labels.

Tip

Using one of the available AutoFormats is always an option for improving the appearance of a form, but an AutoFormat doesn't provide the control you can achieve by setting properties in Design view and in Layout view.

To modify the controls in the form:

1. Select the **Number of Invoices** label and the **Invoice Amount Total** label; in the Font group on the Design tab, click the arrow for the **Font Color** button 🅰; click the **Blue** color (row 7, column 8) in the Standard Colors palette; and then in the Font group on the Design tab, click the **Bold** button 𝐁. The labels' captions now use a bold, blue font.

Next, you'll set properties for the Select Contract label in the Form Header section.

▶ **2.** Select the **Select Contract** label in the Form Header section, set the label's color to **Red** (row 7, column 2 in the Standard Colors palette), and then set the font style to bold.

Next, you'll set the label's Special Effect property to a raised effect. The **Special Effect property** specifies the type of special effect applied to a control in a form or report. The choices for this property are Flat, Raised, Sunken, Etched, Shadowed, and Chiseled.

▶ **3.** In the Controls group on the Design tab, click the arrow for the **Special Effect** button ⬜ , and then click **Special Effect: Raised**. The label now has a raised special effect, and the label's caption now uses a bold, red font.

Next, you'll set the Special Effect property for the bound control labels to a sunken effect.

▶ **4.** Select the **Contract Num** label, **Contract Amt** label, **Signing Date** label, **Start Date** label, **Customer ID** label, and **Contract Type** label, set the controls' Special Effect property to **Special Effect: Sunken**, and then deselect all controls.

Trouble? If setting the Sunken effect does not work, repeat Step 4 and set the selected controls' Special Effect property to Special Effect: Shadowed, and then repeat Step 4 and set the selected controls' Special Effect property to Special Effect: Sunken.

Finally, you'll set the background color of the Form Header section, the Detail section, the Select Contract combo box, and the two calculated controls. You can use the **Fill/Back Color button** in the Font group on the Design tab to change the background color of a control, section, or object (form or report).

▶ **5.** Click the Form Header's section bar, and in the Font group on the Design tab, click the arrow for the **Fill/Back Color** button 🎨 ; and then click the **Access Theme 2** color (row 2, column 2) in the Access Theme Colors palette. The Form Header's background color changes to the Access Theme 2 color.

▶ **6.** Click the Detail section's section bar, and in the Font Group on the Design tab, click the **Fill/Back Color** button to change the Detail section's background color to the **Access Theme 2** color.

▶ **7.** Select the **Select Contract** combo box, **Number of Invoices** text box, and the **Invoice Amount Total** text box, set the selected controls' background color to the **Access Theme 2** color, and then deselect all controls by clicking to the right of the Detail section's grid. See Figure 6-51.

Completed custom form in Design view | Figure 6-51

8. Switch to Form view, and then click the **ContractNum** text box to deselect the value. See Figure 6-52.

Completed custom form in Form view | Figure 6-52

Trouble? Depending on which control has the focus in the form, the CustomerID combo box's background color might be white or it might be the background color of the Detail section.

▶ **9.** Test the form by tabbing from field to field, navigating from record to record, and using the Select Contract combo box to find records, making sure you don't change any field values and observing that the calculated controls display the correct values.

You've completed the custom form.

▶ **10.** Save your form design changes, close the form, close the Panorama database, make a backup copy of the database, open the **Panorama** database, compact and repair the database, close the database, and then exit Access.

The custom form you created will make it easier for Sarah and her staff to work with contract and invoice data in the Panorama database.

Review | **Session 6.3 Quick Check**

1. To create a combo box to find records in a form with the Combo Box Wizard, the form's record source must be a(n) _____ .
2. You use the _____ tool to add a subform to a form.
3. To calculate subtotals and overall totals in a form or report, you use the _____ function.
4. The Control Source property setting can be either a(n) _____ or a(n) _____ .
5. Explain the difference between the Tab Stop property and tab order.
6. What is focus?
7. The _____ property has settings such as Raised and Sunken.

Tutorial Summary | Review

In this tutorial, you examined general form design guidelines and learned how to use them in planning a custom form. You learned how to change a lookup field back to a Text field, to print database relationships, and to use the Documenter. You created a datasheet form, a multiple items form, and a split form, and you modified a form in Layout view. After creating a blank bound form, you learned how to add bound controls to a form, and how to select, move, align, resize, delete, and rename controls. You also learned how to add and delete form headers and footers, how to add a combo box to display and update a field and a combo box to find records, how to add a subform to a form, how to add calculated controls to a subform and a main form, and how to change the tab order in a form. Finally, you learned how to improve the visual appearance of a form.

Key Terms

Anchor property	Detail section	rulers
bound control	Display Control property	section bar
bound form	Documenter	section selector
calculated control	Fill/Back Color button	sizing handle
Caption property	focus	Special Effect property
combo box	Form Footer section	Split Form tool
Combo Box tool	Form Header section	stacked layout
control	form selector	Subform/Subreport tool
control layout	grid	Sum function
Control Margins property	label	tab order
Control Padding property	Line tool	Tab Stop property
Control Source property	move handle	tabular layout
Control Wizard	Multiple Items tool	Text Box tool
ControlTip Text property	Name property	unbound control
Count function	Record Source property	unbound form
custom form	Rectangle tool	Visible property
Datasheet tool	Row Source property	

Practice	**Review Assignments**

Practice the skills you learned in the tutorial using the same case scenario.

Data File needed for the Review Assignments: Products.accdb (*cont. from Tutorial 5*)

Sarah wants you to create several forms, including a custom form that displays and updates companies and the products they offer. You'll do so by completing the following:

1. Open the **Products** database located in the Level.02\Review folder provided with your Data Files.

2. Remove the lookup feature from the CompanyID field in the **tblProduct** table, and resize the Company ID column to its best fit.

3. Edit the relationship between the primary tblCompany and related tblProduct tables to enforce referential integrity and to cascade update related fields. Create the relationship report, and then save the report as **rptRelationshipsForProducts**.

4. Use the Documenter to document the qryContactList query. Select all query options; use the Names, Data Types, and Sizes option for fields; and use the Names and Fields option for indexes. Print the report produced by the Documenter.

5. Use the Datasheet tool to create a form based on the tblProduct table, and then save the form as **frmProductDatasheet**.

6. Use the Multiple Items tool to create a form based on the qryCompanyList query, and then save the form as **frmCompanyListMultipleItems**.

7. Use the Split Form tool to create a split form based on the tblProduct table, and then make the following changes to the form in Layout view.

    a. Remove the Unit control from the stacked layout, and then anchor it to the bottom left.

    b. Remove the five controls in the right column from the stacked layout, and then anchor the group to the bottom right.

    c. Remove the ProductType and Price controls from the stacked layout, move them to the top right, and then anchor them to the top right.

    d. Reduce the widths of the ProductID and CompanyID text boxes to a reasonable size.

    e. Save the modifiied form as **frmProductSplitForm**.

8. Use Figure 6-53 and the following steps to create a custom form named **frmCompaniesWithProducts** based on the tblCompany and tblProduct tables.

Figure 6-53

a. Place the fields from the tblCompany table at the top of the Detail section. Delete the Contact Last Name label and change the caption for the Contact First Name label to **Contact:**.

b. Move the fields into two columns in the Detail section, resizing and aligning controls, as necessary.

c. Add the title in the Form Header section.

d. Make sure the form's Record Source property is set to tblCompany, and then add a combo box in the Form Header section to find CompanyName field values. In the wizard steps, select the CompanyName and CompanyID fields, and hide the key column. Resize and move the control.

e. Add a subform based on the tblProduct table, include only the fields shown in Figure 6-53, link with CompanyID, name the subform **frmPartialProductSubform**, delete the subform label, and resize the columns in the subform to their best fit and resize and position the subform.

f. Add a calculated control that displays the number of products displayed in the subform. Set the calculated control's Tab Stop property to No, and the ControlTip Text property to **Calculated number of products**.

g. Add a line in the Form Header section, and add a rectangle around the calculated control and its label, setting the line thickness of both controls to the line style with the ScreenTip 3 pt.

h. Use the Dark Label Text font (row 1, column 3 in the Access Theme Colors palette) for all labels, and use the Background fill color (row 1, column 5 in the Access Theme Colors palette) for the sections, the calculated control, and the Select Company combo box.

i. Make sure the tab order is top-to-bottom, left-to-right for the main form text boxes.

9. Close the Products database without exiting Access, make a backup copy of the database, open the **Products** database, compact and repair the database, close the database, and then exit Access.

Challenge | **Case Problem 1**

Apply the skills you learned in the tutorial to create a custom form for a small music school.

Data File needed for this Case Problem: Contract.accdb (*cont. from Tutorial 5*)

Pine Hill Music School   Yuka wants you to create several forms, including a custom form that displays and updates the school's music contracts with students. You'll do so by completing the following:

1. Open the **Contract** database located in the Level.02\Case1 folder provided with your Data Files.
2. Remove the lookup feature from the TeacherID field in the **tblContract** table, and then resize the Teacher ID column to its best fit.
3. Define a one-to-many relationship between the primary tblTeacher table and the related tblContract table. Select the referential integrity option and the cascade updates option for this relationship.
4. Use the Documenter to document the tblContract table. Select all table options; use the Names, Data Types, and Sizes option for fields; and use the Names and Fields option for indexes. Print the report produced by the Documenter.
5. Use the Multiple Items tool to create a form based on the qryLessonsByTeacher query, change the title to **Lessons by Teacher**, and then save the form as **frmLessonsByTeacherMultipleItems**.
6. Use the Split Form tool to create a split form based on the qryLessonsByTeacher query, and then make the following changes to the form in Layout view.
   a. Reduce the widths of all six text boxes to a reasonable size.
   b. Remove the LessonType, LessonLength, and MonthlyLessonCost controls from the stacked layout, move these three controls to the right and then to the top of the form, and then anchor them to the top right.
   c. Select the MonthlyLessonCost control and its label, and then anchor them to the bottom right.
   d. Remove the ContractEndDate control from the stacked layout, and then anchor the control to the bottom left.
   e. Change the title to **Lessons by Teacher**, and then save the modifiied form as **frmLessonsByTeacherSplitForm**.
7. Use Figure 6-54 and the following steps to create a custom form named **frmContract** based on the tblContract table.

Figure 6-54

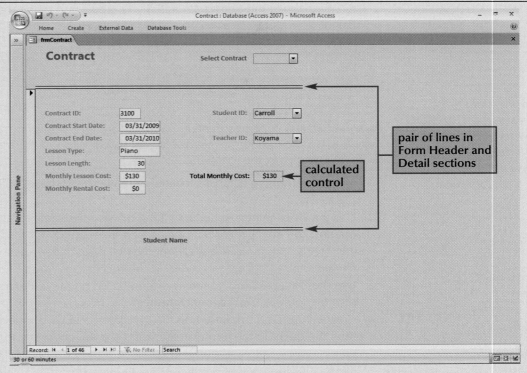

a. For the StudentID combo box, select the LastName, FirstName, and StudentID fields, in order; and sort in ascending order by the LastName field and then by the FirstName field.

b. For the TeacherID combo box, select the LastName, FirstName, and TeacherID fields, in order; and sort in ascending order by the LastName field and then by the FirstName field.

c. Make sure the form's Record Source property is set to tblContract, and then add a combo box in the Form Header section to find ContractID field values.

⊕ EXPLORE

d. Add a calculated control that displays the total of the MonthlyLessonCost and MonthlyRentalCost fields. Set the calculated control's Tab Stop property to No and format the values as currency with no decimal places.

⊕ EXPLORE

e. Add a line in the Form Header section, add a second line below it, and then add a second pair of lines near the bottom of the Detail section. Set the line thickness of all lines to the line setting with the ScreenTip 1 pt.

⊕ EXPLORE

f. Use the Label tool to add your name below the pair of lines at the bottom of the Detail section.

g. For the labels in the Details section, except for the Total Monthly Cost label and the label displaying your name, use the Red font (row 7, column 2 in the Standard Colors palette).

h. For the title, the Select Contract label, and the label displaying your name, use the Dark Red font (row 7, column 1 in the Standard Colors palette).

i. For the background color of the bound controls in the Detail section, use the Background fill color (row 1, column 5 in the Access Theme Colors palette). For the background fill color of the sections, the calculated control, and the Select Contract combo box, use the Brown 3 color (row 4, column 10 in the Standard Colors palette).

j. Make sure the tab order is top-to-bottom, left-to-right for the main form text boxes.

8. Close the Contract database without exiting Access, make a backup copy of the database, open the **Contract** database, compact and repair the database, close the database, and then exit Access.

| Create | **Case Problem 2** |

Use the skills you learned in the tutorial to work with the data for a health and fitness center and to create a custom form.

Data File needed for this Case Problem: Training.accdb (*cont. from Tutorial 5*)

Parkhurst Health & Fitness Center Martha Parkhurst wants you to create several forms, including two custom forms that display and update data in the Training database. You'll do so by completing the following:

1. Open the **Training** database located in the Level.02\Case2 folder provided with your Data Files.

2. Use the Documenter to document the qryMemberNames query. Select all query options; use the Names, Data Types, and Sizes option for fields; and use the Names and Fields option for indexes. Print the first page of the report produced by the Documenter.

3. Use the Datasheet tool to create a form based on the tblProgram table, and then save the form as **frmProgramDatasheet**.

⊕EXPLORE

4. Create a custom form based on the qryUpcomingExpirations query. Display all fields from the query in the form. Create your own design for the form. Add a label to the bottom of the Detail section that contains your first and last names. Change the label's font so that your name appears in bold, blue text. Change the ExpirationDate text box format so that the field value displays in bold, red text. Save the form as **frmUpcomingExpirations**.

5. Use Figure 6-55 and the following steps to create a custom form named **frmProgramsAndMembers** based on the tblProgram and tblMember tables.

Figure 6-55

a. Selected fields from the **tblMember** table appear in a subform named **frmProgramMemberSubform**.

b. The calculated control displays the total number of records that appear in the subform. Set the calculated control's ControlTip Text property to **Total number of members in this program**. Set the calculated control's Tab Stop property to No.

c. Apply an appropriate AutoFormat to the form.

d. View the completed form.

6. Close the Training database without exiting Access, make a backup copy of the database, open the **Training** database, compact and repair the database, close the database, and then exit Access.

Create | **Case Problem 3**

Use the skills you learned in the tutorial to work with a database that contains data about an agency that recycles household goods and to create a custom form.

Data File needed for this Case Problem: Agency.accdb (*cont. from Tutorial 5*)

Rossi Recycling Group Mary Rossi asks you to create several forms, including a custom form for the Agency database so that she can better track donations for the agency. You'll do so by completing the following:

1. Open the **Agency** database located in the Level.02\Case3 folder provided with your Data Files.

2. Use the Documenter to document the tblDonor table. Select all table options; use the Names, Data Types, and Sizes option for fields; and use the Names and Fields option for indexes. Print the report produced by the Documenter.

3. Use the Multiple Items tool to create a form based on the qryDonorPhoneList query, change the title to **Donor Phone List**, and then save the form as **frmDonorPhoneListMultipleItems**.

4. Use the Split Form tool to create a split form based on the tblDonor table, and then make the following changes to the form in Layout view.
   a. Reduce the widths of all five text boxes to a reasonable size.
   b. Remove the FirstName, LastName, and Phone controls from the stacked layout, move them to the top right, and then anchor them to the top right.
   c. Change the title to **Donor**, and then save the modifiied form as **frmDonorSplitForm**.
5. Use Figure 6-56 and the following steps to create a custom form named **frmDonorDonations** based on the tblDonor and tblDonation tables.

Figure 6-56

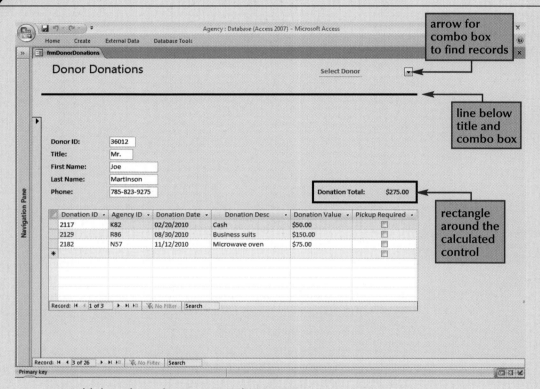

   a. Add the title in the Form Header section.
   b. Make sure the form's Record Source property is set to tblDonor, and then add a combo box in the Form Header section to find DonorID field values. In the wizard steps, select the DonorID field. Format the label using a bold, Red font (row 7, column 2 in the Standard Colors palette) and the Chiseled special effect.
   c. Add a subform based on the tblDonation table, name the subform **frmDonorDonationSubform**, delete the subform label, and resize the columns in the subform to their best fit and resize and position the subform.

⊕ EXPLORE

   d. Add a calculated control that displays the total of the DonationValue field displayed in the subform with the Currency format. Set the calculated control's Tab Stop property to No, and the Border Style property to Transparent.
   e. Add a line in the Form Header section, and add a rectangle around the calculated control and its label, setting the line thickness of both controls to the line style with the ScreenTip 3 pt.
   f. Use the background color Aqua Blue 2 (row 3, column 9 in the Standard Colors palette) for the sections, the calculated control, and the Select Donor combo box.
   g. Make sure the tab order is top-to-bottom for the main form text boxes.

6. Close the Agency database without exiting Access, make a backup copy of the database, open the **Agency** database, compact and repair the database, close the database, and then exit Access.

| Create | **Case Problem 4** |

Use the skills you learned in the tutorial to work with the data for a luxury property rental company and to create two custom forms.

Data File needed for this Case Problem: Vacation.accdb (*cont. from Tutorial 5*)

GEM Ultimate Vacations   Griffin and Emma MacElroy want you to create several forms, including a custom form that displays and updates guest and reservation data in the Vacation database. You'll do so by completing the following:

1. Open the **Vacation** database located in the Level.02\Case4 folder provided with your Data Files.
2. Remove the lookup feature from the PropertyID field in the **tblReservation** table.
3. Edit the relationship between the primary tblProperty and related tblReservation tables to enforce referential integrity and to cascade update related fields. Create the relationship report, and then save the report as **rptRelationshipsForVacation**.
4. Use the Documenter to document the qryIllinoisGuests query. Select all query options; use the Names, Data Types, and Sizes option for fields; and use the Nothing option for indexes. Print the report produced by the Documenter.
5. Use the Datasheet tool to create a form based on the qryGuestTripDates query, and then save the form as **frmGuestTripDates**.

⊕ EXPLORE

6. Create a custom form based on the qryRentalCost query. Display all fields in the form. Use your own design for the form, but use the title **Reserved Trips** in the Form Header section, and use the Label tool to add your name to the Form Header section. Save the form as **frmRentalCost**.
7. Use Figure 6-57 and the following steps to create a custom form named **frmGuestsWithReservations** based on the tblGuest and tblReservation tables.

Figure 6-57

a. Add the title in the Form Header section.

b. Make sure the form's Record Source property is set to tblGuest and then add a combo box in the Form Header section to find GuestID field values.

c. Add a subform based on the tblReservation table, name the subform **frmGuestAndReservationSubform**, delete the subform label, and resize the columns in the subform to their best fit and resize and position the subform.

⊕ **EXPLORE**

d. Add a calculated control that displays the total of the People field displayed in the subform. Set the calculated control's Tab Stop property to No, and set the label's and calculated control's Border Style property to Transparent.

e. Add a line in the Form Header section, and add a rectangle around the calculated control and its label, setting the line thickness of both controls to the line style with the ScreenTip 3 pt.

f. Use the Background fill color (row 1, column 5 in the Access Theme Colors palette) for the sections and the calculated control.

g. Use the Raised special effect for the labels in the Detail section and the Form Header section.

h. Make sure the tab order is top-to-bottom and left-to-right for the main form text boxes.

8. Close the Vacation database without exiting Access, make a backup copy of the database, open the **Vacation** database, compact and repair the database, close the database, and then exit Access.

Create | Case Problem 5

Use the skills you learned in this tutorial to work with the data for an Internet service provider.

Data File needed for this Case Problem: ACE.accdb (*cont. from Tutorial 5*)

Always Connected Everyday   Chris and Pat Dixon want you to create several forms, including a custom form that displays and updates data in the ACE database. You'll do so by completing the following:

1. Open the **ACE** database located in the Level.02\Case5 folder provided with your Data Files.
2. In Tutorial 5, you created a lookup field in the tblCustomer table. Remove the lookup feature from this field.
3. Make sure that the table relationship enforces referential integrity and cascade updates related fields. Create the relationship report, and then save the report as **rptRelationshipsForACE**.
4. Use the Documenter to document one of your forms. Select all form options and use the Names option for sections and controls. Print the report produced by the Documenter.
5. In Tutorial 5, you created forms to display and update the data in the ACE database. Review these forms, and develop a consistent design strategy that you'll use to customize all the forms. Your design strategy should include the use of combo boxes for foreign keys and for searching, calculated controls, and visual effects.
6. Using your form design strategy, customize all the forms in the ACE database.
7. Close the ACE database without exiting Access, make a backup copy of the database, open the **ACE** database, compact and repair the database, close the database, and then exit Access.

Research | Internet Assignments

Use the Internet to find and work with data related to the topics presented in this tutorial.

The purpose of the Internet Assignments is to challenge you to find information on the Internet that you can use to work effectively with this software. The actual assignments are updated and maintained on the Course Technology Web site. Log on to the Internet and use your Web browser to go to the Student Online Companion for New Perspectives Office 2007 at **www.course.com/np/office2007**. Then navigate to the Internet Assignments for this tutorial.

Assess | SAM Assessment and Training

If you have a SAM user profile, you may have access to hands-on instruction, practice, and assessment of the skills covered in this tutorial. Log in to your SAM account (**http://sam2007.course.com**) to launch any assigned training activities or exams that relate to the skills covered in this tutorial.

Review | Quick Check Answers

Session 6.1

1. forms
2. Row Source
3. An Access tool that creates detailed documentation of the objects in a database.

4. A form tool that creates a customizable form that displays multiple records from a source table or query in a datasheet format.

5. A form that displays a form's data in Form view and Datasheet view at the same time; the views are synchronized with each other at all times.

6. Anchor

Session 6.2

1. A bound form has a table or query as its record source, and is used to maintain and display table data.

2. A bound control is connected to a field in the database; an unbound control is not.

3. grid

4. move

5. Click the text box to select it, position the pointer anywhere on the border of the text box (but not on a move or sizing handle), and then drag the text box and its attached label.

6. Select the control, position the pointer on a sizing handle, and then drag the pointer in the appropriate direction until it is the desired size.

7. combo box

8. Right-click the label, click Properties on the shortcut menu, click the All tab, and then change the entry in the Caption text box.

9. The Form Header section lets you add titles, instructions, command buttons, and other controls to the top of a form. This section of the form does not change as you navigate through the records.

Session 6.3

1. table or query

2. Subform/Subreport

3. Sum

4. field name, expression

5. The Tab Stop property specifies whether users can use the Tab key to move to a control on a form. Tab order is the order in which you move from control to control, or change the focus, in a form when you press the Tab key.

6. Focus refers to the control that is currently active and awaiting user action; focus also refers to the object and record that is currently active.

7. Special Effect

Ending Data Files

Level.02 → Tutorial — Panorama.accdb

Review — Products.accdb

Case1 — Contract.accdb

Case2 — Training.accdb

Case3 — Agency.accdb

Case4 — Vacation.accdb

Case5 — ACE.accdb

Objectives

Session 7.1
- View, filter, and copy report information in Report view
- Modify a report in Layout view
- Modify a report in Design view

Session 7.2
- Design and create a custom report
- Sort and group data in a report
- Add, move, resize, and align controls in a report
- Add lines to a report
- Hide duplicate values in a report

Session 7.3
- Add the date, page numbers, and title to a report
- Create and modify mailing labels

Creating Custom Reports

Creating Reports with Information About Contracts and Invoices

Case | Belmont Landscapes

At a recent staff meeting, Sarah Fisher indicated that she would like to make some changes to an existing report in the database. She also requested a new report that she can use to produce a printed list of all invoices for all contracts.

In this tutorial, you will modify an existing report and create the new report for Sarah. In modifying and building these reports, you will use many Access report customization features, including grouping data, calculating totals, and adding lines to separate report sections. These features will enhance Sarah's reports and make them easier to read and use.

Starting Data Files

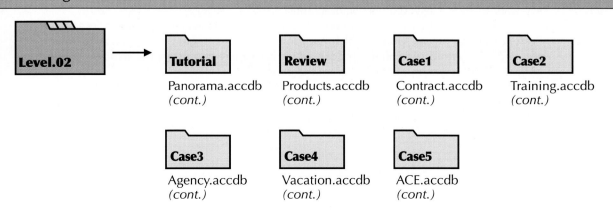

Level.02 →

Tutorial
Panorama.accdb
(cont.)

Review
Products.accdb
(cont.)

Case1
Contract.accdb
(cont.)

Case2
Training.accdb
(cont.)

Case3
Agency.accdb
(cont.)

Case4
Vacation.accdb
(cont.)

Case5
ACE.accdb
(cont.)

Session 7.1

Customizing Existing Reports

A report is a formatted printout (or screen display) of the contents of one or more tables in a database. Although you can format and print data using datasheets, queries, and forms, reports offer greater flexibility and provide a more professional, readable appearance. For example, the staff at Belmont Landscapes can create reports from the database for billing statements and mailing labels, but they could not use datasheets, queries, and forms for the same purposes.

Before Lucia Perez joined Belmont Landscapes to enhance the Panorama database, Sarah Fisher and her staff created two reports. Sarah used the Report tool to create the rptContract report and the Report Wizard to create the rptCustomersAndContracts report. One of Sarah's staff members modified the rptCustomersAndContracts report in Layout view by modifying the title, moving and resizing fields, changing the font color of field names, inserting a picture, and using conditional formatting to format values in the ContractAmt field that exceed $25,000 in a red font. The rptCustomersAndContracts report is an example of a custom report. When you modify a report created by the Report tool or the Report Wizard in Layout view or in Design view, or when you create a report from scratch in Layout view or in Design view, you produce a **custom report**. You need to produce a custom report whenever the Report tool or the Report Wizard cannot automatically create the specific report you need, or when you need to fine-tune an existing report to fix formatting problems or to add controls and special features.

Sarah asks Lucia to review the rptContract report, make improvements to it, and demonstrate features that Sarah's staff can use when working with reports.

Viewing a Report in Report View

You can view reports on screen in Print Preview, Layout view, Design view, and Report view. You've already viewed and worked with reports in Print Preview and Layout view, and you'll find that making modifications in Design view for reports is similar to making changes in Design view for forms. **Report view** provides an interactive view of a report. You can use Report view to view the contents of a report and to apply a filter to the data in a report. You can also copy selected portions of the report to the Clipboard and use the selected data in another program.

InSight	Choosing the View to Use for a Report

You can view a report on screen using Report view, Print Preview, Layout view, or Design view. Which view you choose depends on what you intend to do with the report and its data.

- Use Report view when you want to filter the report data before printing a report, or when you want to copy a selected portion of a report.
- Use Print Preview when you want to see what a report will look like when it is printed. Print Preview is the only view in which you can navigate the pages of a report, zoom in or out, and view a **multiple-column report**, which is a report that prints the same collection of field values in two or more sets across the page.
- Use Layout view when you want to modify a report while seeing actual report data.
- Use Design view when you want to fine-tune a report's design, or when you want to add lines, rectangles, and other controls that are available only in Design view.

You'll open the rptContract report in Report view and show Sarah how she can interact with the report in this view.

To interact with the rptContract report in Report view:

▶ **1.** Start Access, and then open the **Panorama** database in the Level.02\Tutorial folder provided with your Data Files.

Trouble? If the Security Warning is displayed below the Ribbon, either the Panorama database is not located in the Level.02\Tutorial folder or you did not designate that folder as a trusted folder. Make sure you opened the database in the Level.02\Tutorial folder, and make sure that it's a trusted folder.

▶ **2.** Open the Navigation Pane, scroll down the Navigation Pane (if necessary), right-click **rptContract**, click **Open** on the shortcut menu, and then close the Navigation Pane. The rptContract report opens in Report view and the Navigation Pane closes. See Figure 7-1.

Tip

Double-clicking a report name in the Navigation Pane opens the report in Report view.

Report displayed in Report view | **Figure 7-1**

In Report view, you can view the live version of the report prior to printing it, just as you can do in Print Preview. Unlike Print Preview, you can apply filters to the report before printing it. You'll show Sarah how to apply filters to the rptContract report.

▶ **3.** In the first report detail line for Contract Num 3011, right-click **Residential landscape plan** in the Contract Type column to open the shortcut menu, and then point to **Text Filters**. A submenu of filter options for the Text field opens. See Figure 7-2.

Figure 7-2 **Filter options for a Text field in Report view**

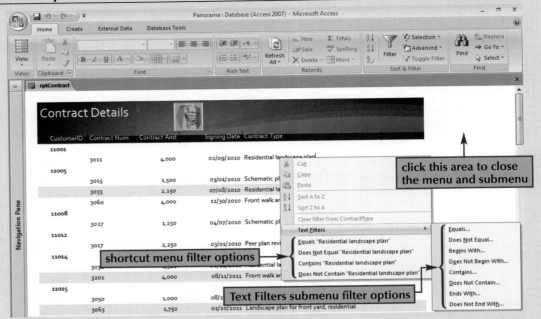

The filter options that appear on the shortcut menu depend on the selected field's data type and the selected value. Because you clicked the ContractType field value without selecting a portion of the value, the shortcut menu displays filter options—various conditions using the value "Residential landscape plan"—for the entire ContractType field value. You'll close the menus and select a portion of the ContractNum field value to show Sarah a different way of filtering the report.

▶ **4.** Click an unused portion of the window (see Figure 7-2) to close the menus, and in the report detail line for Contract Num 3011, double-click **Residential** in the Contract Type column to select it, right-click **Residential**, and then point to **Text Filters** on the shortcut menu. The filter options now apply to the selected text.

Notice that the filter options on the shortcut menu include options such as "Begins With" and "Does Not Begin With," because the text you selected is at the beginning of the field value in the Contract Type column.

▶ **5.** Click **Contains "Residential"** on the shortcut menu. The report content changes to display only those contracts that contain the word "residential" in the Contract Type column.

▶ **6.** Double-click the word **residential** in the Contract Type column for the report detail line for Contract Num 3015 to select it, right-click **residential** to open the shortcut menu, and then point to **Text Filters**. The filter options on the shortcut menu now include the "Ends With" and "Does Not End With" options, because the text you selected is at the end of the field value in the Contract Type column.

Sarah wants to view only those contracts whose Contract Type column equals "residential landscape plan."

▶ **7.** Click an unused portion of the window to close the menus, and in the report detail line for Contract Num 3011, right-click **Residential landscape plan** in the Contract Type column, and then click **Equals "Residential landscape plan"** on the shortcut menu. Only the five contracts that contain the selected phrase are displayed in the report. See Figure 7-3.

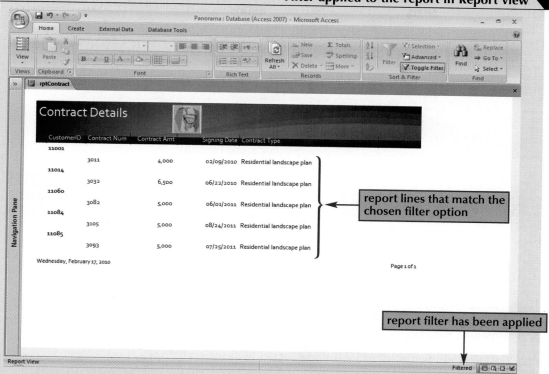

report lines that match the chosen filter option

report filter has been applied

Sarah can print the filtered report, or she can select the entire filtered report or a portion of the filtered report. Then she can copy the selection to the Clipboard and paste it into another program, such as a Word document or an Excel spreadsheet. You'll show Sarah how to copy the entire filtered report to the Clipboard.

8. Click to the left of the Contract Details title at the top of the report (but don't click in the Navigation Pane), drag down to the bottom of the report, release the mouse button to select the entire report, and then in the Clipboard group on the Home tab, point to the **Copy** button. See Figure 7-4.

Tip

To select a portion of the report instead of the entire report, click to the left of the top of the selection and drag down to the bottom of the selection.

Figure 7-4   **After selecting the entire report in Report view**

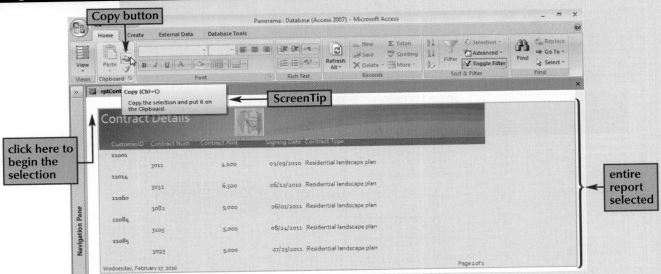

If you needed to copy the selection to the Clipboard, you would click the Copy button (see Figure 7-4). Sarah doesn't need to copy the selection, so you'll show her how to remove the filter from the report.

▶ 9. Click to the left of the Contract Details title at the top of the report to select the top portion of the report and to deselect the rest of the report, right-click **Residential landscape plan** in any report detail line in the Contract Type column, and then click **Clear filter from ContractType**. Access removes the filter and displays the complete report.

▶ 10. Scroll down the report, and notice that some field values in the Contract Type column are not fully displayed and that no grand total of the ContractAmt field values is displayed at the end of the report.

Sarah wants you to enlarge the Contract Type column in the rptContract report so that all field values are fully displayed. She also wants you to insert a space in the CustomerID column heading, remove the report's AutoFormat, format the ContractAmt field values using the Currency format, and add a grand total of the ContractAmt field values. These changes will make the report more useful for Sarah.

Enhancing and Correcting Reports Created by the Report Tool and the Report Wizard | InSight

Creating a report using the Report tool or the Report Wizard can save time, but you should review the report to determine if you need to make any of the following types of common enhancements and corrections:

- Change the report title from the report object name (with an rpt prefix and no spaces) to one that has meaning to the users.
- Reduce the widths of the date and page number controls, and move the controls so that they are not printed on a separate page.
- Review the report in Print Preview and, if the report displays excess pages, adjust the page margins and the placement of controls.
- Verify that all controls are large enough to fully display their values.

Modifying a Report in Layout View

You can make all the report changes Sarah wants in Layout view. Modifying a report in Layout view is similar to modifying a form in Layout view.

To view the report in Layout view:

1. On the status bar, click the **Layout View** button 🖽 , and then scroll to the top of the report (if necessary). See Figure 7-5.

Viewing the report in Layout view | Figure 7-5

Tip

You can also switch views by right-clicking the object tab, and then clicking the view option on the shortcut menu.

Trouble? If the Group, Sort, and Total pane is not open at the bottom of the screen, click the Group & Sort button in the Grouping & Totals group on the Format tab.

Because the rptContract report has a grouping field and a sort field, the Group & Sort button is selected, and the Group, Sort, and Total pane is open at the bottom of the screen. In the **Group, Sort, and Total pane**, you can modify the report's grouping fields and sort fields, and the report calculations for the groups. A **grouping field** is a report sort field that includes a Group Header section before a group of records having the same sort field value and a Group Footer section after the group of records. A **Group Header section** usually displays the group name and the sort field value for the group. A **Group Footer section** usually displays subtotals or counts for the records in that group. The rptContract report's grouping field is the CustomerID field, which is displayed in a Group Header section that precedes the set of contracts for the customer; the grouping field does not have a Group Footer section. The ContractNum field is a secondary sort key, as shown in the Group, Sort, and Total pane.

Because you don't need to change the grouping or sort fields for the report, you'll close the pane and then make Sarah's modifications to the report.

To modify the report in Layout view:

1. In the Grouping & Totals group on the Format tab, click the **Group & Sort** button to close the Group, Sort, and Total pane.

   First, you'll increase the height of the Contract Type column.

2. Scroll down the report to CustomerID 11083, which has the longest field value in the Contract Type column, click the **ContractType** field value for ContractNum 3043, move the pointer to the bottom edge of the selected value, and when the pointer changes to a ↕ shape, drag down the bottom edge to increase the height to display two lines. See Figure 7-6. After you make a resizing adjustment to the control, the portion of the report you're using as a basis for the resizing might move off the screen, and you might have to scroll back to it.

| Figure 7-6 | After resizing the Contract Type column |

Next, you'll change the format of the field values in the Contract Amt column to Currency.

3. Right-click any value in the Contract Amt column to open the shortcut menu, click **Properties** to open the property sheet, set the Format property to **Currency**, and then close the property sheet.

When Lucia made her initial modifications to the tables, queries, forms, and reports in the Panorama database, she failed to change the first column heading in the rptContract report to Customer ID (with a space) when she modified the report. Although Lucia had set the Caption property for the CustomerID field in the tblContract table to Customer ID before she modified the rptContract report, Caption property changes do not propagate to existing forms and reports. However, a Caption property setting propagates to all new forms and reports.

4. Scroll to the top of the report (if necessary), double-click the **CustomerID** column heading, insert a space before "ID," and then press the **Enter** key.

Sarah intends to print the rptContract report periodically in the future, and she finds the AutoFormat at the beginning of the report distracting and unnecessary in a printed report. You'll remove the AutoFormat from the report.

5. In the AutoFormat group on the Format tab, click the **AutoFormat** button to open the AutoFormat gallery, and then click the **None** button (row 3, column 4). The AutoFormat gallery closes, and the AutoFormat is removed from the report. See Figure 7-7.

After removing the AutoFormat from the report ◄ **Figure 7-7**

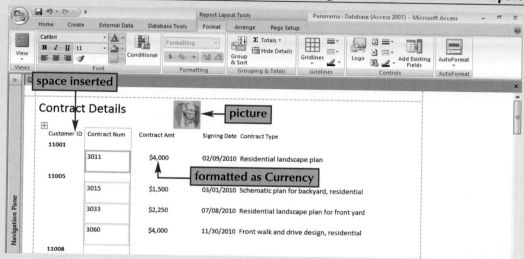

Sarah notes that the picture at the top of the report isn't needed now that you've removed the AutoFormat, so you'll delete it.

6. Right-click the picture at the top of the report to open the shortcut menu, and then click **Delete** to remove the picture.

Removing the AutoFormat also removed the alternate background color setting in the detailed contract lines, and Sarah wants you to restore this feature.

7. Click to the left of **3011** in the Contract Num column to select the detail lines, click the arrow on the **Alternate Fill/Back Color** button to display the gallery of available colors, and then in the Access Theme Colors palette, click the **Background** color (row 1, column 5). The Background color is applied to alternate detail lines in the report.

Sarah's last change to the report is to add a grand total of the ContractAmt field values. First, you must select the Contract Amt column or one of the values in the column.

▶ 8. In the detail line for ContractNum 3011, click **$4,000** in the Contract Amt column, and then in the Grouping & Totals group on the Format tab, click the **Totals** button to display the Totals menu. See Figure 7-8.

Figure 7-8 | **Displaying options on the Totals menu**

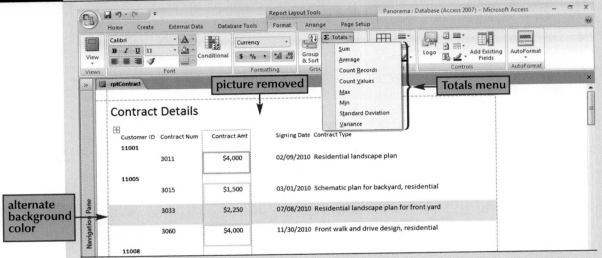

You select one of the eight aggregate functions on the Totals menu to summarize values in the selected column. To calculate and display the grand total contract amount, you'll select the Sum aggregate function.

▶ 9. Click **Sum** on the Totals menu, and then scroll to the bottom of the report. The grand total of the ContractAmt field values ($1,758,075) is displayed at the end of the report, as are subtotals for each group of contracts for each CustomerID field value ($19,000 for the last customer). See Figure 7-9.

Figure 7-9 | **After adding subtotals and a grand total of the ContractAmt field values**

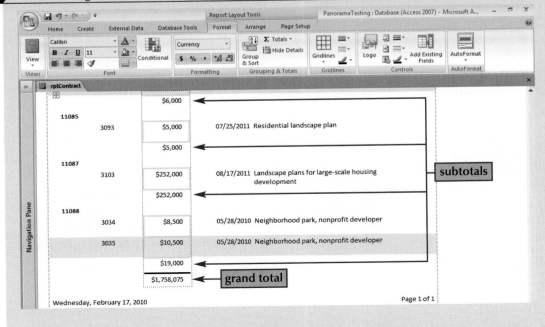

When you use an aggregate function in Layout view, Access adds the results of the function to the end of the report and adds subtotals for each grouping field. Because each customer has few contracts, Sarah asks you to remove the subtotals from the report.

▶ **10.** Right-click the **$19,000** subtotal to open the shortcut menu, click **Delete** to remove the subtotals, and then scroll to the end of the report. Although you deleted the subtotals, the grand total still appears at the end of the report.

Sarah wants to review the rptContract report in Print Preview.

▶ **11.** Save your report changes, switch to Print Preview, and then scroll through the report, ending on the last page of the report.

You can use the Zoom control on the status bar to zoom in or out the report view in 10% increments (click the Zoom In or Zoom Out buttons) or in variable increments (drag the Zoom slider control).

▶ **12.** Click the **Zoom In** button ⊕ on the status bar to increase the zoom percentage to 110%. See Figure 7-10.

Viewing the rptContract report in Print Preview | Figure 7-10

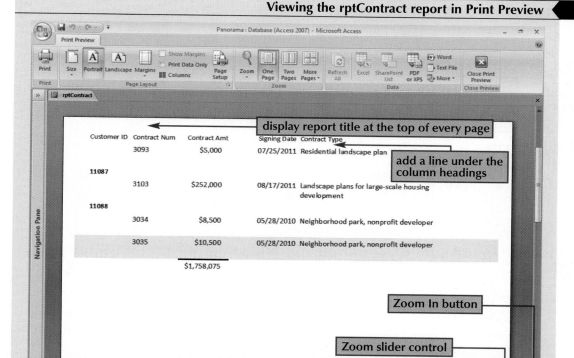

Trouble? Depending on the printer you are using, the last page of your report might differ. If so, don't worry. Different printers format reports in different ways, sometimes affecting the total number of pages and the number of records printed per page.

Sarah identifies two additional modifications she wants you to make to the report. She wants you to add a line below the column heading labels to separate them from the following detail report lines, and she wants the report title to be displayed at the top of every page, not just on the first page of the report.

Modifying a Report in Design View

Unlike the modifications you made to the report in Layout view, you can't use Layout view for Sarah's two new modifications. You must make these modifications in Design view. Design view for reports is similar to Design view for forms, which you used in Tutorial 6 to customize forms.

To view the report in Design view:

▶ **1.** Switch to display the report in Design view. See Figure 7-11.

Figure 7-11 ▶ **rptContract report in Design view**

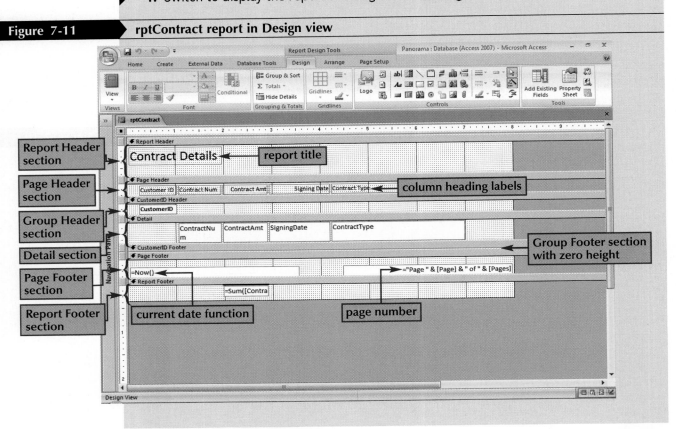

Notice that Design view for a report has most of the same components as Design view for a form. For example, Design view for forms and reports includes horizontal and vertical rulers, grids in each section, and similar buttons in groups on the Design tab.

Design view for the rptContract report displays seven sections: the Report Header section contains the report title, the Page Header section contains column heading labels, the Group Header section (CustomerID Header) contains the CustomerID grouping field, the Detail section contains the bound controls to display the field values for each record in the record source (tblContract), the Group Footer section (CustomerID Footer) has zero height and isn't displayed in the report, the Page Footer section contains the current date and the page number, and the Report Footer section contains a horizontal line above the Sum function for the grand total of the ContactAmt field values.

Each Access report can have the seven different sections described in Figure 7-12.

Access report sections ◄ Figure 7-12

Report Section	Description
Report Header	Appears once at the beginning of a report. Use it for report titles, company logos, report introductions, and cover pages.
Page Header	Appears at the top of each page of a report. Use it for column headings, report titles, page numbers, and report dates. If your report has a Report Header section, it precedes the first Page Header section.
Group Header	Appears before each group of records that has the same sort field value. Use it to print the group name and the field value that all records in the group have in common. A report can have up to 10 grouping levels.
Detail	Appears once for each record in the underlying table or query. Use it to print selected fields from the table or query and to print calculated values.
Group Footer	Appears after each group of records that has the same sort field value. It is usually used to print totals for the group.
Report Footer	Appears once at the end of the report. Use it for report totals and other summary information.
Page Footer	Appears at the bottom of each page of a report. Use it for page numbers and brief explanations of symbols or abbreviations. If your report has a Report Footer section, it precedes the Page Footer section on the last page of the report.

You don't have to include all seven sections in a report. When you design a report, you determine which sections to include and what information to place in each section. Figure 7-13 shows a sample report produced from the Panorama database; it includes all seven sections.

Figure 7-13 — Sample report showing the seven sections of a report

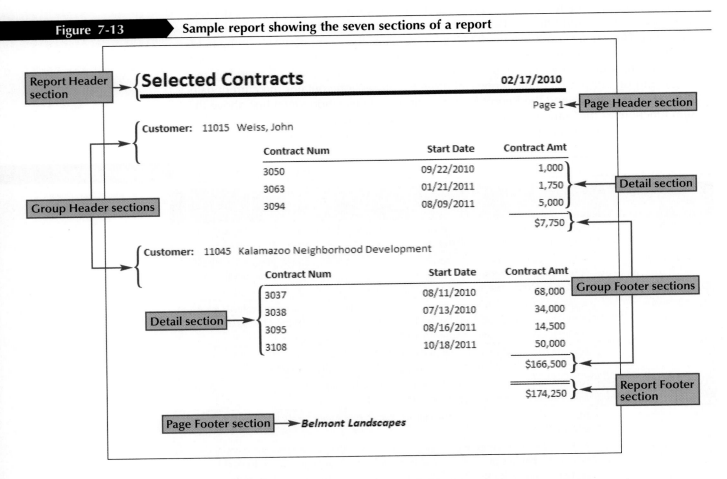

The Report tool used six of the seven report sections to create the rptContract report for Sarah. To make Sarah's changes to the report, you need to increase the height of the Page Header section, move the column heading labels down in the section, add a line under the column heading labels, cut the report title from the Report Header section and paste it in the Page Header section, move the report title, and then resize the Report Header and Page Header sections.

To modify the report in Design view:

▶ 1. Place the pointer on the bottom edge of the Page Header section. When the pointer changes to a ✛ shape, drag the section's edge down until it is at the 1-inch mark on the vertical ruler.

Before you can move the column heading labels down in the Page Header section, you need to remove them and their related text boxes from the tabular layout. Recall that a tabular layout is a control layout arranged in a datasheet format. If you don't remove all the controls from the tabular layout before moving the labels, some of the controls that remain in the tabular layout might shift position or undergo unintended property changes.

▶ 2. Use **Shift + Click** to select all five labels in the Page Header section, the **CustomerID** text box in the CustomerID Header section, the four text boxes in the Detail section, and the grand total text box in the Report Footer section, and then click the **Arrange** tab on the Ribbon. See Figure 7-14.

3. In the Control Layout group on the Arrange tab, click the **Remove** button to remove all selected controls from the tabular layout.

4. Use **Shift + Click** to deselect the **CustomerID** text box in the CustomerID Header section, the four text boxes in the Detail section, and the grand total text box in the Report Footer section, leaving only the five labels selected, and then use the ↓ key to move the labels down in the Page Header section until the tops of the labels are at the 0.625-inch mark on the vertical ruler.

Next, you'll add a line under the labels.

5. Click to the right of the grid in the Page Header section to deselect all controls, click the **Design** tab on the Ribbon, and then in the Controls group on the Design tab, click the **Line** button ⟍.

6. Position the pointer's plus symbol (+) at the lower-left corner of the Customer ID label in the Page Header section, hold down the **Shift** key, drag a horizontal line from left to right, so the end of the line aligns with the right edge of "Contract Type" in the Contract Type label box, release the mouse button, and then release the **Shift** key.

7. In the Controls group on the Design tab, click the **Line Thickness** button ☰▾, click the line with the ScreenTip **1 pt** in the list, and then deselect the control.

8. Reduce the height of the Page Header section by dragging the bottom of the section up until it touches the bottom of the line you just added.

Finally, you'll cut the report title from the Report Header section and paste it in the Page Header section, and then remove the Report Header section.

9. Right-click the report title in the Report Header section to open the shortcut menu, click **Cut** to delete the control and place it on the Clipboard, right-click the **Page Header** section bar to select that section and open the shortcut menu, and then click **Paste**. The report title is pasted in the upper-left corner of the Page Header section.

Tip

If you want to make sure you draw a straight horizontal or vertical line, press the Shift key before you start drawing the line and release the Shift key after you've created it.

▶ **10.** Drag the bottom of the Report Header section all the way up to the Report Header section bar to remove the section from the report. See Figure 7-15.

Figure 7-15 ▶ **After modifying the rptContract report in Design view**

▶ **11.** Save your report changes, switch to Print Preview, and then scroll through the report, ending on the last page of the report. See Figure 7-16.

Figure 7-16 ▶ **The modified rptContract report in Print Preview**

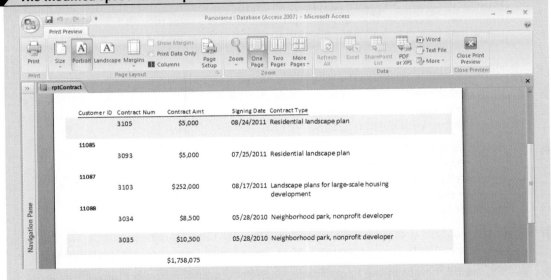

▶ **12.** Close the report.

▶ **13.** If you are not continuing on to the next session, close the Panorama database, and then exit Access.

Now that you have completed the changes to the rptContract report, you'll create a custom report for Sarah in the next session.

Session 7.1 Quick Check | Review

1. What is a custom report?
2. You can view a report in Report view. What other actions can you perform in Report view?
3. What is a grouping field?
4. Describe the seven sections of an Access report.

Session 7.2

Designing a Custom Report

Before you create a custom report, you should first plan the report's contents and appearance.

Guidelines for Designing a Report | InSight

When you plan a report, you should keep in mind the following report design guidelines:

- Determine the purpose of and record source for the report. Recall that the record source is a table or query that provides the fields for a form or report. If the report displays detailed information (a **detail report**), such as a list of all contracts, then the report will display fields from the record source in the Detail section. If the report displays only summary information (a **summary report**), such as total contracts by city, then no detailed information appears; only grand totals and possibly subtotals appear based on calculations using fields from the record source.
- Determine the sort order for the information in the report.
- Identify any grouping fields in the report.

At the same time you are designing a report, you should keep in mind the following report formatting guidelines:

- Balance the report's attractiveness against its readability and economy. Keep in mind that an attractive, readable two-page report is more economical than a report of three pages or more. Unlike forms, which usually display one record at a time in the main form, reports display multiple records. Instead of arranging fields vertically as you do in a form, you usually position fields horizontally across the page in a report. Typically, you single space the detail lines in a report. At the same time, make sure to include enough white space between columns so the values do not overlap or run together.
- Group related fields and position them in a meaningful, logical order. For example, position identifying fields, such as names and codes, on the left. Group together all location fields, such as street and city, and position them in their customary order.
- Identify each column of field values with a column heading label that names the field.
- Include the report title, page number, and date on every page of the report.
- Identify the end of a report either by displaying grand totals or an end-of-report message.
- Use few colors, fonts, and graphics to keep the report uncluttered and to keep the focus on the information.
- Use a consistent style for all reports in a database.

After working with Sarah and her staff to determine their requirements for a new report, Lucia prepared a paper design for a custom report to display invoices grouped by invoice item. Lucia then used her paper design to create the report shown in Figure 7-17.

Figure 7-17 ▷ **Lucia's design for the custom report**

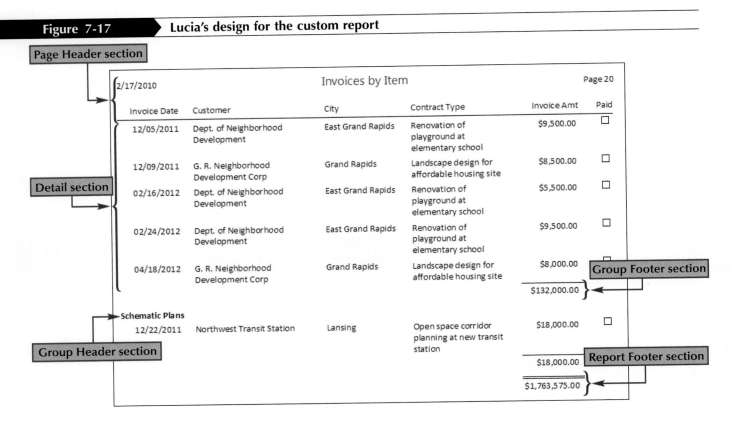

The custom report will list the records for all invoices and will contain five sections:

- The Page Header section contains the report title ("Invoices by Item") centered between the current date on the left and the page number on the right. A horizontal line separates the column heading labels from the rest of the report page. From your work with the Report tool and the Report Wizard, you know that, by default, Access places the report title in the Report Header section and the date and page number in the Page Footer section. Sarah prefers the date, report title, and page number to appear at the top of each page, so you need to place this information in the custom report's Page Header section.
- The InvoiceItem field value from the tblInvoice table is displayed in a Group Header section.
- The Detail section contains the InvoiceDate, InvoiceAmt, and InvoicePaid field values from the tblInvoice table; the ContractType field value from the tblContract table; the City field value from the tblCustomer table; and the Customer calculated field value from the qryCustomersByName query. The detail records are sorted in ascending value by the InvoiceDate field.
- A subtotal of the InvoiceAmt field values is displayed below a line in the a Group Footer section.
- The grand total of the InvoiceAmt field values is displayed below a double line in the Report Footer section.

Before you start creating the custom report, you need to create a query that'll serve as the record source for the report.

Creating a Query for a Custom Report

The data for a report or form can come from a single table, from a single query based on one or more tables, or from multiple tables and/or queries. Sarah's report will contain data from the tblInvoice, tblContract, and tblCustomer tables, and from the qryCustomersByName query. You'll use the Simple Query Wizard to create a query to retrieve all the data required for the custom report and to serve as the report's record source.

Tip

For reports and forms that use data from multiple tables and/or queries, you should create a query to serve as the record source. If the report or form requirements change, you can easily add fields, including calculated fields, to the query.

To create the query using the Simple Query Wizard:

▶ 1. If you took a break after the previous session, make sure that the Panorama database is open and the Navigation Pane is closed.

▶ 2. Click the **Create** tab on the Ribbon, in the Other group on the Create tab, click the **Query Wizard** button, make sure **Simple Query Wizard** is selected, and then click the **OK** button. The first Simple Query Wizard dialog box opens.

   You need to select fields from the tblInvoice, tblContract, and tblCustomer tables, and from the qryCustomersByName query, in that order.

▶ 3. Make sure **Table: tblInvoice** is selected in the Tables/Queries box, and then move the **InvoiceItem**, **InvoiceDate**, **InvoiceAmt**, and **InvoicePaid** fields, in that order, to the Selected Fields list box.

▶ 4. Select **Table: tblContract** in the Tables/Queries box, and then move the **ContractType** field to the Selected Fields list box.

▶ 5. Select **Table: tblCustomer** in the Tables/Queries box, and then move the **City** field to the Selected Fields list box.

▶ 6. Select **Query: qryCustomersByName** in the Tables/Queries box, move the **Customer** calculated field to the Selected Fields list box, and then click the **Next** button.

▶ 7. Make sure the **Detail (shows every field of every record)** option button is selected, and then click the **Next** button to open the final Simple Query Wizard dialog box.

   After entering the query name and creating the query, you'll need to set the sort fields for the query.

▶ 8. Change the query name to **qryInvoicesByItem**, click the **Modify the query design** option button, and then click the **Finish** button.

   The InvoiceItem field will be a grouping field, which means it's the primary sort field, and the InvoiceDate field is the secondary sort field.

▶ 9. Set the InvoiceItem Sort text box to **Ascending**, set the InvoiceDate Sort text box to **Ascending**, save your query changes, and then click below the field lists and above the design grid to deselect all values. The completed query contains seven fields from three tables and one query and has two sort fields, the InvoiceItem primary sort field and the InvoiceDate secondary sort field. See Figure 7-18.

Figure 7-18 | Finished qryInvoicesByItem query in Design view

Trouble? After you've finished creating the query and close it, if you later open the query in Design view, you'll see the thicker join lines with referential integrity enforced connecting the tblCustomer and tblContract table field lists and the tblContract and tblInvoice table field lists.

Before closing the query, you'll run it to view the query recordset.

▶ **10.** Run the query, which displays 172 records, and then close the query.

You'll use the qryInvoicesByItem query as the record source for Lucia's custom report.

Creating a Custom Report

You could use the Report Wizard to create the report and then modify it to match the report design. However, because you need to customize several components of the report, you will create a custom report in Layout view, and then switch between Layout and Design view to fine-tune the report. As the first step to creating the report, you need to display a blank report in Layout view.

Reference Window | **Creating a Blank Report in Layout View**

- Click the Create tab on the Ribbon.
- In the Reports group on the Create tab, click the Blank Report button to open a blank report in Layout view.

Making Report Design Modifications

You perform operations in Layout and Design views for reports the same as you perform operations in these views for forms. These operations become easier with practice. Remember to use the Undo button, back up your database frequently, save your report changes frequently, work from a copy of the report for complicated design changes, and compact and repair the database on a regular basis. You can also display the report in Print Preview at any time to view your progress on the report.

The record source for the report will the qryInvoicesByItem query. You'll set the record source after you create a blank report in Layout view.

To create a blank report and add bound controls in Layout view:

▶ **1.** Click the **Create** tab on the Ribbon, and then in the Reports group on the Create tab, click the **Blank Report** button. A new report opens in Layout view. In addition, the Field List pane and the Group, Sort, and Total pane open. See Figure 7-19.

Blank report in Layout view **Figure 7-19**

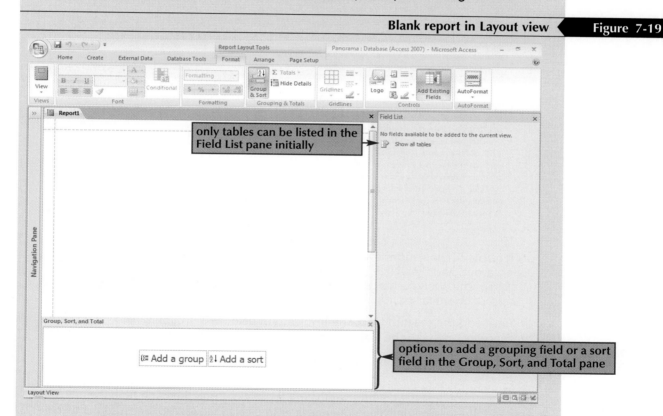

Trouble? If the Group, Sort, and Total pane is not open on your screen, click the Group & Sort button in the Grouping & Totals group on the Format tab.

▶ **2.** Click the **Arrange** tab on the Ribbon, and then in the Tools group on the Arrange tab, click the **Property Sheet** button to open the property sheet for the report.

▶ **3.** In the property sheet, click the **Record Source** arrow, click **qryInvoicesByItem**, and then close the property sheet.

4. Click the **Format** tab on the Ribbon, and then in the Controls group on the Format tab, click the **Add Existing Fields** button to open the Field List pane. The Field List pane displays the seven fields in the qryInvoicesByItem query, which is the record source for the report.

   Referring to Lucia's report design, you'll add six of the seven fields to the report in a tabular layout, which is the default control layout when you add fields to a report in Layout view.

5. Double-click **InvoiceDate** in the Field List pane, and then in order, double-click **Customer**, **City**, **ContractType**, **InvoiceAmt**, and **InvoicePaid** in the Field List pane. The six bound controls are displayed in a tabular layout in the report. See Figure 7-20.

Figure 7-20 | **After adding fields to the report in Layout view**

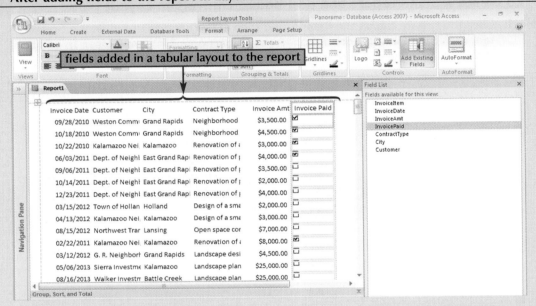

   Trouble? If you add the wrong field to the report, right-click the field in the tabular layout, and then click Delete on the shortcut menu to delete it. If you add a field in the wrong order, click the field in the tabular layout, and then drag it to its correct columnar position.

   You'll add the seventh field, the InvoiceItem field, as a grouping field, so you are done working with the Field List pane.

6. Close the Field List pane, and then save the report as **rptInvoicesByItem**.

Next, you'll adjust the column widths in Layout view, and then fine-tune the adjustments and the spacing between columns later in Design view. Also, because the Invoice Amt and Invoice Paid columns are adjacent, you can change the rightmost column heading to Paid without losing any meaning and to save space.

To resize and rename columns in Layout view:

1. Click **Customer** to select the column, and then drag the right edge of the control to increase its width. See Figure 7-21.

2. Repeat Step 1 to increase the width of the **City** column and the **Contract Type** column. See Figure 7-21.

3. Double-click **Invoice Paid** in the rightmost column, delete **Invoice** and the following space, and then press the **Enter** key.

4. Drag the right edge of the **Paid** control to the left to decrease the column's width. See Figure 7-21.

After resizing and renaming columns in Layout view | Figure 7-21

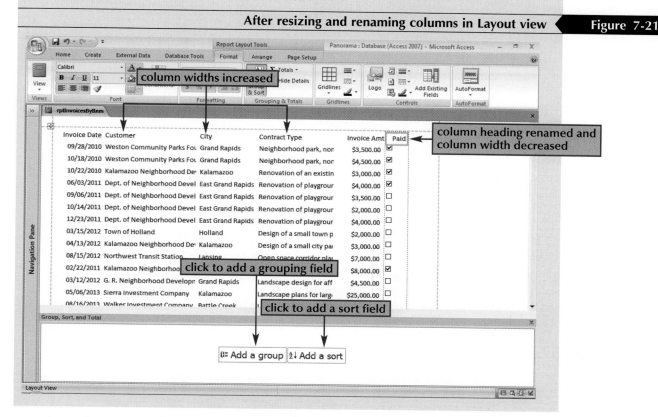

According to Lucia's plan for the report (see Figure 7-17), the InvoiceItem field is a grouping field that is displayed in a Group Header section. Subtotals for the InvoiceAmt field are displayed in a Group Footer section for each InvoiceItem field value.

Sorting and Grouping Data in a Report

Access lets you organize records in a report by sorting them using one or more sort fields. Each sort field can also be a grouping field. If you specify a sort field as a grouping field, you can include a Group Header section and a Group Footer section for the group. A Group Header section typically includes the name of the group, and a Group Footer section typically includes a count or subtotal for records in that group. Some reports have a Group Header section but not a Group Footer section, some reports have a Group Footer section but not a Group Header section, and some reports have both sections or have neither section.

You use the Group, Sort, and Total pane to select sort fields and grouping fields for a report. Each report can have up to 10 sort fields, and any of its sort fields can also be grouping fields.

Sorting and Grouping Data in a Report

- Display the report in Layout or Design view.
- If necessary, click the Group & Sort button in the Grouping & Totals group on the Format tab in Layout view or the Design tab in Design view to display the Group, Sort, and Total pane.
- To select a grouping field, click the Add a group button in the Group, Sort, and Total pane, and then click the grouping field in the list. To set additional properties for the grouping field, click the More button on the grouping field band.
- To select a sort field that is not a grouping field, click the Add a sort button in the Group, Sort, and Total pane, and then click the sort field in the list. To set additional properties for the sort field, click the More button on the sort field band.

In Lucia's report design, the InvoiceItem field is a grouping field, and the InvoiceDate field is a sort field. The InvoiceItem field value is displayed in a Group Header section, but not its label. The sum of the InvoiceAmt field values is displayed in the Group Footer section for the InvoiceItem grouping field. Next, you'll select the grouping field and the sort field and set their properties.

To select and set the properties for the grouping field and the sort field:

▶ 1. In the Group, Sort, and Total pane, click the **Add a group** button, and then click **InvoiceItem** in the list. Access adds a Group Header section to the report with InvoiceItem as the grouping field, and adds a group band in the Group, Sort, and Total pane. See Figure 7-22.

| Figure 7-22 | After selecting InvoiceItem as a grouping field in Layout view |

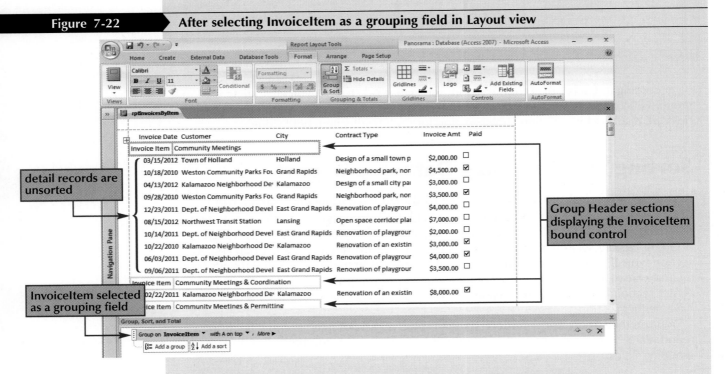

detail records are unsorted

InvoiceItem selected as a grouping field

Group Header sections displaying the InvoiceItem bound control

InvoiceItem is now a bound control in the report in a Group Header section that displays a field value text box and its attached label. The group band in the Group, Sort, and Total pane contains the name of the grouping field (InvoiceItem), the sort order ("with A on top" to indicate ascending), and the More option, which you click to display more options for the grouping field. You can click the "with A on top" arrow to change to descending sort order ("with Z on top").

Notice that the detail records are unsorted, and Lucia's design specifies an ascending sort on the InvoiceDate field. Next, you'll select this field as a secondary sort field; the InvoiceItem grouping field is the primary sort field.

▶ **2.** In the Group, Sort, and Total pane, click the **Add a sort** button, and then click **InvoiceDate** in the list. Access displays the detail records in ascending InvoiceDate order, and adds a sort band for the InvoiceDate field in the Group, Sort, and Total pane.

Next, you'll display all the options for the InvoiceItem grouping field, and set grouping options as shown in Lucia's report design.

▶ **3.** Click ⫶ to the left of the group band to select it, and then click **More** to expand the band and display all group options. See Figure 7-23.

After expanding the group band   ◀   **Figure 7-23**

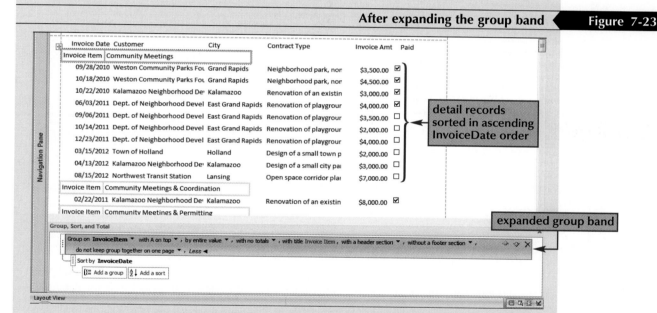

Reviewing Lucia's report design (see Figure 7-17), you need to delete the InvoiceItem label, add a Group Footer section, add a grand total and subtotals for the InvoiceAmt field values to the Group Footer section, and set the Keep Together property. The **Keep Together property** prints a group header on a page only if there is enough room on the page to print the first detail record for the group; otherwise, the group header prints at the top of the next page.

▶ **4.** In the "with title Invoice Item" option, click the **Invoice Item** link to open the Zoom dialog box, press the **Delete** key to delete the expression, and then click the **OK** button. The Invoice Item label is deleted from the report, and the option in the group band changes to "with title click to add."

▶ **5.** Click the **do not keep group together on one page** arrow, and then click **keep header and first record together on one page**.

▶ **6.** Click the **without a footer section** arrow, and then click **with a footer section**. Access adds a Group Footer section for the InvoiceItem grouping field, but the report doesn't display this new section until you add controls to it.

▶ **7.** Click the **with no totals** arrow to open the Totals menu, click the **Total On** arrow, click **InvoiceAmt**, make sure **Sum** is selected in the Type box, click the **Show Grand Total** check box, click the **Show in group footer** check box, and then click an empty area of the group band to close the menu. Access adds InvoiceAmt subtotals to the report. See Figure 7-24.

Figure 7-24 **After setting properties in the group band**

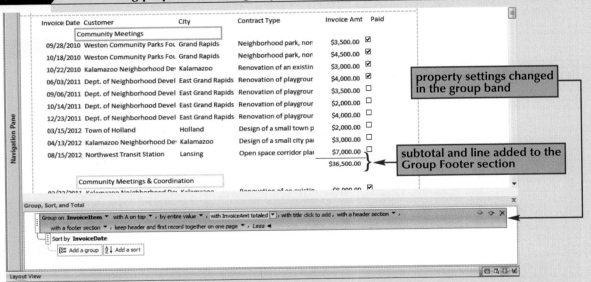

Similar to the sound form design strategy you followed in the previous tutorial, you should frequently save your report changes and review the report in Print Preview.

▶ **8.** Save your report changes, switch to Print Preview, and review every page until you reach the end of the report—noticing in particular the details of the report format and the effects of the Keep Together property. See Figure 7-25.

Figure 7-25

Last page of the custom report in Print Preview

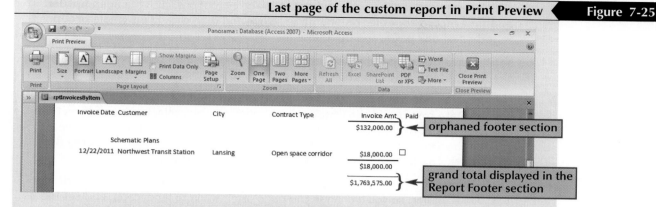

Trouble? Depending on the printer you are using, the last page of your report might differ.

The grand total of the InvoiceAmt field values is displayed at the end of the report. Also, as shown in Figure 7-25, it's possible for subtotals, which you added to the Group Footer section, to appear in an orphaned footer section. An **orphaned footer section** appears by itself at the top of a page, and the detail lines for the section appear on the previous page. When you set the Keep Together property for the grouping field, you set it to keep the group and the first detail record together on one page to prevent an **orphaned header section**, which is a section that appears by itself at the bottom of a page. To prevent both types of orphaned sections, you'll set the Keep Together property to keep the whole group together on one page.

In addition, you need to fine-tune the sizes of the text boxes in the Detail section, adjust the spacing between columns, and make other adjustments to the current content of the report design before adding a report title, the date, and page numbers to the Page Header section. You'll make most of these report design changes in Design view.

Working with Controls in Design View

Compared to Layout view, Design view gives you greater control over the placement and sizing of controls, and lets you add and manipulate many more controls, but at the expense of not being able to see live data in the controls to guide you as you make changes.

You'll switch to Design view to move and resize controls in the report.

To move and resize controls in the report:

▶ 1. Switch to Design view. The report has five sections: the Page Header section contains the six column heading labels, the InvoiceItem Header section (a Group Header section) contains the InvoiceItem text box, the Detail section contains the six bound controls, the InvoiceItem Footer section (a Group Footer section) contains a line and the subtotal text box, and the Report Footer section contains a line and the grand total text box.

The Group, Sort, and Total pane is still open, so first you'll change the Keep Together property setting.

2. In the Group, Sort, and Total pane, click ⫶ to the left of the group band to select it, click **More** to expand the band and display all group options, click the **keep header and first record together on one page** arrow, and then click **keep whole group together on one page**, and then close the Group, Sort, and Total pane.

You'll start improving the report by moving the InvoiceItem text box to the left in the InvoiceItem Header section and setting its font to bold.

3. Select the **InvoiceItem** text box in the InvoiceItem Header section and the **InvoiceDate** text box in the Detail section, align the two selected controls on their left edges, hold down the **Shift** key, click the **InvoiceDate** text box to deselect it, release the **Shift** key, and then in the Font group on the Design tab, click the **Bold** button ⧉. The InvoiceItem text box is displayed as bold text.

The report width is 8 inches, and Sarah will want to print the report on standard 8.5" × 11" paper, so you'll change the page orientation to landscape, and set the left and right margin widths to 1.5 inches each.

4. Click the **Page Setup** tab on the Ribbon, and in the Page Layout group on the Page Setup tab, click the **Page Setup** button to open the Page Setup dialog box, click the **Page** tab, click the **Landscape** option button, click the **Print Options** tab, set the Top and Bottom margin properties to **0.7** and the Left and Right margin properties to **1.5**, and then click the **OK** button.

The text boxes in the Detail section are crowded together with little space between them. Your reports shouldn't have too much space between columns, but reports are easier to read when the columns are separated more than they are in the rptInvoicesByItem report. Sometimes the amount of spacing is dictated by the users of the report, but mostly it's the report designer's choice to make. First, you'll remove the Paid label and the InvoicePaid text box from the tabular layout, resize them, and move them to the right.

5. Select the **Paid** label in the Page Header section and the **InvoicePaid** text box (it contains a check box) in the Detail section, right-click one of the selected controls to open the shortcut menu, point to **Layout**, click **Remove** to remove both controls from the tabular layout, deselect the **InvoicePaid** text box, right-click an edge of the **Paid** label to open the shortcut menu, point to **Size**, click **To Fit**, and then move the label to the right until its right edge is at the 8-inch mark on the horizontal ruler.

6. Click the **InvoicePaid** text box in the Detail section, decrease its width until it's slightly wider than the check box inside it, and then move it to the right until the check box is centered under the Paid label. See Figure 7-26.

To move the remaining bound controls, you first need to remove them from the tabular layout.

7. Select the **InvoiceAmt** text box and the other three controls in that column, right-click the **InvoiceAmt** text box, point to **Layout** on the shortcut menu, click **Remove**, deselect all controls except the **Invoice Amt** label in the Page Header section, right-click the **Invoice Amt** label, point to **Size** on the shortcut menu, click **To Fit**, select all controls in the column, right-click one of the selected controls, point to **Align** on the shortcut menu, click **Right**, and then move the selected controls to the right. See Figure 7-26.

8. Refer to Figure 7-26 and repeat Step 7 for the **ContractType**, **City**, and **Customer** bound controls, in that order, but do not align the bound controls on their right edges. See Figure 7-26.

After resizing and moving controls in Design view   Figure 7-26

You resized the Customer and ContractType text boxes in Layout view, but you did not resize them wide enough to display the entire field value in all cases. For the Customer and ContractType text boxes, you'll set their Can Grow property to Yes. The **Can Grow property**, when set to Yes, expands a text box vertically to fit the field value when the report is printed, previewed, or viewed in Layout and Report views.

▶ **9.** Select the **Customer** and **ContractType** text boxes in the Detail section, open the property sheet, click the **Format** tab in the property sheet, scroll down the property sheet, set the Can Grow property to **Yes** (if necessary), close the property sheet, and then save your report changes.

▶ **10.** Switch to Print Preview, and review every page of the report, ending on the last page of the report. See Figure 7-27.

Tip

You can select two or more controls, and then set common properties for the selected controls, instead of setting them one control at a time.

Reviewing the report changes in Print Preview   Figure 7-27

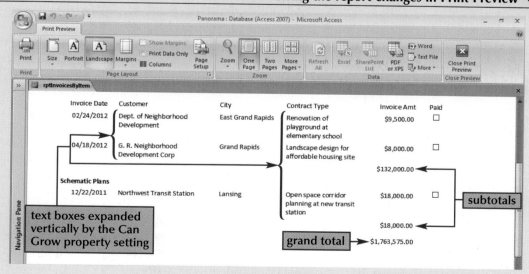

The groups stay together on one page, except for the Schematic Plan group, which has too many lines to fit on one page. The Can Grow property correctly expands the height of the Customer and ContractType text boxes. Also, the lines that were displayed above the subtotals and grand total are no longer displayed. You'll add those lines back in the report.

Adding Lines to a Report

You've used the Line tool to add lines to a form. You can also use the Line tool to add lines to a report, and you'll use the Line tool to add a single line above the subtotal control and a double line above the grand total control.

You'll switch to Design view to add the lines to the report.

To add lines to the report:

▶ **1.** Switch to Design view.

▶ **2.** In the Controls group on the Design tab, click the **Line** button $\searchow$, position the pointer's plus symbol (+) at the upper-left corner of the subtotal text box in the InvoiceItem Footer section, hold down the **Shift** key, drag a horizontal line from left to right, so the end of the line aligns with the upper-right corner of the subtotal text box, release the mouse button, and then release the **Shift** key.

▶ **3.** Click the **grand total** text box in the Report Footer section, and then press the ↓ key four times to move the control down slightly in the section, and then deselect all controls.

▶ **4.** In the Controls group on the Design tab, click the **Line** button $\searchow$, position the pointer's plus symbol (+) at the grid dot just above the upper-left corner of the grand total text box in the Report Footer section, hold down the **Shift** key, drag a horizontal line from left to right, so the end of the line aligns with the right edge of the grand total text box, release the mouse button, and then release the **Shift** key.

Next, you'll copy and paste the line in the Report Footer section, and then align the copied line into position.

▶ **5.** Right-click the selected line in the Report Footer section, and then click **Copy** on the shortcut menu.

▶ **6.** Right-click the Report Footer section bar, and then click **Paste** on the shortcut menu. A copy of the line is pasted in the upper-left corner of the Report Footer section.

▶ **7.** Press the ↓ key twice to move the copied line down slightly in the section, hold down the **Shift** key, click the original line in the Report Footer section to select both lines, release the **Shift** key, right-click the copied line, point to **Align**, and then click **Right**. A double line is now positioned above the grand total text box.

▶ **8.** Save your report changes, switch to Print Preview, and then navigate to the last page of the report. See Figure 7-28.

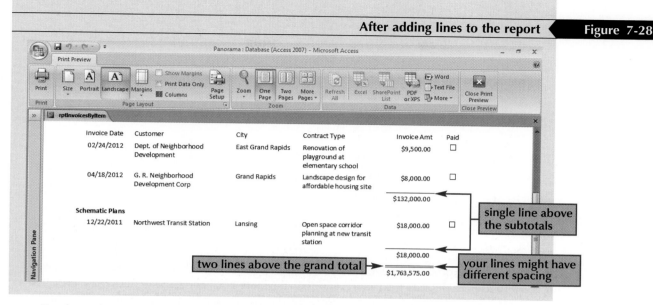

After adding lines to the report

Figure 7-28

For the rptInvoicesByItem report, the InvoiceDate field is a sort field. Two or more consecutive detail report lines can have the same InvoiceDate field value. In these cases, Sarah wants the InvoiceDate field value printed for the first detail line but not for subsequent detail lines because she believes it makes the printed information easier to read.

Hiding Duplicate Values in a Report

You use the **Hide Duplicates property** to hide a control in a report when the control's value is the same as that of the preceding record in the group.

Hiding Duplicate Values in a Report | Reference Window

- Display the report in Layout or Design view.
- Open the property sheet for the field whose duplicate values you want to hide, set the Hide Duplicates property to Yes, and then close the property sheet.

Your next design change to the report is to hide duplicate InvoiceDate field values in the Detail section. This change will make the report easier to read.

To hide the duplicate InvoiceDate field values:

▶ **1.** Switch to Design view, and then click below the Report Footer section to deselect all controls.

▶ **2.** Open the property sheet for the **InvoiceDate** text box in the Detail section.

▶ **3.** Click the **All** tab (if necessary), click the right side of the **Hide Duplicates** text box, and then click **Yes**. See Figure 7-29.

Tip

For properties in the property sheet that offer a list of choices, you can double-click the property name to cycle through the options in the list.

Figure 7-29 ▶ **Hiding duplicate field values**

4. Close the property sheet, save your report changes, switch to Print Preview, navigate to the last page of the report, and then navigate back one page (if necessary) until you see the two invoice records for 08/25/2011. The InvoiceDate value is hidden for the second of the two consecutive records with a 08/25/2011 date. See Figure 7-30.

Figure 7-30 ▶ **Report in Print Preview with hidden duplicate values**

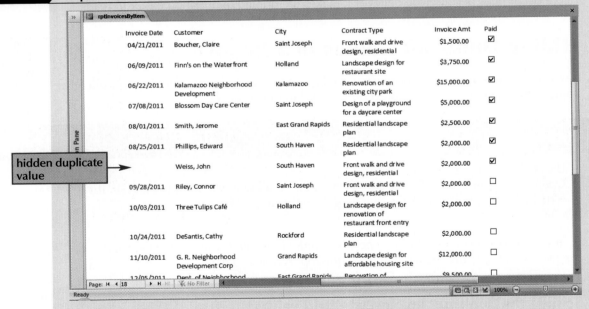

5. If you are not continuing on to the next session, close the Panorama database, and then exit Access.

You have completed the Detail section of the custom report. In the next session, you will complete the custom report according to Lucia's design by adding controls to the Page Header section.

1. What is a detail report? a summary report?
2. The _____ property prints a group header on a page only if there is enough room on the page to print the first detail record for the group; otherwise, the group header prints at the top of the next page.
3. A(n) _____ section appears by itself at the top of a page, and the detail lines for the section appear on the previous page.
4. The _____ property, when set to Yes, expands a text box vertically to fit the field value when a report is printed, previewed, or viewed in Layout and Report views.
5. Why might you want to hide duplicate values in a report?

Session 7.3

Adding the Date to a Report

According to Lucia's design, the rptInvoicesByItem report includes the date in the Page Header section, along with the report title, the page number, the column heading labels, and a line under the labels.

Placing the Report Title, Date, and Page Number in the Page Header Section | InSight

When you use the Report tool or the Report Wizard to create a report, the report title is displayed in the Report Header section and the page number is displayed in the Page Footer section. However, the date (and time) is displayed in the Report Header section when you use the Report tool and in the Page Footer section when you use the Report Wizard. Because you should create reports that display controls in consistent positions, you have to move the date control for reports created by the Report tool or by the Report Wizard so the date is displayed in the same section for all reports.

Although company standards vary, a common report standard places the report title, date, and page number on the same line in the Page Header section. Using one line saves vertical space in the report compared to placing some controls in the Page Header section and others in the Page Footer section. Placing the report title in the Page Header section, instead of in the Report Header section, allows users to identify the report title on any page without having to turn to the first page.

To add the date to a report, you can click the Date & Time button in the Controls group on the Ribbon, and Access will insert the Date function in a text box without an attached label at the right edge of the Report Header section. The **Date function** returns the current date. The format of the Date function is =*Date()*. The equal sign (=) indicates that what follows it is an expression; *Date* is the name of the function; and the empty set of parentheses indicates a function rather than simple text.

Reference Window | **Adding the Date and Time to a Report**

- Display the report in Layout or Design view.
- In the Controls group on the Design tab in Design view, or on the Format tab in Layout view, click the Date & Time button to open the Date and Time dialog box.
- To display the date, click the Include Date check box, and then click one of the three date option buttons.
- To display the time, click the Include Time check box, and then click one of the three time option buttons.
- Click the OK button.

According to Lucia's design for the report, the date appears at the left edge of the Page Header section, so you'll need to add the date to the report, and then cut the date from the Report Header section and paste it into the Page Header section.

To add the date to the Page Header section:

▶ 1. If you took a break after the previous session, make sure that the Panorama database is open, that the rptInvoicesByItem report is open in Print Preview, and that the Navigation Pane is closed.

You can add the current date in Layout or Design view. Because you can't cut and paste controls between sections in Layout view, you'll add the date in Design view. First, you'll move the column heading labels down in the Page Header section to make room for the controls you'll be adding above them.

▶ 2. Switch to Design view, increase the height of the Page Header section until the bottom edge of the section is at the 1-inch mark on the vertical ruler, select all six labels in the Page Header section, and then use the ↓ key to move the labels down until the tops of the labels are at the 0.5-inch mark on the vertical ruler.

Lucia's report design has a horizontal line under the labels that you'll add next.

▶ 3. In the Controls group on the Design tab, click the **Line** button ◺ , position the pointer's plus symbol (+) at the lower-left corner of the Invoice Date label in the Page Header section, hold down the **Shift** key, drag a horizontal line from left to right so the end of the line aligns with the right edge of the Paid label, release the mouse button, and then release the **Shift** key.

▶ 4. Reduce the height of the Page Header section by dragging the bottom of the section up until it touches the bottom of the line you just added.

▶ 5. In the Controls group on the Design tab, click the **Date & Time** button 📑 to open the Date and Time dialog box, make sure the **Include Date** check box is checked and the **Include Time** check box is unchecked, and then click the third date option button. See Figure 7-31.

6. Click the **OK** button. The Date function is added to the Report Header section. See Figure 7-32.

The default size for the Date function text box must accommodate long dates and long times, so the text box is much wider than needed for the date that'll appear in the custom report. You'll decrease its width before moving it to the Page Header section.

7. Click the **Date function** text box, decrease its width from the left to one inch total, right-click an edge of the Date function text box to open the shortcut menu, click **Cut** to delete the control, right-click the **Page Header** section bar to select that section and open the shortcut menu, and then click **Paste**. The Date function text box is pasted in the upper-left corner of the Page Header section.

8. Save your report changes, and then switch to Print Preview to view the date in the Page Header section. See Figure 7-33.

Tip

When you print, preview, or view the report in Report or Layout view, the current date is displayed instead of the Date function that appears in the text box in Design view.

Figure 7-33 **Viewing the date in Print Preview**

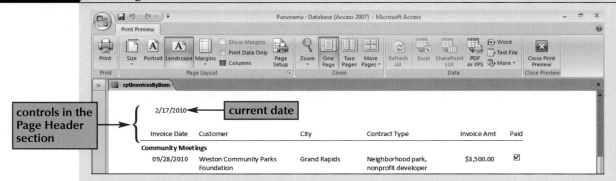

controls in the Page Header section

current date

Trouble? Your year might appear with two digits instead of four digits as shown in Figure 7-33. Your date format might also differ, depending on your computer's date settings. These differences do not cause any problems.

You'll left-align the date in the text box in Design view.

▶ 9. Switch to Design view, make sure the Date function text box is selected, and then in the Font group on the Design tab, click the **Align Text Left** button.

You are now ready to add page numbers to the Page Header section.

Adding Page Numbers to a Report

You can display page numbers in a report by including an expression in the Page Header or Page Footer section. You can click the Insert Page Number button in the Controls group in Layout or Design view to add a page number expression to a report. The inserted page number expression automatically displays the correct page number on each page of a report.

Reference Window | **Adding Page Numbers to a Report**

- Display the report in Layout or Design view.
- In the Controls group on the Design tab in Design view, or on the Format tab in Layout view, click the Insert Page Number button to open the Page Numbers dialog box.
- Select the format, position, and alignment options you want.
- Select whether you want to display the page number on the first page.
- Click the OK button to place the page number expression in the report.

Lucia's design shows the page number displayed on the right side of the Page Header section, on the same line with the date.

To add page numbers in the Page Header section:

▶ 1. In the Controls group on the Design tab, click the **Insert Page Number** button. The Page Numbers dialog box opens.

You use the Format options to specify the format of the page number. Sarah wants page numbers to appear as Page 1, Page 2, and so on. This is the Page N format option. You use the Position options to place the page numbers at the top of the page in the Page Header section or at the bottom of the page in the Page Footer section. Lucia's design shows page numbers at the top of the page.

▶ **2.** Make sure that the **Page N** option button in the Format section and that the **Top of Page [Header]** option button in the Position section are both selected.

The report design shows page numbers at the right side of the page. You can specify this placement in the Alignment list box.

▶ **3.** Click the **Alignment** arrow, and then click **Right**.

▶ **4.** Make sure the **Show Number on First Page** check box is checked, so the page number prints on the first page and all other pages as well. See Figure 7-34.

Completed Page Numbers dialog box ◀ Figure 7-34

▶ **5.** Click the **OK** button. The text box shown in Figure 7-35 appears in the upper-right corner of the Page Header section. The expression =*"Page " & [Page]* in the text box means that the printed report will show the word "Page" followed by a space and the page number.

Page number expression added to the Page Header section ◀ Figure 7-35

The page number text box is much wider than needed for the page number expression that'll appear in the custom report. You'll decrease its width and right-align it.

▶ **6.** Click the **Page Number** text box, decrease its width from the left to one inch total, and then in the Font group on the Design tab, click the **Align Text Right** button.

▶ **7.** Save your report changes, and then switch to Print Preview. See Figure 7-36.

Figure 7-36 | Date and page number in the Page Header section

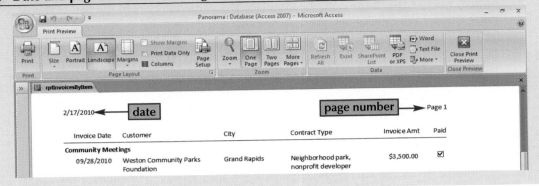

Now you are ready to add the title to the Page Header section.

Adding a Title to a Report

Lucia's report design includes the title "Invoices by Item," which you'll add to the Page Header section centered between the date and the page number.

To add the title to the Page Header section:

1. Switch to Design view.

2. In the Controls group on the Design tab, click the **Title** button. The title "rptInvoicesByItem," which is name of the report object, appears in the Report Header section in 18-point font.

   To match Lucia's design, you need to change the title, set its font size to 14 points, move it to the Page Header section, and then resize the Report Header section to zero height. The title is selected, so typing the new title will replace the current title.

3. Type **Invoices by Item**, press the **Enter** key, click the **Font Size** arrow, and then click **14**.

4. Right-click an edge of the title, point to **Size**, and then click **To Fit**.

5. Right-click an edge of the title, click **Cut**, right-click the **Page Header** section bar, and then click **Paste**. The title is pasted in the upper-left corner of the Page Header section, and the Error Checking Options button appears to the right of the report title.

6. Position the pointer on the **Error Checking Options** button. A ScreenTip is displayed and describes the potential error. See Figure 7-37.

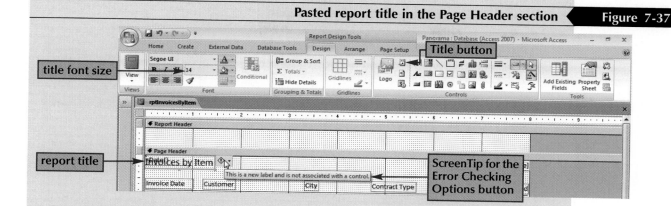

Pasted report title in the Page Header section | Figure 7-37

The ScreenTip indicates that the report title, which is a label control, is not associated with any bound or calculated control. Because you don't want a label that contains a report title to be associated with another control, you can ignore this potential error.

▶ **7.** Click the **Error Checking Options** button ◈, and then click **Ignore Error**.

The report title is still selected, so you can move it so that it's centered between the date and the page number. Because the report title is positioned on top of the date control, there's a chance you might inadvertently also select the date control when you try to drag the report title into position, so you should use the → key to move the report title.

▶ **8.** Move the report title control to the right until it's centered between the date and page number controls.

Finally, you'll align the date, report title, and page number controls on their bottom edges.

▶ **9.** Select the date, report title, and page number controls in the Page Header section, right-click one of the selected controls, point to **Align**, and then click **Bottom**.

▶ **10.** Drag the bottom edge of the Report Header section up all the way to the Report Header section bar to remove the section from the report, and then save your report changes. You completed the design of the custom report. See Figure 7-38.

Figure 7-38 | Completed design of the rptInvoicesByItem report

> **11.** Switch to Print Preview to review the completed report, and then navigate to the last page of the report. See Figure 7-39.

Figure 7-39 | Completed rptInvoicesByItem report in Print Preview

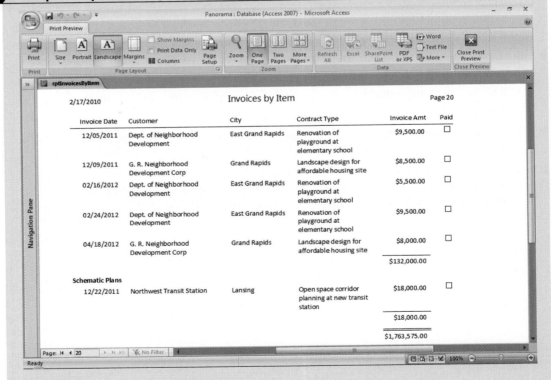

> **12.** Close the report.

Next, Sarah wants you to create mailing labels that can be used to address materials to Belmont Landscapes' customers.

Creating Mailing Labels

Sarah needs a set of mailing labels printed for all customers so she can mail a marketing brochure and other materials to them. The tblCustomer table contains the name and address information that will serve as the record source for the labels. Each mailing label will have the same format: first name and last name on the first line; company name (if it exists for the customer) on the second line; address on the third line; and city, state, and zip code on the fourth line.

You could create a custom report to produce the mailing labels, but using the Label Wizard is an easier and faster way to produce them. The **Label Wizard** provides templates for hundreds of standard label formats, each of which is uniquely identified by a label manufacturer's name and number. These templates specify the dimensions and arrangement of labels on each page. Standard label formats can have between one and five labels across a page; the number of labels printed on a single page also varies. Sarah's mailing labels are Avery number C2163; each sheet has 12 1.5-inch by 3.9-inch labels arranged in two columns and six rows on the page.

Creating Mailing Labels and Other Labels | Reference Window

- In the Navigation Pane, click the table or query that'll serve as the record source for the labels.
- In the Reports group on the Create tab, click the Labels button to start the Label Wizard and open its first dialog box.
- Select the label manufacturer and its product number, and then click the Next button.
- Select the label font, color, and style, and then click the Next button.
- Construct the label content by selecting the fields from the record source and specifying their placement and spacing on the label, and then click the Next button.
- Select one or more optional sort fields, click the Next button, specify the report name, and then click the Finish button.

You'll use the Label Wizard to create a report to produce mailing labels for all customers.

To use the Label Wizard to create the mailing label report:

1. Open the Navigation Pane, click **tblCustomer** to make it the current object that'll serve as the record source for the labels, close the Navigation Pane, and then click the **Create** tab on the Ribbon.

2. In the Reports group on the Create tab, click the **Labels** button. The first Label Wizard dialog box opens and asks you to select the standard or custom label you'll use.

3. Make sure that the **English** option button is selected in the Unit of Measure section, that the **Sheet feed** option button is selected in the Label Type section, and that **Avery** is selected in the Filter by manufacturer list box, and then click **C2163** in the Product number list box. See Figure 7-40.

Figure 7-40 ▶ **Selecting a standard label**

Because the labels are already filtered for the Avery manufacturer, the top list box shows the Avery product number, dimensions, and number of labels across the page for each of its standard label formats. You can display the dimensions in the list in either inches or millimeters by choosing the appropriate option in the Unit of Measure section. You can also specify in the Label Type section whether the labels are on individual sheets or are continuous forms.

▶ 4. Click the **Next** button to open the second Label Wizard dialog box, in which you choose font specifications for the labels.

Sarah wants the labels to use 10-point Arial with a medium font weight and without italics or underlines. The font weight determines how light or dark the characters will print; you can choose from nine values ranging from thin to heavy.

▶ 5. If necessary, select **Arial** for the font name, **10** for the font size, and **Medium** for the font weight; make sure the Italic and the Underline check boxes are not checked and that black is the text color; and then click the **Next** button to open the third Label Wizard dialog box, from which you select the data to appear on the labels.

Sarah wants the mailing labels to print the FirstName and LastName fields on the first line; the Company field on the second line; the Address field on the third line; and the City, State, and Zip fields on the fourth line. One space will separate the FirstName and LastName fields, the City and State fields, and the State and Zip fields.

▶ 6. Click **FirstName** in the Available fields list box, click the > button to move the field to the Prototype label box, press the **spacebar**, click **LastName** in the Available fields list box (if necessary), and then click the > button (see Figure 7-41). The braces around the field names in the Prototype label box indicate that the name represents a field rather than text that you entered.

   Trouble? If you select the wrong field or type the wrong text, highlight the incorrect item in the Prototype label box, press the Delete key to remove the item, and then select the correct field or type the correct text.

▶ 7. Press the **Enter** key to move to the next line in the Prototype label box, and then use Figure 7-41 to complete the entries in the Prototype label box. Make sure you press the **spacebar** after selecting the City field and the State field.

Completed label prototype | **Figure 7-41**

8. Click the **Next** button to open the fourth Label Wizard dialog box, in which you choose the sort fields for the labels.

   Sarah wants Zip to be the primary sort field and LastName to be the secondary sort field.

9. Select the **Zip** field as the primary sort field, select the **LastName** field as the secondary sort field, and then click the **Next** button to open the last Label Wizard dialog box, in which you enter a name for the report.

10. Change the report name to **rptCustomerMailingLabels**, and then click the **Finish** button. Access saves the report as rptCustomerMailingLabels and then opens the first page of the report in Print Preview. Note that two columns of labels appear across the page. See Figure 7-42.

Previewing the label content and sequence | **Figure 7-42**

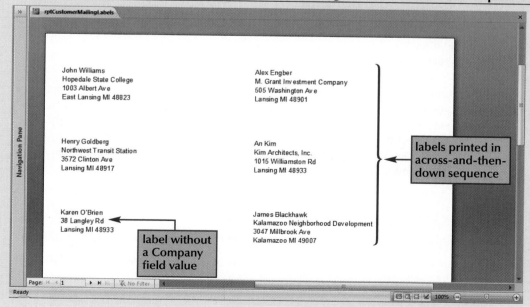

The rptCustomerMailingLabels report is a multiple-column report. The labels will be printed in ascending order by zip code and then in ascending order by last name. The first label will be printed in the upper-left corner on the first page, the second label will be printed to its right, the third label will be printed under the first label, and so on. This style of multiple-column report is the across-and-then-down layout. Instead, Sarah wants the labels to print with the "down, then across" layout—the first label is printed, the second label is printed under the first, and so on. After the bottom label in the first column is printed, the next label is printed at the top of the second column. The "down, then across" layout is also called **newspaper-style columns**, or **snaking columns**.

To change the layout of the mailing label report:

▶ **1.** Switch to Design view. The Detail section, the only section in the report, is sized for a single label.

First, you'll change the layout to snaking columns.

▶ **2.** Click the **Page Setup** tab on the Ribbon, click the **Page Setup** button in the Page Layout group, and then click the **Columns** tab. The Page Setup dialog box displays the Columns options for the report. See Figure 7-43.

| Figure 7-43 | Column options in the Page Setup dialog box |

The Columns options in the Page Setup dialog box let you change the properties of a multiple-column report. In the Grid Settings section, you specify the number of column sets and the row and column spacing between the column sets. In the Column Size section, you specify the width and height of each column set. In the Column Layout section, you select between the "down, then across" and the "across, then down" layouts.

You can now change the layout for the labels.

Tip

When you select a label using a manufacturer's name and product code, the options in the Grid Settings and Column Size sections are set for you automatically based on your selection.

▶ **3.** Click the **Down, then Across** option button, and then click the **OK** button.

You've finished the report changes, so you can now save and preview the report.

▶ **4.** Save your report design changes, and then switch to Print Preview. The labels appear in the snaking-columns layout.

You've finished all work on Sarah's reports.

▶ **5.** Close the report, close the Panorama database, make a backup copy of the database, open the **Panorama** database, compact and repair the database, close the database, and then exit Access.

Sarah is very pleased with the modified report and the two new reports, which will provide her with improved information and help expedite her written communications with customers.

Session 7.3 Quick Check | Review

1. What is the function and its format to print the current date in a report?
2. How do you insert a page number in the Page Header section?
3. Clicking the Title button in the Controls group on the Design tab adds a report title to the _____ section.
4. What is a multiple-column report?

Tutorial Summary | Review

In this tutorial, you viewed a report created by the Report tool in Report view, filtered and copied information in the report, and customized the report in Layout view and Design view. You then examined general report design guidelines, learned how to use the guidelines in planning a custom report, and created a query to serve as the record source for the report. In creating the custom report, you sorted and grouped data; added fields and modified report controls; added lines; and added the date, page numbers, and a title. Finally, you created mailing labels.

Key Terms

Can Grow property	Group, Sort, and Total pane	newspaper-style columns
custom report	grouping field	orphaned footer section
Date function	Hide Duplicates property	orphaned header section
detail report	Keep Together property	Report view
Group Footer section	Label Wizard	snaking columns
Group Header section	multiple-column report	summary report

| Practice | **Review Assignments** |

Practice the skills you learned in the tutorial using the same case scenario.

Data File needed for the Review Assignments: Products.accdb (*cont. from Tutorial 6*)

Sarah wants you to create a custom report for the Products database that prints all companies and the products they offer. She also wants you to customize an existing report. You will perform the tasks for Sarah by completing the following steps:

1. Open the **Products** database located in the Level.02\Review folder provided with your Data Files.
2. Modify the **rptProductsByCompany** report. Figure 7-45 shows a sample of the last page of the completed report. Refer to the figure as you modify the report.

Figure 7-44

a. Change the Caption property for the report so that it matches the report name.
b. To fit the report on three pages, you might have to change Page Setup properties and reduce the width of the report in Design view after moving the page number to the left.
c. Use the Label tool in the Controls group on the Ribbon to add a label that contains the text **total products** to the right of the count of the total number of products displayed in the Report Footer section.

3. After you've completed and saved your modifications to the rptProductsByCompany report, filter the report in Report view, selecting all records that contain the word "soil" in the ProductType field. Copy the entire filtered report and paste it into a new Word document. Save the document as **rptProductsByCompanyCopy** in the Level.02\Review folder provided with your Data Files. Close Word, and then close the report without saving changes.

4. Create a query that displays the ProductType and CompanyName fields from the tblCompany table, and the ProductType, Price, and Unit fields from the tblProduct table. Sort in ascending order by the first three fields in the query, and then save the query as **qryCompanyProducts**.

5. Create a custom report based on the qryCompanyProducts query. Figure 7-46 shows a sample of the last page of the completed report. Refer to the figure as you create the report.

Figure 7-45

a. Save the report as **rptProductsAvailable**.
b. The ProductType field (from the tblCompany table) is a grouping field.
c. Hide duplicate values for the CompanyName field.
d. Use the Label tool in the Controls group on the Ribbon to add labels for the subtotals, the grand total, and your name.
e. Keep the whole group together on one page.

6. Create a mailing label report according to the following instructions:
a. Use the tblCompany table as the record source.
b. Use Avery C2160 labels, and use the default font and color.
c. For the prototype label, add the ContactFirstName, a space, and ContactLastName on the first line; the CompanyName on the second line; the Address on the third line; and the City, a space, State, a space, and Zip on the fourth line.
d. Sort by Zip and then by CompanyName, and then enter the report name **rptCompanyMailingLabels**.

7. Close the Products database without exiting Access, make a backup copy of the database, open the **Products** database, compact and repair the database, close the database, and then exit Access.

Create | Case Problem 1

Use the skills you learned in the tutorial to work with the data in a database for a small music school.

Data File needed for this Case Problem: Contract.accdb (*cont. from Tutorial 6*)

Pine Hill Music School   Yuka wants you to modify an existing report and to create a custom report and mailing labels for the Contract database. You'll do so by completing the following:

1. Open the **Contract** database located in the Level.02\Case1 folder provided with your Data Files.
2. Modify the **rptStudentContracts** report. Figure 7-47 shows a sample of the last page of the completed report. Refer to the figure as you modify the report.

Figure 7-46

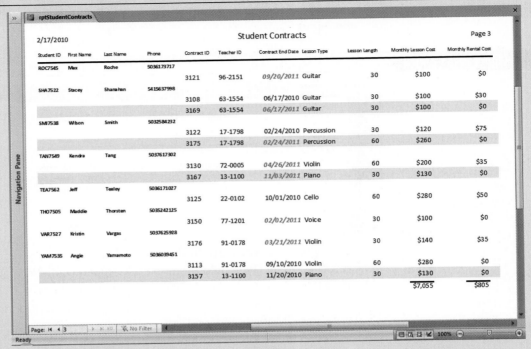

a. Change the conditional formatting rule for the ContractEndDate field to display the date in red, bold, italic font when the date is more recent than 1/1/2011.

b. Add controls to the last page of the report that calculate the total monthly lesson cost and total monthly rental cost below the correct columns.

3. Create a query that displays the LastName and FirstName fields from the tblTeacher table, the LessonType field from the tblContract table, the FirstName and LastName fields from the tblStudent table, and the MonthlyLessonCost and MonthlyRentalCost fields from the tblContract table. Sort in ascending order by the first three fields in the query, and then save the query as **qryTeacherLessons**.

4. Create a custom report based on the qryTeacherLessons query. Figure 7-48 shows a sample of the last page of the completed report. Refer to the figure as you create the report.

Figure 7-47

a. Save the report as **rptTeacherLessons**.
b. The LastName field (from the tblTeacher table) is a grouping field.
c. The LessonType field is a sort field, and the LastName field (from the tblStudent table) is a sort field.
d. Hide duplicate values for the LessonType field.
e. Add the FirstName field (from the tblTeacher table) to the Group Header section, and then delete its attached label.

5. Create a mailing label report according to the following instructions:

⊕EXPLORE

a. Use the tblStudent table as the record source.
b. Use Avery C2160 labels, use a larger font size and a heavier font weight, and use the other default font and color options.
c. For the prototype label, place FirstName, a space, and LastName on the first line; Address on the second line; and City, a space, State, a space, and Zip on the third line.
d. Sort by Zip and then by LastName, and then enter the report name **rptStudentMailingLabels**.
e. Change the mailing label layout to snaking columns.

6. Close the Contract database without exiting Access, make a backup copy of the database, open the **Contract** database, compact and repair the database, close the database, and then exit Access.

Apply | **Case Problem 2**

Apply what you learned in the tutorial to work with the data for a health and fitness center.

Data File needed for this Case Problem: Training.accdb (*cont. from Tutorial 6*)

Parkhurst Health & Fitness Center   Martha Parkhurst wants you to create a custom report and mailing labels for the Training database. The custom report will be based on the results of a query you will create. You will create the query, the custom report, and the mailing labels by completing the following steps:

1. Open the **Training** database located in the Level.02\Case2 folder provided with your Data Files.
2. Create a query that displays the ProgramID, ProgramType, and MonthlyFee fields from the tblProgram table, and the MembershipStatus, FirstName, and LastName fields from the tblMember table. Sort in ascending order by the ProgramID, MembershipStatus, and LastName fields, and then save the query as **qryProgramMembership**.
3. Create a custom report based on the qryProgramMembership query. Figure 7-49 shows a sample of the last page of the completed report. Refer to the figure as you create the report.

Figure 7-48

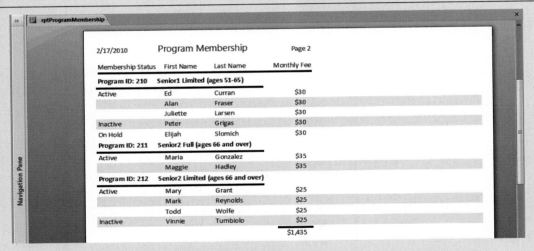

a. Save the report as **rptProgramMembership**.
b. The ProgramID field is a grouping field.
c. The MembershipStatus field is a sort field, and the LastName field is a sort field.
d. Hide duplicate values for the MembershipStatus field.
e. Add the ProgramType field to the Group Header section, and then delete its attached label.

4. Use the following instructions to create the mailing labels:
   a. Use the tblMember table as the record source for the mailing labels.
   b. Use Avery C2160 labels, and use the default font and color.
   c. For the prototype label, place FirstName, a space, and LastName on the first line; Street on the second line; and City, a space, State, a space, and Zip on the third line.
   d. Sort by Zip and then by LastName, and then type the report name **rptMemberLabels**.

5. Close the Training database with out exiting Access, make a backup copy of the database, open the **Training** database, compact and repair the database, close the database, and then exit Access.

| Apply | **Case Problem 3** |

Apply what you learned in the tutorial to work with a database that contains data about an agency that recycles household goods.

Data File needed for this Case Problem: Agency.accdb (*cont. from Tutorial 6*)

Rossi Recycling Group   Mary Rossi asks you to create a custom report for the Agency database so that she can better track donations made by donors and to create mailing labels. You'll do so by completing the following:

1. Open the **Agency** database located in the Level.02\Case3 folder provided with your Data Files.
2. Create a query that displays the DonationDesc, DonationDate, and DonationValue fields from the tblDonation table, and the FirstName and LastName fields from the tblDonor table. Sort in ascending order by the DonationDesc, DonationDate, and LastName fields, and then save the query as **qryDonorDonations**.
3. Create a custom report based on the qryDonorDonations query. Figure 7-50 shows a sample of the last page of the completed report. Refer to the figure as you create the report.

Figure 7-49

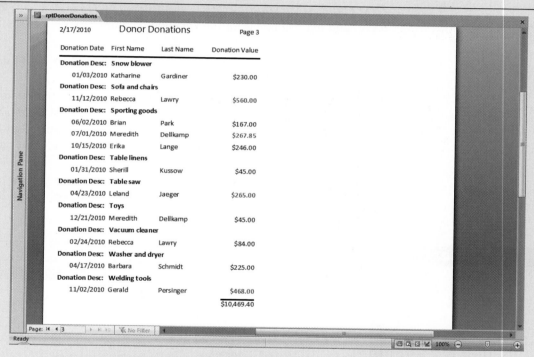

a. Save the report as **rptDonorDonations**.
b. The DonationDesc field is a grouping field.
c. The DonationDate field is a sort field, and the LastName field is a sort field.
d. Hide duplicate values for the DonationDate field.

⊕ EXPLORE

e. Create a conditional formatting rule for the DonationValue field to display the value in blue, bold font when the amount is more than $250.
4. After you've created and saved the rptDonorDonations report, filter the report in Report view, selecting all records whose LastName field value is "Park." Copy the entire filtered report and paste it into a new Word document. Save the document as **rptDonorDonationsCopy**. Close Word, and then close the report without saving it.

5. Use the following instructions to create the mailing labels:
   a. Use the tblAgency table as the record source for the mailing labels.
   b. Use Avery C2160 labels, and use the default font and color.
   c. For the prototype label, place ContactFirstName, a space, and ContactLastName on the first line; AgencyName on the second line; Address on the third line; and City, a space, State, a space, and Zip on the fourth line.
   d. Sort by Zip and then by ContactLastName, and then type the report name **rptAgencyLabels**.
   e. Change the mailing label layout to snaking columns.
6. Close the Agency database without exiting Access, make a backup copy of the database, open the **Agency** database, compact and repair the database, close the database, and then exit Access.

Create	**Case Problem 4**

Use the skills you've learned in this tutorial to work with the data for a luxury property rental company.

Data File needed for this Case Problem: Vacation.accdb (*cont. from Tutorial 6*)

GEM Ultimate Vacations   Griffin and Emma MacElroy want you to create a custom report and mailing labels for the Vacation database. You will create the custom report and the mailing labels by completing the following steps:

1. Open the **Vacation** database located in the Level.02\Case4 folder provided with your Data Files.
2. Create a query that displays the PropertyName and Country fields from the tblProperty table, the StateProv field from the tblGuest table, and the StartDate, EndDate, and People fields from the tblReservation table. Sort in ascending order by the PropertyName, StateProv, and StartDate fields, and then save the query as **qryPropertyReservations**.
3. Create a custom report based on the qryPropertyReservations query. Figure 7-51 shows a sample of the last page of the completed report. Refer to the figure as you create the report.

Figure 7-50

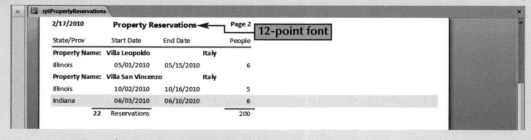

   a. Save the report as **rptPropertyReservations**.
   b. The PropertyName field is a grouping field.
   c. The StateProv field is a sort field, and the StartDate field is a sort field.
   d. Hide duplicate values for the StateProv field.
    EXPLORE
   e. Add the Country field to the Group Header section.
4. Use the following instructions to create the mailing labels:
   a. Use the tblGuest table as the record source for the mailing labels.

    b. Use Avery C2163 labels, with the default font and color settings. (*Hint*: Be certain the English option button is selected in the Unit of Measure section.)

    c. For the prototype label, place GuestFirstName, a space, and GuestLastName on the first line; Address on the second line; City, a space, StateProv, a space, and PostalCode on the third line; and Country on the fourth line.

    d. Sort by PostalCode, then by GuestLastName, and then enter the report name **rptGuestLabels**.

    e. Change the mailing label layout to snaking columns.

⊕ **EXPLORE**

5. Make a copy of the rptPropertyReservations report. For the copy use the name **rptPropertyReservationsSummary**. Read Access Help to find out how to create a summary report. Modify the rptPropertyReservationsSummary report as follows:

    a. Delete the column heading labels, move up the line in the Page Header section to just below the remaining controls, and then reduce the height of the section.

    b. Add subtotals for the number of reservations and number of people.

    c. Change the report to a summary report.

6. Close the Vacation database without exiting Access, make a backup copy of the database, open the **Vacation** database, compact and repair the database, close the database, and then exit Access.

Create	Case Problem 5

Work with the skills you've learned in the tutorial to work with data for an Internet service provider.

Data File needed for this Case Problem: ACE.accdb (*cont. from Tutorial 6*)

Always Connected Everyday   Chris and Pat Dixon want you to create a custom report and mailing labels for the ACE database. You'll do so by completing the following:

1. Open the **ACE** database located in the Level.02\Case5 folder provided with your Data Files.

2. Create a query to serve as the record source for the custom report shown in Figure 7-52, and then save the query as **qryAccessPlanCustomers**.

3. Create a custom report based on the qryAccessPlanCustomers query. Figure 7-52 shows a sample of the completed report. Refer to the figure as you create the report. Save the report as **rptAccessPlanCustomers**.

Figure 7-51

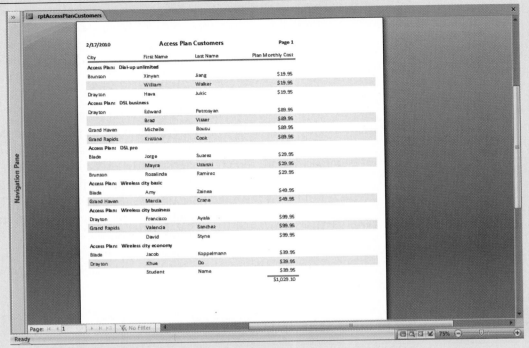

4. After you've created the rptAccessPlanCustomers report, filter the report in Report view, selecting all records that contain a specific value in the city field. Copy the entire filtered report and paste it into a new Word document. Save the document as **rptAccessPlanCustomersCopy**.

5. Use the tblCustomer table as the record source for the mailing labels. Choose appropriate options in the Label Wizard, change the mailing label layout to snaking columns, and save the report as **rptCustomerLabels**.

6. Close the ACE database without exiting Access, make a backup copy of the database, open the **ACE** database, compact and repair the database, close the database, and then exit Access.

Research | **Internet Assignments**

Use the Internet to find and work with data related to the topics presented in this tutorial.

The purpose of the Internet Assignments is to challenge you to find information on the Internet that you can use to work effectively with this software. The actual assignments are updated and maintained on the Course Technology Web site. Log on to the Internet and use your Web browser to go to the Student Online Companion for New Perspectives Office 2007 at **www.course.com/np/office2007**. Then navigate to the Internet Assignments for this tutorial.

Assess | **SAM Assessment and Training**

If you have a SAM user profile, you may have access to hands-on instruction, practice, and assessment of the skills covered in this tutorial. Log in to your SAM account (**http://sam2007.course.com**) to launch any assigned training activities or exams that relate to the skills covered in this tutorial.

Session 7.1

1. A custom report is a report created by the Report tool or the Report Wizard and that you modify in Layout or Design view, or a report you create from scratch in Layout or Design view.

2. You can apply a filter or you can copy selected portions of the report to the Clipboard.

3. A report sort field that includes a Group Header section before a group of records having the same sort field value and that includes a Group Footer section after the group of records.

4. The Report Header section appears once at the beginning of a report. The Page Header section appears at the top of each page of a report. The Group Header section appears once at the beginning of a new group of records. The Detail section appears once for each record in the underlying table or query. The Group Footer section appears once at the end of a group of records. The Report Footer section appears once at the end of a report. The Page Footer section appears at the bottom of each page of a report.

Session 7.2

1. A detail report is a report that displays fields from the record source in the Detail section. A summary report is a report that displays only summary information, such as grand totals and subtotals.

2. Keep Together

3. orphaned footer

4. Can Grow

5. Hiding duplicate values makes a report easier to read; duplicate values clutter the report.

Session 7.3

1. =Date()

2. Click the Insert Page Number button in the Controls group in Layout or Design view; specify the format, position, and alignment of the page number; and then click the OK button.

3. Report Header

4. A multiple-column report prints the same collection of data in two or more sets across the page.

Ending Data Files

Level.02 →

Tutorial
Panorama.accdb

Review
Products.accdb and
rptProductsByCompanyCopy.docx

Case1
Contract.accdb

Case2
Training.accdb

Case3
Agency.accdb and
rptDonorDonationsCopy.docx

Case4
Vacation.accdb

Case5
ACE.accdb and
rptAccessPlanCustomersCopy.docx

Objectives

Session 8.1
- Export an Access table to an HTML document and view the document
- Import a CSV file as an Access table
- Use the Table Analyzer
- Import and export XML files
- Save and run import and export specifications

Session 8.2
- Create a multi-page form using a tab control
- Embed a chart in a form
- Create and modify PivotTables and PivotCharts
- Link data from an Excel worksheet

Sharing, Integrating, and Analyzing Data

Importing, Exporting, Linking, and Analyzing Data in the Panorama Database

Case | Belmont Landscapes

Oren Belmont, Sarah Fisher, and Taylor Sico are pleased with the design and contents of the Panorama database. Oren feels that other employees would benefit from gaining access to the Panorama database and by sharing data among the different programs employees use. Oren and Sarah would also like to be able to analyze the data in the database.

In this tutorial, you will show Oren and Sarah how to import, export, link, and embed data. You will also introduce them to the charting, PivotTable, and Pivot-Chart features of Access.

Starting Data Files

Level.02 →

Tutorial
BelmLogo.gif
BelmTemp.htm
Panorama.accdb *(cont.)*
Products.xlsx
tblCustomerBilling.csv
tblProspect.xml

Review
Ads.xlsx
BelmLogo.gif
BelmTemp.htm
Payables.csv
Products.accdb *(cont.)*
tblPayments.xml

Case1
Contract.accdb *(cont.)*
Instrument.csv
Room.xlsx

Case2
CreditCard.xml
ParkLogo.gif
ParkTemp.htm
Schedule.xlsx
Training.accdb *(cont.)*

Case3
Agency.accdb *(cont.)*
Facility.csv

Case4
Personnel.xlsx
Vacation.accdb *(cont.)*
Works.xml

Case5
ACE.accdb *(cont.)*

Session 8.1

Using the Web

The **Internet** is a worldwide collection of millions of interconnected computers and computer networks that share resources. The **World Wide Web** (or the **Web**) is a vast collection of digital documents available on the Internet. Each digital document on the Web is called a **Web page**, each computer on which an individual or company stores Web pages for access on the Internet is called a **Web server**, and each computer requesting a Web page from a Web server is called a **Web client**. Each Web page is assigned an Internet address, which is also called a **Uniform Resource Locator** (**URL**); the URL identifies where the Web page is stored—the location of the Web server and the name and location of the Web page on the server. For example, http://www.course.com/catalog/default.html is a URL that identifies the Web server (www.course.com), the location path (catalog) on the Web server, and the Web page name (default.html). The beginning of the URL (http) specifies the **Hypertext Transfer Protocol** (**HTTP**), which is the data communication method used by Web clients and Web servers to exchange data over the Internet. To view a Web page, you use a computer program called a **Web browser**, such as Microsoft Internet Explorer or Mozilla Firefox. After you start a Web browser, you enter the Web page's URL. The Web browser uses the URL to find and retrieve the Web page, and then displays it on your computer screen.

Each Web page is a text document that contains the necessary codes, called **tags**, that the Web browser interprets to position and format the text in the Web page. A Web page can also contain tags for links to audio files to be played, to graphics and animations to be displayed on the screen, and to other files, which are sent along with the Web page by the Web server. A Web page can also contain tags for **hyperlinks**, which connect Web pages to other Web pages or Web sites or to a location in the same Web page. When you click hyperlink text, the linked page opens. Hyperlinks connect Web pages throughout the Internet.

Web pages are usually created using a programming language called **Hypertext Markup Language** (**HTML**). You can create a Web page by typing all the necessary HTML tags into a text document, called an **HTML document**, and saving the document with the .htm or .html file extension. You can also use a program, such as ColdFusion or Adobe Dreamweaver, to create the HTML documents for Web pages without needing to learn HTML. Many programs, including Access, have built-in tools that convert and export objects, such as tables and queries, to HTML documents.

Tip

An intranet is an internal company network that uses software tools and languages, such as HTML, that typically are used on the Internet and the Web. The company that manages or owns the intranet restricts access to it by using passwords.

Exporting an Access Query to an HTML Document

Oren wants to display the customer contact data in the qryCustomersByName query on the company's intranet so that all employees working in the office are able to access it. To store the data on the company's intranet, you'll create a Web page version of the qryCustomersByName query.

Creating the necessary HTML document to provide Oren with the information he wants is not as difficult as it might appear at first. You can use Access to export the query and convert it to an HTML document automatically.

Exporting an Access Query to an HTML Document | Reference Window

- In the Navigation Pane, right-click the object (table, query, form, or report) you want to export, point to Export on the shortcut menu, and then click HTML Document.

or

- In the Navigation Pane, click the object (table, query, form, or report) you want to export, click the External Data tab on the Ribbon, click the More button in the Export group on the External Data tab, and then click HTML Document.
- Enter the filename in the File name text box of the Export - HTML Document dialog box, click the Browse button, select the location where you want to save the file, and then click the Save button.
- Click the Export data with formatting and layout check box to retain most formatting and layout information, check the other two check boxes, as necessary, and then click the OK button.
- If using a template, click the Select a HTML Template check box in the HTML Output Options dialog box, click the Browse button, select the location for the template, click the template filename, and then click the OK button.
- Click the OK button.
- Click the Close button to close the Export - HTML Document dialog box.

To complete the following steps, you need to use Access and a Web browser. The steps in this tutorial are written for Internet Explorer, the Web browser used at Belmont Landscapes. If you use another browser, the steps you need to complete might be slightly different.

You'll export the qryCustomersByName query as an HTML document.

To export the qryCustomersByName query as an HTML document:

▶ 1. Start Access, and then open the **Panorama** database in the Level.02\Tutorial folder provided with your Data Files.

▶ 2. Open the Navigation Pane (if necessary), right-click **qryCustomersByName** to display the shortcut menu, point to **Export**, and then click **HTML Document**. The Export - HTML Document dialog box opens.

▶ 3. Select the text in the File name text box, and then type **Customers by Name**. See Figure 8-1.

Figure 8-1   **Export - HTML Document dialog box**

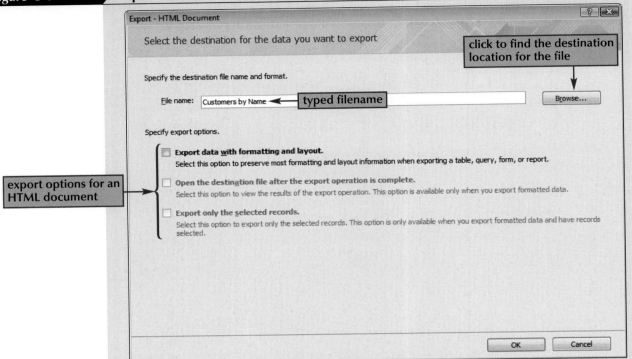

Tip

You should always select the "Export data with formatting and layout" option. Not selecting this option results in an HTML document that's poorly formatted and difficult to read.

The dialog box provides options for exporting the data with formatting and layout, opening the exported file after the export operation is complete, and exporting selected records from the source object (available only when you selected records in an object instead of the object on the Navigation Pane). You need to select the option for exporting the data with formatting and layout and the destination location for the exported file.

4. Click the **Export data with formatting and layout** check box, click the **Browse** button, navigate to and open the **Level.02\Tutorial** folder, and then click the **Save** button in the File Save dialog box. The File Save dialog box closes, and the File name text box displays the path to your Data Files and the filename Customers by Name.html.

5. Click the **OK** button. The Export - HTML Document dialog box closes and the HTML Output Options dialog box opens.

This dialog box lets you specify an HTML template or use the default format when saving the object. An **HTML template** is a file that contains HTML instructions for creating a Web page with both text and graphics, together with special instructions that tell Access where to place the Access data in the Web page. Lucia used a text-editing program to create an HTML template named BelmTemp that you'll use to create the Customers by Name HTML document. The template will automatically insert a Belmont Landscapes logo in all Web pages created with it. You need to locate Lucia's template file in your Data Files.

6. If necessary, click the **Select a HTML Template** check box to select it.

7. Click the **Browse** button to open the HTML Template to Use dialog box, navigate to and open the **Level.02\Tutorial** folder, click **BelmTemp**, and then click the **OK** button. Access closes the HTML Template to Use dialog box, returns to the HTML Output Options dialog box, and displays the location and filename for the HTML template. See Figure 8-2.

HTML Output Options dialog box | Figure 8-2

Trouble? If BelmTemp does not appear in the Level.02\Tutorial folder when you open the HTML Template to Use dialog box, click the Cancel button to return to the HTML Output Options dialog box so you can specify the template filename manually. In the HTML Template text box, type the full path to the BelmTemp.htm file in the Level.02\Tutorial folder—for example, C:\Level.02\Tutorial\BelmTemp.htm.

8. Click the **OK** button. The HTML Output Options dialog box closes, the HTML document named Customers by Name is saved in the Level.02\Tutorial folder, and the Export - HTML Document dialog box asks if you want to save the export steps. You won't save these export steps.

9. Click the **Close** button in the dialog box to close it without saving the steps.

Now you can view the Web page.

Viewing an HTML Document Using Internet Explorer

Oren asks to see the Web page you created. You can view the HTML document that you created using any Web browser. You'll view it using Internet Explorer.

To view the qryCustomersByName query Web page:

1. Open Windows Explorer, and then navigate to and open the **Level.02\Tutorial** folder, which is where you saved the exported HTML document.

2. Right-click **Customers by Name** in the file list to open the shortcut menu, click **Open With**, click **Internet Explorer** in the list of programs in the Open With dialog box, and then click the **OK** button. Internet Explorer starts and opens the Customers by Name Web page. See Figure 8-3.

Figure 8-3 | **qryCustomersByName query in the Internet Explorer window**

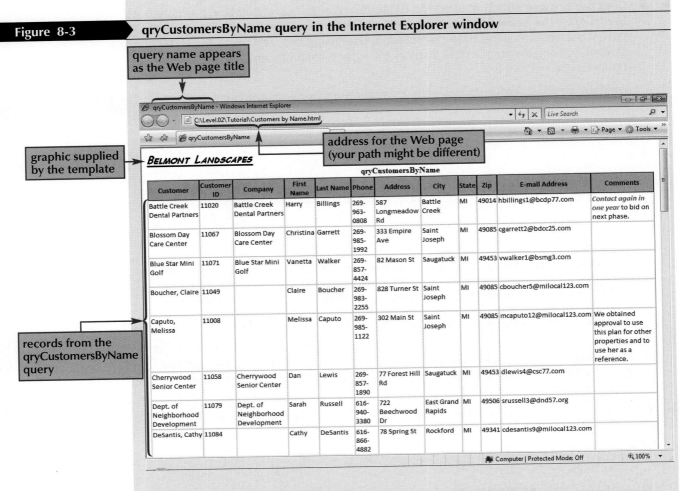

Changes that employees make to the Panorama database will not appear in the Customers by Name Web page that you created because it is a **static Web page**—that is, it reflects the state of the qryCustomersByName query in the Panorama database at the time you created it. If data in the qryCustomersByName query changes, you will need to export the query as an HTML document again.

Because this static Web page is not linked to the qryCustomersByName query on which it is based, you cannot use your browser to make changes to its data. Before closing the Customers by Name Web page, you'll try to change one of its field values.

To attempt to change a field value, and then close the browser:

► 1. Double-click **MI** in the State column for the first record (Battle Creek Dental Partners), and then type **NY**. The value of MI remains highlighted and unchanged, because the Customers by Name Web page is a static page.

► 2. Click the **Close** button ❎ on the Internet Explorer window title bar to close it and to return to Windows Explorer.

▶ **3.** Click the **Close** button ⊠ on the Windows Explorer window title bar to close it and to return to Access.

Trouble? If the Access window is not active on your screen, click the Microsoft Access program button on the taskbar.

Sarah has a file containing customer billing addresses that she needs to add to the Panorama database. Instead of typing these billing addresses into new records, she asks you to import the data into the Panorama database.

Importing a CSV File as an Access Table

For most customers, the Address, City, State, and Zip fields in the tblCustomer table identify both the customer's location and billing address, which is where Belmont Landscapes sends the customer's invoices. In a few cases, however, the billing address is different from the location address; in addition, the company name used for billing purposes might be different from the company name stored in the tblCustomer table. Sarah has been maintaining an Excel workbook containing customer billing data, and she's exported the data to a CSV file. A **CSV (comma-separated values) file** is a text file in which commas separate values, and each line is a record containing the same number of values in the same positions.

Access can import data from a CSV file directly into a database table. Sarah's CSV file is named tblCustomerBilling, and you'll import it as a table with the same name into the Panorama database.

Importing a CSV File as an Access Table | Reference Window

- Click the External Data tab on the Ribbon.
- In the Import group on the External Data tab, click the Text File button to open the Get External Data - Text File dialog box.
- Click the Browse button in the dialog box, navigate to the location where the file to import is stored, click the filename, and then click the Open button.
- Click the Import the source data into a new table in the current database option button, and then click the OK button.
- In the Import Text Wizard dialog box, click the Delimited option button, and then click the Next button.
- Make sure the Comma option button is selected. If appropriate, click the First Row Contains Field Names check box to select it, and then click the Next button.
- For each field, select the column, type its field name, and select its data type, and then click the Next button.
- Choose the appropriate option button to let Access create a primary key, to choose your own primary key, or to avoid setting a primary key, click the Next button, type the table name, and then click the Finish button.

Now you will import the tblCustomerBilling.csv file as an Access database table.

To import the CSV file as an Access table:

▶ **1.** Click the **External Data** tab on the Ribbon, and then in the Import group on the External Data tab, click the **Text File** button (with the ScreenTip "Import text file") to open the Get External Data - Text File dialog box.

▶ **2.** Click the **Browse** button, navigate to and open the **Level.02\Tutorial** folder, click **tblCustomerBilling**, click the **Open** button, and then click the **Import the source data into a new table in the current database** option button. The selected path and filename appears in the File name text box. See Figure 8-4.

Figure 8-4 **Get External Data - Text File dialog box**

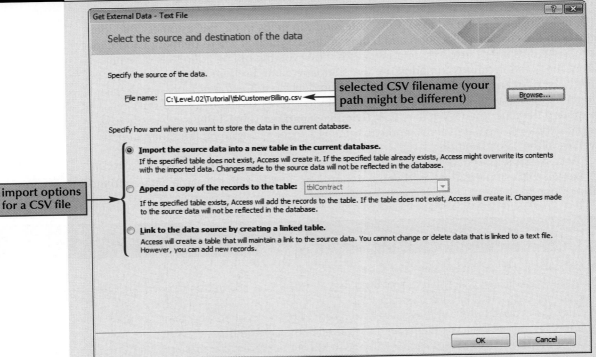

import options for a CSV file

The dialog box provides options for importing the data into a new table in the database, appending a copy of the data to an existing table in the database, and linking to the source data. In the future, Sarah wants to maintain the customer billing data in the Panorama database, instead of using her Excel workbook, so you'll import the data into a new table.

▶ **3.** Click the **OK** button to open the first Import Text Wizard dialog box, in which you designate how to identify the separation between field values in each line in the source data. The choices are the use of commas, tabs, or another character to separate, or delimit, the values, or the use of fixed width columns with spaces between each column. The wizard has correctly identified that values are delimited by commas.

▶ **4.** Click the **Next** button to open the second Import Text Wizard dialog box, in which you verify the delimiter for values in each line. See Figure 8-5.

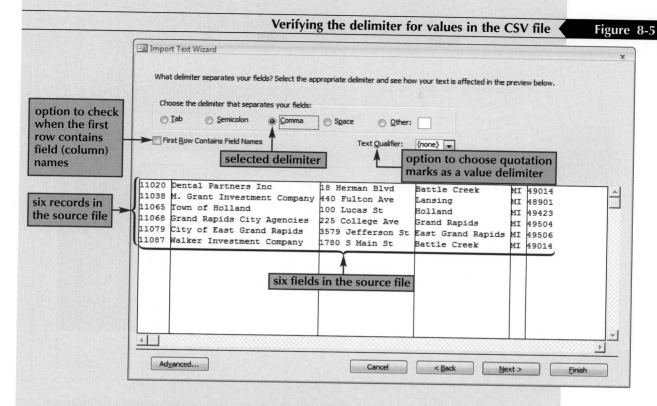

Verifying the delimiter for values in the CSV file — Figure 8-5

The CSV source file contains six records with six fields in each record. A comma serves as the delimiter for values in each line, so the Comma option button is selected. The first row in the source file contains the first record, not field names, so the First Row Contains Field Names check box is not checked. If the source file uses either single quotation marks or double quotation marks to enclose values, you would click the Text Qualifier arrow to choose the appropriate option.

5. Click the **Next** button to open the third Import Text Wizard dialog box, in which you enter the field name and set other properties for the imported fields. You will import all fields from the source file and use the default data type and indexed settings for each field.

6. Type **CustomerID** in the Field Name text box, and then click **Field2** in the table list. CustomerID (partially hidden) is the heading for the first column in the table list, and the second column is selected.

7. Repeat Step 6 for the rightmost five columns, typing **BillingCompany**, **BillingAddress**, **BillingCity**, **BillingState**, and **BillingZip** in the Field Name text box. See Figure 8-6.

Figure 8-6 **After setting field names for the six fields in the source file**

> 8. Click the **Next** button to open the fourth Import Text Wizard dialog box, in which you select the primary key for the imported table. CustomerID, the first column, will be the primary key.

> 9. Click the **Choose my own primary key** option button, make sure **CustomerID** appears in the list box for the option, click the **Next** button, click the **I would like a wizard to analyze my table after importing the data** check box, and then click the **Finish** button. An Import Text Wizard dialog box opens asking if you want to analyze the table.

After importing data and creating a new table, you can use the Import Text Wizard to analyze the imported table. When you choose this option, you start the Table Analyzer.

Analyzing a Table with the Table Analyzer

Tip
Read the Normalization section in the appendix titled "Relational Databases and Database Design" for more information about normalization and third normal form.

The **Table Analyzer** analyzes a single table and, if necessary, splits it into two or more tables that are in third normal form. The Table Analyzer looks for redundant data in the table. When the Table Analyzer encounters redundant data, it removes redundant fields from the table and then places the redundant fields in new tables.

To use the Table Analyzer to analyze the imported table:

▶ 1. Click the **Yes** button to close the dialog box and to open the first Table Analyzer Wizard dialog box. The diagram and explanation in this dialog box describe the problem when duplicate data is stored in a table.

▶ 2. Click the first **Show me an example** button ⟦»⟧, read the explanation, close the example box, click the second **Show me an example** button ⟦»⟧, read the explanation, close the example box, and then click the **Next** button to open the second Table Analyzer Wizard dialog box. The diagram and explanation in this dialog box describe how the Table Analyzer solves the duplicate data problem.

▶ 3. Click the first **Show me an example** button ⟦»⟧, read the explanation, close the example box, click the second **Show me an example** button ⟦»⟧, read the explanation, close the example box, and then click the **Next** button to open the third Table Analyzer Wizard dialog box. In this dialog box, you choose whether to let the wizard decide which fields go in what tables, if the table is not already normalized. You'll let the wizard decide.

▶ 4. Make sure the **Yes, let the wizard decide** option button is selected, and then click the **Next** button. A message box informs you that the wizard does not recommend splitting the table because the table is normalized and does not contain redundant data.

▶ 5. Click the **Cancel** button to close the message box, exit the wizard, and return to the Get External Data - Text File dialog box, in which you are asked if you want to save the import steps. You don't need to save these steps because you're importing the data only this one time.

▶ 6. Click the **Close** button to close the dialog box.

Tip

You can start the Table Analyzer directly by clicking the Database Tools tab, and then clicking the Analyze Table button in the Analyze group.

The TblCustomerBilling table is now listed in the Tables section in the Navigation Pane. You'll rename the table to change the initial letter to lowercase, and then open the table to verify the import results.

To rename and open the imported TblCustomerBilling table:

▶ 1. Right-click **TblCustomerBilling** in the Navigation Pane, click **Rename**, press the **Home** key, press the **Delete** key, type the letter **t**, and then press the **Enter** key to change the table name to tblCustomerBilling.

▶ 2. Double-click **tblCustomerBilling** in the Navigation Pane to open the table datasheet, resize all columns to their best fit, and then click **11020** in the first row in the CustomerID column to deselect all values. See Figure 8-7.

Imported tblCustomerBilling table datasheet ◀ Figure 8-7

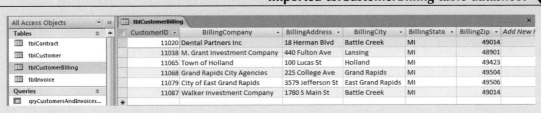

CustomerID	BillingCompany	BillingAddress	BillingCity	BillingState	BillingZip	Add New F
11020	Dental Partners Inc	18 Herman Blvd	Battle Creek	MI	49014	
11038	M. Grant Investment Company	440 Fulton Ave	Lansing	MI	48901	
11065	Town of Holland	100 Lucas St	Holland	MI	49423	
11068	Grand Rapids City Agencies	225 College Ave	Grand Rapids	MI	49504	
11079	City of East Grand Rapids	3579 Jefferson St	East Grand Rapids	MI	49506	
11087	Walker Investment Company	1780 S Main St	Battle Creek	MI	49014	

▶ 3. Save and close the table.

Sarah has some additional data that she wants to import into the Panorama database. The data is stored in XML format.

Using XML

Belmont Landscapes has contacts in the building trade industry and gets customer leads from builders when they sell new homes. One of the builders has several prospective customers available to Sarah in an XML document, which she wants to add to the Panorama database. **XML** (**Extensible Markup Language**) is a programming language that is similar in format to HTML, but is more customizable and suited to the exchange of data between different programs. Unlike HTML, which uses a fixed set of tags to describe the appearance of a Web page, developers can customize XML to describe the data it contains and how that data should be structured.

Importing an XML File as an Access Table

Access can import data from an XML file directly into a database table. Sarah's XML file is named tblProspect, and you'll import it as a table with the same name into the Panorama database.

Reference Window | **Importing an XML File as an Access Table**

- Click the External Data tab on the Ribbon.
- In the Import group on the External Data tab, click the XML File button to open the Get External Data - XML File dialog box.
- Click the Browse button, navigate to the location for the XML file, click the XML filename, and then click the Open button.
- Click the OK button in the Get External Data - XML File dialog box, click the table name in the Import XML dialog box, click the appropriate option button in the Import Options section, and then click the OK button.
- Click the Close button.

or

- If you need to save the import steps, click the Save import steps check box, enter a name for the saved steps in the Save as text box, and then click the Save Import button.

Now you will import the tblProspect.xml document as an Access database table.

To import the XML document as an Access table:

▶ 1. Click the **External Data** tab on the Ribbon (if necessary), and then in the Import group on the External Data tab, click the **XML File** button (with the ScreenTip "Import XML file"). The Get External Data - XML File dialog box opens.

▶ 2. Click the **Browse** button, navigate to and open the **Level.02\Tutorial** folder, click **tblProspect**, and then click the **Open** button. The selected path and filename now appear in the File name text box.

▶ 3. Click the **OK** button. The Import XML dialog box opens. See Figure 8-8.

Import XML dialog box Figure 8-8

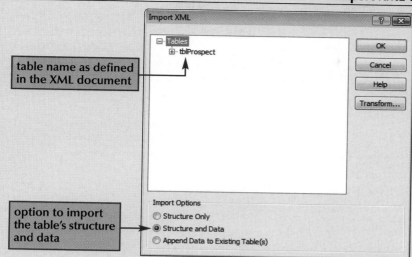

From the XML file, you can import only the table structure to a new table, import the table structure and data to a new table, or append the data in the XML file to an existing table. You'll import the table structure and data to a new table named tblProspect.

▶ **4.** Make sure the **Structure and Data** option button is selected, click **tblProspect** in the list box, and then click the **OK** button. The Import XML dialog box closes, and the last Get External Data - XML File dialog box is displayed.

Before reviewing the imported table, you'll save the import steps.

Saving and Running Import Specifications

If you need to repeat the same import procedure many times, you can save the steps for the procedure and expedite future imports by running the saved import steps without using a wizard. Because the builder intends to send Sarah additional lists of prospective customers in the future, you'll save the import steps for Sarah.

To save and run the XML file import steps:

▶ **1.** Click the **Save import steps** check box. The dialog box expands to display additional options for the save operation. See Figure 8-9.

Figure 8-9 Saving the import steps

In the expanded dialog box, you can accept the default name for the saved import steps or choose one that you create, and you can enter an optional description. If the import will occur on a set schedule, you can also create a reminder task in Microsoft Outlook. You'll accept the default name for the saved steps, and you won't enter a description or schedule an Outlook task.

▶ **2.** Click the **Save Import** button. The import steps are saved as Import-tblProspect, the Get External Data - XML File dialog box closes, the tblProspect file is imported to the Panorama database, and the table is now listed in the Navigation Pane.

You'll now show Sarah how she can run the saved steps when she receives customer prospects from the builder in the future.

▶ **3.** In the Import group on the External Data tab, click the **Saved Imports** button. The Manage Data Tasks dialog box opens. See Figure 8-10.

Manage Data Tasks dialog box | Figure 8-10

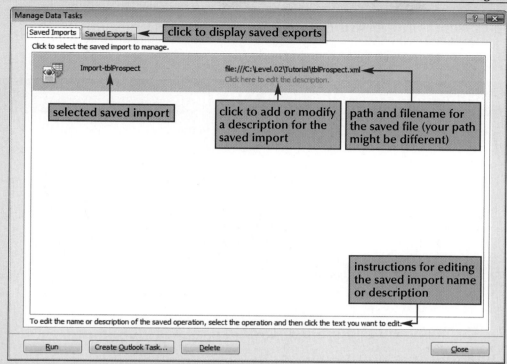

In this dialog box, you can change the saved import name, add or change its description, create an Outlook task for the saved import, run a saved import, or delete a saved import. You can also manage any saved export by clicking the Saved Exports tab. You'll add a description for the saved procedure and review the list of saved exports.

▶ **4.** Click the **Click here to edit the description** link to open an editing box, type **Builder's XML file of customer prospects**, click an unused portion of the orange selection band to close the editing box and accept the typed description, and then click the **Saved Exports** tab. You have not saved any export steps, so no saved exports are displayed.

▶ **5.** Click the **Close** button to close the Manage Data Tasks dialog box.

▶ **6.** Double-click the **tblProspect** table in the Navigation Pane to open the table datasheet, close the Navigation Pane, resize all columns to their best fit, and then click **12001** in the first row in the CustomerID column to deselect all values. See Figure 8-11.

Imported tblProspect table datasheet | Figure 8-11

▶ **7.** Save and close the table.

Sarah next asks you to export the tblInvoice table as an XML file.

Exporting an Access Table as an XML File

Belmont Landscapes uses an accounting package that accepts the data in XML files as input for making accounting entries. Sarah wants to test this capability by exporting the tblInvoice table as an XML file and giving the XML file to the company's accounting manager for testing with the accounting package.

Reference Window	**Exporting an Access Table as an XML File**

- Right-click the object (table, query, form, or report) in the Navigation Pane, point to Export, and then click XML File.

or

- Click the object (table, query, form, or report) in the Navigation Pane. In the Export group on the External Data tab, click the More button, and then click XML File.
- Click the Browse button in the Export - XML File dialog box, navigate to the location where you will save the XML file, and then click the Save button.
- Click the OK button in the dialog box, select the options in the Export XML dialog box or click the More Options button and select the options in the expanded Export XML dialog box, and then click the OK button.
- Click the Close button.

or

- If you need to save the export steps, click the Save export steps check box, enter a name for the saved steps in the Save as text box, and then click the Save Export button.

InSight	**Importing and Exporting Data**

You've imported data from an Excel workbook and a text file (TXT extension) in Tutorial 2 and from a text file (CSV extension) and an XML file in this tutorial. Additional Access options include importing an object from another Access database, importing data from other databases (ODBC databases such as SQL Server, dBASE, and Paradox), and importing a Lotus 1-2-3 file, an HTML document, an Outlook folder, or a SharePoint list.

In addition to exporting Access objects as an XML file or an HTML document, Access includes options for exporting data to another Access database, other databases (ODBC database, dBASE, or Paradox), an Excel workbook, a Lotus 1-2-3 file, a text file, a Word document, or a SharePoint list. You can also "export" table or query data to Word's mail merge feature, or export a report to a snapshot file (SNP extension) so you can view it with the Microsoft Snapshot Viewer available from the Microsoft Download Center.

Also available from the Microsoft Download Center is the Microsoft Save as PDF or XPS add-in that you can download and install to export and save objects as PDF or XPS files. Installing this download adds a "PDF or XPS" button in the Export group on the External Data tab. PDF (Portable Document Format) and XPS (XML Paper Specification) are file formats that render reports and other objects in a form viewable on any computer using the free Adobe Reader program for PDF files and an XPS reader program, such as Windows Presentation Foundation, for XPS files.

The steps you follow for all import and export options work similar to the import and export steps you've used in this tutorial and in Tutorial 2. For example, to save an object as an XPS file, right-click the name of the object you want to export in the Navigation Pane, point to Export on the shortcut menu, click PDF or XPS, navigate to the folder where you want to store the file, click the Save as type arrow, click XPS Document, click the Publish button, and then click the Close button.

You can now export the tblInvoice table as an XML file.

To export the tblInvoice table as an XML file:

▶ **1.** Open the Navigation Pane, right-click **tblInvoice** in the Navigation Pane, point to **Export** on the shortcut menu, and then click **XML File**. The Export - XML File dialog box opens.

▶ **2.** Click the **Browse** button, navigate to and open the **Level.02\Tutorial** folder, and then click the **Save** button. The selected path and filename now appears in the File name text box in the Export - XML File dialog box.

▶ **3.** Click the **OK** button. The Export XML dialog box opens.

   Clicking the More Options button in the Export XML dialog box expands the dialog box and lets you view and change detailed options for exporting a database object to an XML file.

▶ **4.** Click the **More Options** button to reveal detailed export options in the Export XML dialog box. See Figure 8-12.

Data tab in the Export XML dialog box ◀ **Figure 8-12**

The Export Data check box, the Export Location text box, and the Records To Export option group display the selections you made in the previous step. You're exporting all records from the tblInvoice table, including the data in the records and the structure of the table, to the tblInvoice.xml file in the Level.02\Tutorial folder. The encoding option determines how characters will be represented in the exported XML file. The encoding choices are UTF-8, which uses 8 bits to represent each character, and UTF-16, which uses 16 bits to represent each character. You can also click the Transforms button if you have a special file that contains instructions for changing the exported data.

The accounting package doesn't have a transform file and requires the default encoding, but Sarah wants to review the tables that contain lookup data.

▶ **5.** Click the **plus box** to the left of [Lookup Data]. The tblContract table contains lookup data because it's the primary table in the one-to-many relationship with the related tblInvoice table. The accounting package requirements don't include any lookup data from the tblContract table, so make sure the tblContract check box is not checked.

   The Data tab settings are correct, so you'll verify the Schema tab settings.

6. Click the **Schema** tab. See Figure 8-13.

Figure 8-13 **Schema tab in the Export XML dialog box**

option to export the table structure

option to include the table structure in the XML file

Along with the data from the tblInvoice table, you'll be exporting its table structure, including information about the table's primary key, indexes, and table and field properties. You can include this information in a separate **XSD** (**XML Structure Definition**) file, or you can embed the information in the XML file. The accounting package expects a single XML file, so you'll embed the structure information in the XML file.

7. Click the **Embed schema in exported XML data document** option button to select that option and to dim the "Create separate schema document" text box, and then click the **Presentation** tab.

The Presentation tab options let you export a separate **XSL** (**Extensible Stylesheet Language**) file containing the format specifications for the tblInvoice table data. Unlike HTML, XML provides no screen formatting information. An XSL file provides formatting instructions so that a browser or another program can display the data in the XML file in a readable way. The accounting package will import the tblInvoice table data directly into its computer program, which contains its own formatting instructions, so you will not export an XSL file.

8. Make sure that the **Export Presentation (HTML 4.0 Sample XSL)** check box is not checked, and then click the **OK** button. Access closes the Export XML dialog box, exports the data in the tblInvoice table as an XML file in the Level.02\Tutorial folder, and returns you to the final Export - XML File dialog box.

Sarah plans to make further tests exporting the tblInvoice table as an XML file, so you'll save the export steps.

Saving and Running Export Specifications

Saving the steps to export the tblInvoice table as an XML file will save time and eliminate errors when Sarah repeats the export procedure. You'll save the export steps and then show Sarah how to run the saved export steps.

To save and run the XML file export steps:

▶ **1.** Click the **Save export steps** check box. The dialog box expands to display additional options for the save operation.

The expanded dialog box has the same options you saw earlier when you saved the XML import steps. You'll enter a description, and you won't create an Outlook task because Sarah will be running the saved export steps on an as needed basis.

▶ **2.** In the Description text box, type **XML file accounting entries from the tblInvoice table**. See Figure 8-14.

Saving the export steps ◀ Figure 8-14

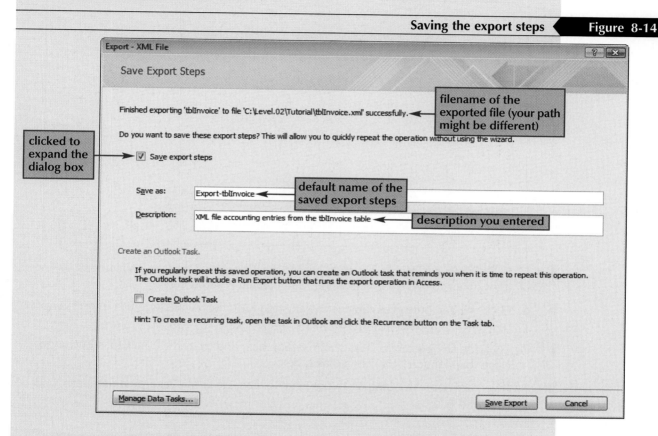

▶ **3.** Click the **Save Export** button. The export steps are saved as Export-tblInvoice, the Export - XML File dialog box closes, and the tblInvoice table is exported as an XML file named tblInvoice.

You'll now show Sarah how she can to run the saved steps.

▶ **4.** Click the **External Data** tab on the Ribbon (if necessary), and in the Export group on the External Data tab, click the **Saved Exports** button. The Manage Data Tasks dialog box opens. See Figure 8-15.

Figure 8-15 | **Manage Data Tasks dialog box**

5. Click the **Run** button. The saved procedure runs, and a message box opens, asking if you want to replace the existing XML file you created earlier.

6. Click the **Yes** button to replace the existing XML file. A message box informs you that the export was completed successfully.

7. Click the **OK** button to close the message box, and then click the **Close** button to close the Manage Data Tasks dialog box.

8. If you are not continuing on to the next session, close the Panorama database, and then exit Access.

You've imported and exported data, analyzed a table's design, and saved and run import and export specifications. In the next session, you will analyze data by working with a chart, PivotTable, PivotChart, and linked data, and you will add a tab control to a form.

Review | **Session 8.1 Quick Check**

1. What is the World Wide Web, and what do you use to view the information it provides?
2. What is a hyperlink?
3. What is HTML?
4. What is an HTML template?
5. What is a static Web page?
6. What is a CSV file?
7. What is the Table Analyzer?
8. _____ is a programming language that describes data and its structure.

Session 8.2

Creating a Multi-page Form Using a Tab Control

You can create a multi-page form in two ways: use the **Page Break tool** to insert a page break control in the form, or use the **Tab Control tool** to insert a control that's called a tab control. If you insert a page break control in a form, users can move between the form pages by pressing the Page Up and Page Down keys. If you use a tab control, the control appears with tabs at the top, with one tab for each page. Users can switch between pages by clicking the tabs.

Sarah wants to include a tab control with two pages in the frmContractsAndInvoices form. The first page of the tab control will contain the frmInvoiceSubform subform that is currently positioned at the bottom of the frmContractsAndInvoices form. The second page of the tab control will contain a chart showing the invoice amounts for the invoices associated with the displayed contract.

To expedite placing the subform in the tab control, you'll cut the subform from the form, add the tab control, and then paste the subform into the left tab on the tab control. You need to perform these steps in Design view.

To add the tab control to the form:

▶ 1. If you took a break after the previous session, make sure that the Panorama database is open and the Navigation Pane is open.

▶ 2. Open the **frmContractsAndInvoices** form in Design view, and then close the Navigation Pane.

▶ 3. Right-click the top edge of the subform control to open the shortcut menu, and then click **Cut** to delete the subform control and place it on the Clipboard.

   Trouble? If you do not see Subform in New Window as one of the options on the shortcut menu, you did not click the top edge of the subform control correctly. Right-click the top edge of the subform control until you see this option on the shortcut menu, and then repeat Step 3.

▶ 4. In the Controls group on the Design tab, click the **Tab Control** button ☐.

▶ 5. Position the + portion of the pointer in the Detail section three grid dots from the left edge of the grid and at the 2.5-inch mark on the vertical ruler, and then click the mouse button. Access places a tab control with two pages in the form.

▶ 6. Right-click the left tab, and then click **Paste** on the shortcut menu. The subform is pasted in the tab control. See Figure 8-16.

Figure 8-16 Subform on the tab control in the Detail section

> **7.** Save your form design changes, switch to Form view, and then click **3011** in the ContractNum text box to deselect all controls. The left tab, which represents the first page in the tab control, is the active tab. See Figure 8-17.

Figure 8-17 Subform on the tab control in Form view

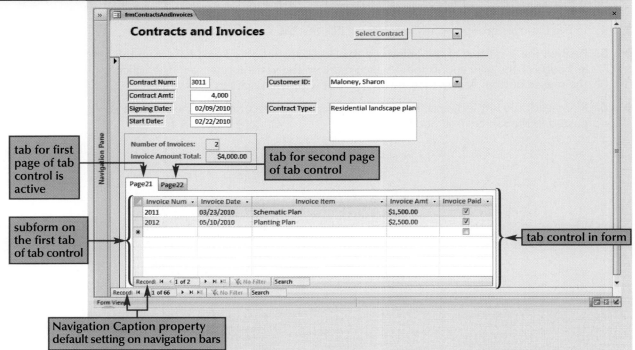

The subform is now displayed on the first page of the tab control and its design is the same as it was before you cut and pasted it to the tab control.

▶ **8.** Click the right tab of the tab control to display the second page, which is empty because you haven't added any controls to it yet.

After viewing the form in Form view, Sarah asks you to edit the labels for the tabs in the tab control, so they indicate the contents of each page. Also, Sarah's staff finds the two sets of navigation buttons confusing—they waste time determining which set of navigation buttons applies to the subform and which to the main form. You'll set the Navigation Caption property for the main form and the subform. The **Navigation Caption property** lets you change the navigation label from the word "Record" to another value. Because the main form displays data about contracts and the subform displays data about invoices, you'll change the Navigation Caption property for the main form to "Contract" and for the subform to "Invoice."

To change the captions for the tabs and the navigation buttons:

▶ **1.** Switch to Design view.

▶ **2.** Click the **form selector** for the main form to select the form control in the main form, open the property sheet to display the properties for the selected form control, click the **Navigation Caption** text box, and then type **Contract**. See Figure 8-18.

Setting the Navigation Caption property for the main form ◀ **Figure 8-18**

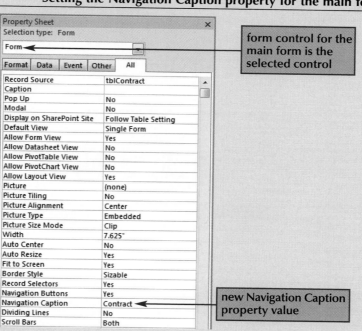

Property Sheet	×
Selection type: Form	

Form ◀ *form control for the main form is the selected control*

Format | Data | Event | Other | **All**

Record Source	tblContract
Caption	
Pop Up	No
Modal	No
Display on SharePoint Site	Follow Table Setting
Default View	Single Form
Allow Form View	Yes
Allow Datasheet View	No
Allow PivotTable View	No
Allow PivotChart View	No
Allow Layout View	Yes
Picture	(none)
Picture Tiling	No
Picture Alignment	Center
Picture Type	Embedded
Picture Size Mode	Clip
Width	7.625"
Auto Center	No
Auto Resize	Yes
Fit to Screen	Yes
Border Style	Sizable
Record Selectors	Yes
Navigation Buttons	Yes
Navigation Caption	Contract ◀ *new Navigation Caption property value*
Dividing Lines	No
Scroll Bars	Both

▶ **3.** Click the **form selector** for the subform to select the subform, click the **form selector** for the subform again to select the form control in the subform and display the properties for the selected form control, click the **Navigation Caption** text box, and then type **Invoice**. Navigation buttons don't appear in Design view, so you won't see the effects of the Navigation Caption property settings until you switch to Form view.

▶ **4.** Click the left tab in the subform to select it, and then type **Invoice Data** in the Caption text box on the property sheet. See Figure 8-19.

Figure 8-19 **Setting the Caption property for the left tab**

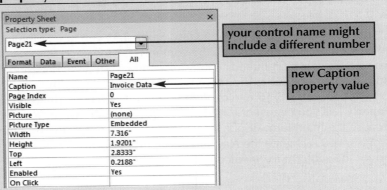

your control name might include a different number

new Caption property value

▶ **5.** Click the right tab in the subform to select it, type **Invoice Chart** in the Caption text box, and then close the property sheet.

▶ **6.** Save your form design changes, switch to Form view, and then click **3011** in the ContractNum text box to deselect all controls. The tabs and the navigation buttons now display the new caption values. See Figure 8-20.

Figure 8-20 **Subform on the tab control in Form view**

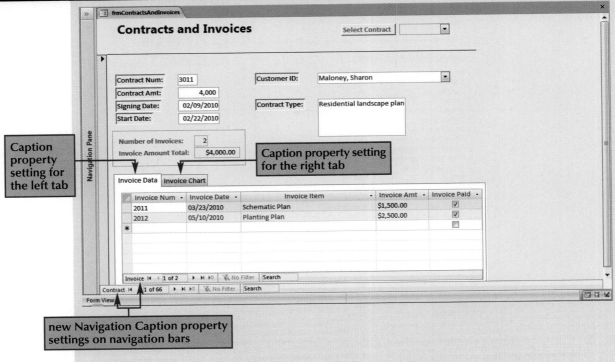

Caption property setting for the left tab

Caption property setting for the right tab

new Navigation Caption property settings on navigation bars

Sarah wants you to add a simple chart to the second page of the tab control.

Integrating Access with Other Programs

When you create a form or report in Access, you include more than just the data from the record source table or query. You've added controls such as lines, rectangles, tab controls, and graphics in your forms and reports to improve their appearance and usability. You can also add charts, drawings, and other objects to your forms and reports, but Access doesn't have the capability to create them. Instead, you create these other objects using other programs and then place them in a form or report using the appropriate integration method.

When you integrate information between programs, the program containing the original information, or object, is called the **source program**, and the program in which you place the information created by the source program is called the **destination program**. Access offers three ways for you to integrate objects created by other programs.

- **Importing**. When you import an object, you include the contents of a file in a new table or append it to an existing table, or you include the contents of the file in a form, report, or field. For example, in Tutorial 2 you added a picture to a form, or imported it into the form, and in this tutorial you imported CSV and XML files as new tables in the Panorama database. The imported picture is a file with a .bmp extension that was created by a graphics program, and the CSV and XML files were created by other programs. Once an object is imported, it has no relation to the program in which it was created. Any changes made to the object using the source program are not reflected in the imported objects.
- **Embedding**. When you embed an object in a form, report, or field, you preserve its connection to the source program, which enables you to edit the object, if necessary, using the features of the source program. Any changes you make to the object are reflected only in the form, report, or field in which it is embedded; the changes do not affect the original object in the file from which it was embedded. Likewise, if you start the source program outside Access and make any changes to the original object, these changes are not reflected in the embedded object.
- **Linking**. When you link an object to a form, report, or field, you include a connection in the destination program to the original file maintained by the source program; you do not store data from the file in the destination program. Any changes you made to the original file using the source program are reflected in the linked file version in the destination program.

InSight | **Importing, Embedding, and Linking Data**

How do you decide which method to use when you need to use data stored in another format in Access? You import a file as a new table or append the records in the file to an existing table when you intend to use Access to maintain the data and no longer need an updated version of the data with the source program. You link to the data when the source program will continue to maintain the data in the file, and you need to use an updated version of the file at all times in the destination program. When linking to the data, you can also maintain the data using the destination program, and the source program will always use the updated version of the file.

For objects in forms or reports, you import an object (such as a picture) when you want a copy of the object in your form or report and you don't intend to make any changes to the object. You embed or link an object when you want a copy of the object in your form or report and you intend to edit the object using the source program in the future. You embed the object when you do not want your edits to the object in the destination program to affect any other copies of the object used by other programs. You link the object when you want your edits to the object in the destination program to affect the object used by other programs.

Sarah wants you to embed a chart on the second page of the tab control.

Embedding a Chart in a Form

The Chart Wizard in Access helps you to embed a chart in a form or report. The chart is actually created by another program, Microsoft Graph, but the Chart Wizard does the work of embedding the chart. After embeddng the chart in a form or report, you can edit it using the Microsoft Graph program.

Reference Window | **Embedding a Chart in a Form**

- In the Controls group on the Design tab in Design view, click the Insert Chart button.
- Position the + portion of the pointer where you want to position the upper-left corner of the chart, and then click the mouse button to start the Chart Wizard.
- Select the record source, fields, and chart type.
- Edit the chart contents, and select the fields that link the object and chart, if necessary.
- Enter a chart title, select whether to include a legend, and then click the Finish button.

The tblInvoice table contains the information needed for the chart Sarah wants you to include in the form's right tab in the tab control.

To add a chart in the tab control and start the Chart Wizard:

▶ **1.** Switch to Design view, and then click the **Invoice Chart** tab on the tab control, if necessary.

▶ **2.** In the Controls group on the Design tab, click the **Insert Chart** button 📊 , and then move the pointer to the tab control. When the pointer is inside the tab control, the rectangular portion of the tab control you can use to place controls is filled in black.

▶ **3.** Position the + portion of the pointer in the upper-left corner of the black portion of the tab control, and then click the mouse button. Access places a chart control in the form and opens the first Chart Wizard dialog box, in which you select the record source for the chart.

Sarah wants the chart to provide her staff with a simple visual display of the relative proportions of the invoice amounts for the invoices for the currently displayed contract. You'll use the tblInvoice table as the record source for the chart and select the InvoiceDate and InvoiceAmt fields as the fields to use in the chart.

To create the chart with the Chart Wizard:

▶ **1.** Click **Table: tblInvoice** in the list box, and then click the **Next** button to display the second Chart Wizard dialog box.

▶ **2.** Select the **InvoiceDate** and the **InvoiceAmt** fields, and then click the **Next** button to display the third Chart Wizard dialog box, in which you choose the chart type.

▶ **3.** Click the **Pie Chart** button (row 4, column 1) to select the pie chart as the chart type to use for Sarah's chart. See Figure 8-21.

Selecting the chart type ◀   **Figure 8-21**

click to select the Pie Chart chart type

description of the selected chart type

▶ **4.** Click the **Next** button to display the next Chart Wizard dialog box, in which you preview the chart and modify the data and its placement in the chart. Because visualizing the chart from the displayed preview is difficult, you'll use the default layout based on the two selected fields. You can easily modify the chart after you create it.

Tip

The box on the right displays a brief description of the selected chart type.

Tip

The record source for a primary main form must have a one-to-many relationship to the record source for a related subform or chart. The subform or chart object has its Link Master Fields property set to the primary key in the record source to the main form. Its Link Child Fields property is set to the foreign key in the record source to the subform or chart.

5. Click the **Next** button to display the next Chart Wizard dialog box, in which you choose the fields that link records in the main form, which uses the tblContract table as its record source, to records in the chart, which uses the tblInvoice table as its record source. ContractNum is the common field linking these two tables, and you can use that field as the linking field even though you didn't select it as a field for the chart.

6. Click the **Next** button to display the final dialog box, in which you enter the title that will appear at the top of the chart and choose whether to include a legend in the chart.

7. Type **Invoices for this Contract**, make sure the **Yes, display a legend** option button is selected, and then click the **Finish** button. The completed chart appears in the tab control.

   You'll view the form in Form view, where it's easier to assess the chart's appearance.

8. Save your form design changes, switch to Form view, navigate to record 5 in the main form, notice the four contracts displayed in the subform, click the **Invoice Chart** tab to display the chart, and then scroll down the form (if necessary). See Figure 8-22.

| Figure 8-22 | Embedded chart in Form view |

After viewing the chart, Sarah decides it needs some modifications. She wants you to change the chart type from a pie chart to a bar chart, remove the legend, and modify the chart's background color. You'll make these changes by switching to Design view, and then you'll start Microsoft Graph so you can edit the chart.

To edit the chart using Microsoft Graph:

▶ 1. Switch to Design view, right-click an edge of the chart object to open the shortcut menu, point to **Chart Object**, and then click **Open**. Microsoft Graph starts and displays the chart. See Figure 8-23.

Editing the chart with Microsoft Graph | Figure 8-23

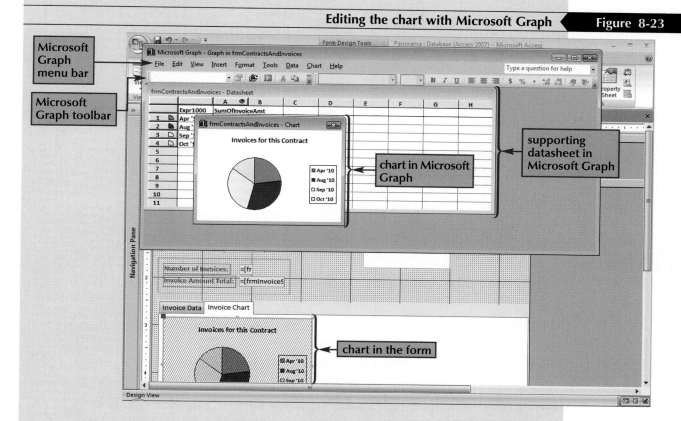

Microsoft Graph is the source program that the Chart Wizard used to create the chart. Because the chart was embedded in the form, editing the chart object starts Graph and allows you to edit the chart using the Graph menu bar and toolbar. In addition to displaying the selected chart, the Graph window displays a datasheet, which contains the data on which the chart is based. You'll now make Sarah's chart changes using Graph.

▶ 2. Click **Chart** on the Graph menu bar, click **Chart Type** to open the Chart Type dialog box, and then click **Column** in the Chart type list box to display the types of column charts. See Figure 8-24.

Figure 8-24   Chart Type dialog box

selected chart type

click to create a custom chart type

subtypes of the selected chart type

description of selected chart subtype

click and hold to view sample of selected chart subtype

The Column chart is the selected chart type, and the Clustered Column chart is the default chart subtype (row 1, column 1). A description of the selected chart sub-type appears below the chart subtypes. You can create a custom chart by clicking the Custom Types tab. If you click and hold down the Press and Hold to View Sample button, you'll see a sample of the selected subtype.

3. Click the **Press and Hold to View Sample** button to view a sample of the chart, release the mouse button, and then click the **OK** button to close the dialog box and change the chart to a column chart in the Graph window and in the form.

4. Click **Chart** on the Graph menu bar, click **Chart Options** to open the Chart Options dialog box, click the **Legend** tab to display the chart's legend options, click the **Show legend** check box to clear it, and then click the **OK** button. The legend is removed from the chart object in the Graph window and in the form.

To change the color or other properties of a chart control—the chart background (or chart area), axes, labels to the left of the y-axis, labels below the x-axis, or data markers (columnar bars for a column chart)—you need to double-click the control.

5. In the Graph window, double-click one of the blue data markers inside the chart to open the Format Data Series dialog box, and then click the orange box (row 2, column 2) in the color palette in the Area section. See Figure 8-25.

Tip

A data marker is a bar, dot, segment, or other symbol that represents a single data value.

Format Data Series dialog box ◄ Figure 8-25

The sample color in the dialog box changes to orange to match the selected color in the color palette.

▶ **6.** Click the **OK** button to close the dialog box and to change the color of the data markers in the chart in the Graph window and in the form to orange.

▶ **7.** In the Graph window, double-click the white chart background to open the Format Chart Area dialog box, click the light orange box (row 5, column 2) in the color palette in the Area section, and then click the **OK** button. The background color changes to light orange in the chart in the Graph window and in the form.

▶ **8.** Click **File** on the Graph menu bar, and then click **Exit & Return to frmContractsAndInvoices** to exit Graph and return to the form.

▶ **9.** Save your form design changes, switch to Form view, navigate to record 5 in the main form, click the **Invoice Chart** tab to display the chart, and then scroll down the form (if necessary). See Figure 8-26.

Figure 8-26	Completed chart in Form view

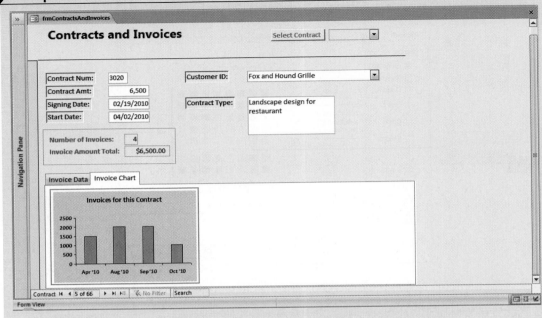

▶ **10.** Close the form.

Sarah wants to know if Access has other charting and data analysis tools. You'll show her how to create a PivotTable and a PivotChart.

Creating and Using a PivotTable

Sarah wants to be able to analyze Belmont Landscapes' business in a flexible way. You can use PivotTables to provide the flexible analysis that Sarah needs. A **PivotTable** is an interactive table that lets you analyze data dynamically. You can use a PivotTable to view and organize data from a database, look for summary or detail information, and dynamically change the contents and organization of the table. Figure 8-27 shows a PivotTable.

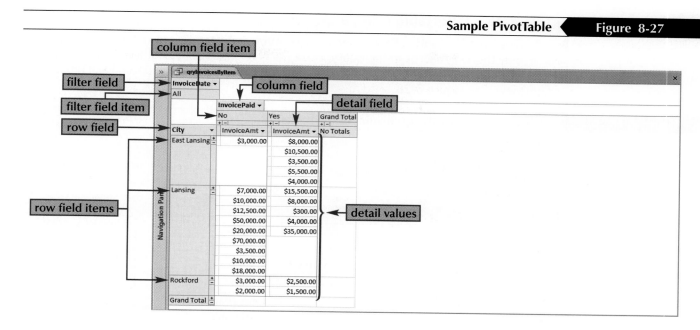

Sample PivotTable | **Figure 8-27**

A PivotTable contains the following basic components:

- The **detail area**, consisting of a **detail field** and **detail values**, provides details or totals from a database table or query. In Figure 8-27, the detail field is the InvoiceAmt field from the tblInvoice table, and the detail values are the InvoiceAmt field values.
- The **row area**, consisting of a **row field** and **row field items**, provides row groupings in the PivotTable. In Figure 8-27, the row field is the City field from the tblCustomer table, and the row field items are the City field values.
- The **column area**, consisting of a **column field** and **column field items**, provides column groupings in the PivotTable. In Figure 8-27, the column field is the InvoicePaid field from the tblInvoice table, and the column field items are the InvoicePaid field values.
- The **filter area**, consisting of a **filter field** and **filter field items**, lets you restrict which data appears in the PivotTable. In Figure 8-27, the filter field is the InvoiceDate field from the tblInvoice table, and the filter field item is "All" dates, which means that all InvoiceDate field values are represented in the PivotTable.
- All the PivotTable areas—detail area, row area, column area, and filter area—can have multiple fields with multiple field items.

When you work with PivotTables, you use another program, the **Office PivotTable Component**, which is one of the **Office Web Components** that are part of Office 2007. Therefore, you can use PivotTables with other programs such as Excel. You can create PivotTables with Access tables and queries; the PivotTable view with these Access objects provides this capability.

Creating a PivotTable

Sarah wants to analyze invoice amounts by city and by invoice date in various ways. You'll create a PivotTable using the qryInvoicesByItem query to let her perform this analysis.

To create a PivotTable using a query:

▶ **1.** Open the Navigation Pane, open the **qryInvoicesByItem** query datasheet to display the 172 records in the query, close the Navigation Pane, right-click the **qryInvoicesByItem** tab, and then click **PivotTable View** to switch to PivotTable view. See Figure 8-28.

Figure 8-28	PivotTable view for the qryInvoicesByItem query

To create a PivotTable, you click a field in the PivotTable Field List pane to select it, and then drag it to one of the four drop areas—row, column, filter, or totals/detail—or click the Add to button at the bottom of the PivotTable Field List pane after selecting one of the four drop areas in the list to the right of the Add to button.

Sarah wants to use the InvoicePaid field as the column field, the City field as the row field, the InvoiceDate field as the filter field, and the InvoiceAmt field as the detail field.

▶ **2.** Click **InvoicePaid** in the PivotTable Field List pane, click the **arrow** on the list box to the right of the Add to button in the PivotTable Field List pane, click **Column Area** in the list, and then click the **Add to** button. Access places the InvoicePaid field and its field values in the column drop area.

▶ **3.** Repeat Step 2 to add the **City** field to the row drop area, the **InvoiceDate** field to the filter drop area, and the **InvoiceAmt** field to the totals or detail drop area. The four selected fields are bold in the PivotTable Field List pane and appear as components in the PivotTable. See Figure 8-29.

After adding the four fields to the PivotTable ◄ Figure 8-29

The PivotTable displays all the InvoiceAmt field values from the source query organized by city and invoice status (unpaid or paid).

4. Close the PivotTable Field List pane.

Sarah can filter the PivotTable using one or more of the four selected fields. She can also add total fields and hide the detail values in the PivotTable.

Filtering and Summarizing Data in a PivotTable

A **total field** summarizes values from a source field. For example, Sarah can add subtotals and a grand total of the InvoiceAmt field values to the PivotTable. You'll show Sarah how to filter data in the PivotTable and how to add subtotals by city and a grand total for the InvoiceAmt field values.

To filter data and add a total field in a PivotTable:

▶ 1. Click the **City** arrow, click the **All** check box to clear all the selections, click the **East Lansing** check box, click the **Lansing** check box, click the **Rockford** check box, and then click the **OK** button. Access applies the City filter and display total invoice amounts for the three selected cities. See Figure 8-30.

| Figure 8-30 | Filtering data by city |

Tip

You've applied a filter to the row field. In a similar way, you can apply filters to the column, filter, and detail fields.

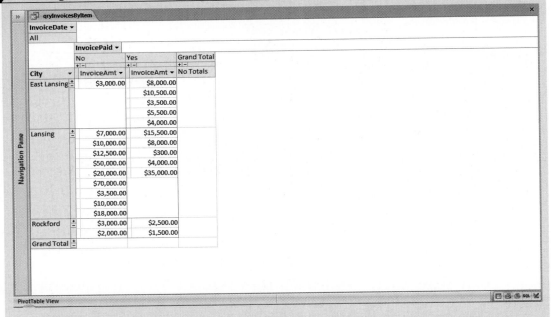

The applied City filter displays all the InvoiceAmt field values from the source query for the cities of East Lansing, Lansing, and Rockford.

▶ 2. Click one of the **InvoiceAmt** column heading labels; in the Tools group on the Design tab, click the **AutoCalc** button, click **Sum**, and then click to the right of the PivotTable to deselect all values. Access adds a new row for each city in the PivotTable that displays the city's InvoiceAmt total and a new row at the bottom of the PivotTable that displays the grand total for the displayed InvoiceAmt values. See Figure 8-31.

After adding the total field to the PivotTable | Figure 8-31

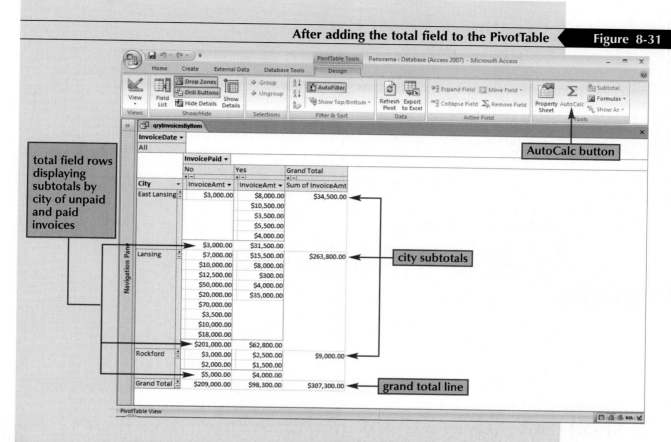

3. In the Show/Hide group on the Design tab, click the **Hide Details** button. Access hides the detail lines and displays only the subtotal and grand total lines in the PivotTable. See Figure 8-32.

Subtotals and grand total displayed in the PivotTable | Figure 8-32

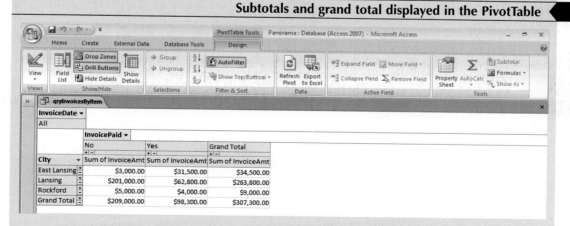

4. In the Show/Hide group on the Design tab, click the **Show Details** button. Access shows the detail lines and the subtotal and grand total lines in the PivotTable for the cities of East Lansing, Lansing, and Rockford.

Sarah asks if you can display the filtered PivotTable data in a chart. You'll switch to PivotChart view to satisfy Sarah's request.

Creating a PivotChart

Office 2007 provides the **Office PivotChart Component** to assist you in adding a chart to a table or query. Using the Office PivotChart Component, you can create a **PivotChart**, an interactive chart that provides capabilities similar to a PivotTable. You can open a table or query, switch to PivotChart view, add fields to the PivotChart's drop areas, just as you did when you created the PivotTable, and then filter the data in the PivotChart. When you create a PivotChart, you can switch to PivotTable view to view and further filter the charted data in a PivotTable. Likewise, after creating a PivotTable, you can switch to PivotChart view to view and further filter the tabular data in a PivotChart.

You'll switch to PivotChart view to show Sarah the PivotChart of the PivotTable data.

To switch to PivotChart view:

1. Right-click the **qryInvoicesByItem** tab, and then click **PivotChart View** on the shortcut menu to switch to PivotChart view. See Figure 8-33.

Figure 8-33   Filtered PivotTable data in a PivotChart

A PivotChart contains the following basic components:

- The **plot area** provides a background for the data markers and gridlines. A **data marker** is a bar, dot, segment, or other symbol that represents a single data value. The **data field**, which is the Sum of InvoiceAmt field in Figure 8-33, identifies which values the data markers represent and identifies each value displayed as a **value axis label**. Each **gridline**, which appears in Figure 8-33 as one of the horizontal lines in the plot area, makes it easier to see the values represented by the data markers.

- The **category field** identifies each value that's displayed as a **category axis label**; each category axis label identifies an individual data marker. In Figure 8-33, the City field is the category field; East Lansing, Lansing, and Rockford are the category axis labels. The data markers show the total unpaid and paid InvoiceAmt field values for each city.
- The **filter field** lets you restrict which data appears in the PivotChart. In Figure 8-33, the filter field is the InvoiceDate field. The "All" value below InvoiceDate indicates that no filter has been applied to the filter field.
- The **series field** identifies the data markers' subdivisions or splits. In Figure 8-33, the InvoicePaid field is the series field, and each pair of data markers represent the two values for the InvoicePaid field. (The series field is not visible in Figure 8-33) The left data marker represents unpaid invoices, and the right data marker represents paid invoices. An optional **legend** provides a list of the series field values and how these values are indicated on the data markers. (Figure 8-33 does not include a legend.)

Next, you'll show Sarah how to modify the PivotChart.

To modify the PivotChart:

1. Close the Chart Field List pane. The InvoicePaid field, which is the series field for the PivotChart, is now visible to the right of the PivotChart.

2. In the Show/Hide group on the Design tab, click the **Legend** button. A legend is displayed below the InvoicePaid field and indicates that the blue bars represent unpaid invoices (No value) and the red bars represent paid invoices (Yes value).

   Sarah wants to change the City filter to display data for Grand Rapids, Holland, Kalamazoo, and Lansing.

3. Click the **City** arrow, click the **East Lansing** check box to clear it, click the **Rockford** check box to clear it, click the **Grand Rapids** check box to select it, click the **Holland** check box to select it, click the **Kalamazoo** check box to select it, and then click the **OK** button. Access applies the City filter, displays total invoice amounts for the four selected cities, and changes the scale of the vertical axis and its value axis labels. See Figure 8-34.

Figure 8-34 | **After changing the City filter and displaying the legend**

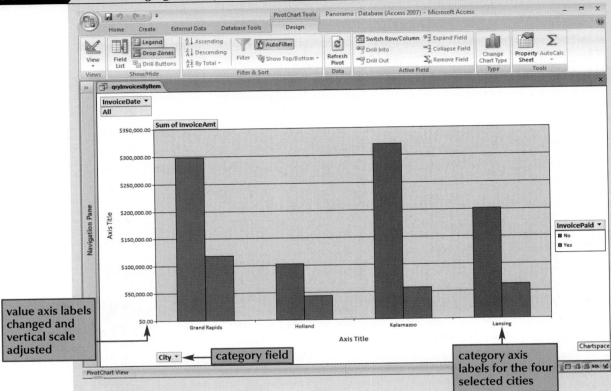

value axis labels changed and vertical scale adjusted

category field

category axis labels for the four selected cities

Sarah wants to change the PivotChart from a column chart to a bar chart to take advantage of the screen width, and she wants to change the colors of the data markers.

▶ **4.** Click in the white portion of the chart (if necessary) to deselect any chart control, and then in the Type group on the Design tab, click the **Change Chart Type** button, click **Bar** in the left list, and then click the **Clustered Bar** chart (row 1, column 1) in the right list. The chart changes from a clustered column chart to a clustered bar chart.

▶ **5.** In the chart, click the red data marker for Lansing, hold down the **Shift** key, click the red data marker for Lansing a second time, and then release the **Shift** key. All red data markers are now selected, and any property change you make in the Properties dialog box will apply to all four red data markers.

▶ **6.** Click the **Border/Fill** tab in the Properties dialog box, click the **Fill Color** arrow, and then click the **DodgerBlue** color (row 3, column 4) in the color palette. The four selected data markers change to the selected DodgerBlue color. See Figure 8-35.

▶ **7.** Repeat Steps 5-6, selecting the other four data markers (the lower data marker in each set), and clicking the **Tomato** color (row 8, column 13), and then click the **Fill Color** arrow to display the color palette. The four selected data markers change to the Tomato color. See Figure 8-35.

After changing the chart type and data marker colors | Figure 8-35

▶ 8. Close the Properties dialog box, save your PivotTable and PivotChart changes, and then close the query.

▶ 9. Open the Navigation Pane, open the **qryInvoicesByItem** query datasheet to display the 172 records in the query, switch to PivotChart view to display the saved PivotChart, switch to PivotTable view to display the saved PivotTable, and then close the query.

Sarah's staff maintains an Excel worksheet that tracks the products Belmont Landscapes has used for its landscaping projects. Sarah want to use the product data in the Panorama database.

Linking Data from an Excel Worksheet

Sarah's staff has extensive experience working with Excel and prefers to maintain the data in the Products worksheet using Excel. However, Sarah needs to reference the products data in the Panorama database, and the data she's referencing must always be the current version of the worksheet data. Importing the Excel worksheet data as an Access table would provide Sarah with data that's quickly out of date unless she repeats the import steps each time the data in the Excel worksheet changes. Because Sarah doesn't need to update the products data in the Panorama database, you'll link to the worksheet from the database. When the staff changes the Products worksheet, the changes will be reflected automatically in the linked version of the table in the database. At the same time, Sarah won't be able to update the products data from the Panorama database, which ensures that only the staff members responsible for maintaing the Excel worksheet can update the data.

You'll now link to the data in the Excel worksheet.

To link to the data in the Excel worksheet:

▶ 1. Click the **External Data** tab on the Ribbon, and then in the Import group on the External Data tab, click the **Excel** button (with the ScreenTip "Import Excel spreadsheet"). The Get External Data - Excel Spreadsheet dialog box opens.

▶ **2.** Click the **Browse** button, navigate to and open the **Level.02\Tutorial** folder, click **Products**, click the **Open** button, and then click the **Link to the data source by creating a linked table** option button. The selected path and filename now appear in the File name text box, and you've set the option to link to the data instead of importing or appending the data. See Figure 8-36.

| Figure 8-36 | Linking to data in an Excel worksheet |

▶ **3.** Click the **OK** button. The Link Spreadsheet Wizard dialog box opens. See Figure 8-37.

| Figure 8-37 | Linking to data in an Excel worksheet |

The first row in the worksheet contains column heading names, and each row in the worksheet represents the data about a single product.

▶ **4.** Click the **Next** button to open the next Link Spreadsheet Wizard dialog box, in which you choose a name for the linked table. You'll use the default table name tblProduct.

▶ **5.** Click the **Finish** button. A message box informs you that you've created a linking table to the Excel worksheet file.

▶ **6.** Click the **OK** button to close the message box and complete the linking steps. The tblProduct table now appears in the Navigation Pane. The icon to the left of the table name 🔗 identifies the table as a linked table.

You can open and view the tblProduct table and use fields from the linked table in queries, forms, and reports, but you can't update the products data using the Panorama database. You can update the products data only from the Excel worksheet.

Next, you'll show Sarah how the worksheet and the linked table interact.

To update the Excel worksheet and view the data in the linked table:

▶ **1.** Open Windows Explorer, navigate to and open the **Level.02\Tutorial** folder, right-click **Products**, click **Open With** on the shortcut menu, click **Microsoft Office Excel**, and then click the **OK** button. The Products workbook opens and displays the tblProduct worksheet.

▶ **2.** Click the **Microsoft Office Access** program button on the taskbar to switch to the Panorama database, and then open the **tblProduct** datasheet. The fields and records in the tblProduct table display the same data as the Excel worksheet.

▶ **3.** Select **Yellow** in the first record's Color column, and then type **G**. A warning sound chimes, the message "This Recordset is not updateable" is displayed on the status bar, and the value is not changed.

▶ **4.** Click the **Microsoft Excel** program button on the taskbar to switch to the Products workbook, select **Yellow** in cell F2, type **Green**, and then press the **Enter** key. The value in cell F2 changes from Yellow to Green.

▶ **5.** Click the **Microsoft Office Access** program button on the taskbar to switch to the Panorama database. The first row's Color field value is now Green, because this is the newly changed value in the Excel worksheet.

You've completed your work for Sarah and her staff.

▶ **6.** Close the table.

▶ **7.** Click the **Microsoft Excel** program button on the taskbar to switch to the Products workbook, save your worksheet change, and then exit Excel.

▶ **8.** Close the Panorama database, make a backup copy of the database, open the **Panorama** database, compact and repair the database, close the database, and then exit Access.

Knowing how to create charts, PivotTables, and PivotCharts and how to link to data maintained by other programs will make it easier for Sarah and her staff to anlayze their operations and to work efficiently in managing data.

Review | **Session 8.2 Quick Check**

1. The _____ property lets you change the navigation label from the word "Record" to another value.
2. When you use the Microsoft Graph program to create and change charts in a form or report, you must _____ the chart.
3. What is a PivotTable?
4. Within a PivotTable you can choose fields form the field list to be a column field, a row field, a detail field, or a(n) _____ field.
5. In a PivotChart, the _____ field identifies which values are shown as value axis labels.
6. You can show/hide a legend for the _____ field in a PivotChart.

Review | **Tutorial Summary**

In this tutorial, you learned how to share and integrate data. You exported an Access query to an HTML document and then used a Web browser to view the document. You imported a CSV file as an Access table, imported and exported XML files, used the Table Analyzer, and saved and executed import and export specifications. Then you created a multi-page form using a tab control, embedded a chart in one of the tab control's pages, and modified the chart. Finally, you created and modified a PivotTable and a PivotChart and linked data from an Excel worksheet.

Key Terms

category axis label	Hypertext Markup	static Web page
category field	Language (HTML)	Tab Control tool
column area	Hypertext Transfer	Table Analyzer
column field	Protocol (HTTP)	tag
column field items	importing	total field
CSV (comma-separated	Internet	Uniform Resource
values) file	legend	Locator (URL)
data field	linking	value axis label
data marker	Navigation Caption property	Web
destination program	Office PivotChart Component	Web browser
detail area	Office PivotTable Component	Web client
detail field	Office Web Component	Web page
detail values	Page Break tool	Web server
embedding	PivotChart	World Wide Web
filter area	PivotTable	XML (Extensible Markup
filter field	plot area	Language)
filter field items	row area	XSD (XML Structure
gridline	row field	Definition)
HTML document	row field items	XSL (Extensible Stylesheet
HTML template	series field	Language)
hyperlink	source program	

Practice	**Review Assignments**

Practice the skills you learned in the tutorial using the same case scenario.

Data Files needed for the Review Assignments: Ads.xlsx, BelmLogo.gif, BelmTemp.htm, Payables.csv, Products.accdb (*cont. from Tutorial 7*), and tblPayments.xml

Sarah wants you to integrate the data in the Products database with other programs and she wants to be able to analyze the data in the database. You'll help her achieve these goals by completing the following:

1. Open the **Products** database located in the Level.02\Review folder provided with your Data Files.

2. Export the qryCompanyList query as an HTML document to the Level.02\Review folder, using the HTML template file named BelmTemp, which is located in the Level.02\Review folder, and saving the file as **qryCompanyList**. Do not save the export steps.

3. Import the CSV file named Payables, which is located in the Level.02\Review folder, as a new table in the database. Choose your own primary key, name the table **tblPayables**, run the Table Analyzer, and record the Table Analyzer's recommendation. Do not save the import steps.

4. Import the XML file named tblPayments, which is located in the Level.02\Review folder, as a new table named **tblPayments** in the database. Save the import steps.

5. Export the tblCompany table as an XML file named **tblCompany** to the Level.02\Review folder; do not create a separate XSD file. Save the export steps.

6. Link to the Ads workbook, which is located in the Level.02\Review folder, using **tblAd** as the table name. Change the cost of the flyer for Ad Num 5 to **$300**.

7. Modify the **frmCompaniesWithProducts** form in the following ways:
   a. Add a tab control to the bottom of the Detail section, and place the existing subform on the first page of the tab control.
   b. Change the caption for the left tab to **Product Data** and for the right tab to **Product Chart**.
   c. Change the caption for the main form's navigation buttons to **Company** and for the subform's navigation buttons to **Product**.
   d. Add a chart to the second page of the tab control. Use the tblProduct table as the record source, select the ProductType, Price, and Unit fields, use the 3-D Column Chart type, include a legend, and use **Products Offered** as the chart title.
   e. Change the chart to a Clustered Column chart, and change the blue colored data marker to pink.

8. Open the **tblPayments** table and create a PivotTable with PaymentAmt as the detail field, PaymentDate as the column field, CompanyID as the row field, and PaymentID as the filter field.

9. Switch to PivotChart view. Filter the CompanyID field, selecting BAC200, BEL273, and CHE802, select PaymentAmt as the data field, display the legend, and then save the table.

10. Close the Products database without exiting Access, make a backup copy of the database, open the **Products** database, compact and repair the database, close the database, and then exit Access.

| Challenge | **Case Problem 1** |

Apply the skills you learned in the tutorial to import and export data and create charts for a small music school.

Data Files needed for this Case Problem: Contract.accdb (*cont. from Tutorial 7*), Instrument.csv, and Room.xlsx

Pine Hill Music School Yuka wants you to integrate the data in the Contract database with other programs, and she wants to be able to analyze the data in the database. You'll help her achieve these goals by completing the following:

1. Open the **Contract** database located in the Level.02\Case1 folder provided with your Data Files.

⊕ EXPLORE

2. Export the rptTeacherLessons report as an HTML document to the Level.02\Case1 folder; do not use a template or save the export steps. Use your Web browser to open the **rptTeacherLessons** HTML document. Then scroll to the bottom of the page; use the First, Previous, Next, and Last links to navigate through the document.

3. Import the CSV file named Instrument, which is located in the Level.02\Case1 folder, as a new table in the database. Choose your own primary key, name the table **tblInstrument**, run the Table Analyzer, and record the Table Analyzer's recommendation, but do not accept the recommendation. Do not save the import steps.

4. Export the tblTeacher table as an XML file named **tblTeacher** to the Level.02\Case1 folder; do not create a separate XSD file. Save the export steps.

5. Link to the Room workbook, which is located in the Level.02\Case1 folder, using **tblRoom** as the table name. Add a new record to the Room workbook as follows: Room Num **5**, Rental Cost **$25**, and Type **Private**.

6. Open the qryLessonsByTeacher query, and create a PivotTable with MonthlyLessonCost as the detail field, LessonType as the column field, LastName as the row field, and LessonLength as the filter field. Filter the LessonType field, selecting Guitar, Piano, and Saxophone. Add subtotals and a grand total for the MonthlyLessonCost field values.

7. Switch to PivotChart view. Display the legend (if necessary), change the color of the Saxophone data markers to yellow, and then save the query.

8. Close the Contract database without exiting Access, make a backup copy of the database, open the **Contract** database, compact and repair the database, close the database, and then exit Access.

| Create | **Case Problem 2** |

Use the skills you learned in the tutorial to analyze the data for a health and fitness center.

Data Files needed for this Case Problem: CreditCard.xml, ParkLogo.gif, ParkTemp.htm, Schedule.xlsx, and Training.accdb (*cont. from Tutorial 7*)

Parkhurst Health & Fitness Center Martha Parkhurst wants you to integrate the data in the Training database with other programs, and she wants to be able to analyze the data in the database. You'll help her achieve these goals by completing the following:

1. Open the **Training** database located in the Level.02\Case2 folder provided with your Data Files.

2. Export the qryPhysicalsNeeded query as an HTML document to the Level.02\Case2 folder, using the HTML template file named ParkTemp, which is located in the Level.02\Case2 folder, and saving the file as **qryPhysicalsNeeded**. Save the export steps.

✦ EXPLORE

3. Export the rptProgramMembership report as an HTML document to the Level.02\Case2 folder; do not use a template or save the export steps. Use your Web browser to open the **rptProgramMembership** HTML document. Then scroll to the bottom of the page; use the First, Previous, Next, and Last links to navigate through the document.

4. Import the XML file named CreditCard, which is located in the Level.02\Case2 folder, as a new table named **tblCreditCard**. Save the import steps.

5. Export the tblProgram table as an XML file named **tblProgram** to the Level.02\Case2 folder; do not create a separate XSD file. Save the export steps.

6. Link to the Schedule workbook, which is located in the Level.02\Case2 folder, using **tblSchedule** as the table name. For ClassID 301, change the ClassDay value to **F**.

7. Modify the **frmProgramsAndMembers** form in the following ways:
   a. Add a tab control to the bottom of the Detail section, and place the existing subform on the first page of the tab control.
   b. Change the caption for the left tab to **Member Data** and for the right tab to **Member Chart**.
   c. Change the caption for the main form's navigation buttons to **Program** and for the subform's navigation buttons to **Member**.
   d. Add a chart to the second page of the tab control. Use the tblMember table as the record source, select the ProgramID and MembershipStatus fields, use the Clustered Column chart type, include a legend, and use **Membership Status** as the chart title.
   e. Change the color of the right data marker (or the middle data marker, depending on whether you see two or three data markers) to red.

8. Open the **qryMonthlyFeeStatus** query and create a PivotTable with MonthlyFee as the detail field, MonthlyFeeStatus as the column field, LastName as the row field, and ProgramType as the filter field. Add subtotals and a grand total of the MonthlyFee values, hide the details, and filter the ProgramType field to display only programs for juniors.

9. Switch to PivotChart view for the qryMonthlyFeeStatus query. Change the chart type to Clustered Bar, display the legend, change the data markers to colors of your choice, and then save the query.

10. Close the Training database without exiting Access, make a backup copy of the database, open the **Training** database, compact and repair the database, close the database, and then exit Access.

| Create | **Case Problem 3** |

Use the skills you learned in the tutorial to integrate and analyze data about an agency that recycles household goods.

Data Files needed for this Case Problem: Agency.accdb (*cont. from Tutorial 7*) and Facility.csv

Rossi Recycling Group Mary Rossi wants you to integrate the data in the Agency database with other programs, and she wants to be able to analyze the data in the database. You'll help her achieve these goals by completing the following:

1. Open the **Agency** database located in the Level.02\Case3 folder provided with your Data Files.

2. Export the qryNetDonationsCrosstab query as an HTML document to the Level.02\Case3 folder; do not use a template. Save the file as **qryNetDonationsCrosstab**. Save the export steps.

⊕ EXPLORE

3. Export the frmDonationInfo form as an HTML document to the Level.02\Case3 folder; do not use a template or save the export steps. Use your Web browser to open the **frmDonationInfo** HTML document and review its contents.

⊕ EXPLORE

4. Import the CSV file named Facility, which is located in the Level.02\Case3 folder, as a new table in the database. Choose your own primary key, name the table **tblTemporary**, and run the Table Analyzer. Accept the Table Analyzer's recommendations, rename the tables as **tblStorage** and **tblFacility**, make sure each table has the correct primary key, and let the Table Analzyer create a query. Do not save the import steps. Review the tblTemporary query, review the tblTemporary table (it might be named tblTemporary_OLD), and then review the tblStorage and tblFacility tables.

5. Export the tblDonation table as an XML file named **tblDonation** to the Level.02\Case3 folder; do not create a separate XSD file. Save the export steps.

6. Modify the **frmDonorDonations** form in the following ways:
   a. Add a tab control to the bottom of the Detail section, and place the existing subform on the first page of the tab control.
   b. Change the caption for the left tab to **Donation Data** and for the right tab to **Donation Chart**.
   c. Change the caption for the main form's navigation buttons to **Donor** and for the subform's navigation buttons to **Donation**.
   d. Add a chart to the second page of the tab control. Use the tblDonation table as the record source; select the AgencyID, DonationValue, PickupRequired, and DonationDate fields; use the 3-D Column Chart type; include a legend; and use **Donations by Agency** as the chart title.
   e. Change the chart to a Clustered Bar chart, and change the color of the maroon data marker to red.

7. Open the **qryNetDonations** query and create a PivotTable with NetDonation as the detail field, AgencyName as the column field, DonationDesc as the row field, and PickupRequired as the filter field. Filter the DonationDesc field to display only cash donations.

8. Switch to PivotChart view. Select NetDonation as the data field, filter the AgencyName by removing the first five agencies, leaving the data for five agencies in the chart, display the legend, change the chart type to Clustered Bar, and then save the query.

9. Close the Agency database without exiting Access, make a backup copy of the database, open the **Agency** database, compact and repair the database, close the database, and then exit Access.

Create | **Case Problem 4**

Use the skills you learned in the tutorial to analyze the data for a luxury property rental company.

Data Files needed for this Case Problem: Personnel.xlsx, Vacation.accdb (*cont. from Tutorial 7*)**, and Works.xml**

GEM Ultimate Vacations Griffin and Emma MacElroy want you to integrate the data in the Vacation database with other programs, and they want to be able to analyze the data in the database. You'll help them achieve these goals by completing the following:

1. Open the **Vacation** database located in the Level.02\Case4 folder provided with your Data Files.

2. Export the qryPropertiesByRate query as an HTML document to the Level.02\Case4 folder; do not use a template. Save the file as **qryPropertiesByRate**. Save the export steps.

3. Import the XML file named Works, which is located in the Level.02\Case4 folder, as a new table in the database named **tblWorks**. Save the import steps.

4. Export the qryPropertyReservations query as an XML file named **qryPropertyReservations** to the Level.02\Case4 folder; do not create a separate XSD file. Save the export steps.

5. Link to the Personnel workbook, which is located in the Level.02\Case4 folder, using **tblPersonnel** as the table name. Change the name in the fourth record from Edward Leary to **Marie Leary**.

6. Modify the **frmGuestsWithReservations** form in the following ways:
   a. Add a tab control to the bottom of the Detail section, and place the existing subform on the first page of the tab control.
   b. Change the caption for the left tab to **Reservation Data** and for the right tab to **Reservation Chart**.
   c. Change the caption for the main form's navigation buttons to **Guest** and for the subform's navigation buttons to **Reservation**.
   d. Add a chart to the second page of the tab control. Use the tblReservation table as the record source, select the StartDate, PropertyID, and RentalRate fields, use the Column Chart chart type, include a legend, and use **Reservations** as the chart title.

7. Open the **qryGuestsAndReservations** query, and create a PivotTable with RentalRate as the detail field, StateProv as the column field, the Quarters component of the StartDate By Month entry in the PivotTable Field List as the row field, and PropertyID as the filter field. Add subtotals and a grand total of the RentalRate field, and then hide the details.

8. Switch to PivotChart view. Display the legend, change the green color to yellow, and then save the query.

9. Close the Vacation database without exiting Access, make a backup copy of the database, open the **Vacation** database, compact and repair the database, close the database, and then exit Access.

| Create | **Case Problem 5** |

Use the skills you learned in this tutorial to integrate and analyze the data for an Internet service provider.

Data File needed for this Case Problem: ACE.accdb (*cont. from Tutorial 7*)

Always Connected Everyday Chris and Pat Aquino want you to integrate the data in the ACE database with other programs, and they want to be able to analyze the data in the database. You'll help them achieve these goals by completing the following:

1. Open the **ACE** database located in the Level.02\Case5 folder provided with your Data Files.

2. Export the tblAccessPlan table as an HTML document to the Level.02\Case5 folder; do not use a template or save the import steps. Save the file as **tblAccessPlan**.

⊕ EXPLORE

3. Export the rptAccessPlanCustomers report as an HTML document to the Level.02\Case5 folder; do not use a template or save the export steps. Use your Web browser to open and review the HTML document.

4. Export the tblCustomer table as an XML file named **tblCustomer** to the Level.02\Case5 folder; do not create a separate XSD file. Save the export steps.

5. Modify one of the existing forms or create a new form so that the form uses a tab control. Change the caption for the navigation buttons, and set the captions for the tab labels.

6. For one of the existing queries (or create a new query), create a PivotTable, add subtotals and a grand total, apply a filter, and hide details. In PivotChart view, display the legend and make any other appropriate changes.

7. Close the ACE database without exiting Access, make a backup copy of the database, open the **ACE** database, compact and repair the database, close the database, and then exit Access.

Research | Internet Assignments

Use the Internet to find and work with data related to the topics presented in this tutorial.

The purpose of the Internet Assignments is to challenge you to find information on the Internet that you can use to work effectively with this software. The actual assignments are updated and maintained on the Course Technology Web site. Log on to the Internet and use your Web browser to go to the Student Online Companion for New Perspectives Office 2007 at **www.course.com/np/office2007**. Then navigate to the Internet Assignments for this tutorial.

Assess | SAM Assessment and Training

If you have a SAM user profile, you may have access to hands-on instruction, practice, and assessment of the skills covered in this tutorial. Log in to your SAM account (**http://sam2007.course.com**) to launch any assigned training activities or exams that relate to the skills covered in this tutorial.

Review | Quick Check Answers

Session 8.1

1. a vast collection of digital documents available on the Internet; Web browser
2. links one Web page to another Web page or Web site, or to another location in the same Web page
3. language used to create most Web pages
4. An HTML template is a file that contains HTML instructions for creating a Web page with both text and graphics, together with special instructions that tell Access where to place the Access data in the page.
5. shows the state of the database at the time the page was created; any subsequent changes made to the database object, such as updates to field values in records, are not reflected in a static Web page
6. a text file in which commas separate values, and each line is a record containing the same number of values in the same positions
7. an Access tool that analyzes a single table and, if necessary, splits it into two or more tables that are in third normal form
8. XML (Extensible Markup Language)

Session 8.2

1. Navigation Caption
2. embed
3. an interactive table that lets you analyze data dynamically
4. filter
5. data
6. series

Ending Data Files

Level.02 → **Tutorial**

Customers by Name.html
Panorama.accdb
Products.xlsx
tblInvoice.xml

Review

Ads.xlsx
Products.accdb
qryCompanyList.html
tblCompany.xml

Case1

Contract.accdb
Room.xlsx
rptTeacherLessons.html
rptTeacherLessonsPage2.html
tblTeacher.xml

Case2

qryPhysicalsNeeded.html
rptProgramMembership.html
rptProgramMembershipPage2.html
Schedule.xlsx
tblProgram.xml
Training.accdb

Case3

Agency.accdb
frmDonationInfo.html
qryNetDonationsCrosstab.html
tblDonation.xml

Case4

Personnel.xlsx
qryPropertiesByRate.html
qryPropertyReservations.xml
Vacation.accdb

Case5

ACE.accdb
rptAccessPlanCustomers.html
tblAccessPlan.html
tblCustomer.xml

Reality Check

You interact with databases whenever you place an order on the Internet, check out at a retail store or restaurant, verify your bank account balance, or register for classes. Most businesses use databases, and you can also use databases to track data in your personal life. Examples of personal database use include tracking personal collections, such as DVDs or books; hobby data, such as family histories or antiques; or items related to sports teams, theater clubs, or other organizations to which you might belong. In this exercise, you'll use Access to create a database that will contain information of your choice, using the Access skills and features you've learned in these tutorials.

Note: Please be sure *not* to include any personal information of a sensitive nature in the database you create to be submitted to your instructor for this exercise. Later on, you can update the data in your database with such information for your own personal use.

1. Create a new Access database to contain personal data you want to track. (If you completed Tutorials 1-4 of this book and the Reality Check at the end of Tutorial 4, you can use and enhance the database you've already created, and you can skip this step.) The database must include two or more tables that you can join through one-to-many relationships. Define the properties for each field in each table. Make sure you include a mix of data types for the fields (for example, do not include only Text fields in each table). Specify a primary key for each table, define the table relationships and enforce referential integrity, and enter records in each table.
2. Create queries that include at least the following: pattern query match, list-of-values match, parameter, crosstab, find duplicates, find unmatched, and the use of a conditional value in a calculated field.
3. For one or more fields, apply an input mask and specify field validation rules.
4. Create a split form and modify the form.
5. Create a custom form that uses at least the following: combo box for a lookup, combo box to find records, subform, lines and rectangles, and a tab control. Add one or more calculated controls to the main form based on the subform's calculated control(s), and add a chart, if appropriate. Check the main form's tab order, and improve the form's appearance.
6. Create a custom report that uses at least the following: grouping field, sort field(s), lines, and rectangles. Hide duplicates, and add the date, page numbers, and a report title.
7. Export two or more objects in different formats, and save the step specifications.
8. Create a PivotTable and PivotChart for one of the tables or queries.
9. Designate a trusted folder, backup the database, and compact and repair it.
10. Submit your completed database to your instructor as requested. Include printouts of any database objects, if required.

Objectives

- Learn the characteristics of a table
- Learn about primary, candidate, alternate, composite, and foreign keys
- Study one-to-one, one-to-many, and many-to-many relationships
- Learn to describe tables and relationships with entity-relationship diagrams and with a shorthand method
- Study database integrity constraints for primary keys, referential integrity, and domains
- Learn about determinants, functional dependencies, anomalies, and normalization
- Understand the differences among natural, artificial, and surrogate keys
- Learn about naming conventions

Relational Databases and Database Design

Appendix

This appendix introduces you to the basics of database design. Before trying to master this material, be sure you understand the following concepts: data, information, field, field value, record, table, relational database, common field, database management system (DBMS), and relational database management system (RDBMS).

There are no starting Data Files needed for this appendix.

Tables

A relational database stores its data in tables. A **table** is a two-dimensional structure made up of rows and columns. The terms table, **record** (row), and **field** (column) are the popular names for the more formal terms **relation** (table), **tuple** (row), and **attribute** (column), as shown in Figure A-1.

Figure A-1	A table (relation) consisting of records and fields

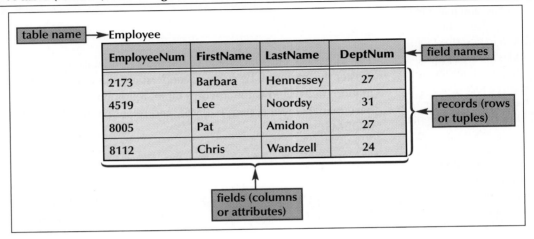

The Employee table shown in Figure A-1 is an example of a relational database table, a two-dimensional structure with the following characteristics:

- Each row is unique. Because no two rows are the same, you can easily locate and update specific data. For example, you can locate the row for EmployeeNum 8005 and change the FirstName value, Pat, the LastName value, Amidon, or the DeptNum value, 27.
- The order of the rows is unimportant. You can add or view rows in any order. For example, you can view the rows in LastName order instead of EmployeeNum order.
- Each table entry contains a single value. At the intersection of each row and column, you cannot have more than one value. For example, each row in Figure A-1 contains one EmployeeNum value, one FirstName value, one LastName value, and one DeptNum value.
- The order of the columns is unimportant. You can add or view columns in any order.
- Each column has a unique name called the **field name**. The field name allows you to access a specific column without needing to know its position within the table.
- The entries in a column are from the same domain. A **domain** is a set of values from which one or more columns (fields) draw their actual values. A domain can be broad, such as "all legitimate last names of people" for the LastName column, or narrow, such as "24, 27, or 31" for the DeptNum column. The domain of "all legitimate dates" could be shared by the BirthDate, StartDate, and TerminationDate columns in a company's employee table.
- Each row in a table describes, or shows the characteristics of, an entity. An **entity** is a person, place, object, event, or idea for which you want to store and process data. For example, EmployeeNum, FirstName, LastName, and DeptNum are characteristics of the employees of a company. The Employee table represents all the employee entities and their characteristics. That is, each row of the Employee table describes a different employee of the company using the characteristics of EmployeeNum, FirstName, LastName, and DeptNum. The Employee table includes only characteristics of employees. Other tables would exist for the company's other entities. For example, a Department table would describe the company's departments and a Position table would describe the company's job positions.

Knowing the characteristics of a table leads directly to a definition of a relational database. A **relational database** is a collection of tables (relations).

Note that this book uses singular table names, such as Employee and Department, but some people use plural table names, such as Employees and Departments. You can use either singular table names or plural table names, as long as you consistently use the style you choose.

Keys

Primary keys ensure that each row in a table is unique. A **primary key** is a column, or a collection of columns, whose values uniquely identify each row in a table. In addition to being *unique*, a primary key must be *minimal* (that is, contain no unnecessary extra columns) and must not change in value. For example, in Figure A-2 the State table contains one record per state and uses the StateAbbrev column as its primary key.

A table and its keys | Figure A-2

State				
StateAbbrev	**StateName**	**EnteredUnionOrder**	**StateBird**	**StatePopulation**
CT	Connecticut	5	American robin	3,510,297
MI	Michigan	26	robin	10,120,860
SD	South Dakota	40	pheasant	775,933
TN	Tennessee	16	mockingbird	5,962,959
TX	Texas	28	mockingbird	22,859,968

Could any other column, or collection of columns, be the primary key of the State table?

- Could the StateBird column serve as the primary key? No, because the StateBird column does not have unique values (for example, the mockingbird is the state bird of more than one state).
- Could the StatePopulation column serve as the primary key? No, because the StatePopulation column values change periodically and are not guaranteed to be unique.
- Could the StateAbbrev and StateName columns together serve as the primary key? No, because the combination of these two columns is not minimal. Something less, such as the StateAbbrev column by itself, can serve as the primary key.
- Could the StateName column serve as the primary key? Yes, because the StateName column has unique values. In a similar way, you could select the EnteredUnionOrder column as the primary key for the State table. One column, or a collection of columns, that can serve as a primary key is called a **candidate key**. The candidate keys for the State table are the StateAbbrev column, the StateName column, and the EnteredUnionOrder column. You choose one of the candidate keys to be the primary key, and each remaining candidate key is called an **alternate key**. The StateAbbrev column is the State table's primary key in Figure A-2, so the StateName and EnteredUnionOrder columns become alternate keys in the table.

Figure A-3 shows a City table containing the fields StateAbbrev, CityName, and CityPopulation.

primary key

City

StateAbbrev	CityName	CityPopulation
CT	Hartford	124,397
CT	Madison	18,812
CT	Portland	9,543
MI	Lansing	115,518
SD	Madison	6,223
SD	Pierre	14,052
TN	Nashville	549,110
TX	Austin	690,252
TX	Portland	16,219

What is the primary key for the City table? The values for the CityPopulation column periodically change and are not guaranteed to be unique, so the CityPopulation column cannot be the primary key. Because the values for each of the other two columns are not unique, the StateAbbrev column alone cannot be the primary key and neither can the CityName column (for example, there are two cities named Madison and two cities named Portland). The primary key is the combination of the StateAbbrev and CityName columns. Both columns together are needed to identify—uniquely and minimally—each row in the City table. A multiple-column primary key is called a **composite key** or a **concatenated key**.

The StateAbbrev column in the City table is also a foreign key. A **foreign key** is a column, or a collection of columns, in one table in which each column value must match the value of the primary key of some table or must be null. A **null** is the absence of a value in a particular table entry. A null value is not blank, nor zero, nor any other value. You give a null value to a column value when you do not know its value or when a value does not apply. As shown in Figure A-4, the values in the City table's StateAbbrev column match the values in the State table's StateAbbrev column. Thus, the StateAbbrev column, the primary key of the State table, is a foreign key in the City table. Although the field name StateAbbrev is the same in both tables, the names could be different. However, all experts use the same name for a field stored in two or more tables to broadcast clearly that they store similar values.

StateAbbrev as a primary key (State table) and a foreign key (City table) ◄ **Figure A-4**

primary key (State table)

State

StateAbbrev	StateName	EnteredUnionOrder	StateBird	StatePopulation
CT	Connecticut	5	American robin	3,510,297
MI	Michigan	26	robin	10,120,860
SD	South Dakota	40	pheasant	775,933
TN	Tennessee	16	mockingbird	5,962,959
TX	Texas	28	mockingbird	22,859,968

composite primary key (City table)

City

foreign key ►

StateAbbrev	CityName	CityPopulation
CT	Hartford	124,397
CT	Madison	18,812
CT	Portland	9,543
MI	Lansing	115,518
SD	Madison	6,223
SD	Pierre	14,052
TN	Nashville	549,110
TX	Austin	690,252
TX	Portland	16,219

A **nonkey field** is a field that is not part of the primary key. In the two tables shown in Figure A-4, all fields are nonkey fields except the StateAbbrev field in the State and City tables and the CityName field in the City table. *Key* is an ambiguous word because it can refer to a primary, candidate, alternate, or foreign key. When the word key appears alone, however, it means primary key and the definition for a nonkey field consequently makes sense.

Relationships

In a database, a table can be associated with another table in one of three ways: a one-to-many relationship, a many-to-many relationship, or a one-to-one relationship.

One-to-Many Relationship

The Department and Employee tables, shown in Figure A-5, have a one-to-many relationship. A **one-to-many relationship** (abbreviated **1:M** or **1:N**) exists between two tables when each row in the first table (sometimes called the **primary table**) matches many rows in the second table and each row in the second table (sometimes called the **related table**) matches at most one row in the first table. "Many" can mean zero rows, one row, or two or more rows. The DeptNum field, which is a foreign key in the Employee table and the primary key in the Department table, is the common field that ties together the rows of the two tables. Each department has many employees; and each employee works in exactly one department or hasn't been assigned to a department, if the DeptNum field value for that employee is null.

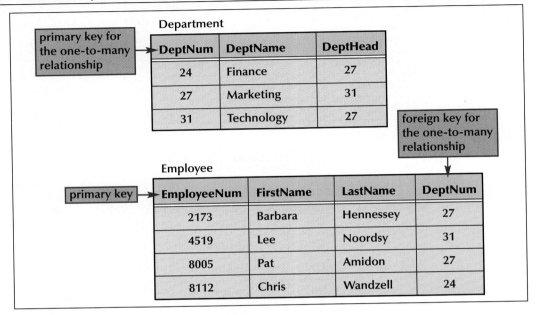

Many-to-Many Relationship

In Figure A-6, the Employee table (with the EmployeeNum field as its primary key) and the Position table (with the PositionID field as its primary key) have a many-to-many relationship. A **many-to-many relationship** (abbreviated as **M:N**) exists between two tables when each row in the first table matches many rows in the second table and each row in the second table matches many rows in the first table. In a relational database, you must use a third table (often called an **intersection table**, **junction table**, or **link table**) to serve as a bridge between the two many-to-many tables; the third table has the primary keys of the two many-to-many tables as its primary key. The original tables now each have a one-to-many relationship with the new table. The EmployeeNum and PositionID fields represent the primary key of the Employment table that is shown in Figure A-6. The EmployeeNum field, which is a foreign key in the Employment table and the primary key in the Employee table, is the common field that ties together the rows of the Employee and Employment tables. Likewise, the PositionID field is the common field for the Position and Employment tables. Each employee has served in many different positions within the company over time, and each position in the company has been filled by many different employees over time.

Employee

primary key
(Employee
table)

EmployeeNum	FirstName	LastName	DeptNum
2173	Barbara	Hennessey	27
4519	Lee	Noordsy	31
8005	Pat	Amidon	27
8112	Chris	Wandzell	24

Position

primary key
(Position table)

PositionID	PositionDesc	PayGrade
1	Director	45
2	Manager	40
3	Analyst	30
4	Clerk	20

composite key of the
intersection table

Employment

foreign keys related
to the Employee and
Position tables

EmployeeNum	PositionID	StartDate	EndDate
2173	2	12/14/2008	
4519	1	04/23/2010	
4519	3	11/11/2004	04/22/2010
8005	3	06/05/2009	08/25/2010
8005	4	07/02/2007	06/04/2009
8112	1	12/15/2009	
8112	2	10/04/2008	12/14/2009

One-to-One Relationship

In Figure A-5, recall that there's a one-to-many relationship between the Department table (the primary table) and the Employee table (the related table). Each department has many employees, and each employee works in one department. The DeptNum field in the Employee table serves as a foreign key to connect records in that table to records with matching DeptNum field values in the Department table.

Furthermore, each department has a single employee who serves as the head of the department, and each employee either serves as the head of a department or simply works in a department without being the department head. Therefore, the Department and Employee tables not only have a one-to-many relationship, but these two tables also have a second relationship, a one-to-one relationship. A **one-to-one relationship** (abbreviated **1:1**) exists between two tables when each row in each table has at most one matching row in the other table. As shown in Figure A-7, each DeptHead field value in the Department table represents the employee number in the Employee table of the employee who heads the department. In other words, each DeptHead field value in the Department table matches exactly one EmployeeNum field value in the Employee table. At the same time, each EmployeeNum field value in the Employee table matches at most one DeptHead field value in the Department table—matching one DeptHead field value if the employee is a department head, or matching zero DeptHead field values if the employee is not a department head. For this one-to-one relationship, the EmployeeNum field in the Employee table and the DeptHead field in the Department table are the fields that link the two tables, with the DeptHead field serving as a foreign key in the Department table and the EmployeeNum field serving as a primary key in the Employee table.

Some database designers might use EmployeeNum instead of DeptHead as the field name for the foreign key in the Department table, because they both represent the employee number for the employees of the company. However, DeptHead better identifies the purpose of the field and would more commonly be used as the field name.

Figure A-7 ▸ **A one-to-one relationship**

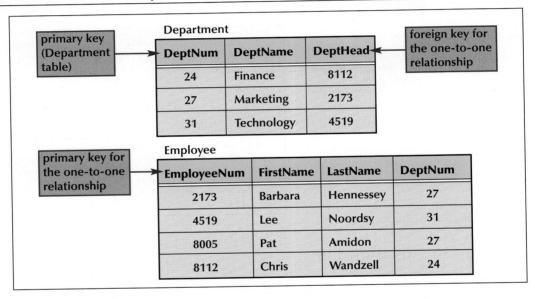

Entity Subtype

Suppose the company awards annual bonuses to a small number of employees who fill director positions in selected departments. As shown in Figure A-8, you could store the Bonus field in the Employee table, because a bonus is an attribute associated with employees. The Bonus field would contain either the amount of the employee's bonus (record 4 in the Employee table) or a null value for employees without bonuses (records 1 through 3 in the Employee table).

Bonus field added to the Employee table ◄ **Figure A-8**

Employee

EmployeeNum	FirstName	LastName	DeptNum	Bonus
2173	Barbara	Hennessey	27	
4519	Lee	Noordsy	31	
8005	Pat	Amidon	27	
8112	Chris	Wandzell	24	$20,000

nulls for these Bonus field values

Bonus field value for the fourth record

Figure A-9 shows an alternative approach, in which the Bonus field is placed in a separate table, the EmployeeBonus table. The EmployeeBonus table's primary key is the EmployeeNum field, and the table contains one row for each employee earning a bonus. Because some employees do not earn a bonus, the EmployeeBonus table has fewer rows than the Employee table. However, each row in the EmployeeBonus table has a matching row in the Employee table, with the EmployeeNum field serving as the common field; the EmployeeNum field is the primary key in the Employee table and is a foreign key in the EmployeeBonus table.

Storing bonus values in a separate table, an entity subtype ◄ **Figure A-9**

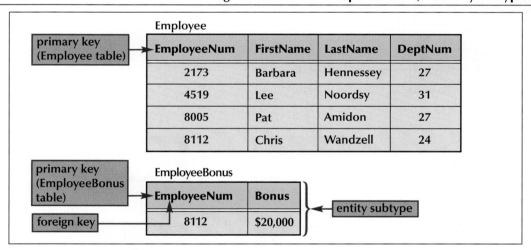

primary key (Employee table)

Employee

EmployeeNum	FirstName	LastName	DeptNum
2173	Barbara	Hennessey	27
4519	Lee	Noordsy	31
8005	Pat	Amidon	27
8112	Chris	Wandzell	24

primary key (EmployeeBonus table)

EmployeeBonus

EmployeeNum	Bonus
8112	$20,000

foreign key

entity subtype

The EmployeeBonus table, in this situation, is called an **entity subtype**, a table whose primary key is a foreign key to a second table and whose fields are additional fields for the second table. Database designers create an entity subtype in two situations. In the first situation, some users might need access to all employee fields, including employee bonuses, while other employees might need access to all employee fields except bonuses. Because most database management systems allow you to control which tables a user can access, you can specify that some users can access both tables and that other users can access the Employee table but not the EmployeeBonus table, keeping the employee bonus information hidden from the latter group. In the second situation, you can create an entity subtype when a table has fields that could have nulls, as was the case for the Bonus field stored in the Employee table in Figure A-8. You should be aware that database experts are currently debating the validity of the use of nulls in relational databases, and many experts insist that you should never use nulls. This warning against nulls is partly based on the inconsistent way different RDBMSs treat nulls and partly due to the lack of a firm theoretical foundation for how to use nulls. In any case, entity subtypes are an alternative to the use of nulls.

Entity-Relationship Diagrams

A common shorthand method for describing tables is to write the table name followed by its fields in parentheses, underlining the fields that represent the primary key and identifying the foreign keys for a table immediately after the table. Using this method, the tables that appear in Figures A-5 through A-7 and Figure A-9 are described in the following way:

Department (<u>DeptNum</u>, DeptName, DeptHead)
    Foreign key: DeptHead to Employee table
Employee (<u>EmployeeNum</u>, FirstName, LastName, DeptNum)
    Foreign key: DeptNum to Department table
Position (<u>PositionID</u>, PositionDesc, PayGrade)
Employment (<u>EmployeeNum</u>, <u>PositionID</u>, StartDate, EndDate)
    Foreign key: EmployeeNum to Employee table
    Foreign key: PositionID to Position table
EmployeeBonus (<u>EmployeeNum</u>, Bonus)
    Foreign key: EmployeeNum to Employee table

Another popular way to describe tables *and their relationships* is with entity-relationship diagrams. An **entity-relationship diagram (ERD)** shows a database's entities and the relationships among the entities in a symbolic, visual way. In an entity-relationship diagram, an entity and a table are equivalent. Figure A-10 shows an entity-relationship diagram for the tables that appear in Figures A-5 through A-7 and Figure A-9.

Figure A-10	An entity-relationship diagram

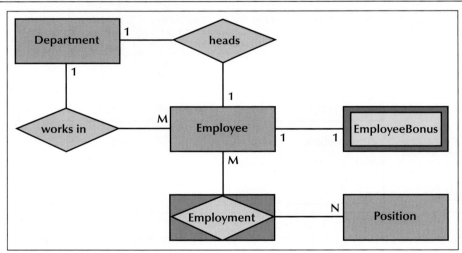

Entity-relationship diagrams have the following characteristics:

- Entities, or tables, appear in rectangles, and relationships appear in diamonds. The entity name appears inside the rectangle, and a verb describing the relationship appears inside the diamond. For example, the Employee rectangle is connected to the Department rectangle by the "works in" diamond and is read: "an employee works in a department."
- The 1 by the Department entity and the M by the Employee entity identify a one-to-many relationship between these two entities. In a similar manner, a many-to-many relationship exists between the Employee and Position entities and one-to-one relationships exist between the Department and Employee entities and between the Employee and EmployeeBonus entities.

- A diamond inside a rectangle defines a composite entity. A **composite entity** is a relationship that has the characteristics of an entity. For example, Employment connects the Employee and Position entities in a many-to-many relationship and acts as an entity by containing the StartDate and EndDate fields, along with the composite key of the EmployeeNum and PositionID fields.
- An entity subtype, for example, EmployeeBonus, appears in a double rectangle and is connected without an intervening diamond directly to its related entity, Employee.

You can also show fields in an ERD by placing each individual field in a bubble connected to its entity or relationship. However, typical ERDs have large numbers of entities and relationships, so including the fields might confuse rather than clarify the ERD.

Integrity Constraints

A database has **integrity** if its data follows certain rules; each rule is called an **integrity constraint**. The ideal is to have the DBMS enforce all integrity constraints. If a DBMS can enforce some integrity constraints but not others, the other integrity constraints must be enforced by other programs or by the people who use the DBMS. Integrity constraints can be divided into three groups: primary key constraints, foreign key constraints, and domain integrity constraints.

- One primary key constraint is inherent in the definition of a primary key, which says that the primary key must be unique. The **entity integrity constraint** says that the primary key cannot be null. For a composite key, none of the individual fields can be null. The uniqueness and nonnull properties of a primary key ensure that you can reference any data value in a database by supplying its table name, field name, and primary key value.
- Foreign keys provide the mechanism for forming a relationship between two tables, and referential integrity ensures that only valid relationships exist. **Referential integrity** is the constraint specifying that each nonnull foreign key value must match a primary key value in the primary table. Specifically, referential integrity means that you cannot add a row with an unmatched foreign key value. Referential integrity also means that you cannot change or delete the related primary key value and leave the foreign key orphaned. In some RDBMSs, if you try to change or delete a primary key value, you can specify one of these options: restricted, cascades, or nullifies. If you specify **restricted**, the DBMS updates or deletes the value only if there are no matching foreign key values. If you choose **cascades** and then change a primary key value, the DBMS changes the matching foreign key values to the new primary key value, or, if you delete a primary key value, the DBMS also deletes the matching foreign key rows. If you choose **nullifies** and then change or delete a primary key value, the DBMS sets all matching foreign key values to null.
- Recall that a domain is a set of values from which one or more fields draw their actual values. A **domain integrity constraint** is a rule you specify for a field. By choosing a data type for a field, you impose a constraint on the set of values allowed for the field. You can create specific validation rules for a field to limit its domain further. As you make a field's domain definition more precise, you exclude more and more unacceptable values for the field. For example, in the State table, shown in Figures A-2 and A-4, you could define the domain for the EnteredUnionOrder field to be a unique integer between 1 and 50 and the domain for the StateBird field to be any name containing 25 or fewer characters.

Dependencies and Determinants

Tables are related to other tables. Fields are also related to other fields. Consider the modified Employee table shown in Figure A-11. Its description is:

Employee (<u>EmployeeNum</u>, <u>PositionID</u>, LastName, PositionDesc, StartDate, HealthPlan, PlanDesc)

Figure A-11
A table combining fields from three tables

				primary key		

Employee

EmployeeNum	PositionID	LastName	PositionDesc	StartDate	HealthPlan	PlanDesc
2173	2	Hennessey	Manager	12/14/2008	B	Managed HMO
4519	1	Noordsy	Director	04/23/2010	A	Managed PPO
4519	3	Noordsy	Analyst	11/11/2004	A	Managed PPO
8005	3	Amidon	Analyst	06/05/2009	C	Health Savings
8005	4	Amidon	Clerk	07/02/2007	C	Health Savings
8112	1	Wandzell	Director	12/15/2009	A	Managed PPO
8112	2	Wandzell	Manager	10/04/2008	A	Managed PPO

The modified Employee table combines several fields from the Employee, Position, and Employment tables that appeared in Figure A-6. The EmployeeNum and LastName fields are from the Employee table. The PositionID and PositionDesc fields are from the Position table. The EmployeeNum, PositionID, and StartDate fields are from the Employment table. The HealthPlan and PlanDesc fields are new fields for the Employee table, whose primary key is now the combination of the EmployeeNum and PositionID fields.

In the Employee table, each field is related to other fields. To determine field relationships, you ask "Does a value for a particular field give me a single value for another field?" If the answer is Yes, then the two fields are related. For example, a value for the EmployeeNum field determines a single value for the LastName field, and a value for the LastName field depends on the value of the EmployeeNum field. In database discussions, the word functionally is used, as in: "EmployeeNum functionally determines LastName" and "LastName is functionally dependent on EmployeeNum." In this case, EmployeeNum is called a determinant. A **determinant** is a field, or a collection of fields, whose values determine the values of another field. A field is functionally dependent on another field (or a collection of fields) if that other field is a determinant for it.

You can graphically show a table's functional dependencies and determinants in a **bubble diagram**; a bubble diagram is also called a **data model diagram** and a **functional dependency diagram**. Figure A-12 shows the bubble diagram for the Employee table shown in Figure A-11.

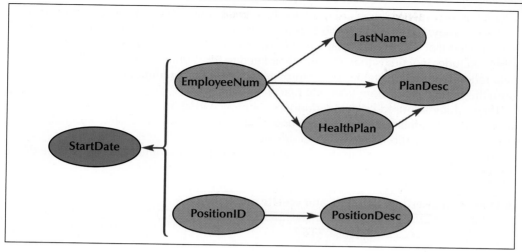

You can read the bubble diagram in Figure A-12 as follows:

- The EmployeeNum field is a determinant for the LastName, HealthPlan, and PlanDesc fields.
- The PositionID field is a determinant for the PositionDesc field.
- The StartDate field is functionally dependent on the EmployeeNum and PositionID fields together.
- The HealthPlan field is a determinant for the PlanDesc field.

Note that EmployeeNum and PositionID together is a determinant for the StartDate field and for all fields that depend on the EmployeeNum field alone and the PositionID field alone. Some experts include these additional fields and some don't. The previous list of determinants does not include these additional fields.

An alternative way to show determinants is to list the determinant, a right arrow, and then the dependent fields, separated by commas. Using this alternative, the determinants shown in Figure A-12 are:

EmployeeNum → LastName, HealthPlan, PlanDesc
PositionID → PositionDesc
EmployeeNum, PositionID → StartDate
HealthPlan → PlanDesc

Only the StartDate field is functionally dependent on the table's full primary key, the EmployeeNum and PositionID fields. The LastName, HealthPlan, and PlanDesc fields have partial dependencies because they are functionally dependent on the EmployeeNum field, which is part of the primary key. A **partial dependency** is a functional dependency on part of the primary key, instead of the entire primary key. Does another partial dependency exist in the Employee table? Yes, the PositionDesc field has a partial dependency on the PositionID field.

Because the EmployeeNum field is a determinant of both the HealthPlan and PlanDesc fields, and the HealthPlan field is a determinant of the PlanDesc field, the HealthPlan and PlanDesc fields have a transitive dependency. A **transitive dependency** is a functional dependency between two nonkey fields, which are both dependent on a third field.

How do you know which functional dependencies exist among a collection of fields, and how do you recognize partial and transitive dependencies? The answers lie with the questions you ask as you gather the requirements for a database application. For each field and entity, you must gain an accurate understanding of its meaning and relationships in the context of the application. **Semantic object modeling** is an entire area of study within the database field devoted to the meanings and relationships of data.

Anomalies

When you use a DBMS, you are more likely to get results you can trust if you create your tables carefully. For example, problems might occur with tables that have partial and transitive dependencies, whereas you won't have as much trouble if you ensure that your tables include only fields that are directly related to each other. Also, when you remove data redundancy from a table, you improve that table. **Data redundancy** occurs when you store the same data in more than one place.

The problems caused by data redundancy and by partial and transitive dependencies are called **anomalies** because they are undesirable irregularities of tables. Anomalies are of three types: insertion, deletion, and update.

To examine the effects of these anomalies, consider the modified Employee table that is shown again in Figure A-13.

Figure A-13	A table with insertion, deletion, and update anomalies

Employee

EmployeeNum	PositionID	LastName	PositionDesc	StartDate	HealthPlan	PlanDesc
2173	2	Hennessey	Manager	12/14/2008	B	Managed HMO
4519	1	Noordsy	Director	04/23/2010	A	Managed PPO
4519	3	Noordsy	Analyst	11/11/2004	A	Managed PPO
8005	3	Amidon	Analyst	06/05/2009	C	Health Savings
8005	4	Amidon	Clerk	07/02/2007	C	Health Savings
8112	1	Wandzell	Director	12/15/2009	A	Managed PPO
8112	2	Wandzell	Manager	10/04/2008	A	Managed PPO

- An **insertion anomaly** occurs when you cannot add a record to a table because you do not know the entire primary key value. For example, you cannot add the new employee Cathy Corbett with an EmployeeNum of 3322 to the Employee table if you do not know her position in the company. Entity integrity prevents you from leaving any part of a primary key null. Because the PositionID field is part of the primary key, you cannot leave it null. To add the new employee, your only option is to make up a PositionID field value, until you determine the correct position. This solution misrepresents the facts and is unacceptable, if a better approach is available.

- A **deletion anomaly** occurs when you delete data from a table and unintentionally lose other critical data. For example, if you delete EmployeeNum 2173 because Hennessey is no longer an employee, you also lose the only instance of HealthPlan B in the database. Thus, you no longer know that HealthPlan B is the "Managed HMO" plan.

- An **update anomaly** occurs when you change one field value and either the DBMS must make more than one change to the database or else the database ends up containing inconsistent data. For example, if you change a LastName, HealthPlan, or PlanDesc field value for EmployeeNum 8005, the DBMS must change multiple rows of the Employee table. If the DBMS fails to change all the rows, the LastName, HealthPlan, or PlanDesc field now has different values in the database and is inconsistent.

Normalization

Database design is the process of determining the content and structure of data in a database in order to support some activity on behalf of a user or group of users. After you have determined the collection of fields users need to support an activity, you need to determine the precise tables needed for the collection of fields and then place those fields into the correct tables. Crucial to good database design is understanding the functional dependencies of all fields; recognizing the anomalies caused by data redundancy, partial dependencies, and transitive dependencies when they exist; and knowing how to eliminate the anomalies. Failure to eliminate anomalies leads to data redundancy and can cause data integrity and other problems as your database grows in size.

The process of identifying and eliminating anomalies is called **normalization**. Using normalization, you start with a collection of tables, apply sets of rules to eliminate anomalies, and produce a new collection of problem-free tables. The sets of rules are called **normal forms**. Of special interest for our purposes are the first three normal forms: first normal form, second normal form, and third normal form. First normal form improves the design of your tables, second normal form improves the first normal form design, and third normal form applies even more stringent rules to produce an even better design. Note that normal forms beyond third normal form exist; these higher normal forms can improve a database design in some situations but won't be covered in this section.

First Normal Form

Consider the Employee table shown in Figure A-14. For each employee, the table contains EmployeeNum, which is the primary key; the employee's first name, last name, health plan code and description; and the ID, description, pay grade, and start date of each position held by the employee. For example, Barbara Hennessey has held one position, while the other three employees have held two positions. Because each entry in a table must contain a single value, the structure shown in Figure A-14 does not meet the requirements for a table, or relation; therefore, it is called an **unnormalized relation**. The set of fields that includes the PositionID, PositionDesc, PayGrade, and StartDate fields, which can have more than one value, is called a **repeating group**.

Repeating group of data in an unnormalized Employee table ◄ **Figure A-14**

Employee

EmployeeNum	PositionID	FirstName	LastName	PositionDesc	PayGrade	StartDate	HealthPlan	PlanDesc
2173	2	Barbara	Hennessey	Manager	40	12/14/2008	B	Managed HMO
4519	1 3	Lee	Noordsy	Director Analyst	45 30	04/23/2010 11/11/2004	A	Managed PPO
8005	3 4	Pat	Amidon	Analyst Clerk	30 20	06/05/2009 07/02/2007	C	Health Savings
8112	1 2	Chris	Wandzell	Director Manager	45 40	12/15/2009 10/04/2008	A	Managed PPO

First normal form addresses this repeating-group situation. A table is in **first normal form (1NF)** if it does not contain repeating groups. To remove a repeating group and convert to first normal form, you expand the primary key to include the primary key of the repeating group, forming a composite key. Performing the conversion step produces the 1NF table shown in Figure A-15.

| Figure A-15 | After conversion to 1NF |

Employee

primary key

EmployeeNum	PositionID	FirstName	LastName	PositionDesc	PayGrade	StartDate	HealthPlan	PlanDesc
2173	2	Barbara	Hennessey	Manager	40	12/14/2008	B	Managed HMO
4519	1	Lee	Noordsy	Director	45	04/23/2010	A	Managed PPO
4519	3	Lee	Noordsy	Analyst	30	11/11/2004	A	Managed PPO
8005	3	Pat	Amidon	Analyst	30	06/05/2009	C	Health Savings
8005	4	Pat	Amidon	Clerk	20	07/02/2007	C	Health Savings
8112	1	Chris	Wandzell	Director	45	12/15/2009	A	Managed PPO
8112	2	Chris	Wandzell	Manager	40	10/04/2008	A	Managed PPO

The alternative way to describe the 1NF table is:

Employee (<u>EmployeeNum</u>, <u>PositionID</u>, FirstName, LastName, PositionDesc, PayGrade, StartDate, HealthPlan, PlanDesc)

The Employee table is now a true table and has a composite key. The table, however, suffers from insertion, deletion, and update anomalies. (As an exercise, find examples of the three anomalies in the table.) The EmployeeNum field is a determinant for the FirstName, LastName, HealthPlan, and PlanDesc fields, so partial dependencies exist in the Employee table. It is these partial dependencies that cause the anomalies in the Employee table, and second normal form addresses the partial-dependency problem.

Second Normal Form

A table in 1NF is in **second normal form (2NF)** if it does not contain any partial dependencies. To remove partial dependencies from a table and convert it to second normal form, you perform two steps. First, identify the functional dependencies for every field in the table. Second, if necessary, create new tables and place each field in a table, so that the field is functionally dependent on the entire primary key, not part of the primary key. If you need to create new tables, restrict them to ones with a primary key that is a subset of the original composite key. Note that partial dependencies occur only when you have a composite key; a table in first normal form with a single-field primary key is automatically in second normal form.

First, identifying the functional dependencies leads to the following determinants for the Employee table:

EmployeeNum → FirstName, LastName, HealthPlan, PlanDesc
PositionID → PositionDesc, PayGrade
EmployeeNum, PositionID → StartDate
HealthPlan → PlanDesc

The EmployeeNum field is a determinant for the FirstName, LastName, HealthPlan, and PlanDesc fields. The PositionID field is a determinant for the PositionDesc and PayGrade fields. The HealthPlan field is a determinant for the PlanDesc field. The composite key EmployeeNum and PositionID is a determinant for the StartDate field. Performing the second step in the conversion from first normal form to second form produces the three 2NF tables shown in Figure A-16.

After conversion to 2NF | **Figure A-16**

Employee

primary key →	EmployeeNum	FirstName	LastName	HealthPlan	PlanDesc
	2173	Barbara	Hennessey	B	Managed HMO
	4519	Lee	Noordsy	A	Managed PPO
	8005	Pat	Amidon	C	Health Savings
	8112	Chris	Wandzell	A	Managed PPO

Position

primary key →	PositionID	PositionDesc	PayGrade
	1	Director	45
	2	Manager	40
	3	Analyst	30
	4	Clerk	20

Employment

	primary key

EmployeeNum	PositionID	StartDate
2173	2	12/14/2008
4519	1	04/23/2010
4519	3	11/11/2004
8005	3	06/05/2009
8005	4	07/02/2007
8112	1	12/15/2009
8112	2	10/04/2008

The alternative way to describe the 2NF tables is:

Employee (EmployeeNum, FirstName, LastName, HealthPlan, PlanDesc)
Position (PositionID, PositionDesc, PayGrade)
Employment (EmployeeNum, PositionID, StartDate)
    Foreign key: EmployeeNum to Employee table
    Foreign key: PositionID to Position table

All three tables are in second normal form. Do anomalies still exist? The Position and Employment tables show no anomalies, but the Employee table suffers from anomalies caused by the transitive dependency between the HealthPlan and PlanDesc fields. (As an exercise, find examples of the three anomalies caused by the transitive dependency.) That is, the HealthPlan field is a determinant for the PlanDesc field, and the EmployeeNum field is a determinant for the HealthPlan and PlanDesc fields. Third normal form addresses the transitive-dependency problem.

Third Normal Form

A table in 2NF is in **third normal form (3NF)** if every determinant is a candidate key. This definition for 3NF is referred to as **Boyce-Codd normal form (BCNF)** and is an improvement over the original version of 3NF. What are the determinants in the Employee table? The EmployeeNum and HealthPlan fields are the determinants; however, the EmployeeNum field is a candidate key because it's the table's primary key, and the HealthPlan field is not a candidate key. Therefore, the Employee table is in second normal form, but it is not in third normal form.

To convert a table to third normal form, remove the fields that depend on the non-candidate-key determinant and place them into a new table with the determinant as the primary key. For the Employee table, the PlanDesc field depends on the HealthPlan field, which is a non-candidate-key determinant. Thus, you remove the PlanDesc field from the table, create a new HealthBenefits table, place the PlanDesc field in the HealthBenefits table, and then make the HealthPlan field the primary key of the HealthBenefits table. Note that only the PlanDesc field is removed from the Employee table; the HealthPlan field remains as a foreign key in the Employee table. Figure A-17 shows the database design for the four 3NF tables.

Figure A-17	After conversion to 3NF

The alternative way to describe the 3NF relations is:

HealthBenefits (HealthPlan, PlanDesc)
Employee (EmployeeNum, FirstName, LastName, HealthPlan)
    Foreign key: HealthPlan to HealthBenefits table
Position (PositionID, PositionDesc, PayGrade)
Employment (EmployeeNum, PositionID, StartDate)
    Foreign key: EmployeeNum to Employee table
    Foreign key: PositionID to Position table

The four tables have no anomalies because you have eliminated all the data redundancy, partial dependencies, and transitive dependencies. Normalization provides the framework for eliminating anomalies and delivering an optimal database design, which you should always strive to achieve. You should be aware, however, that experts sometimes denormalize tables to improve database performance—specifically, to decrease the time it takes the database to respond to a user's commands and requests. Typically, when you denormalize tables, you combine separate tables into one table to reduce the need for the DBMS to join the separate tables to process queries and other informational requests. When you denormalize a table, you reintroduce redundancy to the table. At the same time, you reintroduce anomalies. Thus, improving performance exposes a database to potential integrity problems. Only database experts should denormalize tables, but even experts first complete the normalization of their tables.

Natural, Artificial, and Surrogate Keys

When you complete the design of a database, your tables should be in third normal form, free of anomalies and redundancy. Some tables, such as the State table (see Figure A-2), have obvious third normal form designs with obvious primary keys. The State table's description is:

State (StateAbbrev, StateName, EnteredUnionOrder, StateBird, StatePopulation)

Recall that the candidate keys for the State table are StateAbbrev, StateName, and EnteredUnionOrder. Choosing the StateAbbrev field as the State table's primary key makes the StateName and EnteredUnionOrder fields alternate keys. Primary keys such as the StateAbbrev field are sometimes called natural keys. A **natural key** (also called a **logical key** or an **intelligent key**) is a primary key that consists of a field, or a collection of fields, that is an inherent characteristic of the entity described by the table and that is visible to users. Other examples of natural keys are the ISBN (International Standard Book Number) for a book, the SSN (Social Security number) for a U.S. individual, the UPC (Universal Product Code) for a product, and the VIN (vehicle identification number) for a vehicle.

Is the PositionID field, which is the primary key for the Position table (see Figure A-17), a natural key? No, the PositionID field is not an inherent characteristic of a position. Instead, the PositionID field has been added to the Position table only as a way to identify each position uniquely. The PositionID field is an **artificial key**, which is a field that you add to a table to serve solely as the primary key and that is visible to users.

Another reason for using an artificial key arises in tables that allow duplicate records. Although relational database theory and most experts do not allow duplicate records in a table, consider a database that tracks donors and their donations. Figure A-18 shows a Donor table with an artificial key of DonorID and with the DonorFirstName and DonorLastName fields. Some cash donations are anonymous, which accounts for the fourth record in the Donor table. Figure A-18 also shows the Donation table with the DonorID field, a foreign key to the Donor table, and the DonationDate and DonationAmt fields.

Figure A-18 | **Donor and Donation tables**

What is the primary key of the Donation table? No single field is unique, and neither is any combination of fields. For example, on 10/10/2011 two anonymous donors (DonorID value of 4) donated $50 each. You need to add an artificial key, DonationID for example, to the Donation table. The addition of the artificial key makes every record in the Donation table unique, as shown in Figure A-19.

Donation table after adding DonationID, an artificial key — **Figure A-19**

Donation

artificial key →

DonationID	DonorID	DonationDate	DonationAmt
1	1	10/12/2010	$50.00
2	1	09/30/2011	$50.00
3	2	10/03/2011	$75.00
4	4	10/10/2011	$50.00
5	4	10/10/2011	$50.00
6	4	10/11/2011	$25.00
7	5	10/13/2011	$50.00

The descriptions of the Donor and Donation tables now are:

Donor (DonorID, DonorFirstName, DonorLastName)
Donation (DonationID, DonorID, DonationDate, DonationAmt)
    Foreign key: DonorID to Donor table

For another common situation, consider the 3NF tables you reviewed in the previous section (see Figure A-17) that have the following descriptions:

HealthBenefits (HealthPlan, PlanDesc)
Employee (EmployeeNum, FirstName, LastName, HealthPlan)
    Foreign key: HealthPlan to HealthBenefits table
Position (PositionID, PositionDesc, PayGrade)
Employment (EmployeeNum, PositionID, StartDate)
    Foreign key: EmployeeNum to Employee table
    Foreign key: PositionID to Position table

Recall that a primary key must be unique, must be minimal, and must not change in value. In theory, primary keys don't change in value. However, in practice, you might have to change EmployeeNum field values that you incorrectly entered in the Employment table. Further, if you need to change an EmployeeNum field value in the Employee table, the change must cascade to the EmployeeNum field values in the Employment table. Also, changes to a PositionID field value in the Position table must cascade to the Employment table. For these and other reasons, many experts add surrogate keys to their tables. A **surrogate key** (also called a **synthetic key**) is a system-generated primary key that is hidden from users. Usually you can use an automatic numbering data type, such as the Access AutoNumber data type, for a surrogate key. Figure A-20 shows the four tables with surrogate keys added to three of the four tables.

Figure A-20   Using surrogate keys

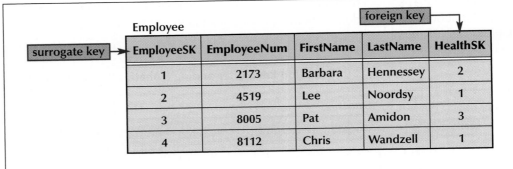

Employee

surrogate key →

foreign key

EmployeeSK	EmployeeNum	FirstName	LastName	HealthSK
1	2173	Barbara	Hennessey	2
2	4519	Lee	Noordsy	1
3	8005	Pat	Amidon	3
4	8112	Chris	Wandzell	1

HealthBenefits

surrogate key →

HealthSK	HealthPlan	PlanDesc
1	A	Managed PPO
2	B	Managed HMO
3	C	Health Savings

Position

artificial key →

PositionID	PositionDesc	PayGrade
1	Director	45
2	Manager	40
3	Analyst	30
4	Clerk	20

Employment

surrogate key →

foreign key

EmploymentSK	EmployeeSK	PositionID	StartDate
1	1	2	12/14/2008
1	2	1	04/23/2010
1	4	3	11/11/2004
2	2	3	06/05/2009
3	1	4	07/02/2007
3	2	1	12/15/2009
4	3	2	10/04/2008

The HealthSK field replaces the HealthPlan field as a foreign key in the Employee table, and the EmployeeSK field replaces the EmployeeNum field in the Employment table. When you change an incorrectly entered EmployeeNum field value in the Employee table, you don't need to cascade the change to the Employment table. When you change an incorrectly entered HealthPlan field value in the HealthBenefits table, you don't have to cascade the change to the Employee table.

As you design a database, you should *not* consider the use of surrogate keys, and you should use an artificial key only for the rare table that has duplicate records. At the point when you implement a database, you might choose to use artificial and surrogate keys, but be aware that database experts debate their use and effectiveness. Some of the trade-offs between natural and surrogate keys that you need to consider are:

- Use surrogate keys to avoid cascading updates to foreign key values. Surrogate keys can also replace lengthier foreign keys when those foreign keys reference composite fields.
- You don't need a surrogate key for a table whose primary key is not used as a foreign key in another table, because cascading updates is not an issue.
- Tables with surrogate keys require more joins than do tables with natural keys. For example, if you need to know all employees with a HealthPlan field value of A, the surrogate key in Figure A-20 requires that you join the Employee and HealthBenefits tables to answer the question. Using natural keys as shown in Figure A-17, the HealthPlan field appears in the Employee table, so no join is necessary.
- Although surrogate keys are meant to be hidden from users, they cannot be hidden from users who create SQL statements and use other ad hoc tools.
- Because you need a unique index for the natural key and a unique index for the surrogate key, your database size is larger and index maintenance takes more time when you use a surrogate key. On the other hand, a foreign key using a surrogate key is usually smaller than a foreign key using a natural key, especially when the natural key is a composite key, so those indexes are smaller and faster to access for lookups and joins.

Microsoft Access Naming Conventions

In the early 1980s, Microsoft's Charles Simonyi introduced an identifier naming convention that became known as Hungarian notation. Microsoft and other companies use this naming convention for variable, control, and other object naming in Basic, Visual Basic, and other programming languages. When Access was introduced in the early 1990s, Stan Leszynski and Greg Reddick adapted Hungarian notation for Microsoft Access databases; their guidelines became known as the Leszynski/Reddick naming conventions. In recent years, the Leszynski naming conventions, the Reddick naming conventions, and other naming conventions have been published. Individuals and companies have created their own Access naming conventions, but many are based on the Leszynski/Reddick naming conventions, as are the naming conventions covered in this section.

An Access database can contain thousands of objects, fields, controls, and other items, and keeping track of their names and what they represent is a difficult task. Consequently, you should use naming conventions that identify the type and purpose of each item in an Access database. You can use naming conventions that identify items generally or very specifically.

For objects, include a prefix tag to identify the type of object, as shown in Figure A-21. In each example in Figure A-21, the final object name consists of a three-character tag prefixed to the base object name. The form name of frmEmployeesAndPositions, for example, consists of the frm tag and the EmployeesAndPositions base form name.

Figure A-21 ▶ **Object naming tags**

Object type	Tag	Example
Form	frm	frmEmployeesAndPositions
Macro	mcr	mcrCalculations
Module	bas	basCalculations
Query	qry	qryEmployee
Report	rpt	rptEmployeesAndPositions
Table	tbl	tblEmployee

The tags in Figure A-21 identify each object type in general. If you want to identify object types more specifically, you could expand Figure A-21 to include tags such as fsub for a subform, qxtb for a crosstab query, tlkp for a lookup table, rsub for a subreport, and so on.

For controls in forms and reports, a general naming convention uses lbl as a prefix tag for labels and ctl as a prefix tag for other types of controls. For more specific naming conventions for controls, you'd use a specific prefix tag for each type of control. Figure A-22 shows the prefix tag for some common controls in forms and reports.

Control naming tags | Figure A-22

Control type	Tag
Check box	chk
Combo box	cbo
Command button	cmd
Image	img
Label	lbl
Line	lin
List box	lst
Option button	opt
PivotTable	pvt
Rectangle	shp
Subform/Subreport	sub
Text box	txt

Some database developers use a prefix tag for each field name to identify the field's data type (for example, dtm for Date/Time, num for Number, and chr for Text or Character), others use a prefix tag for each field name to identify in which table the field is located (for example, emp for the Employee table and pos for the Position table), and still others don't use a prefix tag for field names.

You might use suffix tags for controls that might otherwise have identical names. For example, if you have two text boxes in a form for calculated controls that display the average and the sum of the OrderAmt field, both could legitimately be named txtOrderAmt unless you used suffix tags to name them txtOrderAmtAvg and txtOrderAmtSum.

You should ensure that any name you use does not duplicate a property name or any keyword Access reserves for special purposes. In general, you can avoid property and keyword name conflicts by using two-word field, control, and object names. For example, use StudentName instead of Name, and use OrderDate instead of Date to avoid name conflicts.

All database developers avoid spaces in names, mainly because spaces are not allowed in server database management systems (DBMSs), such as SQL Server, Oracle, and DB2. If you are prototyping a Microsoft Access database that you'll migrate to one of these server DBMSs, or if future requirements might force a migration, you should restrict your Access identifier names so that they conform to the rules common to them all. Figure A-23 shows the identifier naming rules for Access, SQL Server, Oracle, and DB2.

Figure A-23 Identifier naming rules for common database management systems

Identifier naming rule	Access	SQL Server	Oracle	DB2
Maximum character length	64	30	30	30
Allowable characters	Letters, digits, space, and special characters, except for period (.), exclamation point (!), accent grave (`), and square brackets ([ ])	Letters, digits, dollar sign ($), underscore (_), number symbol (#), and at symbol (@)	Letters, digits, dollar sign ($), underscore (_), and number symbol (#)	Letters, digits, at symbol (@), dollar sign ($), underscore (_), and number symbol (#)
Special rules		No spaces; first character must be a letter or at symbol (@)	No spaces; first character must be a letter; stored in the database in uppercase	No spaces; first character must be a letter, at symbol (@), dollar sign ($), or number symbol (#); stored in the database in uppercase

Appendix Summary | Review

In this appendix, you learned about tables and their characteristics, keys (primary, candidate, alternate, composite, and foreign), relationships (one-to-many, many-to-many, one-to-one, and entity subtypes), entity-relationship diagrams, integrity constraints (entity, referential, and domain), dependencies and determinants, and anomalies. You also learned how to design a database using normalization to place all tables in third normal form. Finally, you learned about natural, artificial, and surrogate keys, and you examined naming conventions.

Key Terms

alternate key
anomalies
artificial key
attribute
Boyce-Codd normal
    form (BCNF)
bubble diagram
candidate key
cascades
composite entity
composite key
concatenated key
data model diagram
data redundancy
database design
deletion anomaly
determinant
domain
domain integrity constraint
entity
entity integrity constraint
entity subtype

entity-relationship
    diagram (ERD)
field
field name
first normal form (1NF)
foreign key
functional dependency
    diagram
insertion anomaly
integrity
integrity constraint
intelligent key
intersection table
junction table
link table
logical key
many-to-many
    relationship (M:N)
natural key
nonkey field
normal forms
normalization
null

nullifies
one-to-many
    relationship (1:M or 1:N)
one-to-one relationship (1:1)
partial dependency
primary key
primary table
record
referential integrity
related table
relation
relational database
repeating group
restricted
second normal form (2NF)
semantic object modeling
surrogate key
synthetic key
table
third normal form (3NF)
transitive dependency
tuple
unnormalized relation
update anomaly

1. What are the formal names for a table, for a row, and for a column? What are the popular names for a row and for a column?
2. What is a domain?
3. What is an entity?
4. What is the relationship between a primary key and a candidate key?
5. What is a composite key?
6. What is a foreign key?
7. Look for an example of a one-to-one relationship, an example of a one-to-many relationship, and an example of a many-to-many relationship in a newspaper, magazine, book, or everyday situation you encounter. For each one, name the entities and select the primary and foreign keys.
8. When do you use an entity subtype?
9. What is a composite entity in an entity-relationship diagram?
10. What is the entity integrity constraint?
11. What is referential integrity?
12. What does the cascades option, which is used with referential integrity, accomplish?
13. What are partial and transitive dependencies?
14. What three types of anomalies can be exhibited by a table, and what problems do they cause?
15. Figure A-24 shows the Employee, Position, and Employment tables with primary keys EmployeeNum, PositionID, and both EmployeeNum and PositionID, respectively. Which two integrity constraints do these tables violate and why?

Figure A-24

Employee

EmployeeNum	ClientName	LastName	HealthPlan
2173	Barbara	Hennessey	B
4519	Lee	Noordsy	A
8005	Pat	Amidon	C
8112	Chris	Wandzell	A

Position

PositionID	PositionDes	PayGrade
1	Director	45
2	Manager	40
3	Analyst	30
4	Clerk	20

Employment

EmployeeNum	PositionID	StartDate
2173	2	12/14/2008
4519	1	04/23/2010
4519		11/11/2004
8005	3	06/05/2009
8005	4	07/02/2007
8112	1	12/15/2009
9876	2	10/04/2008

16. The State and City tables, shown in Figure A-4, are described as follows:
    State (StateAbbrev, StateName, EnteredUnionOrder, StateBird,
        StatePopulation)
    City (StateAbbrev, CityName, CityPopulation)
        Foreign key: StateAbbrev to State table
    Add the field named CountyName for the county or counties in a state containing the city to this database, justify where you placed it (that is, in an existing table or in a new one), and draw the entity-relationship diagram for all the entities. Counties for some of the cities shown in Figure A-4 are Travis and Williamson counties for Austin TX; Hartford county for Hartford CT; Clinton, Eaton, and Ingham counties for Lansing MI; Davidson county for Nashville TN; Hughes county for Pierre SD; and Nueces and San Patricio counties for Portland TX.

17. Suppose you have a table for a dance studio. The fields are dancer's identification number, dancer's name, dancer's address, dancer's telephone number, class identification number, day that the class meets, time that the class meets, instructor name, and instructor identification number. Assume that each dancer takes one class, each class meets only once a week and has one instructor, and each instructor can teach more than one class. In what normal form is the table currently, given the following alternative description?

    Dancer (<u>DancerID</u>, DancerName, DancerAddr, DancerPhone, ClassID, ClassDay, ClassTime, InstrName, InstrID)

    Convert this relation to third normal form and represent the design using the alternative description method.

18. Store the following fields for a library database: AuthorCode, AuthorName, BookTitle, BorrowerAddress, BorrowerName, BorrowerCardNumber, CopiesOfBook, ISBN (International Standard Book Number), LoanDate, PublisherCode, PublisherName, and PublisherAddress. A one-to-many relationship exists between publishers and books. Many-to-many relationships exist between authors and books and between borrowers and books.

    a. Name the entities for the library database.

    b. Create the tables for the library database and describe them using the alternative method. Be sure the tables are in third normal form.

    c. Draw an entity-relationship diagram for the library database.

19. In the following database, which consists of the Department and Employee tables, add one record to the end of the Employee table that violates both the entity integrity constraint and the referential integrity constraint.

Figure A-25

Department

DeptID	DeptName	Location
M	Marketing	New York
R	Research	Houston
S	Sales	Chicago

Employee

EmployeeID	EmployeeName	DeptID
1111	Sue	R
2222	Pam	M
3333	Bob	S
4444	Chris	S
5555	Pat	R
6666	Meg	R

20. Consider the following table:

    Patient (PatientID, PatientName, BalanceOwed, DoctorID, DoctorName, ServiceCode, ServiceDesc, ServiceFee, ServiceDate)

    This is a table concerning data about patients of doctors at a clinic and the services the doctors perform for their patients. The following dependencies exist in the Patient table:

    PatientID → PatientName, BalanceOwed

    DoctorID → DoctorName

    ServiceCode → ServiceDesc, ServiceFee

    PatientID, DoctorID, ServiceCode → PatientName, BalanceOwed, DoctorName, ServiceDesc, ServiceFee, ServiceDate

    a. Based on the dependencies, convert the Patient table to first normal form.

    b. Next, convert the Patient table to third normal form.

21. Suppose you need to track data for mountain climbing expeditions. Each member of an expedition is called a climber, and one of the climbers is named to lead an expedition. Climbers can be members of many expeditions over time. The climbers in each expedition attempt to ascend one or more peaks by scaling one of the many faces of the peaks. The data you need to track includes the name of the expedition, the leader of the expedition, and comments about the expedition; the first name, last name, nationality, birth date, death date, and comments about each climber; the name, location, height, and comments about each peak; the name and comments about each face of a peak; comments about each climber for each expedition; and the highest height reached and the date for each ascent attempt by a climber on a face with commentary.

    a. Create the tables for the expedition database and describe them using the alternative method. Be sure the tables are in third normal form.

    b. Draw an entity-relationship diagram for the expedition database.

22. What is the difference among natural, artificial, and surrogate keys?

23. Why should you use naming conventions for the identifiers in a database?

Ending Data Files

There are no ending Data Files needed for this appendix.

Glossary/Index

E

editing charts using Microsoft Graph, AC 417–420

editing mode The mode in which you can insert or delete characters in a field value based on the location of the insertion point. AC 100

embedding Creating or copying an object in a form, report, or field and preserving the object's connection to the source program, which enables you to edit the object, if necessary, using the features of the source program. AC 413, AC 414

    charts in forms, AC 414–420

Enter Parameter Value dialog box, AC 216

entity A person, place, object, event, or idea for which you want to store and process data. AC A2

    composite, AC A4, AC A11

entity integrity The condition that exists when a primary key has been specified for a table, whereby Access forces you to enter a value for the primary key field in every record in the table. AC 61

entity integrity constraint The rule that none of the individual fields comprising the primary key can contain nulls. AC A11

entity subtype A table whose primary key is a foreign key to a second table and whose fields are additional fields for the second table. AC A8–A9

entity-relationship diagram (ERD) A symbolic, visual way to show a database's entities and the relationships among the entities. AC A10–A11

equal sign (=), Date function, AC 365

ERD. See entity-relationship diagram

exact match A type of query in which the value in the specified field must match the condition exactly in order for the record to be included in the query results. AC 119–121

Excel. See Microsoft Office Excel 2007

exclamation point (!), wildcard character, AC 167

exiting programs, OFF 28–29

expand indicator In a datasheet, the plus sign that lets you display the related records in the subdatasheet. AC 103

explanations, Memo field, AC 244–246

Export - HTML Document dialog box, AC 391–392

Export XML dialog box, AC 405

exporting, AC 404

    Access tables as XML files, AC 404–406

    queries to HTML documents, AC 390–393

    saving and running export specifications, AC 406–408

expression A statement containing a combination of database fields, constants, and operators that you define in a query to perform a calculation. AC 133

Expression Builder An Access tool that makes it easy for you to create an expression in a query by providing boxes for entering the expression, buttons for common operators, and lists of expression elements, such as table and field names. AC 133, AC 309

Extensible Markup Language. See XML

Extensible Stylesheet Language. See XSL

F

F1 key The function key you press to display Help information, such as for the current property in Table Design view. AC 55

F2 key The function key you press to switch between navigation mode and editing mode. AC 100

F6 key The function key you press to move between the Table Design grid and the Field Properties pane of the Table window in Design view. AC 65, AC 76

field A single characteristic or attribute of a person, place, object, event, or idea. AC 2, AC A2

    adding to forms, AC 283–284

    adding to tables, AC 63–64

    assigning data types, AC 49–50

    calculated. See calculated field

    category, PivotChart, AC 427

    changing data type in Design view, AC 76–79

    changing format in Datasheet view, AC 52–54

    changing lookup field to text field, AC 264–266

    changing properties, AC 64–65

    comments and explanations in Memo fields, AC 244–246

    common. See common field

    data, PivotChart, AC 426

    defining in Design view, AC 55–61

    deleting from table structure, AC 74–75

    detail, PivotTable, AC 421

    determining properties, AC 48

    entering names, AC 11–12

    filter, PivotChart, AC 427

    filter, PivotTable, AC 421

    identifying needed fields, AC 46

    lookup, AC 231–235

    modifying data type, AC 51–52

    moving, AC 62–63

    moving in Layout view, AC 163–164

    names, AC 133

    naming, AC 48, AC 203–204

    nonkey, AC A5

    primary key, data type, AC 10–11

    primary key, renaming, AC 9–10

    related, grouping into tables, AC 46

    renaming in Design view, AC 75–76

    reports, resizing in Layout view, AC 183–184

    row, PivotTable, AC 421

    series, PivotChart, AC 427

    setting properties, AC 48–50

    sort, AC 112, AC 113

    total, PivotTable, AC 423–425

field list A small window listing the fields contained in a table. AC 84, AC 106

field name The unique name for a column in a table. The table name allows you to access a specific column without needing to know its position within the table. AC A2

Field Properties pane The part of the Table window in Design view that contains the properties for the selected field. AC 55

field selector In a datasheet, the column heading (also called the column selector), which you click to select the entire column. AC 12

Field Size property The property that defines a field's maximum storage size for text, number, and AutoNumber fields. AC 50

field validation rule Setting the Validation Rule and Validation Text properties for a field to verify its values by comparing them to a constant or a set of constants. AC 241–243

    duplicate, hiding in reports, AC 363–364

file

    closing, OFF 21

    earlier versions of Office, OFF 19

    new, creating, OFF 22

    open, switching between, OFF 5

    opening, OFF 21–22

    printing, OFF 27–28

    saving, OFF 18–21

file extension A multi-character code that Office appends to a filename to identify the program in which that file was created. The default file extensions are .docx for Word, .xlsx for Excel, .pptx for PowerPoint, and .accdb for Access. OFF 19

filename The name you provide when you save a file and the name you associate with that file. OFF 19

Fill/Back Color button A button in the Font group on the Design tab that you use to change the background color of an object (form or report) or of a specific section or control in the object. AC 318

filter A set of restrictions you place on the records in an open datasheet or form to temporarily isolate a subset of the records. AC 116–118

filter area The portion of a PivotTable or PivotChart, consisting of a filter field and filter field items, that lets you restrict which data to display. AC 421

Filter By Form A filtering technique that changes the datasheet to display empty fields, allowing you to select a value from a list in any blank field to apply a filter that selects only those records containing that value. AC 116

Filter By Selection A filtering technique that lets you select all or part of a field value in a datasheet or form, and then display only those records that contain the selected value in the field. AC 116–118

filter field A field in a PivotTable's or PivotChart's filter area that you use to filter the displayed data. AC 421, AC 426

filter field items The values in a PivotTable's or PivotChart's column area that identify the filter you applied to the displayed data. AC 421

filtering

    AutoFilter, AC 209–211

    data in PivotTable, AC 423–425

Find command A command you use to search for data in a form or datasheet so that you can display only those records you want to view. AC 101–102

I

ID column The default field Access creates to serve as the primary key field for all new tables. AC 8

IIf function A function that returns one of two values based on whether the condition being tested is true or false. Also called the Immediate If function. AC 212–213, AC 225

Immediate If function. *See* IIf function

import a table To copy a table, including its structure, field definitions, and field values, from one Access database to another. AC 68
  adding data to tables by importing text files, AC 79–81
  creating tables by importing existing table structure, AC 71–79
  from Excel worksheet to Access, AC 68–71

importing Including the contents of a file in a new table or appending the contents to an existing table, or including the contents of the file in a form, report, or field. AC 404, AC 413, AC 414
  CSV files as Access tables, AC 395–399
  saving and running import specifications, AC 401–403
  XML files as Access tables, AC 400–401

In comparison operator A comparison operator that defines a condition with a list of two or more values for a field. If a record's field value matches one value from the list of defined values, then Access selects and includes that record in the query results. AC 207

input mask A field property to define a predefined format used to enter and display data in a field. AC 235–239
  characters, AC 237

Input Mask Wizard An Access tool that guides you in creating an input mask for a field. AC 236–237

insertion anomaly The inability to add a record to a table because you do not know the entire primary key value. AC A14

Integer The Field Size property that stores whole numbers from -32,768 to 32,767 in two bytes. AC 50

integration The ability to share information between programs through OLE. OFF 3

integrity A database has integrity if its data follows certain rules, known as integrity constraints. AC A11
  referential, AC A11

integrity constraint A rule that must be followed by data in a database. AC A11

intelligent key. *See* natural key

Internet A worldwide collection of millions of interconnected computers and computer networks that share resources. AC 390
  Internet Explorer, viewing HTML documents, AC 393–395

intersection table A table that connects two other tables having a many-to-many relationship; its primary key is a composite key, consisting of the primary keys of the other two tables. AC A6

IsNull function A function that tests a field value or an expression for a null value; if the field value or expression is null, the result is true; otherwise, the result is false. AC 212

J

join To relate tables through a common field. AC 81–82

join line In the Relationships window, the line that connects the common field that joins two tables. AC 86

junction table. *See* intersection table

K

Keep Together property A property for a group in a report to keep parts of the group together on the same page. Settings for the property are "do not keep together on one page" (default), "keep whole group together on one page" (prints the group header, detail, and group footers on the same page), and "keep header and first record together on one page" (prints the group header on a page only if it can also print the first detail record). For a section, this property specifies whether the section starts printing on a new page if the entire section doesn't fit entirely on the current page. AC 357

key
  artificial, AC A20
  composite (concatenated), AC A4
  foreign, AC A4, AC A5
  natural (intelligent, logical), AC A19
  primary, AC A3–A4, AC A5, AC A19–A23

keyboard shortcut A combination of keys you press to perform a command. OFF 12

keystroke
  editing mode, AC 100
  navigation mode, AC 100

L

label An unbound control that displays text. AC 283
  changing caption, AC 292
  deleting, AC 289

Label Wizard An Access tool that asks you a series of questions, and then creates a mailing label report based on your answers. AC 373–375

layout
  control, AC 275
  stacked, AC 276
  tabular, AC 276

Layout view An Access view in which you can make design changes to a form or report while it is displaying data so that you can immediately *see* the effects of changing the design. AC 28, AC 157
  creating custom reports, AC 352–355
  modifying form design, AC 157–164
  modifying report design, AC 181–185
  modifying reports, AC 339–343
  modifying split forms, AC 274–277
  resizing fields in reports, AC 183–184

legend A box in a chart or PivotChart that lists the series field values and how these values are indicated on the data markers. AC 427

Like comparison operator A comparison operator that selects records by matching field values to a specific pattern that includes one or more wildcard characters. AC 205

line
  adding in forms, AC 315–316
  adding to reports, AC 362–363
  changing in forms, AC 161–162
  straight, drawing in reports, AC 347

Line tool A tool that you use to add a line to a form or report in Design view. AC 315–316

link table. *See* intersection table

linking Creating a connection in the destination program to the original file maintained by the source program; you do not store data from the file in the destination program. Any changes you make to the original file using the source program are reflected in the linked file version in the destination program. AC 413, AC 414
  data from Excel worksheet, AC 429–433

list-of-values match A selection of records whose value for the designated field matches one of two or more simple condition values. AC 207–208

literal display character A special character that automatically appears in specific positions of a field value, usually associated with the field's input mask. AC 235–236

Live Preview An Office feature that shows the results you would achieve in your file, such as the effects of formatting options on a document's appearance, if you click the option to which you are pointing. OFF 13

logical key. *See* natural key

logical operator In a query, an operator that allows you to combine two or more conditions. AC 128–132
  Not logical operator, AC 208–209

Long Integer The Field Size property that stores whole numbers from -2,147,483,648 to 2,147,483,647 in four bytes. AC 50

lookup field A foreign key field that lets you optionally display the foreign key value and other field values from the related record in the primary table. Also known as a Lookup Wizard field. AC 231–235
  changing to text field, AC 264–266
  Lookup Wizard data type, AC 49

Lookup Wizard field. *See* lookup field

M

mailing label, creating, AC 373–377

main form In a form based on two tables, the form that contains data from the primary table. AC 172–175

maintain (a database). *See* update (a database)
Manage Data Tasks dialog box, AC 408

Task Reference

TASK	PAGE #	RECOMMENDED METHOD
Access, start	AC 5	Click ⊕, click All Programs, click Microsoft Office, click Microsoft Office Access 2007
Aggregate functions, use in a datasheet	AC 138	Open table or query in Datasheet view, in Records group on Home tab click Totals button, click Total field row, click function
Aggregate functions, use in a query	AC 139	Display the query in Design view, click Totals button in the Show/Hide group on the Query Tools Design tab
AutoFilter, use in a table or query datasheet	AC 209	Click arrow on column heading, click filter option
AutoFormat, change	AC 157	*See* Reference Window: Changing a Form's AutoFormat
Caption, change for a form's navigation bar	AC 8	Click the form selector, open the property sheet, type the value in the Navigation Caption text box, press Enter
Caption, change for a label	AC 292	*See* Reference Window: Changing a Label's Caption
Calculated field, add to a query	AC 133	*See* Reference Window: Using Expression Builder
Chart, edit with Microsoft Graph	AC 8	In Design view, right-click the chart's edge, point to Chart Object, click Open, make desired changes, click File, click Exit & Return
Chart, embed in a form or report	AC 8	*See* Reference Window: Embedding a Chart in a Form or Report
Color, change an object's background	AC 318	Click the object, click the arrow for 🖌, click the desired color
Column, resize width in a datasheet	AC 12	Double-click ✛ on the right border of the column heading
Combo box, add to a form	AC 299	*See* Reference Window: Adding a Combo Box to Find Records
Control, anchor in a form	AC 277	In Layout view, select the control(s) to anchor, click Arrange tab, click Anchoring button in Position group, click option in gallery
Control, apply special effect	AC 317	Select the control, click the arrow for ⬚, click the special effect
Control, delete	AC 289	Right-click the control, click Delete
Control layout, remove control from in a form	AC 276	In Layout view, click ⊕, select the control, click Arrange tab, click Remove button in Control Layout Group
Control, move in a form	AC 285	*See* Reference Window: Selecting and Moving Controls
Control, resize in a form	AC 289	*See* Reference Window: Resizing a Control
Control, select	AC 285	*See* Reference Window: Selecting and Moving Controls
Control tip property, set for a form control	AC 312	In Layout view, right-click the control, click Properties, click Other tab, type the tip in the ControlTip Text property, press Enter
Controls, align selected	AC 287	Right-click one of the selected controls, point to Align, click desired alignment
Crosstab query, create	AC 219	*See* Reference Window: Using the Crosstab Query Wizard
CSV file, import as an Access table	AC 8	*See* Reference Window: Importing a CSV File as an Access Table
Data, find	AC 166	*See* Reference Window: Finding Data in a Form or Datasheet
Data, group in a report	AC 356	*See* Reference Window: Sorting and Grouping Data in a Report
Data, sort in a report	AC 356	*See* Reference Window: Sorting and Grouping Data in a Report
Database, compact and repair	AC 34	*See* Reference Window: Compacting and Repairing a Database
Database, compact on close	AC 34	Click 🖭, click Access Options, click Current Database, click Compact on Close

TASK	PAGE #	RECOMMENDED METHOD
Database, create a blank	AC 6	Start Access, click Blank database, type the database name, select the drive and folder, click OK, click Create
Database, open	AC 20	*See* Reference Window: Opening a Database
Datasheet view for tables, switch to	AC 77	In the Views group on the Table Tools Design tab, click View button
Date and time, add to a report	AC 366	*See* Reference Window: Adding the Date and Time to a Report
Design view, switch to	AC 65	In Views group on Home tab, click View button arrow, click Design View
Documenter, use	AC 267	*See* Reference Window: Using the Documenter
Duplicate values, hide	AC 363	*See* Reference Window: Hiding Duplicate Values in a Report
Excel worksheet, link data from	AC 8	Click External Data tab, click Excel button in Import group, click Browse, select the workbook, click Open, click Link to the data source by creating a linked table, click OK, follow the steps in the Link Spreadsheet Wizard
Export steps, save	AC 8	Click Save export steps check box in Export dialog box, click Save Export
Field, add to a form or report	AC 283	In Design view, click Add Existing Fields button in Tools group, click the record source, double-click the field
Field, add to a table	AC 63	*See* Reference Window: Adding a Field Between Two Existing Fields
Field, define in a table	AC 55	*See* Reference Window: Defining a Field in Design View
Field, delete from a table	AC 74	*See* Reference Window: Deleting a Field from a Table Structure
Field, move to a new location in a table	AC 78	Display the table in Design view, click the field's row selector, drag the field with the pointer
Field property change, update	AC 77	Click ⬚, select option for updating field property
File, close	OFF 21	Click ⬚, click Close
File, open	OFF 22	*See* Reference Window: Opening an Existing File or Creating a New File
File, print	OFF 27	*See* Reference Window: Printing a File
File, save	OFF 18	*See* Reference Window: Saving a File
File, switch between open	OFF 5	Click the taskbar button for the file you want to make active
Filter By Selection, activate	AC 116	*See* Reference Window: Using Filter By Selection
Find duplicates query, create	AC 226	*See* Reference Window: Using the Find Duplicates Query Wizard
Find unmatched query, create	AC 227	*See* Reference Window: Using the Find Unmatched Query Wizard
Form, create a custom	AC 282	*See* Reference Window: Creating a Form in Design View
Form, create using the Datasheet tool	AC 270	Select record source in Navigation Pane, click Create tab, click More Forms button in Forms group, click Datasheet
Form, create using the Multiple Items tool	AC 271	Select record source in Navigation Pane, click Create tab, click Multiple Items button in Forms group
Form, create using the Split Form tool	AC 273	Select record source in Navigation Pane, click Create tab, click Split Form button in Forms group
Form, select in Design view	AC 299	Click the form selector
Form Footer, add	AC 296	*See* Reference Window: Adding and Removing Form Header and Form Footer Sections
Form Footer, remove	AC 296	*See* Reference Window: Adding and Removing Form Header and Form Footer Sections
Form Header, add	AC 296	*See* Reference Window: Adding and Removing Form Header and Form Footer Sections

TASK	PAGE #	RECOMMENDED METHOD
Form Header, remove	AC 296	*See* Reference Window: Adding and Removing Form Header and Form Footer Sections
Form Wizard, activate	AC 172	Click Create tab, click More Forms button in Forms group, click Form Wizard, choose the table or query for the form, select fields, click Next
Help task pane, use	OFF 24	*See* Reference Window: Getting Help
HTML document, export an object as	AC 8	*See* Reference Window: Exporting an Access Object to an HTML Access Document
Import steps, save	AC 8	Click Save import steps check box in Import dialog box, click Save Import
Input Mask Wizard, activate	AC 235	Click the field's Input Mask text box, click [...], specify your choices in the Input Mask Wizard dialog boxes
Legend, add to PivotChart	AC 8	Click Design tab, click Legend button in Show/Hide group
Line, add to a form or report	AC 315	*See* Reference Window: Adding a Line to a Form or Report
Lookup field, change to Text field	AC 265	Display the table in Design view, select the field, click the Lookup tab, set the Display Control property to Text Box
Lookup field, create	AC 231	Click the Data Type arrow, click Lookup Wizard, specify your choices in the Lookup Wizard dialog boxes
Mailing labels, create	AC 373	*See* Reference Window: Creating Mailing Labels and Other Labels
Memo field, change properties of	AC 245	Display the table in Design view, select the memo field, click the Text Format property or click the Append Only property
Multiple-column report, modify	AC 376	In Design view, click Page Setup tab, click Page Setup button, click the Columns tab, set the column options, click OK
Object, open	AC 17	Double-click object in Navigation Pane
Object, save	AC 16	Click [💾], type the object name, click OK
Object dependencies, identify	AC 239	Click Database Tools tab, click Object Dependencies button in Show/Hide group, click the object, click [+]
Office program, start	OFF 3	*See* Reference Window: Starting Office Programs
Padding, change in a form control	AC 277	In Layout view, click the control, click Arrange tab, click Control Padding button, click the desired setting
Page numbers, add to a report	AC 368	*See* Reference Window: Adding Page Numbers to a Report
Parameter query, create	AC 215	*See* Reference Window: Creating a Parameter Query
Picture, insert in a form	AC 184	In Layout view, in Controls group on Form Layout Tools Format tab, click Logo button, select the picture file, click OK
PivotChart, add to a table or query	AC 8	Open the table or query in Datasheet view, right-click the object tab, click PivotChart View, drag the fields from the Field List pane into the PivotChart
PivotTable, add a total field	AC 8	Click a detail field's column heading, click Design tab, click AutoCalc button in Tools group, click an aggregate option
PivotTable, add to a table or query	AC 8	Open the table or query in Datasheet view, right-click the object tab, click PivotTable View, drag the fields from the Field List pane into the PivotTable
PivotTable, show or hide details	AC 8	Click Design tab, click Show Details or Hide Details in Show/Hide group
Primary key, specify	AC 61	*See* Reference Window: Specifying a Primary Key in Design View

TASK	PAGE #	RECOMMENDED METHOD
Program, Office, exit	OFF 28	Click ☒ on the title bar
Programs, Office, open	OFF 3	*See* Reference Window: Starting Office Programs
Programs, switch between open	OFF 5	Click the taskbar button for the program you want to make active
Property sheet, open	AC 136	Right-click the object or control, click Properties
Property sheet, open or close for a form or report control	AC 214	Select the control, click Design tab, click Property Sheet button in Show/Hide group
Query datasheet, sort	AC 114	*See* Reference Window: Sorting a Query Datasheet
Query, define	AC 120	Click Create tab, click Query Design button in Other group
Query, run	AC 121	Double-click query in Navigation Pane or, in Results group on Query Tools Design tab, click Run button
Query results, sort	AC 114	*See* Reference Window: Sorting a Query Datasheet
Record, add a new one	AC 16	In Records group on Home tab, click New button
Record, delete	AC 102	*See* Reference Window: Deleting a Record
Record, move to first	AC 23	Click ◄◄
Record, move to last	AC 23	Click ►►|
Record, move to next	AC 23	Click ►
Record, move to previous	AC 23	Click ◄
Records, print selected in a form	AC 171	Click ⊕, point to Print, click Print, click Selected Record(s), click OK
Records, redisplay all after filter	AC 118	In Sort & Filter group on Home tab, click Toggle Filter button
Rectangle, add to a form or report	AC 316	*See* Reference Window: Adding a Rectangle to a Form or Report
Report, create a custom	AC 353	*See* Reference Window: Creating a Blank Report in Layout View
Report, filter in Report view	AC 335	Right-click the value to filter, point to Text Filters, click filter option
Report, select and copy data in Report view	AC 337	Click the top of the selection, drag to the end of the selection, click Home tab, click ▣ in Clipboard group
Report, print all	AC 32	*See* Reference Window: Printing a Report
Report, print specific pages of	AC 187–188	Click Print Preview tab, click Print button in Print group, click Pages, enter number of pages to print in From and To boxes, click OK
Report Wizard, activate	AC 177	Click Create tab, click Report Wizard button in Reports group, choose the table or query for the report, select fields, click Next
Saved export, run	AC 8	Click External Data tab, click Saved Exports button in Export group, click the saved export, click Run
Saved import, run	AC 8	Click External Data tab, click Saved Imports button in Import group, click the saved import, click Run
Sort, specify ascending in datasheet	AC 113	Click column heading arrow, click Sort A to Z
Sort, specify descending in datasheet	AC 113	Click column heading arrow, click Sort Z to A
Spacing, change in a form control	AC 277	In Layout view, click the control, click Arrange tab, click Control Margins button in Control Layout group, click the desired setting
Subform, open in a new window	AC 305	Right-click the subform, click Subform in New Window
Subform/Subreport Wizard, activate	AC 302	Make sure ◪ is selected, click ▤, click in the grid at the upper-left corner for the subform/subreport

TASK	PAGE #	RECOMMENDED METHOD
Tab Control, add to a form	AC 8	Click Design tab, click Tab Control button in Controls group, click in the grid at the upper-left corner for the tab control
Tab order, change in a form	AC 313	In Design view, click Arrange tab, click Tab Order button in Control Layout group, drag the rows into the desired order, click OK
Tab Stop property, change for a form control	AC 312	In Layout view, right-click the control, click Properties, click Other tab, set the Tab Stop property
Table, analyze	AC 8	Select the table, click Database Tools tab, click Analyze Table button in Analyze group
Table, create in a database in Datasheet View	AC 8	*See* Reference Window: Creating a Table in Datasheet View
Table, open in a database	AC 17	Double-click table in Navigation Pane
Table, save in a database	AC 15	*See* Reference Window: Saving a Table
Template, use an HTML	AC 8	Click the Export data with formatting and layout check box in the Export - HTML Document dialog box, click the Select a HTML Template check box, click Browse, select template, click OK
Title, add to a form or report	AC 296	In Controls group, click Title button, click in the grid at the upper-left corner for the title, type the title, press Enter
Top values query, create	AC 229	*See* Reference Window: Creating a Top Values Query
Totals, calculating in a report	AC 343	In Layout view, click any value in the column to calculate, click Format tab, click Totals button in Groupings & Totals group, click Sum
Trusted folder, create	AC 246	Click 🔘, click Access Options, click Trust Center, click Trust Center Settings, click Trusted Locations, click Add new location, click Browse, navigate to the desired folder, click OK four times
Validation Rule property, set	AC 243	Display the table in Design view, select the field, enter the rule in the Validation Rule text box
Validation Text property, set	AC 241	Display the table in Design view, select the field, enter the text in the Validation Text text box
Window, close	OFF 6	Click [X] or click X
Window, maximize	OFF 7	Click [□] or click □
Window, minimize	OFF 7	Click [▬] or click ▬
Window, restore	OFF 7	Click [▣] or click ▢
Workspace, zoom	OFF 8	*See* Reference Window: Zooming the Workspace
XML file, export an Access object to an	AC 8	*See* Reference Window: Exporting and Access Object as an XML File
XML file, import as a table	AC 8	*See* Reference Window: Importing an XML File as an Access Table